# CCIE Enterprise
# Infrastructure I

T0100780

Narbik Kocharians

**Cisco Press**

# CCIE Enterprise Infrastructure Foundation

Narbik Kocharians

Copyright© 2023 Pearson Education, Inc.

Published by: Cisco Press

1 2022

Library of Congress Control Number: 2022902108

ISBN-13: 978-0-13-737424-3

ISBN-10: 0-13-737424-0

## Warning and Disclaimer

## Trademark Acknowledgments

## Special Sales

For information about buying this title in bulk quantities, or for special sales opportunities (which may include electronic versions; custom cover designs; and content particular to your business, training goals, marketing focus, or branding interests), please contact our corporate sales department at corpsales@pearsoned.com or (800) 382-3419.

For government sales inquiries, please contact governmentsales@pearsoned.com.

For questions about sales outside the U.S., please contact intlcs@pearson.com.

# Feedback Information

At Cisco Press, our goal is to create in-depth technical books of the highest quality and value. Each book is crafted with care and precision, undergoing rigorous development that involves the unique expertise of members from the professional technical community.

Readers' feedback is a natural continuation of this process. If you have any comments regarding how we could improve the quality of this book, or otherwise alter it to better suit your needs, you can contact us through email at feedback@ciscopress.com. Please make sure to include the book title and ISBN in your message.

We greatly appreciate your assistance.

**Editor-in-Chief:** Mark Taub

**Alliances Manager, Cisco Press:** Arezou Gol

**Director, ITP Product Management:** Brett Bartow

**Executive Editor:** James Manly

**Managing Editor:** Sandra Schroeder

**Development Editor:** Ellie Bru

**Project Editor:** Mandie Frank

**Copy Editor:** Kitty Wilson

**Technical Editors:** Sarah Anand; Dante McNeil

**Editorial Assistant:** Cindy Teeters

**Designer:** Chuti Prasertsith

**Composition:** codeMantra

**Indexer:** Timothy Wright

**Proofreader:** Donna E. Mulder

**CISCO**

| Americas Headquarters | Asia Pacific Headquarters | Europe Headquarters |
| --- | --- | --- |
| Cisco Systems, Inc. | Cisco Systems (USA) Pte. Ltd. | Cisco Systems International BV |
| San Jose, CA | Singapore | Amsterdam, The Netherlands |

Cisco has more than 200 offices worldwide. Addresses, phone numbers, and fax numbers are listed on the Cisco Website at **www.cisco.com/go/offices.**

CCDE, CCENT, Cisco Eos, Cisco HealthPresence, the Cisco logo, Cisco Lumin, Cisco Nexus, Cisco StadiumVision, Cisco TelePresence, Cisco WebEx, DCE, and Welcome to the Human Network are trademarks; Changing the Way We Work, Live, Play, and Learn and Cisco Store are service marks; and Access Registrar, Aironet, AsyncOS, Bringing the Meeting To You, Catalyst, CCDA, CCDP, CCIE, CCIP, CCNA, CCNP, CCSP, CCVP, Cisco, the Cisco Certified Internetwork Expert logo, Cisco IOS, Cisco Press, Cisco Systems, Cisco Systems Capital, the Cisco Systems logo, Cisco Unity, Collaboration Without Limitation, EtherFast, EtherSwitch, Event Center, Fast Step, Follow Me Browsing, FormShare, GigaDrive, HomeLink, Internet Quotient, IOS, iPhone, iQuick Study, IronPort, the IronPort logo, LightStream, Linksys, MediaTone, MeetingPlace, MeetingPlace Chime Sound, MGX, Networkers, Networking Academy, Network Registrar, PCNow, PIX, PowerPanels, ProConnect, ScriptShare, SenderBase, SMARTnet, Spectrum Expert, StackWise, The Fastest Way to Increase Your Internet Quotient, TransPath, WebEx, and the WebEx logo are registered trademarks of Cisco Systems, Inc. and/or its affiliates in the United States and certain other countries.

All other trademarks mentioned in this document or website are the property of their respective owners. The use of the word partner does not imply a partnership relationship between Cisco and any other company. (0812R)

## Credits

Unnumbered figures on pages 860-861          PuTTY

# Pearson's Commitment to Diversity, Equity, and Inclusion

Pearson is dedicated to creating bias-free content that reflects the diversity of all learners. We embrace the many dimensions of diversity, including but not limited to race, ethnicity, gender, socioeconomic status, ability, age, sexual orientation, and religious or political beliefs.

Education is a powerful force for equity and change in our world. It has the potential to deliver opportunities that improve lives and enable economic mobility. As we work with authors to create content for every product and service, we acknowledge our responsibility to demonstrate inclusivity and incorporate diverse scholarship so that everyone can achieve their potential through learning. As the world's leading learning company, we have a duty to help drive change and live up to our purpose to help more people create a better life for themselves and to create a better world.

Our ambition is to purposefully contribute to a world where

- Everyone has an equitable and lifelong opportunity to succeed through learning

- Our educational products and services are inclusive and represent the rich diversity of learners

- Our educational content accurately reflects the histories and experiences of the learners we serve

- Our educational content prompts deeper discussions with learners and motivates them to expand their own learning (and worldview)

While we work hard to present unbiased content, we want to hear from you about any concerns or needs with this Pearson product so that we can investigate and address them.

Please contact us with concerns about any potential bias at https://www.pearson.com/report-bias.html.

## About the Author

**Narbik Kocharians,** CCIE No. 12410 (Routing and Switching, Service Provider, and Security) is a triple CCIE with more than 46 years of experience in this industry. He has designed, implemented, and supported numerous small, mid-size, and large enterprise networks.

Narbik is the president of Micronics Networking and Training, Inc. (www.Micronics Training.com), where almost all Cisco-authorized and custom courses are conducted, including CCIE-DC, CCIE-SP, CCIE-Enterprise Infrastructure, CCDE, ACI, and many more.

# About the Technical Reviewers

**Sarah Anand** has been affiliated with different networking technologies, including Cisco-specific implementations, for 7 years, with a focus on routing/switching and service provider technologies. Currently she works as a technical writer and editor, training network engineers in vendor-specific and industry-standard technologies. She has a degree in computer science and enjoys spending free time exploring passions in web design and search engine optimization.

**Dante McNeil** has 10 years of IT networking experience in the nonprofit, enterprise, K–12, and higher education spaces, with a focus on advanced networking implementations and Cisco technologies. He also spends time writing and creating network training content for networking engineers. He holds a bachelor of science degree in computing information sciences from Jacksonville University. In his spare time, he enjoys roller coasters, video games, and road trips.

## Dedications

I would like to dedicate this book to my beautiful wife, Janet, my children and their spouses, Chris and Nona (aka Siroon Achik), Patrick and Diana (aka Bestelik Jan), Alexandra (aka Achiko) and Sevak, and Daniel (aka Chompolik), as well as our first grandson, Matthew (aka Jigar), whom I LOVE so much, he brightens my day every morning!

I would like to acknowledge with gratitude the support, sacrifice, and love of my family for making this book possible. I thank God for the health and wisdom that He has instilled in me, my lovely family, my first grandson Mathew, and my father, who was my best friend.

# Acknowledgments

A very special thanks to James and Eleanor. I remember brainstorming with James for hours about this book, and eventually he came up with the ultimate solution. I would like to thank Eleanor for having a tremendous amount of patience and professionalism.

I would also like to thank my tech editors, Sarah Anand and Dante McNeil, two gifted network engineers with a tremendous amount of knowledge. God willing, I will be working with these two champions for a long time to come. They are not CCIEs yet, but their knowledge is on par with the best CCIEs out there.

# Contents at a Glance

# Reader Services

**Register your copy** at www.ciscopress.com/title/ISBN for convenient access to downloads, updates, and corrections as they become available. To start the registration process, go to www.ciscopress.com/register and log in or create an account*. Enter the product ISBN 9780137374243 and click Submit. When the process is complete, you will find any available bonus content under Registered Products.

*Be sure to check the box that you would like to hear from us to receive exclusive discounts on future editions of this product.

# Contents

## Command Syntax Conventions

The conventions used to present command syntax in this book are the same conventions used in the IOS Command Reference. The Command Reference describes these conventions as follows:

- **Boldface** indicates commands and keywords that are entered literally as shown. In actual configuration examples and output (not general command syntax), boldface indicates commands that are manually input by the user (such as a **show** command).

- *Italic* indicates arguments for which you supply actual values.

- Vertical bars (|) separate alternative, mutually exclusive elements.

- Square brackets ([ ]) indicate an optional element.

- Braces ({ }) indicate a required choice.

- Braces within brackets ([{ }]) indicate a required choice within an optional element.

# Introduction

Enterprise networking has undergone many small changes over the years, building from simple shared bus LANs to intricate routing and switching architectures and wireless communications. Behind all of this is a need to ensure high reliability, agility, and speed. Through the decades, many different networking technologies, from physical connections to software protocols, have been created to assist enterprise networks in reaching those goals. For seasoned networking veterans, working with the various protocols and architectures is second nature. However, those who are just starting to build their careers and trying to study more advanced areas of network engineering may be overwhelmed by the multitude of routing protocols, Layer 2 features, and new buzzwords like "software-defined."

This book is written as a foundation guide for the most common enterprise networking concepts that are required for a network engineer looking to move forward to more advanced aspects of networking. It combines aspects of theory instruction with practical application. Topics such as LAN switching, IP routing, and overlay networking technologies such as DMVPN are explained as foundational topics, including examples. Each chapter also functions as a lab manual with a task-oriented structure. Lab scenarios are presented as either configuration objectives, troubleshooting scenarios, or design scenarios. Each lab scenario includes full solutions and explanations. For beginner to intermediate readers, the solutions can be read while solving the tasks. Advanced readers can challenge their knowledge and skills by solving tasks first and then comparing their solutions to the ones provided in this book.

This book is not meant to be an exhaustive study of all the included technologies. It is meant to provide enough information on all topics to allow you to speak intelligently about each technology and even implement some of the configurations, if necessary, in your own environment. It takes topics from Cisco's CCIE Enterprise Infrastructure certification blueprint but includes some legacy topics, where necessary, to facilitate understanding.

## Who This Book Is For

Although the title of this book is *CCIE Enterprise Infrastructure Foundation*, the target audience is not limited to just those seeking expert-level certification. Any person looking to learn a little bit more about these foundational technologies will find this book very accessible.

This book breaks down complicated topics and provides examples to maximize understanding. It does, however, assume some basic networking knowledge. The following types of readers will get the most out of this book:

■ Those who have completed CCNA certification and are part of the way through their preparation for CCNP Enterprise certification

■ Those who have completed CCNP Enterprise certification and are pursuing CCIE Enterprise Infrastructure certification

■ Those who are currently working in an environment that is implementing specific technologies covered in this book

■ Those who are migrating from another vendor to a Cisco environment and need to understand Cisco configurations for common networking protocols

## How This Book Is Organized

This book is divided into the 11 chapters described here. Every chapter can stand alone and can be used as a reference for the technologies it covers.

## Chapter 1: Switching

Chapter 1 introduces Layer 2 concepts such as preventing loops with Spanning Tree Protocol, segmenting with VLANs, extending VLANs between switches through trunking, and bonding multiple Ethernet links together to increase bandwidth between network nodes. It covers topics such as Spanning Tree Protocol, RSTP, MSTP, VTP and VTP pruning, 802.1Q and ISL trunking, and LACP and PAgP.

## Chapter 2: IP Prefix Lists

Chapter 2 introduces a common route filtering mechanism known as a prefix list. It explains why prefix lists were invented and why they are used over access lists for route filtering. This chapter shows how to write prefix lists and apply them in various routing protocols for filtering routes.

## Chapter 3: RIPv2

Chapter 3 introduces Routing Information Protocol (RIP). RIP may not be included on the exam, but it is a perfect example of a simple distance vector routing protocol that follows all the standard distance vector designs. It focuses on the simplicity of RIP configuration, advanced RIP filtering scenarios, and RIP configuration challenges.

## Chapter 4: EIGRP

Chapter 4 focuses on Cisco's improvement on its own version of Interior Gateway Routing Protocol (IGRP), Enhanced Interior Gateway Routing Protocol (EIGRP). It introduces EIGRP as a distance vector protocol that forms neighbor relationships and keeps a topology table like some other protocols. EIGRP is considered an advanced distance vector protocol that uses more than simple hop counts to learn loop-free paths through a network. This chapter covers EIGRP configuration topics such as EIGRP classic and address family configuration, EIGRP stub routing, and EIGRP with BFD.

## Chapter 5: OSPF

Chapter 5 introduces the Open Shortest Path First (OSPF) routing protocol. It begins with an analysis of how OSPF builds its link-state database (LSDB) with various link-state advertisements (LSA) and uses that information to calculate loop-free routed paths through a network. This chapter also details multiarea OSPF design, filtering, and virtual links. It includes a detailed walkthrough on OSPF's best-path determination to help you understand OSPF's path selection process.

## Chapter 6: BGP

Chapter 6 introduces Border Gateway Protocol (BGP), the protocol that routes the Internet. It explains BGP operation between autonomous systems (external BGP, or eBGP) and within a single autonomous system (internal BGP, or iBGP). Topics covered include BGP session establishment, route reflectors and confederations, aggregation, and filtering. This chapter includes a detailed walkthrough of the BGP best-path determination process.

## Chapter 7: DMVPN

Chapter 7 focuses on Cisco's original SD-WAN technology, known as Dynamic Multipoint VPN (DMVPN). It explains DMVPN from the ground up, introducing concepts such as overlay and underlay networking, the link between DMVPN and NHRP, DMVPN routing using common routing protocols, and different DMVPN designs. It covers DMVPN Phase 1 through Phase 3 configurations, NHRP shortcut switching enhancements, hub-and-spoke networking designs, and (m)GRE tunnels.

## Chapter 8: MPLS and L3VPNs

Chapter 8 introduces Multiprotocol Label Switching (MPLS) and the suite of services MPLS can provide. This chapter begins with an introduction to MPLS labels and Label Distribution Protocol (LDP). It also introduces the most common MPLS service, MPLS Layer 3 VPN (L3VPN). Topics covered include CE and PE routers, MPLS core configuration, LDP session establishment, BGP route targets and route distinguishers, and exchange of IGP routes between two sites connected by an MPLS L3VPN.

## Chapter 9: IPv6

Chapter 9 introduces Internet Protocol Version 6 (IPv6), which is the successor to IPv4 due to its massive address space. It also details IPv6 address types, assignment, and configuration. Topics covered include IPv6 NDP, IPv6 SLAAC, DMVPN for IPv6, OSPF for IPv6 (OSPFv3), EIGRP for IPv6, and BGP for IPv6.

## Chapter 10: SD-WAN

Chapter 10 introduces Cisco's new SD-WAN platform, which is based on its acquisition of Viptela. This chapter details basic SD-WAN components, such as vSmart, vManage, and vBond, as well as the setup and configuration required to join vEdge routers to an SD-WAN solution. Topics covered include onboarding WAN edge devices, unicast routing, segmentation, vManage device templates, ZTP, and application-aware policies.

## Chapter 11: SD-Access

Chapter 11 introduces Cisco's SD-Access solution for creating scalable, automated, and resilient enterprise fabric. This chapter covers configuration of the SD-Access policy engine as well as SDA design and implementation. Topics covered include Cisco ISE, pxGrid, XMPP, SDA hierarchy global IP pools, DNAC, and LAN automation.

# Before Starting the First Chapter

## Bookmark the Companion Website

The companion website contains the config files, topology diagrams, CLI output, and explanations for the labs in this book. These elements are essential and a fundamental part of your learning experience. To use this book effectively, you need to have them. Use the config files, reference the topology diagrams, and work through the labs while checking your work against the CLI output on the companion website. At the end of each lab, read through the explanations for further insight.

To access the book's companion website, simply follow these steps:

1.  Go to www.ciscopress.com/register.

2.  Enter the print book **ISBN: 9780137374243.**

3.  Answer the security question to validate you purchase.

4.  Go to your account page.

5.  Click on the **Registered Product** tab.

6.  Under the book listings, click on **Access Bonus Content** link.

If you have any issues accessing the companion website, you can contact our support team by going to http://pearsonitp.echelp.org.

# Chapter 1

# Switching

## Lab 1: Configuring Trunks

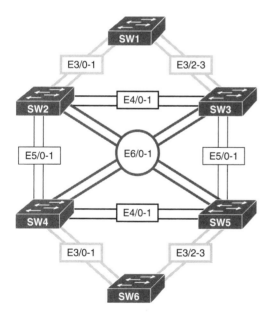

What is covered in this lab:

This lab focuses mainly on configuring trunk links and VLANs and controlling which VLANs are allowed on a particular trunk link. This lab covers the following topics: dynamic trunks, basic VTP operation, how to modify the allowed VLAN lists on trunk links, and VTP pruning.

This lab should be conducted on the Enterprise POD.

## Task 1

Shut down all ports on all six switches and configure the VTP domain name to be **TST**.

## Task 2

Configure the following hostnames:

Second switch: SW2

Third switch: SW3

Fourth switch: SW4

Fifth switch: SW5

## Task 3

Configure a dot1q trunk between SW3 and SW5 using their E5/0 interfaces, based on the following policy:

SW3, E5/0

This port should be configured into a permanent trunk mode, and it should negotiate to convert the neighboring interface into a trunk.

SW5, E5/0

This port should be configured to actively attempt to convert the link to a trunk. You should not configure **switchport trunk encapsulation dot1q** on this port.

## Task 4

Configure a trunk between SW3 and SW5, using their E5/1 interfaces. You should use an industry-standard protocol for the trunk encapsulation, based on the following policy:

SW3, E5/1

This port should be configured into permanent trunk mode, and it should negotiate to convert the neighboring interface into a trunk.

SW5, E5/1

This port should be configured to negotiate a trunk only if it receives negotiation packets from a neighboring port; this port should never start the negotiation process. You should not configure **switchport trunk encapsulation dot1q** on this port.

## Task 5

Configure a trunk link between SW4 and SW5, using their E4/0 interfaces. These ports should be configured to negotiate the neighboring interface into a dot1q trunk, but they should not be in permanent trunk mode.

## Task 6

Configure a dot1q trunk between SW4 and SW5, using their E4/1 interfaces, based on the following policy:

SW4, E4/1

This port should be configured to actively attempt to convert the link to a trunk. This port should not be in permanent trunk mode.

SW5, E4/1

This port should be configured to negotiate a trunk only if it receives negotiation packets from a neighboring port; this port should never start the negotiation process or be configured with the **switchport trunk encapsulation dot1q** command.

## Task 7

Configure a dot1q trunk between SW3 and SW4, using their E6/0 interfaces; these switches should be configured into permanent trunk mode and negotiate the neighboring interface into a trunk.

## Task 8

Configure a dot1q trunk between SW3 and SW4, using their E6/1 interfaces. These ports should not use DTP to negotiate a trunk.

## Task 9

Configure trunking on the E4/0-1 interfaces of SW2 and SW3, the E5/0-1 interfaces on SW2 and SW4, and the E6/0-1 interfaces of SW2 and SW5. These ports should be in permanent trunk mode.

## Task 10

Configure the following VLANs on SW2 and ensure that they are propagated to the other switches:

VLANs 2–10, 100, 200, 300, 400, 230, 350, 450, 240, 250, and 340

## Task 11

Configure the trunks based on the following policy:

| Policy Item | Trunk Interface | Between Switches | Allowed VLAN/s |
| --- | --- | --- | --- |
| 1 | E4/1 | SW2 ←→ SW3 | Only 230 |
| 2 | E5/0 | SW3 ←→ SW5 | Only 350 |
| 3 | E4/0 | SW4 ←→ SW5 | Only 450 |
| 4 | E5/0 | SW2 ←→ SW4 | Only 240 |
| 5 | E6/0 | SW2 ←→ SW5 | Only 250 |
| 6 | E6/0 | SW3 ←→ SW4 | Only 340 |

## Task 12

Add VLANs to the allowed list of the trunks, based on the following chart:

| Policy Item | Trunk Interface | Between Switches | Add to the Allowed VLAN/s |
| --- | --- | --- | --- |
| 1 | E4/1 | SW2 ←→ SW3 | 100 |
| 2 | E5/0 | SW3 ←→ SW5 | 200 |
| 3 | E4/0 | SW4 ←→ SW5 | 300 |
| 4 | E6/0 | SW2 ←→ SW5 | 400 |

## Task 13

Remove VLANs from the allowed list of trunks, based on the following chart:

| Policy Item | Trunk Interface | Between Switches | Allowed VLAN/s |
| --- | --- | --- | --- |
| 1 | E5/1 | SW2 ←→ SW4 | Remove 1, 4 – 10 only |
| 2 | E5/1 | SW3 ←→ SW5 | Remove 2, 4 – 10 only |

## Task 14

Configure SW2, SW3, and SW5, based on the following chart:

| Policy Item | Trunk Interface | Between Switches | Allowed VLAN/s |
| --- | --- | --- | --- |
| 1 | E4/0 | SW2 ←→ SW3 | None |
| 2 | E6/1 | SW2 ←→ SW5 | None |

## Task 15

Configure SW2, SW4, and SW5, based on the following chart:

| Policy Item | Trunk Interface | Between Switches | Allowed VLAN/s |
|---|---|---|---|
| 1 | E4/1 | SW4 ⟵→ SW5 | All except 450 |
| 2 | E5/1 | SW2 ⟵→ SW4 | All except 240 |

## Task 16

Configure SW3 and SW4, based on the following chart. You may override some of the previous tasks to accomplish this task.

| Policy Item | Trunk Interface | Between Switches | Allowed VLAN/s |
|---|---|---|---|
| 1 | E6/0 | SW3 ⟵→ SW4 | All |
| 2 | E6/1 | SW3 ⟵→ SW4 | All |

## Task 17

Erase the config.text and vlan.dat files on SW1-5 and reload them before proceeding to the next task.

## Task 18

Configure SW2 and SW3 based on the following policies:

- Configure the hostnames of Switch 2 and Switch 3 to be SW2 and SW3, respectively.

- Shut down all the ports on SW2 and SW3.

- Configure a dot1q trunk between SW2 and SW3 using port E4/0.

- Ensure that both switches belong to the VTP domain TST.

## Task 19

Configure VLAN 100 on SW2 and assign its E0/1 interface to this VLAN.

## VTP Pruning

In Task 10, it was explained that VTP is a protocol that can be used to synchronize the VLAN databases between switches that participate in the same VTP domain. VTP uses three message types to achieve this synchronization: **summary advertisement**, **advertisement request**, and **subset advertisements**. This synchronization process makes it such that an administrator only needs to configure VLANs on a single VTP server switch and have those configurations propagated for synchronization to all remaining switches in the VTP domain.

VTP can be used for more than simple VLAN database synchronization. It can be used to reduce unnecessary broadcast flooded traffic originating in a specific VLAN from entering sections of the network that do not require that VLAN traffic. For example, the sample topology from Task 10 is examined:

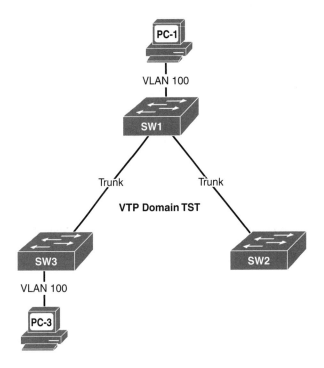

In this topology, the interfaces connecting Switch-1 to Switch-2 and Switch-3 are configured as trunk links. All three switches belong to the same VTP domain, **TST**.

Previously, VLAN 100 was created on Switch-1. Switch-1 propagated information about this VLAN to Switch-2 and Switch-3 using VTP. Looking at the diagram, notice only Switch-1 and Switch-3 have interfaces connected to hosts in VLAN 100. Switch-2 does not have any interfaces connected to VLAN 100. Since Switch-2 has no interfaces in VLAN 100, there is no need for it to receive broadcast traffic originating from hosts in VLAN 100 connected to other switches in the network. Recall, ARP requests are broadcasted to all devices in the same VLAN. They are generated by end hosts to resolve the MAC address of a target device.

When PC-1 needs to reach PC-3 in the topology, it starts by sending a broadcast ARP frame to learn PC-3's MAC address. The following packet capture shows that the ARP frame was broadcasted to both Switch-2 and Switch-3:

---

**On Switch-3:**

```
Frame 4990: 64 bytes on wire (512 bits), 64 bytes captured (512 bits) on interface 0
Ethernet II, Src: aa:bb:cc:00:04:20 (aa:bb:cc:00:04:20), Dst: Broadcast
  (ff:ff:ff:ff:ff:ff)
802.1Q Virtual LAN, PRI: 0, DEI: 0, ID: 100
Address Resolution Protocol (request)
   Hardware type: Ethernet (1)
   Protocol type: IPv4 (0x0800)
   Hardware size: 6
   Protocol size: 4
   Opcode: request (1)
   Sender MAC address: aa:bb:cc:00:04:20 (aa:bb:cc:00:04:20)
   Sender IP address: 100.1.1.1
   Target MAC address: 00:00:00_00:00:00 (00:00:00:00:00:00)
   Target IP address: 100.1.1.2
```

**On Switch-2:**

```
Frame 4134: 64 bytes on wire (512 bits), 64 bytes captured (512 bits) on interface 0
Ethernet II, Src: aa:bb:cc:00:04:20 (aa:bb:cc:00:04:20), Dst: aa:bb:cc:00:05:10
  (aa:bb:cc:00:05:10)
802.1Q Virtual LAN, PRI: 0, DEI: 0, ID: 100
Address Resolution Protocol (request)
   Hardware type: Ethernet (1)
   Protocol type: IPv4 (0x0800)
   Hardware size: 6
   Protocol size: 4
   Opcode: request (1)
   Sender MAC address: aa:bb:cc:00:04:20 (aa:bb:cc:00:04:20)
   Sender IP address: 100.1.1.1
   Target MAC address: aa:bb:cc:00:05:10 (aa:bb:cc:00:05:10)
   Target IP address: 100.1.1.2
```

---

Switch-2 has received the broadcast traffic even though it will ultimately drop it because it does not have any hosts in that VLAN. The VLAN 100 broadcast in this case was unnecessarily broadcasted to Switch-2. This unnecessary broadcast occurred because Switch-1 included VLAN 100 in its allowed VLAN list for the trunk link connected to Switch-2, as shown here:

```
Switch-1# show interfaces trunk

Port          Mode              Encapsulation  Status        Native vlan
Et0/0         on                802.1q         trunking      1
Et0/1         on                802.1q         trunking      1


Port          Vlans allowed on trunk
Et0/0         1-4094
Et0/1         1-4094


Port          Vlans allowed and active in management domain
Et0/0         1,100,200
Et0/1         1,100,200


Port          Vlans in spanning tree forwarding state and not pruned
Et0/0         1,100
Et0/1         1,100 ! VLAN 100 is allowed on the trunk link to Switch-2
```

This inclusion extends VLAN 100's broadcast domain to Switch-2. One way to stop the unnecessary broadcast of VLAN 100 traffic to Switch-2 is to manually remove VLAN 100 from the Switch-1/Switch-2 trunk link by using the **switchport trunk allowed-vlan remove 100** command in interface configuration mode. This process, called *manual pruning*, is demonstrated extensively in previous tasks.

The problem with manual pruning is that if a host were connected to Switch-2 in VLAN 100, that VLAN would need to be manually added to the allowed VLAN list on the Switch-1/Switch-2 trunk link again. Multiply this process by hundreds of VLANs and potentially hundreds of clients moving around in the network, and it is clear that this manual pruning process can cause high administrative overhead.

This is where **VTP pruning** comes into play. VTP pruning is a feature of VTP that allows dynamic pruning of VLANs from trunk links where the VLAN traffic is not needed. The process utilizes a fourth VTP message type, called the **VTP membership advertisement**, or **VMA**. These are basically VTP Join/Prune messages.

The basic process for VTP pruning is that a switch sends a VMA for all VLANs for which it is interested in receiving traffic. The switch makes this determination based on whether or not it contains any interfaces that are currently associated with a VLAN that exists in the local switch's VLAN database.

Once again, referring back to the sample topology shown earlier, when VTP pruning is enabled on all the switches, they exchange VMAs with each other. Because Switch-3 is interested in receiving traffic for VLAN 100, its VMA includes VLAN 1 and VLAN 100, as shown in the following capture.

**Note**   VLAN 1 is pruning ineligible, which means this VLAN will always be included in the advertised active VLAN field and cannot be removed.

---

**From Switch-3:**

```
VLAN Trunking Protocol
    Version: 0x01
    Code: Join/Prune Message (0x04)
    Reserved: 00
    Management Domain Length: 3
    Management Domain: TST
    First VLAN ID: 0
    Last VLAN ID: 1007
    Advertised active (i.e. not pruned) VLANs
        VLAN: 1
        VLAN: 100
```

The **Advertised active (i.e. not pruned) VLANs** field indicates the VLANs for which Switch-3 is interested in receiving traffic. Any VLAN that is not assigned to an interface on Switch-3 is omitted from this list. For example, the VMA sent from Switch-2 to Switch-1 includes only VLAN 1. This is because Switch-2 does not have any interfaces assigned to VLAN 100, and thus it has no need for VLAN 100 traffic. Any traffic sent by Switch-1 to Switch-2 in VLAN 100 would inevitably be a futile effort since Switch-2 would end up dropping the traffic anyway.

---

**From Switch-2:**

```
VLAN Trunking Protocol
    Version: 0x01
    Code: Join/Prune Message (0x04)
    Reserved: 00
    Management Domain Length: 3
    Management Domain: TST
    First VLAN ID: 0
    Last VLAN ID: 1007
    Advertised active (i.e. not pruned) VLANs
        VLAN: 1
```

The following shows the state of the **show interface trunk** output on Switch-1. As a
result of the VMA message exchanges, Switch-1 will now send traffic for VLAN 100 out
its trunk link E0/0 to Switch-3 only.

```
Switch-1# show interfaces trunk

Port         Mode            Encapsulation  Status       Native vlan
Et0/0        on              802.1q         trunking     1
Et0/1        on              802.1q         trunking     1


Port         Vlans allowed on trunk
Et0/0        1-4094
Et0/1        1-4094


Port         Vlans allowed and active in management domain
Et0/0        1,100,200
Et0/1        1,100,200


Port         Vlans in spanning tree forwarding state and not pruned
Et0/0        1,100 ! VLAN 1 and 100 allowed to Switch-2
Et0/1        1 ! Only VLAN 1 allowed to Switch-2
```

VTP pruning is disabled by default and can be enabled by using the **vtp pruning** command in global configuration mode. VTP keeps a list of VLANs that are allowed to be
dynamically pruned; it is called the **pruning-eligible list** or the **pruning VLANs enabled
list**, depending on the **show** command being used. This list can be seen using the **show
interface switchport** command, as shown here:

```
Switch-1# show int e0/0 switchport | in Pruning
Pruning VLANs Enabled: 2-1001
```

The pruning-eligible list can be modified much like the allowed VLAN list of a trunk link
with the **switchport trunk pruning vlan** command and the following additional parameters:

```
Switch-1(config-if)# switchport trunk pruning vlan ?
  WORD    VLAN IDs of the allowed VLANs when this port is in trunking mode
  add     add VLANs to the current list
  except  all VLANs except the following
  none    no VLANs
  remove  remove VLANs from the current list
```

The result of this command can be seen with the sample topology shown earlier.
Before any configuration changes are made, the **show interface e0/1 pruning** command

output on Switch-1 reveals that it is pruning VLAN 100 on the E0/1 trunk link connected to Switch-2. This is a result of the missing VLAN 100 in the VMA sent by Switch-2, as shown here:

```
Switch-1# show interface e0/1 pruning

Port                  Vlans pruned for lack of request by neighbor
Et0/1                 100


Port                  Vlan traffic requested of neighbor
Et0/1                 1,100
```

Next, VLAN 200 is configured on Switch-2. The pruning-eligible list on Switch-2 is then modified to include only VLAN 200 with the **switchport trunk pruning vlan 200** command:

```
Switch-2(config-if)# vlan 200
Switch-2(config-vlan)# exit
Switch-2(config)# interface e0/1
Switch-2(config-if)# switchport trunk pruning vlan 200
```

Notice how the pruning-eligible list on Switch-2 shows only VLAN 200:

```
Switch-2# show interface e0/1 switchport | in Pruning
Pruning VLANs Enabled: 200
```

The result of this configuration is that all other VLANs are now considered to be pruning ineligible. As a result, the VMA sent by Switch-2 to Switch-1 will include VLAN 100, thus preventing Switch-1 from pruning this VLAN off the trunk link connected to Switch-2. You can see this in the following packet capture, where VLAN 100 is included in the **Advertised active (i.e. not pruned) VLANs** field:

```
VLAN Trunking Protocol
   Version: 0x01
   Code: Join/Prune Message (0x04)
   Reserved: 00
   Management Domain Length: 3
   Management Domain: TST
   First VLAN ID: 0
   Last VLAN ID: 1007
   Advertised active (i.e. not pruned) VLANs
      VLAN: 1
      VLAN: 100
```

Tasks 20 through 27 pertain to VTP pruning for the lab topology.

## Task 20

Configure the switches such that they restrict flooded traffic to those trunk links the traffic must use to access the appropriate network device(s).

## Task 21

Configure VLANs 200, 300, 400, 500, and 600 on SW2 and ensure that these VLANs are propagated to SW3.

## Task 22

Configure the E3/3 interface of SW3 in VLAN 100.

## Task 23

Configure the switches such that only VLAN 300 is pruned.

## Task 24

Configure the switches such that VLAN 200 is also pruned. You should not use the command from the previous task to accomplish this task.

## Task 25

Configure SW2 and SW3 such that none of the VLANs are pruned.

## Task 26

Configure SW2 and SW3 such that all configured VLANs in the VLAN database are pruned.

## Task 27

Configure SW2 and SW3 such that VLAN 200 is no longer pruned; do not use a command that was used before to accomplish this task.

## Task 28

Erase the vlan.dat and config.text files and reload the switches before proceeding to the next lab.

# Lab 2: Configuring EtherChannels

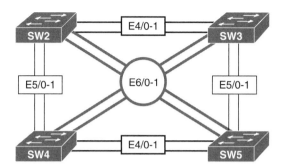

## This lab should be conducted on the Enterprise POD.

### Task 1

Configure the hostname of the switches based on the provided diagram. Ensure that all the ports of these four switches are in shutdown mode. Configure these four switches in a VTP domain called **TST**.

### Task 2

Configure ports E4/0 and E4/1 on SW2 and SW3 as trunk links, using an industry-standard protocol. These links should appear to Spanning Tree Protocol as a single link. If one of the links fails, the traffic should use the other link, without any interruption. The ports on SW2 should be configured such that they only respond to PAgP packets and never start the negotiation process.

### Task 3

Configure ports E5/0 and E5/1 on SW2 and SW4 as trunk links, using an industry-standard protocol. These links should appear to Spanning Tree Protocol as a single link. If one of the links fails, the traffic should use the other link, without any interruption. These ports should *not* negotiate an etherchannel by exchanging **LACP** or **PAgP** protocols to accomplish this task.

### Task 4

Ensure that all the EtherChannels created on SW2 are load balanced based on the destination MAC address.

## Task 5

Configure ports E6/0 and E6/1 on SW3 and SW4 as a single Layer 3 link; SW3 should be configured with the IP address 34.1.1.3/24, and SW4 should be configured with the IP address 34.1.1.4/24. These ports should not negotiate LACP or PAgP.

## Task 6

Erase the startup configuration and vlan.dat files before proceeding to the next lab.

# Lab 3: Introducing Spanning Tree Protocol

This section is designed to teach basic to advanced concepts of Spanning Tree Protocol-.

It utilizes a common topology over which each version of Spanning Tree Protocol is configured with a given set of requirements and restraints. The requirements and restraints are engineered to explain the behaviors of each version of Spanning Tree Protocol, highlighting the important limitations and enhancements of each feature.

This lab is entirely focused on Spanning Tree Protocol technologies and assumes basic knowledge of the following:

- Trunking configuration

- VLAN configuration and usage

- Layer 2 link aggregation

- IP address configuration

- Basic IP connectivity testing

> **Note**   The solutions provided in this lab are not all inclusive. There may be many ways to solve each task. All alternate solutions are acceptable, provided that they do not violate previous restraints or tasks.

### 802.1D Per-VLAN Spanning Tree Protocol

This lab should be conducted on the Mock Rack.

*Initial Lab Setup*

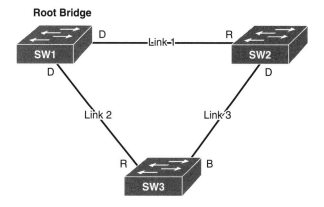

## Task 1

Change the hostname on each switch to SW#, where # is the number of the switch (for example, Switch 1 = SW1).

## Task 2

Ensure that only the following ports on the switches are in an up/up state:

- SW1
    - E2/1-2
    - E3/1-2
- SW2
    - E1/1-2
    - E3/1-2
    - E4/1-2
    - E5/1-2
- SW3
    - E1/1-2
    - E2/1-2
    - E4/1-2
    - E5/1-2
- SW4
    - E2/1-2
    - E3/1-2
    - E6/1-2

- SW5
    - E2/1-2
    - E3/1-2
    - E6/1-2
- SW6
    - E4/1-2
    - E5/1-2

## Task 3

Configure VLANs 10, 20, 30, and 40 on each switch, using any method.

## Task 4

Configure trunk ports on all up/up interfaces.

# Configuration Tasks: 802.1D

Before getting into the tasks, it helps to review the basic operation of Spanning Tree Protocol and some of the terms that will be used throughout the solution guide. These concepts will be fleshed out more throughout the guide.

802.1D Spanning Tree Protocol is the protocol that is run between switches used to prevent Layer 2 bridging loops. Loops can form in Layer 2 networks because the Layer 2 Ethernet frame format does not contain any maximum hop count limitation, such as the TTL field in the IP header. This omission of maximum hop count means a single Ethernet frame can be forwarded infinitely throughout a switched network. This is particularly dangerous when the frame being forwarded is a broadcast frame.

Switches are called *transparent bridges* because they abstract the physical network design from the end stations connecting to the LAN. In the past, all stations connected to a Layer 2 LAN were physically connected to the same physical electrical bus via a repeater. Only one station could speak on the segment at a time, and all stations were considered directly connected. This setup was called a *single collision domain* because there was a possibility that two stations would transmit at the same time, and those transmissions could collide.

Later, bridges came about that allowed intelligent learning. An ethernet Bridge would be used to combine two Layer 2 network segments into a single Layer 2 network. Bridges learned MAC addresses and only forwarded traffic between the two network segments when necessary. This operation was transparent to the end stations, because as far as the stations could detect, they directly connected to the remote stations they were communicating with. The ethernet bridge in this way creates two separate collision domains.

An ethernet switch is basically a multiport bridge. Instead of learning MAC addresses only on two ports, a switch learns MAC addresses on all ports and forwards traffic based on destination MAC addresses to destination ports. If two ethernet frames are destined to the same port, the switch will buffer one frame while forwarding the other. Because not all traffic forwarded across the LAN segment is repeated to all ports, the switch achieves a single collision domain between each port on the switch and the stations connected to those ports.

For the switch to do this, it must first learn which MAC addresses are reachable off its various ports. To do so, the switch reads the source MAC address of all frames it receives and records it associated to the receiving port in a MAC address table, also called a **Content Addressable Memory** or **CAM** table. The switch switches traffic between ports by performing a lookup in the CAM table based on the destination MAC address of the ethernet frames. Through this, known unicast traffic can be forwarded only out the port where the intended station exists.

The problem arises when a switch receives a frame destined to a MAC address it has not learned. The switch cannot drop the frame because that would break the LAN communication. Instead, it floods the frame out all ports in the same VLAN on the switch (including trunk ports that carry those VLANs) except the port on which it initially received the frame. This process, known as **unknown unicast flooding**, can cause a loop condition in the switched network with broadcast frames.

**Broadcast frames** are frames that are intended to be received by all stations. They are sent to the well-known broadcast destination MAC address FFFF.FFFF.FFFF. When a switch encounters a broadcast frame, it performs unknown-unicast-type flooding for the frame in question. It sends the traffic out all interfaces except the interface on which it was received. The switch does this because the broadcast MAC address FFFF.FFFF.FFFF will never be the source of an ethernet frame. Because it is never the source of an ethernet frame, the switch will never associate the broadcast MAC address with a receiving port in its CAM table, triggering the unknown unicast flooding behavior.

If there are redundant links in a multi-switch environment, where the chain of interconnected links leads back to the switch that originally forwarded the broadcast traffic, a **broadcast storm** occurs. In a broadcast storm, each receiving switch performs the same unknown-unicast-type flooding on the broadcast packet. The broadcast packet is therefore regenerated and looped endlessly throughout the switched network. This leads to high CPU utilization on the switches and can quickly bring down the entire Layer 2 network.

Spanning Tree Protocol converts a switched network into a shortest-path tree. This tree is constructed by designating a switch as the root of the tree, called the **root bridge**. The root bridge is the only bridge in which all of the ports are considered designated ports. A designated port is a port that is responsible for relaying spanning-tree-related messages downstream from the root bridge to other leaf switches. From the root bridge's perspective, all other switches are downstream from it, and thus it should be designated on all of its ports.

All non-root switches elect a single port to become their root port. The root port is the port that the switch uses to reach the root bridge. This port also receives spanning-tree-related messages on the shortest-path tree to be relayed out all other designated ports on the switch.

Finally, redundant links in the network are put into a blocking state. So-called blocking ports are ports that receive BPDUs from a designated port that is not on the shortest-path tree. In other words, they are alternate looped paths to the root bridge that are longer than the path used by the root port. Blocking ports do not send BPDUs in traditional Spanning Tree Protocol; instead, a blocking port receives a constant flow of BPDUs from the neighboring designated port.

Through this system of designated, root, and blocking ports, STP creates a loop-free network. Broadcast frames and frames undergoing unknown unicast flooding travel the shortest path from leaf switch to root switch and are blocked (dropped) on redundant links.

### Task 1

Configure all switches to run 802.1D Spanning Tree Protocol.

### Task 2

Ensure that SW1 is the root for every VLAN.

### Task 3

Ensure that all switches wait a total of 10 seconds in the listening and learning states before moving a port to forwarding.

### Task 4

Ensure that if the current root bridge fails, SW2 becomes the new root bridge for all VLANs.

### Task 5

Ensure that SW2's and SW3's E1/2 interface is used as the root port for all VLANs. Do not modify cost to achieve this.

### Task 6

Ensure that SW5 uses its E3/1 port as the root port for VLANs 10 and 30. Do not modify SW2 to achieve this.

## Task 7

Ensure that SW4 uses its E3/1 port as root port for VLANs 20 and 40. Do not modify SW3 to achieve this.

## Task 8

Ensure that interfaces connected to non-switch hosts come online immediately.

**a.** If SW4 or SW5 detects a switch on these ports when they first come online, they should process the BPDUs normally. Otherwise, it should not process received BPDUs.

**b.** If SW6 detects a switch on one of these ports, it should disable the port.

## Task 9

Ensure that SW6 is able to fully utilize redundant links between neighboring switches. Use a Cisco-specific approach to solve this.

## Task 10

Ensure that SW6's interface toward SW5 is used as the root port for all VLANs. If the link between SW5 and SW6 goes down, SW6 should immediately switch to using its link toward SW4.

## Task 11

Ensure that SW3's interfaces is designated on the SW2/SW3 link for all VLANs.

## Task 12

Ensure that SW4 and SW5 can recover from an indirect link failure within 10 seconds. Do not modify spanning-tree timers.

## Task 13

Ensure that SW2 only allows its ports toward SW1 to become root ports.

**Note**   Do not forget to reset the switch configurations to initial configurations upon completing this exercise.

## 802.1w Per-VLAN Rapid Spanning Tree Protocol

So far, we have explored the processes and functionality of traditional Spanning Tree Protocol (also known as 802.1D). The original intent of 802.1D was to ensure that loop-free paths exist in a Layer 2 switched network where redundant links are utilized. 802.1D in its base form accomplishes this goal, but it does so at a price: convergence time. 802.1D utilizes timer-based convergence mechanics, which means ports must receive and evaluate BPDUs to determine the root bridge.

The winning BPDU is stored by each port and relayed out all designated ports on the switch until it is refreshed by the reception of the same BPDU on one of the switch's non-designated (blocking or root) ports. If a port does not receive a BPDU within the Max Age time, the BPDU is aged out, and the topology reconverges. Furthermore, a port that transitions from blocking to forwarding must first pass through listening and learning states.

The entire convergence process for 802.1D, with default timers, can take up to 50 seconds (20 seconds for Max Age time and 30 seconds for transitioning between listening and learning states). As mentioned earlier in the lab, this is a considerable amount of down-time for a modern network. It interferes with host operations such as acquiring a network address to use for data communication.

Recognizing this inefficiency, the IEEE developed the **802.1w** standard, which is also called the **Rapid Spanning Tree Protocol**, or **RSTP**. The goal of RSTP is to drastically reduce the amount of time it takes a network to converge during a convergence event and whenever a switch is newly joined to a network. To do so, RSTP makes a few changes to the 802.1D mechanics:

- BPDUs are sent by all switches independently of reception of the root bridge's BPDU.

- Listening and learning states are combined into a single **learning state**.

- Port roles more clearly define what function a specific port plays in the network.

- Timer-based convergence is replaced by a proposal/agreement process.

In 802.1D, switches do not originate BPDUs. Instead, they relay the received superior BPDU from their root port out their designated ports. This superior BPDU is first origi-nated by the root bridge and acts as the heartbeat of the spanning tree. 802.1w modi-fies this behavior. All RSTP-compliant switches generate their best stored BPDUs out all of their designated ports at each hello interval, regardless of whether or not one was received on the root ports. This transforms the BPDU from being a measurement of the activity of the root bridge to being a keepalive between two bridges.

This modification of BPDU generation means RSTP can determine if a neighboring switch is active, based on when it last received a BPDU from the neighboring switch. If three Hello intervals of BPDUs are missed (2-second intervals, for 6 seconds total), the switch can immediately act. For blocking ports, that action is to become designated and send its own BPDU. Thus, in order for a blocking port to remain in the blocking state, it must continue to receive superior BPDUs from its upstream designated port.

In addition, the port states were revised. As mentioned earlier in 802.1D, there is little difference between a port that is blocking and a port that is listening or learning. In each of these states, one of three actions is being performed:

- The port is not forwarding traffic (that is, it is discarding traffic).

- The port is learning about the STP topology while not forwarding traffic.

- The port is learning MAC addresses while not forwarding traffic.

The first two actions correspond to the port refusing to process data frames even to the point where MAC addresses are not being learned over the ports. Instead, state information about the spanning-tree topology is being evaluated. These two functions fall within the purview of the blocking and listening states of the original 802.1D. In 802.1w, they are combined into a simple discarding state to signify that data traffic is being discarded while spanning-tree BPDUs are still being processed. The last point corresponds to the switch processing MAC address information to build MAC address tables on the interfaces—a function of the learning state. This function was deemed necessary and has been retained as the learning state in RSTP.

With these modifications, RSTP possesses only three states: **discarding**, **learning**, and **forwarding**. These states describe what the port is actively doing but do not describe what function in the spanning-tree topology these ports serve. This distinction is necessary to allow rapid convergence in special circumstances. For this, RSTP utilizes unused fields in the 802.1D BPDU (the flags field) to carry the port state and new port roles describing both what action the port is taking and what role that port has in the spanning-tree topology.

The port roles are:

- **Root:** The port that receives the best BPDU of all BPDUs received by the local switch

- **Designated:** The port that sends the best BPDU on its LAN segment

- **Alternate:** The port that receives a superior BPDU on the LAN segment; it is a potential replacement for the root port

- **Backup:** The port that receives the superior BPDU of the local switch's own designated port; it is a potential replacement for the switch's own designated port

Of all of the states, root and designated are the same and correspond to the root and designated states in 802.1D. Alternate and backup ports are synonymous with blocking ports in 802.1D, but their roles more clearly define where the port lies in the spanning tree. An alternate port is a port that receives a superior BPDU from another bridge that is not the best BPDU the switch has heard. Such ports provide alternative paths to the current root bridge.

A backup port is a port that is self-looped back to the sending local switch. This port could be connected to the same Layer 2 segment that does not speak Spanning Tree Protocol. For example, if a switch is connected to a set of hosts through a hub, the hub echoes all received frames out all ports except the port on which the frames were originally received. For redundancy, the switch could connect to the hub through two ports. If such a situation occurs, the BPDU sent by the switch on port A connected to the hub would be echoed and received on port B, connected to the same hub. If port A is determined to have the superior BPDU, port B would have the backup role because it provides a redundant path to a LAN segment that does not lead back to the root bridge.

A port in 802.1w can be in any mixture of states and roles. For instance, a port can be in the designated discarding role/state, which means it is a port that the switch believes should be designated but has not transitioned to forwarding. This fact is important for RSTP's convergence algorithm.

In 802.1D, convergence is based on a timer-driven state machine. When a switch comes online, it sends BPDUs claiming to be root. When it receives a superior BPDU, the ports must transition from blocking, to listening, to learning, and finally to forwarding, based on the Forward Delay timer (which defaults to 15 seconds, for 30 seconds total). If a switch were to lose connection to the root port, it would announce itself as root toward its neighbors. The neighbors would ignore this information for the Max Age period (which is 20 seconds by default) before reacting to the topology change. The goal is to allow the network to converge before a port is placed into the forwarding state.

802.1w does not use the same process as 802.1D but uses a newer proposal and agreement process that goes as such:

1. A new link port on a switch tries to move from the blocking state to the forwarding state.

2. The port receives a superior BPDU from the root bridge.

3. All other non-edge ports are blocked on the local switch.

4. Once all other switch ports are blocked, the local switch authorizes the root switch to put its port into the forwarding state.

5. The same process occurs on all of the local switch's remaining non-edge ports.

In **step 1**, the new link initializes in the **designated discarding** state. It exchanges BPDUs with the current root's port (which is also in the designated discarding state). During this time, both switches send a BPDU with the proposal bit set as an indication that they want their ports to become the designated port on the segment. Upon receipt of the superior BPDU at step 2, the local switch knows where its root port lies.

In **step 3**, the switch must ensure no loops can occur in the network based on this new information. To do so, it places all of its non-edge ports into the discarding state; this is called synchronization. Throughout this process, the root switch's port is still in the designated discarding state.

At **step 4**, the local switch tells the root switch, through a BPDU with the agreement flag set, that the root switch's port can be moved to the designated forwarding state. This happens because the local switch has blocked all of its other non-edge ports, preventing any bridging loops.

At **step 5**, the local switch sends a BPDU with the proposal bit set out all of its remaining designated discarding ports to start the rapid convergence process with other potential spanning-tree bridges downstream from the root. Step 5 repeats the proposal/agreement process with each switch to which the local switch has a direct connection. The same process occurs: The switches exchange proposal BPDUs, the losing switch enters the synchronization state, and it informs the designated switch it can move its port to the designated forwarding state. In this way, the synchronization process flows downstream from the root to the edge of the network.

This process relies heavily on the switch determining which ports are edge ports and which are non-edge ports. RSTP keeps track of this by assigning an edge variable and link type status to each switch port. The edge variable indicates whether or not the port leads to an end host or sits at the edge of the network. Such ports do not connect to other switches and should not receive BPDUs. If an edge port receives a BPDU, it loses its edge status. Edge ports are allowed to immediately transition to a forwarding state; this is similar to the spanning-tree PortFast feature.

*Link type* refers to whether or not the switch port can use rapid transitions, as previously indicated. There are two link types: point-to-point and shared. A point-to-point link is connected to exactly one other RSTP-compliant switch. A shared port is connected to a shared LAN segment that utilizes hubs or repeaters and cannot transition rapidly, as in the previous proposal agreement process.

Switches attempt to detect link type by using the duplex setting of the interface: Half-duplex is considered shared, and full-duplex is considered point-to-point.

802.1w also achieves rapid convergence by modifying what constitutes a topology change in the network. In 802.1D, loss of a port or a port transitioning to blocking is considered a topology change event. In 802.1w, only a non-edge (blocking or alternate) port transitioning to the forwarding state generates a topology change event. The reason is that the new non-edge port offers a new path in the network, and the remaining switches should synchronize their MAC address tables accordingly to reflect the change. The TC-while timer is started on the switch initiating the topology change. During this time, the switch sends BPDUs with the TC flag set out all of its designated and root ports.

Switches that receive these BPDUs immediately age out all MAC addresses on all ports except where the TC BPDU was received. This mechanism allows rapid transition of the topology because TC BPDUs are originated by the switch experiencing the topology change event and are not initiated by the root bridge, as is the case in 802.1D.

Finally, because BPDUs are necessary for a blocking port to remain blocking, if a blocking port receives an inferior BPDU, it can react immediately to the information. This is in contrast to the 802.1D specification, which requires the stored BPDU on a port to age out before the switch converges the topology. In 802.1w, the switch receiving the inferior BPDU can infer that a topology change event has occurred somewhere in the network.

If a functioning root port exists on the switch receiving an inferior BPDU, it can simply respond with a proposal BPDU on its formerly blocking port, asking to be set to designated. This allows the failed switch to recover rapidly. If there is no functioning root port (meaning the inferior BPDU was received on a root port), the switch can assume that it should be the new root switch and indicates that with all of its remaining, now downstream, neighbors.

These are the key enhancements to 802.1D built into 802.1w. Some of them may sound familiar as they relate to many of the Cisco enhancement features to 802.1D, such as PortFast and Backbone Fast. The following lab demonstrates these enhancement features of 802.1w and contrasts them with their 802.1D equivalents.

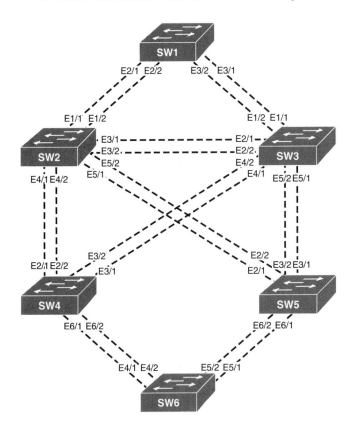

## This lab should be conducted on the Mock Rack.

# Initial Configuration:

## Task 1

Change the hostname on each switch to SW#, where # is the number of the switch (for example, Switch 1 = SW1).

## Task 2

Ensure that only the following ports on the switches are in an up/up state:

- SW1
  - E2/1-2
  - E3/1-2
- SW2
  - E1/1-2
  - E3/1-2
  - E4/1-2
  - E5/1-2
- SW3
  - E1/1-2
  - E2/1-2
  - E4/1-2
  - E5/1-2
- SW4
  - E2/1-2
  - E3/1-2
  - E6/1-2
- SW5
  - E2/1-2
  - E3/1-2
  - E6/1-2
- SW6
  - E4/1-2
  - E5/1-2

### Task 3

Configure VLANs 10, 20, 30, and 40 on each switch, using any method.

### Task 4

Configure trunk ports on all up/up interfaces.

## 802.1w Configuration Tasks

### Task 1

Configure all switches to run 802.1w Rapid Spanning Tree Protocol.

### Task 2

Ensure that SW1 is the root for all VLANs.

### Task 3

Ensure that if the current root bridge fails, SW2 becomes the new root for all VLANs.

### Task 4

Ensure that SW2's and SW3's E1/2 interface is used as the root port for all VLANs. Do not modify cost to achieve this.

### Task 5

Ensure that SW5 uses the following ports as root:

- E2/1 for VLAN 10
- E2/2 for VLAN 20
- E3/1 for VLAN 30
- E3/2 for VLAN 40

Do not modify SW5 to achieve any of this.

### Task 6

Ensure that SW4 uses its E3/1 port as the root port for VLAN 20.

### Task 7

Ensure that RSTP features are enabled on all ports.

## Task 8

Ensure that interfaces connected to non-switch hosts come online immediately.

**a.** If SW4 or SW5 detects a switch on these ports when it first comes online, it should process the BPDUs normally. Otherwise, it should not process received BPDUs.

**b.** If SW6 detects a switch on one of these ports, it should disable the port.

## Task 9

**a.** Ensure that SW6's links toward SW5 are used as the root port for all VLANs except VLAN 10. If the link between SW5 and SW6 goes down, SW6 should immediately switch to using one of its links toward SW4 as the single root port.

## Task 10

Ensure that SW4 and SW5 can recover from an indirect link failure within 10 seconds. Do not modify the spanning-tree timers.

One of the major drawbacks of 802.1D spanning tree was the timer-based convergence mechanisms. If a designated bridge loses its connection to the root, it will begin advertising itself as the root bridge to all of its connected ports. A downstream port in the blocking state would receive these inferior BPDUs. In 802.1D, the blocking port would completely ignore the information until the stored BPDU from the real root on that blocking port expires (in 20 seconds, based on the default Max Age timer). Then the switch signals a topology change event, and the port transitions to the forwarding state. The entire process can take up to 50 seconds with default timers.

The Cisco Backbone Fast feature was created to help this process by utilizing the RLQ protocol when a blocking port suddenly starts receiving inferior BPDUs. The RLQ messages are sent out in order to determine if a path to the root exists on the switch. If a path is found, the previously blocked port can bypass the Max Age timer and begin the transition to the forwarding state, cutting 20 seconds of convergence time.

RSTP incorporates this function through its behavior of immediately accepting inferior BPDUs that are received on a discarding port. An inferior BPDU being received on a discarding port signifies that a topology change has occurred somewhere in the network. Either the current root has failed and the local switch has stale information or the upstream designated bridge has lost its connection to the root. In either case, the spanning-tree topology needs to reconverge and can do so rapidly by using the proposal/agreement processes.

Since this feature is built into RSTP, there is no configuration needed to accomplish this task.

> **Note**   Do not forget to reset the switch configurations to initial configurations upon completing this exercise.

## 802.1s Multiple Spanning Tree Protocol

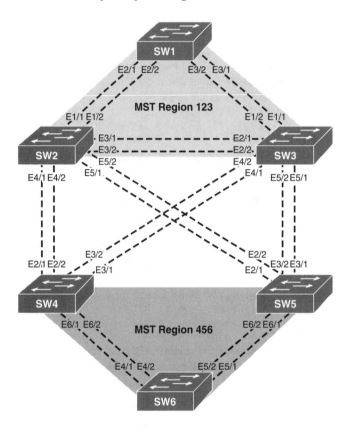

## This lab should be conducted on the Mock Rack.

## Initial Configuration:

### Task 1

Change the hostname on each switch to SW#, where # is the number of the switch (for example, Switch 1 = SW1).

## Task 2

Ensure that only the following ports on the switches are in an up/up state:

- SW1
  - E2/1-2
  - E3/1-2
- SW2
  - E1/1-2
  - E3/1-2
  - E4/1-2
  - E5/1-2
- SW3
  - E1/1-2
  - E2/1-2
  - E4/1-2
  - E5/1-2
- SW4
  - E2/1-2
  - E3/1-2
  - E6/1-2
- SW5
  - E2/1-2
  - E3/1-2
  - E6/1-2
- SW6
  - E4/1-2
  - E5/1-2

## Task 3

Configure VLANs 10, 20, 30, and 40 on each switch, using any method.

## Task 4

Configure trunk ports on all up/up interfaces.

# Let's Explore 802.1s

One of the major drawbacks to spanning tree, be it the 802.1D Spanning Tree Protocol or RSTP, is the fact that redundant links are blocked in the network, making their bandwidth useless unless a failover event occurs. Cisco alleviated this impact by implementing PVST/+ and PVRST/+, which allow administrators to load balance individual VLANs on trunk links to better utilize the bandwidth.

The issue with this approach is that the switch must calculate a separate spanning tree for each VLAN independently. As the total number of VLANs grows, the switch spends more processor cycles calculating the spanning-tree topology. This is inefficient as the total number of possible spanning-tree topologies is limited by the total number of switches and links in the network. If there are only three switches in the network, then there are effectively only three total topologies that can exist: one topology with each switch as the root of the spanning tree. If there are a total of four VLANs in the same sample network, it is reasonable to say that the fourth VLAN spanning-tree calculation yields a redundant result to one of the previous three.

The IEEE 802.1s Multiple Spanning Tree Protocol (MST) standard mitigates this by providing a standards-based way to run different instances of Spanning Tree Protocol on a single switch. Instead of running a single instance for each VLAN, the administrator can define the instances of Spanning Tree Protocol that will be run and their parameters, such as priority and costs. Multiple VLANs are mapped to the configured instances, allowing one instance to represent one or many VLANs.

With this construct, an administrator can group together VLANs with similar pathing requirements in a single instance rather than tuning individual VLAN-specific spanning-tree instance settings. It is even possible to map all VLANs to a single instance and reduce spanning-tree processing overhead for all VLANs. Doing this reduces the computational load on the switches in the network.

The most noticeable way a switch saves computational cycles is through MST's use of a single BPDU for all instances. Instead of explicitly sending a BPDU for each VLAN or each instance containing VLAN-to-instance mapping information, MST exchanges a single BPDU. This BPDU contains information about the root bridge and special M-records. These M-records carry the spanning-tree topology information for all instances configured on the switch.

A switch running MST must be explicitly configured with the VLAN-to-instance mapping in its MST configuration. The MST configuration first gives the MST process a name. This process name is similar to the EIGRP autonomous system number. Then, the process is explicitly given a revision number. Finally, the VLAN-to-instance mapping is configured.

**Note**    Unlike with EIGRP, there can be only one MST process running multiple instances at a time on a switch. Cisco documentation calls the MST process an *MST instance*, but for clarity between MST instances that have VLANs mapped to them, the term *process* is used in this lab.

In order to operate, an MST network needs to be configured with the instances that exist in the network and what VLANs are mapped to those instances. If, for example, instance 1 on SWA contains VLAN 1 but instance 10 on SWB contains VLAN 1, SWA and SWB could come to different conclusions about whether or not the port is forwarding or blocking for both VLANs. However, because no explicit VLAN-to-Instance mapping information is carried between switches, there is no way for two switches to know whether or not they are configured similarly for MST operation.

MST validates VLAN-to-instance mapping consistency between two bridges by including the MST process, the revision number, and a digest of the MST VLAN-to-instance mapping table in the BPDU. If the received BPDU matches a switch's internal configuration, the switch knows it can trust the information contained in the M-records of the BPDU. The set of switches in a network that all have matching MST process names, revision numbers, and VLAN-to-instance mapping tables is called an *MST region*. Multiple MST regions can exist in a network. Topology changes in one region do not affect other regions. Also, each region builds an internal spanning tree separately as well as cooperatively (between neighboring regions) with other regions to form one loop-free path throughout the entire switched network.

Within a region, there always exists MST instance 0, which is called IST0. This instance is the only instance that interacts with other regions and is the instance to which all VLANs are initially mapped when MST is first enabled on a switch. IST0 elects a root bridge called the *IST0 root*. A non-root switch calculates a loop-free path from itself to the IST0 root. This ensures that no matter how many instances are added or VLANs are moved around, there is always at least one loop-free path in the MST topology.

Switches exchange IST0 BPDUs that contain the M-records for all other instances in the MST region. Using these records, independent spanning-tree topologies can be calculated for each instance.

IST0 and M-records help create a loop-free path within an MST region. MST uses a separate process to help negotiate a loop-free path between different MST regions. Switches that connect to neighboring switches in different regions are called *MST boundary switches*. The specific port that the local switch shares with the remote neighboring switch in a different region is called the *boundary port*. On boundary ports, MST only exchanges IST0 BPDU information. This makes sense because IST0 always exists within the MST region and is guaranteed to be loop free at all times. The receiving switch compares the IST0 bridge information to determine if it is superior or inferior to its own IST0 BPDU. This spanning tree running between regions is called the common spanning tree, or CST.

It helps at this point to consider two MST regions as single switches. Because the boundary switches hide the internal M-record topology from switches in different MST regions, the topology becomes very simple from the receiving switch's perspective. Because the receiving switch cannot ensure that VLANs are mapped to the same instances as its own, the receiving switch must make a blocking/forwarding decision on its boundary port for all VLANs. This is the only way to ensure a loop-free path to the remote MST region. The MST boundary switches only compare the IST0 information received from other MST boundary switches. The boundary switches analyze this information and make forwarding or discarding decisions for all VLANs on the boundary ports.

MST interacts with regular 802.1D spanning-tree regions in a similar way. A boundary switch compares a received BPDU with its own IST0 BPDU to make a forwarding or discarding decision for all VLANs on the boundary port. This process ensures that redundant inter-region links are blocked between regions and not internally within a specific region—in the same way a switch blocks ports between switches and not links within the switch itself.

MST interacts with PVST regions a bit differently. This interaction is explained further later on in this solution guide.

## Task 1

Configure all the switches to utilize the following spanning-tree configuration for SW1, SW2, and SW3:

- MST is the operational mode.
- The region name is 123.
- The revision number is 1.
- Configure the following instance-to-VLAN mappings:
  - Instance 1: VLANs 10–19
  - Instance 2: VLANs 20–29
  - Instance 3: VLANs 30–39
  - Instance 4: VLANs 40–49

## Task 2

Configure all the switches to utilize the following spanning-tree configuration for SW4, SW5, and SW6:

- MST is the operational mode.
- The region name is 456.
- The revision number is 1.

- Configure the following instance-to-VLAN mappings:

  - Instance 1: VLAN 10

  - Instance 2: VLAN 20

  - Instance 3: VLAN 30

  - Instance 4: VLAN 40

## Task 3

Ensure that SW1 is the root for the entire topology.

## Task 4

Configure Region 123 as follows:

- SW1 should be the IST root for Instances 1 and 4.

- SW2 should be the IST root for Instance 2.

- SW3 should be the IST root for Instance 3.

Configure Region 456 as follows:

- SW6 should be the IST root for all instances except Instance 0.

- SW5 should be the regional root.

# Chapter 2

# IP Prefix Lists

## Lab 1: Prefix Lists

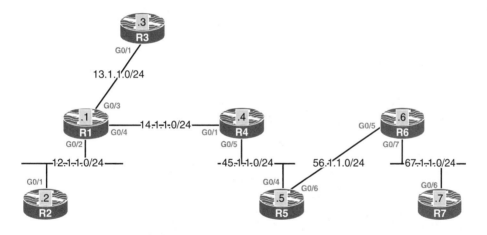

<u>This lab should be conducted on the Enterprise POD.</u>

<u>Lab Setup:</u>

If you are using EVE-NG, and you have imported the EVE-NG topology from the **EVE-NG-Topology** folder, ignore the following tasks and use "**Lab 1-Prefix-Lists**" from the "**IP Prefix-lists**" folder in EVE-NG.

To copy and paste the initial configurations, go to the **Initial-config** folder → IP-Prefix-list folder → **Lab-1**.

## Task 1

Configure R1 to filter 192.1.1.32/27 (an OSPF process ID 1 route) using a prefix list through its G0/2 interface.

## Task 2

Configure R1 such that it only permits class A networks that are not subnetted and filter the rest of the prefixes/networks. These are RIPv2 routes advertised by R3.

## Task 3

Configure R4 such that it only allows class B networks that are not subnetted. These are OSPF routes advertised by R1.

## Task 4

Configure R5 such that it only allows class C networks that are not subnetted. These are EIGRP routes that are advertised by R4.

## Task 5

Configure R4 such that it denies networks 10.4.4.33/27 and 10.4.5.65/26 and allows the rest of the networks. You should configure a minimum number of lines in the prefix list to accomplish this task. These are the RIPv2 routes advertised by R5.

## Task 6

Configure R5 to inject a default route in the RIP routing domain. If this configuration is successful, R4 should see the default route in its routing table.

## Task 7

R4 should be configured to filter the default route injected in the previous task.

## Task 8

Configure R6 to filter any networks with a prefix length of 26 or less. These are OSPF routes advertised by R5.

## Task 9

Reconfigure R6 to filter any networks with a prefix length of 26 or greater. These are OSPF routes received from R5.

## Task 10

Configure R7 to filter the following networks:

- 146.1.2.129/25

- 146.1.3.193/26

- 146.1.4.225/27

- 6.1.4.225/27

- 6.1.5.241/28

You should configure only three prefix list statements. These are EIGRP routes advertised by R6.

## Task 11

Erase the startup configuration and reload the routers before proceeding to the next lab.

# Chapter 3

# RIPv2

## Lab 1: Configuring RIPv2

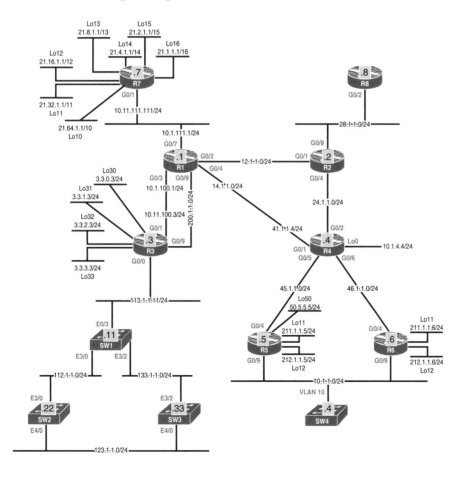

<u>This lab should be conducted on the Enterprise POD.</u>

<u>Lab Setup:</u>

If you are using EVE-NG, and you have imported the EVE-NG topology from the **EVE-NG-Topology** folder, ignore the following tasks and use **Lab 1-Configuring RIPv2** in the **RIPv2** folder in EVE-NG.

To copy and paste the initial configurations, go to the **Initial-config** folder → **RIPv2** folder → **Lab-1**.

## Task 1

Configure RIPv2 on all routers and switches. Advertise their directly connected interfaces in this routing domain. These devices *should not* have a classful nature. If this configuration is successful, the routers and switches should successfully exchange routes.

Use the following policy when configuring this task:

1. R7 and R1 *must* use two static routes for reachability.

2. R1 and R4 *must not* use a static route(s). R1 *cannot* use any solution that's used in the previous policy or the next ones to provide reachability. You are allowed to disable the sanity check.

3. You *cannot* use PBR to resolve any of the policies in this task.

4. The IP addresses configured on all the devices in the topology are correct.

## Task 2

1. Configure R4 such that it sends RIPv2 updates out of its G0/3 interface to a broadcast destination.

   a. Do not change RIP's version.

2. Ensure that R1 is configured to send unicast updates to its neighboring router R7.

## Task 3

Configure the following loopback interfaces on R3. Starting with network 30.3.0.0/24, this router should *only* advertise every other third octet network (for example, x.x.0.x, x.x.2.x, x.x.4.x). These are networks 30.3.0.0, 30.3.2.0, 30.3.4.0, 30.3.6.0, 30.3.8.0, and 30.3.10.0/24.

| | |
|---|---|
| int lo0 = 30.3.0.1 /24 | int lo6 = 30.3.6.1 /24 |
| int lo1 = 30.3.1.1 /24 | int lo7 = 30.3.7.1 /24 |
| int lo2 = 30.3.2.1 /24 | int lo8 = 30.3.8.1 /24 |
| int lo3 = 30.3.3.1 /24 | int lo9 = 30.3.9.1 /24 |
| int lo4 = 30.3.4.1 /24 | int lo10 = 30.3.10.1 /24 |
| int lo5 = 30.3.5.1 /24 | |

## Lab Setup:

If you are using EVE-NG, and you have imported the EVE-NG topology from the **EVE-NG-Topology** folder, ignore the following tasks.

To copy and paste the initial configurations, go to the **Initial-config** folder → **RIPv2** folder → **Lab-1-Task3**.

## Task 4

Configure the following loopback interfaces on R6. Starting with network 60.6.0.0/24, this router should *only* advertise every eighth third octet subnet (for example, x.x.0.x, x.x.8.x, x.x.16.x).

| | |
|---|---|
| int lo0 = 60.6.0.1 /24 | int lo6 = 60.6.6.1 /24 |
| int lo1 = 60.6.1.1 /24 | int lo7 = 60.6.7.1 /24 |
| int lo2 = 60.6.2.1 /24 | int lo8 = 60.6.8.1 /24 |
| int lo3 = 60.6.3.1 /24 | int lo9 = 60.6.9.1 /24 |
| int lo4 = 60.6.4.1 /24 | int lo10 = 60.6.10.1 /24 |
| int lo5 = 60.6.5.1 /24 | |

## Lab Setup:

If you are using EVE-NG, and you have imported the EVE-NG topology from the **EVE-NG-Topology** folder, ignore the following tasks.

To copy and paste the initial configurations, go to the **Initial-config** folder → **RIPv2** folder → **Lab-1-Task4**.

## Task 5

Configure the following loopback interfaces on R4. This router should be configured such that it *only* advertises the even-numbered hosts of the odd third octet networks of these loopback interfaces plus all other networks (for example, x.x.1.x, x.x.3.x, x.x.5.x).

## Lab Setup:

If you are using EVE-NG, and you have imported the EVE-NG topology from the **EVE-NG-Topology** folder, ignore the following tasks.

To copy and paste the initial configurations, go to the **Initial-config** folder → **RIPv2** folder → **Lab-1-Task5**.

| **int lo1** | **int lo6** |
|---|---|
| ip addr 40.4.1.1 255.255.255.0 | ip addr 40.4.6.1 255.255.255.0 |
| ip addr 40.4.1.2 255.255.255.255 sec | ip addr 40.4.6.2 255.255.255.255 sec |
| ip addr 40.4.1.3 255.255.255.255 sec | ip addr 40.4.6.3 255.255.255.255 sec |
| ip addr 40.4.1.4 255.255.255.255 sec | ip addr 40.4.6.4 255.255.255.255 sec |
| ip addr 40.4.1.5 255.255.255.255 sec | ip addr 40.4.6.5 255.255.255.255 sec |
| ip addr 40.4.1.6 255.255.255.255 sec | ip addr 40.4.6.6 255.255.255.255 sec |
| ip addr 40.4.1.7 255.255.255.255 sec | ip addr 40.4.6.7 255.255.255.255 sec |
| ip addr 40.4.1.8 255.255.255.255 sec | ip addr 40.4.6.8 255.255.255.255 sec |
| ip addr 40.4.1.9 255.255.255.255 sec | ip addr 40.4.6.9 255.255.255.255 sec |
| ip addr 40.4.1.10 255.255.255.255 sec | ip addr 40.4.6.10 255.255.255.255 sec |
| **int lo2** | **int lo7** |
| ip addr 40.4.2.1 255.255.255.0 | ip addr 40.4.7.1 255.255.255.0 |
| ip addr 40.4.2.2 255.255.255.255 sec | ip addr 40.4.7.2 255.255.255.255 sec |
| ip addr 40.4.2.3 255.255.255.255 sec | ip addr 40.4.7.3 255.255.255.255 sec |
| ip addr 40.4.2.4 255.255.255.255 sec | ip addr 40.4.7.4 255.255.255.255 sec |
| ip addr 40.4.2.5 255.255.255.255 sec | ip addr 40.4.7.5 255.255.255.255 sec |
| ip addr 40.4.2.6 255.255.255.255 sec | ip addr 40.4.7.6 255.255.255.255 sec |
| ip addr 40.4.2.7 255.255.255.255 sec | ip addr 40.4.7.7 255.255.255.255 sec |
| ip addr 40.4.2.8 255.255.255.255 sec | ip addr 40.4.7.8 255.255.255.255 sec |
| ip addr 40.4.2.9 255.255.255.255 sec | ip addr 40.4.7.9 255.255.255.255 sec |
| ip addr 40.4.2.10 255.255.255.255 sec | ip addr 40.4.7.10 255.255.255.255 sec |

| **int lo3** | **int lo8** |
|---|---|
| ip addr 40.4.3.1 255.255.255.0 | ip addr 40.4.8.1 255.255.255.0 |
| ip addr 40.4.3.2 255.255.255.255 sec | ip addr 40.4.8.2 255.255.255.255 sec |
| ip addr 40.4.3.3 255.255.255.255 sec | ip addr 40.4.8.3 255.255.255.255 sec |
| ip addr 40.4.3.4 255.255.255.255 sec | ip addr 40.4.8.4 255.255.255.255 sec |
| ip addr 40.4.3.5 255.255.255.255 sec | ip addr 40.4.8.5 255.255.255.255 sec |
| ip addr 40.4.3.6 255.255.255.255 sec | ip addr 40.4.8.6 255.255.255.255 sec |
| ip addr 40.4.3.7 255.255.255.255 sec | ip addr 40.4.8.7 255.255.255.255 sec |
| ip addr 40.4.3.8 255.255.255.255 sec | ip addr 40.4.8.8 255.255.255.255 sec |
| ip addr 40.4.3.9 255.255.255.255 sec | ip addr 40.4.8.9 255.255.255.255 sec |
| ip addr 40.4.3.10 255.255.255.255 sec | ip addr 40.4.8.10 255.255.255.255 sec |

| **int lo4** | **int lo9** |
|---|---|
| ip addr 40.4.4.1 255.255.255.0 | ip addr 40.4.9.1 255.255.255.0 |
| ip addr 40.4.4.2 255.255.255.255 sec | ip addr 40.4.9.2 255.255.255.255 sec |
| ip addr 40.4.4.3 255.255.255.255 sec | ip addr 40.4.9.3 255.255.255.255 sec |
| ip addr 40.4.4.4 255.255.255.255 sec | ip addr 40.4.9.4 255.255.255.255 sec |
| ip addr 40.4.4.5 255.255.255.255 sec | ip addr 40.4.9.5 255.255.255.255 sec |
| ip addr 40.4.4.6 255.255.255.255 sec | ip addr 40.4.9.6 255.255.255.255 sec |
| ip addr 40.4.4.7 255.255.255.255 sec | ip addr 40.4.9.7 255.255.255.255 sec |
| ip addr 40.4.4.8 255.255.255.255 sec | ip addr 40.4.9.8 255.255.255.255 sec |
| ip addr 40.4.4.9 255.255.255.255 sec | ip addr 40.4.9.9 255.255.255.255 sec |
| ip addr 40.4.4.10 255.255.255.255 sec | ip addr 40.4.9.10 255.255.255.255 sec |

| int lo5 | int lo10 |
|---|---|
| ip addr 40.4.5.1 255.255.255.0 | ip addr 40.4.10.1 255.255.255.0 |
| ip addr 40.4.5.2 255.255.255.255 sec | ip addr 40.4.10.2 255.255.255.255 sec |
| ip addr 40.4.5.3 255.255.255.255 sec | ip addr 40.4.10.3 255.255.255.255 sec |
| ip addr 40.4.5.4 255.255.255.255 sec | ip addr 40.4.10.4 255.255.255.255 sec |
| ip addr 40.4.5.5 255.255.255.255 sec | ip addr 40.4.10.5 255.255.255.255 sec |
| ip addr 40.4.5.6 255.255.255.255 sec | ip addr 40.4.10.6 255.255.255.255 sec |
| ip addr 40.4.5.7 255.255.255.255 sec | ip addr 40.4.10.7 255.255.255.255 sec |
| ip addr 40.4.5.8 255.255.255.255 sec | ip addr 40.4.10.8 255.255.255.255 sec |
| ip addr 40.4.5.9 255.255.255.255 sec | ip addr 40.4.10.9 255.255.255.255 sec |
| ip addr 40.4.5.10 255.255.255.255 sec | ip addr 40.4.10.10 255.255.255.255 sec |

## Task 6

Configure the routers and switches in this routing domain based on the following timers:

- Periodic updates are sent every 30 seconds.
- Routers and switches should declare a route invalid after 1.5 minutes.
- Routers and switches should suppress routing information regarding a better path for 1.5 minutes.
- Routers and switches should flush routes 30 seconds after they are invalid.
- Routers and switches should postpone their periodic updates by 100 milliseconds.

## Task 7

Since R1 is a very fast router, configure it such that it adds an inter-packet delay of 50 milliseconds between the updates.

## Task 8

Configure R2 to set the number of received but _not_ yet processed RIP update packets in the RIP input queue to 100.

## Task 9

Configure all routers to suppress a flash update when a topology change occurs 10 seconds before a regular update.

## Task 10

Configure R1 and R2 to authenticate their routing updates through their direct connection. Configure these two routers to use the unencrypted key **ccie** for this purpose.

## Task 11

Configure R5, R6, and SW4 to use authentication with the strongest authentication method available to RIPv2. These routers should use Micronic? as their password.

## Task 12

Configure R1 to accept existing and future routes that have a prefix length of 10 to 14. These routes should be received from R7 _only_. _Do not_ use an access list(s) or a **neighbor** command to accomplish this task.

## Task 13

Configure R7 to inject a default route.

## Task 14

Configure R4 to filter the default route injected by R7.

## Task 15

Configure SW4 such that it always prefers to reach network 10.1.4.0/24 through R6.

1. SW4 should use R5 when R6 is down.

2. Restrictions: _Do not_ use an offset list to accomplish this task.

## Task 16

Configure SW4 to filter network 50.5.5.0/24. _Do not_ use an access list to accomplish this task.

### Task 17

Configure R4 such that it injects a default route into the RIPv2 routing domain.

1. Restrictions:

    a. This default route should _not_ be given to R6.

    b. _Do not_ configure R6 to accomplish this task. R5 should _only_ have a default route from R4.

### Task 18

Configure R3 to summarize its Loopback Lo0–Lo3, Lo30–Lo33 and advertise two summary routes into the RIP routing domain.

### Task 19

Configure Lo200 with the IP address 120.2.2.2/24 on SW2. This switch should advertise this network in the RIPv2 routing domain. Configure SW1 such that this network is never advertised to any router downstream/beyond SW4, as those are future devices connected to SW4.

### Task 20

Erase the startup configuration of the routers, the startup configuration, and the VLAN. dat file for each switch and reload the devices before proceeding to the next lab.

## Lab 2: Helper Map

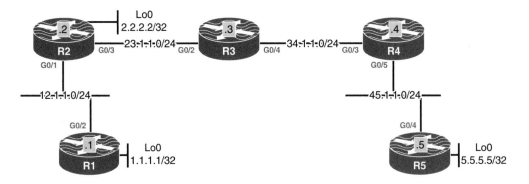

## This lab should be conducted on the Enterprise POD.

## Lab Setup:

If you are using EVE-NG, and you have imported the EVE-NG topology from the **EVE-NG-Topology** folder, ignore the following tasks and use **Lab 2-Helper-map** in the **RIPv2** folder in EVE-NG.

To copy and paste the initial configurations, go to the **Initial-config** folder → **RIPv2** folder → **Lab-2**.

## Task 1

Configure OSPF Area 0 on the following interfaces:

- The G0/1, G0/3, and loopback0 interfaces of R2
- All directly connected interfaces of R3
- The G0/3 interface of R4

## Task 2

Configure RIPv2 on the:

- Lo0 and G0/2 interfaces of R1
- G0/4 interface on R5

Disable auto-summarization on these devices.

## Task 3

Configure multicasting on the appropriate routers such that R5 receives all the RIPv2 updates from R1.

- R2 should be configured as the RP and the BSR router. This router should use its loopback interface as the source of all its BSR messages.
- You must use 224.1.1.1 to accomplish this task.
- Restrictions:
  - **a.** *Do not* run multiple unicast routing protocols on any of the routers.
  - **b.** *Do not* configure GRE, IPnIP, MPLS, LDP, or any type of tunneling to accomplish this task.

## Task 4

Erase the startup configuration and reload the routers before proceeding to the next lab.

## Lab 3: RIPv2 Challenge Lab

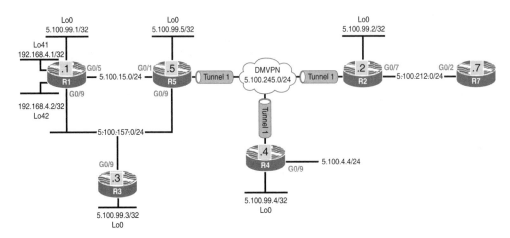

## This lab should be conducted on the Enterprise POD.

## Lab Setup:

If you are using EVE-NG, and you have imported the EVE-NG topology from the **EVE-NG-Topology** folder, ignore the following tickets and use **Lab 3-RIPv2 Challenge Lab** in the **RIPv2** folder in EVE-NG.

To copy and paste the initial configurations, go to the **Initial-config** folder → **RIPv2** folder → **Lab-3**.

### Ticket 1

R1 is configured to filter its Lo41. However, this interface is still reachable from R5.

- ▣ Restrictions:

    **a.** *Do not* configure another access list, prefix list, or route map.

    **b.** Use only two commands to accomplish this task.

### Ticket 2

R7 is configured to filter all even third octet networks (for example, x.x.2.x, x.x.4.x, x.x.6.x) with the mask /24. However, this has affected all routes, and none of them are reachable from R2.

## Ticket 3

R4 can't reach R1's Lo42 using its Lo0 as the source:

■ Use a single command to fix this problem.

## Ticket 4

R2 is configured to filter its G0/7 interface with the IP address 5.100.212.2/24, but R5 can't reach R2's Lo0.

## Ticket 5

R4 can't reach R2's Lo0 interface.

■ Restrictions:

   **a.** *Do not* configure the **neighbor** command.

   **b.** *Do not* change the DMVPN phase or configure DMVPN in a dynamic manner.

## Ticket 6

R3 can't ping R1's Lo0.

## Ticket 7

R3 is configured to filter all routes received from R5. However, the routes are still there. *Do not* use another method to fix this problem; correct the existing problem.

## Ticket 8

R7 should *not* have any RIPv2 routes in its routing table. You *must* configure an outbound filter using a standard numbered ACL and a **distribute-list** command on the G0/7 interface of R2 to accomplish this task. You are allowed to remove one command.

## Ticket 9

Erase the startup configuration and reload the devices before proceeding to the next lab.

# Chapter 4

# EIGRP

## Lab 1: EIGRP Named Mode

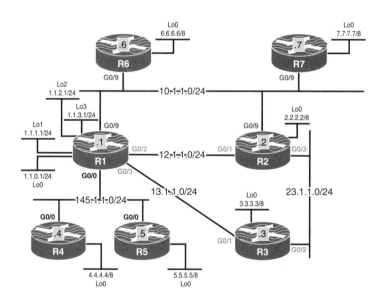

This lab should be conducted on the Enterprise POD.

## Lab Setup:

If you are using EVE-NG, and you have imported the EVE-NG topology from the **EVE-NG-Topology** folder, ignore the following tasks and use **Lab 1-EIGRP Named Mode** in the **EIGRP** folder in EVE-NG.

To copy and paste the initial configurations, go to the **Initial-config** folder → **EIGRP** folder → **Lab-1**.

## Task 1

Configure EIGRP on R1, R2, and R3 based on the following policy:

| Router | Interface | AS Number |
|--------|-----------|-----------|
| R1 | G0/9 | 200 |
|    | G0/0 | 100 |
|    | G0/2 | 100 |
|    | G0/3 | 100 |
|    | Loopback0–Loopback3 | 100 |
| R2 | G0/9 | 200 |
|    | G0/1 | 100 |
|    | G0/3 | 100 |
|    | Loopback0 | 100 |
| R3 | G0/1 | 100 |
|    | G0/2 | 100 |
|    | Loopback0 | 100 |

- R1 should be configured to use unicast to establish an EIGRP neighbor adjacency with R2.

- R1 should use multicast to establish an EIGRP neighbor adjacency with R3.

- R1, R2, and R3 should use an EIGRP named mode configuration to accomplish this task.

## Task 2

Configure R4 and R5 in EIGRP AS 100. You must use named mode to accomplish this task.

## Task 3

Configure R1, R4, and R5 to use unicast to establish their EIGRP neighbor adjacency.

## Task 4

Configure R6 in EIGRP AS 200. This router should run EIGRP AS 200 on its G0/9 and Loopback0 interfaces. You should use an EIGRP named mode configuration to accomplish this task.

## Task 5

Configure OSPF Area 0 on R6's G0/9 and R7's G0/9 and Loopback0 interfaces. The router ID of these routers should be configured as 0.0.0.$x$, where $x$ is the router number.

## Task 6

Configure R6 to redistribute OSPF into EIGRP such that R1 and R2 go directly to R7 to reach the 7.0.0.0/8 network.

## Task 7

Configure the hello interval of all routers in AS 200 to be twice the default hello interval.

## Task 8

Configure R4 such that in the worst-case scenario, it uses 10% of the bandwidth for its EIGRP updates. This policy should apply to the existing and future interfaces.

## Task 9

Configure R1 to summarize its loopback interfaces and advertise a single summary in the EIGRP AS 100 routing domain.

## Task 10

Configure R1 to limit the number of received prefixes from R5 to 10. R1 should be configured to receive a warning message once 50% of this threshold is reached and a warning message for every additional route that exceeds the threshold. You should configure Lo1–Lo10 on R5 by copying and pasting the initial configuration, called **EIGRP-Lab-1-Task10**.

## Task 11

Configure R1 to limit the number of prefixes received from R4 to five. R1 should be configured to tear down the adjacency if R4 exceeds the specified threshold. Copy and paste the **EIGRP-Lab-1-Task11** initial configuration on R4.

### Task 12

Erase the startup configuration and reload the routers before proceeding to the next lab.

## Lab 2: EIGRP and Bidirectional Forwarding Detection (BFD)

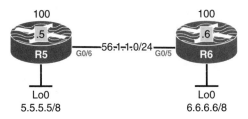

### Task 1

Configure the routers based on the previous diagram. _Do not_ configure any routing protocol.

### Task 2

Configure EIGRP AS 100 on all directly connected interfaces of these two routers and ensure reachability. R5 should be configured using EIGRP classical mode, and R6 should use the EIGRP named mode configuration style.

### Task 3

Configure and test BFD on these two routers.

### Task 4

Erase the startup configuration of these two routers and reload the devices before proceeding to the next lab.

# Lab 3: EIGRP Stub

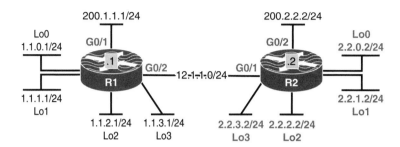

## Lab Setup:

If you are using EVE-NG, and you have imported the EVE-NG topology from the **EVE-NG-Topology** folder, ignore the following tasks and use **Lab 3-EIGRP Stub** in the **EIGRP** folder in EVE-NG.

To copy and paste the initial configurations, go to the **Initial-config** folder → **EIGRP** folder → **Lab-3**.

## Task 1

Configure EIGRP AS 100 on the G0/2 and G0/1 interfaces of R1 and R2, respectively, as well as on all loopback interfaces of these two routers. On R1 configure EIGRP using the classic mode, and on R2 configure EIGRP in named mode to accomplish this task. _Do not_ run EIGRP on the G0/1 interface of R1 or the G0/2 interface of R2.

## Task 2

Configure R1 and R2 to summarize their loopback interfaces in EIGRP.

## Task 3

Configure the following static routes on R1 and R2 and redistribute them into EIGRP:

- On R1: 11.0.0.0/8 via G0/1
- On R2: 22.0.0.0/8 via G0/2

## Task 4

Advertise the G0/1 interface of R1 and the G0/2 interface of R2 into RIPv2 and disable auto-summarization. You should redistribute RIPv2 into EIGRP and use any metric for the redistributed routes.

## Task 5

Configure EIGRP stub routing on R1 by using the command **eigrp stub connected.** Test this option and verify the routes in the routing tables of both routers.

## Task 6

Remove the **eigrp stub connected** option configured in the previous task and reconfigure EIGRP stub routing on R1 by using the **eigrp stub summary** command. Test this option and verify the routes in the routing tables of both routers.

## Task 7

Remove the **eigrp stub summary** option configured in the previous task and reconfigure EIGRP stub routing on R1 by using the command **eigrp stub static.** Test this option and verify the routes in the routing tables of both routers.

## Task 8

Remove the **eigrp stub static** option configured in the previous task and reconfigure EIGRP stub routing on R1 by using the command **eigrp stub redistributed.** Test this option and verify the routes in the routing tables of both routers.

## Task 9

Remove the **eigrp stub redistributed** option configured in the previous task and reconfigure EIGRP stub routing on R1 by using the command **eigrp stub receive-only.** Test this option and verify the routes in the routing tables of both routers.

## Task 10

Remove the **eigrp stub receive-only** option configured in the previous task and recon-figure EIGRP stub routing on R1 by using the command **eigrp stub**. Test this option and verify the routes in the routing tables of both routers.

## Task 11

Erase the startup configuration and reload the routers before proceeding to the next lab.

# Lab 4: EIGRP Filtering

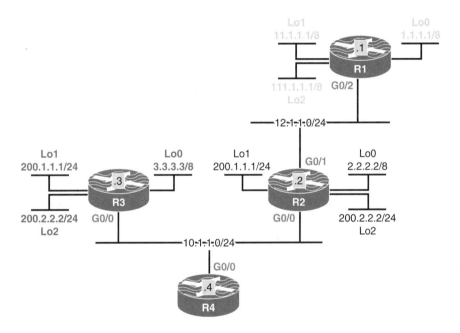

## Lab Setup:

If you are using EVE-NG, and you have imported the EVE-NG topology from the **EVE-NG-Topology** folder, ignore the following tasks and use **Lab 4-EIGRP Filtering** in the **EIGRP** folder in EVE-NG.

To copy and paste the initial configurations, go to the **Initial-config** folder → **EIGRP** folder → **Lab-4**.

## Task 1

Configure EIGRP 100 on all routers and advertise their directly connected links into EIGRP.

## Task 2

Configure R4 such that it filters existing (1.0.0.0/8, 11.0.0.0/8, and 111.0.0.0/8) and future networks behind R1. _Do not_ use **distribute-list**, **access-list**, **prefix-list**, or **route-map** to accomplish this task.

## Task 3

Configure R4 such that it uses R2 as its only connection to network 200.1.1.0 /24. You should use an access list to accomplish this task.

## Task 4

Configure R4 such that it takes R3 to reach network 200.2.2.0 /24. R4 should _only_ use R2 as the next hop to reach network 200.2.2.0/24 when R3 is down. You should use a standard access list to accomplish this task.

## Task 5

Filter network 2.0.0.0/8 on R4. _Do not_ use **distribute-list** or **route-map** to accomplish this task.

## Task 6

Configure R4 to filter network 3.0.0.0/8.

## Task 7

Erase the startup configuration and reload the routers before proceeding to the next task.

# Lab 5: Advanced EIGRP Lab

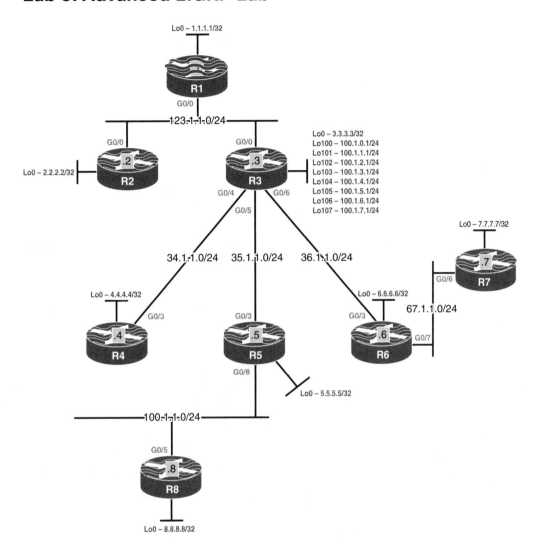

## Lab Setup:

If you are using EVE-NG, and you have imported the EVE-NG topology from the **EVE-NG-Topology** folder, ignore the following tasks and use **Lab 5-Advanced EIGRP Lab** in the **EIGRP** folder in EVE-NG.

To copy and paste the initial configurations, go to the **Initial-config** folder → **EIGRP** folder → **Lab-5**.

## Task 1

Configure the G0/0 interfaces of R1, R2, and R3 in EIGRP AS 100. These routers should be configured to advertise their Lo0 interfaces in this AS, using the following policy:

- These routers should be configured to reach each other's loopback interface/s by going through R1.

- *Do not* use Policy-based Routing (PBR) or configure another AS to accomplish this task.

## Task 2

Configure R3's G0/4, G0/5, and G0/6 in AS 300. Configure R4's, R5's, and R6's G0/3 and loopback 0 interfaces in this AS.

Configure R3 to summarize its Lo100–Lo107.

The summary route should be advertised to R4, R5, and R6 based on the following policy:

- R4 should receive the summary *only*.

- R5 should receive the summary plus network 100.1.3.0 /24.

- R6 should receive the summary plus all the specific routes.

- Configure the minimum number of **ip summary-address** commands possible to accomplish this task.

## Task 3

Configure EIGRP 300 on R4's Lo134 and Lo135 and advertise a single summary in AS 300.

## Task 4

**Configure the G0/7 and Lo0 interfaces of R6 and the G0/6 and loopback 0 interfaces on R7 for EIGRP in AS 67.**

R7 should be configured to advertise its Lo130, such that the command **show ip route eigrp 67** on R6 produces the following output:

```
D EX   130.3.0.0/16 [170/130816] via 67.1.1.7, 00:00:16,
GigabitEthernet0/7
```

R7 should use **redistribute static** to accomplish this task. *Do not* configure a static route to accomplish this task.

## Task 5

Configure the routers in AS 67 such that they log neighbor warning messages and repeat the warning messages every 10 minutes. You should disable logging of neighbor changes for this AS.

## Task 6

Configure the routers in AS 67 such that a dead neighbor is detected within 3 seconds.

## Task 7

Routers in AS 100 should be configured to use **Bandwidth** and *not* **Bandwidth + DLY** when calculating their composite metric.

## Task 8

Configure R2 such that EIGRP *never* uses more than 25% of its G0/0 link's bandwidth.

## Task 9

Configure the G0/8 interface of R5 and the G0/5 and the Lo0 interfaces of R8 in AS 500.

## Task 10

Configure R5 to inject a default route in AS 500 based on the following policy:

- R5 should be configured to inject a default route plus networks 4.0.0.0/8 and 6.0.0.0/8 from AS 300.

## Task 11

Erase the startup configuration and reload the routers before proceeding to the next task.

## Lab 6: EIGRP Authentication

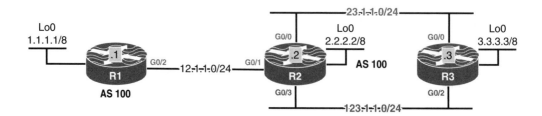

## Lab Setup:

If you are using EVE-NG, and you have imported the EVE-NG topology from the **EVE-NG-Topology** folder, ignore the following tasks and use **Lab 6-EIGRP Authentication** in the **EIGRP** folder in EVE-NG.

To copy and paste the initial configurations, go to the **Initial-config** folder → **EIGRP** folder → **Lab-6**.

## Task 1

Configure EIGRP based on the previous diagram. If this configuration is successful, these routers should be able to see and have reachability to all routes. You should use named mode configuration style when configuring R2 and R3 and classic EIGRP configuration style when configuring R1 to accomplish this task.

## Task 2

Configure R2 to authenticate all existing and future directly connected interfaces using the strongest authentication method available. Use the minimum number of commands and **CCIE** as the password to accomplish this task.

- R2 should authenticate R1 using MD5 and **Cisco** as the password.

- In the future, R3 may have other neighbors that won't need authentication.

## Task 3

Erase the startup configuration and reload the routers before proceeding to the next lab.

# Lab 7: EIGRP Challenge Lab

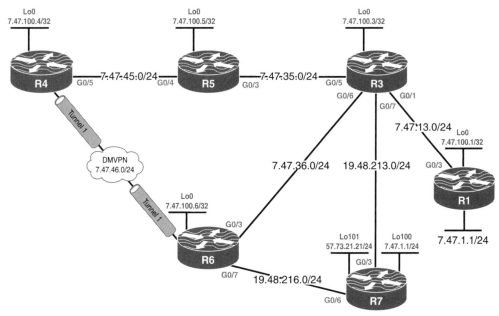

## Lab Setup:

If you are using EVE-NG, and you have imported the EVE-NG topology from the
**EVE-NG-Topology** folder, ignore the following tasks and use **Lab 7-EIGRP Challenge
Lab** in the **EIGRP** folder in EVE-NG.

To copy and paste the initial configurations, go to the **Initial-config** folder → **EIGRP**
folder → **Lab-7.**

**NOTE**   _Do not_ access R7 at all. You should _only_ fix the problem identified in the ticket.

## Ticket 1

R1 can't reach R3's Lo0. You must configure R1 to fix the problem.

## Ticket 2

R6 does _not_ have a stable EIGRP adjacency with R4. _Do not_ use an EIGRP command to
fix this ticket.

## Ticket 3

When R3's G0/1, G0/7, and G0/6 are down, R3 can't reach R4's Lo0. _Do not_ remove any commands to fix this ticket.

## Ticket 4

R1's Lo0 should always have reachability to R4's Lo0 and G0/5 interfaces, but it does not. You should fix this problem without configuring R1 or R4. You should _not_ remove any commands to resolve this ticket.

## Ticket 5

R3 is configured to use multiple paths to R4's Lo0. However, it's using only one of the paths.

## Ticket 6

R6 can't reach R7's Lo101.

## Ticket 7

R3 should establish a EIGRP adjacency with R8 over its G0/8 interface. You should make configuration changes on R3 only.

## Ticket 8

Erase the startup configuration and reload the devices before proceeding to the next lab.

# Chapter 5

# OSPF

## Lab 1: Running OSPF on the Interfaces

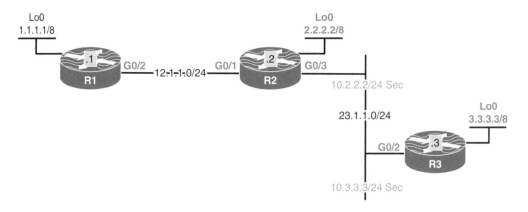

This lab should be conducted on the Enterprise POD.

Lab Setup:

If you are using EVE-NG, and you have imported the EVE-NG topology from the EVE-NG-Topology folder, ignore the following tasks and use Lab 1-Running OSPF on the Interfaces in the OSPF folder in EVE-NG.

To copy and paste the initial configurations, go to the Initial-config folder → OSPF folder → Lab-1.

## Task 1

Configure OSPF Area 0 on all directly connected interfaces in the previous topology, including the secondary IP addresses.

- Do not use the **network** command to accomplish this task.
- The loopback interfaces should be advertised with their correct mask.
- If this configuration is performed successfully, each router will have reachability to all routes within the previous topology.
- The OSPF RID should be configured based on the Lo0 interface of these three routers.

## Task 2

Configure R2 and R3 such that the secondary IP addresses are not advertised into OSPF.

- *Do not* use filtering, a route map, an access list, or a prefix list.
- *Do not* remove any commands.
- Use a minimum number of commands to accomplish this task.

## Task 3

R3 is getting flooded with LSA Type 6 packets. Ensure that R3 does not generate a syslog message for this LSA type.

## Task 4

To ensure fast detection of a neighbor being down, configure R2 and R3 to send their hellos every 250 milliseconds with a hold time of 1 second for their Ethernet link.

## Task 5

Ensure that these routers look up DNS names for use in most of the OSPF **show** commands. Test this task to ensure proper operation. Since there are no DNS servers in this lab, you should use the local routers for DNS lookups.

## Task 6

Configure R2 such that if it does not receive an acknowledgment from R3 for a given LSA, it waits 10 seconds before it re-sends that given LSA.

## Task 7

Configure R1 and R2 such that when there is a topology change in Area 0 for LSA Types 1 and 2, the entire SPT is *not* recomputed. This should *only* occur for the affected part/s of the tree.

## Task 8

Erase the startup configuration and reload the routers before proceeding to the next lab.

# Lab 2: OSPF Broadcast Networks

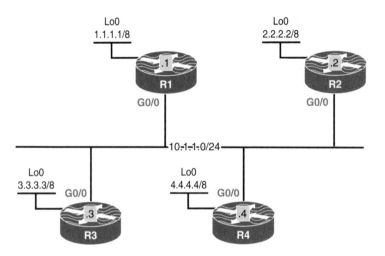

This lab should be conducted on the Enterprise POD.

Lab Setup:

If you are using EVE-NG, and you have imported the EVE-NG topology from the **EVE-NG-Topology** folder, ignore the following tasks and use **Lab 2-OSPF Broadcast Network** in the **OSPF** folder in EVE-NG.

To copy and paste the initial configurations, go to the **Initial-config** folder → **OSPF** folder→ **Lab-2**.

## Task 1

Configure OSPF Area 0 on all routers and their directly connected interfaces. Ensure that Loopback0 interfaces are advertised with their correct mask. You should configure the OSPF router IDs to be 0.0.0.x, where x is the router number.

## Task 2

## Lab Setup:

Erase the configuration of all routers and SW1. To copy and paste the initial configurations, go to the **Initial-config** folder → **OSPF** folder→ **Lab-2-Task-2**.

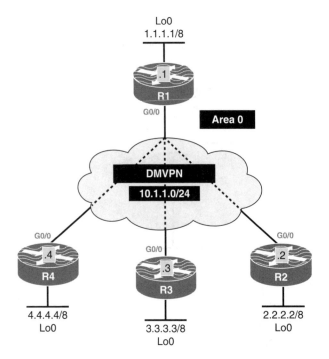

Configure OSPF on the tunnel and Loopback0 interfaces of all routers, based on the following policy:

- R1 is the hub, and R2, R3, and R4 are configured as spokes. *Do not* change the topology.

- Configure the tunnel interfaces of all routers to be OSPF broadcast network type.

- The loopback interfaces should be advertised with their correct mask.

- Configure the router IDs of R1, R2, R3, and R4 to be 0.0.0.1, 0.0.0.2, 0.0.0.3, and 0.0.0.4, respectively.

- You should use static maps on the DMVPN network.

- Spokes should traverse the hub to reach all networks.

## Task 3

Erase the startup configuration of the routers, the config.text file, and the VLAN.dat file of each switch and reload the devices before proceeding to the next lab.

# Lab 3: OSPF Non-broadcast Networks

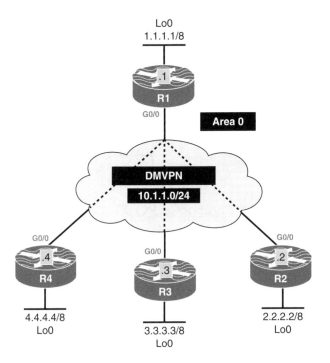

This lab should be conducted on the Enterprise POD.

Lab Setup:

If you are using EVE-NG, and you have imported the EVE-NG topology from the **EVE-NG-Topology** folder, ignore the following tasks and use **Lab 3-OSPF Non-Broadcast Networks** in the **OSPF** folder in EVE-NG.

To copy and paste the initial configurations, go to the **Initial-config** folder → **OSPF** folder→ **Lab-3**.

## Task 1

Configure OSPF Area 0 on all routers and their directly connected interfaces. You should configure the tunnel interfaces as the OSPF non-broadcast network type. Configure the OSPF router IDs to be 0.0.0.x, where x is the router number.

### Task 2

Erase the startup configuration of the routers, the config.text file, and the VLAN.dat file of each switch and reload the devices before proceeding to the next lab.

# Lab 4: OSPF Point-to-Point Networks

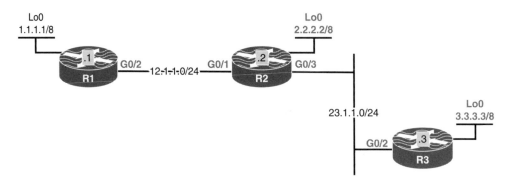

This lab should be conducted on the Enterprise POD.

Lab Setup:

If you are using EVE-NG, and you have imported the EVE-NG topology from the **EVE-NG-Topology** folder, ignore the following tasks and use **Lab 4-OSPF Point-to-Point Networks** in the **OSPF** folder in EVE-NG.

To copy and paste the initial configurations, go to the **Initial-config** folder → **OSPF** folder→ **Lab-4**.

### Task 1

Configure OSPF on all routers and run their directly connected interfaces in Area 0, based on the following policy:

- The Loopback0 interfaces of these routers should be advertised with their correct mask.

- Use 0.0.0.1, 0.0.0.2, and 0.0.0.3 as the router IDs of R1, R2, and R3, respectively.

- There should *not* be any DR/BDR election on any of the links.

- *Do not* configure point-to-multipoint or point-to-multipoint non-broadcast on any of the links.

## Task 2

Erase the startup configuration of the routers, the config.text file, and the VLAN.dat file of each switch and reload the devices before proceeding to the next lab.

# Lab 5: OSPF Point-to-Multipoint and Point-to-Multipoint Non-broadcast Networks

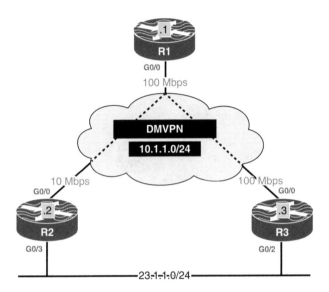

## This lab should be conducted on the Enterprise POD.

## Lab Setup:

If you are using EVE-NG, and you have imported the EVE-NG topology from the **EVE-NG-Topology** folder, ignore the following tasks and use **Lab 5-OSPF Point-to-Multipoint & Point-to-Multipoint Non-broadcast Networks** in the **OSPF** folder in EVE-NG.

To copy and paste the initial configurations, go to the **Initial-config** folder → **OSPF** folder→ **Lab-5.**

## Task 1

Configure OSPF Area 0 on all links in the previous topology. The OSPF router IDs of all routers should be 0.0.0.$x$, where $x$ is the router number. If this configuration is performed successfully, the routers in this topology should have full NLRI to every network in this topology. The tunnel interface of these routers should not perform DR/BDR election.

## Task 2

Since R2's connection to the cloud is 10 Mbps and R3's connection is 100 Mbps, R1 should *not* perform equal-cost load sharing. R1 should go through R3 to reach network 23.1.1.0/24. *Do not* configure **PBR** or the **IP ospf cost** command to accomplish this task.

## Task 3

Erase the startup configuration of the routers, the config.text file, and the VLAN.dat file of each switch and reload the devices before proceeding to the next lab.

# Lab 6: OSPF Area Types

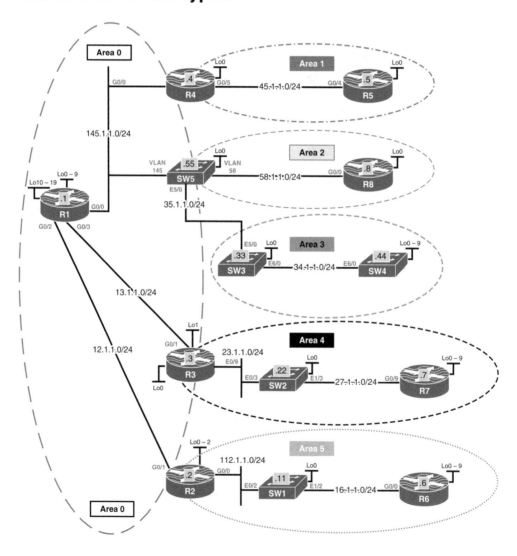

## This lab should be conducted on the Enterprise POD.

## Lab Setup:

If you are using EVE-NG, and you have imported the EVE-NG topology from the **EVE-NG-Topology** folder, ignore the following tasks and use **Lab 6-OSPF Area Types** in the **OSPF** folder in EVE-NG.

To copy and paste the initial configurations, go to the **Initial-config** folder → **OSPF** folder→ **Lab-6**.

## Lab rules:

- All loopback interfaces are configured with **ip ospf network point-to-point**.

- Configure the OSPF router IDs of the routers based on the following chart:

| | | |
|---|---|---|
| R1: 0.0.0.1 | R2: 0.0.0.2 | R3: 0.0.0.3 |
| R4: 0.0.0.4 | R5: 0.0.0.5 | R6: 0.0.0.6 |
| R7: 0.0.0.7 | R8: 0.0.0.8 | SW1: 0.0.0.11 |
| SW2: 0.0.0.22 | SW3: 0.0.0.33 | SW4: 0.0.0.44 |
| SW5: 0.0.0.55 | | |

## Task 1

Configure the Lo0 and G0/4 interfaces of R5 and G0/5 and the Lo0 interface of R4 in Area 1.

## Task 2

Configure the G0/0 and Lo0 interfaces of R8 and the VLAN58 interface of SW5 in Area 2.

## Task 3

Configure the following interfaces for OSPF Area 3:

- E6/0 interface on SW4

- E6/0, E5/0, and Loopback0 interfaces on SW3

- E5/0 interface on SW5

Ensure that SW4 is configured to redistribute its Loopback0 through Loopback9 interfaces into this routing domain.

## Task 4

Configure the following interfaces in Area 4:

**1.** R7's G0/9 interface

**2.** SW2's Lo0, E1/3, and E0/3 interfaces

**3.** R3's G0/9 interface

Ensure that R7 is configured to redistribute the networks on its Loopback0 through Loopback9 interfaces into this routing domain.

## Task 5

Configure the following interfaces in Area 5:

- R6's G0/0 interface
- SW1's Lo0, E1/2, and E0/2 interfaces
- R2's Loopback0 through Loopback2 and G0/0 interfaces

Ensure that R6 is configured to redistribute its Loopback0 through Loopback9 interfaces into this routing domain.

## Task 6

Configure the following interfaces in Area 0:

- R1's Loopback0 through Loopback9, G0/0, G0/3, and G0/2 interfaces
    - R1 must be configured to redistribute its Lo10–Lo19 in this routing domain.
- R4's G0/0 interface
- SW5's VLAN145 and Loopback0 interfaces
- R3's G0/1 and Loopback 0 interfaces
- R2's G0/1 interface

Restrictions:

- R4 should *not* use a **network** command to run its G0/0 interface in Area 0.
- This router should *not* advertise any secondary IP address/es configured under its G0/0 interface.
- *Do not* configure any kind of filtering to accomplish this task.

## Task 7

Ensure that the routers in Area 1 do not have any OSPF external routes in their routing table; these routers should not have LSA Types 4 or 5 in their LSDB.

## Task 8

Configure Area 2 such that existing and future external and inter-area routes are *never* seen in the routing tables of these routers. These routers should *not* have LSA Types 3, 4, or 5 in their LSDB, but these routers should have full reachability to the inter-area and external networks redistributed in this routing domain.

**Restriction:**

■ *Do not* use an ACL or a prefix list to accomplish this task.

## Task 9

Configure the routers in Area 3 based on the following policy:

■ The routers must maintain existing and future inter-area routes in their routing tables.

■ The routers *should not* have LSA Types 4 or 5 in their OSPF link state database.

■ The routers *should not* have reachability to the routes redistributed in the other areas of this routing domain.

■ The routers should have reachability to the routes redistributed in their own area.

## Task 10

Configure the routers in Area 4 based on the following policy:

■ The routers of this area *should* have LSA Type 3 in their OSPF link state database.

■ The routers of this area *should not* have LSA Types 4 or 5 in their OSPF link state database.

■ The routers *must* have reachability to the existing and future routes redistributed in the other areas of this routing domain, except for the external networks redistributed in Area 3.

■ The routers should have reachability to the networks redistributed in their own area.

## Task 11

Implement the following policy for the routers in Area 5:

- The routers must have reachability to the routes redistributed in this routing domain.

- The routers *should not* maintain LSA Type 3 in the OSPF link state database.

- The routers *should not* maintain LSA Types 4 or 5 in their OSPF link state database.

## Task 12

Determine whether the routers in Area 0 maintain LSA Type 4 in their OSPF link state database.

## Task 13

Configure R3 to redistribute its Lo1 interface such that existing and future redistributed routes by this router are *only* injected into Area 0 and *not* into Area 4. *Do not* configure an ACL or a prefix list to accomplish this task.

## Task 14

Configure the following ABRs so that the default route that they inject has an OSPF cost based on the following table:

| ABR/Area | OSPF Cost of the Injected Default Route |
| --- | --- |
| R4/Area 1 | 40 |
| R9/Area 2 | 133 |
| R3/Area 4 | 30 |
| R2/Area 5 | 20 |

## Task 15

Erase the startup configuration of the routers, the config.text file, and the VLAN.dat file of each switch and reload the devices before proceeding to the next lab.

# Lab 7: OSPF Filtering

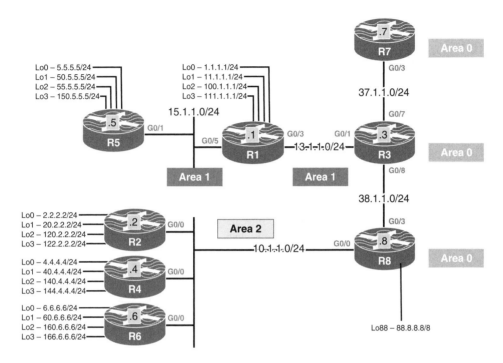

## This lab should be conducted on the Enterprise POD.

## Lab Setup:

If you are using EVE-NG, and you have imported the EVE-NG topology from the **EVE-NG-Topology** folder, ignore the following tasks and use **Lab 7-OSPF Filtering** in the **OSPF** folder in EVE-NG.

To copy and paste the initial configurations, go to the **Initial-config** folder → **OSPF** folder→ **Lab-7.**

## Pre-configuration:

- OSPF is configured on all routers, and all loopback interfaces are configured with their correct masks.

- OSPF router IDs are configured as 0.0.0.$x$, where $x$ is the router number.

## Task 1

Configure R1 and R3 such that the link connecting them to each other is *not* advertised into OSPF. R1 and R3 should still maintain their OSPF adjacency through this interface.

## Task 2

Configure R5 such that it _only_ advertises its Lo0 and Lo1 interface addresses into OSPF.
_Do not_ remove or modify the **network** command/s configured in the router configuration
mode. You should use two different solutions: one for the Lo0 interface and a second one
for the Lo1 interface.

## Task 3

Configure R3 to redistribute all OSPF prefixes into BGP AS 100. R8 should redistribute
its Lo88 into OSPF interfaces such that R7 filters network 88.0.0.0 /8 from getting into its
BGP table.

## Task 4

Configure LSA Type 3 filtering on R3 to filter network 1.1.1.0 /24 from the rest of the
OSPF domain. You should reference Area 1 when accomplishing this task.

## Task 5

Configure LSA Type 3 filtering on R8 to filter network 5.5.5.0 /24 from getting into
Area 2.

## Task 6

Configure LSA Type 3 filtering on R8 to filter network 50.5.5.0 /24. You should reference
Area 0 when accomplishing this task.

## Task 7

Configure R8 such that network 100.1.1.0 /24 is _not_ advertised to the routers in Area 2.
_Do not_ use the following to accomplish this task:

- A distribute list, an area filter list, distance, a route map, an access list, or a prefix list

## Task 8

Configure R3 such that network 111.1.1.0 /24 is _not_ advertised to routers in Area 0 or
Area 2. _Do not_ add any static routes, use a filter list, or use a distribute list to accomplish
this task.

## Task 9

Enable OSPF Area 2 on the G0/9 interfaces of R2, R4, and R6.

## Task 10

Configure R2, R4, and R6 based on the following policy:

- R2 should redistribute networks 120.2.2.0 /24 and 122.2.2.0 /24 as OSPF external Type 1 networks.

- R2 should redistribute its Lo0 and Lo1 interfaces into the OSPF routing domain.

- R4 should redistribute networks 140.4.4.0 /24 and 144.4.4.0 /24 as OSPF external Type 1 networks.

- R4 should redistribute its Lo0 and Lo1 interfaces into the OSPF routing domain.

## Task 11

Configure R2 and R6 to redistribute their Lo0 interfaces. Configure the appropriate routers such that the routers in Area 2 can see networks 2.2.2.0 /24, 4.4.4.0 /24, and 6.6.6.0 /24 in their routing tables. The routers in the other areas, however, should _not_ have these networks in their routing table.

## Task 12

Configure R2 to filter network 122.2.2.0 /24. The other routers should _not_ have this route in their routing table or database.

- _Do not_ use **summary-address** to accomplish this task.

- _Do not_ modify the redistribution parameters to accomplish this task.

## Task 13

Configure R2 to filter existing and future inter-area and/or intra-area routes from its routing table. Use the smallest number of commands possible to accomplish this task.

## Task 14

Configure R4 to filter existing and future routes that have an OSPF cost of 20 from its routing table.

## Task 15

Configure R6 to filter the default route injected by the ABR by R8 from its routing table.

## Task 16

Configure R5 to filter network 1.1.1.0 /24. _Do not_ use **distribute-list** to accomplish this task.

## Task 17

Configure R1 to filter existing and future external routes. _Do not_ configure an access list, a route map, or a prefix list to accomplish this task.

## Task 18

Configure R7 to filter existing and future intra-area routes. _Do not_ configure a route map, an access list, or a prefix list to accomplish this task.

## Task 19

Configure R5 to filter existing and future intra-area routes. _Do not_ configure a route map, an access list, or a prefix list to accomplish this task.

## Task 20

Erase the startup configuration of the routers, the config.text file, and the VLAN.dat file of each switch and reload the devices before proceeding to the next lab.

# Lab 8: OSPF Summarization

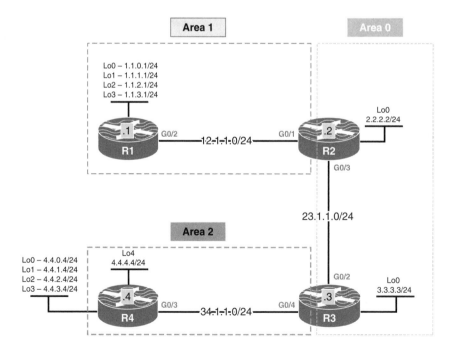

## This lab should be conducted on the Enterprise POD.

## Lab Setup:

If you are using EVE-NG, and you have imported the EVE-NG topology from the **EVE-NG-Topology** folder, ignore the following tasks and use **Lab 8-OSPF Summarization** in the **OSPF** folder in EVE-NG.

To copy and paste the initial configurations, go to the **Initial-config** folder → **OSPF** folder→ **Lab-8**.

## Task 1

Configure the routers as follows:

- R4 should redistribute the four loopback interfaces (4.4.0.4 /24−4.4.3.4 /24) into the OSPF routing domain.

- R4 should advertise its Loopback4 and G0/3 interfaces in Area 2.

- R1 should advertise all of its interfaces in OSPF Area 1. Use a minimum number of commands to accomplish this.

- R2 should advertise its Loopback0 and G0/3 interfaces in Area 0. It should advertise its G0/1 interface in Area 1.

- R3 should advertise its Loopback0 and G0/2 interfaces in Area 0. It should advertise its G0/4 interface in Area 2.

- R1 should use 0.0.0.1, R2 should use 0.0.0.2, R3 should use 0.0.0.3, and R4 should use 0.0.0.4 as their OSPF router IDs.

## Task 2

Configure the appropriate router in Area 2 to summarize all external (E2) routes.

## Task 3

Configure the appropriate router in Area 1 to summarize the following four networks and only advertise a single summary route:

- 1.1.0.0 /24

- 1.1.1.0 /24

- 1.1.2.0 /24

- 1.1.3.0 /24

## Task 4

Ensure that the routers do _not_ install a null 0 route in the routing table when they summarize routes. You should show two ways to accomplish this task.

## Task 5

Reconfigure Area 2 such that the routers within Area 2 see all the specific routes, but the routers in Area 0 and Area 1 see only a single summary route.

## Task 6

In Area 1, configure R1 to advertise its loopback interfaces with their correct mask. You should use a minimum number of commands to accomplish this request. Configure the appropriate router such that the summary route (1.1.0.0/22) plus subnet 1.1.2.0/24 is advertised to other areas.

## Task 7

In Area 2, configure the appropriate router(s) such that R3 advertises the summary plus one of the specific routes (4.4.0.4/24).

## Task 8

Erase the startup configuration and reload the routers before proceeding to the next lab.

# Lab 9: Virtual Links and GRE Tunnels

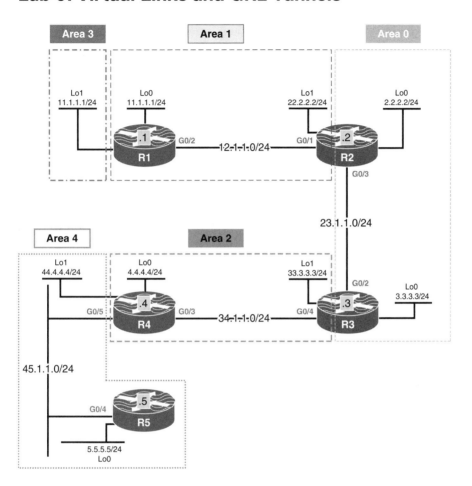

This lab should be conducted on the Enterprise POD.

## Lab Setup:

If you are using EVE-NG, and you have imported the EVE-NG topology from the **EVE-NG-Topology** folder, ignore the following tasks and use **Lab 9-Virtual-links and GRE Tunnels** in the **OSPF** folder in EVE-NG.

To copy and paste the initial configurations, go to the **Initial-config** folder → OSPF folder→ **Lab-9**.

## Task 1

Configure the routers in the previous diagram based on the following chart. The loop-back interfaces should be advertised with their correct masks. You may not see all the networks in every router.

| Router | Router ID | Interface – Area |
|--------|-----------|------------------|
| R1 | 0.0.0.1 | Lo0 – Area 1 |
| | | lo1 – Area 3 |
| | | G0/2 – Area 1 |
| R2 | 0.0.0.2 | Lo0 – Area 0 |
| | | lo1 – Area 1 |
| | | G0/1 – Area 1 |
| | | G0/3 – Area 0 |
| R3 | 0.0.0.3 | Lo0 – Area 0 |
| | | lo1 – Area 2 |
| | | G0/2 – Area 0 |
| | | G0/4 – Area 2 |
| R4 | 0.0.0.4 | Lo0 – Area 2 |
| | | lo1 – Area 4 |
| | | G0/3 – Area 2 |
| | | G0/5 – Area 4 |
| R5 | 0.0.0.5 | Lo0 – Area 4 |
| | | G0/4 – Area 4 |

## Task 2

Ensure that the networks advertised in Area 3 are reachable by the other routers. *Do not* use a GRE tunnel to accomplish this task.

## Task 3

Ensure that the networks in Area 4 are reachable by the other routers. You should use a GRE tunnel to accomplish this task. The IP address of the tunnel should be based on the Lo1 interfaces of R3 and R4. *Do not* reconfigure the Loopback1 interfaces of these two routers.

## Task 4

Erase the startup configuration and reload the routers before proceeding to the next lab.

# Lab 10: Default Route Injection

Lo2 – 2.2.2.2/8
Lo3 – 3.3.3.3/8
Lo5 – 5.5.5.5/8
Lo6 – 6.6.6.6/8

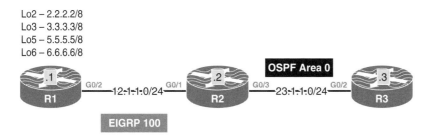

## This lab should be conducted on the Enterprise POD.

## Task 1

Configure the routers in the previous topology. _Do not_ configure any routing protocols.

## Task 2

Configure EIGRP AS 100 on R1 and all of its directly connected interfaces and R2's G0/1 interface.

## Task 3

Configure OSPF on R3's G0/2 interface and R2's G0/3 interface in Area 0.

## Task 4

Configure R2 to inject a default route into the OSPF routing domain if network 2.0.0.0/8 _or_ 3.0.0.0/8 is up.

## Task 5

Remove the configurations from the previous task and configure the appropriate router/s based on the following policy:

- R2 should inject a default route into the OSPF routing domain _only_ if networks 2.0.0.0/8 and 3.0.0.0/8 are both up.

- _Do not_ use route maps, access lists, or prefix lists to complete this task.

## Task 6

Remove the configurations from the previous task and configure the appropriate router/s based on the following policy:

■ R2 should inject a default route into the OSPF routing domain _only_ if network 2.0.0.0/8 is up and network 3.0.0.0/8 is down.

## Task 7

Remove the configurations from the previous task and configure the appropriate router/s based on the following policy:

■ R2 should inject a default route into the OSPF routing domain _only_ if networks 2.0.0.0/8 and 3.0.0.0/8 are both up.

■ R2 should _not_ configure a static default route.

■ R2 should configure a prefix list to accomplish this task.

## Task 8

Remove the configurations from the previous task and configure the appropriate router/s, based on the following policy:

■ R2 should inject a default route into the OSPF routing domain if network 2.0.0.0/8 is up

AND

■ Network 3.0.0.0/8 is down

AND

■ Networks 5.0.0.0/8 OR 6.0.0.0/8 are both up.

## Task 9

Erase the startup configuration and reload the devices before proceeding to the next lab.

# Lab 11: OSPF Authentication

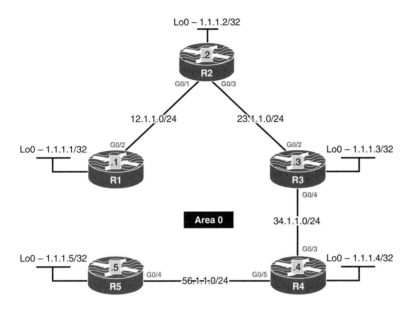

## This lab should be conducted on the Enterprise POD.

## Lab Setup:

If you are using EVE-NG, and you have imported the EVE-NG topology from the **EVE-NG-Topology** folder, ignore the following tasks and use **Lab 11-OSPF Authentication** in the **OSPF** folder in EVE-NG.

To copy and paste the initial configurations, go to the **Initial-config** folder → **OSPF** folder→ **Lab-11**.

## Task 1

Configure the directly connected interfaces of all routers in Area 0. The router IDs of the routers in this area should be configured as $0.0.0.x$, where $x$ is the router number.

## Task 2

Configure plaintext authentication on all the links connecting the routers in this area. You *must* use a router configuration command as part of the solution in resolving this task. Use **aaa** as the password for this authentication.

## Task 3

Remove the authentication configuration from the previous task and ensure that every router sees every route advertised in Area 0.

## Task 4

Configure MD5 authentication on all the links in Area 0. You should use a router configuration command as part of the solution to this task. Use ccc as the password for this authentication.

## Task 5

Remove the authentication configuration from the previous task and ensure that every router sees every route advertised in Area 0.

## Task 6

Configure MD5 authentication on the link connecting R1 to R2. You should use a router configuration command as part of the solution to this task. The password should be ccie.

## Task 7

Reconfigure the authentication password on R1 and R2 to be **CCIE12**, without interrupting the link's operation. _Do not_ remove any commands to accomplish this task.

## Task 8

Configure MD5 authentication on the link that connects R4 to R5, using **Cisco45** as the password. You should _not_ use a router configuration mode to accomplish this task.

## Task 9

Reconfigure OSPF areas based on the following chart:

| Router | Interface | Area |
| --- | --- | --- |
| R1 | G0/2 | 0 |
| | Loopback0 | 0 |
| R2 | G0/1 | 0 |
| | G0/3 | 1 |
| | Loopback0 | 1 |
| R3 | G0/2 | 1 |
| | G0/4 | 2 |
| | Loopback0 | 2 |
| R4 | G0/3 | 2 |
| | G0/5 | 3 |
| | Loopback0 | 3 |

| Router | Interface | Area |
|--------|-----------|------|
| R5 | G0/4 | 3 |
| | Loopback0 | 3 |

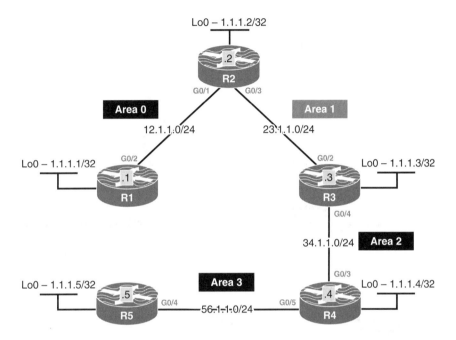

## Task 10

Configure MD5 authentication on the link between R1 and R2 in Area 0. The password for this authentication should be set to **Micronics**. You should use router configuration mode to accomplish this task.

## Task 11

Configure the strongest authentication between R4 and R5. Configure the password to be **PSWD**.

## Task 12

Erase the startup configuration and reload the routers before proceeding to the next lab.

# Lab 12: OSPF Best-Path Determination

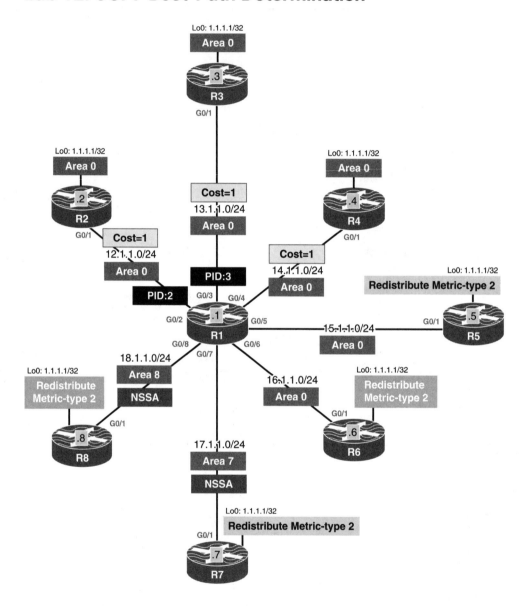

## This lab should be conducted on the Enterprise POD.

## Lab Setup:

If you are using EVE-NG, and you have imported the EVE-NG topology from the **EVE-NG-Topology** folder, ignore the following tasks and use **Lab 12-OSPF Bestpath Determination** in the **OSPF** folder in EVE-NG.

To copy and paste the initial configurations, go to the **Initial-config** folder → **OSPF** folder→ **Lab-12**.

## Task 1

Configure OSPF on the routers in the previous topology based on the following policy:

- Configure OSPF Area 0 on the link connecting R1 to R2. R2 should run OSPF Area 0 on all of its directly connected interfaces. R1 should use OSPF PID 12, and R2 should use OSPF PID 1.

- Configure OSPF Area 0 on the link connecting R1 to R3. R3 should run OSPF Area 0 on all of its directly connected interfaces. R1 should use OSPF PID 13, and R3 should use OSPF PID 1.

- Configure OSPF Area 0 on the link connecting R1 to R4. R4 should run OSPF Area 0 on its G0/1 interface and Area 4 on its Loopback0 interface.

- Configure OSPF Area 0 on the link connecting R1 to R5. R5 should redistribute its Loopback0 interface as external Type 2 in this routing domain.

- Configure OSPF Area 0 on the link connecting R1 to R6. R6 should redistribute its Loopback0 interface as external Type 1 in this routing domain.

- Configure OSPF Area 7 on the link connecting R1 to R7. Area 7 should be configured as an NSSA. R7 should redistribute its Loopback0 interface as external Type 2 in this routing domain.

- Configure OSPF Area 8 on the link connecting R1 to R8. Area 8 should be configured as an NSSA. R8 should redistribute its Loopback0 interface as external Type 1 in this routing domain.

## Task 2

Walk through OSPF best-path determination.

## Task 3

Erase the startup configuration and reload the routers before proceeding to the next lab.

# Lab 13: OSPF Challenge Lab

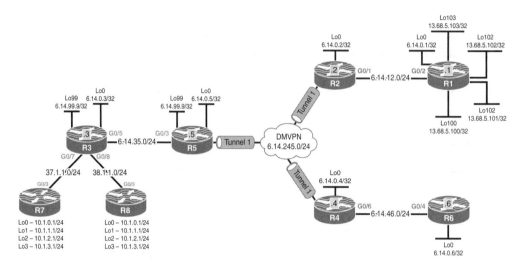

## This lab should be conducted on the Enterprise POD.

## Lab Setup:

If you are using EVE-NG, and you have imported the EVE-NG topology from the **EVE-NG-Topology** folder, ignore the following tickets and use **Lab 13-OSPF Challenge Lab** in the **OSPF** folder in EVE-NG.

To copy and paste the initial configurations, go to the **Initial-config** folder → **OSPF** folder→ **Lab-13**.

Rules:

■ The DMVPN should *not* be changed to dynamic.

■ You should *only* fix the problem that is specified in the ticket.

## Ticket 1

R5 can't ping R3's Lo0 interface.

## Ticket 2

R2 can't reach R5's Lo0 interface. *There should be a DR*. Do not use **neighbor** command when fixing this problem.

## Ticket 3

R1 can't ping R5's Lo0 interface. You *must* use an OSPF command to fix this problem.

## Ticket 4

R4 is configured to filter R3's Lo0 interface from reaching R6. R6 should have reachability to all loopback interfaces in this topology except R3's Lo0 interface. However, this is *not* the case. R6 should not get *any* error messages regarding tunnel interfaces. Use two other commands to fix other problems on R6. R6 should not have 6.14.0.3/32 in its routing table after you fix the other problems.

## Ticket 5

R5 is configured to inject a default route if R3's Lo0 interface is reachable. However, R5 is *not* injecting a default route. You can remove and reconfigure a command on the appropriate router once, but you *must* use the same method.

## Ticket 6

R2 is configured to summarize R1's loopback interfaces (Lo100–Lo103). However, R5 can see all the specific routes of the summary in its routing table. *Do not* remove any commands to accomplish this task.

## Ticket 7

R3 is participating in another OSPF routing domain, using the process ID 378. R3 has two neighboring routers, R7 and R8. R7 and R8 are both summarizing their identical specific routes. R3 should use R7 and *not* R8 to reach the summary route. If router R7 is down, then R3 should go through R8 to reach the summary. *Do not* use the following on any router to accomplish this task:

- Cost
- Bandwidth
- Static routes
- PBR
- Any kind of tunneling
- Running extra routing process

## Ticket 8

Erase the startup configuration and reload the devices before proceeding to the next lab.

# Chapter 6

# BGP

## Lab 1: Establishing a BGP Session Using the Correct TTL Value

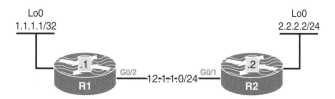

Lo0
1.1.1.1/32

Lo0
2.2.2.2/24

.1   G0/2 —12.1.1.0/24— G0/1   .2

R1                                R2

<u>This lab should be conducted on the Enterprise POD.</u>

### BGP Peering Session Overview

BGP, unlike other routing protocols, such as OSPF and EIGRP, does not implement its own transport when forming neighbor relationships (also called *peer relationships* in BGP terminology) with other BGP-speaking routers. Instead, BGP leverages TCP as its transport protocol, running over the well-known BGP TCP port 179. This means that in order for a BGP peering session to come up between two routers, they must first establish a TCP session with each other. Thus, BGP session establishment is a two-step process, where the first step is establishing a TCP session and the second step is exchanging BGP-specific information to build the BGP peering session.

TCP sessions operate on a client/server model. The server listens for connection attempts on a specific TCP port number. The client attempts to establish TCP sessions to the port number on which the server is listening. The client sends a TCP synchronization (TCP SYN) message to the listening server indicating that it would like to begin sending data to the server. The server responds with a TCP synchronization acknowledgment (TCP SYN ACK) message confirming it received the client's request and is ready to receive data over the connection. The client finally responds with a simple TCP acknowledgment (TCP ACK) message to acknowledge that it received the server's SYN-ACK packet. From this point on, the client can begin sending data to the server as TCP segments. This process is known as the TCP three-way handshake.

When BGP is enabled on a router, the router begins listening for TCP server connection attempts on port 179. When the router is configured to peer with a particular neighbor (using the **neighbor** command in BGP router configuration mode), it attempts to establish a TCP connection with the configured neighbor by sending a TCP SYN to the potential neighbor. This process is also known as an *active open attempt*. The TCP SYN packet is sent with the source IP address of the outgoing interface the router uses to reach the neighbor, the destination IP address of the potential neighbor, and the destination TCP port 179. In this situation, the router is acting as a TCP client, attempting to connect to a TCP server at port 179.

The remote neighbor listens for connections coming in on TCP port 179. When it receives the TCP SYN packet, it checks its own BGP configuration to verify that the connection attempt is being made from an IP address that is designated as a potential BGP peer by using the **neighbor** command in its own BGP configuration. If it finds a match, it responds with a TCP SYN-ACK message; otherwise, it resets the TCP session. At the same time, the server is also sending its own TCP SYN packets to its configured neighbor in an attempt to establish a BGP peering session with it.

Because BGP routers both passively listen for TCP connections and actively attempt to create TCP sessions to configured neighbors, they act as both TCP clients and servers during the TCP exchange. If two neighbors both receive and send a TCP SYN connection to each other, the one with the higher BGP identifier (or BGP router ID) becomes the TCP client, and the one with the lower BGP router ID becomes the TCP server.

Once the TCP session is established, the routers begin the BGP peering session establishment phase, determining the type of BGP peering and exchanging capabilities. Neighbors are identified by their IP addresses and BGP autonomous system numbers (ASNs):

- If a peer's ASN matches the local ASN, it is considered to be an internal BGP (iBGP) peer.

- If a peer's ASN does not match the local ASN, it is considered to be an external BGP (eBGP) peer.

The two peers also exchange BGP capabilities used to negotiate the keepalive (hello) interval, hold timer value, and other session parameters. If the receiving BGP peer finds a parameter unacceptable, then the BGP peering session does not come up.

This is the basic process used to establish a BGP session between two routers. The following labs address the subtleties in how this interaction occurs. The key point to remember is that BGP uses TCP as transport and it is therefore bound by the rules of TCP regarding how it operates. Due to this reliance on TCP, BGP session establishment has two phases: TCP session establishment and BGP peering session establishment.

## Task 1

Configure appropriate IP addressing as indicated in the diagram above.

## Task 2

Configure R1 and R2 to become eBGP neighbors. They should use their Loopback0 interfaces as the peering addresses.

## Task 3

Reconfigure the above BGP peering such that R1 and R2 are able to become eBGP peers without using the **disable-connected-check** command. Ensure that the TTL value of sent packets is as low as possible. Use a BGP-related command to accomplish this task.

## Task 4

Reconfigure R1 and R2 such that they form an eBGP peering with each other. Ensure that the TTL value of any received BGP packet is no less than 253. Do not use the **disable-connected-check** command.

## Task 5

Configure R1 and R2 to become eBGP peers. Do not use **disable-connected-check**, **ebgp-multihop**, or **ttl-security** to accomplish this task. Do not configure any tunneling mechanisms or IRB to accomplish this task.

## Task 6

Reload the routers and configure the following topology.

## Task 7

Configure R1 and R3 with an eBGP session using their Loopback0 interfaces.

## Task 8

Reconfigure R1 and R3 with an eBGP session without modifying the TTL value, configuring IRB, or using GRE or IPnIP tunneling mechanisms.

## Task 9

Erase the startup configuration and reload the routers before proceeding to the next lab.

# Lab 2: Establishing Neighbor Adjacency Using Different Methods

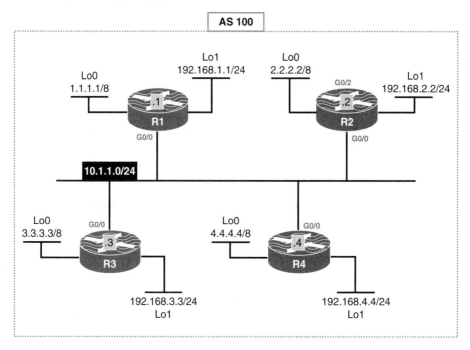

### This lab should be conducted on the Enterprise POD.

### Lab Setup:

If you are using EVE-NG, and you have imported the EVE-NG topology from the EVE-NG-Topology folder, ignore the following and use **Lab-2-T1-4-Establishing Peering session Using Different Methods** in the BGP folder in EVE-NG.

To copy and paste the initial configurations, go to the **initial-config** folder → **BGP** folder → **Lab-2-T1-4.**

## Task 1

Configure R1 through R4 in AS 100.

- Ensure that these routers create an iBGP peering session with each other in a full mesh manner.

- Ensure that these routers advertise their Loopback0 interfaces in this AS.

## Task 2

Reconfigure the routers based on the following policy:

- Keep R1 in AS 100.

- Configure R2, R3, and R4 in AS 200, 300, and 400, respectively.

A full mesh BGP peering session must be configured between these routers. Advertise Loopback0 on each router into BGP.

## Task 3

Reconfigure all the routers in AS 100. Use the following policy for their iBGP peering sessions:

- Enable authentication between the peers, using cisco as the password.

- Ensure that the peering session is established based on the Loopback0 interface's IP address.

- Ensure that these routers only advertise their Loopback1 interface in BGP.

- Provide reachability to the Loopback0 interfaces using RIPv2.

- Ensure that peering sessions between the routers are established only if they are running BGP Version 4.

- Use peer groups to accomplish this task.

## Task 4

Remove the BGP configuration from the routers and reconfigure all four routers in AS 100 using peer session templates. You should configure the following two templates to accomplish this task:

- Common template

    - This template should contain the **neighbor version 4** and **neighbor password** commands.

    - This template should be applied to all neighbors.

- iBGP template

  - This template should contain the **neighbor update-source** and **neighbor remote-as** commands.

  - This template should be applied to all iBGP neighbors.

You should advertise the Loopback1 interface in BGP and use Loopback0 for establishing the peering sessions. Do not remove RIPv2's configuration.

## Task 5

Erase the startup configurations and reload the routers before continuing to Task 6.

## Task 6

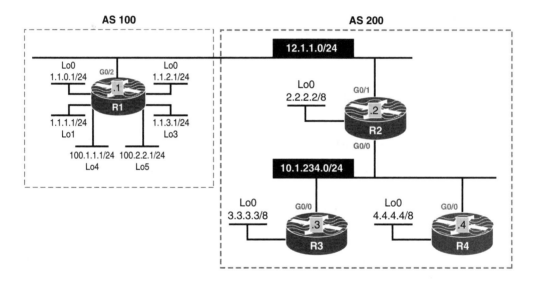

## Lab Setup:

If you are using EVE-NG, and you have imported the EVE-NG topology from the **EVE-NG-Topology** folder, then ignore the following and use **Lab-2-T6-7-Establishing Peering session Using Different Methods** in the BGP folder in EVE-NG.

To copy and paste the initial configurations, go to the **initial-config** folder → **BGP** folder → **Lab-2-T6-7.**

Configure the routers based on the following policy:

- Ensure that R1 in AS 100 establishes an eBGP peering session with R2 in AS 200. Ensure that R1 advertises all of its loopback interfaces in AS 100.

- Ensure that R2, R3, and R4 are configured in AS 200. Ensure that these routers establish iBGP peering sessions in a full mesh manner and advertise their Loopback0 interfaces in AS 200.

- Configure the BGP router IDs of the routers as follows:

  - R1: 10.1.1.1

  - R2: 10.2.2.2

  - R3: 10.3.3.3

  - R4: 10.4.4.4

- Ensure that the loopback interfaces on R4 and R3 have reachability to the networks advertised by R1.

## Task 7

Configure R2 to provide reachability to R3 and R4 by changing the next hop IP address for all the networks advertised by R1 to the IP address of its G0/0 interface. Use a template so that future policies can be implemented once in that template and make sure it affects R3 and R4. Do not use peer groups to accomplish this task.

## Task 8

Erase the startup configuration and reload the routers before proceeding to the next lab.

# Lab 3: Route Reflectors

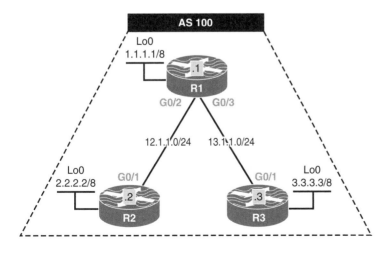

## This lab should be conducted on the Enterprise POD.

## Lab Setup:

If you are using EVE-NG, and you have imported the EVE-NG topology from the **EVE-NG-Topology** folder, ignore the following and use **Lab-3-T1-3-Route Reflectors** in the **BGP** folder in EVE-NG.

To copy and paste the initial configurations, go to the **initial-config** folder → **BGP** folder → **Lab-3-T1-2**.

## Task 1

Configure BGP AS 100 on all routers and ensure that the routers can successfully establish an iBGP peering session with each other. These routers should only advertise their Loopback0 interface in BGP.

## Task 2

Management emails you, stating that within the next 12 months, 20 additional routers will be added to this AS. In order to minimize the number of peering sessions within this AS, you decide to implement route reflectors. Configure R1 as a route reflector for this AS. You must remove OSPF.

## Task 3

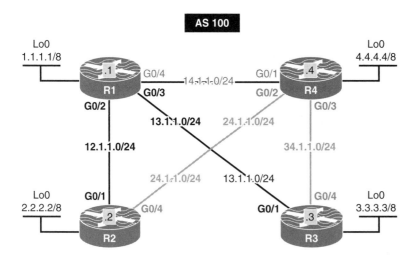

Do not erase the existing configuration. Add the following configuration to the existing configuration.

After implementing the route reflector, you realize that if the route reflector is down, the entire network is dysfunctional; therefore, you decide to add R4 as the second route reflector for redundancy. Ensure that the routers can reach the advertised networks and the redundancy is operational. R4 should advertise its Lo0 interface in BGP.

## Task 4

Erase the startup configuration and reload the routers. Reconfigure the routers based on the following topology. Do not configure BGP.

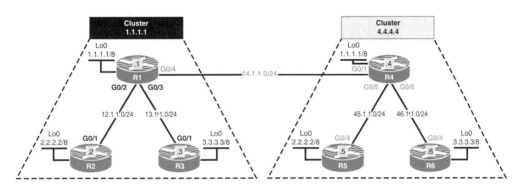

## Lab Setup:

If you are using EVE-NG, and you have imported the EVE-NG topology from the **EVE-NG-Topology** folder, ignore the following and use **Lab-3-T4-Route Reflectors** in the **BGP** folder in EVE-NG.

To copy and paste the initial configurations, go to the **initial-config** folder → **BGP** folder → **Lab-3-T4**.

## Task 5

Configure BGP on R1 through R6, based on the following policy:

- Ensure that all routers belong to AS 100.

- Configure R1 as the route reflector for routers R2 and R3.

- Configure R4 to be the route reflector for routers R5 and R6.

- Configure R1 and R4 to have an iBGP peering session between them.

- Advertise the networks on the Loopback0 interface on every router into BGP.

- Ensure that reachability for the links is provided through OSPF. The OSPF router ID should be set to 0.0.0.$x$, where $x$ is the router number.

## Task 6

Erase the startup configuration and reload the routers before proceeding to the next lab.

## Lab 4: BGP Confederation

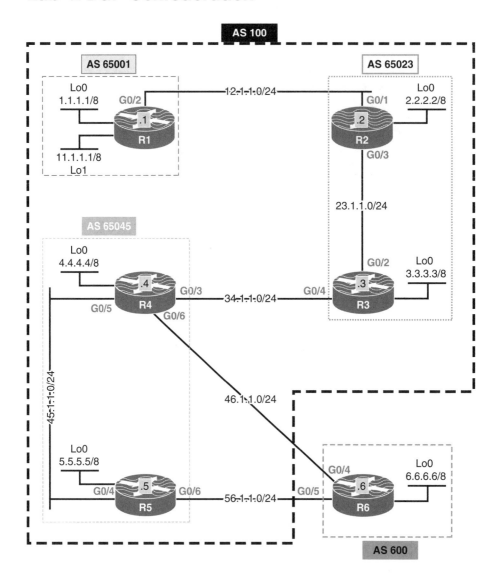

This lab should be conducted on the Enterprise POD.

Lab Setup:

If you are using EVE-NG, and you have imported the EVE-NG topology from the **EVE-NG-Topology** folder, ignore the following and use **Lab-4-BGP Confederation** in the **BGP** folder in EVE-NG.

To copy and paste the initial configurations, go to the **initial-config** folder → **BGP folder** → **Lab-4.txt**.

## Task 1

Configure BGP peering on the routers as follows:

- Ensure that R1 in AS 65001 can establish an eBGP peering session with R2 in AS 65023.

- Ensure that R2 in AS 65023 can establish an iBGP peering session with R3.

- Ensure that R3 in AS 65023 can establish an eBGP peering session with R4 in AS 65045.

- Ensure that R4 in AS 65045 can establish an iBGP peering session with R5.

- Ensure that R4 and R5 can establish an eBGP peering session with R6 in AS 600.

- Provide reachability to the links in AS 100 using EIGRP AS 1.

- Ensure that these routers advertise their loopback interfaces in BGP.

- Configure R1, R2, R3, R4, and R5 in AS 100.

## Task 2

Change the default local preference attribute on R5 to 500 and on R4 to 400.

## Task 3

Configure R6 such that when it advertises its network 6.0.0.0/8 to routers R4 and R5 in AS 65045, the routers in AS 65045 do not advertise this network to any of their existing and future eBGP peers.

## Task 4

Erase the startup configuration and reload the routers before proceeding to the next lab.

# Lab 5: BGP Backdoor and Conditional Advertisement

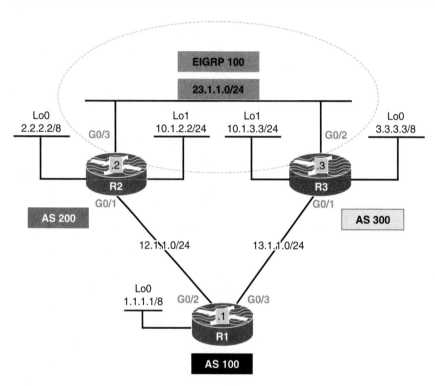

## This lab should be conducted on the Enterprise POD.

## Lab Setup:

If you are using EVE-NG, and you have imported the EVE-NG topology from the **EVE-NG-Topology** folder, ignore the following and use **Lab-5-T1-6-BGP Backdoor and Conditional Advertisement** in the **BGP** folder in EVE-NG.

To copy and paste the initial configurations, go to the **initial-config** folder → **BGP** folder → **Lab-5-T1-6.**

## Task 1

Configure R1 in AS 100 to establish an eBGP peering session with R2 and R3 in AS 200 and 300, respectively.

## Task 2

Configure R1, R2, and R3 to advertise their Loopback0 interface in BGP.

## Task 3

Configure RIPv2 and EIGRP AS 100 on the routers based on the following rules:

- Configure RIPv2 on the networks 12.1.1.0/24 and 13.1.1.0/24. Disable auto-summarization.

- Configure EIGRP AS 100 on R2's G0/3 and R3's G0/2 and their Loopback1 interfaces.

## Task 4

The network 23.1.1.0/24 is not advertised in BGP. This means if the link between R2 and R3 goes down, these routers will not be able to reach each other's Loopback1 interfaces, even though there is a redundant link between these two routers through BGP. Therefore, the administrator of R2 and R3 decided that the Loopback1 interfaces of R2 and R3 should be advertised in BGP for redundancy. Configure these routers to accommodate this decision.

## Task 5

After implementing the previous task, the administrators realized that the traffic between networks 10.1.2.0/24 and 10.1.3.0/24 was taking a suboptimal path and was not using the direct path between routers R2 and R3.

Implement a BGP solution to fix this problem. You should not use the **distance**, PBR, or any global configuration mode command to accomplish this task.

## Task 6

Remove the IP addresses from the G0/3 interface of R2 and G0/2 interface of R3 and ensure that both the G0/2 and G0/3 interfaces are in an administratively down state. Also remove the Loopback1 interfaces from these two routers.

## Task 7

Reconfigure the routers based on the following topology.

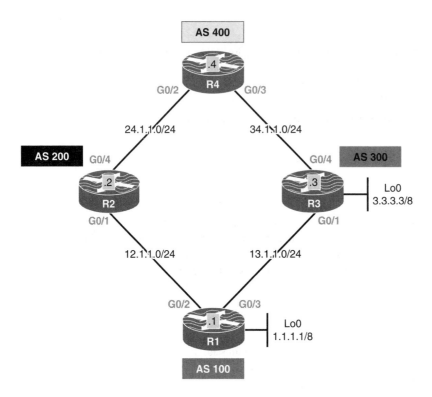

## Lab Setup:

If you are using EVE-NG, and you have imported the EVE-NG topology from the EVE-NG-Topology folder, ignore the following and use **Lab-5-T7-10-BGP Backdoor and Conditional Advertisement** in the **BGP** folder in EVE-NG.

To copy and paste the initial configurations, go to the **initial-config** folder → **BGP** folder → **Lab-5-T7-10**.

Configure BGP based on the above topology. You must use the directly connected IP addresses to establish the peering.

## Task 8

Ensure that R1, which is connected to AS 200 and AS 300, uses AS 300 as its primary service provider. Configure the following policy:

■ If network 3.0.0.0/8 from AS 300 is up and is advertised to R1, R1 should not advertise its network 1.0.0.0/8 to R2 in AS 200.

■ R1 should advertise network 1.0.0.0/8 to R2 only if network 3.0.0.0/8 is down and R1 is no longer receiving this network from AS 300.

## Task 9

Remove the configuration commands entered in the previous task before you proceed to the next task. Ensure that the routers have the advertised networks in their BGP tables.

## Task 10

Configure R2 and R1 such that R1 advertises the network 200.1.1.0/24.

Restrictions:

- Do not configure another interface or logical interface with this IP address to accomplish this task.

- Do not use the **network** command or configure redistribution to complete this task.

- Upon completion of this task, this network may not be reachable.

## Task 11

Erase the startup configuration and reload the routers before proceeding to the next lab.

# Lab 6: BGP Aggregation

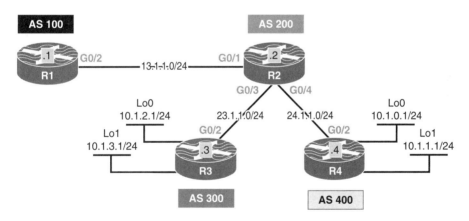

## This lab should be conducted on the Enterprise POD.

## Lab Setup:

If you are using EVE-NG, and you have imported the EVE-NG topology from the **EVE-NG-Topology** folder, ignore the following and use **Lab-6- BGP Aggregation** in the **BGP** folder in EVE-NG.

To copy and paste the initial configurations, go to the **initial-config** folder → **BGP** folder → **Lab-6.txt**.

## Task 1

R3 is configured in AS 300, and R4 is configured in AS 400. Configure R3 and R4 to advertise their loopback interfaces in BGP. If this configuration is done successfully, R2 in AS 200 should see four prefixes in its BGP table. You should use **network** statements to accomplish this task.

## Task 2

Configure R2 to aggregate all four prefixes received from AS 300 and AS 400. Ensure that R2 can advertise the aggregate route to existing and future neighbor(s). Configure a BGP peering session between R2 and R1. If this configuration is performed successfully, R1 in AS 100 should only receive a single prefix representing the four prefixes.

## Task 3

Configure R2 such that R1 in AS 100 can see the AS numbers where some or all the specific prefixes originated. Do not directly attach a route map to a neighbor or prefix in order to accomplish this.

## Task 4

Configure R2 such that only R1 in AS 100 and R4 in AS 400 accept the aggregate. The other AS(es) in this topology (such as AS 300) should receive the aggregate route, but they should discard it.

## Task 5

Configure R2 to advertise the aggregate plus 10.1.2.0/24 prefix to R1 and R4.

## Task 6

Configure R2 to advertise 10.1.3.0/24 to R1 only. R4 should not receive this prefix.

## Task 7

Erase the startup configuration of the routers and reload the devices before proceeding to the next lab.

# Lab 7: BGP Filtering

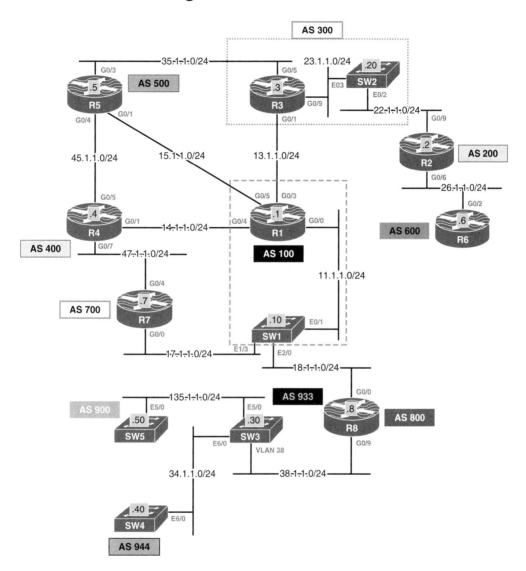

This lab should be conducted on the Enterprise POD.

Lab Setup:

If you are using EVE-NG, and you have imported the EVE-NG topology from the
**EVE-NG-Topology** folder, ignore the following and use **Lab-7- BGP Filtering** in the **BGP**
folder in EVE-NG.

To copy and paste the initial configurations, go to the **initial-config** folder → **BGP folder** → **Lab-7**.

The following loopback interfaces are preconfigured on the routers:

| Router | Loopback0 | Loopback200 |
| --- | --- | --- |
| R1 | 1.1.1.1/8 | 200.1.1.1/32 |
| R2 | 2.2.2.2/8 | 200.1.1.2/32 |
| R3 | 3.3.3.3/8 | 200.1.1.3/32 |
| R4 | 4.4.4.4/8 | 200.1.1.4/32 |
| R5 | 5.5.5.5/8 | 200.1.1.5/32 |
| R6 | 6.6.6.6/8 | 200.1.1.6/32 |
| R7 | 7.7.7.7/8 | 200.1.1.7/32 |
| R8 | 8.8.8.8/8 | 200.1.1.8/32 |
| SW1 | 10.1.1.10/8 | 200.1.1.10/32 |
| SW2 | 20.1.1.20/8 | 200.1.1.20/32 |
| SW3 | 30.1.1.30/8 | 200.1.1.30/32 |
| SW4 | 40.1.1.40/8 | 200.1.1.40/32 |
| SW5 | 50.1.1.50/8 | 200.1.1.50/32 |

OSPF PID 1 is preconfigured to provide reachability.

## Task 1

Establish a BGP peering session on the devices based on the diagram. The BGP sessions must be established based on the Loopback0 interfaces of the devices. These devices should advertise their Lo200 interface in BGP.

## Task 2

Configure R2 such that AS 300 and AS 600 do not use AS 200 as a transit AS.

## Task 3

Configure SW4 such that it filters any prefix(es) that has originated or traversed AS 200. Do not use a route map to accomplish this task.

## Task 4

Configure SW5 to filter any prefix(es) that has originated in AS 400.

## Task 5

Configure R5 to filter paths that have AS 800 as the second AS in the AS-Path.

## Task 6

Configure R8 in AS 800 to *only* allow prefixes from existing and future autonomous systems that are directly connected.

## Task 7

Configure SW1 to filter any prefix(es) that originated in AS 200 and traversed through AS 300.

## Task 8

Configure R7 to prepend its AS number four additional times when it advertises its Loopback200 interface to its directly connected neighbors.

## Task 9

Configure R4 to filter any prefix(es) that has prepended the AS number multiple times.

## Task 10

Configure R6 to filter all prefixes that were received by and originated in AS 200.

## Task 11

Configure SW4 to filter the prefixes that originated from AS 933's directly connected neighbors. This should not override the previous policy implemented in Task 4.

## Task 12

Configure R7 such that it discards paths for any prefix(es) that has more than two AS hops.

## Task 13

Configure R3 to advertise network 30.3.3.0/24. This network is a static route to Null0 that was part of the initial configuration file.

## Task 14

Ensure that R1 is configured such that if the number of routes received from R3 exceeds 10, it shuts down the neighbor (R3). R1 should generate a console warning message when 80% of this threshold is reached. If the adjacency goes down because of this policy, R1 should restart the adjacency after 1 minute and check the number of routes; if they still exceed the threshold, the adjacency should once again go down, and the cycle should repeat.

## Task 15

Configure SW4 to advertise networks 40.0.0.0/8 through 49.0.0.0/8, which were preconfigured in SW4's routing table as static routes pointing to Null0.

### Task 16

Since SW3 is running low on system resources, it cannot handle networks advertised by SW4 in the previous task. Configure the appropriate device(s) such that networks 40.0.0.0/8 through 49.0.0.0/8 are filtered.

### Task 17

Erase the startup configuration on all routers and switches, delete vlan.dat on all switches, and reload all devices before proceeding to the next lab.

## Lab 8: BGP Load Balancing

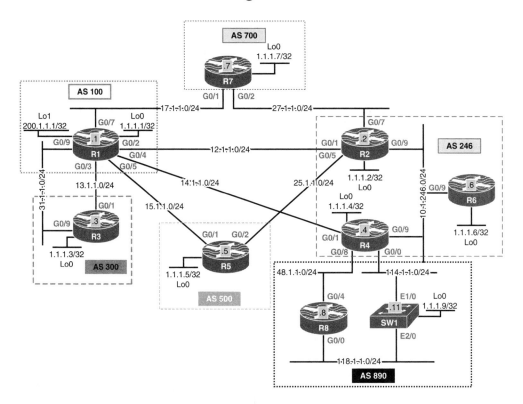

### This lab should be conducted on the Enterprise POD.

### Lab Setup:

If you are using EVE-NG, and you have imported the EVE-NG topology from the **EVE-NG-Topology** folder, ignore the following and use **Lab-8- BGP Load Balancing** in the **BGP** folder in EVE-NG.

To copy and paste the initial configurations, go to the **initial-config** folder → **BGP** folder → **Lab-8.txt.**

## Task 1

Configure R1 in AS 100 to establish a peering session with R3 in AS 300. These two routers should be configured such that they load share:

- R1 should use its G0/9 and G0/3 interfaces.

- R3 should use its G0/9 and G0/1 interfaces.

Underlying reachability should be provided with RIPv2.

## Task 2

Configure the following:

- Configure R2, R4, and R6 with full mesh iBGP peering in AS 246.

  - Configure R8 and SW1 for iBGP peerings in AS 890. The peerings should be established over their Loopback0 interfaces.

- Configure R4 in AS 246 such that it performs load sharing between the two eBGP neighbors (R8 and SW1) to reach the 118.1.1.0/24 network.

## Task 3

Configure R1 to advertise its Lo1 interface in BGP. Configure the appropriate router(s) such that R6 performs unequal-cost load sharing for R1's Lo1, based on the bandwidth of the R1–R2 and R1–R4 connections. Configure the appropriate BGP peering to accomplish this task.

## Task 4

Configure eBGP peerings between the following routers:

- R7–R1

- R7–R2

- R1–R5

- R2–R5

Configure R7 to advertise its Lo0 interface into AS 700. Configure the appropriate router such that R5 in AS 500 load shares between R1 and R2 to reach the Loopback0 interface of R7 in AS 700.

## Task 5

Erase the startup configuration and reload the devices before proceeding to the next lab.

## Lab 9: Remove-Private-AS: A Walkthrough

<u>This lab should be conducted on the Enterprise POD.</u>

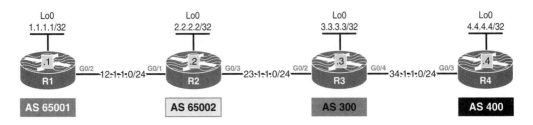

Erase the startup configuration and reload the routers before proceeding with this lab.

The following configurations handle IP addressing and BGP peerings on the devices in the topology:

### On R1:

```
R1(config)#interface lo0
R1(config-if)#ip address 1.1.1.1 255.255.255.255

R1(config)#interface g0/2
R1(config-if)#ip address 12.1.1.1 255.255.255.0
R1(config-if)#no shut


R1(config)#router bgp 65001
R1(config-router)#neighbor 12.1.1.2 remote-as 65002
R1(config-router)#network 1.1.1.1 mask 255.255.255.255
```

### On R2:

```
R2(config)#interface lo0
R2(config-if)#ip address 2.2.2.2 255.255.255.255

R2(config)#interface g0/1
R2(config-if)#ip address 12.1.1.2 255.255.255.0
R2(config-if)#no shut

R2(config-if)#interface g0/3
R2(config-if)#ip address 23.1.1.2 255.255.255.0
R2(config-if)#no shut

R2(config)#router bgp 65002
R2(config-router)#neighbor 12.1.1.1 remote-as 65001
```

```
R2(config-router)#neighbor 23.1.1.3 remote-as 300
R2(config-router)#network 2.2.2.2 mask 255.255.255.255
```

You should see the following console message:

```
%BGP-5-ADJCHANGE: neighbor 12.1.1.1 Up
```

## On R3:

```
R3(config)#interface lo0
R3(config-if)#ip address 3.3.3.3 255.255.255.255

R3(config)#interface g0/2
R3(config-if)#ip address 23.1.1.3 255.255.255.0
R3(config-if)#no shut

R3(config)#interface g0/4
R3(config-if)#ip address 34.1.1.3 255.255.255.0
R3(config-if)#no shut

R3(config)#router bgp 300
R3(config-router)#network 3.3.3.3 mask 255.255.255.255
R3(config-router)#neighbor 23.1.1.2 remote-as 65002
R3(config-router)#neighbor 34.1.1.4 remote-as 400
```

You should see the following console message:

```
%BGP-5-ADJCHANGE: neighbor 23.1.1.2 Up
```

## On R4:

```
R4(config)#interface lo0
R4(config-if)#ip address 4.4.4.4 255.255.255.255

R4(config)#interface g0/3
R4(config-if)#ip address 34.1.1.4 255.255.255.0
R4(config-if)#no shut

R4(config)#router bgp 400
R4(config-router)#network 4.4.4.4 mask 255.255.255.255
R4(config-router)#neighbor 34.1.1.3 remote-as 300
```

You should see the following console message:

```
%BGP-5-ADJCHANGE: neighbor 34.1.1.3 Up
```

The **show ip bgp** command is issued on R4 to verify the BGP paths the router learns:

```
R4#show ip bgp | begin Net

     Network           Next Hop      Metric LocPrf Weight Path
 *>  1.1.1.1/32        34.1.1.3                      0 300 65002 65001 i
 *>  2.2.2.2/32        34.1.1.3                      0 300 65002 i
 *>  3.3.3.3/32        34.1.1.3         0            0 300 i
 *>  4.4.4.4/32        0.0.0.0          0        32768 i
```

A ping from R4's loopback address 4.4.4.4 to R1's address 1.1.1.1 is issued to verify reachability:

```
R4#ping 1.1.1.1 source 4.4.4.4

Type escape sequence to abort.
Sending 5, 100-byte ICMP Echos to 1.1.1.1, timeout is 2 seconds:
Packet sent with a source address of 4.4.4.4
!!!!!
Success rate is 100 percent (5/5), round-trip min/avg/max = 5/26/109 ms
```

This topology has been created to demonstrate the differences between private and public ASNs. Every organization that participates in the global BGP routing table is assigned an autonomous system number (ASN). The ASNs are prepended to paths that an organization either passes on or originates. The original BGP RFC defined a 16-bit field to carry the ASN, which means there are a total of 65536 (0–65535) ASNs in the 16-bit ASN space. In order to participate in the global BGP table, an organization must apply for a BGP ASN from its local registry.

There are situations in which an organization might wish to run BGP privately for its own internal network or might need to run BGP with its service provider in order to advertise its own public IP address space to the global BGP table. This is similar to how organizations need to use IP addresses within their own private networks for devices and use other techniques such as proxy servers or Network Address Translation to provide Internet connectivity to the end devices. This is why the private IP address ranges from RFC 1918 were created.

Based on RFC 1930, BGP has a reserved range of ASNs for private use: 64512–65535. This means these ASNs should not be used on the global BGP table for Internet routes.

**Note**   RFC 6793 introduces 4-octet (32-bit) ASNs, and subsequent RFCs define different ranges of public/private ASNs for 4-octet ASNs. This lab focuses on 16-bit ASNs to show the basic concepts.

Observing the BGP table on R4, the AS_PATH attributes for the 1.1.1.1 and 2.2.2.2 networks both include the private ASNs 65002 and 65001 in addition to the public ASN 300. R3 and R4 in the topology are the only routers configured with public ASNs; therefore, private ASNs should not be exchanged between them.

R3 can be configured to remove the private ASNs and advertise the prefixes on behalf of its customer using the **remove-private-as** command appended to its **neighbor** command to R4. To examine this, the following configuration demonstrates removal of these private ASNs on R3 with the **neighbor 34.1.1.4 remove-private-as** command:

**<u>On R3:</u>**

```
R3(config)#router bgp 300
R3(config-router)#neighbor 34.1.1.4 remove-private-as
```

The command results in the router removing all occurrence of private ASNs in the AS_ PATH attribute. Following is the packet capture for the BGP routing update sent by R3 to R4 that verifies this:

Internet Protocol Version 4, Src: 34.1.1.3, Dst: 34.1.1.4

Transmission Control Protocol, Src Port: 45745, Dst Port: 179, Seq: 262, Ack: 20, Len: 179

Border Gateway Protocol - UPDATE Message

   Marker: ffffffffffffffffffffffffffffffff

   Length: 48

  Type: UPDATE Message (2)

   Withdrawn Routes Length: 0

   Total Path Attribute Length: 20

   Path attributes

      Path Attribute - ORIGIN: IGP

      Path Attribute - AS_PATH: 300

      Path Attribute - NEXT_HOP: 34.1.1.3

   Network Layer Reachability Information (NLRI)

      2.2.2.2/32

Border Gateway Protocol - UPDATE Message

   Marker: ffffffffffffffffffffffffffffffff

   Length: 48

  Type: UPDATE Message (2)

   Withdrawn Routes Length: 0

Total Path Attribute Length: 20

Path attributes

   Path Attribute - ORIGIN: IGP

   Path Attribute - AS_PATH: 300

   Path Attribute - NEXT_HOP: 34.1.1.3

      Flags: 0x40, Transitive, Well-known, Complete

      Type Code: NEXT_HOP (3)

      Length: 4

      Next hop: 34.1.1.3

   Network Layer Reachability Information (NLRI)

      1.1.1.1/32

Border Gateway Protocol - UPDATE Message

Border Gateway Protocol - UPDATE Message

R4's BGP table is also verified below. Notice that, unlike in the earlier output, the private ASNs 65002 and 65001 no longer show up in the AS_PATH attribute:

**On R4:**

```
R4#show ip bgp | begin Net

     Network          Next Hop         Metric LocPrf Weight Path
 *>  1.1.1.1/32       34.1.1.3                          0 300 i
 *>  2.2.2.2/32       34.1.1.3                          0 300 i
 *>  3.3.3.3/32       34.1.1.3         0                0 300 i
 *>  4.4.4.4/32       0.0.0.0          0            32768 i
```

The topology is modified as shown below in order to demonstrate another scenario. The BGP configuration from earlier is removed from R1, R2, and R3. R1 is reconfigured in AS 65001. R2 now belongs to the public AS 200.

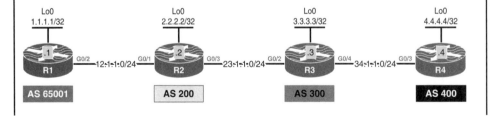

The following commands remove the BGP configuration from R1, R2, and R3:

## On R1:

```
R1(config)#no router bgp 65001
```

## On R2:

```
R2(config)#no router bgp 65002
```

## On R3:

```
R3(config)#no router bgp 300
```

The following commands reconfigure the eBGP peerings based on the diagram above:

## On R1:

```
R1(config)#router bgp 65001
R1(config-router)#neighbor 12.1.1.2 remote-as 200
R1(config-router)#network 1.1.1.1 mask 255.255.255.255
```

## On R2:

```
R2(config)#router bgp 200
R2(config-router)#neighbor 23.1.1.3 remote-as 300
R2(config-router)#neighbor 12.1.1.1 remote-as 65001
R2(config-router)#network 2.2.2.2 mask 255.255.255.255
```

You should see the following console message:

```
%BGP-5-ADJCHANGE: neighbor 12.1.1.1 Up
```

## On R3:

```
R3(config)#router bgp 300
R3(config-router)#network 3.3.3.3 mask 255.255.255.255
R3(config-router)#neighbor 34.1.1.4 remote-as 400
R3(config-router)#neighbor 23.1.1.2 remote-as 200
```

You should see the following console message:

```
%BGP-5-ADJCHANGE: neighbor 34.1.1.4 Up
%BGP-5-ADJCHANGE: neighbor 23.1.1.2 Up
```

In R4's BGP table, notice that the path to 1.1.1.1/32 has the private ASN 65001 included in the AS_PATH attribute:

**On R4:**

```
R4#show ip bgp | begin Net

     Network          Next Hop       Metric LocPrf Weight Path
 *>  1.1.1.1/32       34.1.1.3                     0 300 200 65001 i
 *>  2.2.2.2/32       34.1.1.3                     0 300 200 i
 *>  3.3.3.3/32       34.1.1.3       0             0 300 i
 *>  4.4.4.4/32       0.0.0.0        0         32768 i
```

Much as in the earlier scenario, the **neighbor 34.1.1.4 remove-private-as** command is issued on R3 to remove the private ASN 65001:

**On R3:**

```
R3(config)#router bgp 300
R3(config-router)#neighbor 34.1.1.4 remove-private-as
```

```
R3#clear ip bgp *
```

After using **clear ip bgp** * on R3, the BGP table on R4 is shown again. Unlike earlier, the command has no effect. The private ASN 65001 still exists for the path to the 1.1.1.1/32 prefix:

**On R4:**

```
R4#show ip bgp | begin Net

     Network          Next Hop       Metric LocPrf Weight Path
 *>  1.1.1.1/32       34.1.1.3                     0 300 200 65001 i
 *>  2.2.2.2/32       34.1.1.3                     0 300 200 i
 *>  3.3.3.3/32       34.1.1.3       0             0 300 i
 *>  4.4.4.4/32       0.0.0.0        0         32768 i
```

This scenario is different from the previous one in a key area. In the previous scenario, R3 received only private ASNs in the AS_PATH attribute for paths received from R2. In this scenario, R3 receives a combination of public and private ASNs in the AS_PATH attribute for paths received from R2. It is this distinction that causes the behavior above. Cisco documents this situation as follows:

*If the AS path includes both private and public AS numbers, the software considers this to be a configuration error and does not remove the private AS numbers.*

Since the AS_PATH attribute for the 1.1.1.1/32 network contains both the public and private ASNs, the software on R3 fails to remove the private ASN. This was the behavior in IOS versions prior to 15.1(2)T. IOS Versions 15.1(2)T and later introduced a command that modifies this behavior. You can explicitly tell the router to remove the private by appending the **all** keyword to the end of the **remove-private-as** command, as shown below:

### On R3:

```
R3(config)#router bgp 300
R3(config-router)#neighbor 34.1.1.4 remove-private-as all
```

```
R3#clear ip bgp * soft out
```

After issuing a **clear ip bgp * soft out** on R3, R4's BGP table verifies that the private ASN is no longer included in the AS_PATH attribute for the 1.1.1.1/32 network:

### On R4:

```
R4#show ip bgp | begin Net
```

|    | Network      | Next Hop | Metric | LocPrf | Weight | Path      |
|----|--------------|----------|--------|--------|--------|-----------|
| *> | 1.1.1.1/32   | 34.1.1.3 |        |        | 0      | 300 200 i |
| *> | 2.2.2.2/32   | 34.1.1.3 |        |        | 0      | 300 200 i |
| *> | 3.3.3.3/32   | 34.1.1.3 | 0      |        | 0      | 300 i     |
| *> | 4.4.4.4/32   | 0.0.0.0  | 0      |        | 32768  | i         |

The routers are reconfigured according to the topology below to demonstrate another scenario:

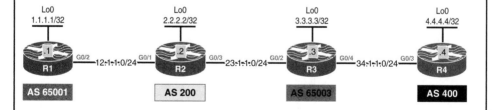

### On R4:

```
R4(config)#no router bgp 400
```

**On R3:**

```
R3(config)#no router bgp 300
```

**On R2:**

```
R2(config)#no router bgp 200
```

**On R1:**

```
R1(config)#no router bgp 65001

R1(config)#router bgp 65001
R1(config-router)#network 1.1.1.1 mask 255.255.255.255
R1(config-router)#neighbor 12.1.1.2 remote-as 200
```

**On R2:**

```
R2(config)#router bgp 200
R2(config-router)#network 2.2.2.2 mask 255.255.255.255
R2(config-router)#neighbor 23.1.1.3 remote-as 65003
R2(config-router)#neighbor 12.1.1.1 remote-as 65001
```

You should see the following console message:

```
%BGP-5-ADJCHANGE: neighbor 12.1.1.1 Up
```

**On R3:**

```
R3(config)#router bgp 65003
R3(config-router)#network 3.3.3.3 mask 255.255.255.255
R3(config-router)#neighbor 34.1.1.4 remote-as 400
R3(config-router)#neighbor 23.1.1.2 remote-as 200
```

You should see the following console message:

```
%BGP-5-ADJCHANGE: neighbor 23.1.1.2 Up
```

**On R4:**

```
R4(config)#router bgp 400
R4(config-router)#network 4.4.4.4 mask 255.255.255.255
R4(config-router)#neighbor 34.1.1.3 remote-as 65003
```

You should see the following console message:

```
%BGP-5-ADJCHANGE: neighbor 34.1.1.3 Up
```

Now the **show ip bgp** command is issued on R4:

```
R4#show ip bgp | begin Net
```

```
     Network          Next Hop      Metric LocPrf Weight Path
 *>   1.1.1.1/32       34.1.1.3                      0 65003 200 65001 i
 *>   2.2.2.2/32       34.1.1.3                      0 65003 200 i
 *>   3.3.3.3/32       34.1.1.3      0               0 65003 i
 *>   4.4.4.4/32       0.0.0.0       0           32768 i
```

Here, R4 receives private ASNs in the AS_PATH attribute for paths received from R3 once again. The **neighbor 34.1.1.4 remove-private-as** command is once again issued to have R3 remove the private ASNs from the BGP routing updates to R4:

## On R3:

```
R3(config)#router bgp 65003
R3(config-router)#neighbor 34.1.1.4 remove-private-as
```

```
R3#clear ip bgp * soft out
```

As expected, the command doesn't work. The private ASNs still exist in the AS_PATH attributes of the 1.1.1.1, 2.2.2.2, and 3.3.3.3 networks:

## On R4:

```
R4#show ip bgp | begin Net
```

```
     Network          Next Hop      Metric LocPrf Weight Path
 *>   1.1.1.1/32       34.1.1.3                      0 65003 200 65001 i
 *>   2.2.2.2/32       34.1.1.3                      0 65003 200 i
 *>   3.3.3.3/32       34.1.1.3      0               0 65003 i
 *>   4.4.4.4/32       0.0.0.0       0           32768 i
```

The result is expected because the AS_PATH attribute that R3 receives contains both public and private ASNs. As in the previous example, by default the software considers this an error and does not remove the private ASNs. The simple solution here should be to add the **all** parameter. Doing so, however, causes the following message on R3:

## On R3:

```
R3(config)#router bgp 65003
R3(config-router)#neighbor 34.1.1.4 remove-private-as all
```

```
%BGP: Private AS cannot be removed for local private as
```

This message is the router's way of kindly letting you know that using the **all** command in this case would mean removing the local private AS as well. In other words, when R3 advertises paths to R4, it must add its own ASN to the AS_PATH attribute. R3's ASN is 65003 in this case. Using the AS_PATH attribute for the path to the 1.1.1.1/32 prefix as an example, R3 will add its own ASN to the AS_PATH attribute, yielding the AS_PATH attribute value 65003 200 65001. After adding this information, if configured with the **remove-private-as all** command on its peering to R4, it must remove all private ASNs. This means the only ASN that would remain is AS 200, which is NOT R3's ASN. This is where the problem begins.

Whenever a router removes the private ASNs from an AS_PATH attribute, it is taking on responsibility for advertising those paths into the global BGP table on behalf of the autonomous systems that have only private ASNs. In other words, when R3 removes the private ASNs from the path to the 1.1.1.1/32 network when advertising to R4, it is abstracting those ASNs that are private and representing them as being advertised by its own AS. If R3 removes its own private ASN during this process, then it would appear to R4 that the paths are actually coming from AS 200 on R2. This can have negative impacts on the global BGP topology.

If, for example, R3 had other peers with public ASNs, paths R3 advertised to R4 could loop back to R3 through those other peers. This is because R3 has removed its own ASN from the AS_PATH attribute and has broken the primary loop-detection mechanism for BGP.

Removing ASNs from the AS_PATH attribute comes at a cost in the BGP table. The AS_PATH attribute is supposed to be a record of all autonomous systems a path passes through. This way, routing information loops can be detected and blocked at AS boundaries (which happens when an AS receives a BGP update with its own ASN in the AS_PATH attribute). Each advertising AS adds its ASN to the AS_PATH attribute. When this information is removed, the loop detection is broken.

Breaking the loop detection doesn't matter for stub autonomous systems, which are autonomous systems that do not provide transit for Internet traffic. Such an autonomous system is typically a customer peered with a single ISP. The ISP participates in global BGP routing and has its own public ASN. Since the ISP customer is only peered with the ISP, it is okay for the ISP to remove the public ASN from paths received for customer prefixes and advertise its own ASN to other public BGP peers it has. There is no way for the customer to receive a looped path because that would mean the ISP itself would have to receive a looped path first.

Thus the proper design for removing private ASNs is as presented in earlier scenarios. The router removing the private ASNs needs to have its own public ASN assigned that it prepends to the outgoing paths advertised to its neighbor. In this scenario, the router receiving the public ASNs is acting as a service provider, filtering out the private ASNs and advertising the paths in the public BGP table on behalf of its customers.

If a customer is multihomed to two ISPs, the customer should have its own public ASN that it advertises to its own ISPs. If it uses a private ASN and both providers remove it, the customer AS could potentially receive a looped path, depending on local best-path decision policies in transit autonomous systems between the two ISPs. (The path from ISP1 is advertised to ISP2 and then advertised to the customer again.)

For these reasons, IOS alerts of this condition and rejects the **all** parameter whenever the local ASN is also a private ASN. This is proven by the BGP configuration on R3 lacking the **all** parameter:

```
R3#show run | section router bgp

router bgp 65003
 bgp log-neighbor-changes
 network 3.3.3.3 mask 255.255.255.255
 neighbor 23.1.1.2 remote-as 200
 neighbor 34.1.1.4 remote-as 400
 neighbor 34.1.1.4 remove-private-as
```

The routers are modified for the following topology.

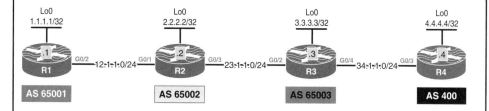

## On R4:

```
R4(config)#no router bgp 400
```

## On R3:

```
R3(config)#no router bgp 300
```

## On R2:

```
R2(config)#no router bgp 200
```

## On R1:

```
R1(config)#no router bgp 65001
```

```
R1(config)#router bgp 65001
R1(config-router)#network 1.1.1.1 mask 255.255.255.255
R1(config-router)#neighbor 12.1.1.2 remote-as 65002
```

**On R2:**

```
R2(config)#router bgp 65002
R2(config-router)#network 2.2.2.2 mask 255.255.255.255
R2(config-router)#neighbor 23.1.1.3 remot 65003
R2(config-router)#neighbor 12.1.1.1 remot 65001
```

You should see the following console message:

```
%BGP-5-ADJCHANGE: neighbor 12.1.1.1 Up
```

**On R3:**

```
R3(config)#router bgp 65003
R3(config-router)#network 3.3.3.3 mask 255.255.255.255
R3(config-router)#neighbor 34.1.1.4 remote-as 400
R3(config-router)#neighbor 23.1.1.2 remote-as 65002
```

You should see the following console message:

```
%BGP-5-ADJCHANGE: neighbor 23.1.1.2 Up
```

**On R4:**

```
R4(config)#router bgp 400
R4(config-router)#network 4.4.4.4 mask 255.255.255.255
R4(config-router)#neighbor 34.1.1.3 remote-as 65003
```

You should see the following console message:

```
%BGP-5-ADJCHANGE: neighbor 34.1.1.3 Up
```

In this scenario, all routers except for R4 are using private ASNs. R4's BGP table shows the following:

```
R4#show ip bgp | begin Net

      Network          Next Hop      Metric LocPrf Weight Path
  *>  1.1.1.1/32       34.1.1.3                  0 65003 65002 65001 i
  *>  2.2.2.2/32       34.1.1.3                  0 65003 65002 i
  *>  3.3.3.3/32       34.1.1.3         0        0 65003 i
  *>  4.4.4.4/32       0.0.0.0          0    32768 i
```

R3 will once again be tasked with removing the private ASNs from the AS_PATH attribute it received from R2 before advertising to R4 using the **remove-private-as** command:

## On R3:

```
R3(config)#router bgp 65003
R3(config-router)#neighbor 34.1.1.4 remove-private-as
```

After R3 re-sends its updates (when it is forced to do so by the **clear ip bgp * soft out** command), R4's BGP table shows the following:

```
R3#clear ip bgp * soft out
```

## On R4:

```
R4#show ip bgp | begin Net

      Network          Next Hop         Metric LocPrf Weight Path
  *>  1.1.1.1/32       34.1.1.3                     0 65003 i
  *>  2.2.2.2/32       34.1.1.3                     0 65003 i
  *>  3.3.3.3/32       34.1.1.3         0           0 65003 i
  *>  4.4.4.4/32       0.0.0.0          0       32768 i
```

Notice that in this situation, R3 successfully removed the private ASNs 65002 and 65001. Its own private ASN, 65003, remains. This behavior is consistent with the previous examples. Since there are no public ASNs in the AS_PATH attribute on the paths R3 receives from R2, R3 can remove all private ASNs except its own by using just the regular **remove-private-as** command. It doesn't attempt to remove its own private ASN because the **all** parameter has not been issued. If it were to be added, the IOS software on R3 would return the following error:

## On R3:

```
R3(config)#router bgp 65003
R3(config-router)#neighbor 34.1.1.4 remove-private-as all
```

```
%BGP: Private AS cannot be removed for local private as
```

This error occurs for the same reason as in the previous task: R3 cannot remove its own ASN from the AS_PATH attribute. In this case, doing so would actually make R3 advertise a blank AS_PATH attribute to R4. With the configuration as is, from R4's perspective, R3 has originated paths to the 1.1.1.1, 2.2.2.2, and 3.3.3.3 prefixes.

A final scenario for removing private ASNs is shown here:

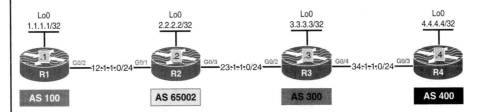

The routers are modified to reflect this topology.

## On R4:

```
R4(config)#no router bgp 400
```

## On R3:

```
R3(config)#no router bgp 65003
```

## On R2:

```
R2(config)#no router bgp 65002
```

## On R1:

```
R1(config)#no router bgp 65001
R1(config)#router bgp 100
R1(config-router)#network 1.1.1.1 mask 255.255.255.255
R1(config-router)#neighbor 12.1.1.2 remote-as 65002
```

## On R2:

```
R2(config)#router bgp 65002
R2(config-router)#network 2.2.2.2 mask 255.255.255.255
```

```
R2(config-router)#neighbor 23.1.1.3 remote-as 300
R2(config-router)#neighbor 12.1.1.1 remote-as 100
```

You should see the following console message:

```
%BGP-5-ADJCHANGE: neighbor 12.1.1.1 Up
```

## On R3:

```
R3(config)#router bgp 300
R3(config-router)#network 3.3.3.3 mask 255.255.255.255
R3(config-router)#neighbor 34.1.1.4 remote-as 400
R3(config-router)#neighbor 23.1.1.2 remote-as 65002
```

You should see the following console message:

```
%BGP-5-ADJCHANGE: neighbor 23.1.1.2 Up
```

## On R4:

```
R4(config)#router bgp 400
R4(config-router)#network 4.4.4.4 mask 255.255.255.255
R4(config-router)#neighbor 34.1.1.3 remote-as 300
```

You should see the following console message:

```
%BGP-5-ADJCHANGE: neighbor 34.1.1.3 Up
```

## To verify the configuration:

```
R4#show ip bgp | begin Net

     Network          Next Hop          Metric LocPrf Weight Path
 *>  1.1.1.1/32       34.1.1.3                        0 300 65002 100 i
 *>  2.2.2.2/32       34.1.1.3                        0 300 65002 i
 *>  3.3.3.3/32       34.1.1.3          0             0 300 i
 *>  4.4.4.4/32       0.0.0.0           0         32768 i
```

In this topology, AS 65002 exists between AS 100 and AS 300. It advertises paths to AS 300. AS 300 needs to remove the private ASN from the paths as it advertises to

AS 400. The **show ip bgp | begin Net** command on R4 in AS 400 confirms the received private ASNs:

## On R4:

```
R4#show ip bgp | begin Net
```

| | Network | Next Hop | Metric | LocPrf | Weight | Path |
|---|---|---|---|---|---|---|
| *> | 1.1.1.1/32 | 34.1.1.3 | | | 0 | 300 65002 100 i |
| *> | 2.2.2.2/32 | 34.1.1.3 | | | 0 | 300 i |
| *> | 3.3.3.3/32 | 34.1.1.3 | 0 | | 0 | 300 i |
| *> | 4.4.4.4/32 | 0.0.0.0 | 0 | | 32768 | i |

Building on results from prior examples, it's clear that just issuing the **remove-private-as** command will not be sufficient to complete the task. This is because the private ASN exists in the middle of the AS_PATH attribute. To implement the required task changes, the **remove-private-as all** command will be used on R3's neighbor command to R4:

## On R3:

```
R3(config)#router bgp 300
R3(config-router)#neighbor 34.1.1.4 remove-private-as all
```

After clearing the BGP updates outbound on R3, R4's BGP table shows the following:

```
R3#clear ip bgp * soft out
```

## On R4:

```
R4#show ip bgp | begin Net
```

| | Network | Next Hop | Metric | LocPrf | Weight | Path |
|---|---|---|---|---|---|---|
| *> | 1.1.1.1/32 | 34.1.1.3 | | | 0 | 300 100 i |
| *> | 2.2.2.2/32 | 34.1.1.3 | | | 0 | 300 i |
| *> | 3.3.3.3/32 | 34.1.1.3 | 0 | | 0 | 300 i |
| *> | 4.4.4.4/32 | 0.0.0.0 | 0 | | 32768 | i |

R3 removes the private ASNs from the middle of the AS_PATH attribute. From R4's perspective, R3 receives the path from AS 100. R4 has no knowledge of AS 65002 sitting in between. R3 has advertised the path on behalf of AS 65002.

To summarize this section, the **remove-private-as** command attached to a neighbor will remove all private ASNs from an AS_PATH attribute as long as there are only private ASNs in the AS_PATH attribute. Otherwise, the **all** parameter should be added to the command. The **all** parameter removes all private ASNs in the AS_PATH attribute only if the local ASN is a public ASN.

# Lab 10: AS Migration

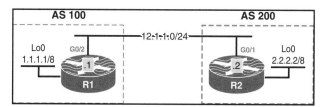

## This lab should be conducted on the Enterprise POD.

## Lab Setup:

If you are using EVE-NG, and you have imported the EVE-NG topology from the **EVE-NG-Topology** folder, ignore the following and use **Lab-10- AS Migration** in the **BGP** folder in EVE-NG.

To copy and paste the initial configurations, go to the **initial-config** folder → **BGP** folder → **Lab-10**.

## Task 1

Configure R1 in AS 100 to establish an eBGP session with R2 in AS 200. Ensure that these routers advertise their Loopback0 interfaces.

## Task 2

Configure R1 in AS 111 to establish an eBGP peering session with R2 in AS 200 such that the output of the **show ip bgp** command on these two routers will be identical to the following:

### On R1:

```
R1#show ip bgp | begin Network
   Network          Next Hop         Metric LocPrf Weight Path
*> 1.0.0.0          0.0.0.0               0         32768 i
*> 2.0.0.0          12.1.1.2              0             0 100 200 i
```

### On R2:

```
R2#show ip bgp | begin Network
   Network          Next Hop         Metric LocPrf Weight Path
*> 1.0.0.0          12.1.1.1              0             0 100 111 i
*> 2.0.0.0          0.0.0.0               0         32768 i
```

## Task 3

Configure R1 such that when R2 advertises network 2.0.0.0/8, the output of the **show ip bgp** command on R1 resembles the following. Do not remove any commands to accomplish this task.

**<u>On R1:</u>**

```
R1#show ip bgp | begin Network
   Network          Next Hop         Metric LocPrf Weight Path
*> 1.0.0.0          0.0.0.0               0         32768 i
*> 2.0.0.0          12.1.1.2              0             0 200 i
```

## Task 4

Configure R1 such that the output of the **show ip bgp** command on R2 is identical to the following. Do not remove any commands to accomplish this task.

**<u>On R2:</u>**

```
R2#show ip bgp | begin Network
   Network          Next Hop         Metric LocPrf Weight Path
*> 1.0.0.0          12.1.1.1              0             0 100 i
*> 2.0.0.0          0.0.0.0               0         32768 i
```

## Task 5

Configure R1 such that R2 can establish an eBGP peering session with R1 using AS 111 or AS 100.

## Task 6

Erase the startup configuration and reload the routers before proceeding to the next lab.

# Lab 11: BGP Best-Path Algorithm: A Walkthrough

<u>This lab should be conducted on the MOCK LAB POD.</u>

<u>Lab Setup:</u>

<u>If you are using EVE-NG, and you have imported the EVE-NG topology from the **EVE-NG-Topology** folder, ignore the following and use **Lab-11- BGP BestPath Algorithm a Walk Through** in the **BGP** folder in EVE-NG.</u>

<u>To copy and paste the initial configurations, go to the **initial-config** folder → **BGP** folder → **Lab-11**.</u>

## Introduction

This lab follows a guided lab format focused on explaining the BGP best-path algorithm. The lab explores how and why BGP uses such an algorithm for making decisions about which paths should be added to the local RIB of a router. The lab begins with a brief introduction to core BGP concepts and then elaborates on BGP path attributes as they relate to the processing of the BGP best-path algorithm. These examples are demonstrated in a sample topology with real output from IOS devices. The lab assumes a basic understanding of configuring BGP peers and knowledge of the difference between an internal peer and an external peer.

## Building Blocks of BGP

To understand BGP's place in the modern network, you must first be familiar with the concept of autonomous systems. An autonomous system (AS) is a set of networking equipment that belongs to the same governing body. The Internet is composed of many autonomous systems. Each AS advertises the locations and names of resources, such as websites, FTP servers, or other services, that are made available across the public Internet. In order to exchange this routing information dynamically, a routing protocol was needed that can be run between these autonomous system.

BGP is the routing protocol of choice for carrying these routes. It is the successor to EGP, which was the original exterior gateway protocol. BGP added many features the EGP lacked. BGP gained this position because it was engineered to be scalable, flexible, stable, and tunable. BGP maintains these four features through its unique operation.

## Path Vector

Routing protocols can generally be classified into two categories: link-state and distance vector protocols. Link-state routing protocols operate by advertising the status of connected links—such as cost and what other devices are connected to those links—to neighboring routers. Neighboring routers then use this information to build a graph of the overall network topology. Routes are calculated as shortest path computations against points on the resulting graph. Distance vector protocols operate by advertising to a neighboring router all networks reachable by the local router and the local router's cost to each network.

In both link-state and distance vector protocols, the prefixes are advertised based on the physical connections of the network. These connections have static metrics assigned to them that are aggregated along the way. The metric can be cost, delay, bandwidth, or any other quantifiable value. It is important to note that these characteristics are attached to the physical links of the network. As a result, if a link goes down or is added to the network, the aggregate metric values contained in the routing updates need to be updated accordingly. This adds a degree of instability to the overall network design.

Such instability would cause constant route updates across the public Internet. If an internal link in AS A goes down, for example, AS B does not need to be aware of it. It is up to AS A to route around the failure. For this reason, BGP needs a different way to calculate best paths that doesn't rely on metrics attached to physical links. Instead, BGP uses the concept of paths.

Rather than describing links of an internal network, BGP describes virtual paths through an AS. When a BGP peer advertises a prefix, it isn't advertising a physical connection but advertising the availability of a path that can be used to transit traffic. BGP peers exchange path information with each other and glean reachability information for all available paths between all autonomous systems participating in the global Internet routing table.

This advertisement and collection of different paths is one of the reasons BGP is called a *path vector* protocol. Rather than make decisions based on a calculated link-state graph or explicitly advertise all prefixes with metric assignments, BGP advertises paths. What kind of path, where the path goes, which BGP router advertised the path, which BGP router is the next step in the path, and how the path was first learned are all issues that are addressed through *BGP path attributes*.

## Controlling Routing to Paths

The entire reason BGP advertises routing information as paths is to provide mechanisms to control traffic flow. When speaking about BGP routing, there are two kinds of traffic flows: local traffic and transit traffic. Local traffic is traffic that originates or is destined to a node (that is, a host, a server, or another network device) within the local AS. Transit traffic is traffic that originates outside the local AS and is destined to another AS that is external to the local AS. A *transit AS* is an AS that acts as an intermediary point between two or more autonomous systems.

Think of it like a business that spans a large geographic region containing multiple buildings. That business requires roads to connect all of its buildings together to allow employees and supplies to enter and leave the establishment. The business also requires a road that allows access to the main road utilized by all other citizens. Within the business's compound, traffic traveling the internal roads is always destined for a building owned by the company. A normal citizen looking for access to another business would not go through this business to reach their destination. This business does not provide transit for any other businesses on its own local roads.

Some businesses are located in shared geographic areas where internal connections allow access to two separate businesses. Each business has a separate connection to the main road. The difference is, if a citizen wishes to access Business B, it could use Business A's connection to the main road, pass through Business A's internal roads, and access Business B. In this case, Business A has become a transit business because it can carry traffic that neither originates from nor is destined to a building it controls.

Using BGP, a network administrator can set policies, based on their own autonomous system's corporate policies, regarding whether an AS is a transit AS and how traffic is sent and received from the Internet. These policies are similar to a business employing a gate at their main connection to the road. The security guards at the gate can deny or allow traffic based on a configured set of rules (policies); these rules are based on the attributes of the car wishing to transit the business. BGP paths have the same system of attributes assigned to each potential path. These attributes, called *path attributes*, are the main way administrators can influence the path selection process.

## Path Attributes

BGP path attributes are descriptors attached to a BGP path that describe what kind of path it is. These descriptors include the destination network, the originating router, and the list of all autonomous systems that are traversed along the path. Each attribute is classified as one of the following:

■ **Well-known mandatory:** The attribute should be understood by all BGP-speaking routers and included in all BGP updates.

■ **Well-known discretionary:** The attribute should be understood by all BGP-speaking routers and may not be included in all BGP updates.

■ **Optional transitive:** The attribute does not have to be understood by all BGP-speaking routers and can be included in a BGP update.

■ **Optional non-transitive:** The attribute does not have to be understood by all BGP-speaking routers and should not be sent in any BGP updates.

For example, the BGP AS_PATH attribute is a well-known mandatory attribute. It must be included in all BGP updates and must be understood by all BGP implementations. The ORIGINATOR_ID attribute, however, is an optional non-transitive attribute. All BGP-speaking routers do not need to understand the ORIGINATOR_ID attribute, and it should not be sent in any update messages to other BGP peers.

Path attributes provide the framework for BGP's decision-making algorithm when it encounters two paths to the same destination and can be modified by the administrator to achieve specific traffic flow goals.

## Modifying Path Attributes

Let's go back to the earlier example of the business with a security gate. If the business has two entrances—one for customers and one for freight trucks—the business could, in its advertisements to the city, specify that preference. The business would be modifying its advertisements outbound toward the rest of the city but would be affecting how the rest of the city entered its own establishment.

The same business can have a policy that all goods delivered to customers with large orders should leave out the freight entrance as well. Such orders are marked as they are received by the business to keep them separate from normal orders. In this case, the order received inbound from the customer determines how the company utilizes its exits outbound toward the city.

This concept can be applied to how path attributes are modified and advertised between BGP peers. Path attributes can be modified inbound as they enter the BGP table or as the local BGP router advertises the path outbound toward another BGP peer. These modifications are advertised in inbound (received from a BGP peer) and outbound (sent to a BGP peer) BGP update advertisements.

In general, outbound path attribute updates affect how traffic enters the AS, and inbound path attribute updates affect how traffic leaves the AS. The exact effect of a particular change depends on the specific attribute being modified and its position with regard to BGP's decision-making algorithm.

## The Best-Path Algorithm

By default, BGP can only advertise a single path to its BGP peers. This path, called the *best path*, is the same path that is sent to be potentially installed in the local router's RIB. A common occurrence in routing protocols is receiving several advertisements for the same destination. IGPs utilize metrics as tie-breakers in this event, but BGP does not have a concept of traditional metrics. Instead, it relies on the path attributes to make its routing decisions.

BGP consumes the information provided in path attributes in order to choose a best path from among several competing paths. It does so in a step-by-step elimination process, in which a particular attribute is compared between the two competing paths, and preference is given to a specific value of that attribute. If the values tie, BGP continues to the next step in the algorithm.

Assuming that the next hop IP address specified in the BGP updates is reachable by the local router, the BGP best-path algorithm step-by-step process occurs as follows:

1. Prefer the path with the higher WEIGHT attribute.

2. Prefer the path with the higher LOCAL_PREF attribute.

3. Prefer locally originated routes.

4. Prefer the path with the lowest total AS_PATH attribute length.

5. Prefer the path that is directly injected into BGP over paths that are learned from EGP. Prefer the path that originates from EGP over a path that has unknown or incomplete ORIGIN information.

6. Prefer the path with the lowest MED value.

7. Prefer a path learned externally over a path learned internally.

8. Prefer the path for which the metric to the next hop on the local router is lowest.

9. If all of the above tie, consider using both paths but continuing to evaluate the best path.

10. If two competing paths are both external paths, prefer the path that was learned first.

11. Prefer the path with the lowest BGP router ID.

12. Prefer the path with the shorter CLUSTER length.

13. Prefer the path learned from the peer with the lowest peering IP address.

This algorithm provides two important things to the operation of BGP. First, it ensures that no matter what different set of path attributes two competing paths have, there will always be a single best path chosen. Second, it allows an administrator to manipulate the path attributes in order to influence BGP's best-path decision.

The remainder of this lab examines all the steps of the BGP decision-making algorithm and how specific path attributes can be modified to influence BGP's decision making. It also specifies cases where inbound and outbound make a difference in specific traffic flows.

The topology for this lab is located in the **initial-config** folder → **BGP** folder, **BGP-Topology.pdf.**

The following section describes the topology setup. The initial configurations for all the switches and routers are found in the initial configuration folder.

[--L2 Switching--]

1. SW1 - SW5 are used for this topology

   a. R1, R2, R3, R4, R5, R6, R7, R8 are connected to SW1

   b. R9 and R10 are connected to SW2

   c. R11, R12, R13, R14, and R15 are connected to SW3

   d. R21 is connected to SW4

   e. R16, R17, R18, R19, and R20 are connected to SW5

2. The routers to switch connections are configured to run as trunk ports

3. All x/1 (x - Switch number) interfaces between the switches are configured to run as trunk ports

   [--IP Addressing--]

1. Configure IPv4 addresses on the physical and logical interfaces as indicated in the diagram

   a. Each router in the topology is configured with loopback 1 interface. The IP address format for the loopback 1 interface is x.x.x.x/32 where x is the router number. Eg. R20's loopback 1 address is configured with an IP address of 20.20.20.20/32

   [--BGP Configuration--]

1. AS 300

   a. All BGP peerings within AS 300 are established over Loopback 1 interfaces. AS 300 is subdivided as:

      i.   R1 and R2 are iBGP peers in sub confederation 312

      ii.  R4 and R5 are iBGP peers in sub confederation 345

      iii. R7 and R8 are iBGP peers in sub confederation 378

      iv.  R3 and R6 are iBGP peers in sub confederation 336

      v.  R1 and R4 are eBGP confederation peers

      vi.  R2 and R3 are eBGP confederation peers

      vii.  R3 and R4 are eBGP confederation peers

      viii. R5 and R7 are eBGP confederation peers

      ix.  R6 and R8 are eBGP confederation peers

2. AS 100

   a.  R19 and R20 use their loopback 1 interface for the iBGP peering session between them

3. AS 200

   a.  R16, R17, and R18 use their loopback 1 interface for the iBGP peering session between them

4. AS 400

   a.  All routers in AS 400 use their loopback 1 interfaces for their iBGP peerings

   b.  R11 reflects routes to R10 and R14

   c.  R12 reflects routes to R9, R10, R11, and R13

   d.  R13 reflects routes to R14 and R15

   e.  R9 and R10 are iBGP peers

5. eBGP Peerings are established between:

   a.  R2 - R20

   b.  R2 - R16

   c.  R2 - R10

   d.  R3 - R10

   e.  R6 - R11

   f.  R18 - R19

   g.  R10 - R17

   h.  R9 - R17

## Step 1: WEIGHT

**Note**   Before starting this section, revert the configuration on all the routers to the base initial configuration files provided with the lab.

The first step, holding the highest precedence over all other steps, in the best-path algorithm involves comparing a path attribute called the WEIGHT attribute. The WEIGHT attribute is a Cisco-proprietary attribute, and therefore, this step is performed only on Cisco routers. It is represented by a 16-bit number with a valid range of 0 to 65,535. The attribute is an optional, non-transitive attribute, meaning its value is only significant to the local router and will not be exchanged with neighboring BGP routers in UPDATE messages.

By default, the router will set the WEIGHT for all paths it injects into the BGP table through either **network**, **redistribute**, or **aggregate-address** commands to 32768. Paths introduced into the BGP table are considered local paths, and an example can be seen in the **show ip bgp 110.19.1.1** output on R19 below:

---

**On R19:**

```
R19#show run | section router bgp

router bgp 100
 bgp log-neighbor-changes
 network 110.19.1.1 mask 255.255.255.255

R19#show ip bgp 110.19.1.1

BGP routing table entry for 110.19.1.1/32, version 2
Paths: (1 available, best #1, table default)
  Advertised to update-groups:
     1           2
  Refresh Epoch 1
  Local
    0.0.0.0 from 0.0.0.0 (19.19.19.19)
      Origin IGP, metric 0, localpref 100, weight 32768, valid,
sourced, local, best
      rx pathid: 0, tx pathid: 0x0
```

---

R19 is configured to inject a path to the 110.19.1.1 network into BGP. This path is flagged in its BGP table as a local route.

All other paths received through BGP updates have their WEIGHT attributes initialized at 0. These defaults can be modified per neighbor or per prefix. The non-transitive property of the WEIGHT attribute carries the implication that it is not possible to set it in the outbound direction for a neighbor. If such a configuration is ever attempted, the router kindly reminds you of this fact with the message *"% 'WEIGHT' used as BGP outbound route-map, set weight not supported."* The non-transitive restriction leaves only two ways of manually setting the weight attribute on a router:

- Attached to the **neighbor** command using the **neighbor x.x.x.x weight** *weight* command

- Attached to the **neighbor** command using an inbound route map with the **set weight** clause

The non-transitive property of the WEIGHT attribute also ensures that a router cannot influence the WEIGHT value of its BGP peer. The WEIGHT attribute's position as first in the best-path algorithm and its inability to be affected by neighboring BGP routers give the administrator complete control over what the local router ultimately chooses as its best path, regardless of the interactions of other path attributes.

The WEIGHT attribute can be utilized to force the local router to prefer one path over another in its BGP table. When deciding between two paths to the same prefix in the BGP table, the router will choose the path with the higher WEIGHT value. This preference for choosing higher weight values means that all prefixes originated by the router itself (through the **network**, **redistribute**, or **aggregate-address** commands) will be preferred over all other routers by default due to their default weight setting of 32,768.

This point can be observed below. R20 is configured to inject paths to the 110.20.1.1 and 110.20.2.1 prefixes into its BGP table using a **network** command:

---

**On R20:**

```
router bgp 100
 network 110.20.1.1 mask 255.255.255.255
 network 110.20.2.1 mask 255.255.255.255


R20#show ip bgp

BGP table version is 16, local router ID is 20.20.20.20
Status codes: s suppressed, d damped, h history, * valid, > best,
i - internal,
             r RIB-failure, S Stale, m multipath, b backup-path,
f RT-Filter,
             x best-external, a additional-path, c RIB-compressed,
Origin codes: i - IGP, e - EGP, ? - incomplete
RPKI validation codes: V valid, I invalid, N Not found
    Network          Next Hop        Metric LocPrf Weight Path
 *>i 110.19.1.1/32    19.19.19.19          0    100      0 i
 *>i 110.19.2.1/32    19.19.19.19          0    100      0 i
 *>  110.20.1.1/32    0.0.0.0              0         32768 i
 *>  110.20.2.1/32    0.0.0.0              0         32768 i
 *>i 120.18.1.1/32    19.19.19.19          0    100      0 200 i
 *                    200.2.20.2                          0 300 200 i
 *>i 120.18.2.1/32    19.19.19.19          0    100      0 200 i
 *                    200.2.20.2                          0 300 200 i
 *>  130.7.1.1/32     200.2.20.2                          0 300 i
 * i 140.15.1.1/32    19.19.19.19          0    100      0 200 400 i
 *>                   200.2.20.2                          0 300 400 i
 * i 140.15.2.1/32    19.19.19.19          0    100      0 200 400 i
 *>                   200.2.20.2                          0 300 400 i
```

The WEIGHT values for those paths (highlighted in red) have been set to 32768 in the output. In contrast, the WEIGHT values for the BGP paths learned from R19 and R2 (110.19.1.1/32, 110.19.2.1/32, 120.18.1.1/32, and 120.18.2.1/32) are set to 0.

As stated above, the administrator can manually modify the WEIGHT attribute for a particular path to influence the local outbound routing decision in the BGP table. In the output above, R20 learns paths to the 120.18.1.1 and 120.18.2.1 prefixes from its iBGP neighbor R19 and eBGP neighbor R2. Because the WEIGHT values for these paths are tied, the path via R19 is chosen as best because it has a shorter AS_PATH attribute length (step 4 in the best-path algorithm, explained in detail later). To demonstrate the WEIGHT attribute's higher precedence over the AS_PATH attribute length, R20 will be configured to prefer the path via R2 instead of R19 for the 120.18.1.1 prefix.

Recall that the WEIGHT value can be assigned directly with the **neighbor x.x.x.x weight** command. However, this would apply to all routes learned from that neighbor, which is not the desired outcome of this example. Instead, a route map will be configured using the **set weight** clause. The route map uses a prefix list to target only the 120.18.1.1 prefix. This route map will be applied to the R20/R2 **neighbor** peering statement in the inbound direction, as shown below.

**Note**   The **neighbor x.x.x.x weight** command and an inbound route map can be used simultaneously to set WEIGHT for paths coming from a particular neighbor.

In such a situation, the inbound route map takes precedence over the global **neighbor x.x.x.x weight** command. Any path to a prefix that is not matched by the inbound route map will receive the WEIGHT set by the **neighbor x.x.x.x weight** command.

In the following configuration, the prefix 120.18.1.1 is first identified and permitted in a prefix list called 123. Then a route map called tst is created that references the 123 prefix list. This route map contains the **set weight** parameter with a value of 32768. The route map is then appended to the **neighbor** statement for the eBGP peer 200.2.20.2 in the inbound direction:

---

**On R20:**

```
R20(config)#ip prefix-list 123 permit 120.18.1.1/32

R20(config)#route-map tst permit 10
R20(config-route-map)#match ip address prefix 123
R20(config-route-map)#set weight 32768
R20(config)#route-map tst permit 90

R20(config)#router bgp 100
R20(config-router)#neighbor 200.2.20.2 route-map tst in
```

**Note**   The relationship between route maps and prefix lists (and access lists) has two fundamental properties:

- The prefix list or access list identifies prefixes that will be manipulated by the route map.

- The route map manipulates, permits, or denies those prefixes (or paths to prefixes, in the case of BGP) from being advertised or accepted by the local router.

When using prefix lists or access lists for BGP path attribute modifications, the following rules apply:

- A **permit** action in a prefix list indicates a prefix that will be matched.

- A **deny** action in a prefix list indicates prefixes that will not be matched.

Similarly, when working with route maps for the same purpose, the following rules apply:

- A **permit** route map statement allows the path to be accepted or advertised if it matches all **match** clauses.

- A **deny** route map statement disallows the path from being accepted or advertised if it matches all **match** clauses.

The implicit deny at the end of a prefix list or access list prevents all prefixes that are not matched by a **permit** statement from being manipulated by that particular route map statement. Those that are not matched by the prefix list or access list will still be able to be processed by subsequent route map statements.

The implicit deny at the end of a route map prevents all prefixes that are not matched by any route map statement to be filtered out or blocked from being advertised or accepted. For this reason, it is important to include an empty **permit** route map statement (containing no **match** clauses) at the end of a route map to ensure that unaffected prefixes are allowed to safely pass through to be advertised or accepted.

With the above configured, **clear ip bgp * soft in** is issued on R20. R20 sends a route refresh message to all its neighbors, which is an indication to them to re-send their routing advertisements. When R20 receives the refreshed BGP updates, it processes the inbound route map configuration, assigning the WEIGHT value of 32768 to R2's path for the prefix 120.18.1.1.

Since the WEIGHT value has higher precedence than the AS_PATH attribute, R20 chooses the path via R2 as best. Notice that the best path to 120.18.2.1 has not been affected. Traffic destined to the 120.18.1.1 network from R20 will now transit AS 300, and traffic destined to the 120.18.2.1 network from R20 will be sent to R19.

```
R20#show ip bgp regexp _200$

BGP table version is 48, local router ID is 20.20.20.20
Status codes: s suppressed, d damped, h history, * valid, > best,
i - internal,
            r RIB-failure, S Stale, m multipath, b backup-path,
f RT-Filter,
            x best-external, a additional-path, c RIB-compressed,
Origin codes: i - IGP, e - EGP, ? - incomplete
RPKI validation codes: V valid, I invalid, N Not found

     Network          Next Hop          Metric LocPrf Weight Path
 *>  120.18.1.1/32    200.2.20.2                      32768 300 200 i
 * i                  19.19.19.19       0     100     0 200 i
 *   120.18.2.1/32    200.2.20.2                      0 300 200 i
 *>i                  19.19.19.19       0     100     0 200 i
```

Observing R20's advertisement of the 120.18.1.1 network to R19 helps confirm the non-transitive property of the WEIGHT attribute. A quick look at R19's BGP table for its paths to the 120.18.1.1/32 prefix reveals a missing WEIGHT value for the path received from R20:

**On R19:**

```
R19#show ip bgp 120.18.1.1

BGP routing table entry for 120.18.1.1/32, version 6
Paths: (2 available, best #2, table default)
  Advertised to update-groups:
     2
  Refresh Epoch 2
  300 200
    20.20.20.20 (metric 11) from 20.20.20.20 (20.20.20.20)
      Origin IGP, metric 0, localpref 100,[weight value of 0 should be
here but isn't], valid, internal
      rx pathid: 0, tx pathid: 0
  Refresh Epoch 1
  200
    200.18.19.18 from 200.18.19.18 (18.18.18.18)
      Origin IGP, metric 0, localpref 100, valid, external, best
      rx pathid: 0, tx pathid: 0x0
```

The missing WEIGHT value is a result of how Cisco IOS chooses to display path attributes in the long format of the **show ip bgp x.xx.x.x** command. The router shows a weight value only if it has a value over 0. Paths with a WEIGHT value of 0 do not report this value in the long version of the command. The 0 WEIGHT value is, however, reported in the short version **show ip bgp** command output shown below:

```
R19#show ip bgp | begin Net

    Network          Next Hop         Metric LocPrf Weight Path
*>  110.19.1.1/32    0.0.0.0          0             32768 i
*>  110.19.2.1/32    0.0.0.0          0             32768 i
*>i 110.20.1.1/32    20.20.20.20      0      100        0 i
*>i 110.20.2.1/32    20.20.20.20      0      100        0 i
* i 120.18.1.1/32    20.20.20.20      0      100        0 300 200 i
*>                   200.18.19.18     0                 0 200 i
*>  120.18.2.1/32    200.18.19.18     0                 0 200 i
*   130.7.1.1/32     200.18.19.18                       0 200 300 i
*>i                  20.20.20.20      0      100        0 300 i
* i 140.15.1.1/32    20.20.20.20      0      100        0 300 400 i
*>                   200.18.19.18                       0 200 400 i
* i 140.15.2.1/32    20.20.20.20      0      100        0 300 400 i
*>                   200.18.19.18                       0 200 400 i
```

The output above confirms that R19 has a WEIGHT value of 0 for all paths to the 120.18.1.1/32 network, including the path it receives from R20. This fact can further be seen by the packet capture below:

```
Internet Protocol Version 4, Src: 20.20.20.20, Dst: 19.19.19.19
Transmission Control Protocol, Src Port: 179, Dst Port: 24627, Seq:
43, Ack: 43, Len: 283
Border Gateway Protocol - UPDATE Message
    Marker: ffffffffffffffffffffffffffffffff
    Length: 66
    Type: UPDATE Message (2)
   Withdrawn Routes Length: 0
    Total Path Attribute Length: 38
    Path attributes
        Path Attribute - ORIGIN: IGP
        Path Attribute - AS_PATH: 300 200
        Path Attribute - NEXT_HOP: 20.20.20.20
        Path Attribute - MULTI_EXIT_DISC: 0
        Path Attribute - LOCAL_PREF: 100
```

```
    Network Layer Reachability Information (NLRI)
        120.18.1.1/32
Border Gateway Protocol - UPDATE Message
Border Gateway Protocol - UPDATE Message
Border Gateway Protocol - UPDATE Message
```

The key point to notice in the capture is there is no "Path Attribute - WEIGHT" section in the packet capture, which proves that R20 did not advertise the WEIGHT value to R19.

All of the above pieces of evidence confirm that the WEIGHT value is not exchanged between neighbors. R19 chooses the path received from R18 over the one received from R20 for the same prefix due to the lower AS_PATH attribute.

## Step 2: Local Preference

**Note**   Before starting this section, revert the configuration on all routers to the base initial configuration files provided with the lab.

Local preference, or LOCAL_PREF, is the next step in the BGP best-path algorithm. Unlike WEIGHT, local preference is a well-known discretionary BGP attribute, meaning all implementations of BGP should understand the local preference attribute. It is a 32-bit number ranging from 0 to 4,294,967,295. As with WEIGHT, higher values are preferred over lower ones. The default local preference value for received paths that have no explicit local preference defined is 100.

Local preference is used by the local AS to signify a global preference for a specific path that should be used within the AS. To serve this purpose, local preference has what is known as *limited transitive capabilities*.

Limited transit capability signifies that Local Preference can be sent in BGP updates, but routers only send it in specific situations. It is only sent in BGP updates to iBGP peers and is never sent to eBGP peers. This limited transit functionality is what allows Local Preference to be used to define preferred paths for prefixes in the entire AS and affect the entire AS's outbound routing decisions. Local Preference's limited transit capability does not apply to confederation eBGP peers as documented in RFC 4271:

### 5.1.5.   LOCAL_PREF

LOCAL_PREF is a well-known attribute that SHALL be included in all UPDATE messages that a given BGP speaker sends to other internal peers. A BGP speaker MUST NOT include this attribute in UPDATE messages it sends to external peers, except in the case of BGP Confederations.

This is because BGP confederations are simply subdivisions of a large AS. Confederations are typically implemented to reduce the iBGP full-mesh scaling issues as the number of iBGP routers grows within the AS. These subdivisions are known as sub-autonomous systems. Even though the AS has been divided into sub-autonomous systems, the routing inside the AS remains unchanged. The routers within the AS should still all agree on all outbound routing decisions.

For example, in AS 300, the policy could be such that outbound traffic destined to AS 400 should exit R2 or R6. This policy could be enforced using local preference and can be set on R2 or R6 in the inbound direction for routes received from AS 400. To maintain consistent routing within the AS, this local preference value should be communicated to R4 even though it is in a different sub-AS within AS 300.

Local preference can be set in the following manner using a route map with the **set local-preference** clause:

- **Inbound** from any BGP peer
- **Outbound** to iBGP peers only

An example will help illustrate the implications of each option. In this case, we examine AS 300's choice of best path to reach the 120.18.1.1/32 prefix. A path to this prefix is received by edge routers R2, R3, and R6 in the network from their eBGP peers. These routers will advertise the same path to their confederation iBGP and eBGP peers. This act of advertising the prefix makes R2, R3, and R6 potential exit points for traffic destined to 120.18.1.1/32. Traffic will be funneled from the internal routers R1, R4, R5, R7, and R8 toward R2, R3, or R6, based on which path the AS decides is the best path.

> **Note**   In the paragraph above, R1, R4, R5, R7, and R8 are called *internal routers* to signify the fact that they do not have any true eBGP peers. They only have confederation iBGP or eBGP peers that exist within AS 300. Not having true eBGP peers from which external paths can be learned means they will not receive any external paths. This makes them ineligible to be exit points for any traffic.
>
> Alternatively, R2, R3, and R6 are called *edge routers* because they have eBGP peerings and sit on the edge of the network. Being positioned as such, these routers will learn external paths and advertise them as internal paths inside AS 300.

BGP will only select a single best path to be submitted to the routing table by default. This means only the path from R2, R3, or R6 will be chosen as best by all routers in the topology. Next, we examine each edge router and internal router R8's path selection decision.

R2 in AS 300 has multiple paths to reach 120.18.1.1/32 and 120.18.2.1/32. The output below shows that it currently uses the direct path from R16 as its best path due to the shorter AS_PATH attribute length.

## On R2:

```
R2#show ip bgp regex _200$

BGP table version is 28, local router ID is 2.2.2.2
Status codes: s suppressed, d damped, h history, * valid, > best,
i - internal,
             r RIB-failure, S Stale, m multipath, b backup-path,
f RT-Filter,
             x best-external, a additional-path, c RIB-compressed,
Origin codes: i - IGP, e - EGP, ? - incomplete
RPKI validation codes: V valid, I invalid, N Not found

     Network          Next Hop            Metric LocPrf Weight Path
 *   120.18.1.1/32    200.2.20.20                    0 100 200 i
 *                    200.2.10.10                    0 400 200 i
 *>                   200.2.16.16                    0 200 i
 *   120.18.2.1/32    200.2.20.20                    0 100 200 i
 *                    200.2.10.10                    0 400 200 i
 *>                   200.2.16.16                    0 200 i
```

R2 advertises this selected best path to all of its BGP neighbors, setting itself as the next hop because it has been configured with the **next-hop-self** setting on all of its iBGP peers. Of those neighbors, R3, as an edge router, is most notable for this exercise. R3 receives the paths from R2 and R10. It compares the two paths and chooses R2's path due to the shorter AS_PATH attribute, as shown below. As a result, R3's routing table entry for the 120.18.1.1/32 network shows R2 as the next hop.

## On R3:

```
R3#show ip bgp regex _200$

--- omitted ---
     Network          Next Hop          Metric LocPrf Weight Path
 *   120.18.1.1/32    200.3.10.10                      0 400 200 i
 *>                   2.2.2.2               0    100    0 (312) 200 i
 *   120.18.2.1/32    200.3.10.10                      0 400 200 i
 *>                   2.2.2.2               0    100    0 (312) 200 i
```

```
R3#show ip route bgp

--- omitted ---
Gateway of last resort is not set

      110.0.0.0/32 is subnetted, 2 subnets
B        110.19.1.1 [200/0] via 2.2.2.2, 00:27:47
B        110.19.2.1 [200/0] via 2.2.2.2, 00:27:47
      120.0.0.0/32 is subnetted, 2 subnets
B        120.18.1.1 [200/0] via 2.2.2.2, 00:27:16
B        120.18.2.1 [200/0] via 2.2.2.2, 00:27:16

--- omitted ---
```

R3 then advertises this chosen best path to R6 with itself as next hop because it has been
configured with the **next-hop-self** setting on all of its BGP peers. R6 has received a path
to the same prefix from R11. It compares the two paths and selects the path from R3 as
best because of the AS_PATH attribute length again. Just as in R3's case, R6's routing
table reflects R3 as its next hop to reach the 120.18.1.1/32 prefix as well:

**On R6:**

```
R6#show ip bgp regex _200$

--- omitted ---
     Network          Next Hop          Metric LocPrf Weight Path
*>i 120.18.1.1/32     3.3.3.3              0     100       0 (312) 200 i
*                     200.6.11.11                           0 400 200 i
*>i 120.18.2.1/32     3.3.3.3              0     100       0 (312) 200 i
*                     200.6.11.11                           0 400 200 i

R6#show ip route bgp

--- omitted ---
Gateway of last resort is not set

      110.0.0.0/32 is subnetted, 2 subnets
B        110.19.1.1 [200/0] via 3.3.3.3, 00:30:18
B        110.19.2.1 [200/0] via 3.3.3.3, 00:30:18
      120.0.0.0/32 is subnetted, 2 subnets
B        120.18.1.1 [200/0] via 3.3.3.3, 00:29:50
B        120.18.2.1 [200/0] via 3.3.3.3, 00:29:50
```

Finally, R6 advertises this same path to its confed-eBGP peer R8, as shown below. It also sets the next hop to itself because it has been configured with the **next-hop-self** setting on all of its BGP peers. R8 only receives a single path to this prefix from R6, so it marks it as best and installs a route in its routing table pointing to R6 as the next hop:

---

### On R8:

```
R8#show ip bgp regexp _200$

BGP table version is 32, local router ID is 8.8.8.8
Status codes: s suppressed, d damped, h history, * valid, > best,
i - internal,
            r RIB-failure, S Stale, m multipath, b backup-path,
f RT-Filter,
            x best-external, a additional-path, c RIB-compressed,
Origin codes: i - IGP, e - EGP, ? - incomplete
RPKI validation codes: V valid, I invalid, N Not found

     Network          Next Hop      Metric LocPrf Weight Path
 *>  120.18.1.1/32    6.6.6.6            0    100      0 (336 312) 200 i
 *>  120.18.2.1/32    6.6.6.6            0    100      0 (336 312) 200 i

R8#show ip route bgp | begin Gateway
Gateway of last resort is not set

      110.0.0.0/32 is subnetted, 2 subnets
B        110.19.1.1 [200/0] via 6.6.6.6, 00:31:22
B        110.19.2.1 [200/0] via 6.6.6.6, 00:31:22
      120.0.0.0/32 is subnetted, 2 subnets
B        120.18.1.1 [200/0] via 6.6.6.6, 00:31:10
B        120.18.2.1 [200/0] via 6.6.6.6, 00:31:10
```

---

**Note**   The path on R3 and R6 may not seem shorter because the AS_PATH is listed as **(312) 200**. The numbers in parentheses represent the confederation sub-ASNs the path traverses more specifically forming the **AS_CONFED_SEQUENCE**. The AS_CONFED_SEQUENCE is ignored whenever making best-path decisions in BGP. The guide goes into more detail on this fact in the AS_PATH section.

From the above outputs, it is concluded that R8 uses R6 as the next hop to reach the 120.18.1.1/32 prefix, R6 uses R3, and R3 uses R2. Traffic flowing from R8 to the 120.18.1.1/32 prefix flows R8 → R6 → R3 → R2, as shown in the traceroute below:

```
R8#traceroute 120.18.1.1

Type escape sequence to abort.
Tracing the route to 120.18.1.1
VRF info: (vrf in name/id, vrf out name/id)
  1 30.6.8.6 1 msec 1 msec 1 msec
  2 30.3.6.3 1 msec 1 msec 1 msec
  3 30.2.3.2 2 msec 2 msec 1 msec
  4  *  *  *
```

The traffic only exits the AS at the edge router R2, indicated by the * * * output of the traceroute. This output signifies that the traceroute fails after the R2 router hop. The failure occurs because AS 200 does not have a route to reach R8 and cannot route the traceroute probe back to R8.

No matter which edge router first receives traffic destined to the 120.18.1.1/32 network, it eventually ends up at R2 because R6 forwards it to R3, and R3 ultimately forwards to R2. Thus, the exit point for traffic destined to the 120.18.1.1/32 network in AS 300 is R2.

The following sections show what happens when the administrator attempts to make R6 become the preferred exit point for the 120.18.1.1/32 prefix by modifying the local preference attribute R6 advertises to its neighbors. These sections examine the change made in the **outbound** direction and again in the **inbound** direction. Each example uses the following **prefix-list/route-map** combination to set the local preference advertised by R6 to other routers in AS 300, in an attempt to ensure that all other routers accept R6's path as the best path. The only difference is the choice of inbound/outbound direction and to which BGP neighbor the route map is applied:

```
On R6:

R6(config)#ip prefix-list 123 permit 120.18.1.1/32

R6(config)#route-map tst permit 10
R6(config-route-map)#match ip address prefix 123
R6(config-route-map)#set local-preference 200
R6(config)#route-map tst permit 90
```

### Local Preference Outbound

In this section, the administrator chooses to apply the change in the outbound direction on R6. R6 will only advertise the selected path with the modified LOCAL_PREF value to neighbors where the route map is applied.

In order to attempt to change outbound to affect all the other routers in AS 300's best-path decision, the change will be applied on every neighbor command for R6's peers within AS 300. In this case, it is applied to R3 and R8 in the outbound direction, as shown:

---

**On R6:**

```
R6(config)#router bgp 336
R6(config-router)#neighbor 3.3.3.3 route-map tst out
R6(config-router)#neighbor 8.8.8.8 route-map tst out

R6#clear ip bgp * soft
```

---

After the changes have been made, the BGP table is refreshed by issuing the **clear ip bgp * soft** command. As a result, R6 re-sends the updates to R3 and R8 with the modified LOCAL_PREF value 200, as shown in the packet capture below:

---

```
Internet Protocol Version 4, Src: 6.6.6.6, Dst: 8.8.8.8
Transmission Control Protocol, Src Port: 29995, Dst Port: 179, Seq:
24, Ack: 20, Len: 387
Border Gateway Protocol - UPDATE Message
Border Gateway Protocol - UPDATE Message
    Marker: ffffffffffffffffffffffffffffffff
    Length: 72
    Type: UPDATE Message (2)
    Withdrawn Routes Length: 0
    Total Path Attribute Length: 44
    Path attributes
        Path Attribute - ORIGIN: IGP
        Path Attribute - AS_PATH: (336 312) 200
        Path Attribute - NEXT_HOP: 6.6.6.6
        Path Attribute - MULTI_EXIT_DISC: 0
        Path Attribute - LOCAL_PREF: 200
    Network Layer Reachability Information (NLRI)
        120.18.1.1/32
```

The expectation at this point is that all of the routers in AS 300 now choose to use R6 to reach the designated prefix 120.18.1.1/32. A quick glance at R8's BGP table seems promising:

**On R8:**

```
R8#show ip bgp regexp _200$

BGP table version is 33, local router ID is 8.8.8.8
Status codes: s suppressed, d damped, h history, * valid, > best,
i - internal,
            r RIB-failure, S Stale, m multipath, b backup-path,
f RT-Filter,
            x best-external, a additional-path, c RIB-compressed,
Origin codes: i - IGP, e - EGP, ? - incomplete
RPKI validation codes: V valid, I invalid, N Not found

     Network          Next Hop     Metric LocPrf Weight Path
 *>  120.18.1.1/32    6.6.6.6        0     200     0 (336 312) 200 i
 *>  120.18.2.1/32    6.6.6.6        0     100     0 (336 312) 200 i
```

R8's BGP table reflects the changes made on R6. The path to 120.18.1.1/32 now has a local preference value of 200. This proves that even though R8 is a confed-eBGP peer to R6, R6 still communicates the local preference changes to R8, in compliance with the RFC excerpt mentioned earlier.

The problem, however, comes in whenever R3's BGP table is examined:

**On R3:**

```
R3#show ip bgp regexp _200$

--- omitted ---
     Network          Next Hop     Metric LocPrf Weight Path
 *>  120.18.1.1/32    2.2.2.2        0     100     0 (312) 200 i
 *                    200.3.10.10                  0 400 200 i
 *>  120.18.2.1/32    2.2.2.2        0     100     0 (312) 200 i
 *                    200.3.10.10                  0 400 200 i
```

R3's BGP table contains no noticeable changes. It continues to use R2's path as the best path to reach the prefix 120.18.1.1/32. Why does R3 seemingly ignore R6's advertisements? The answer lies in R6's BGP table, shown on the next page:

**On R6:**

```
R6#show ip bgp regexp _200$

--- omitted---

    Network           Next Hop        Metric LocPrf Weight Path
*>i 120.18.1.1/32     3.3.3.3              0    100      0 (312) 200 i
*                     200.6.11.11                        0 400 200 i
*   120.18.2.1/32     200.6.11.11                        0 400 200 i
*>i                   3.3.3.3              0    100      0 (312) 200 i
```

This table reveals that, although R6 has advertised a modified local preference value to its neighbors, its own BGP table is unchanged by the outbound policy. The reason is that outbound modifications to path attributes do not affect the local router's BGP table. R6 still chooses R3 as its best path due to the shorter AS_PATH attribute length. As a result, R6 will not advertise R3's path back to R3 because R3 is a confederation internal peer. The iBGP split-horizon rule prevents R6 from advertising an internal route to an internal peer. This fact is proven by observing R6's advertised routes to R3 below, using the command **show ip bgp neighbors 3.3.3.3 advertised-routes**:

```
R6#show ip bgp neighbors 3.3.3.3 advertised-routes

BGP table version is 27, local router ID is 6.6.6.6
Status codes: s suppressed, d damped, h history, * valid, > best,
i - internal,
            r RIB-failure, S Stale, m multipath, b backup-path,
f RT-Filter,
            x best-external, a additional-path, c RIB-compressed,
Origin codes: i - IGP, e - EGP, ? - incomplete
RPKI validation codes: V valid, I invalid, N Not found
    Network           Next Hop            Metric LocPrf Weight Path
*>  140.15.1.1/32     200.6.11.11                          0 400 i
*>  140.15.2.1/32     200.6.11.11                          0 400 i
```

**Note**    A BGP router follows different rules for advertising paths depending on whether the peer is an internal or external peer. In the above, R3 and R6 have a confederation internal BGP peering with each other. Such peerings act like internal peerings. The **show ip bgp neighbor 3.3.3.3** command on R6 confirms the two peers are connected via an internal link:

```
R6#show ip bgp neighbors 3.3.3.3
BGP neighbor is 3.3.3.3,  remote AS 336, internal link
  BGP version 4, remote router ID 3.3.3.3
  Neighbor under common administration
  BGP state = Established, up for 6d00h
  Last read 00:00:22, last write 00:00:24, hold time is 180, keepalive
  interval is 60 seconds
  Neighbor sessions:
    1 active, is not multisession capable (disabled)
```

The reasoning behind this lies in how BGP advertises routes. For external (eBGP) peers, the router prepends its own ASN to the AS_PATH attribute in the UPDATE message sent to the external peer. For internal (iBGP or confederation iBGP) peers, this AS_PATH prepend is not performed.

Recall that BGP uses the AS_PATH attribute for loop prevention. Paths received with the router's own ASN in the AS_PATH attribute are rejected. Therefore the AS_PATH is not prepended with the router's ASN when advertising to other internal peers.

The side effect of this is there is no way for the internal peer to verify the path is not a looped path. The only sure way to prevent a loop is for the receiving peer to never advertise the received internal path to another internal peer. This is the iBGP split-horizon rule.

To mitigate this, iBGP peers should be fully meshed (all internal BGP routers peer with all other internal BGP routers), employ route reflection, or use confederations.

AS 300 has decided to employ confederations to bypass this requirement. Confederations are implemented by breaking up the AS into multiple sub-ASes. These ASes have their own ASN, which is recorded in the AS_CONFED_SEQUENCE attribute of paths advertised between sub-ASes. The AS_CONFED_SEQUENCE attribute is used in lieu of the AS_PATH attribute for loop prevention.

R6 does, however, advertise the path to R8. You might think that R3 should still receive the path from R6 through the R8 → R7 → R5 → R4 path. Following that path leads to the correct answer:

1. First, R3 selects R2's path as the best path to reach the 120.18.1.1/32 prefix. The AS_CONFED_SEQUENCE at this point is (312). R3 advertises this best path to R6.

2. R6 receives the path and chooses it as its best path. It advertises the path to R8 with the modified LOCAL_PREF value of 200 and the AS_CONFED_SEQUENCE value (336 312).

3. R8 receives the path as well and chooses it as its best path. It advertises to R7, retaining the received LOCAL_PREF of 200 and the AS_CONFED_SEQUENCE value (336 312).

4. R7 receives the path and marks it as the best path. It advertises the path to R5 with the retained LOCAL_PREF value 200 and the modified AS_CONFED_SEQUENCE value (378 336 312).

5. R5 receives the path, marks it as best, and advertises to R4, retaining the received LOCAL_PREF value 200 and the AS_CONFED_SEQUENCE value (378 336 312).

6. R4 receives the path and marks it as best. It advertises the path to R1 and R3 with the retained LOCAL_PREF value 200 and the AS_CONFED_SEQUENCE value (345 378 336 312).

What happens next is critical to this example. Both R3 and R1 receive the path from R4 in a BGP update. They examine the AS_CONFED_SEQUENCE attribute, only to find their own sub-ASN in the sequence. For this reason, both R1 and R3 deny the update. This is proven on R3 through the following debug message:

```
BGP(0): 4.4.4.4 rcv UPDATE w/ attr: nexthop 6.6.6.6, origin i, local-
pref 200, metric 0, originator 0.0.0.0, merged path (345 378 336 312)
200, AS_PATH , community , extended community , SSA attribute
BGPSSA ssacount is 0

BGP(0): 4.4.4.4 rcv UPDATE about 120.18.1.1/32 -- DENIED due to:
AS-PATH contains our own AS;
```

Notice that the path is received from 4.4.4.4, with the LOCAL_PREF value 200 and the indicated AS_CONFED_SEQUENCE clearly containing R3's sub-ASN 336. The same occurs on R1. Both R1 and R3 are forced to deny the path, in compliance with standard BGP confederation rules. These rules protect the topology from a loop situation that could occur as a result of modifying the LOCAL_PREF value outbound on R6.

All in all, modifying the LOCAL_PREF value outbound on R6 does not result in the desired outcome because R6 does not affect the change itself. R6 continues to use the same path through R3 to reach the 120.18.1.1/32 prefix, triggering a sequence of events that ultimately leads to the state reported above.

While there may be specific use cases where setting the local preference in this manner is a desirable outcome, it should be done with caution and careful examination due to the fact that suboptimal routing and control/data plane loops can result in such changes. It is also true that R6 could also manipulate its own BGP table to remedy the problem. It is far easier to simply apply the change inbound, as specified in the next section.

**Note**   The potential for suboptimal routing can be observed in the case of R5. R5 chooses the path received from R7 as the best path. When it installs the path in its BGP table, the
next hop points to R6's 6.6.6.6 address. When R5 needs to route a packet, it must recurse
to an exit interface of the next hop 6.6.6.6:

```
R5#show ip route bgp | in 120.18.1.1
B         120.18.1.1 [200/0] via 6.6.6.6, 00:49:06
```

R5's routing table has two equal-cost paths to reach 6.6.6.6—one through R4 and one
through R7—as shown below:

```
R5#show ip cef 6.6.6.6
6.6.6.6/32
   nexthop 30.4.5.4 Ethernet0/0.45
   nexthop 30.5.7.7 Ethernet0/0.57
```

Because R6 currently uses R3 as its best path and R3 uses R2 as its best path, the ultimate
exit point is R2. With the current state of R5' table, R5 has the potential to send packets
on an R4 → R3 → R2 path OR an R7 → R8 → R6 → R3 → R2 path.

The path through R7 is the suboptimal path, traversing four routers to reach R2, and the
path through R4 is more optimal, traversing only two routers to reach R2.

### Local Preference Inbound

The preceding section demonstrated how an outbound policy that modified the local
preference value on R6 for the 120.18.1.1 prefix did not change the LOCAL_PREF value
on R6. As a result, R6's best-path decision remained unaffected, and R6 continued to use
the path from R3 as best. The effects of the change were seen only on R4, R5, R7, and
R8, which all decided to use the path from R6 as their best paths. The net result is that R6
was not chosen as the preferred exit path in AS 300, and the modifications performed on
R6 made suboptimal routing a possibility.

To force R6 to become the new exit point, rather than setting the local preference outbound
toward its neighbors, the local preference in this case is set inbound as R6 receives the path
from its eBGP peer R11. This change is made by first removing the previous outbound configuration and applying the route map tst inbound on the neighborship to R11, as shown below:

**On R6:**

```
R6(config)#router bgp 336

R6(config-router)#no neighbor 3.3.3.3 route-map tst out
R6(config-router)#no neighbor 8.8.8.8 route-map tst out

R6#clear ip bgp * soft
R6(config)#router bgp 336
R6(config-router)#neighbor 200.6.11.11 route-map tst in
```

After performing a soft clear of the BGP table, R6 assigns the LOCAL_PREF value 200 to the path to the 120.18.1.1/32 received from R11, as shown below:

```
R6#clear ip bgp * soft

R6#show ip bgp regexp _200$

--- omitted ---
    Network            Next Hop          Metric LocPrf Weight Path
 *>  120.18.1.1/32     200.6.11.11              200      0 400 200 i
 *   120.18.2.1/32     200.6.11.11                       0 400 200 i
 *>i                   3.3.3.3            0      100      0 (312) 200 i
```

The output above contrasts with the output observed in the outbound section. Here, the path to 120.18.1.1/32 exists in R6's BGP table, with a LOCAL_PREF value 200, whereas in the outbound section, there was no noticeable change in R6's BGP table following the policy modification.

R6 can now act on the new LOCAL_PREF setting and choose the path received from R11 as the best path. As shown with the **debug ip bgp update** output below from R3 and R8, R6 advertises this best path to all of its BGP neighbors, this time including R3 because the received path from R11 is an external path, not an internal one.

**On R3:**

```
BGP(0): 6.6.6.6 rcvd UPDATE w/ attr: nexthop 6.6.6.6, origin i,
localpref 200, metric 0, merged path 400 200, AS_PATH

BGP(0): 6.6.6.6 rcvd 120.18.1.1/32
```

**On R8:**

```
BGP(0): 6.6.6.6 rcvd UPDATE w/ attr: nexthop 6.6.6.6, origin i,
localpref 200, metric 0, merged path (336) 400 200, AS_PATH

Scode_l20:07:09.543: BGP(0): 6.6.6.6 rcvd 120.18.1.1/32
```

Because R3 chooses R6's path as its best path, it advertises this path to R2 and R4, its confed-eBGP neighbors:

**On R3:**

```
R3#show ip bgp regexp _200$

BGP table version is 26, local router ID is 3.3.3.3
```

```
Status codes: s suppressed, d damped, h history, * valid, > best,
i - internal,
            r RIB-failure, S Stale, m multipath, b backup-path,
f RT-Filter,
            x best-external, a additional-path, c RIB-compressed,
Origin codes: i - IGP, e - EGP, ? - incomplete
RPKI validation codes: V valid, I invalid, N Not found

     Network            Next Hop         Metric LocPrf Weight Path
 *>i 120.18.1.1/32      6.6.6.6               0    200      0 400 200 i
 *                      200.3.10.10                         0 400 200 i
 *>  120.18.2.1/32      2.2.2.2               0    100      0 (312) 200 i
 *                      200.3.10.10                         0 400 200 i
```

In the following example, R2 receives R3's new best path with LOCAL_PREF set to 200, even though it is a confed-eBGP peer of R3. R2 chooses this path as best and will advertise it on to its BGP peers as well.

**On R2:**

```
R2#show ip bgp regexp _200$

BGP table version is 22, local router ID is 2.2.2.2
Status codes: s suppressed, d damped, h history, * valid, > best,
i - internal,
            r RIB-failure, S Stale, m multipath, b backup-path,
f RT-Filter,
            x best-external, a additional-path, c RIB-compressed,
Origin codes: i - IGP, e - EGP, ? - incomplete
RPKI validation codes: V valid, I invalid, N Not found

     Network            Next Hop      Metric LocPrf Weight Path
 *>  120.18.1.1/32      3.3.3.3            0    200      0 (336) 400 200 i
 *                      200.2.16.16                     0 200 i
 *                      200.2.10.10                     0 400 200 i
 *                      200.2.20.20                     0 100 200 i
 *>  120.18.2.1/32      200.2.16.16                     0 200 i
 *                      200.2.10.10                     0 400 200 i
 *                      200.2.2                         0 100 200 i
```

This process continues until all routers in the AS receive the path originally advertised by R6. The other routers will choose this path as best, resulting in the entire AS 300 agreeing that R6 should be the exit point for the 120.18.1.1/32 network.

**Note**   Reviewing the BGP table on R6 after the inbound policy change reveals that an interesting dichotomy exists between the BGP table's current state and the state of the BGP table before the policy change was made.

**R6 Before:**

```
R6#show ip bgp regex _200$
--- omitted ---
    Network            Next Hop        Metric LocPrf Weight Path
 *>i 120.18.1.1/32     3.3.3.3              0    100      0 (312) 200 i
 *                     200.6.11.11                        0 400 200 i
 *>i 120.18.2.1/32     3.3.3.3              0    100      0 (312) 200 i
 *                     200.6.11.11                        0 400 200 i
```

**R6 After:**

```
R6#show ip bgp regexp _200$
--- omitted ---
    Network            Next Hop        Metric LocPrf Weight Path
 *>  120.18.1.1/32     200.6.11.11            200         0 400 200 i
 *   120.18.2.1/32     200.6.11.11                        0 400 200 i
 *>i                   3.3.3.3              0    100      0 (312) 200 i
```

Before any changes were made, R6 received two paths to the 120.18.1.1/32 prefix, one from R3 and one from R11. After the changes were made, however, R6 only receives a single path.

The sequence of events that brought this change is as follows:

1. R6 first receives the two paths (from R11 and R3).

2. Because R6's modified policy sets the local preference to 200 for the path received from R11, R6 chooses this path as best over the path received from R3.

3. R6 advertises its best path, with local preference 200, to R3.

4. R3 compares this newly received path from R6 to its other received paths for the same prefix. Namely, the path it received from R2, which is its current best path.

5. R3 selects the path from R6 as the best path because of the local preference.

6. R3 now advertises R6's path to all of its BGP neighbors. At the same time R3 withdraws the path from R6.

Through this sequence of events, R3 discovers a better path to 120.18.1.1/32 through R6. This new path replaces its previous best path through R2. Because R3 has replaced its best path, it needs to update all of its neighbors about the new path change. To do so,

*Continued*

R3 must withdraw the path from R2 it advertised to all of its neighbors, and then advertise the new path to R6. It will not, however, advertise R6's path to R6 again because it is an internal path. A BGP router does not advertise internal paths to iBGP peers.

A debug performed on R6 during this transition proves R3 withdraws its path from R6 and doesn't advertise a new path to R6 again:

```
19:00:42.568: BGP(0): 3.3.3.3 rcv UPDATE about 120.18.1.1/32 --
withdrawn
The final table on R3 is as follows:
R3#show ip bgp regexp _200$
BGP table version is 26, local router ID is 3.3.3.3
Status codes: s suppressed, d damped, h history, * valid, >
best,
i - internal,
            r RIB-failure, S Stale, m multipath, b backup-
path,
f RT-Filter,
            x best-external, a additional-path, c RIB-
compressed,
Origin codes: i - IGP, e - EGP, ? - incomplete
RPKI validation codes: V valid, I invalid, N Not found

      Network          Next Hop        Metric LocPrf Weight Path
 *>i 120.18.1.1/32     6.6.6.6           0     200      0 400 200 i
 *                     200.3.10.10                      0 400 200 i
 *>  120.18.2.1/32     2.2.2.2           0     100      0 (312)
200 i
 *                     200.3.10.10                      0 400 200 i
```

A quick glance at the BGP table on R20 helps prove that local preference, while communicated to iBGP and confed-eBGP peers, is not communicated to true eBGP peers. In fact, the LOCAL_PREF attribute isn't even included in the UPDATE packet sent from R2 to R20, as evidenced by the packet capture below:

```
Internet Protocol Version 4, Src: 200.2.20.2, Dst: 200.2.20.20
Transmission Control Protocol, Src Port: 179, Dst Port: 59790, Seq:
43, Ack: 20, Len: 293
Border Gateway Protocol - UPDATE Message
Border Gateway Protocol - UPDATE Message
Border Gateway Protocol - UPDATE Message
   Marker: ffffffffffffffffffffffffffffffff
   Length: 52
   Type: UPDATE Message (2)
```

```
    Withdrawn Routes Length: 0
    Total Path Attribute Length: 24
    Path attributes !LOCAL_PREF is missing here
        Path Attribute - ORIGIN: IGP
        Path Attribute - AS_PATH: 300 200
        Path Attribute - NEXT_HOP: 200.2.20.2
    Network Layer Reachability Information (NLRI)
        120.18.2.1/32
```

The BGP table shows the path received from R2, but without the local preference modifications:

**On R20:**

```
R20#show ip bgp regexp _200$

BGP table version is 17, local router ID is 20.20.20.20
Status codes: s suppressed, d damped, h history, * valid, > best,
i - internal,
            r RIB-failure, S Stale, m multipath, b backup-path,
f RT-Filter,
            x best-external, a additional-path, c RIB-compressed,
Origin codes: i - IGP, e - EGP, ? - incomplete
RPKI validation codes: V valid, I invalid, N Not found

     Network          Next Hop         Metric LocPrf Weight Path
 *   120.18.1.1/32    200.2.20.2                    0 300 400 200 i
 *>i                  19.19.19.19        0    100    0 200 i
 *   120.18.2.1/32    200.2.20.2                    0 300 200 i
 *>i                  19.19.19.19        0    100    0 200 i
```

Above, it appears as though there is no local preference value assigned to the path received from R2. In reality, IOS does not show the local preference value if it has not been modified from the default in the **show ip bgp** output for external prefixes. As stated earlier, the default LOCAL_PREF value is 100. The detailed **show ip bgp 128.18.1.1** output confirms the default LOCAL_PREF setting:

```
R20#show ip bgp 120.18.1.1
BGP routing table entry for 120.18.1.1/32, version 48
Paths: (2 available, best #1, table default)
  Advertised to update-groups:
     1
  Refresh Epoch 13
  200
```

```
    19.19.19.19 (metric 11) from 19.19.19.19 (110.19.2.1)
      Origin IGP, metric 0, localpref 100, valid, internal, best
      rx pathid: 0, tx pathid: 0x0
  Refresh Epoch 13
  300 400 200
    200.2.20.2 from 200.2.20.2 (2.2.2.2)
      Origin IGP, localpref 100, valid, external
      rx pathid: 0, tx pathid: 0
```

## Step 3: Locally Originated

**Note**   Before starting this section, revert the configuration on all the routers to the base
initial configuration files provided with the lab.

Step 3 of the BGP best-path algorithm makes a distinction between locally originated
paths and paths received from other BGP peers. As mentioned earlier, in BGP, a locally
originated path is a path that was injected into the BGP table using either the **network**,
**redistribute**, or **aggregate-address** command. By default, the BGP router should prefer
to use paths that it locally originates over any path received by another BGP peer if the
previous steps in the BGP best-path algorithm resulted in a tie.

To demonstrate this preference, R16 has been chosen. Currently R16 chooses to use the
path from R18 to reach the 120.18.1.1/32 prefix. Because this path has not been locally
originated by R16 and instead was received from R18, it is a prime candidate for this
demonstration.

---

**On R16:**

```
R16#show ip bgp regex ^$

BGP table version is 36, local router ID is 16.16.16.16
Status codes: s suppressed, d damped, h history, * valid, > best,
i - internal,
            r RIB-failure, S Stale, m multipath, b backup-path,
f RT-Filter,
            x best-external, a additional-path, c RIB-compressed,
Origin codes: i - IGP, e - EGP, ? - incomplete
RPKI validation codes: V valid, I invalid, N Not found

    Network          Next Hop          Metric LocPrf Weight Path
 *>i 120.18.1.1/32    18.18.18.18            0    100      0 i
 *>i 120.18.2.1/32    18.18.18.18            0    100      0 i
```

On R16, a static route to Null0 is created for the 120.18.1.1/32 prefix, as shown below. Such a route is called a *discard route* because Null0 is a discard interface on a Cisco router. Any traffic sent to the Null0 interface is silently discarded by the router. Creating such a route for the 120.18.1.1/32 prefix populates a route in the routing table that directs traffic sent to the 120.18.1.1/32 prefix to the Null0 interface. This simply means all traffic sent to the 120.18.1.1/32 prefix will be discarded. This route is then injected into the BGP table by matching it with a **network** command on R16:

---

**On R16:**

```
R16(config)#ip route 120.18.1.1 255.255.255.255 null0

R16(config)#router bgp 200
R16(config-router)#network 120.18.1.1 mask 255.255.255.255
```
The results of this configuration can be seen in the output below:
```
R16#show ip bgp regexp ^$

--- omitted ---


     Network          Next Hop           Metric LocPrf Weight Path
 *>  120.18.1.1/32    0.0.0.0                 0           32768 i
 * i                  18.18.18.18             0    100        0 i
 *>i 120.18.2.1/32    18.18.18.18             0    100        0 i


R16#show ip bgp 120.18.1.1

BGP routing table entry for 120.18.1.1/32, version 19
Paths: (2 available, best #1, table default)
  Advertised to update-groups:
     1        2
  Refresh Epoch 1
  Local
    0.0.0.0 from 0.0.0.0 (16.16.16.16)
      Origin IGP, metric 0, localpref 100, weight 32768, valid,
sourced, local, best
      rx pathid: 0, tx pathid: 0x0
  Refresh Epoch 1
  Local
    18.18.18.18 (metric 11) from 18.18.18.18 (18.18.18.18)
      Origin IGP, metric 0, localpref 100, valid, internal
      rx pathid: 0, tx pathid: 0
```

R16 chooses the locally sourced path to Null0 instead of the one received from R18. However, the reason it chooses this path is not because of step 3 of the best-path algorithm. Instead, it's because of step 1.

Recall that step 1 of the best-path algorithm prefers paths with higher WEIGHT values. By default, Cisco IOS assigns a local weight of 32768 to all locally originated paths in the BGP table. In doing so, Cisco guarantees that locally originated paths will be preferred over all received paths to the same prefix. In order to properly test the step 3 preference, the WEIGHT attribute for the locally originated path needs to be set to 0 to match the default WEIGHT values for received paths.

A route map is therefore created that sets WEIGHT to 0. Unlike most other changes made in this document, the route map is applied to the **network** command instead of to a **neighbor** statement. Route maps applied to **network** commands affect only the specific prefix being injected using the **network** command. More importantly, any path attributes modified by the route map are reflected in the BGP table of the local router. It is not necessary to specify an **in** or **out** direction when applying a route map directly to the **network** command. It is always applied in the **in** direction. The configuration commands used are shown below:

---

**On R16:**

```
R16(config)#route-map tst permit 10
R16(config-route-map)#set weight 0

R16(config)#router bgp 200
R16(config-router)#network 120.18.1.1 mask 255.255.255.255 route-map tst
```

---

After applying the changes, R16's BGP tables reflect the following:

```
R16#show ip bgp regex ^$

--- omitted ---
     Network          Next Hop         Metric LocPrf Weight Path
 *>  120.18.1.1/32    0.0.0.0               0             0 i
 * i                  18.18.18.18           0    100      0 i
 *>i 120.18.2.1/32    18.18.18.18           0    100      0 i
```

```
R16#show ip bgp 120.18.1.1

BGP routing table entry for 120.18.1.1/32, version 18
Paths: (2 available, best #1, table default)
  Advertised to update-groups:
     1          2
  Refresh Epoch 1
  Local
    0.0.0.0 from 0.0.0.0 (16.16.16.16)
      Origin IGP, metric 0, localpref 100, valid, sourced, local, best
      rx pathid: 0, tx pathid: 0x0
  Refresh Epoch 1
  Local
    18.18.18.18 (metric 11) from 18.18.18.18 (18.18.18.18)
      Origin IGP, metric 0, localpref 100, valid, internal
      rx pathid: 0, tx pathid: 0
```

With the WEIGHT and LOCAL_PREF values being equal, R16 still prefers its own locally sourced path to the prefix due to step 3 in the best-path algorithm. It is important to note that this configuration was implemented as a proof-of-concept to demonstrate step 3 of the best-path algorithm processes. It is not recommended to implement this configuration in a production environment because traffic may be blackholed unintentionally as a result.

## Step 4: AS_PATH

**Note**  Before starting this section, revert the configuration on all the routers to the base initial configuration files provided with the lab.

In the first three steps of the BGP best-path algorithm, determinations are made based on administrative preferences or how the paths were inserted into the BGP table. While each step is instrumental in creating policies, the steps do not really describe much about measurable characteristics in the path itself, as a distance vector or link-state routing protocol would.

The fourth step in the BGP best-path algorithm deals with the length of the AS_PATH attribute. Specifically, when deciding between two paths, BGP should choose the path with the shorter AS_PATH attribute length. The reasoning for this preference is grounded in the assumption that a shorter AS_PATH attribute length indicates that the path goes through fewer autonomous systems and therefore is a shorter path to the destination prefix.

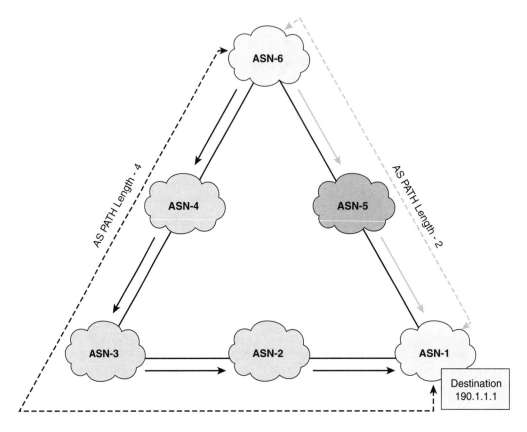

This assumption is based on how the AS_PATH attribute is set. When a BGP router originates a path to a prefix, the AS_PATH attribute is empty. Whenever the BGP router advertises the same path to an external neighbor, it prepends its local ASN, such as ASN1, to the AS_PATH attribute. The external peer receives the path and stores it in its BGP table with the new AS_PATH attribute value of ASN1. When the same external peer advertises the path to one if its own external peers, it prepends its ASN, ASN2, to the existing AS_PATH attribute value. Now the AS_PATH attribute has two values: ASN2 and ASN1.

Following suit, the third external peer receives the path with AS_PATH attribute values ASN2 and ASN1. Whenever it advertises the path along again, it prepends its ASN, ASN3, to the AS_PATH attribute, resulting in the AS_PATH attribute length ASN3, ASN2, and ASN1. This process continues as the path is advertised from external peer to external peer. Each successive peer prepends its own ASN to the AS_PATH attribute length.

The prepending process ensures that when a BGP peer receives a path from its external peer, the AS_PATH attribute is presented in order from first ASN hop to originating ASN hop. By looking at the AS_PATH attribute of a BGP prefix in the BGP table, it is possible to determine every AS that has received and forwarded the path.

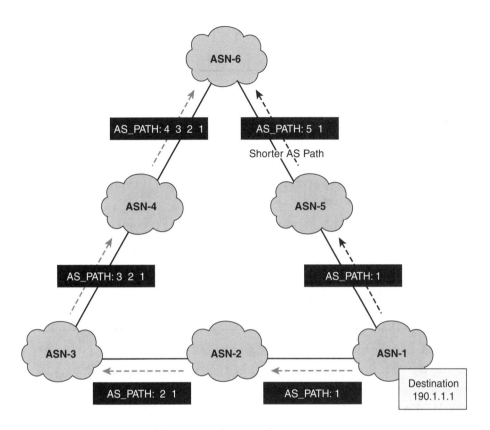

Notice the use of the term **external BGP peer** in the prepending process above. This terminology is important because the prepending process only occurs when a path is advertised between external BGP peers. When a BGP router advertises a prefix to an internal BGP peer, it does not automatically modify the AS_PATH attribute in any way. This behavior makes sense, based on the purpose of the AS_PATH attribute.

The AS_PATH attribute is a well-known, mandatory attribute. Its primary purpose is to record the ASNs a path follows in order to prevent routing loops between autonomous systems. Whenever a BGP router receives a path from its external BGP peer, it checks the AS_PATH attribute for any occurrence of its own ASN. If the path contains the local ASN, the router rejects the path and will not install it in its BGP table, assuming the path passes through the local router's own ASN.

For example, say that **debug bgp updates** is enabled on R20. Then R2 is forced to re-send its best paths to all of its BGP neighbors, including R20. R20 receives an UPDATE with path information for its 110.19.1.1/32 and 110.19.2.1/32 prefixes. It rejects the update it receives from R2, however, because the ASN 100 is contained in the AS_PATH attribute:

---

**On R20:**

```
R20#debug ip bgp updates
```

**On R2:**

```
R2#clear ip bgp * soft out
```

**On R20:**

```
BGP(0): 200.2.20.2 rcv UPDATE about 110.19.1.1/32 -- DENIED due to:
AS-PATH contains our own AS;
BGP(0): 200.2.20.2 rcv UPDATE about 110.19.2.1/32 -- DENIED due to:
AS-PATH contains our own AS;
```

---

This check has been instituted to prevent external routing loops in BGP.

Because the AS_PATH is designed to record AS hops, it makes sense for internal peers not to perform prepending when advertising paths amongst themselves because no AS boundary has been crossed.

The AS_PATH attribute can be modified using **set as-path prepend** *[asn1 asn2 asn3]* for the route map. The route map is then applied to a **neighbor** command in the outbound or inbound direction. The effects of this command are different, depending on which direction it is set. To demonstrate these differences, R10 and R9 from AS 400 along with R17 from AS 200 will be used as an example, with interest focused on the 140.15.1.1/32 and 140.15.2.1/32 prefixes. R17 receives these prefixes from R9 and R10 with an AS_PATH attribute of 400, as shown below:

---

**On R17:**

```
R17#show ip bgp regex _400$

--- omitted ---

    Network          Next Hop        Metric LocPrf Weight Path
 *  140.15.1.1/32    200.9.17.9                       0 400 i
 *>                  200.10.17.10                      0 400 i
 *  140.15.2.1/32    200.9.17.9                        0 400 i
 *>                  200.10.17.10                      0 400 i
```

The Wireshark capture below shows the AS_PATH attribute in the UPDATE message received by R17 from R10, and R9 contains the ASN 400 as the AS_SEQUENCE:

---

### On R10:

```
Internet Protocol Version 4, Src: 200.10.17.10, Dst: 200.10.17.17
Transmission Control Protocol, Src Port: 60843, Dst Port: 179,
Seq: 100, Ack: 96, Len: 231
Border Gateway Protocol - UPDATE Message
    Marker: ffffffffffffffffffffffffffffffff
    Length: 53
    Type: UPDATE Message (2)
    Withdrawn Routes Length: 0
    Total Path Attribute Length: 20
        Path Attribute - AS_PATH: 400
            Flags: 0x40, Transitive, Well-known, Complete
            Type Code: AS_PATH (2)
            Length: 6
            AS Path segment: 400
                Segment type: AS_SEQUENCE (2)
                Segment length (number of ASN): 1
                AS4: 400
        Path Attribute - NEXT_HOP: 200.10.17.10
            Flags: 0x40, Transitive, Well-known, Complete
            Type Code: NEXT_HOP (3)
            Length: 4
            Next hop: 200.10.17.10
    Network Layer Reachability Information (NLRI)
        140.15.1.1/32
        140.15.2.1/32
```

---

### On R9:

```
Internet Protocol Version 4, Src: 200.9.17.9, Dst: 200.9.17.17
Transmission Control Protocol, Src Port: 59690, Dst Port: 179,
Seq: 96, Ack: 220, Len: 204
Border Gateway Protocol - UPDATE Message
    Marker: ffffffffffffffffffffffffffffffff
    Length: 53
    Type: UPDATE Message (2)
    Withdrawn Routes Length: 0
    Total Path Attribute Length: 20
        Path Attribute - AS_PATH: 400
            Flags: 0x40, Transitive, Well-known, Complete
            Type Code: AS_PATH (2)
```

```
        Length: 6
        AS Path segment: 400
            Segment type: AS_SEQUENCE (2)
            Segment length (number of ASN): 1
            AS4: 400
    Path Attribute - NEXT_HOP: 200.9.17.9
        Flags: 0x40, Transitive, Well-known, Complete
        Type Code: NEXT_HOP (3)
        Length: 4
        Next hop: 200.9.17.9
Network Layer Reachability Information (NLRI)
    140.15.1.1/32
    140.15.2.1/32
```

R17 receives two paths for each 140.15.1.1 and 140.15.1.2. By default, R17 prefers which-ever route it received first, which in this example is R10's path.

**Note**   The above output may vary depending on the order in which R17 received the updates from R9 and R10. This is because all attributes between the two paths will tie. In such a situation, BGP will simply select the path that was received first as the best path because it is the older path. In this lab, that path was received from R10.

If the current best-path selection is R9 instead, to better align with the examples in this lab, simply shut down the neighbor connection between R17 and R9 by using the following command sequence:

```
R17(config)#router bgp 200
R17(config-router)#neighbor 200.9.17.9 shutdown


22:02:17.293: %BGP-5-NBR_RESET: Neighbor 200.9.17.9 reset (Admin.
shutdown)
22:02:17.298: %BGP-5-ADJCHANGE: neighbor 200.9.17.9 Down Admin.
shutdown
22:02:17.298: %BGP_SESSION-5-ADJCHANGE: neighbor 200.9.17.9 IPv4
Unicast topology base removed from session  Admin. shutdown
```

Doing so causes R17 to clear out R9's path in its BGP table and install the path through R10. When R9 is brought back up, R10 will remain the best path because it will be the older route:

```
R17(config-router)#no neighbor 200.9.17.9 shutdown
*Jun  5 22:02:31.164: %BGP-5-ADJCHANGE: neighbor 200.9.17.9 Up
```

Details behind this path selection behavior are explained in step 10 of this lab.

AS 400 has a specific application that utilizes the 140.15.1.1/32 address. Because of internal politics, traffic for this application needs to come into the AS via R9 whenever possible. The goal will be for R17 to prefer to use the path through R9 to reach the 140.15.1.1/32 prefix instead of R10 using only the AS_PATH attribute.

The following sections demonstrate solutions for this scenario that involve prepending AS_PATH outbound and inbound.

### AS_PATH Outbound

The more common way of using the AS_PATH attribute is in the outbound direction. Typically, an AS will prepend its own ASN to make certain paths less favorable to the rest of the global BGP table. Recall that a shorter AS_PATH attribute length is preferred over longer ones. Thus, in order to influence R17 to choose the path through R9, R10 needs to prepend its path when it advertises it to R17 to make it longer. Once applied, for R17, R10's path will be less preferable than R9's path because the AS_PATH attribute will be longer.

To apply the AS_PATH attribute in the outbound direction, a prefix list is created to identify the 140.15.1.1/32 network. This prefix list is then added to a route map with the **set as-path prepend** option. The route map is then applied in the outbound direction on the R10/R17 **neighbor** command. The following configuration on R10 configures R10 to prepend ASN 400 to the beginning of the AS_PATH attribute one time:

```
On R10:


R10(config)#ip prefix-list 123 permit 140.15.1.1/32

R10(config)#route-map tst permit 10
R10(config-route-map)#match ip address prefix 123
R10(config-route-map)#set as-path prepend 400

R10(config)#route-map tst permit 90
R10(config-route-map)#router bgp 400
R10(config-router)#neighbor 200.10.17.17 route-map tst out

R10#clear ip bgp * soft out
```

The effects of this command can be seen with a before/after view of R17's BGP table. First, the AS_PATH attribute length ties (containing a single 400) between the paths received from R9 and R10. After initiating the change and performing a **clear ip bgp \***

**soft out** on R10, R10 advertises its path to R17 with a modified AS_PATH attribute, shown in the packet capture of the UPDATE packet sent by R10 to R17 below:

```
Internet Protocol Version 4, Src: 200.10.17.10, Dst: 200.10.17.17
Transmission Control Protocol, Src Port: 179, Dst Port: 23911, Seq: 1,
Ack: 20, Len: 204
Border Gateway Protocol - UPDATE Message
    Marker: ffffffffffffffffffffffffffffffff
    Length: 52
    Type: UPDATE Message (2)
    Withdrawn Routes Length: 0
    Total Path Attribute Length: 24
    Path attributes
        Path Attribute - AS_PATH: 400 400
            Flags: 0x40, Transitive, Well-known, Complete
            Type Code: AS_PATH (2)
            Length: 10
            AS Path segment: 400 400
                Segment type: AS_SEQUENCE (2)
                Segment length (number of ASN): 2
                AS4: 400
                AS4: 400
        Path Attribute - NEXT_HOP: 200.10.17.10
            Flags: 0x40, Transitive, Well-known, Complete
            Type Code: NEXT_HOP (3)
            Length: 4
            Next hop: 200.10.17.10
    Network Layer Reachability Information (NLRI)
        140.15.1.1/32
```

As a result, R17 now prefers R9's path because the AS_PATH attribute length is shorter, as evidenced by the before and after views of R17's BGP table:

```
R17 Before the changes were made:


R17#show ip bgp regex _400$

--- omitted ---


     Network          Next Hop          Metric LocPrf Weight Path
 *   140.15.1.1/32    200.9.17.9                           0 400 i
 *>                   200.10.17.10                          0 400 i
```

```
 *    140.15.2.1/32    200.9.17.9                                    0 400 i
 *>                    200.10.17.10                                  0 400 i
```

**On R17:**

```
R17#show ip bgp regex _400$

--- omitted ---

     Network           Next Hop         Metric LocPrf Weight Path
 *>  140.15.1.1/32     200.9.17.9                         0 400 i
 *                     200.10.17.10                       0 400 400 i
 *   140.15.2.1/32     200.9.17.9                         0 400 i
 *>                    200.10.17.10                       0 400 i
```

**Note**   When configuring AS_PATH prepending, it's important to keep in mind these three rules:

- The router will always prepend its own ASN to the AS_PATH attribute as the leftmost ASN in the AS_PATH attribute.

- The AS_PATH attribute is prepended with the exact values in order, as entered in the **set as-path prepend** command, in addition to the normal AS_PATH prepending that happens whenever an eBGP peer advertises to another eBGP peer.

- It is wise to use only the local ASN when prepending in the outbound direction.

The first point reinforces the fact that the **set as-path prepend** command does not replace the router's own ASN. The router will always prepend its own ASN to the path as the leftmost ASN in the path.

The second point is better serviced with an example. In the example above, the **set as-path** command contains only a single 400. When R10 advertised the path to the prefix 140.15.1.1/32 to R17, it first performed its normal prepending, adding a single 400 to the AS_PATH attribute length. Then, because of the outbound route map applied, it added an additional 400 to the advertisement, creating an AS_PATH attribute of 400 400. If the command **set as-path 400 400** were used instead, the result would be an AS_PATH attribute of 400 400 400.

The last point is a best practice rooted in the simple fact that if an AS decides to prepend another ASN to a BGP path, if the path reaches that ASN, the path would be denied, and all autonomous systems that rely on that AS for their Internet routes will not have the path that was prepended. This occurs because of the default loop prevention mechanisms employed by BGP.

For example, if R10 above prepended the ASN 200 to R17 instead of prepending 400, as shown in the configuration below, R17 would receive the BGP update message and see an occurrence of its own ASN in the AS_PATH attribute. This is shown in the capture below:

```
R10:
ip prefix-list PREPEND seq 5 permit 140.15.1.1/32
```

*Continued*

```
!
route-map PREPEND permit 10
 match ip address prefix-list PREPEND
 set as-path prepend 200
route-map PREPEND permit 20
!
router bgp 400
 neighbor 200.10.17.17 route-map PREPEND out
```

**BGP Update message from R10 to R17:**

```
Internet Protocol Version 4, Src: 200.10.17.10, Dst: 200.10.17.17
Transmission Control Protocol, Src Port: 60843, Dst Port: 179, Seq:
455, Ack: 91, Len: 204
Border Gateway Protocol - UPDATE Message
   Marker: ffffffffffffffffffffffffffffffff
   Length: 52
   Type: UPDATE Message (2)
   Withdrawn Routes Length: 0
   Total Path Attribute Length: 24
   Path attributes
       Path Attribute - ORIGIN: IGP
           Flags: 0x40, Transitive, Well-known, Complete
           Type Code: ORIGIN (1)
           Length: 1
           Origin: IGP (0)
       Path Attribute - AS_PATH: 400 200
           Flags: 0x40, Transitive, Well-known, Complete
           Type Code: AS_PATH (2)
           Length: 10
           AS Path segment: 400 200
               Segment type: AS_SEQUENCE (2)
               Segment length (number of ASN): 2
               AS4: 400
               AS4: 200
   Network Layer Reachability Information (NLRI)
       140.15.1.1/32
```

Note, in compliance with the three rules above, R10 advertises the AS_PATH as "400 200",
keeping its own ASN as the leftmost ASN in the AS_PATH. R17 would deny the path
because the AS_PATH would contain "400 200". Because R17 is a member of AS 200, it
will not accept the path. This can be confirmed by turning on **debug ip bgp updates** on
R17:

```
16:46:39.466: BGP(0): 200.10.17.10 rcv UPDATE about
140.15.1.1/32 -- DENIED due to: AS-PATH contains our own AS;
```

Any AS that peers with AS 200 will not receive the path, resulting in whatever resource is made available using the 140.15.1.1/32 to be unavailable to them.

However, prepending with the local ASN does not suffer from this problem and is the recommended way to affect outbound AS_PATH manipulation.

The AS_PATH attribute can only be modified outbound toward eBGP neighbors, as in the example above. It cannot be modified outbound toward iBGP neighbors. BGP routers do not modify the AS_PATH attribute for paths advertised to iBGP peers at all, even when explicitly set using a route map. This is proven in the example below.

R10 will attempt to advertise the 130.7.1.1/32 prefix to its iBGP neighbor R12 by prepending the ASN 400:

---

**R10 and R12 before AS_PATH prepending configuration:**

**On R10:**

```
R10#show ip bgp regexp _300$
--- omitted ---

     Network          Next Hop        Metric LocPrf Weight Path
 * i 130.7.1.1/32     11.11.11.11          0    100      0 300 i
 *                    200.10.17.17                       0 200 300 i
 *                    200.3.10.3                         0 300 i
 *>                   200.2.10.2                         0 300 i
```

! Depending on the order of received UPDATES, R10 may receive the path through R3 before the path through R2. In such a situation, R10 may choose R3's path as best since it is the older route.

**On R12:**

```
R12#show ip bgp regexp _300$

--- omitted ---

   Network          Next Hop        Metric LocPrf Weight Path
 * i 130.7.1.1/32    11.11.11.11          0    100      0 300 i
 *>i                 10.10.10.10          0    100      0 300 i
```

**On R10:**

```
R10(config)#ip prefix-list PREPEND permit 130.7.1.1/32

R10(config)#route-map PREPEND permit 10
R10(config-route-map)#match ip address prefix PREPEND
R10(config-route-map)#set as-path prepend 400
R10(config)#route-map PREPEND permit 20

R10(config-route-map)#router bgp 400
R10(config-router)#neighbor 12.12.12.12 route-map PREPEND out

R10#clear ip bgp *
```

**On R10:**

```
R10#show ip bgp regexp _300$

--- omitted ---

     Network          Next Hop          Metric LocPrf Weight Path
  * i 130.7.1.1/32    11.11.11.11          0     100     0 300 i
  *                   200.10.17.17                        0 200 300 i
  *                   200.3.10.3                          0 300 i
  *>                  200.2.10.2                          0 300 i
```

**On R12:**

```
R12#show ip bgp regexp _300$

--- omitted ---
     Network          Next Hop          Metric LocPrf Weight Path
  * i 130.7.1.1/32    11.11.11.11          0     100     0 300 i
  *>i                 10.10.10.10          0     100     0 300 i
```

Notice above that even though the route map PREPEND_R12 sets the AS_PATH prepend, it does not work toward R10's iBGP neighbor R12. BGP peers do not modify the

AS_PATH attribute when advertising a path to an internal peer. This can also be seen in the capture below:

```
Internet Protocol Version 4, Src: 10.10.10.10, Dst: 9.9.9.9
Transmission Control Protocol, Src Port: 12201, Dst Port: 179, Seq:
20, Ack: 20, Len: 233
Border Gateway Protocol - UPDATE Message
    Marker: ffffffffffffffffffffffffffffffff
    Length: 62
    Type: UPDATE Message (2)
    Withdrawn Routes Length: 0
    Total Path Attribute Length: 34
    Path attributes
        Path Attribute - AS_PATH: 300
            Flags: 0x40, Transitive, Well-known, Complete
            Type Code: AS_PATH (2)
            Length: 6
            AS Path segment: 300
                Segment type: AS_SEQUENCE (2)
                Segment length (number of ASN): 1
                AS4: 300
    Network Layer Reachability Information (NLRI)
        130.7.1.1/32
```

# AS_PATH Inbound

**Note**  Before starting this section, revert the configuration on all routers to the base initial configuration files provided with the lab.

The AS_PATH attribute can also be modified in the inbound direction on a BGP router. It is uncommon to do this, but it is a valid configuration. When the AS_PATH attribute is modified inbound, it affects the local AS and any other AS to which the local AS is peered. The above AS_PATH attribute modification can be made by simply reversing where the configuration is being made. Instead of setting the AS_PATH attribute outbound toward R17, R17 will set it for the path to 140.15.1.1/32 received from R10 inbound.

This time, R17 is configured with the same route map and prefix list combination as in the outbound example. The route map is then applied in the **in** direction on the **neighbor** command for R17's peering with R10, as shown on the next page:

---

**R17 before AS_PATH prepending:**

```
R17#show ip bgp regex _400$

--- omitted ---

     Network            Next Hop         Metric LocPrf Weight Path
  *   140.15.1.1/32      200.9.17.9                         0 400 i
  *>                     200.10.17.10                        0 400 i
  *   140.15.2.1/32      200.9.17.9                         0 400 i
  *>                     200.10.17.10                        0 400 i
```

---

**Note**   R17 chooses the path via R10 as best because it received it before R9's path. The results may vary in lab testing, depending on whose path is received first by R17.

---

**R17 AS_PATH prepending configuration:**

```
R17(config)#ip prefix-list PREPEND permit 140.15.1.1/32

R17(config)#route-map PREPEND per 10
R17(config-route-map)#match ip address prefix PREPEND
R17(config-route-map)#set as-path prepend 400
R17(config)#route-map PREPEND permit 90

R17(config)#router bgp 200
R17(config-router)#neighbor 200.10.17.10 route-map PREPEND in

R17#show ip bgp regex _400$

--- omitted ---

     Network            Next Hop         Metric LocPrf Weight Path
  *   140.15.1.1/32      200.10.17.10                        0 400 400 i
  *>                     200.9.17.9                          0 400 i
  *   140.15.2.1/32      200.10.17.10                        0 400 i
  *>                     200.9.17.9                          0 400 i
```

---

Here, the net result is the same: R17 prefers the path from R9 to enter AS 400. A special note about prepending inbound is that, unlike with outbound prepending, it is possible to prepend with the local ASN or the peer's ASN without negative impact to the global BGP table. In this example, R17 could prepend the ASNs 200 or 400 to achieve this result.

However, care should be taken to ensure that only the local ASN or the peer's ASN is used in the inbound prepending. If another ASN is used, it could cause that path to be rejected by the AS that actually owns that particular ASN.

### AS_PATH in Confederations

**Loop Prevention Within the AS**    The examples above dealt heavily with the subject of how the AS_PATH attribute is communicated between BGP routers. One key aspect of this is that the AS_PATH attribute is not prepended when advertised between iBGP peers. This section deals with the implications of that behavior. Because the AS_PATH attribute is not prepended between iBGP peers, there is no way for all routers in the AS to prevent loops from forming from within the AS. The default loop-prevention mechanism is broken because it relies on the presence of the AS's own ASN.

iBGP peers have to rely on another loop-prevention mechanism to compensate for this deficiency and must first advertise external paths to their iBGP neighbors as internal paths. With the paths designated as internal paths, all iBGP routers then must follow the rule that they are not to advertise internal paths to other internal peers. This rule is often called the iBGP split-horizon rule in the networking community. The process works as follows:

1. A BGP router receives a path from its eBGP peer.

2. The BGP router checks for loops, using the AS_PATH attribute.

3. After passing the AS_PATH attribute check, the path is accepted into the BGP table and marked as best (after the best-path algorithm is run).

4. The BGP router advertises the same external path as an internal path to its iBGP peers.

5. The iBGP peers cannot advertise the same path to each other, resulting in the only path coming from the original BGP router that received the prefix.

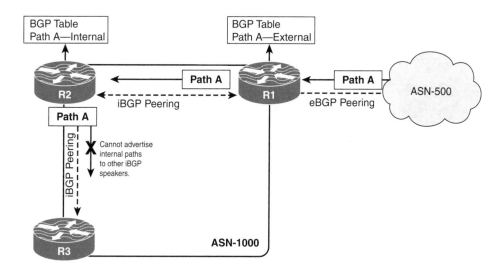

This sequence of events ensures that no loops are formed inside the AS whenever BGP peers advertise internal prefixes. The unfortunate side effect of this configuration is that, in order to ensure that all iBGP peers receive all internal updates, all the BGP routers inside the AS should be iBGP peers with each other. In other words, there should be a full mesh of iBGP peers within the AS; otherwise, all routers may not receive all prefixes.

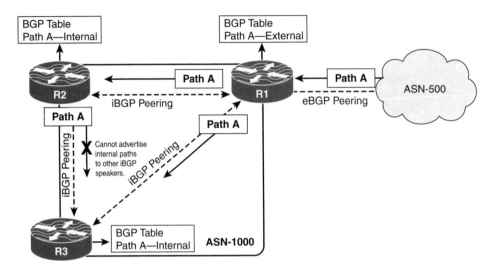

This requirement can cause issues with scalability within the AS as the number of peerings grows when new BGP routers are added to the AS. Two methods are generally used to handle this scalability problem: **route reflection** and **confederations**. Route reflection involves designating a BGP router as a route reflector. The route reflector serves a set of clients. When advertising internal prefixes, the route reflector is able to relax the iBGP split-horizon rule and advertise internal prefixes to other internal routers. (Route reflection will be explained further in later steps of the BGP best-path algorithm.)

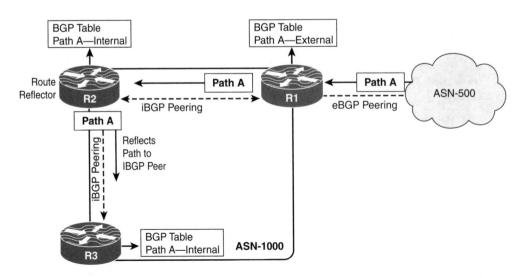

The method most applicable to the AS_PATH attribute is confederations, which deserves more explanation here.

Confederations introduce a new kind of path attribute called the AS_CONFED_SEQUENCE segment. This segment behaves similarly to the AS_SEQUENCE segment but is specific to how confederations function. Rather than simply allowing certain routers to relax the iBGP split-horizon rule, confederations break up the AS into multiple sub-autonomous systems. These sub-autonomous systems are assigned their own sub-ASNs. Routers belonging to two different sub-autonomous systems form a special kind of eBGP peering called a *confederation eBGP peering*. A router is allowed to advertise a received internal prefix to its confederation external BGP peers, as shown below.

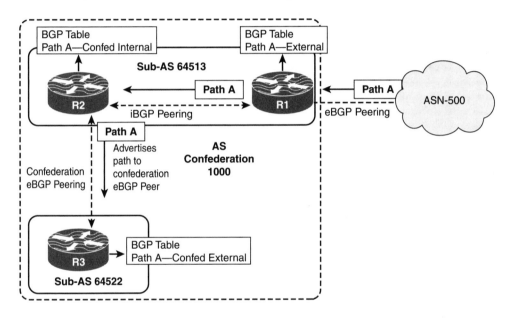

**Advertising Paths Within Confederations**  Confederation eBGP peers are able to advertise internal paths between each other, as confederation external paths. When doing so, they prepend their sub-ASNs to the AS_CONFED_SEQUENCE segment of the path. The process is similar to how regular eBGP peers prepend their local ASNs to paths advertised to other external peers. The purpose for this prepending is also identical to the purpose with regular eBGP peers. By prepending the local sub-ASN to the AS_CONFED_SEQUENCE, the original BGP loop-prevention check is restored. When a router receives a confederation external path from a confed-eBGP neighbor, it first checks the AS_CONFED_SEQUENCE segment for its own local ASN. If the ASN is found, then the path is denied by the local router.

The AS_CONFED_SEQUENCE and AS_SEQUENCE segments are separate segments within the AS_PATH attribute that are combined in the **show ip bgp** output under the Path column, as shown in the packet capture text and **show ip bgp** output from an exchange between R2 and R3 in the lab topology:

**Packet Capture of an UPDATE message from R2 to R3:**

```
Frame 723: 586 bytes on wire (4688 bits), 586 bytes captured (4688
bits) on interface 0
Ethernet II, Src: aa:bb:cc:00:02:00 (aa:bb:cc:00:02:00), Dst:
aa:bb:cc:00:03:00 (aa:bb:cc:00:03:00)
802.1Q Virtual LAN, PRI: 0, DEI: 0, ID: 23
Internet Protocol Version 4, Src: 2.2.2.2, Dst: 3.3.3.3
Transmission Control Protocol, Src Port: 179, Dst Port: 11176, Seq:
62, Ack: 570, Len: 528
Border Gateway Protocol - UPDATE Message
    Marker: ffffffffffffffffffffffffffffffff
    Length: 73
    Type: UPDATE Message (2)
    Withdrawn Routes Length: 0
    Total Path Attribute Length: 40
    Path attributes
        Path Attribute - ORIGIN: IGP
            Flags: 0x40, Transitive, Well-known, Complete
            Type Code: ORIGIN (1)
            Length: 1
            Origin: IGP (0)
        Path Attribute - AS_PATH: (312) 400
            Flags: 0x40, Transitive, Well-known, Complete
            Type Code: AS_PATH (2)
            Length: 12
            AS Path segment: (312)
                Segment type: AS_CONFED_SEQUENCE (3)
                Segment length (number of ASN): 1
                AS4: 312
            AS Path segment: 400
                Segment type: AS_SEQUENCE (2)
                Segment length (number of ASN): 1
                AS4: 400
    --output omitted--
    Network Layer Reachability Information (NLRI)
        140.15.1.1/32
            NLRI prefix length: 32
            NLRI prefix: 140.15.1.1
        140.15.2.1/32
            NLRI prefix length: 32
            NLRI prefix: 140.15.2.1
```

Here, R2 sends an UPDATE message, advertising a path to reach the 140.15.1.1/32 and 140.15.2.1/32 prefixes. The AS_PATH attribute is included in the UPDATE message as expected because the AS_PATH attribute is a well-known mandatory attribute. Within the AS_PATH attribute are the AS_CONFED_SEQUENCE attribute, highlighted in red, and the AS_SEQUENCE attribute, highlighted in blue. R2, belonging to sub-AS 312, prepends (312) to the AS_CONFED_SEQUENCE attribute before advertising the path to R3.

Notice how the AS_CONFED_SEQUENCE value is written in parenthesis. This coincides with how the AS_PATH attribute is represented in R3's BGP table for the same prefixes in the output below. Again, the AS_SEQUENCE is highlighted in blue, and the AS_CONFED_SEQUENCE is highlighted in red:

**On R3:**

```
R3#show ip bgp regexp _400$

--- omitted---

     Network            Next Hop          Metric LocPrf Weight Path
*    140.15.1.1/32      2.2.2.2           0      100    0 (312) 400 i
* i                     6.6.6.6           0      100    0 400 i
*>                      200.3.10.10                     0 400 i
*    140.15.2.1/32      2.2.2.2           0      100    0 (312) 400 i
* i                     6.6.6.6           0      100    0 400 i
*>                      200.3.10.10                     0 400 i
```

R3 itself is a member of sub-AS 336. The AS_PATH attribute does not include sub-AS 336 in the AS_CONFED_SEQUENCE attribute, allowing R3 to accept the path as advertised from R2. R3 also receives the same paths from R4, as shown in the packet capture below:

**Packet Capture of an UPDATE Message from R4 to R3:**

```
Internet Protocol Version 4, Src: 4.4.4.4, Dst: 3.3.3.3
Transmission Control Protocol, Src Port: 38522, Dst Port: 179,
Seq: 81, Ack: 570, Len: 485
Border Gateway Protocol - UPDATE Message
    Marker: ffffffffffffffffffffffffffffffff
    Length: 77
    Type: UPDATE Message (2)
    Withdrawn Routes Length: 0
    Total Path Attribute Length: 44
    Path attributes
        Path Attribute - AS_PATH: (345 336) 400
            Flags: 0x40, Transitive, Well-known, Complete
            Type Code: AS_PATH (2)
            Length: 16
```

```
            AS Path segment: (345 336)
                Segment type: AS_CONFED_SEQUENCE (3)
                Segment length (number of ASN): 2
                AS4: 345
                AS4: 336
            AS Path segment: 400
                Segment type: AS_SEQUENCE (2)
                Segment length (number of ASN): 1
                AS4: 400
    Network Layer Reachability Information (NLRI)
        140.15.1.1/32
            NLRI prefix length: 32
            NLRI prefix: 140.15.1.1
        140.15.2.1/32
            NLRI prefix length: 32
            NLRI prefix: 140.15.2.1
```

In the above, R4 is advertising R3's path back to R3. It does so because R4 and R3 are confederation eBGP peers. The iBGP split-horizon rule does not apply and R4 will advertise all of its best paths to R3 even if it has selected the path through R3 as best (as in this situation). This behavior is the same as how a BGP router with a normal eBGP peering would advertise a path back to its neighboring eBGP peer.

R4 advertises the path with AS_CONFED_SEQUENCE (345 336). When this advertisement reaches R3, it fails the AS_PATH attribute check at the sub-AS boundary, and R3 denies the path because its own ASN, 336, is contained in the AS_CONFED_SEQUENCE. The **debug ip bgp updates** output below illustrates this process:

```
BGP(0): 4.4.4.4 rcv UPDATE about 140.15.1.1/32 -- DENIED due to:
AS-PATH contains our own AS; NEXTHOP is our own address;

BGP(0): 4.4.4.4 rcv UPDATE about 140.15.2.1/32 -- DENIED due to:
AS-PATH contains our own AS; NEXTHOP is our own address;
```

We have just looked at the process by which paths are exchanged between routers belonging to different sub-autonomous systems. Routers within a single sub-AS can exchange paths as well but are considered confederation iBGP peers. Confederation iBGP peers are constrained by the same rules as normal iBGP peers. They are unable to advertise internal paths, called confederation internal paths, with each other, and they do not prepend the local sub-ASN to the AS_CONFED_SEQUENCE when advertising paths with each other.

The final point that deserves highlighting in this section regarding confederations is how confederations are represented to external autonomous systems. When a BGP router belonging to a confederation advertises a path to a true external peer, it strips off the

AS_CONFED_SEQUENCE segment from the AS_PATH attribute and prepends the main ASN to the AS_SEQUENCE segment. As an example, see the advertisement of the 140.15.1.1/32 prefix from R2 to R20 below:

```
On R20:


R20#show ip bgp regexp _400$

--- omitted ---

    Network              Next Hop          Metric LocPrf Weight Path
 * i 140.15.1.1/32       19.19.19.19           0    100      0 200 400 i
 *>                      200.2.20.2                          0 300 400 i
 * i 140.15.2.1/32       19.19.19.19           0    100      0 200 400 i
 *>                      200.2.20.2                          0 300 400 i
```

This can be verified with a Wireshark capture showing the BGP update message sent by R2 to R20. Notice the missing AS_CONFED_SEQUENCE segment:

```
Internet Protocol Version 4, Src: 200.2.20.2, Dst: 200.2.20.20
Transmission Control Protocol, Src Port: 32403, Dst Port: 179,
Seq: 96, Ack: 410, Len: 299
Border Gateway Protocol - UPDATE Message
    Marker: ffffffffffffffffffffffffffffffff
    Length: 57
    Type: UPDATE Message (2)
    Withdrawn Routes Length: 0
    Total Path Attribute Length: 24
    Path attributes
        Path Attribute - ORIGIN: IGP
            Flags: 0x40, Transitive, Well-known, Complete
            Type Code: ORIGIN (1)
            Length: 1
            Origin: IGP (0)
        Path Attribute - AS_PATH: 300 400
            Flags: 0x40, Transitive, Well-known, Complete
            Type Code: AS_PATH (2)
            Length: 10
            AS Path segment: 300 400
                Segment type: AS_SEQUENCE (2)
                Segment length (number of ASN): 2
```

```
                    AS4: 300
                    AS4: 400
        Path Attribute - NEXT_HOP: 200.2.20.2
            Flags: 0x40, Transitive, Well-known, Complete
            Type Code: NEXT_HOP (3)
            Length: 4
            Next hop: 200.2.20.2
    Network Layer Reachability Information (NLRI)
        140.15.1.1/32
        140.15.2.1/32
```

This function is implemented because routers in completely different autonomous systems have no use for the information contained in the AS_CONFED_SEQUENCE attribute. The information is germane only to the local AS. By performing the stripping and prepending, the confederation is represented as a single AS to all other BGP-speaking routers in different autonomous systems.

### AS_PATH Processing Within the Confederation

**Note**    Before starting this section, revert the configuration on all routers to the base initial configuration files provided with the lab.

As shown in the sections above, the AS_CONFED_SEQUENCE segment within the AS_PATH attribute is primarily used for loop prevention. AS_CONFED_SEQUENCE does not contribute to the overall AS_PATH attribute length comparison used in step 4 of the best-path algorithm. Only the AS_SEQUENCE segment is compared for the AS_PATH attribute length selection criteria. R4 receives two paths for both the 120.18.1.1/32 and 120.18.2.1/32 prefixes, as shown below:

**On R4:**

```
R4#show ip bgp regex 200$

BGP table version is 16, local router ID is 4.4.4.4
Status codes: s suppressed, d damped, h history, * valid, > best,
i - internal,
            r RIB-failure, S Stale, m multipath, b backup-path,
f RT-Filter,
            x best-external, a additional-path, c RIB-compressed,
Origin codes: i - IGP, e - EGP, ? - incomplete
RPKI validation codes: V valid, I invalid, N Not found
```

```
      Network           Next Hop   Metric LocPrf Weight Path
 *    120.18.1.1/32     2.2.2.2         0    100      0 (312) 200 i
 *>                     3.3.3.3         0    100      0 (336 312) 200 i
 *    120.18.2.1/32     2.2.2.2         0    100      0 (312) 200 i
 *>                     3.3.3.3         0    100      0 (336 312) 200 i
```

The path to next hop R2 has a single sub-AS (312) in the AS_CONFED_SEQUENCE segment. The path to the next hop R3 has two sub-autonomous systems (336 312). Technically, the path to next hop R2 has the shorter total AS_CONFED_SEQUENCE length and should be considered best.

R4, however, chooses the path to next hop R3 as best, even though the AS_CONFED_ SEQUENCE segment is longer than the path to next hop R2. This proves that the AS_CONFED_SEQUENCE segment is not considered as part of the AS_PATH attribute length.

When R4 makes the comparison between the two paths, it considers the AS_PATH attribute length a tie, with an AS_SEQUENCE segment value of 200. The deciding factor is then the IGP metric to the next hop, as shown in the output below:

**On R4:**

```
R4#show ip bgp 120.18.1.1

BGP routing table entry for 120.18.1.1/32, version 12
Paths: (2 available, best #2, table default)
  Advertised to update-groups:
     1          2
  Refresh Epoch 1
  (312) 200
    2.2.2.2 (metric 21) from 1.1.1.1 (1.1.1.1)
      Origin IGP, metric 0, localpref 100, valid, confed-external
      rx pathid: 0, tx pathid: 0
  Refresh Epoch 1
  (336 312) 200
    3.3.3.3 (metric 11) from 3.3.3.3 (3.3.3.3)
      Origin IGP, metric 0, localpref 100, valid, confed-external,
best
      rx pathid: 0, tx pathid: 0x0

R4#show ip bgp 120.18.2.1

BGP routing table entry for 120.18.2.1/32, version 13
```

```
Paths: (2 available, best #2, table default)
  Advertised to update-groups:
     1         2
  Refresh Epoch 1
  (312) 200
    2.2.2.2 (metric 21) from 1.1.1.1 (1.1.1.1)
      Origin IGP, metric 0, localpref 100, valid, confed-external
      rx pathid: 0, tx pathid: 0
  Refresh Epoch 1
  (336 312) 200
    3.3.3.3 (metric 11) from 3.3.3.3 (3.3.3.3)
      Origin IGP, metric 0, localpref 100, valid, confed-external,
best
      rx pathid: 0, tx pathid: 0x0
```

In this case, the **metric** expressed in the **show ip bgp** output above was taken directly from R4's IGP metrics for the same prefixes:

---

**On R4:**

```
R4#show ip route ospf | i 2.2.2.2|3.3.3.3

O        2.2.2.2 [110/21] via 30.3.4.3, 00:44:07, Ethernet0/0.34
O        3.3.3.3 [110/11] via 30.3.4.3, 00:44:07, Ethernet0/0.34
```

---

This metric is assigned to the paths through the route recursion process in IOS routing. Because R4 has a lower metric to reach next hop R3, it chooses to use the path with next hop R3 as its best path, assuming that it has an overall shorter or more preferred internal route to reach it. More about this determination is revealed in step 8 of the BGP best-path process.

This behavior of ignoring the AS_CONFED_SEQUENCE for best-path calculations follows with the functionality specified in RFC 5065 Section 5.3, point 3:

### 5.3.  AS_PATH and Path Selection

*Path selection criteria for information received from members inside*

*a confederation MUST follow the same rules used for information*

*received from members inside the same autonomous system, as specified*

*in [BGP-4].*

*In addition, the following rules SHALL be applied:*

*--- omitted for brevity ---*

*3) When comparing routes using AS_PATH length, CONFED_SEQUENCE and CONFED_SETs SHOULD NOT be counted.*

### as-path ignore

The command **bgp bestpath as-path ignore** is a hidden command that allows a BGP router to ignore the AS_PATH attribute length in its decision-making process. It causes the router to completely skip step 4 of the best-path algorithm and ignore the AS_PATH length comparison. R2 is chosen below to demonstrate the use of this command:

```
On R2:


R2#show ip bgp 120.18.1.1

BGP routing table entry for 120.18.1.1/32, version 20
Paths: (3 available, best #1, table default)
  Advertised to update-groups:
     8          9          10
  Refresh Epoch 1
  200
    200.2.16.16 from 200.2.16.16 (16.16.16.16)
      Origin IGP, localpref 100, valid, external, best
      rx pathid: 0, tx pathid: 0x0
  Refresh Epoch 1
  100 200
    200.2.20.20 from 200.2.20.20 (20.20.20.20)
      Origin IGP, localpref 100, valid, external
      rx pathid: 0, tx pathid: 0
  Refresh Epoch 2
  400 200
    200.2.10.10 from 200.2.10.10 (10.10.10.10)
      Origin IGP, localpref 100, valid, external
      rx pathid: 0, tx pathid: 0
```

Here, R2 chooses to use the path from R16 to reach the 120.18.1.1 prefix because it has the lower AS_PATH length compared to its other paths received from R20 and R10. R2 is then modified with the **bgp bestpath as-path ignore** command. Then, the peering between R2 and R16 is reset, resulting in the following after clearing the BGP peering to R16:

---

**On R2:**

```
R2(config)#router bgp 312
R2(config-router)#bgp bestpath as-path ignore

R2#clear ip bgp 200.2.16.16

%BGP-5-ADJCHANGE: neighbor 200.2.16.16 Down User reset
%BGP_SESSION-5-ADJCHANGE: neighbor 200.2.16.16 IPv4 Unicast topology
base removed from session  User reset

%BGP-5-ADJCHANGE: neighbor 200.2.16.16 Up


R2#show ip bgp 120.18.1.1

BGP routing table entry for 120.18.1.1/32, version 6
Paths: (4 available, best #3, table default)
  Advertised to update-groups:
     8          9          10
  Refresh Epoch 1
  200
    200.2.16.16 from 200.2.16.16 (16.16.16.16)
      Origin IGP, localpref 100, valid, external
      rx pathid: 0, tx pathid: 0
  Refresh Epoch 1
  100 200
    200.2.20.20 from 200.2.20.20 (20.20.20.20)
      Origin IGP, localpref 100, valid, external
      rx pathid: 0, tx pathid: 0
  Refresh Epoch 2
  400 200
    200.2.10.10 from 200.2.10.10 (10.10.10.10)
      Origin IGP, localpref 100, valid, external, best
      rx pathid: 0, tx pathid: 0x0
  Refresh Epoch 2
  (336) 400 200
    3.3.3.3 (metric 11) from 3.3.3.3 (3.3.3.3)
      Origin IGP, metric 0, localpref 100, valid, confed-external
      rx pathid: 0, tx pathid: 0
```

After the change is implemented, R2 adjusts its decision making. When the neighborship to R16 is reset, R2 loses its best path. It then reevaluates its decision between R10 and R20. R2 chooses R10's path as best because it has a lower router ID (10.10.10.10) than R20 (20.20.20.20).

After selecting the path from R10 as the best path, the R2/R16 peering comes up. After this, R16 advertises its path to R2 again. R2 runs the best-path algorithm. This time, because it is configured with the **bgp bestpath as-path ignore** command, it ignores step 4 of the best-path algorithm. Now, the paths from R16, R10, and R20 tie. Since R2 has already marked R10 as its best path, it follows step 10 of the best-path algorithm and continues to use R10 as its best path, preferring its older route.

---

**Note**   When R2 chooses R10 as its best path, it advertises this new path selection to R3. Before all the madness, R3 chose R2 as its best path because of the lower AS_PATH length shown below:

```
R3#show ip bgp 120.18.1.1
BGP routing table entry for 120.18.1.1/32, version 27
Paths: (3 available, best #2, table default)
  Advertised to update-groups:
     1            2            3
  Refresh Epoch 2
  (345 312) 200
    2.2.2.2 (metric 11) from 4.4.4.4 (4.4.4.4)
      Origin IGP, metric 0, localpref 100, valid, confed-external
      rx pathid: 0, tx pathid: 0
  Refresh Epoch 1
  (312) 200
    2.2.2.2 (metric 11) from 2.2.2.2 (2.2.2.2)
      Origin IGP, metric 0, localpref 100, valid, confed-external,
 best
      rx pathid: 0, tx pathid: 0x0
  Refresh Epoch 2
  400 200
    200.3.10.10 from 200.3.10.10 (10.10.10.10)
      Origin IGP, localpref 100, valid, external
      rx pathid: 0, tx pathid: 0
```

---

When R2 advertises the new path through R10, the AS_PATH attribute ties between R2's path and the path R3 receives from R10 itself. With the AS_PATH as a tie, R3 chooses the path from R10 as best because it is an external path over its confederation external path received from R2. This is in compliance with confederation route selection rules that are explained in RFC 5065.

R3 advertises this path to R2, as shown in the outputs above. R2 will choose its external path received from R10 over the confederation external path received from R3, just as R3 itself did.

More details about this path selection are provided in step 7 of the best-path algorithm.

It's important to keep in mind that the **bgp bestpath as-path ignore** command does not disable the loop-prevention check. Before accepting the path, the router still checks the AS_PATH attribute to ensure that its own ASN does not appear. The effects of this command only apply to whether the router considers AS_PATH length in its decision-making process.

## Step 5: Origin Code

> **Note**   Before starting this section, revert the configuration on all routers to the base initial configuration files provided with the lab.

The fifth step in the BGP best-path decision algorithm relates to how the path was first injected into the BGP table. This attribute is known as the well-known mandatory ORIGIN attribute. The ORIGIN attribute is defined as having one of three values: IGP, EGP, or INCOMPLETE.

The ORIGIN value of IGP signifies that the path was first injected into the BGP table directly by the originating router. In Cisco IOS, paths that are injected into the BGP process in the following ways are given the ORIGIN code IGP:

1. Using a **network** command in the BGP process

2. As the result of the **aggregate-address** command where the **as-set** option is not used

3. As the result of the **aggregate-address** command with the **as-set** option used and all component paths have an ORIGIN code of IGP

A value of EGP signifies that the path was originally injected into an EGP process by a legacy EGP-only-speaking router. Finally, a value of INCOMPLETE signifies that there is no authoritative origin information for the path.

The INCOMPLETE origin code requires a bit more explanation than the first two. Paths with origin of INCOMPLETE are typically for NLRI that have been redistributed into BGP from another routing source. The INCOMPLETE origin code also applies to NLRI that are injected into BGP using an **aggregate-address** command along with the **as-set** option, if any component path covered by the aggregate has an INCOMPLETE origin.

These origins are shown in the **show ip bgp** output under the Path column with values of **e**, **i** or **?**, as shown below:

---

**On Any Router:**

```
Router#show ip bgp
BGP table version is 14, local router ID is 100.1.1.1
Status codes: s suppressed, d damped, h history, * valid, > best,
i - internal,
            r RIB-failure, S Stale, m multipath, b backup-path,
f RT-Filter,
```

```
                  x best-external, a additional-path, c RIB-compressed,
Origin codes: i - IGP, e - EGP, ? - incomplete
RPKI validation codes: V valid, I invalid, N Not found
     Network          Next Hop        Metric LocPrf Weight Path
 *>  1.11.1.1/32      200.2.16.16                        0 200 100 i
 *>  2.22.2.2/32      0.0.0.0               0         32768 ?
```

In the output above, the i and ? to the far right of the AS_PATH information indicates the origin of the path.

Because redistributed information is external to the BGP process, BGP has less granular information about the path compared to a path that was directly injected into BGP originally. The BGP best-path algorithm prefers to trust paths that were originated directly by BGP (containing code IGP) or EGP over such paths.

The ORIGIN attribute of a particular path can be changed by using the **set origin** argument in a route map. The BGP best-path algorithm prefers ORIGIN code IGP over EGP and code EGP over INCOMPLETE.

R19 is chosen to demonstrate this path preference. It has two potential paths it can use to reach the 140.15.1.1/32 prefix: one from R18 and another from R20.

---

**On R19:**

```
R19#show ip bgp 140.15.1.1

BGP routing table entry for 140.15.1.1/32, version 10
Paths: (2 available, best #1, table default)
  Advertised to update-groups:
     2
  Refresh Epoch 1
  200 400
    200.18.19.18 from 200.18.19.18 (18.18.18.18)
      Origin IGP, localpref 100, valid, external, best
      rx pathid: 0, tx pathid: 0x0
  Refresh Epoch 1
  300 400
    20.20.20.20 (metric 11) from 20.20.20.20 (20.20.20.20)
      Origin IGP, metric 0, localpref 100, valid, internal
      rx pathid: 0, tx pathid: 0
```

Without any further modifications, R19 chooses the path through R18 because it is an external path, and all steps prior tie; that is, the WEIGHT, LOCAL_PREF, locally originated, AS_PATH, and ORIGIN steps all tie.

The packet capture shows the BGP update message sent by R18 to R19, where the ORIGIN code for the 140.15.1.1 network is set to IGP. The code is set to IGP by R15 when the network is injected into BGP using the **network** command. This code is preserved in UPDATE messages as it is exchanged between BGP routers.

```
Internet Protocol Version 4, Src: 200.18.19.18, Dst: 200.18.19.19
Transmission Control Protocol, Src Port: 40092, Dst Port: 179,
Seq: 24, Ack: 24, Len: 192
Border Gateway Protocol - UPDATE Message
    Marker: ffffffffffffffffffffffffffffffff
    Length: 57
    Type: UPDATE Message (2)
    Withdrawn Routes Length: 0
    Total Path Attribute Length: 24
    Path attributes
        Path Attribute - ORIGIN: IGP
            Flags: 0x40, Transitive, Well-known, Complete
                0... .... = Optional: Not set
                .1.. .... = Transitive: Set
                ..0. .... = Partial: Not set
                ...0 .... = Extended-Length: Not set
                .... 0000 = Unused: 0x0
            Type Code: ORIGIN (1)
            Length: 1
            Origin: IGP (0)
    Network Layer Reachability Information (NLRI)
        140.15.1.1/32
        140.15.2.1/32
```

The path preference for the 140.15.1.1 prefix on R19 can be changed by modifying the ORIGIN value of the path received from R18 to INCOMPLETE. This method is implemented below on R19.

A prefix list 123 permitting the 140.15.1.1/32 prefix is first configured. This prefix list is then referenced inside the route map TST. The **set origin code** command under the route map sets the origin code to INCOMPLETE. An empty permit route map statement allows for all other prefixes to pass through. Finally, the route map TST is appended to the neighbor 200.18.19.18 statement in an inbound direction:

---

**On R19:**

```
R19(config)#ip prefix-list 123 permit 140.15.1.1/32

R19(config)#route-map TST per 10
R19(config-route-map)#match ip address prefix 123
R19(config-route-map)#set origin incomplete
R19(config)#route-map TST permit 90

R19(config)#router bgp 100
R19(config-router)#neighbor 200.18.19.18 route-map TST in

R19#clear ip bgp * soft in

R19#show ip bgp 140.15.1.1

BGP routing table entry for 140.15.1.1/32, version 30
Paths: (2 available, best #2, table default)
  Advertised to update-groups:
     1
  Refresh Epoch 2
  200 400
    200.18.19.18 from 200.18.19.18 (120.18.2.1)
      Origin incomplete, localpref 100, valid, external
      rx pathid: 0, tx pathid: 0
  Refresh Epoch 2
  300 400
    20.20.20.20 (metric 11) from 20.20.20.20 (20.20.20.20)
      Origin IGP, metric 0, localpref 100, valid, internal, best
      rx pathid: 0, tx pathid: 0x0
```

---

**clear ip bgp * soft in** is then issued on R19, causing R18 to re-send its BGP routing advertisements to R19. R19 can then apply the newly configured policy that sets the path attribute of the origin code to INCOMPLETE for the 140.15.1.1/32 prefix. With these changes made, R19 now chooses the path through R20 because its ORIGIN code of IGP is a more favorable code than the path through R18 with an incomplete origin code.

## Step 6: MED

The sixth step in the BGP best-path algorithm compares the value of the MED or MULTI_EXIT_DISC attribute. The MED attribute is an optional non-transitive attribute that is used to indicate a preferred entry point into the local AS to a neighboring AS. MED is expressed as a 32-bit unsigned number and is commonly referred to as the *metric* of a BGP path because it behaves in a similar way to IGP metrics.

The MED attribute is set and exchanged in many different ways, depending on a specific set of circumstances. To aid in the explanation, the following adjustments have been made to the original topology:

- The prefix 130.7.1.1 is no longer advertised into BGP on R7.

- The prefix 130.7.1.1 is advertised into OSPF Area 0 on R7.

- R2 and R3 advertise the 130.7.1.1 prefix into BGP using a **network** statement.

- R1 has been configured to set the WEIGHT value to 100 for the path to the 130.7.1.1 network it receives from R4.

```
On R7:

R7(config)#router bgp 378
R7(config-router)#no network 130.7.1.1 mask 255.255.255.255

R7(config-router)#interface lo10
R7(config-if)#ip ospf 1 area 0

On R2:

R2(config)#router bgp 312
R2(config-router)#network 130.7.1.1 mask 255.255.255.255


On R3:

R3(config)#router bgp 336
R3(config-router)#network 130.7.1.1 mask 255.255.255.255
```

**On R1:**

```
R1(config)#ip prefix-list 123 permit 130.7.1.1/32

R1(config)#route-map TST permit 10
R1(config-route-map)#match ip address prefix 123
R1(config-route-map)#set weight 100
R1(config)#route-map TST permit 90

R1(config)#router bgp 312
R1(config-router)#neighbor 4.4.4.4 route-map TST in
```

After making the changes, R2 and R3 now receive the prefix 130.7.1.1 through OSPF instead of through BGP. On R2 and R3, the **network** command matches this OSPF-learned route. The result is that R2 and R3 originate the BGP prefix 130.7.1.1 into BGP instead of R7. R1 will prefer the path advertised to it from R4 by R3 and advertise it to R2. With this setup, the different ways in which MED is set can be examined.

### How MED Is Set

The BGP table on R2 helps reveal one way that MED can initially be set:

**On R2:**

```
R2#show ip bgp
---omitted---
     Network          Next Hop          Metric LocPrf Weight Path
 * i 130.7.1.1/32     3.3.3.3              31    100     0 (345 336) i
 *                    3.3.3.3              31    100     0 (336) i
 *>                   30.1.2.1             41            32768 i

R2#show ip bgp 130.7.1.1
BGP routing table entry for 130.7.1.1/32, version 20
Paths: (3 available, best #3, table default)
  Advertised to update-groups:
     1          2          3
  Refresh Epoch 5
  (345 336)
    3.3.3.3 (metric 11) from 1.1.1.1 (1.1.1.1)
      Origin IGP, metric 31, localpref 100, valid, confed-internal
      rx pathid: 0, tx pathid: 0
```

```
Refresh Epoch 6
(336)
   3.3.3.3 (metric 11) from 3.3.3.3 (3.3.3.3)
      Origin IGP, metric 31, localpref 100, valid, confed-external
      rx pathid: 0, tx pathid: 0
Refresh Epoch 1
Local
   30.1.2.1 from 0.0.0.0 (2.2.2.2)
      Origin IGP, metric 41, localpref 100, weight 32768, valid,
sourced, local, best
      rx pathid: 0, tx pathid: 0x0
```

**Note**   Depending on the IOS version, the next hop value for the locally injected path to the 130.7.1.1 network may not match the output above. The reason behind this is because R2 has two equal-cost OSPF paths to reach this network in its routing table, 30.1.2.1 and 30.2.3.3. BGP will select only one next hop as the next hop it adds to the BGP table. In older IOS versions such as 15.4, when multiple IGP next hops exist, the router next hop IP address will be the lowest IP address, 30.1.2.1. In case of newer IOS versions such as 15.7, IOS chooses to display the higher next hop IP address, 30.2.3.3.

R2's BGP table in the output above shows three paths for the 130.7.1.1 network: one from R1, one from R3, and one locally injected by R2 itself. R2 chooses its own locally originated path as best due to the WEIGHT attribute, as discussed in step 1.

Looking at the MED value of each path, the paths received from R1 and R3 both have a MED value set to 31. The locally injected path has a MED value of 41. These values were not randomly generated by BGP. Instead, they correspond to the IGP metric used to reach the destination prefix. This case can be proven on R2 by examining the following **show ip route** output for the 130.7.1.1 prefix:

```
R2#show ip route 130.7.1.1

Routing entry for 130.7.1.1/32
  Known via "ospf 1", distance 110, metric 41, type intra area
  Advertised by bgp 312
  Last update from 30.1.2.1 on Ethernet0/0.12, 01:59:48 ago
  Routing Descriptor Blocks:
  * 30.2.3.3, from 7.7.7.7, 01:59:48 ago, via Ethernet0/0.23
      Route metric is 41, traffic share count is 1
    30.1.2.1, from 7.7.7.7, 01:59:48 ago, via Ethernet0/0.12
      Route metric is 41, traffic share count is 1
```

By default, MED is set to whatever the internal metric is to reach that specific prefix whenever the router originates a prefix into BGP. In the case of the 130.7.1.1 prefix, R2's metric to reach the prefix is its OSPF cost of 41. Thus, this metric value is copied into the MED attribute of the BGP prefix when matched with the **network** command in BGP configuration. The same is true whenever a route is redistributed from another routing source into BGP, using the **redistribute** command. MED can also be set manually using a route map with the **set metric** option included. The metric value chosen will be sent in the BGP update as the new MED value.

### How MED Is Communicated

The above proved that MED is initially set based on the local router's metric to the target prefix. R2 inserted a MED value of 41 for its locally originated path to the 130.7.1.1 prefix because its internal OSPF cost to reach that prefix was also 41. If the examination continues to the paths received from both R1 and R3, however, there seems to be a contradiction:

```
R2#show ip bgp

 * i   130.7.1.1/32    3.3.3.3      31    100      0 (345 336) i
 *                     3.3.3.3      31    100      0 (336) i
 *>                    30.1.2.1     41          32768 i
```

**Note**  Depending on the IOS version, the next hop IP address for the best path may differ. In older IOS versions such as 15.4, when multiple IGP next hops exist, the router next hop IP address (highlighted in yellow above) will be the lowest IP address. In case of newer IOS versions such as 15.7, IOS chooses to display the higher next hop IP address. In which case, the highlighted output might show 30.2.3.3.

The MED values assigned to R1's and R3's paths are listed as 31 instead of 41. Why isn't MED set to 41 on R2 for the other two paths? The answer lies in which router originated the path to next hop 3.3.3.3 in BGP. In this case, that router is R3.

The simple explanation is that R3 is also configured to inject the 130.7.1.1/32 prefix into BGP, using a **network** command. R3's own OSPF cost to reach the 130.7.1.1/32 prefix is 31, as shown below:

```
R3#show ip route ospf | section 130.7.1.1

O       130.7.1.1 [110/31] via 30.3.6.6, 00:23:21, Ethernet0/0.36
                  [110/31] via 30.3.4.4, 00:23:21, Ethernet0/0.34
```

```
R3#show ip bgp 130.7.1.1

BGP routing table entry for 130.7.1.1/32, version 27
Paths: (2 available, best #2, table default)
  Advertised to update-groups:
     1          2          3
  Refresh Epoch 1
  (312)
    2.2.2.2 (metric 11) from 2.2.2.2 (2.2.2.2)
      Origin IGP, metric 41, localpref 100, valid, confed-external
      rx pathid: 0, tx pathid: 0
  Refresh Epoch 1
  Local
    30.3.4.4 from 0.0.0.0 (3.3.3.3)
      Origin IGP, metric 31, localpref 100, weight 32768, valid,
sourced, local, best
      rx pathid: 0, tx pathid: 0x0
```

Just like R2, R3 will inject its internal metric from its routing table (OSPF cost 31) as the MED value for the BGP path. This MED value will stick with R3's path as it is advertised from peer to peer within the AS.

The process is as follows:

1. R3 injects the 130.7.1.1/32 prefix into its BGP table with MED value 31 and marks it as the best path. It advertises this prefix to R2 and R4, its confederation external BGP peers, and to R6, its confederation internal BGP peer.

2. R4 also marks R3's path as the best path and advertises the same path to R1 with the same MED value of 31.

3. R1 receives R3's path from R4 with the original MED value of 31 and marks it as the best path. R1 then advertises R3's path to R2 as well with the retained MED value.

R2 receives two paths to the prefix with next hop 3.3.3.3—one from R1 and one from R3—both with the metric 31.

The sequence of events above shows how MED values are communicated between confederation internal and external BGP peers unchanged. The path advertised by R3 travels from R4 to R1 to R2, retaining its original MED value of 31 throughout its journey.

MED is not limited to confederation peers; it is also communicated to normal iBGP peers and even eBGP peers under certain circumstances. To illustrate this, R20's BGP table is examined below:

```
R20#show ip bgp 130.7.1.1

BGP routing table entry for 130.7.1.1/32, version 22
Paths: (1 available, best #1, table default)
```

```
Advertised to update-groups:
    2
 Refresh Epoch 1
 300
    200.2.20.2 from 200.2.20.2 (2.2.2.2)
      Origin IGP, metric 41, localpref 100, valid, external, best
      rx pathid: 0, tx pathid: 0x0
```

R20 also receives a path from R2 with MED value set to 41, the same MED value R2 set for its locally originated path to the same prefix. A packet capture of the BGP update message sent to R20 by R2 for the 130.7.1.1 prefix below confirms this:

```
Internet Protocol Version 4, Src: 200.2.20.2, Dst: 200.2.20.20
Transmission Control Protocol, Src Port: 25684, Dst Port: 179,
Seq: 24, Ack: 240, Len: 306
Border Gateway Protocol - UPDATE Message
    Marker: ffffffffffffffffffffffffffffffff
    Length: 55
    Type: UPDATE Message (2)
    Withdrawn Routes Length: 0
    Total Path Attribute Length: 27
    Path attributes
        Path Attribute - ORIGIN: IGP
            Flags: 0x40, Transitive, Well-known, Complete
            Type Code: ORIGIN (1)
            Length: 1
            Origin: IGP (0)
        Path Attribute - AS_PATH: 300
            Flags: 0x40, Transitive, Well-known, Complete
            Type Code: AS_PATH (2)
            Length: 6
            AS Path segment: 300
        Path Attribute - NEXT_HOP: 200.2.20.2
            Flags: 0x40, Transitive, Well-known, Complete
            Type Code: NEXT_HOP (3)
            Length: 4
            Next hop: 200.2.20.2
        Path Attribute - MULTI_EXIT_DISC: 41
            Flags: 0x80, Optional, Non-transitive, Complete
            Type Code: MULTI_EXIT_DISC (4)
            Length: 4
            Multiple exit discriminator: 41
    Network Layer Reachability Information (NLRI)
        130.7.1.1/32
```

**Note**  Interestingly, the BGP metric is actually recorded in R20's routing table entry for the prefix 130.7.1.1. In the **show ip route** output below, R20 has a BGP-learned entry for 130.7.1.1 with the AD/metric combination 20/41. The 41 is the same MED value as the path to 130.7.1.1 in R20's BGP table:

**On R20:**

```
R20#show ip route bgp | sec 130.7.1.1

B        130.7.1.1 [20/41] via 200.2.20.2, 00:02:23
         140.15.0.0/32 is subnetted, 2 subnets
```

R20 will also in turn advertise this MED value to R19. This too can be seen with the **show ip bgp 130.7.1.1** output on R19 and the update message from R20 to R19, as shown below:

```
R19#show ip bgp 130.7.1.1

BGP routing table entry for 130.7.1.1/32, version 23
Paths: (2 available, best #2, table default)
  Advertised to update-groups:
     1
  Refresh Epoch 1
  200 300
    200.18.19.18 from 200.18.19.18 (18.18.18.18)
      Origin IGP, localpref 100, valid, external
      rx pathid: 0, tx pathid: 0
  Refresh Epoch 1
  300
    20.20.20.20 (metric 11) from 20.20.20.20 (20.20.20.20)
      Origin IGP, metric 41, localpref 100, valid, internal, best
      rx pathid: 0, tx pathid: 0x0
Internet Protocol Version 4, Src: 20.20.20.20, Dst: 19.19.19.19

Transmission Control Protocol, Src Port: 179, Dst Port: 51761, Seq:
43, Ack: 20, Len: 217
Border Gateway Protocol - UPDATE Message
    Marker: ffffffffffffffffffffffffffffffff
    Length: 62
    Type: UPDATE Message (2)
    Withdrawn Routes Length: 0
    Total Path Attribute Length: 34
    Path attributes
        Path Attribute - ORIGIN: IGP
```

```
            Flags: 0x40, Transitive, Well-known, Complete
            Type Code: ORIGIN (1)
            Length: 1
            Origin: IGP (0)
        Path Attribute - AS_PATH: 300
            Flags: 0x40, Transitive, Well-known, Complete
            Type Code: AS_PATH (2)
            Length: 6
            AS Path segment: 300
        Path Attribute - NEXT_HOP: 20.20.20.20
            Flags: 0x40, Transitive, Well-known, Complete
            Type Code: NEXT_HOP (3)
            Length: 4
            Next hop: 20.20.20.20
        Path Attribute - MULTI_EXIT_DISC: 41
            Flags: 0x80, Optional, Non-transitive, Complete
            Type Code: MULTI_EXIT_DISC (4)
            Length: 4
            Multiple exit discriminator: 41
        Path Attribute - LOCAL_PREF: 100
            Flags: 0x40, Transitive, Well-known, Complete
            Type Code: LOCAL_PREF (5)
            Length: 4
            Local preference: 100
    Network Layer Reachability Information (NLRI)
        130.7.1.1/32
```

A difference occurs whenever R19 advertises the same path to R18. The BGP table on R18 shows a missing MED value instead of the expected value of 41:

```
R18#show ip bgp 130.7.1.1

BGP routing table entry for 130.7.1.1/32, version 25
Paths: (2 available, best #2, table default)
  Advertised to update-groups:
     1
  Refresh Epoch 1
  100 300
    200.18.19.19 from 200.18.19.19 (19.19.19.19)
      Origin IGP, localpref 100, valid, external
      rx pathid: 0, tx pathid: 0
  Refresh Epoch 1
  300
    16.16.16.16 (metric 11) from 16.16.16.16 (16.16.16.16)
```

```
    Origin IGP, metric 41, localpref 100, valid, internal, best
    rx pathid: 0, tx pathid: 0x0
```

A packet capture showing the BGP update message sent by R19 to R18 also reveals the missing MED attribute for the 130.7.1.1/32 prefix:

```
Internet Protocol Version 4, Src: 200.18.19.19, Dst: 200.18.19.18
Transmission Control Protocol, Src Port: 179, Dst Port: 62942,
Seq: 43, Ack: 24, Len: 188
Border Gateway Protocol - UPDATE Message
    Marker: ffffffffffffffffffffffffffffffff
    Length: 52
    Type: UPDATE Message (2)
    Withdrawn Routes Length: 0
    Total Path Attribute Length: 24
    Path attributes
        Path Attribute - ORIGIN: IGP
        Path Attribute - AS_PATH: 100 300
        Path Attribute - NEXT_HOP: 200.18.19.19
    Network Layer Reachability Information (NLRI)
        130.7.1.1/32
```

The reason for this is related to the nature of the MED attribute. Although MED is a transitive attribute, there are restrictions on when MED values are retained when advertised between BGP peers. MED is retained only when advertised to iBGP peers, confederation internal peers, and confederation external peers. MED values are also retained when advertised to eBGP peers, but only if the MED value was not received from another AS. MED values received from a neighboring AS should not be communicated to a different AS. This point is made clear in RFC 4271:

*If received over EBGP, the MULTI_EXIT_DISC attribute MAY be propagated over IBGP to other BGP speakers within the same AS (see also 9.1.2.2). The MULTI_EXIT_ DISC attribute received from a neighboring AS MUST NOT be propagated to other neighboring ASes.*

In compliance with the RFC, R19 strips the MED value from its UPDATE message to R18 because the value was originally set by AS 300. The reasoning behind this behavior is explained by the nature of the MED attribute. MED stands for Multi-Exit Discriminator. The value is intended to represent a degree of preference to the neighboring AS when there are multiple entry points into the local AS. MED accomplishes this task by allowing the neighboring AS a glimpse into the local AS's internal metric structure.

In this example, AS 300 has communicated to AS 100 that it has an internal metric of 41 to reach the prefix 130.7.1.1. If R19 advertises this same preference to R18, R18 will believe that AS 100 is advertising its internal metric, which is not true. The value 41 does not represent AS 100's true internal metric structure. It represents AS 300's internal metric structure. Thus, R19 strips it from the advertisement. A simpler way of stating this requirement is that a BGP router will not advertise the MED value of an internal path to an external peer without administrator intervention.

R18 does receive a path from R16 that has MED set to 41. This is the path R2 sent directly to R16, containing the indicated MED value. The path was communicated in the same manner as from R2 to R20 to R19. This time, because it was received directly from R2 in AS 300, the MED is representative of AS 300's internal metric structure.

### How MED Is Evaluated

Now that we have established how MED is set and communicated between BGP peers, the discussion can turn to how MED is evaluated and influences path selection in the BGP best-path algorithm.

As mentioned, MED is a communication of internal path preferences for a specific prefix between the local AS and its neighboring AS. The neighboring AS can consider this information when making decisions on how to send traffic into the local AS when there are multiple direct entry points from the neighboring AS to the local AS. The lower MED value is preferred between competing entry points, allowing MED to behave in a manner similar to IGP metrics.

To help show this preference, R2, R6, R10, and R11 are examined. First, the BGP table on R10 shows the following paths to reach the 130.7.1.1 prefix:

```
R10#show ip bgp 130.7.1.1

BGP routing table entry for 130.7.1.1/32, version 25
Paths: (5 available, best #5, table default)
  Advertised to update-groups:
     1
  Refresh Epoch 1
  300
    11.11.11.11 (metric 11) from 12.12.12.12 (12.12.12.12)
      Origin IGP, metric 0, localpref 100, valid, internal
      Originator: 11.11.11.11, Cluster list: 12.12.12.12
      rx pathid: 0, tx pathid: 0
  Refresh Epoch 1
  200 300
    200.10.17.17 from 200.10.17.17 (17.17.17.17)
      Origin IGP, localpref 100, valid, external
      rx pathid: 0, tx pathid: 0
  Refresh Epoch 1
```

```
300
  200.3.10.3 from 200.3.10.3 (3.3.3.3)
    Origin IGP, metric 31, localpref 100, valid, external
    rx pathid: 0, tx pathid: 0
Refresh Epoch 1
300
  200.2.10.2 from 200.2.10.2 (2.2.2.2)
    Origin IGP, metric 41, localpref 100, valid, external
    rx pathid: 0, tx pathid: 0
Refresh Epoch 1
300
  11.11.11.11 (metric 11) from 11.11.11.11 (11.11.11.11)
    Origin IGP, metric 0, localpref 100, valid, internal, best
    rx pathid: 0, tx pathid: 0x0
```

In the above, R10 has paths from R2, R3, R11, R12, and R17 to reach the prefix 130.7.1.1. With the default path selection only the paths from R2, R3, R11, and R12 are considered (the path from R17 has a higher AS_PATH length and is least favorable as a result). ORIGIN codes tie between all paths, so the decision lands on the MED attribute. R10 chooses the path from R11 as its best path because its MED value is 0, which is the lowest possible MED value. From where did this MED value of 0

**Note**   Technically, R11's and R12's paths tie on R10. The deciding factor in this case is based on the lower cluster length attribute. Because R11 does not have a cluster length attribute, its path is chosen over R12's. More about this decision-making process is explained in step 12 of the best-path algorithm

**Missing MED Values**   R10 receives a path from R11 with a mysterious MED value of 0. To track down where this MED value comes from, the BGP table on R11 reveals that it learns the path to the 130.7.1.1/32 prefix from R6 with no MED value set:

```
R11#show ip bgp 130.7.1.1

BGP routing table entry for 130.7.1.1/32, version 30
Paths: (1 available, best #1, table default)
  Advertised to update-groups:
     2          3
  Refresh Epoch 1
  300
    200.6.11.6 from 200.6.11.6 (6.6.6.6)
      Origin IGP, localpref 100, valid, external, best
      rx pathid: 0, tx pathid: 0x0
```

R6's BGP table reveals that its path to reach 130.7.1.1/32 has a MED value of 31 set:

```
R6#show ip bgp 130.7.1.1

BGP routing table entry for 130.7.1.1/32, version 29
Paths: (1 available, best #1, table default, RIB-failure(17) - next-
hop mismatch)
  Advertised to update-groups:
     1          3
  Refresh Epoch 1
  Local
    3.3.3.3 (metric 11) from 3.3.3.3 (3.3.3.3)
      Origin IGP, metric 31, localpref 100, valid, confed-internal,
best
      rx pathid: 0, tx pathid: 0x0
```

So why does R11 report a MED value of 0 and not 31 for the same path? Recall that, by default, BGP does not advertise MED values of internal paths to external peers. As a result, R6 strips the MED value from the advertisement to R11. When R11 receives the update with the missing MED value, it advertises it to R10 with a MED value of 0. This is a behavior specific to the Cisco implementation of BGP.

Cisco routers treat missing MED values as 0 values when they are received from eBGP neighbors. Originally, the BGP specification was unclear on what to do with missing MED values. Some implementations set them to maximum value, while others, Cisco included, set them to 0. The impact of this function results in R11's path to reach the 130.7.1.1/32 prefix always being preferred over any path received by R10 for the same prefix.

**BGP MED Missing as Worst**    By default, Cisco routers treat missing MED values as having a value of 0 when received from an external peer. This preference means paths without MED values set will always be preferred over those that do have MED set. Cisco routers, however, include a command that reverses this preference. Instead of considering missing MED values as MED value 0, the router will consider them to have the maximum MED value 4294967295. Such a change ensures that set MED values are always preferred over paths without set MED values. The **bgp bestpath med missing-as-worst** command can be used to activate this behavior.

To demonstrate such a configuration, the network will be configured such that R10 chooses the path through R3 to reach the 130.7.1.1 network by modifying MED alone. To do so, R10 needs to receive the path from R3 with the lowest MED value. However, the path R10 receives from R11 has a MED value of 0, which is the lowest possible value.

By issuing the **bgp bestpath med missing-as-worst** command on R11, R11 will assign all paths with missing MED values the maximum MED value.

---

**On R11:**

```
R11(config)#router bgp 400
R11(config-router)#bgp bestpath med missing-as-worst

R11#clear ip bgp *
```

---

After configuring the above and executing the **clear ip bgp *** command, R11's BGP table for 130.7.1.1 looks as follows:

---

```
R11#show ip bgp 130.7.1.1

BGP routing table entry for 130.7.1.1/32, version 42
BGP Bestpath: med
Paths: (3 available, best #2, table default)
  Advertised to update-groups:
     1          3
  Refresh Epoch 2
  300
    10.10.10.10 (metric 11) from 12.12.12.12 (12.12.12.12)
      Origin IGP, metric 31, localpref 100, valid, internal
      Originator: 10.10.10.10, Cluster list: 12.12.12.12
      rx pathid: 0, tx pathid: 0
  Refresh Epoch 3
  300
    10.10.10.10 (metric 11) from 10.10.10.10 (10.10.10.10)
      Origin IGP, metric 31, localpref 100, valid, internal, best
      rx pathid: 0, tx pathid: 0x0
  Refresh Epoch 2
  300
    200.6.11.6 from 200.6.11.6 (6.6.6.6)
      Origin IGP, metric 4294967295, localpref 100, valid, external
      rx pathid: 0, tx pathid: 0
```

---

What has happened above is that R11 receives three paths to reach the prefix 130.7.1.1—from R12, R10, and R6. Originally, R6's path was assigned a MED value of 0 because it was missing from R6's BGP UPDATE. With the lowest possible MED value, R6's path was chosen. Now that **bgp bestpath med missing-as-worst** has been configured, R11 instead marks R6's path with the highest possible MED value. When evaluating the best-path algorithm again, R11's decision is between paths received from R10 and R12 because their MED values of 31 are much lower than the maximum MED value it has stored for the path received from R6. R10's path is marked best due to step 12 of the best-path algorithm.

## Modifying MED Evaluation

**Note**   Before starting this section, revert the configuration on all routers to the base initial configuration files provided with the lab.

By default, the MED attribute is only evaluated when deciding between two external paths from the same AS. Used in this way, as discussed previously, the remote AS can indicate a degree of preference for which entry point the local AS should use to reach the prefix advertised by the remote AS. If a BGP router receives multiple paths to the same prefix with differing MED values from different autonomous systems, these MED values are ignored during MED evaluation because they cannot be directly compared. The representation of internal metric information from one AS may not be the same as from another. For example, one AS may use monetary cost as its metric, while another uses bandwidth—and these values are not comparable. This is why, under normal circumstances, only MED values received from the same AS are compared.

Equally important, BGP best-path processing follows a top-down model. The first path received is compared to the second, the resulting winner is then compared to the third, and then the fourth, and so on until all available paths to a specific prefix have been evaluated and only a single best path remains. This approach can lead to very different results, depending on the order in which paths are received from external and internal peers.

To demonstrate these differences, the topology is modified in the following manner:

1. R10 has its peerings to R2, R3, R9, R11, R12, and R17 shut down in the BGP configuration.

2. R2 is configured to send a MED value of 200 to R10 for the prefix 110.19.1.1/32.

3. R3 is configured to send a MED value of 300 to R10 for the prefix 110.19.1.1/32.

4. R9 is configured to send a MED value of 100 to R10 for the prefix 1+ 10.19.1.1/32.

5. R17 is configured to send a MED value of 150 to R10 for the prefix 110.19.1.1/32.

6. R10's BGP peerings to R9, R3, R17, and R2 are brought back up—in that order (making sure BGP learns a path to 110.19.1.1/32 from each peer before bringing the next up).

The relevant configuration modifications are shown below:

**On R10:**

```
R10(config)#router bgp 400
R10(config-router)#neighbor 200.10.17.17 shutdown
R10(config-router)#neighbor 200.3.10.3 shutdown
R10(config-router)#neighbor 200.2.10.2 shutdown
R10(config-router)#neighbor 9.9.9.9 shutdown
R10(config-router)#neighbor 11.11.11.11 shutdown
R10(config-router)#neighbor 12.12.12.12 shutdown
```

**On R2:**

```
R2(config)#ip prefix-list 123 permit 110.19.1.1/32

R2(config)#route-map TST permit 10
R2(config-route-map)#match ip address prefix 123
R2(config-route-map)#set metric 200

R2(config)#router bgp 312
R2(config-router)#neighbor 200.2.10.10 route-map TST out
```

**On R3:**

```
R3(config)#ip prefix-list 123 permit 110.19.1.1/32

R3(config)#route-map TST permit 10
R3(config-route-map)#match ip address prefix 123
R3(config-route-map)#set metric 300

R3(config)#router bgp 336
R3(config-router)#neighbor 200.3.10.10 route-map TST out
```

**On R9:**

```
R9(config)#ip prefix-list 123 permit 110.19.1.1/32

R9(config)#route-map TST permit 10
R9(config-route-map)#match ip address prefix 123
R9(config-route-map)#set metric 100

R9(config)#router bgp 400
R9(config-router)#neighbor 10.10.10.10 route-map TST out
```

**On R17:**

```
R17(config)#ip prefix-list 123 permit 110.19.1.1/32

R17(config)#route-map TST permit 10
R17(config-route-map)#match ip address prefix 123
R17(config-route-map)#set metric 150

R17(config)#router bgp 200
R17(config-router)#neighbor 200.10.17.10 route-map TST out
```

**On R10:**

```
R10(config)#router bgp 400

R10(config-router)#no neighbor 9.9.9.9 shutdown
R10(config-router)#no neighbor 200.3.10.3 shutdown
R10(config-router)#no neighbor 200.10.17.17 shutdown
R10(config-router)#no neighbor 200.2.10.2 shutdown
```

As a result of the sequence of configurations, R10's BGP table lists all of the learned paths for the 110.19.1.1/32 prefix in the order presented in the example below. For readability, internal paths are highlighted in orange, external paths are highlighted in green, MED values are highlighted in red, and the AS_PATH attribute is highlighted in purple:

**On R10:**

```
R10#show ip bgp 110.19.1.1

BGP routing table entry for 110.19.1.1/32, version 84
BGP Bestpath: med
Paths: (4 available, best #3, table default)
  Advertised to update-groups:
     6          7
  Refresh Epoch 1
  300 100
    200.2.10.2 from 200.2.10.2 (2.2.2.2)
      Origin IGP, metric 200, localpref 100, valid, external
      rx pathid: 0, tx pathid: 0
  Refresh Epoch 1
  200 100
```

```
    200.10.17.17 from 200.10.17.17 (17.17.17.17)
      Origin IGP, metric 150, localpref 100, valid, external
      rx pathid: 0, tx pathid: 0
  Refresh Epoch 1
  300 100
    200.3.10.3 from 200.3.10.3 (3.3.3.3)
      Origin IGP, metric 300, localpref 100, valid, external, best
      rx pathid: 0, tx pathid: 0x0
  Refresh Epoch 1
  200 100
    9.9.9.9 (metric 11) from 9.9.9.9 (9.9.9.9)
      Origin IGP, metric 100, localpref 100, valid, internal
      rx pathid: 0, tx pathid: 0
```

With the top-down BGP comparison method, the best path is determined as follows:

1. The path from R2 is compared to the path from R17. R17 is chosen as best because it is the older path.

2. The path from R17 is then compared to the path from R3. The path from R3 is chosen as best because it is the older path as well.

3. The path from R3 is compared to the path from R9. The path from R3 is chosen as best because it is an external path.

In this comparison, R3 is chosen as the best path, even though all other paths possess better MED values. MED is not considered because, at every comparison, the paths being compared did not have the same source AS (the first ASN in the AS_PATH). In addition, the R3/R9 comparison does not consider MED because the two paths are not external paths.

BGP best-path processing can be altered to influence a different outcome by forcing the router to always compare MED values, forcing the router to reorganize how the paths were received, or forcing the router to do both. The following sections examine this process with the above setup in mind.

**Always Comparing MED Values**   In the above case, the BGP decision would be vastly different if the MED values were compared between the four competing paths. However, due to the rules regarding MED comparison, MED does not have an effect in the decision-making process.

The **bgp always-compare-med** command changes this behavior. With this command enabled, the MED attribute is always compared between two competing paths, regardless of whether the paths are both external paths or were received from the same AS. The effects can be seen when applied to R10, as shown on the next page.

First, the BGP peering of R10 to R9, R3, R17, and R2 is shut down. The **bgp always-compare-med** command is issued on R10 in BGP router configuration mode. The peerings are once again brought back up in the order R9, R3, R17, and R2:

```
On R10:

R10(config)#router bgp 400

R10(config-router)#neighbor 9.9.9.9 shutdown
R10(config-router)#neighbor 200.3.10.3 shutdown
R10(config-router)#neighbor 200.10.17.17 shutdown
R10(config-router)#neighbor 200.2.10.2 shutdown
R10(config-router)#bgp always-compare-med

! Reestablishing the BGP peerings in order:

R10(config-router)#no neighbor 9.9.9.9 shutdown

%BGP-5-ADJCHANGE: neighbor 9.9.9.9 Up

R10(config-router)#no neighbor 200.3.10.3 shutdown

%BGP-5-ADJCHANGE: neighbor 200.3.10.3 Up

R10(config-router)#no neighbor 200.10.17.17 shutdown

%BGP-5-ADJCHANGE: neighbor 200.10.17.17 Up

R10(config-router)#no neighbor 200.2.10.2 shutdown

%BGP-5-ADJCHANGE: neighbor 200.2.10.2 Up
```

In this run, the result seems to be unexpected regarding normal best-path operation:

```
R10#show ip bgp 110.19.1.1

BGP routing table entry for 110.19.1.1/32, version 85
BGP Bestpath: med
Paths: (4 available, best #4, table default)
  Advertised to update-groupsc:
     7
  Refresh Epoch 1
  300 100
```

```
    200.2.10.2 from 200.2.10.2 (2.2.2.2)
      Origin IGP, metric 200, localpref 100, valid, external
      rx pathid: 0, tx pathid: 0
  Refresh Epoch 1
  200 100
    200.10.17.17 from 200.10.17.17 (17.17.17.17)
      Origin IGP, metric 150, localpref 100, valid, external
      rx pathid: 0, tx pathid: 0
  Refresh Epoch 1
  300 100
    200.3.10.3 from 200.3.10.3 (3.3.3.3)
      Origin IGP, metric 300, localpref 100, valid, external
      rx pathid: 0, tx pathid: 0
  Refresh Epoch 1
  200 100
    9.9.9.9 (metric 11) from 9.9.9.9 (9.9.9.9)
      Origin IGP, metric 100, localpref 100, valid, internal, best
      rx pathid: 0, tx pathid: 0x0
```

In this case, the internal path from R9 is chosen over all three competing external paths. The reason, of course, is because of the command enabled on R10. This time, R10 considers MED in all comparisons, regardless of external or internal status and regardless of whether the paths were received from the same AS. The comparison process for the paths is conducted in this manner:

1. The path from R2 is compared to the path from R17. The path from R17 has a lower MED value than the path from R2. R17's path is preferred.

2. The path from R17 is compared to the path from R3. The path from R17 still has a lower MED value than the path from R3. R17's path is preferred.

3. The path from R17 is compared to the path from R9. The path from R9 has a lower MED value than the path from R17. R9's path is preferred.

The **bgp always-compare-med** option is a powerful command. It is most useful in situations where a set of autonomous systems all agree on how MED values are measured. Typically, MED values received from different autonomous systems are not directly comparable because the MED values are measures of different metrics between the two autonomous systems. If all autonomous systems agree on how MED values are measured, then the MED values become directly comparable once again.

> **Note**   The logic of comparable metrics is not unique to BGP. The same logic is used with OSPF external routes as well. OSPF type 1 external routes will combine the external metric with the internal metric when calculating costs. With a type 1 OSPF external route, it is assumed that the external metric is directly comparable to the internal metrics and thus the metrics can be aggregated together in the OSPF domain.

**More Deterministic MED Evaluation**    There may be cases in which the MED values are not directly comparable, but the administrator wants to ensure that the best MED value possible is represented during the best-path processing of a BGP router. In the original example, the path from R2 has a MED value of 200, and the path from R3 has a MED value of 300. If these paths are compared directly, R2 provides a better path based on MED. Due to the order in which the paths were received, the R2/R3 comparison never happens, and R3 is chosen as the best path.

BGP can be modified to always take into consideration MED values received from the same AS. This modification ensures that the path from the AS with the best MED value is always selected before a comparison with paths from other autonomous systems occurs. In this way, MED's influence on the decision process becomes more deterministic. The **bgp deterministic-med** command activates this feature.

Once configured with the **bgp deterministic-med** command, the router will reorganize its BGP table such that paths received from the same AS are grouped together. MED values are first compared between all paths belonging to the same AS. After this comparison, BGP then compares the winning paths from each AS to each other in a top-down fashion.

To demonstrate, R10 is reset as indicated above. The **bgp always-compare-med** command is removed, and the **bgp deterministic-med** command is then enabled on R10. The results are as follows:

---

**On R10:**

```
R10(config)#router bgp 400
R10(config-router)#no bgp always-compare-med
R10(config-router)#bgp deterministic-med

R10#show ip bgp 110.19.1.1

BGP routing table entry for 110.19.1.1/32, version 87
BGP Bestpath: deterministic-med: med
Paths: (4 available, best #3, table default)
  Advertised to update-groups:
      6          7
  Refresh Epoch 1
  200 100
    9.9.9.9 (metric 11) from 9.9.9.9 (9.9.9.9)
      Origin IGP, metric 100, localpref 100, valid, internal
      rx pathid: 0, tx pathid: 0
  Refresh Epoch 1
  200 100
    200.10.17.17 from 200.10.17.17 (17.17.17.17)
      Origin IGP, metric 150, localpref 100, valid, external
      rx pathid: 0, tx pathid: 0
```

```
Refresh Epoch 1
300 100
  200.2.10.2 from 200.2.10.2 (2.2.2.2)
    Origin IGP, metric 200, localpref 100, valid, external, best
    rx pathid: 0, tx pathid: 0x0
Refresh Epoch 1
300 100
  200.3.10.3 from 200.3.10.3 (3.3.3.3)
    Origin IGP, metric 300, localpref 100, valid, external
    rx pathid: 0, tx pathid: 0
```

Notice in the output above that BGP has actually reorganized the paths based on their source AS. R10 also chooses R2's path as the best path. To come to this conclusion, R10 follows these steps:

1. The path received from R3 is compared to the path received from R2. The path from R2 has a lower MED value than the path from R3. R2's path replaces R3's as the current best path.

2. The path received from R9 is compared to the path received from R17. R17's path is considered best because it is an external path.

3. The path from R17 is compared to the path from R2. MED is not considered because the paths are from different autonomous systems. Processing falls to retaining the current best path over installing a new best path. R2's path is chosen as the best path.

This processing order ensures that R2's path is the chosen path to represent AS 300, even though it is the path that was received last. This processing order creates a more deterministic outcome for paths received from the same AS. The administrator knows the path received with the lower MED value will always be chosen for comparison to other paths in the BGP table.

**Combining the Options**    The final case for modifying the MED processing is a case in which MED values are always compared and are made deterministic. This configuration is achieved by using both **bgp always-compare-med** and **bgp deterministic-med** together. When both options are present, processing first starts by grouping together paths received from the same AS and determining a best path among them. Then all other paths are evaluated in order, with the better MED value winning.

R10's configuration is updated to include both the **bgp always-compare-med** and **bgp deterministic-med** commands. After configuration, it is instructed to do a soft refresh of its BGP table, using the **clear ip bgp * soft** command. The configuration steps and output are shown below:

---

**On R10:**

```
R10(config)#router bgp 400
R10(config-router)#bgp always-compare-med
R10(config-router)#bgp deterministic-med

R10#clear ip bgp *

R10#show ip bgp 110.19.1.1

BGP routing table entry for 110.19.1.1/32, version 96
BGP Bestpath: deterministic-med: med
Paths: (4 available, best #1, table default)
Flag: 0x820
  Advertised to update-groups:
     11
  Refresh Epoch 1
  200 100
    9.9.9.9 (metric 11) from 9.9.9.9 (9.9.9.9)
      Origin IGP, metric 100, localpref 100, valid, internal, best
      rx pathid: 0, tx pathid: 0x0
  Refresh Epoch 1
  200 100
    200.10.17.17 from 200.10.17.17 (17.17.17.17)
      Origin IGP, metric 150, localpref 100, valid, external
      rx pathid: 0, tx pathid: 0
  Refresh Epoch 1
  300 100
    200.2.10.2 from 200.2.10.2 (2.2.2.2)
      Origin IGP, metric 200, localpref 100, valid, external
      rx pathid: 0, tx pathid: 0
  Refresh Epoch 1
  300 100
    200.3.10.3 from 200.3.10.3 (3.3.3.3)
      Origin IGP, metric 300, localpref 100, valid, external
      rx pathid: 0, tx pathid: 0
```

R10 now chooses the path through R9 as the best path. This decision is made using the following process:

1. All paths from the same AS are grouped together.

2. The path from R9 is compared to the path from R17. The path from R9 has the lower MED value and is chosen as the best path from all AS 200 paths.

3. The path from R2 is compared to the path from R3. The path from R2 has the lower MED value and is chosen as the best path from all AS 300 paths.

4. The path from R9 is compared to the path from R2. The path from R9 has the lower MED value and is chosen as the best path overall.

Keep in mind that each of these features, **bgp always-compare-med** and **bgp deterministic-med**, should be configured everywhere to ensure consistent decision making for all BGP routers in the AS. In addition, the **bgp always-compare-med** command is typically used only if a group of autonomous systems all agree on the same measure for assigning MED values.

## Step 7: eBGP over iBGP

> **Note**    Before starting this section, revert the configuration on all routers to the base initial configuration files provided with the lab.

The seventh step in the BGP best-path algorithm gives preference to external paths over internal paths. If no best path has been chosen within the first six steps of the best-path algorithm, BGP will prefer to send traffic on an external path rather than an internal one. Paths received from an eBGP peer are external paths, while paths received from an iBGP peers are internal paths.

This is an important distinction to make. What makes a path internal or external is not the path itself but from which type of BGP peering the path was learned. This means a path can be advertised to the router by an external peer, existing in the local router's BGP table as an external path.

When the router advertises this same path to one of its iBGP peers, the iBGP peer will consider the path an internal path in its own BGP table. The distinction points to the fact that BGP does not advertise routes per se. Instead, it advertises paths and descriptions about those paths. A path learned from an eBGP peer describes a path that is external to the local BGP domain. A path learned from an iBGP peer describes a path inside the local BGP domain. Consider this example:

```
On R19:


R19#show ip bgp 140.15.1.1

BGP routing table entry for 140.15.1.1/32, version 34
Paths: (2 available, best #2, table default)
  Advertised to update-groups:
     2
  Refresh Epoch 1
  300 400
    20.20.20.20 (metric 11) from 20.20.20.20 (20.20.20.20)
      Origin IGP, metric 0, localpref 100, valid, internal
      rx pathid: 0, tx pathid: 0
  Refresh Epoch 1
  200 400
    200.18.19.18 from 200.18.19.18 (18.18.18.18)
      Origin IGP, localpref 100, valid, external, best
      rx pathid: 0, tx pathid: 0x0
```

In this case, R19 has learned two paths to reach the prefix 140.15.1.1/32. Keep in mind that the 140.15.1.1/32 prefix does not exist within R19's local BGP domain (AS 100). However, that does not determine the path types reported in the BGP table. R19 learns one path from its iBGP neighbor R20 and another from its eBGP peer R18. If R19 were to follow the path to R20, the packets would flow toward a BGP router inside the domain first. Thus, it is an internal path. If R19 were to follow the path received from R18, the packets would flow to a BGP router outside, or external to, the domain. Thus the path is an external path.

**Note**   The above statement may seem erroneous when considering multi-hop eBGP peerings. It is possible for a BGP router to form an eBGP peering with a BGP router that is not directly connected to it. In this case, even if following an external path, the packets may flow between multiple internal routers before reaching the appropriate eBGP peer.

BGP does not see the topologies as such. BGP does not concern itself with the inner specific workings of a particular AS. Instead, it is more concerned with routing outside the AS. From BGP's perspective, the AS is treated as a single router. An eBGP peering describes a link between two autonomous systems or two singular routers. From the perspective of how BGP understands the topology, the BGP router is following an external path because it was learned from an external router.

This policy assumes that the administrator has no preference between the two paths in question because the preceding six criteria (WEIGHT, LOCAL_PREF, locally originated versus received from another peer, AS_PATH, ORIGIN, and MED) have tied, and there is no explicit administration-driven preference between the two paths. Thus BGP makes the decision to prefer the external path over the internal one.

This is basically a form of hot-potato routing, where the AS attempts to exit external traffic in the smallest number of internal hops possible. For example, the BGP table on R10 for the 120.18.1.1/32 and 120.18.2.1/32 prefixes reveals the following:

---

**On R10:**

```
R10#show ip bgp regex _200$

BGP table version is 8, local router ID is 10.10.10.10
Status codes: s suppressed, d damped, h history, * valid, > best,
i - internal,
             r RIB-failure, S Stale, m multipath, b backup-path,
f RT-Filter,
             x best-external, a additional-path, c RIB-compressed,
             t secondary path,
Origin codes: i - IGP, e - EGP, ? - incomplete
RPKI validation codes: V valid, I invalid, N Not found

     Network          Next Hop          Metric LocPrf Weight Path
 * i  120.18.1.1/32   9.9.9.9               0    100     0 200 i
 * i                  9.9.9.9               0    100     0 200 i
 *                    200.2.10.2                         0 300 200 i
 *                    200.3.10.3                         0 300 200 i
 *>                   200.10.17.17                        0 200 i
 * i  120.18.2.1/32   9.9.9.9               0    100     0 200 i
 * i                  9.9.9.9               0    100     0 200 i
 *                    200.2.10.2                         0 300 200 i
 *                    200.3.10.3                         0 300 200 i
 *>                   200.10.17.17                        0 200 i
```

---

R10 receives five paths for both prefixes. Paths to next hops 200.3.10.3 and 200.2.10.2 are not considered because of a longer AS_PATH length. For the remaining paths, in accordance with step 7, R10 will choose the paths with the next hop 200.10.17.17 as its best path because it was received from an external peer. The other two remaining paths were received from the internal iBGP peer, R9 (indicated with the i to the left of the prefix).

Thinking about the flow of traffic, with R10 choosing the external path directly to R17, R10 will forward transit traffic for 120.18.1.1/32 and 120.18.2.1/32 directly out the local AS toward the proper destination.

If R10 chose to send to R9 (as indicated in its internal paths), transit traffic traverses an extra hop inside the local AS before ultimately leaving. This is an example of cold-potato routing, where transit traffic is kept local to the AS longer before leaving the AS, possibly leading to latency and internal link utilization.

## Confederations

Recall the concept of confederation internal peers and confederation external peers. Some publications claim that the decision-making algorithm prefers confederation external peers over confederation internal peers. Let's examine these claims from R5's point of view of the 120.18.1.1 prefix:

```
On R5:


R5#show ip bgp 120.18.1.1

BGP routing table entry for 120.18.1.1/32, version 4
Paths: (2 available, best #1, table default)
  Advertised to update-groups:
     1
  Refresh Epoch 1
  (336 312) 200
    3.3.3.3 (metric 21) from 4.4.4.4 (4.4.4.4)
      Origin IGP, metric 0, localpref 100, valid, confed-internal,
best
      rx pathid: 0, tx pathid: 0x0
  Refresh Epoch 1
  (378 336 312) 200
    6.6.6.6 (metric 31) from 7.7.7.7 (7.7.7.7)
      Origin IGP, metric 0, localpref 100, valid, confed-external
      rx pathid: 0, tx pathid: 0
```

Here, R5 receives two paths to 120.18.1.1: one from its confederation iBGP (internal) neighbor R4 and the other from its confederation eBGP (external) neighbor R7. According to the statements from other sources, R5 should prefer the path through R7, but this is not the case, as you can see above. In reality, with all else being equal, the decision falls on the lowest IGP metric to the next hop.

R5's metric to reach next hop 3.3.3.3 is 21, whereas the metric to reach next hop 6.6.6.6 is 31. Since the metric to the next hop 3.3.3.3 is lower than the metric to 6.6.6.6, R5 uses the path from R4.

To prove this point, the metrics will be modified in the topology. This is done by modifying the OSPF cost on the E0/0.45 interface on R5 to 20. With the changes made, the output below reveals a tie in metric to reach both 3.3.3.3 and 6.6.6.6:

```
R5(config)#interface e0/0.45
R5(config-subif)#ip ospf cost 20


R5#show ip bgp 120.18.1.1


BGP routing table entry for 120.18.1.1/32, version 4
Paths: (2 available, best #1, table default)
Flag: 0x100
  Advertised to update-groups:
     1
  Refresh Epoch 1
  (336 312) 200
    3.3.3.3 (metric 31) from 4.4.4.4 (4.4.4.4)
      Origin IGP, metric 0, localpref 100, valid, confed-internal, best
      rx pathid: 0, tx pathid: 0x0
  Refresh Epoch 1
  (378 336 312) 200
    6.6.6.6 (metric 31) from 7.7.7.7 (7.7.7.7)
      Origin IGP, metric 0, localpref 100, valid, confed-external
      rx pathid: 0, tx pathid: 0
```

Because R4's RID 4.4.4.4 is lower than R7's RID 7.7.7.7, R4's path is chosen as best. This fact can once again be proven by modifying the router IDs on both routers such that R7's RID is lower:

**On R7:**

```
R7(config)#router bgp 378
R7(config-router)#bgp router-id 1.1.1.7
```

**On R5:**

```
R5#show ip bgp 120.18.1.1


BGP routing table entry for 120.18.1.1/32, version 14
Paths: (2 available, best #1, table default)
```

```
   Advertised to update-groups:
      2
   Refresh Epoch 1
   (378 336 312) 200
      6.6.6.6 (metric 31) from 7.7.7.7 (1.1.1.7)
        Origin IGP, metric 0, localpref 100, valid, confed-external,
best
        rx pathid: 0, tx pathid: 0x0
   Refresh Epoch 1
   (336 312) 200
      3.3.3.3 (metric 31) from 4.4.4.4 (4.4.4.4)
        Origin IGP, metric 0, localpref 100, valid, confed-internal
        rx pathid: 0, tx pathid: 0
```

With the changes made, the path via R7 is chosen as the best path due the lower RID. The results above should not be surprising as this is the exact behavior described in RFC 5065 Section 5.3, point 4:

*Path selection criteria for information received from members inside a confederation MUST follow the same rules used for information received from members inside the same autonomous system, as specified in [BGP-4].*

*In addition, the following rules SHALL be applied:*

**1)** *If the AS_PATH is internal to the local confederation (i.e., there are only AS_CONFED_\* segments), consider the neighbor AS to be the local AS.*

**2)** *Otherwise, if the first segment in the path that is not an AS_CONFED_SEQUENCE or AS_CONFED_SET is an AS_SEQUENCE, consider the neighbor AS to be the leftmost AS_SEQUENCE AS.*

**3)** *When comparing routes using AS_PATH length, CONFED_SEQUENCE and CONFED_SETs SHOULD NOT be counted.*

**4)** *When comparing routes using the internal (IBGP learned) versus external (EBGP learned) rules, treat a route that is learned from a peer that is in the same confederation (not necessarily the same Member-AS) as "internal".*

This simply means that all peers that are members of the same confederation should be treated as internal peers, regardless of whether they belong to the same member AS. Because R4, R5, and R7 are all members of the confederation AS 300, when comparing paths received from confederation members, the paths are treated as though they are internal paths.

This rule also has the side effect of making eBGP paths preferred over both iBGP and confederation eBGP paths because iBGP and confederation eBGP paths are treated the same.

## Step 8: Lowest IGP Metric to the Next Hop

**Note**   Before starting this section, revert the configuration on all of the routers to the base initial configuration files provided with the lab.

At this stage in the best-path algorithm, BGP is left with two paths that are both either external or internal. Step 8 in the best-path algorithm is a comparison that is based on internal metrics to reach the next hop. In this step, BGP prefers paths to which the local router has a lower metric to reach the BGP next hop. The comparison exists as an enhancement to BGP's hot-potato routing default. By comparing the internal cost to reach the next hop for two similar paths, BGP further ensures that the closest exit is chosen for the traffic.

The IGP metric to the next hop is the aggregate IGP metric, as stored in the local router's RIB. This information is kept up to date with IGP metric changes.

To examine the effects of the IGP next hop on BGP decision making, the 120.18.1.1/32 network is examined within AS 400. The following catalogs the prefix's journey from edge router to internal router:

1. R10 and R9 receive multiple paths for the 120.18.1.1 prefix. They both choose their eBGP paths from R17 as best and advertise them to R12. R10 also advertises its best path to R11.

**On R10:**

```
R10#show ip bgp regexp _200$

BGP table version is 10, local router ID is 10.10.10.10
Status codes: s suppressed, d damped, h history, * valid, > best,
i - internal,
            r RIB-failure, S Stale, m multipath, b backup-path,
f RT-Filter,
            x best-external, a additional-path, c RIB-compressed,
            t secondary path,
Origin codes: i - IGP, e - EGP, ? - incomplete
RPKI validation codes: V valid, I invalid, N Not found

     Network          Next Hop          Metric LocPrf Weight Path
 * i  120.18.1.1/32    9.9.9.9               0    100      0 200 i
 * i                   9.9.9.9               0    100      0 200 i
 *>                    200.10.17.17                         0 200 i
 *                     200.3.10.3                           0 300 200 i
 *                     200.2.10.2                           0 300 200 i
 * i  120.18.2.1/32    9.9.9.9               0    100      0 200 i
 * i                   9.9.9.9               0    100      0 200 i
```

```
*>                       200.10.17.17                        0 200 i
*                        200.3.10.3                          0 300 200 i
*                        200.2.10.2                          0 300 200 i
```

## On R9:

```
R9#show ip bgp regexp _200$

BGP table version is 97, local router ID is 9.9.9.9
Status codes: s suppressed, d damped, h history, * valid, > best,
i - internal,
            r RIB-failure, S Stale, m multipath, b backup-path,
f RT-Filter,
            x best-external, a additional-path, c RIB-compressed,
            t secondary path,
Origin codes: i - IGP, e - EGP, ? - incomplete
RPKI validation codes: V valid, I invalid, N Not found
     Network          Next Hop          Metric LocPrf Weight Path
 * i  120.18.1.1/32   10.10.10.10            0    100      0 200 i
 *>                   200.9.17.17                           0 200 i
 * i  120.18.2.1/32   10.10.10.10            0    100      0 200 i
 *>                   200.9.17.17                           0 200 i
```

2. R12 receives two paths: one from R9 and one from R10. It chooses the one from R9 because of lower RID and advertises it to R11 and R13 (as shown below).

## On R12:

```
R12#show ip bgp 120.18.1.1
BGP routing table entry for 120.18.1.1/32, version 6
Paths: (2 available, best #1, table default)
  Advertised to update-groups:
     1
  Refresh Epoch 1
  200, (Received from a RR-client)
    9.9.9.9 (metric 11) from 9.9.9.9 (9.9.9.9)
      Origin IGP, metric 0, localpref 100, valid, internal, best
      rx pathid: 0, tx pathid: 0x0
  Refresh Epoch 1
  200, (Received from a RR-client)
    10.10.10.10 (metric 11) from 10.10.10.10 (10.10.10.10)
      Origin IGP, metric 0, localpref 100, valid, internal
      rx pathid: 0, tx pathid: 0
```

3. R11 receives three paths: one from R6, one from R10, and one from R12. The path
   through R6 has a longer AS_PATH length and is less preferred. The remaining paths
   from R10 and R12 are compared. The next hop for the path via R10 is 10.10.10.10
   and for the path via R12 is 9.9.9.9. R11 chooses the one from R10 because the metric
   to next hop 10.10.10.10 is lower than the one to next hop 9.9.9.9. R10 advertises the
   path received from R10 to R14.

---

**On R11:**

```
R11#show ip bgp 120.18.1.1
BGP routing table entry for 120.18.1.1/32, version 4
Paths: (3 available, best #3, table default)
  Advertised to update-groups:
     1          3
  Refresh Epoch 1
  200
    9.9.9.9 (metric 21) from 12.12.12.12 (12.12.12.12)
      Origin IGP, metric 0, localpref 100, valid, internal
      Originator: 9.9.9.9, Cluster list: 12.12.12.12
      rx pathid: 0, tx pathid: 0
  Refresh Epoch 1
  300 200
    200.6.11.6 from 200.6.11.6 (6.6.6.6)
      Origin IGP, localpref 100, valid, external
      rx pathid: 0, tx pathid: 0
  Refresh Epoch 1
  200
    10.10.10.10 (metric 11) from 10.10.10.10 (10.10.10.10)
      Origin IGP, metric 0, localpref 100, valid, internal, best
      rx pathid: 0, tx pathid: 0x0
```

---

**Note**  The output above may look odd because the next hop advertised by R12 for the
path to 120.18.1.1 is 9.9.9.9 instead of itself (12.12.12.12). However, this is normal behavior
for BGP routers in a route reflector configuration.

Originally, R9 received the advertisement from R17, its eBGP neighbor. When R9
advertised the path to R12, it set itself as the next hop because it is configured with the
**next-hop-self** command under its **neighbor** command for its peering with R12.

Under normal circumstances, R12 would not advertise the path to R11 because it is an
internal path. R11 is a route reflector client of R12, however, which means R12 can relax its
normal iBGP split-horizon rule and reflect the path to R11.

When a route reflector reflects a path, it does not change the next hop to itself. This is because the route reflector does not insert itself into the data forwarding path unnecessarily. The next hop should be retained as R9 because it was R9 that originally advertised in the internal prefix, and R9 is the edge router to which all other routers in the topology should recurse.

To help better show this interaction, two packet captures are included below:

```
! BGP update message from R9 to R12:

Internet Protocol Version 4, Src: 9.9.9.9, Dst: 12.12.12.12
Transmission Control Protocol, Src Port: 179, Dst Port: 41971, Seq:
66, Ack: 397, Len: 171

Border Gateway Protocol - UPDATE Message
    Marker: ffffffffffffffffffffffffffffffff
    Length: 67
    Type: UPDATE Message (2)
    Withdrawn Routes Length: 0
    Total Path Attribute Length: 34
    Path attributes
Path Attribute - ORIGIN: IGP
Path Attribute - AS_PATH: 200
Path Attribute - NEXT_HOP: 9.9.9.9 Path Attribute - MULTI_EXIT_DISC: 0
Path Attribute - LOCAL_PREF: 100
    Network Layer Reachability Information (NLRI)
        120.18.1.1/32
        120.18.2.1/32
! BGP update message from R12 to R11:

Internet Protocol Version 4, Src: 12.12.12.12, Dst: 11.11.11.11
Transmission Control Protocol, Src Port: 179, Dst Port: 60255, Seq:
24, Ack: 1, Len: 354
Border Gateway Protocol - UPDATE Message
    Marker: ffffffffffffffffffffffffffffffff
    Length: 81
    Type: UPDATE Message (2)
    Withdrawn Routes Length: 0
    Total Path Attribute Length: 48
    Path attributes
Path Attribute - ORIGIN: IGP
Path Attribute - AS_PATH: 200
Path Attribute - NEXT_HOP: 9.9.9.9
Path Attribute - MULTI_EXIT_DISC: 0
Path Attribute - LOCAL_PREF: 100
```

*Continued*

```
Path Attribute - CLUSTER_LIST: 12.12.12.12 Path Attribute -
ORIGINATOR_ID: 9.9.9.9
    Network Layer Reachability Information (NLRI)
        120.18.1.1/32
        120.18.2.1/32
```

R9 advertises itself as next hop to R12 in the first packet capture. In the second capture, R12 continues to advertise R9 as next hop to R11 because it is performing route reflection.

4. R13 receives a single path to the prefix from R12 and advertises it on to R14.

---

**On R13:**

```
R13#show ip bgp 120.18.1.1

BGP routing table entry for 120.18.1.1/32, version 129
Paths: (1 available, best #1, table default)
  Advertised to update-groups:
     2
  Refresh Epoch 1
  200
     9.9.9.9 (metric 21) from 12.12.12.12 (12.12.12.12)
       Origin IGP, metric 0, localpref 100, valid, internal, best
       Originator: 9.9.9.9, Cluster list: 12.12.12.12
       rx pathid: 0, tx pathid: 0x0
```

---

5. R14 has two paths: one path with next hop 10.10.10.10 and the other with next hop 9.9.9.9, shown below. R14 chooses the path through R10 as best because of the lower metric to the next hop 10.10.10.10.

---

**On R14:**

```
R14#show ip bgp 120.18.1.1

BGP routing table entry for 120.18.1.1/32, version 43
Paths: (2 available, best #2, table default)
Flag: 0x100
  Not advertised to any peer
  Refresh Epoch 2
  200
     9.9.9.9 (metric 31) from 13.13.13.13 (13.13.13.13)
       Origin IGP, metric 0, localpref 100, valid, internal
```

```
    Originator: 9.9.9.9, Cluster list: 13.13.13.13, 12.12.12.12
    rx pathid: 0, tx pathid: 0
Refresh Epoch 2
200
  10.10.10.10 (metric 21) from 11.11.11.11 (11.11.11.11)
    Origin IGP, metric 0, localpref 100, valid, internal, best
    Originator: 10.10.10.10, Cluster list: 11.11.11.11
    rx pathid: 0, tx pathid: 0x0
```

In the sequence above, both R11 and R14 make best-path decisions based on their internal IGP metric to reach the next hop for the prefix 120.18.1.1/32.

First, R11 chooses its path from R10 because its metric to the next hop 10.10.10.10 is 1,1 compared to the alternate path through R12, with a next hop of 9.9.9.9 and metric of 21. R14 chooses the path from R11 with metric 21 to reach next hop 10.10.10.10 compared to the path from R13, with a metric of 31, to reach the next hop 9.9.9.9.

All the metrics from the above are calculated based on the cumulative IGP metric to reach the next hop. In this case, the metric used is the OSPF cost for the routes as installed in the routing table, as shown in the output on R14:

```
R14#show ip route 9.9.9.9
Routing entry for 9.9.9.9/32
  Known via "ospf 1", distance 110, metric 31, type intra area
  Last update from 40.11.14.11 on Ethernet0/0.1114, 2d23h ago
  Routing Descriptor Blocks:
  * 40.13.14.13, from 9.9.9.9, 2d23h ago, via Ethernet0/0.1314
      Route metric is 31, traffic share count is 1
    40.11.14.11, from 9.9.9.9, 2d23h ago, via Ethernet0/0.1114
      Route metric is 31, traffic share count is 1

R14#show ip route 10.10.10.10

Routing entry for 10.10.10.10/32
  Known via "ospf 1", distance 110, metric 21, type intra area
  Last update from 40.11.14.11 on Ethernet0/0.1114, 00:51:21 ago
  Routing Descriptor Blocks:
  * 40.11.14.11, from 10.10.10.10, 00:51:21 ago, via Ethernet0/0.1114
      Route metric is 21, traffic share count is 1
```

To manipulate BGP's choice of best path utilizing the IGP metric to the next hop, the administrator can modify the physical link OSPF costs to engineer the desired results. For example, to force R14 to prefer the path through R9 instead of R10, the administrator could change the costs of R12's e0/0.1012 interface and R14's e0/0.1114 interface.

In the following, R12 has its e0/0.1012 interface's cost increased to 20, while R14 has its e0/0.1114 interface's cost increased to 30. The result increases the metric R14 uses to reach the next hop 10.10.10.10 from 20 to 41, as shown below:

```
On R12:


R12(config)#interface e0/0.1012
R12(config-subif)#ip ospf cost 20

On R14:


R14(config)#interface e0/0.1114
R14(config-subif)#ip ospf cost 10


R14#show ip bgp 120.18.1.1

BGP routing table entry for 120.18.1.1/32, version 53
Paths: (2 available, best #1, table default)
  Not advertised to any peer
  Refresh Epoch 2
  200
    9.9.9.9 (metric 31) from 13.13.13.13 (13.13.13.13)
      Origin IGP, metric 0, localpref 100, valid, internal, best
      Originator: 9.9.9.9, Cluster list: 13.13.13.13, 12.12.12.12
      rx pathid: 0, tx pathid: 0x0
  Refresh Epoch 2
  200
    10.10.10.10 (metric 41) from 11.11.11.11 (11.11.11.11)
      Origin IGP, metric 0, localpref 100, valid, internal
      Originator: 10.10.10.10, Cluster list: 11.11.11.11
      rx pathid: 0, tx pathid: 0
```

As a result of the above configuration, R14 now installs the path via R9 as the best path due to the lower metric (31) to reach 9.9.9.9.

## Step 9: Determine if Multiple Paths Exist

> **Note**   Before starting this section, revert the configuration on all routers to the base initial configuration files provided with the lab.

A common phenomenon in IP routing is a situation whereby the router receives multiple equal-cost routes to reach a specific destination. In such a situation, the individual routing protocols can offer both routes to the RIB for load sharing purposes. BGP also includes this functionality, but it is implemented based on two criteria.

First, BGP selects only a single path as the best path to a particular prefix and installs it into the RIB. This setting is limited by what is known as the **maximum path** configuration setting. By default, the maximum path setting is set to 1, which is why only a single path is installed into the RIB from BGP. The **show ip protocols** output below confirms this default setting:

```
On R10:


R10#show ip protocols | section "bgp 400"

Routing Protocol is "bgp 400"
  Outgoing update filter list for all interfaces is not set
  Incoming update filter list for all interfaces is not set
  IGP synchronization is disabled
  Automatic route summarization is disabled
  Neighbor(s):
    Address          FiltIn FiltOut DistIn DistOut Weight RouteMap
    9.9.9.9
    11.11.11.11
    12.12.12.12
    200.2.10.2
    200.3.10.3
    200.10.17.17
  Maximum path: 1
  Routing Information Sources:
    Gateway         Distance      Last Update
    12.12.12.12          200      03:43:11
    200.10.17.17          20      03:43:48
    200.2.10.2            20      03:43:48
  Distance: external 20 internal 200 local 200
```

The administrator must designate the type and quantity of paths that can be considered for multipath. For example, if the administrator designates that only two external paths can be considered to be installed into the RIB, then BGP picks two external paths as multipath and one as best path. Both paths are installed into the RIB.

The **maximum-paths [ibgp | eibgp] [number-of-paths]** command controls the quantity and type of paths that can be used as best paths and can be installed as multiple paths in the RIB. There are three ways this command can be used in BGP router configuration mode:

■ **maximum-paths [number-of-paths]:** Chooses only equal external paths

■ **maximum-paths eibgp [number-of-paths]:** Chooses between a mix of equal external and internal paths

■ **maximum-paths ibgp [number-of-paths]:** Chooses only equal internal paths

For example, let's configure R10 to increase its default number of maximum paths to four by using the command **maximum-paths 4**. With this form of the command, R10 will only select up to four equal-cost paths as multipath in the BGP RIB to be installed in the RIB. The effects of this change are reflected in the **show ip protocols** output on R10:

```
R10(config)#router bgp 400
R10(config-router)#maximum-paths 4

R10#show ip protocols | section bgp

Routing Protocol is "bgp 400"
  Outgoing update filter list for all interfaces is not set
  Incoming update filter list for all interfaces is not set
  IGP synchronization is disabled
  Automatic route summarization is disabled
  Neighbor(s):
    Address           FiltIn FiltOut DistIn DistOut Weight RouteMap
    9.9.9.9
    11.11.11.11
    12.12.12.12
    200.2.10.2
    200.3.10.3
    200.10.17.17
  Maximum path: 4
  Routing Information Sources:
    Gateway         Distance      Last Update
    12.12.12.12          200      00:22:51
    200.2.10.2            20       00:00:09
    200.3.10.3           20       00:22:18
    200.10.17.17         20       00:22:48
  Distance: external 20 internal 200 local 200
```

Now that the BGP default has been modified to allow multiple equal-cost paths to be selected as the best path from the BGP table, the second criterion deals with how BGP determines whether two paths are equal. This is a simple calculation for IGPs, which use metric values to determine what specific route is more preferred over another. If the metric value ties between two routes learned by an IGP, the IGP will automatically list them as candidates for multipath routing. BGP does not use metric values in this way.

As discussed earlier, BGP does not include the concept of traditional metrics, as IGPs do. Instead, it relies on its path attributes to determine degrees of preference for all received paths. Logically speaking, if BGP determined that particular path attributes are equal between two competing paths, then it could provide both paths as routes to the RIB of the local router. The only thing BGP would need to do is determine which path attributes should be equal and integrate such a check into the best-path algorithm it already uses. BGP includes this functionality but with different criteria.

First, it must be established that the BGP algorithm always chooses a single best path. No matter what multipath settings are applied, there is always a solitary best path selected in the BGP table for all prefixes. Any additional paths that are to be installed in the RIB are selected based on how much they match the chosen best path.

Step 9 in the best-path algorithm performs this step. If, for a particular competing path, certain attributes are equal to the current best path, then step 9 calls for a check of the multipath settings for the router. BGP selects as many equal paths as the maximum path settings allow. In the above, R10's maximum path setting was increased to four. Thus, BGP would install up to four paths from the BGP table into the RIB.

So, in short, these are the two criteria for selecting multiple paths in the BGP table:

■ The maximum path setting must be set to allow more than one path.

■ Certain attributes of the path in question must match the same attributes of the current best path.

Although the specific attributes that must match vary depending on which version of the **maximum-paths** command is used, at least the following attributes must be equal to the current best path:

■ WEIGHT

■ LOCAL_PREF

■ AS_PATH length

■ ORIGIN

■ MED

■ AS_PATH SEQUENCE

The next subsections review the specific requirements for each **maximum-paths** command variant.

**External Paths**   In order for BGP to consider two or more external paths as equal-cost paths suitable for multipathing, in addition to the attributes listed above, the following additional requirements must be met:

- The path must be learned from an external or confederation-external BGP neighbor.

- The IGP metric to the next hop should be equal to the best-path IGP metric.

In other words, the path must be an external path or must be learned from an external confederation peer, and the router's own metric to reach the next hop should be the same. These concepts are proven next, using R10. In the following configuration, the previous **maximum-paths 4** command is removed. R10 receives a mix of internal and external paths to reach the 130.7.1.1/32 prefix shown below:

```
R10(config)#router bgp 400
R10(config-router)#no maximum-paths 4

R10#show ip bgp 130.7.1.1

BGP routing table entry for 130.7.1.1/32, version 58
Paths: (4 available, best #3, table default)
  Advertised to update-groups:
     1         2
  Refresh Epoch 2
  300
    11.11.11.11 (metric 11) from 11.11.11.11 (11.11.11.11)
      Origin IGP, metric 0, localpref 100, valid, internal
      rx pathid: 0, tx pathid: 0
  Refresh Epoch 1
  300
    200.3.10.3 from 200.3.10.3 (3.3.3.3)
      Origin IGP, localpref 100, valid, external
      rx pathid: 0, tx pathid: 0
  Refresh Epoch 2
  300
    200.2.10.2 from 200.2.10.2 (2.2.2.2)
      Origin IGP, localpref 100, valid, external, best
      rx pathid: 0, tx pathid: 0x0
  Refresh Epoch 2
  200 300
    200.10.17.17 from 200.10.17.17 (17.17.17.17)
      Origin IGP, localpref 100, valid, external
      rx pathid: 0, tx pathid: 0
```

The path from R17 is not considered a best path because of the longer AS_PATH length. The path from R11 is also not considered the best path because it is an internal BGP route, unlike the external BGP routes received from R2 and R3. The paths from R2 and R3 are identical up to step 10. Without multipath enabled, the decision is based on whichever path is older. In this case, the path received from R2 is older or was marked as best before the path to R3, and thus R10 chooses R2's path as its best path.

**Note**  The results of this best-path calculation are highly dependent upon the timing in which R10 received the paths from R2 and R3. If R10 received both paths at the same time before running the best-path algorithm to select a best path, then R2's path will be chosen over R3's because of its lower BGP RID.

However, if R3's path is received before R2's and marked as best, then R10 will retain R3 as its best path because it is the older route. These concepts are explained in greater detail in steps 10 and 11.

R10 submits the above best path via R2 to the RIB. This can be confirmed with the **show ip route 130.7.1.1** output on R10:

```
R10#show ip route 130.7.1.1

Routing entry for 130.7.1.1/32
  Known via "bgp 400", distance 20, metric 0
  Tag 300, type external
  Last update from 200.2.10.2 00:08:59 ago
  Routing Descriptor Blocks:
  * 200.2.10.2, from 200.2.10.2, 00:08:59 ago
      Route metric is 0, traffic share count is 1
      AS Hops 1
      Route tag 300
      MPLS label: none
```

R10 has an additional path to the same prefix in its BGP RIB that appears to be virtually identical to its best path through R2. However, because the default maximum path setting is 1, it will only install the best path in the RIB. In order for R10 to consider the extra external path, the **maximum-paths 2** command is configured on R10. Remember that the **maximum-paths** command followed by a number only considers external paths for equal-cost multipathing.

```
R10(config)#router bgp 400
R10(config-router)#maximum-paths 2
```

The output of the **show ip protocols** command confirms that the maximum paths setting has taken effect:

```
R10#show ip protocols | s bgp

Routing Protocol is "bgp 400"
  Outgoing update filter list for all interfaces is not set
  Incoming update filter list for all interfaces is not set
  IGP synchronization is disabled
  Automatic route summarization is disabled
  Neighbor(s):
    Address          FiltIn FiltOut DistIn DistOut Weight RouteMap
    9.9.9.9
    11.11.11.11
    12.12.12.12
    200.2.10.2
    200.3.10.3
    200.10.17.17
  Maximum path: 2
  Routing Information Sources:
    Gateway           Distance      Last Update
    12.12.12.12           200        00:29:17
    200.10.17.17           20        00:29:16
    200.3.10.3             20        00:00:54
    200.2.10.2             20        00:20:03
  Distance: external 20 internal 200 local 200
```

With the new maximum path setting in effect, R10's BGP table shows the following:

```
R10#show ip bgp 130.7.1.1

BGP routing table entry for 130.7.1.1/32, version 122
Paths: (4 available, best #3, table default)
Multipath: eBGP
  Advertised to update-groups:
     1          2
  Refresh Epoch 2
  300
    11.11.11.11 (metric 11) from 11.11.11.11 (11.11.11.11)
      Origin IGP, metric 0, localpref 100, valid, internal
      rx pathid: 0, tx pathid: 0
  Refresh Epoch 1
  300
    200.3.10.3 from 200.3.10.3 (3.3.3.3)
```

```
      Origin IGP, localpref 100, valid, external, multipath(oldest)
      rx pathid: 0, tx pathid: 0
  Refresh Epoch 2
  300
    200.2.10.2 from 200.2.10.2 (2.2.2.2)
      Origin IGP, localpref 100, valid, external, multipath, best
      rx pathid: 0, tx pathid: 0x0
  Refresh Epoch 2
  200 300
    200.10.17.17 from 200.10.17.17 (17.17.17.17)
      Origin IGP, localpref 100, valid, external
      rx pathid: 0, tx pathid: 0
```

Now R10 marks the external paths received from R3 and R2 as multipath, with R2's path as best. The multipath designation indicates that R10 has sent both paths to the RIB for multipath installation consideration. This can be seen in R10's routing table for the same prefix:

```
R10#show ip route 130.7.1.1

Routing entry for 130.7.1.1/32
  Known via "bgp 400", distance 20, metric 0
  Tag 300, type external
  Last update from 200.2.10.2 00:00:11 ago
  Routing Descriptor Blocks:
  * 200.3.10.3, from 200.3.10.3, 00:00:11 ago
      Route metric is 0, traffic share count is 1
      AS Hops 1
      Route tag 300
      MPLS label: none
    200.2.10.2, from 200.2.10.2, 00:00:11 ago
      Route metric is 0, traffic share count is 1
      AS Hops 1
      Route tag 300
      MPLS label: none
```

It is important to understand that even though BGP sends both paths to the RIB to be installed, BGP will still only advertise one path as its best path to its other BGP neighbors. To demonstrate this, in this example, R10 has selected R2's path as its best path.

The output of the **show ip bgp neighbor 12.12.12.12 advertised-routes** command shows that this is the same path that R10 advertises to R12 as its iBGP neighbor:

```
R10#show ip bgp neighbor 12.12.12.12 advertised-routes

BGP table version is 27, local router ID is 10.10.10.10
Status codes: s suppressed, d damped, h history, * valid, > best,
i - internal,
              r RIB-failure, S Stale, m multipath, b backup-path,
f RT-Filter,
              x best-external, a additional-path, c RIB-compressed,
Origin codes: i - IGP, e - EGP, ? - incomplete
RPKI validation codes: V valid, I invalid, N Not found

     Network          Next Hop         Metric LocPrf Weight Path
 *>  110.19.1.1/32    200.10.17.17                      0 300 100 i
 *>  110.19.2.1/32    200.10.17.17                      0 300 100 i
 *>  120.18.1.1/32    200.10.17.17                      0 200 i
 *>  120.18.2.1/32    200.10.17.17                      0 200 i
 *>  130.7.1.1/32     200.2.10.2                        0 300 i
```

This behavior is not unlike IGP behavior—specifically with distance vector protocols. Distance vector IGPs advertise only a single route to reach a destination prefix, even if they have multiple routes stored in their IGP topology tables and stored in the RIB. Similarly, BGP advertises a single best path while installing multiple equal-cost paths.

**External and Internal Paths**    The example above shows a configuration where R10 is allowed to install its additional **external** equal-cost path into the RIB. However, if you look again at R10's **show ip bgp 130.7.1.1** output, you see that there is another path that could potentially be installed in the routing table:

```
R10#show ip bgp 130.7.1.1

BGP routing table entry for 130.7.1.1/32, version 27
Paths: (4 available, best #3, table default)
Multipath: eBGP
  Advertised to update-groups:
     2          3
  Refresh Epoch 2
  300
    11.11.11.11 (metric 11) from 11.11.11.11 (11.11.11.11)
      Origin IGP, metric 0, localpref 100, valid, internal
      rx pathid: 0, tx pathid: 0
```

```
Refresh Epoch 1
300
  200.3.10.3 from 200.3.10.3 (3.3.3.3)
    Origin IGP, localpref 100, valid, external, multipath(oldest)
    rx pathid: 0, tx pathid: 0
Refresh Epoch 2
300
  200.2.10.2 from 200.2.10.2 (2.2.2.2)
    Origin IGP, localpref 100, valid, external, multipath, best
    rx pathid: 0, tx pathid: 0x0
Refresh Epoch 2
200 300
  200.10.17.17 from 200.10.17.17 (17.17.17.17)
    Origin IGP, localpref 100, valid, external
    rx pathid: 0, tx pathid: 0
```

The path received from R11 ties with the paths received from R2 and R3 except for one thing: The path received from R11 is an internal path, while the current best path received from R2 is an external path. With the **maximum-paths 2** command, only external paths are considered for multipathing.

If you wanted to include any potential equal path, regardless of whether it was an internal or external path, you would use the **maximum-paths eibgp** command. In this case, the router will designate all paths as multipath candidates if the following attributes are the same as for its current best path:

- WEIGHT
- LOCAL_PREF
- AS_PATH
- ORIGIN
- MED
- AS_PATH SEQUENCE

Basically, the requirements are that steps 1–6 should all result in a tie when compared to the current best path. To configure this command, the **maximum-paths 2** command should be removed from the configuration on R10 and replaced with the **maximum-paths**

**eibgp 3** command. Note that the number increases from 2 to 3. This ensures that three total paths (including the best path) can be marked for multipathing. This configuration is shown below:

---

**R10 After maximum-path eibgp 3:**

```
R10(config)#router bgp 400
R10(config-router)#no maximum-paths 2
R10(config-router)#maximum-paths eibgp 3
R10#show ip bgp 130.7.1.1

BGP routing table entry for 130.7.1.1/32, version 144
Paths: (4 available, best #3, table default)
Multipath: eiBGP
  Advertised to update-groups:
      1         2
  Refresh Epoch 2
  300
     11.11.11.11 (metric 11) from 11.11.11.11 (11.11.11.11)
       Origin IGP, metric 0, localpref 100, valid, internal,
multipath
       rx pathid: 0, tx pathid: 0
  Refresh Epoch 1
  300
    200.3.10.3 from 200.3.10.3 (3.3.3.3)
       Origin IGP, localpref 100, valid, external, multipath(oldest)
       rx pathid: 0, tx pathid: 0
  Refresh Epoch 2
  300
    200.2.10.2 from 200.2.10.2 (2.2.2.2)
       Origin IGP, localpref 100, valid, external, multipath, best
       rx pathid: 0, tx pathid: 0x0
  Refresh Epoch 2
  200 300
    200.10.17.17 from 200.10.17.17 (17.17.17.17)
       Origin IGP, localpref 100, valid, external
       rx pathid: 0, tx pathid: 0
```

---

After you configure this command, the internal path from R11 and the external paths from R2 and R3 are both designated as multipath in the BGP table, as shown above. These paths are once again installed in the routing table, as shown in the output below:

```
R10#show ip route 130.7.1.1

Routing entry for 130.7.1.1/32
  Known via "bgp 400", distance 20, metric 0
  Tag 300, type external
  Last update from 200.2.10.2 00:00:55 ago
  Routing Descriptor Blocks:
  * 200.3.10.3, from 200.3.10.3, 00:00:55 ago
      Route metric is 0, traffic share count is 1
      AS Hops 1
      Route tag 300
      MPLS label: none
    200.2.10.2, from 200.2.10.2, 00:00:55 ago
      Route metric is 0, traffic share count is 1
      AS Hops 1
      Route tag 300
      MPLS label: none
    11.11.11.11, from 11.11.11.11, 00:00:55 ago
      Route metric is 0, traffic share count is 1
      AS Hops 1
      Route tag 300
      MPLS label: none
```

The **maximum-paths eibgp** command includes equal internal and external paths in the calculation, as expressed above. Even though the multipath configuration includes both internal and external paths, there will still be only one best path. In this example, the best path is the path received from R2. All other multipath-capable paths are selected if they contain attributes that are equal to the path R10 received from R2.

**Note**   When entering the **maximum-paths eibgp** command, the following output can be observed:

```
R10(config-router)#maximum-paths eibgp 3

%BGP: This may cause traffic loop if not used properly (command
accepted)
R10(config-router)#
*Jun 28 14:35:08.029: %BGP-4-MULTIPATH_LOOP: This may cause traffic
loop if not used properly (command accepted).
```

*Continued*

This message serves as a warning when you use the eiBGP multihop feature. In certain situations, such as when an iBGP path may have inconsistent next hops that lead back to the calculating router, loops may be formed when using this form of multipathing.

**Note**   Even though AS_PATH SEQUENCE must match exactly for multipath decision making, the **bgp bestpath as-path multipath-relax** hidden command removes this consideration. When configured, the router will consider all paths with the same AS_PATH length—not necessarily the same SEQUENCE—as potential multipath candidates.

Without this command, the AS_PATH SEQUENCE of the multipath candidate must equal the AS_PATH SEQUENCE of the best path.

**Internal Paths**   Finally, the **maximum-paths ibgp** command can be used to have the router select multipath paths for only internally learned paths. When selecting multipath paths for internal paths, the following additional attributes must be the same between the candidate multipath path and the current best path:

- Both paths must be learned from an internal neighbor.

- The IGP metric to the BGP next hop should be equal to the best path.

To demonstrate this feature, R12's BGP table for the 130.7.1.1 prefix is shown below:

```
On R12:


R12#show ip bgp 130.7.1.1

BGP routing table entry for 130.7.1.1/32, version 112
Paths: (2 available, best #1, table default)
  Advertised to update-groups:
     1
  Refresh Epoch 1
  300, (Received from a RR-client)
    10.10.10.10 (metric 11) from 10.10.10.10 (10.10.10.10)
      Origin IGP, metric 0, localpref 100, valid, internal, best
      rx pathid: 0, tx pathid: 0x0
  Refresh Epoch 1
  300, (Received from a RR-client)
    11.11.11.11 (metric 11) from 11.11.11.11 (11.11.11.11)
      Origin IGP, metric 0, localpref 100, valid, internal
      rx pathid: 0, tx pathid: 0
```

Here, R12 receives two iBGP paths to reach the prefix. It has marked its path from R10 as the best path because of the lower BGP RID. For the path through R11, however, all of the required path attributes for multipath are equal with R12's current best path through R10.

The **maximum-paths ibgp 2** command is configured under BGP router configuration mode on R12 to allow R12 to install the extra path through R11 as multipath in the RIB. The results are shown in the output below. R12 designates both internal paths as multipaths, with the path received from R10 as the best path.

---

### On R12:

```
R12(config)#router bgp 400
R12(config-router)#maximum-paths ibgp 2


R12#show ip bgp 130.7.1.1

BGP routing table entry for 130.7.1.1/32, version 120
Paths: (2 available, best #1, table default)
Multipath: iBGP
  Advertised to update-groups:
     1
  Refresh Epoch 1
  300, (Received from a RR-client)
    10.10.10.10 (metric 11) from 10.10.10.10 (10.10.10.10)
      Origin IGP, metric 0, localpref 100, valid, internal, multipath,
best
      rx pathid: 0, tx pathid: 0x0
  Refresh Epoch 1
  300, (Received from a RR-client)
    11.11.11.11 (metric 11) from 11.11.11.11 (11.11.11.11)
      Origin IGP, metric 0, localpref 100, valid, internal,
multipath(oldest)
      rx pathid: 0, tx pathid: 0
```

---

As you have seen in this section, the BGP multipath settings allow BGP to act like a normal IGP and install multiple paths into the routing table if certain attributes are equal to its current best path. When configuring BGP multipathing, the following should be considered:

- Potential multipath paths are compared to the current BGP best path.

- It is not possible to configure **maximum-paths** or **maximum-paths ibgp** along with **maximum-paths eibgp**.

- It is possible to configure **maximum-paths** along with **maximum-paths ibgp**.

The first point is just another friendly reminder that the multipath comparison is made by comparing the path attributes of the additional path to the current BGP best path. If multipathing isn't working, start by verifying that the proper set of attributes matches between the two paths.

The second point enforces the requirement that if both internal and external paths to the same prefix are to be considered for multipathing, it is not possible to enable multipathing for only one set of paths. In other words, the administrator must choose whether only internal or external paths to the same prefix are considered for multipathing. This is because the **maximum-paths eibgp** command would include a subset of the other two commands. Including this subset makes it incompatible for consideration.

On the other hand, the second point emphasizes that it is possible to configure the **maximum-paths** and **maximum-paths ibgp** commands together. This use is not detailed in this document.

## Step 10: Oldest Route

**Note**    Before starting this section, revert the configuration on all routers to the base initial configuration files provided with the lab.

The next steps of the BGP best-path algorithm introduce a series of tie-breaker conditions that are designed to help deterministically choose a best path from two paths that are virtually identical. At this point, the two paths under consideration have similar attributes and are either both external or both internal paths. Step 10 of the best-path algorithm specifically deals with stability between external peers.

Put simply, at this step, BGP prefers an external path that has already become best over any competing external path with the same attributes. This ensures that BGP does not unnecessarily introduce route flaps into the BGP process run with its external peers by informing it of a path that is only superior to the local BGP router's already chosen best path based on criteria following this step.

The **show ip bgp** output lists paths in reverse order from when they were received. That is, paths at the bottom of the list were received first, and paths at the top of the list were received last.

This step only applies to external paths and is skipped if any of the following are true:

- The router ID is the same for multiple paths, indicating that the path was learned from the same router.

- There is currently no best path, indicating that the current best path was lost or has never been selected.

- The **bgp best-path compare-routerid** command has been enabled. This is explained in step 11 of the best-path algorithm.

Because this section is heavily dependent on a specific order of operations, the following has been applied to the topology in order to achieve consistent results:

- The R17/R10 peering is shut down.

- The R17/R10 peering is brought up.

To demonstrate how this step functions, examine the output of the **show ip bgp 140.15.1.1** output on R17:

---

**On R17:**

```
R17(config)#router bgp 200
R17(config-router)#neighbor 200.10.17.10 shutdown

%BGP-5-NBR_RESET: Neighbor 200.10.17.10 reset (Admin. shutdown)

%BGP-5-ADJCHANGE: neighbor 200.10.17.10 Down Admin. shutdown

%BGP_SESSION-5-ADJCHANGE: neighbor 200.10.17.10 IPv4 Unicast topology
base removed from session  Admin. shutdown

R17(config-router)#no neighbor 200.10.17.10 shutdown
```

You should see the following console message:

```
%BGP-5-ADJCHANGE: neighbor 200.10.17.10 Up


R17#show ip bgp 140.15.1.1

BGP routing table entry for 140.15.1.1/32, version 28
Paths: (2 available, best #2, table default)
  Advertised to update-groups:
     1         2
  Refresh Epoch 1
  400
    200.10.17.10 from 200.10.17.10 (10.10.10.10)
      Origin IGP, localpref 100, valid, external
      rx pathid: 0, tx pathid: 0
  Refresh Epoch 1
  400
    200.9.17.9 from 200.9.17.9 (9.9.9.9)
      Origin IGP, localpref 100, valid, external, best
      rx pathid: 0, tx pathid: 0x0
```

R17 receives two paths for the 140.15.1.1/32 prefix: one from R9 and one from R10. Between the two competing prefixes, the WEIGHT, LOCAL_PREF, AS_PATH, ORIGIN, and MED are all tied. In addition, both paths are external paths. The deciding factor between the two paths is that the path from R9 was received first, as indicated by its being the last path listed in the output. Since R9 is the oldest route, BGP prefers R9.

To prove this point, the peering between R17 and R9 is shut down and brought back up again. R17 removes all prefixes learned from R9 as the peering goes down. At this point, the only path R17 has is from R10, which it now considers best. When the peering is restored to R9, R9 advertises its path back to R17. R17 runs the best-path algorithm for the two paths again. The result of the calculation is that R17 will continue to retain its current best path via R10 as its oldest path.

```
R17(config)#router bgp 200
R17(config-router)#neighbor 200.9.17.9 shut


You should see the following console messages:


%BGP-5-NBR_RESET: Neighbor 200.9.17.9 reset (Admin. shutdown)
%BGP-5-ADJCHANGE: neighbor 200.9.17.9 Down Admin. shutdown
%BGP_SESSION-5-ADJCHANGE: neighbor 200.9.17.9 IPv4 Unicast topology
base removed from session  Admin. shutdown


R17(config-router)#no neighbor 200.9.17.9 shut
You should see the following console messages:
%BGP-5-ADJCHANGE: neighbor 200.9.17.9 Up


R17#show ip bgp 140.15.1.1


BGP routing table entry for 140.15.1.1/32, version 20
Paths: (2 available, best #2, table default)
  Advertised to update-groups:
     1         2
  Refresh Epoch 1
  400
    200.9.17.9 from 200.9.17.9 (9.9.9.9)
      Origin IGP, localpref 100, valid, external
      rx pathid: 0, tx pathid: 0
  Refresh Epoch 2
  400
    200.10.17.10 from 200.10.17.10 (10.10.10.10)
      Origin IGP, localpref 100, valid, external, best
      rx pathid: 0, tx pathid: 0x0
```

A key aspect of understanding this step comes whenever the "best" path is not also the oldest path. In the case above, R10's path was retained as best, and it was the oldest path. This provided for a clear basic understanding. To fully grasp the functionality, however, you need to understand the case where the "best" path isn't also the oldest path. The path to the prefix 120.18.1.1/32 on R2 can help demonstrate.

R2 has three paths to reach this prefix. Of those three paths, R2 chooses the path through R16 as its best path because it has the lower AS_PATH length. Before looking at the output on R2, R2's peerings need to be reset as follows:

1. The R20 and R2/R16 peerings are shut down.

2. The R2/20 peering is brought up

3. The R2/R16 peering is brought up.

Now, the output of **show ip bgp 120.18.1.1** on R2 should appear in the following order:

---

**<u>On R2:</u>**

```
R2#show ip bgp 120.18.1.1

BGP routing table entry for 120.18.1.1/32, version 20
Paths: (3 available, best #1, table default)
  Advertised to update-groups:
     8          9          10
  Refresh Epoch 1
  200
    200.2.16.16 from 200.2.16.16 (16.16.16.16)
      Origin IGP, localpref 100, valid, external, best
      rx pathid: 0, tx pathid: 0x0
  Refresh Epoch 1
  100 200
    200.2.20.20 from 200.2.20.20 (20.20.20.20)
      Origin IGP, localpref 100, valid, external
      rx pathid: 0, tx pathid: 0
  Refresh Epoch 2
  400 200
    200.2.10.10 from 200.2.10.10 (10.10.10.10)
      Origin IGP, localpref 100, valid, external
      rx pathid: 0, tx pathid: 0
```

---

In output above, R16's path is chosen as the best path because it has a lower AS_PATH length attribute than the paths received from R10 and R20. This determination is made in step 4 of the best-path algorithm. If step 4 in the AS_PATH algorithm were skipped, then processing would eventually fall to step 10, where BGP would prefer the oldest route.

This scenario can be tested using the **bgp bestpath as-path ignore** command on R2. After making this change, R2 ignores step 4 of the best-path algorithm when evaluating best paths. In this case, the expectation is that R10's path would be chosen because it was received before the path received from R16. However, R2 still chooses R16, as shown below:

```
R2(config)#router bgp 312
R2(config-router)#bgp bestpath as-path ignore

show ip bgp 120.18.1.1
BGP routing table entry for 120.18.1.1/32, version 20
Paths: (3 available, best #1, table default)
  Advertised to update-groups:
     8          9          10
  Refresh Epoch 1
  200
    200.2.16.16 from 200.2.16.16 (16.16.16.16)
      Origin IGP, localpref 100, valid, external, best
      rx pathid: 0, tx pathid: 0x0
  Refresh Epoch 1
  100 200
    200.2.20.20 from 200.2.20.20 (20.20.20.20)
      Origin IGP, localpref 100, valid, external
      rx pathid: 0, tx pathid: 0
  Refresh Epoch 2
  400 200
    200.2.10.10 from 200.2.10.10 (10.10.10.10)
      Origin IGP, localpref 100, valid, external
      rx pathid: 0, tx pathid: 0
```

R2 chooses 16 again because BGP has determined that the three paths are all the same. Since R2 previously marked the path through R16 as best, in compliance with step 10 of the best-path algorithm, R2 will not swap the best path to R10. To do so, R2 would have to first lose R2's path in its BGP table, prompting a new evaluation for the best path, as demonstrated below:

```
! Shutting down the peering between R2 and R16

R2(config)#router bgp 312
R2(config-router)#neighbor 200.2.16.16 shutdown

Neighbor 200.2.16.16 reset (Admin. shutdown)
neighbor 200.2.16.16 Down Admin. Shutdown
```

```
neighbor 200.2.16.16 IPv4 Unicast topology base removed from session
Admin. Shutdown


! Bringing back the peering between R2 and R16

R2(config-router)#no neighbor 200.2.16.16 shutdown
%BGP-5-ADJCHANGE: neighbor 200.2.16.16 Up



R2#show ip bgp 120.18.1.1

BGP routing table entry for 120.18.1.1/32, version 27
Paths: (4 available, best #4, table default)
  Advertised to update-groups:
     1          2          3
  Refresh Epoch 1
  200
    200.2.16.16 from 200.2.16.16 (16.16.16.16)
      Origin IGP, localpref 100, valid, external
      rx pathid: 0, tx pathid: 0
  Refresh Epoch 2
  (336) 400 200
    3.3.3.3 (metric 11) from 3.3.3.3 (3.3.3.3)
      Origin IGP, metric 0, localpref 100, valid, confed-external
      rx pathid: 0, tx pathid: 0
  Refresh Epoch 2
  100 200
    200.2.20.20 from 200.2.20.20 (20.20.20.20)
      Origin IGP, localpref 100, valid, external
      rx pathid: 0, tx pathid: 0
  Refresh Epoch 2
  400 200
    200.2.10.10 from 200.2.10.10 (10.10.10.10)
      Origin IGP, localpref 100, valid, external, best
      rx pathid: 0, tx pathid: 0x0
```

Here, R2 shuts down its peering to R16. This causes it to lose its best path. R2 then decides between the path from R10 and the path from R20 remaining in its BGP table. The path to R10 is chosen between the two paths, but this time it isn't due to the older route but because of step 11, covered below.

R2 skips the oldest-path comparison because when it loses its best path R16, there is no longer an existing best path in its table. As covered above, if there is no current best path, then BGP does not evaluate the oldest route.

During convergence, R2 receives a path from R3 as well. R10's path is preferred over R3's because R10's path is an external path, while R3's path is a confederation-external path. Finally, the R16 peering comes up again, and R2 receives R16's path again. This time, because it is still ignoring AS_PATH calculations, it retains R10 as its best path because R10 is the oldest path.

So step 10 of the best-path algorithm can be put succinctly as follows: *If there is already a current best path, continue using that same best path if all other attributes are equal.* So, it isn't necessarily strictly the oldest path that is always selected; rather, the oldest *best* path is selected.

**Note**   If the **bgp bestpath as-path ignore** command were removed from the configuration and the BGP peering were reset, R10 would again select R16 as its best path. This is proven in the output below:

```
R2:
router bgp 312
 no bgp bestpath as-path ignore
R2#clear ip bgp * soft in
R2#show ip bgp 120.18.1.1
BGP routing table entry for 120.18.1.1/32, version 31
Paths: (3 available, best #1, table default)
  Advertised to update-groups:
     1          2          3
  Refresh Epoch 2
  200
    200.2.16.16 from 200.2.16.16 (16.16.16.16)
      Origin IGP, localpref 100, valid, external, best
      rx pathid: 0, tx pathid: 0x0
  Refresh Epoch 3
  100 200
    200.2.20.20 from 200.2.20.20 (20.20.20.20)
      Origin IGP, localpref 100, valid, external
      rx pathid: 0, tx pathid: 0
  Refresh Epoch 3
  400 200
    200.2.10.10 from 200.2.10.10 (10.10.10.10)
      Origin IGP, localpref 100, valid, external
      rx pathid: 0, tx pathid: 0
```

## Step 11: Lowest Router ID

**Note**   Before starting this section, revert the configuration on all routers to the base initial configuration files provided with the lab.

Step 11 in the best-path algorithm considers the router ID assigned to the BGP router. The BGP router ID is a 32-bit value that is automatically assigned to a router in the following way:

1. If a loopback address exists, the highest IP address of a loopback on the router is used as the BGP router ID

2. The highest IP address assigned to a non-shut physical interface is used as the BGP router ID

The administrator is also given the option to manually set the BGP router ID for better control over its value. This is accomplished using the **bgp router-id** command in BGP router configuration mode.

At this step, BGP prefers the path that was learned from the router with the lower BGP router ID. There isn't much to this particular preference. It is a mostly arbitrary decision—with some interesting caveats. First, to demonstrate the functionality, R12's 120.18.1.1/32 prefix is examined below:

---

**On R12:**

```
R12#show ip bgp 120.18.1.1

BGP routing table entry for 120.18.1.1/32, version 74
Paths: (2 available, best #1, table default)
  Advertised to update-groups:
     1
  Refresh Epoch 1
  200, (Received from a RR-client)
    9.9.9.9 (metric 11) from 9.9.9.9 (9.9.9.9)
      Origin IGP, metric 0, localpref 100, valid, internal, best
      rx pathid: 0, tx pathid: 0x0
  Refresh Epoch 1
  200, (Received from a RR-client)
    10.10.10.10 (metric 11) from 10.10.10.10 (10.10.10.10)
      Origin IGP, metric 0, localpref 100, valid, internal
      rx pathid: 0, tx pathid: 0
```

---

R12 receives two paths to reach this particular prefix: one from R9 with router ID 9.9.9.9 and one from R10 with router ID 10.10.10.10. R12 decides to choose the path with the lower RID as its best path. To prove that lower router ID is the deciding factor, R10's router ID is modified into something lower than R9's in the following configuration:

---

**On R10:**

```
R10(config)#router bgp 400
R10(config-router)#bgp router-id 1.1.1.10
```

You should see the following console messages:

```
%BGP-5-ADJCHANGE: neighbor 9.9.9.9 Down Router ID changed
%BGP_SESSION-5-ADJCHANGE: neighbor 9.9.9.9 IPv4 Unicast topology base
removed from session  Router ID changed
```

---

Changing the router ID on R10 causes R10 to reset all of its BGP sessions. As a result, R12 now chooses the path through R10 as the best path because of its lower BGP router ID.

---

**On R12:**

```
R12#show ip bgp 120.18.1.1

BGP routing table entry for 120.18.1.1/32, version 86
Paths: (2 available, best #1, table default)
  Advertised to update-groups:
     1
  Refresh Epoch 1
  200, (Received from a RR-client)
    10.10.10.10 (metric 11) from 10.10.10.10 (1.1.1.10)
      Origin IGP, metric 0, localpref 100, valid, internal, best
      rx pathid: 0, tx pathid: 0x0
  Refresh Epoch 1
  200, (Received from a RR-client)
    9.9.9.9 (metric 11) from 9.9.9.9 (9.9.9.9)
      Origin IGP, metric 0, localpref 100, valid, internal
      rx pathid: 0, tx pathid: 0
```

---

There are two caveats to how this particular step is processed, both having to do with paths with route reflector attributes attached to them. Route reflectors are an iBGP scaling mechanism whereby a router is designated as a route reflector. The route reflector is statically configured with a set of route reflector clients. When advertising routes to its clients, the route reflector is allowed to relax the iBGP split-horizon rules and advertise internal paths to each of its clients.

When the route reflector reflects a path, it adds attributes to the paths in the UPDATE messages sent to its clients. The two most important attributes are **Originator ID** and **Cluster List**. The route reflector keeps track of which BGP router originally advertised a path to the route reflector. This attribute is important in preventing loops. If a client receives a path with its own BGP router ID in the Originator ID attribute, it will reject the path, preventing loops. This can be seen in the following capture of the UPDATE packet R12 sends to R11:

```
Internet Protocol Version 4, Src: 12.12.12.12, Dst: 11.11.11.11
Transmission Control Protocol, Src Port: 36963, Dst Port: 179,
Seq: 115, Ack: 218, Len: 242
Border Gateway Protocol - UPDATE Message
Border Gateway Protocol - UPDATE Message
    Marker: ffffffffffffffffffffffffffffffff
    Length: 81
    Type: UPDATE Message (2)
    Withdrawn Routes Length: 0
    Total Path Attribute Length: 48
    Path attributes
        Path Attribute - ORIGIN: IGP
        Path Attribute - AS_PATH: 200
        Path Attribute - NEXT_HOP: 10.10.10.10
        Path Attribute - MULTI_EXIT_DISC: 0
        Path Attribute - LOCAL_PREF: 100
        Path Attribute - CLUSTER_LIST: 12.12.12.12
        Path Attribute - ORIGINATOR_ID: 1.1.1.10
    Network Layer Reachability Information (NLRI)
        120.18.1.1/32
        120.18.2.1/32
```

In the UPDATE message above, R12, having selected the path through R10 with new RID 1.1.1.10 as the best path, reflects that path in its BGP UPDATE message to R11. Within the UPDATE message, R12 has added the Cluster List and Originator ID attributes. In this case, Originator ID is given the value of R10's RID 1.1.1.10 because R10 was the originator of the path. Cluster List, on the other hand, lists R12's RID because R12 is a route reflector participating in the route reflector cluster 12.12.12.12.

The Cluster List attribute keeps track of how many route reflector clusters the path has traversed. Multiple route reflectors may exist together in larger iBGP environments. Route reflectors identify themselves using the cluster ID. The cluster ID designates which route reflectors service the same clients and helps prevent loops within the route reflector environment. When a route reflector reflects a path, it adds its own cluster ID to the Cluster Length attribute. Route reflectors will not accept paths with the local cluster ID in the Cluster List attribute.

When processing step 11 of the best-path algorithm, if one of the paths contains route reflector attributes, the Originator ID attribute is used instead of the router ID as the comparison value. The 120.18.1.1 prefix on R11 helps you understand how this comparison works. Before examining the BGP table, first, the competing paths from R10 and R12 need to tie in all steps through step 10. Without modification, R11 will choose the path through R10 because of its lower metric to the next hop. To engineer the tie condition, the **ip ospf cost 20** command is issued on the VLAN 1011 interface on R11 to even out the metrics. In addition, R10's BGP RID is set back to 10.10.10.10:

```
On R10:


R10(config)#router bgp 400
R10(config-router)#bgp router-id 10.10.10.10


On R11:


R11(config)#interface e0/0.1011
R11(config-subif)#ip ospf cost 20


R11#show ip bgp 120.18.1.1

BGP routing table entry for 120.18.1.1/32, version 24
Paths: (3 available, best #2, table default)
  Advertised to update-groups:
     1          3
  Refresh Epoch 1
  300 200
    200.6.11.6 from 200.6.11.6 (6.6.6.6)
      Origin IGP, localpref 100, valid, external
      rx pathid: 0, tx pathid: 0
  Refresh Epoch 1
  200
    9.9.9.9 (metric 21) from 12.12.12.12 (12.12.12.12)
      Origin IGP, metric 0, localpref 100, valid, internal, best
      Originator: 9.9.9.9, Cluster list: 12.12.12.12
      rx pathid: 0, tx pathid: 0x0
  Refresh Epoch 1
  200
    10.10.10.10 (metric 21) from 10.10.10.10 (10.10.10.10)
      Origin IGP, metric 0, localpref 100, valid, internal
      rx pathid: 0, tx pathid: 0
```

Now that the metrics tie, R11 is left to use the lower router ID to determine the best path. In the output above, it seems that R11 has incorrectly chosen R12's path with RID 12.12.12.12 rather than R10's path with router ID 10.10.10.10. This is not the case. The path received from R12 has route reflector attributes. Instead of comparing R12's router ID 12.12.12.12 with R10's RID 10.10.10.10, R11 compares the Originator ID value 9.9.9.9. The Originator ID value 9.9.9.9 is lower than the router ID 10.10.10.10, and R11 chooses R12's path over R10's, as expected.

This decision-making process is outlined in Section 9 of RFC 4456:

## 9. Impact on Route Selection

*The BGP Decision Process Tie Breaking rules (Sect. 9.1.2.2, [1]) are*

*modified as follows:*

*If a route carries the ORIGINATOR_ID attribute,* then in Step f)

*the ORIGINATOR_ID SHOULD be treated as the BGP Identifier of the*

*BGP speaker that has advertised the route.*

The reason for this preference relates to the purpose of the route reflector. The route reflector is used as a route server. Its primary job is to advertise paths on behalf of other internal peers. As a result, it doesn't necessarily have to be in the data plane. In such a capacity, it acts as a control plane device. Thus, the router ID of a reflected path is representative of the route reflector and not the original router. This step of the BGP best-path algorithm attempts to give preference to a specific originator of a path and not the route reflector itself, so the originator ID is preferred over the router ID for paths with route reflector attributes.

The above was a comparison between originator ID and router ID. In cases where both paths are learned from a route reflector, meaning they have route reflector attributes, the originator ID is used in comparison of both paths. For this R14 is used as an example. It learns a path to the 120.18.1.1 /32 network from R11 and R13. Both R11 and R13 are route reflectors serving R14. To even up the metric to reach the next hop between the two paths, the OSPF cost on the VLAN 1114 interface on R14 has been modified to the value 20. In addition, the OSPF cost of R11's e0/0.1011 interface has been returned to default using the **no ip ospf cost 20** command:

**On R11:**

```
R11(config)#interface e0/0.1011
R11(config-subif)#no ip ospf cost 20
```

**On R14:**

```
R14(config)#interface e0/0.1114
R14(config-subif)#ip ospf cost 20

R14#show ip bgp 120.18.1.1

BGP routing table entry for 120.18.1.1/32, version 88
Paths: (2 available, best #2, table default)
  Not advertised to any peer
  Refresh Epoch 1
  200
    10.10.10.10 (metric 31) from 11.11.11.11 (11.11.11.11)
      Origin IGP, metric 0, localpref 100, valid, internal
      Originator: 10.10.10.10, Cluster list: 11.11.11.11
      rx pathid: 0, tx pathid: 0
  Refresh Epoch 1
  200
    9.9.9.9 (metric 31) from 13.13.13.13 (13.13.13.13)
      Origin IGP, metric 0, localpref 100, valid, internal, best
      Originator: 9.9.9.9, Cluster list: 13.13.13.13, 12.12.12.12
      rx pathid: 0, tx pathid: 0x0
```

With the metrics tied, R14 prefers the path with the lower RID, which is R9, as shown above—even though the router ID associated with the path of 13.13.13.13 is higher than the path from R11, which has the router ID 11.11.11.11.

Finally, a special note for this step has to do with whether or not this step is included when comparing external paths. When evaluating external paths, processing typically stops at step 10, where BGP prefers the oldest received path. This requirement can lead to some unpredictable behavior, especially during failure scenarios in the BGP table. The **bgp bestpath compare-routerid** command configures the router to bypass the oldest path check entirely and to always compare the BGP router IDs between two external paths.

As proof of this concept, R17's 140.15.1.1/32 prefix is examined. To begin, R17's peerings to R10 and R9 are shut down. Then, the **bgp bestpath compare-routerid** command is issued on R17. After that, R17's peering to R10 is brought back up.

In this state, R10 advertises the 140.15.1.1/32 prefix to R17. R17 is allowed to mark R10's path as best:

**On R17:**

```
R17#show ip bgp 140.15.1.1
```

```
BGP routing table entry for 140.15.1.1/32, version 24
BGP Bestpath: compare-routerid
Paths: (1 available, best #1, table default)
Flag: 0x820
  Advertised to update-groups: (Pending Update Generation)
     2          3
  Refresh Epoch 2
  400
    200.10.17.10 from 200.10.17.10 (10.10.10.10)
      Origin IGP, localpref 100, valid, external, best
      rx pathid: 0, tx pathid: 0x0
```

At this point, under normal circumstances, when the R9 peering is brought back up, R17 would not switch to R9's path as the best path. The R9 peering is brought back up, and the following is recorded in the BGP table on R17:

```
R17(config-router)#no neighbor 200.9.17.9 shutdown

R17#show ip bgp 140.15.1.1

BGP routing table entry for 140.15.1.1/32, version 26
BGP Bestpath: compare-routerid
Paths: (2 available, best #1, table default)
  Advertised to update-groups:
     2          3
  Refresh Epoch 1
  400
    200.9.17.9 from 200.9.17.9 (9.9.9.9)
      Origin IGP, localpref 100, valid, external, best
      rx pathid: 0, tx pathid: 0x0
  Refresh Epoch 2
  400
    200.10.17.10 from 200.10.17.10 (10.10.10.10)
      Origin IGP, localpref 100, valid, external
      rx pathid: 0, tx pathid: 0
```

R17 marks the path received from R9 as its best path over the path received from R10 due to the **bgp bestpath compare-routerid** command. R17 is forced to always compare the router ID between two external paths, regardless of whether it has a previously learned best path. This feature has the potential to introduce some instability in the BGP process, particularly if R17's peering to R9 flaps. To prevent such instability, BGP features such as route dampening should be employed. This method is not expounded upon in this lab.

## Step 12: Minimum Cluster List Length

**Note**  Before starting this section, revert the configuration on all routers to the base initial configuration files provided with the lab.

This next step in the BGP best-path algorithm provides another tie-breaker mechanism for paths with route reflector attributes. In step 11, the originator IDs of the two paths were compared, with preference given to the lower value. If the two originator IDs tie, then this step considers the Cluster Length attribute. The idea here is that because Cluster Length value is a collection of route reflector clusters that the path has traversed, comparing this value can determine which path traveled the furthest from its originator to the local router. At this step, BGP prefers the path with the lower Cluster Length value.

As an example, we can examine R14's BGP table for the 120.18.1.1/32 prefix:

---

**On R14:**

```
R14#show ip bgp 120.18.1.1

BGP routing table entry for 120.18.1.1/32, version 62
Paths: (2 available, best #1, table default)
  Not advertised to any peer
  Refresh Epoch 1
  200
    10.10.10.10 (metric 21) from 11.11.11.11 (11.11.11.11)
      Origin IGP, metric 0, localpref 100, valid, internal, best
      Originator: 10.10.10.10, Cluster list: 11.11.11.11
      rx pathid: 0, tx pathid: 0x0
  Refresh Epoch 2
  200
    9.9.9.9 (metric 31) from 13.13.13.13 (13.13.13.13)
      Origin IGP, metric 0, localpref 100, valid, internal
      Originator: 9.9.9.9, Cluster list: 13.13.13.13, 12.12.12.12
      rx pathid: 0, tx pathid: 0
```

---

As it stands now, R14 has two paths for the 120.18.1.1 prefix: one from the route reflector R11 and the other from the route reflector R13. Without intervention, the originator IDs are different. To test the impacts of this step, the originator IDs need to tie.

To engineer this tie, R12 needs to prefer the path it learns from R10 over the path learned from R9. Lowering R10's router ID to 1.10.10.10 accomplishes this goal:

**On R10:**

```
R10(config)#router bgp 400
R10(config-router)#bgp router-id 1.10.10.10
```

After you make the changes on R10, R12 properly selects the path from R10 as best and advertises the new path to R13 instead of advertising the path it received from R9:

**On R12:**

```
R12#show ip bgp 120.18.1.1
BGP routing table entry for 120.18.1.1/32, version 86
Paths: (2 available, best #1, table default)
  Advertised to update-groups:
     1
  Refresh Epoch 1
  200, (Received from a RR-client)
    10.10.10.10 (metric 11) from 10.10.10.10 (1.10.10.10)
      Origin IGP, metric 0, localpref 100, valid, internal, best
      rx pathid: 0, tx pathid: 0x0
  Refresh Epoch 3
  200, (Received from a RR-client)
    9.9.9.9 (metric 11) from 9.9.9.9 (9.9.9.9)
      Origin IGP, metric 0, localpref 100, valid, internal
      rx pathid: 0, tx pathid: 0
```

R12 advertises this best path to R13, which in turn advertises it to R14. The results are shown below. R14 receives two paths that both have the originator ID set to 1.10.10.10. Recall that Originator ID is a BGP attribute that is created by the route reflector that carries the router ID of the originator of the route, which is 1.10.10.10 in this case.

**On R14:**

```
R14#show ip bgp 120.18.1.1

BGP routing table entry for 120.18.1.1/32, version 72
Paths: (2 available, best #1, table default)
  Not advertised to any peer
```

```
Refresh Epoch 1
200
  10.10.10.10 (metric 21) from 11.11.11.11 (11.11.11.11)
    Origin IGP, metric 0, localpref 100, valid, internal, best
    Originator: 1.10.10.10, Cluster list: 11.11.11.11
    rx pathid: 0, tx pathid: 0x0
Refresh Epoch 2
200
  10.10.10.10 (metric 21) from 13.13.13.13 (13.13.13.13)
    Origin IGP, metric 0, localpref 100, valid, internal
    Originator: 1.10.10.10, Cluster list: 13.13.13.13, 12.12.12.12
    rx pathid: 0, tx pathid: 0
```

When R14 processes the two paths, the Originator ID values for the two paths tie. R14
falls to step 12 of the best-path algorithm and compares the Cluster Length attributes of
the two paths. The path received from R11 has a smaller Cluster Length value, and so R11
is the best path.

**Note**   You have just seen what happens between paths that both contain route reflector
attributes, but what happens if a router is connected to both a route reflector and a normal
iBGP peer? To answer this question, we can consult R11's BGP table:

R11#**show ip bgp 120.18.1.1**

```
BGP routing table entry for 120.18.1.1/32, version 18
Paths: (3 available, best #1, table default)
  Advertised to update-groups:
     1          2
  Refresh Epoch 1
  200
    10.10.10.10 (metric 11) from 10.10.10.10 (1.10.10.10)
      Origin IGP, metric 0, localpref 100, valid, internal, best
      rx pathid: 0, tx pathid: 0x0
  Refresh Epoch 2
  200
    10.10.10.10 (metric 11) from 12.12.12.12 (12.12.12.12)t
      Origin IGP, metric 0, localpref 100, valid, internal
      Originator: 1.10.10.10, Cluster list: 12.12.12.12
      rx pathid: 0, tx pathid: 0
```

```
Refresh Epoch 1
300 200
  200.6.11.6 from 200.6.11.6 (6.6.6.6)
    Origin IGP, localpref 100, valid, external
    rx pathid: 0, tx pathid: 0
```

R11 learns the prefix 120.18.1.1 from R10 and R12. The originator ID and router ID tie here, so the decision-making process falls to step 12, which focuses on the minimum cluster list length. However, the path received directly from R10 has no cluster list included. This is because R10 is not servicing R11 as a route reflector and is instead a normal iBGP peer to R11. The path received from R12 has route reflector attributes, including Cluster List. RFC 4456 makes concessions for such a situation in Section 9:

### 9. Impact on Route Selection

*The BGP Decision Process Tie Breaking rules (Sect. 9.1.2.2, [1]) are modified as follows:*

*If a route carries the ORIGINATOR_ID attribute, then in Step f) the ORIGINATOR_ID SHOULD be treated as the BGP Identifier of the BGP speaker that has advertised the route.*

*In addition, the following rule SHOULD be inserted between Steps f) and g): a BGP Speaker SHOULD prefer a route with the shorter CLUSTER_LIST length. The CLUSTER_LIST length is zero if a route does not carry the CLUSTER_LIST attribute.*

A path with a missing cluster length is considered to have a Cluster Length value of 0. R10's path has a Cluster Length value of 0 (missing), while R12 has a Cluster Length value of 1. Because 0 is less than 1, R11 chooses R10's path over R12's.

## Step 13: Lowest Neighbor Address

**Note**  Before starting this section, revert the configuration on all routers to the base initial configuration files provided with the lab.

The final factor in deciding a best path between two different paths is the neighbor peering address. At this stage, all other attributes have tied, and an arbitrary decision needs to be made in order for the router to select a best path. This arbitrary decision examines the peering address over which the path was learned. The path that was learned from a neighbor with the lowest peering address is considered the best path.

To see this, we once again examine AS 400. R14 receives two paths to reach the 120.18.1.1/32 prefix:

---

**On R14:**

```
R14#show ip bgp 120.18.1.1

BGP routing table entry for 120.18.1.1/32, version 6
Paths: (2 available, best #2, table default)
  Not advertised to any peer
  Refresh Epoch 1
  200
    9.9.9.9 (metric 31) from 13.13.13.13 (13.13.13.13)
      Origin IGP, metric 0, localpref 100, valid, internal
      Originator: 9.9.9.9, Cluster list: 13.13.13.13, 12.12.12.12
      rx pathid: 0, tx pathid: 0
  Refresh Epoch 1
  200
    10.10.10.10 (metric 21) from 11.11.11.11 (11.11.11.11)
      Origin IGP, metric 0, localpref 100, valid, internal, best
      Originator: 10.10.10.10, Cluster list: 11.11.11.11
      rx pathid: 0, tx pathid: 0x0
```

---

R14 chooses the path from R11 as best because it has a lower metric to the next hop 10.10.10.10. To properly examine the processing of the final step in the BGP best-path algorithm, the two paths R14 receives need to tie for all attributes.

One way to accomplish this is to simply ensure that both paths use the same next hop. This way, the metric to the next hop will be the same for both prefixes. Care must also be taken to ensure that the Originator ID and Cluster Length attributes tie as well. These modifications must happen to the path R11 chooses to send to R14.

R11 receives two paths to reach the 120.18.1.1/32 prefix. Without intervention, R11 chooses the path from R10 with next hop 10.10.10.10 to reach the prefix shown below:

---

**On R11:**

```
R11#show ip bgp 120.18.1.1

BGP routing table entry for 120.18.1.1/32, version 6
Paths: (3 available, best #1, table default)
  Advertised to update-groups:
     1          3
  Refresh Epoch 1
```

```
 200
    10.10.10.10 (metric 11) from 10.10.10.10 (10.10.10.10)
      Origin IGP, metric 0, localpref 100, valid, internal, best
      rx pathid: 0, tx pathid: 0x0
 Refresh Epoch 2
 200
    9.9.9.9 (metric 21) from 12.12.12.12 (12.12.12.12)
      Origin IGP, metric 0, localpref 100, valid, internal
      Originator: 9.9.9.9, Cluster list: 12.12.12.12
      rx pathid: 0, tx pathid: 0
 Refresh Epoch 1
 300 200
    200.6.11.6 from 200.6.11.6 (6.6.6.6)
      Origin IGP, localpref 100, valid, external
      rx pathid: 0, tx pathid: 0
```

R11 receives a path with next hop of 9.9.9.9 (in red) and originator ID of 9.9.9.9 (in green). The path also contains a single cluster ID in the Cluster Length attribute (in purple). These features make R11's path from R12 a prime candidate for being advertised to R14.

R11 needs to choose the path from R12 as its best path. It currently chooses the path from R10 as best due to the lower metric to the next hop. If this metric ties between the paths received from R10 and R12, processing will shift to the lower router ID. This is desirable as the path received from R9 has route reflector attributes, meaning the originator ID will be compared with the router ID of the path received from R10. The originator ID 9.9.9.9 is lower than the router ID 10.10.10.10, making the path received from R9 the best path.

To engineer this decision, the OSPF cost on the e0/0.1011 interface of R11 is increased to 30:

**On R11:**

```
R11(config)#interface e0/0.1011
R11(config-subif)#ip ospf cost 30
```

Now, R11's cost to reach 10.10.10.10 through R10 increases to 31. OSPF chooses to install the route through R12 to reach the next hop with a metric of 21 instead, lowering the BGP metric to the next hop attribute to tie with the path received from R9:

```
R11#show ip bgp 120.18.1.1

BGP routing table entry for 120.18.1.1/32, version 16
Paths: (3 available, best #2, table default)
```

```
Advertised to update-groups:
   1          3
Refresh Epoch 1
200
   10.10.10.10 (metric 21) from 10.10.10.10 (10.10.10.10)
     Origin IGP, metric 0, localpref 100, valid, internal
     rx pathid: 0, tx pathid: 0
Refresh Epoch 2
200
   9.9.9.9 (metric 21) from 12.12.12.12 (12.12.12.12)
     Origin IGP, metric 0, localpref 100, valid, internal, best
     Originator: 9.9.9.9, Cluster list: 12.12.12.12
     rx pathid: 0, tx pathid: 0x0
Refresh Epoch 1
300 200
   200.6.11.6 from 200.6.11.6 (6.6.6.6)
     Origin IGP, localpref 100, valid, external
     rx pathid: 0, tx pathid: 0
```

In the above, R10's path is compared against R9's path. Because the metrics tie, lower Router ID is the deciding tie breaker. R9's path is chosen as best over R10 because the Originator ID attribute (9.9.9.9) is lower than R10's RID 10.10.10.10. R11 then compares R9's path against R6's. R6's path has a longer AS_PATH length and R11 correctly chooses the path through R9 as best.

R11 will advertise this path to R14 as well. Below, R14's BGP table now has two completely equal paths to reach 120.18.1.1/32. All attributes tie up through the Cluster Length attribute.

**On R14:**

```
R14#show ip bgp 120.18.1.1

BGP routing table entry for 120.18.1.1/32, version 78
Paths: (2 available, best #1, table default)
  Not advertised to any peer
  Refresh Epoch 1
  200
     9.9.9.9 (metric 31) from 11.11.11.11 (11.11.11.11)
       Origin IGP, metric 0, localpref 100, valid, internal, best
       Originator: 9.9.9.9, Cluster list: 11.11.11.11, 12.12.12.12
       rx pathid: 0, tx pathid: 0x0
  Refresh Epoch 2
  200
```

```
    9.9.9.9 (metric 31) from 13.13.13.13 (13.13.13.13)
      Origin IGP, metric 0, localpref 100, valid, internal
      Originator: 9.9.9.9, Cluster list: 13.13.13.13, 12.12.12.12
      rx pathid: 0, tx pathid: 0
```

With all attributes tied, processing shifts to the lowest neighbor IP address. In this case, the path from R11 is chosen as best. To prove this decision, the peering address between R14 and R11 is modified in the following steps:

1. A loopback interface is added to R11 with IP address 20.20.20.20/32 and is advertised into OSPF.

2. R11's **neighbor** command for its peering to R14 is modified to source its OPEN messages with the new loopback interface's address (20.20.20.20).

3. R14's peering to R11's 11.11.11.11 address is shut down, and a new peering is created to R11's new 20.20.20.20 address.

These modifications are shown below, in sequence. After the peering to R11 comes up fully, R14 again receives identical paths to reach the 120.18.1.1/32 network. This time, because the peering address to R11 is now 20.20.20.20, when evaluating step 13 of the best-path algorithm, R14 chooses the path through R13 as its best path because the peering address with R13 is now the lowest.

**<u>On R11:</u>**

```
R11(config)#interface lo20
R11(config-if)#ip address 20.20.20.20 255.255.255.255
R11(config-if)#ip ospf 1 area 0

R11(config)#router bgp 400
R11(config-router)#neighbor 14.14.14.14 update-source lo20
```

**<u>On R14:</u>**

```
R14(config)#router bgp 400
R14(config-router)#neighbor 11.11.11.11 shutdown
R14(config-router)#neighbor 20.20.20.20 remote 400
```

You should see the following console message:

```
%BGP-5-ADJCHANGE: neighbor 20.20.20.20 Up
```

**On R14:**

```
R14#show ip bgp 120.18.1.1

BGP routing table entry for 120.18.1.1/32, version 84
Paths: (2 available, best #2, table default)
  Not advertised to any peer
  Refresh Epoch 1
  200
    9.9.9.9 (metric 31) from 20.20.20.20 (11.11.11.11)
      Origin IGP, metric 0, localpref 100, valid, internal
      Originator: 9.9.9.9, Cluster list: 11.11.11.11, 12.12.12.12
      rx pathid: 0, tx pathid: 0
  Refresh Epoch 2
  200
    9.9.9.9 (metric 31) from 13.13.13.13 (13.13.13.13)
      Origin IGP, metric 0, localpref 100, valid, internal, best
      Originator: 9.9.9.9, Cluster list: 13.13.13.13, 12.12.12.12
      rx pathid: 0, tx pathid: 0x0
```

# Chapter 7

# DMVPN

## Introduction to DMVPN

One of the challenges many organizations face is dealing with remote site connectivity. Typically, companies start with a single headquarters office. As the company grows and expands into different locations, these remote locations need to have a means of communicating with each other and the original headquarters location. When sites are geographically separated in such a way, a wide area network (WAN) is needed in order to allow them to interact with each other.

A WAN is a network that spans multiple geographic regions and is typically created by a single service provider or a group of service providers sharing a common interest. The best example of a WAN is the public Internet. The public Internet is a WAN composed of many privately owned organizations and service providers collaborating together to create a global network.

Internet connectivity over the years has moved from being a luxury to being a requirement for continued business operations. It is common for most branch sites to start out with only a single Internet connection in their infancy. Take the example below:

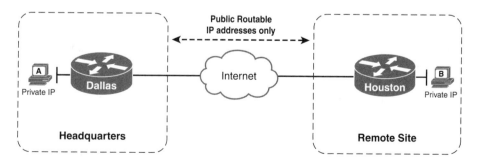

The corporate headquarters office located in Dallas has a remote site located in Houston. Both the headquarters office and remote site have active connections to the public Internet. The company can leverage the existing Internet connection as the WAN transport to exchange information between the networks at the headquarters site and those at the remote site. However, this presents a problem. The public Internet uses public IP addressing, whereas the remote sites use RFC 1918 private addressing. Internet routers are not configured to route RFC 1918 private addresses, which means a packet from Host A in Dallas would not reach Host B in Houston.

Tunneling provides an easy solution to this problem. When the ISP provisions the connection to the Internet, the Dallas and Houston routers are provided with publicly routable IP addressing. Tunneling allows the Dallas router to encapsulate the original IP packet from Host A into an IP packet sourced from Dallas's public IP address and destined to Houston's public IP address. This happens by adding an extra IP header to the existing IP packet called an outer header. The resulting packet is an IP packet that contains the original IP packet with the internal addressing as payload.

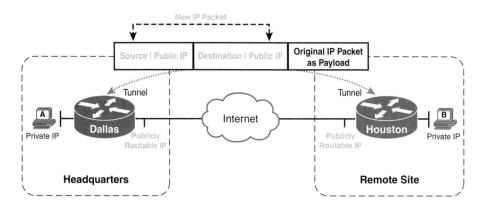

The Internet routers forward the new IP packet just as they would any other traffic, landing it at the Houston router. The Houston router removes the outer IP packet header to expose the original IP packet destined from Host A to Host B. The Houston router can then route the original packet out its LAN interface toward Host B.

What has happened here is that the Dallas and Houston routers have created a virtual network that uses the public Internet as its transport. Such a virtual network is called an **overlay network** because it is dependent on an underlying transport, called the **underlay network**. Traffic flowing through the overlay network is forwarded by the underlay network as opaque data. Without the use of protocol analyzers, the underlay network is unaware of the existence of the overlay. The Dallas and Houston routers are considered the endpoints of the tunnel that forms the overlay network.

Many tunneling technologies can be used to form the overlay network. Probably the most widely used is the **Generic Routing Encapsulation (GRE) tunnel**. A GRE tunnel can support tunneling for a variety of protocols over an IP-based network. It works by inserting an IP and GRE header on top of the original protocol packet, creating a new GRE/IP packet. The resulting GRE/IP packet uses a source/destination pair that is routable over the underlying infrastructure, as described above. The GRE/IP header is known as the **outer header**, and the original protocol header is the **inner header**.

In Cisco IOS, GRE tunnels are configured using tunnel interfaces. A tunnel interface is defined and assigned its own unique IP address, which defines the overlay network. It is then configured with appropriate source and destination IP addresses to use for the GRE tunnel's outer IP header. These addresses should be reachable over the underlay network. For example, if the underlay is provided by the public Internet, then these source and destination addresses should be publicly routable addresses. Typically, the destination IP address should be the address of the remote tunnel endpoint's interface connected to the underlay network. The tunnel overlay addresses of both endpoints should be in the same subnet.

In the following example, the tunnel endpoints on Dallas and Houston form an overlay network in the 10.1.1.0/24 address range. The Dallas router's IP address on the Internet is 11.1.1.1, and the Houston router's is 22.2.2.2. The graphic shows a GRE/IP packet sent from Dallas to Houston.

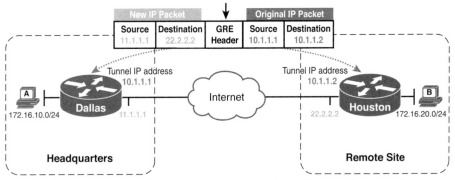

The following commands are used to configure the GRE tunnel between the two routers:

```
Dallas:

interface tunnel1
 ip address 10.1.1.1 255.255.255.0   ! Dallas's overlay address
 tunnel source 11.1.1.1              ! Dallas's underlay address
 tunnel destination 22.2.2.2         ! Houston's underlay address


Houston:

interface tunnel1
 ip address 10.1.1.2 255.255.255.0   ! Houston's overlay address
 tunnel source 22.2.2.2              ! Houston's underlay address
 tunnel destination 11.1.1.1         ! Dallas's underlay address
```

After configuring this, a ping through the overlay network between Dallas and Houston results in the following packet:

```
Internet Protocol Version 4, Src: 11.1.1.1, Dst: 22.2.2.2
Generic Routing Encapsulation (IP)
Internet Protocol Version 4, Src: 10.1.1.1, Dst: 10.1.1.2
Internet Control Message Protocol
```

Notice the top IP header source, 11.1.1.1. It is the same IP address used in Dallas's tunnel source command. The destination IP address is 22.2.2.2, which is the IP address used in Dallas's tunnel destination command. The GRE/IP header uses the values provided from these two commands to build the outer IP header. The next IP header is the original header for ICMP traffic that was delivered through the overlay. 10.1.1.1 is Dallas's overlay address, and 10.1.1.2 is Houston's overlay address.

The tunnel is fully functional. Now the Dallas and Houston routers need a way to direct traffic through their tunnels. Dynamic routing protocols such as EIGRP are a good choice for this. By simply enabling EIGRP on the tunnel and LAN interfaces on the router, the routing table is populated appropriately:

```
Dallas#show ip route | begin Gate
Gateway of last resort is not set

      10.0.0.0/8 is variably subnetted, 2 subnets, 2 masks
C        10.1.1.0/24 is directly connected, Tunnel1
L        10.1.1.1/32 is directly connected, Tunnel1
      11.0.0.0/8 is variably subnetted, 2 subnets, 2 masks
C        11.1.1.0/24 is directly connected, Ethernet0/0
L        11.1.1.1/32 is directly connected, Ethernet0/0
      22.0.0.0/24 is subnetted, 1 subnets
R        22.2.2.0 [120/1] via 11.1.1.2, 00:00:22, Ethernet0/0
      172.16.0.0/16 is variably subnetted, 3 subnets, 2 masks
C        172.16.10.0/24 is directly connected, Loopback1
L        172.16.10.1/32 is directly connected, Loopback1
D        172.16.20.0/24 [90/27008000] via 10.1.1.2, 00:01:03, Tunnel1
```

The routing entry for the 172.16.20.0/24 network lists the tunnel interface 1 as the exit interface. When Dallas routes a packet destined to this network, it forwards to tunnel interface 1 and performs the encapsulation, as shown previously. The Dallas router then performs an additional routing lookup against the new outer tunnel destination IP address (22.2.2.2 in case of Dallas-to-Houston traffic). The second IP lookup carries the requirement that in order for Dallas to successfully route through the tunnel, it must have a route to the remote tunnel endpoint, Houston. In this example, RIP (shown in red) is being used to exchange underlay routing information between the ISP and the Dallas and Houston routers. Using RIP, Dallas has learned a route to 22.2.2.2, which is Houston's underlay address.

The result is that connectivity between the LANs succeeds, as evidenced by this **traceroute** output:

```
Dallas#traceroute 172.16.20.1


Type escape sequence to abort.
Tracing the route to 172.16.20.1
VRF info: (vrf in name/id, vrf out name/id)
  1 10.1.1.2 1 msec 5 msec 5 msec
```

Because of the limitation of setting static source and destination addresses, GRE tunnels are by nature point-to-point tunnels. It is not possible to configure a GRE tunnel to have multiple destinations by default. If the goal is only connecting two sites, then a point-to-point GRE tunnel is a great solution. However, as sites are added, additional point-to-point tunnels are required to connect them. Take the example below, where the company in our example has expanded into a second remote site, in Miami.

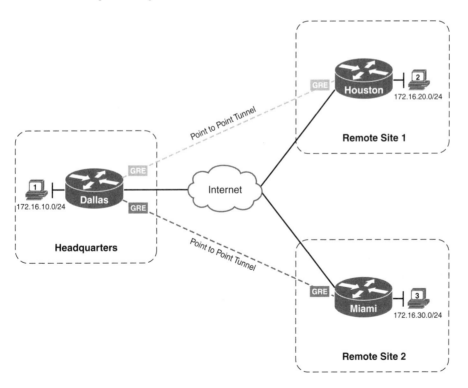

To configure basic connectivity between the two remote sites and the main headquarters site in Dallas, two point-to-point GRE tunnels would need to be configured. In addition, if Houston and Miami required direct communication, a third point-to-point tunnel would be needed. If more sites are added, the number of tunnels grows along with them. In addition to configuring more tunnels, the company would need to ensure that each tunnel exists in a separate subnet, creating multiple isolated overlay networks.

An alternative to configuring multiple point-to-point GRE tunnels is to use **multipoint GRE tunnels** to provide the connectivity desired.

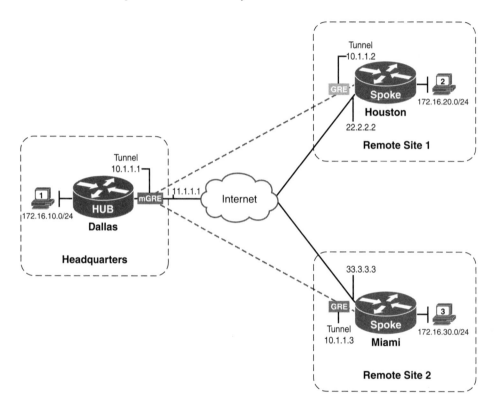

Multipoint GRE (mGRE) tunnels are similar in construction to point-to-point GRE tunnels with the exception of one command: the **tunnel destination** command. Instead of declaring a static destination, no destination is declared, and instead the **tunnel mode gre multipoint** command is issued, as shown in the example below (on the Dallas router):

---

**Dallas:**

```
interface tunnel1
 ip address 10.1.1.1 255.255.255.0
 tunnel source 11.1.1.1
 tunnel destination 22.2.2.2  ! static destination removed
 tunnel mode gre multipoint
```

*How does Dallas know what destination to set for the GRE/IP packet created by the tunnel interface?* The easy answer is that, on its own, there is no way for Dallas to glean the destination address without the help of an additional protocol, such as **Next Hop Resolution Protocol (NHRP)**. NHRP was originally designed to allow routers connected to non-broadcast multiple-access (NBMA) networks to discover the proper next-hop mappings to communicate together. It is specified in RFC 2332. NBMA networks faced a similar issue as mGRE tunnels. In broadcast networks, protocols such as ARP use broadcast or multicast messages to dynamically discover endpoints on the network.

The best example of this is on Ethernet-based networks. Before a station can send to a remote station, it needs to know the MAC address of the remote station to build the Ethernet frame. ARP provides a means by which the sending station can discover and map the Layer 3 address of the receiving station to the receiving station's MAC address, using broadcast packets. This exchange is made possible because Ethernet infrastructure devices (namely switches) provide a means by which a single message can be sent from one station and replicated to all stations connected to the LAN.

In NBMA networks, there is no mechanism for doing this. For example, Dallas cannot simply send a broadcast out of the tunnel interface to dynamically discover the Houston router's address in the underlay for two reasons:

- In order to encapsulate the broadcast using the tunnel interface, Dallas needs to have a destination address for the outer GRE/IP packet.

- Even if Dallas placed a broadcast address in the destination of the IP packet, the underlay network (the public Internet in this case) does not support replication of broadcast packets. The ISP router would simply drop the traffic.

Looking at the two points above, it becomes apparent that by converting the point-to-point GRE tunnel to an mGRE tunnel, the 10.1.1.0/24 overlay network has become an NBMA network. Without the ability to support broadcast communication on the overlay, routers are unable to support broadcast-based network discovery protocols such as ARP, dynamic routing protocol hello messages, and the like. Missing this ability severely stunts the usefulness of mGRE with regard to dynamic scalability. However, with the overlay functioning as an NBMA network, NHRP can step in to glue it back together.

NHRP accomplishes this by keeping a mapping table of Layer 3 overlay addresses to Layer 3 underlay address pairs. For example, the NHRP table on Dallas would include a mapping of 10.1.1.2/22.2.2.2 for the Houston router. When traffic is forwarded out the mGRE interface on Dallas with NHRP configured, Dallas can consult its NHRP table to find the appropriate tunnel destination.

This solution solves the problem of where Dallas can get the information needed to route the packet, but it does not solve how it receives the information. To do so, NHRP organizes the routers connected to the same NHRP NBMA domain into one of two categories. They are either **next hop servers (NHSs)** or **next hop clients (NHCs)**. An NHC is configured with the overlay address of the router acting as the NHS. When a client comes online in an NHRP-enabled NBMA network, it first advertises its own overlay-to-underlay mapping to its configured NHS by using a special **NHRP registration message**. The registration message includes the NHC's overlay and NBMA network layer addressing information. The NHS receives and stores this information in its NHRP table.

All active clients attached to the NHRP-enabled NBMA must register with the NHS. When the client needs to send traffic to another router attached to the NBMA network, the client can send an NHRP resolution message to the NHS router (for which it already has a static mapping), requesting the appropriate mapping information. If the intended router is online, it is in one of two states: It has registered with an NHS (meaning it is a client), or it is an NHS (and contains the appropriate mapping table). In either case, the sending client can logically consult the NHS for the mapping information with a high probability of receiving a reply.

The NHS forwards this resolution request to the proper client, which responds directly to the querying client.

> **Note**   In previous implementations of NHRP on Cisco IOS, the NHS would respond directly to the requesting client. This functionality was changed in later releases as an enhancement to support hierarchical DMVPN setups.

The collection of routers that share NHRP information is known as an *NHRP domain*. An NHRP domain is identified by its NHRP network identifier, which is a configurable numeric value. All routers must be configured with an **NHRP network identifier** in order to process NHRP messages. Doing so allows the router to correlate received NHRP information on multiple interfaces with a specific NHRP domain. This allows multiple interfaces to participate in the same or different NHRP domains as the design requires. The NHRP network identifier is a locally significant value that does NOT have to match between two routers.

To fix the tunnel configuration on the Dallas router, NHRP should be configured on the Dallas and Houston routers. NHS routers should have connectivity to all spokes they will service. Looking at the diagram, the Miami and Houston routers both have GRE tunnel connectivity to the Dallas router. With this information, it makes sense to designate the Dallas router as the NHS for the NHRP domain.

The Houston router is configured with the **ip nhrp nhs 10.1.1.1** command to designate the Dallas router as the proper NHS. Both routers use the **ip nhrp network-id 1** command to enable NHRP messaging on the tunnel interfaces:

**Dallas:**

```
interface Tunnel1
 ip address 10.1.1.1 255.255.255.0
 ip nhrp network-id 1
```

```
 tunnel source 11.1.1.1
 tunnel mode gre multipoint
end
```

**Houston:**

```
interface Tunnel1
 ip address 10.1.1.2 255.255.255.0
 ip nhrp network-id 1
 ip nhrp nhs 10.1.1.1 ! Overlay address of Dallas, the NHS
 tunnel source 22.2.2.2
 tunnel destination 11.1.1.1
end
```

Now a ping through the overlay between Dallas and Houston is successful:

```
Dallas#ping 10.1.1.2
Type escape sequence to abort.
Sending 5, 100-byte ICMP Echos to 10.1.1.2, timeout is 2 seconds:
!!!!!
```

The ping succeeds because Dallas has the necessary overlay-to-underlay mapping information in its NHRP mapping table. The contents of the NHRP mapping table can be displayed using the **show ip nhrp** command:

```
Dallas#show ip nhrp
10.1.1.2/32 via 10.1.1.2 ! Overlay address of Houston
   Tunnel1 created 00:05:15, expire 01:55:29
   Type: dynamic, Flags: unique registered used nhop
   NBMA address: 22.2.2.2 ! Underlay address of Houston
```

**Note**  Houston's NHRP mapping table will be empty. Because it uses a point-to-point GRE tunnel, there is no need for it to store overlay-to-underlay mappings. Its tunnel can only be routed directly to Dallas.

Communication between Dallas and Houston's overlay address is successful, but the communication between their LAN interfaces is not. The routing table on Dallas shown below no longer lists the 172.16.20.0/24 network. EIGRP is still configured on the interfaces, but EIGRP prefixes are not being exchanged.

```
Dallas#show ip route | begin Gate
Gateway of last resort is not set

      10.0.0.0/8 is variably subnetted, 2 subnets, 2 masks
C        10.1.1.0/24 is directly connected, Tunnel1
L        10.1.1.1/32 is directly connected, Tunnel1
      11.0.0.0/8 is variably subnetted, 2 subnets, 2 masks
C        11.1.1.0/24 is directly connected, Ethernet0/0
L        11.1.1.1/32 is directly connected, Ethernet0/0
      22.0.0.0/24 is subnetted, 1 subnets
R        22.2.2.0 [120/1] via 11.1.1.2, 00:00:04, Ethernet0/0
      33.0.0.0/24 is subnetted, 1 subnets
R        33.3.3.0 [120/1] via 11.1.1.2, 00:00:04, Ethernet0/0
      172.16.0.0/16 is variably subnetted, 2 subnets, 2 masks
C        172.16.10.0/24 is directly connected, Loopback1
L        172.16.10.1/32 is directly connected, Loopback1
```

Adding to the difficulties, the EIGRP neighborship between Dallas and Houston is flapping on the Dallas side:

**Dallas:**

```
%DUAL-5-NBRCHANGE: EIGRP-Ipv4 1: Neighbor 10.1.1.2 (Tunnel1) is up:
new adjacency

%DUAL-5-NBRCHANGE: EIGRP-Ipv4 1: Neighbor 10.1.1.2 (Tunnel1) is down:
retry limit exceeded

%DUAL-5-NBRCHANGE: EIGRP-Ipv4 1: Neighbor 10.1.1.2 (Tunnel1) is up:
new adjacency
```

The reason for this is that while NHRP has filled in to provide the tunnel destination, it still has not solved the underlying problem of the overlay being an NBMA network. EIGRP hello messages are multicast between routers. Taking an example of two routers (R1 and R2), the basic EIGRP neighborship process is as follows:

1. R1 and R2 exchange multicast hello messages.

2. R2 receives the hello message and creates a neighbor entry for R1 in its neighbor table in the "pending" state.

3. R2 sends a unicast update message with the "init" bit set to accelerate the hello process.

4. R1 receives the update message with the "init" bit set and sends back an acknowledgment packet.

5. Steps 2–4 are repeated but in reverse.

6. The neighborship is established, and the two routers begin exchanging prefixes.

Through this sequence, both multicast and unicast connectivity is verified between the two EIGRP routers. When the neighborship process above is applied to the mGRE interface on the Dallas router, the Dallas router is unable to tunnel hello packets to the Houston router because the destination address for EIGRP hello packets is 224.0.0.10.

IP addresses in that range are called *multicast IP addresses*. Typically, when EIGRP is enabled on an interface, the router can encode the Ethernet frame with a multicast MAC address that signifies to intermediate devices that this traffic should be forwarded out all switch ports in the same VLAN, much like a broadcast packet. The problem Dallas is facing is that EIGRP is enabled on its mGRE interface. Because the interface is mGRE, Dallas does not have a hard-coded destination address for the GRE/IP header, as explained earlier. As a result, Dallas cannot encode the GRE/IP packet to tunnel the multicast traffic across the underlay. The following events occur:

1. Houston sends a hello packet to Dallas. It can do so because it has a point-to-point GRE tunnel. All traffic through the tunnel goes to Dallas as the statically configured tunnel destination.

2. Dallas receives the hello, initiates the neighbor structure, and sends a unicast update message with the init bit set to Houston.

3. Because Houston has not received a hello packet from Dallas, it does not accept its update packet.

4. Dallas waits to receive an acknowledgment for its update packet sent to Houston and receives none.

5. Dallas clears the neighbor entry for Houston.

6. Houston sends another hello packet to Dallas.

This cycle repeats until Dallas is able to send a multicast hello to Houston. Specifically, because Houston never receives a multicast packet from Dallas (it only receives a unicast packet at step 2), Houston always rejects Dallas's update packet. Dallas can never send a multicast hello packet to Houston because it does not have sufficient forwarding information (that is, destination NBMA address) to send the multicast through its mGRE interface.

Dallas needs a mechanism by which it can associate multicast traffic with a specific NBMA address in order to send the multicast as unicast over the underlay. NHRP solves this problem by storing a separate NHRP table specifically for multicast traffic. This table lists all of the underlay addresses to which multicast traffic should be sent. When the router needs to forward multicast packets out of an NHRP-enabled interface, it replicates the packet as unicast toward each underlay address in the NHRP multicast table. This process, often referred to as **pseudo-multicasting**, is very similar to Frame Relay pseudo-multicasting in Frame Relay hub-and-spoke topologies.

The NHRP multicast table can be configured statically using **ip nhrp map multicast** *underlay-ip-address* command. Such a configuration is tedious on an NHS because there is no telling how many NHRP clients will register mappings with the NHS. So instead, the **ip nhrp map multicast dynamic** command tells the NHS to automatically add a dynamic NHRP multicast entry for every client that registers with the NHS. To solve the connectivity issues between Dallas and Houston, this command is configured on Dallas. Then, the tunnel interface on Houston is flapped to force it to re-register with Dallas. The **show ip nhrp multicast** command verifies the multicast entry on the Dallas router. The EIGRP neighbors come up, and pings are successful between the LAN interfaces again:

```
Dallas#show run interface tunnel1

interface Tunnel1
 ip address 10.1.1.1 255.255.255.0
 no ip redirects
 ip nhrp map multicast dynamic
 ip nhrp network-id 1
 tunnel source 11.1.1.1
 tunnel mode gre multipoint

Houston(config)#interface tunnel1
Houston(config-if)#shut

%LINEPROTO-5-UPDOWN: Line protocol on Interface Tunnel1, changed state
to down
%LINK-5-CHANGED: Interface Tunnel1, changed state to
administratively down

Houston(config-if)#no shut

%LINEPROTO-5-UPDOWN: Line protocol on Interface Tunnel1, changed state
to up
%LINK-3-UPDOWN: Interface Tunnel1, changed state to up

%DUAL-5-NBRCHANGE: EIGRP-Ipv4 1: Neighbor 10.1.1.2 (Tunnel1) is up:
new adjacency

Dallas#show ip nhrp multicast


   I/F     NBMA address
Tunnel1    22.2.2.2         Flags: dynamic          (Enabled)

Dallas#show ip route 172.16.20.0
Routing entry for 172.16.20.0/24
  Known via "eigrp 1", distance 90, metric 27008000, type internal
```

```
  Redistributing via eigrp 1
  Last update from 10.1.1.2 on Tunnel1, 00:00:13 ago
  Routing Descriptor Blocks:
  * 10.1.1.2, from 10.1.1.2, 00:00:13 ago, via Tunnel1
      Route metric is 27008000, traffic share count is 1
      Total delay is 55000 microseconds, minimum bandwidth is 100 Kbit
      Reliability 255/255, minimum MTU 1476 bytes
      Loading 1/255, Hops 1

Dallas#ping 172.16.20.1 source 172.16.10.1

Type escape sequence to abort.
Sending 5, 100-byte ICMP Echos to 172.16.20.1, timeout is 2 seconds:
Packet sent with a source address of 172.16.10.1
!!!!!
```

Taking a step back can help you understand what this seemingly complex configuration has accomplished: Before, static point-to-point GRE tunnels, each representing a separate subnet, were required to form the overlay necessary to connect the Dallas and Houston sites. When the Miami site was added, another tunnel was required to connect Miami to Dallas and, if necessary, to connect Miami with Houston.

The mGRE/NHRP configuration outlined allows only a single tunnel interface to be required per router in order to connect Dallas to Houston and Dallas to Miami. All Miami needs is a point-to-point GRE interface configured with Dallas as the NHRP NHS, and connectivity will be established. Through EIGRP, Miami can also receive routes for the networks behind Dallas as well. Most importantly, the tunnel interfaces on Dallas, Houston, and Miami are all part of the same IP subnet and participate in the same NHRP domain.

The total configuration on Miami to join it to the cloud and the appropriate verification commands are as follows:

**Miami:**

```
interface Tunnel1
 ip address 10.1.1.3 255.255.255.0
 ip nhrp network-id 1
 ip nhrp nhs 10.1.1.1
 tunnel source 33.3.3.3
 tunnel destination 11.1.1.1
end
!
router eigrp 1
 network 10.1.1.0 0.0.0.255
```

```
   network 172.16.30.0 0.0.0.255

Miami#show ip route | begin Gate
Gateway of last resort is not set

     10.0.0.0/8 is variably subnetted, 2 subnets, 2 masks
C       10.1.1.0/24 is directly connected, Tunnel1
L       10.1.1.3/32 is directly connected, Tunnel1
     11.0.0.0/24 is subnetted, 1 subnets
R       11.1.1.0 [120/1] via 33.3.3.1, 00:00:16, Ethernet0/0
     22.0.0.0/24 is subnetted, 1 subnets
R       22.2.2.0 [120/1] via 33.3.3.1, 00:00:16, Ethernet0/0
     33.0.0.0/8 is variably subnetted, 2 subnets, 2 masks
C       33.3.3.0/24 is directly connected, Ethernet0/0
L       33.3.3.3/32 is directly connected, Ethernet0/0
     172.16.0.0/16 is variably subnetted, 3 subnets, 2 masks
D       172.16.10.0/24 [90/27008000] via 10.1.1.1, 00:00:12, Tunnel1
C       172.16.30.0/24 is directly connected, Loopback1
L       172.16.30.1/32 is directly connected, Loopback1

Miami#ping 172.16.10.1 source 172.16.30.1

Type escape sequence to abort.
Sending 5, 100-byte ICMP Echos to 172.16.10.1, timeout is 2 seconds:
Packet sent with a source address of 172.16.30.1
!!!!!
```

In the routing table output above, you can see that Miami receives a route for the LAN behind Dallas (the 172.16.10.0/24 network) but not for the Houston LAN (172.16.20.0/24 network). Dallas appears to not be advertising the Houston LAN to Miami. This reason is not unknown to Distance Vector protocols as it is caused by a concept known as **split horizon**. Split horizon prevents a router from advertising a route for a prefix out the same interface the router uses to reach that prefix. In Dallas's case, it learns the 172.16.20.0/24 route from Houston, which is connected to its tunnel interface. It cannot advertise that same network toward Miami out the same tunnel 1 interface.

To alleviate the problem here, split horizon can be disabled on the tunnel interface of Dallas with the **no ip split-horizon eigrp** command. Notice that Miami now learns of the LAN network behind Houston:

```
Dallas(config)#interface tunnel1
Dallas(config-if)#no ip split-horizon eigrp 1
```

```
%DUAL-5-NBRCHANGE: EIGRP-IPv4 1: Neighbor 10.1.1.3 (Tunnel1) is
resync: split horizon changed

Miami#show ip route eigrp | begin Gateway
Gateway of last resort is not set

      172.16.0.0/16 is variably subnetted, 4 subnets, 2 masks
D        172.16.10.0/24 [90/27008000] via 10.1.1.1, 00:06:57, Tunnel1
D        172.16.20.0/24 [90/28288000] via 10.1.1.1, 00:01:07, Tunnel1
```

A ping between the LAN interfaces of Miami and Houston confirms the connectivity:

```
Miami#ping 172.16.20.1 source 172.16.30.1

Type escape sequence to abort.
Sending 5, 100-byte ICMP Echos to 172.16.20.1, timeout is 2 seconds:
Packet sent with a source address of 172.16.30.1
!!!!!
```

The mGRE/NHRP solution reduces the configuration complexity to something that can be easily scripted out using various tools. Adding a new site to the existing VPN only requires direct configuration of the new devices. The devices come online, register with Dallas, receive their routing updates, and are ready to participate in the overlay network without the need to consult a service provider to provision private WAN circuits.

Using mGRE and NHRP in this way forms the underlying architecture that powers the Dynamic Multipoint VPN (DMVPN) solution. The routers above are actually participating in a DMVPN cloud. It is *dynamic* because routers can be added or removed with minimal configuration. It is *multipoint* because Dallas, as the NHS, can form tunnels to all clients that register with it, using a single multipoint GRE tunnel interface. It is virtually private because it is tunneled over an existing underlay, presenting the illusion of direct connectivity for all of the devices involved.

# DMVPN Mechanics

The section above outlines the use case that DMVPN was created to solve. It also introduces the symbiotic relationship between NHRP and mGRE that forms the building blocks for a DMVPN cloud. This section delves a bit more deeply into the operation and mechanics of a DMVPN cloud.

Although DMVPN uses NHRP for its address resolution, it does not borrow from NHRP terminology but instead uses its own. DMVPN clouds are constructed as **hub-and-spoke** topologies. In a hub-and-spoke topology, networking devices (the spokes) connect through a common, shared network device that acts as the aggregation point for the topology. This common point is termed the **hub** of the hub-and-spoke network.

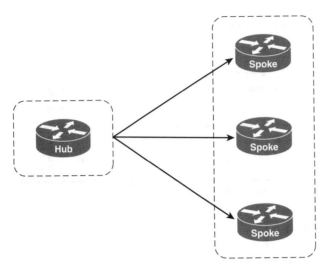

DMVPN clouds are, at their core, hub-and-spoke networks. The DMVPN hub router acts as the central aggregation point for all of the spoke routers that connect to it in its DMVPN cloud. In the NHRP network created in the first section, the Dallas router is considered the hub of the DMVPN cloud, and Houston and Miami routers are the spokes.

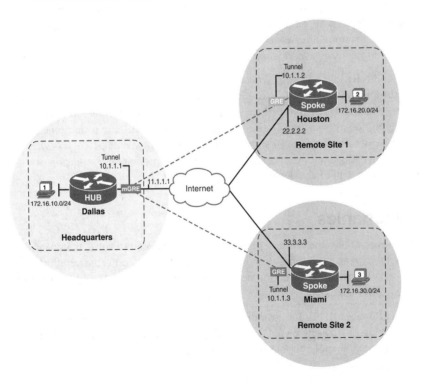

This distinction is important as hubs and spokes have different responsibilities within the DMVPN cloud. DMVPN hub routers also act as NHRP NHS routers that store and receive mapping information from the NHCs. DMVPN spoke routers are the NHRP NHCs, which send their mapping information to a hub router that acts as the spoke routers' NHSs. In the example above, Houston and Miami are the spoke routers that send their NHRP mapping information to the hub router Dallas, through a process called **NHRP registration**.

Going back in time to a point where both Dallas and Houston were first configured and following the entire registration process will help you gain a better understanding of the NHRP registration process. Recall the following configurations on the Dallas and Houston routers from the section above:

---

**On Hub—Dallas:**

```
interface Tunnel1
 ip address 10.1.1.1 255.255.255.0
 no ip split-horizon eigrp 1
 ip nhrp map multicast dynamic
 ip nhrp network-id 1
 tunnel source 11.1.1.1
 tunnel mode gre multipoint
```

**On Spoke—Houston:**

```
interface Tunnel1
 ip address 10.1.1.2 255.255.255.0
 ip nhrp network-id 1
 ip nhrp nhs 10.1.1.1
 tunnel source 22.2.2.2
 tunnel destination 11.1.1.1
```

---

Dallas is configured with an **mGRE** tunnel, while Houston is configured with a **point-to-point** GRE tunnel. EIGRP is also configured to run on the tunnel interfaces of the routers. Finally, EIGRP's split-horizon feature has been disabled on the tunnel interface on Dallas.

Recall that with Dallas being configured with an mGRE tunnel interface, there is no tunnel destination configured for the GRE tunnel interface to use in its GRE tunnel IP header. Without this information, Dallas cannot forward traffic to Houston in the overlay, as evidenced by the unsuccessful **ping** output below:

---

```
Dallas#ping 10.1.1.2

Type escape sequence to abort.
```

```
Sending 5, 100-byte ICMP Echos to 10.1.1.2, timeout is 2 seconds:
.....
Success rate is 0 percent (0/5)
```

NHRP steps in to provide this information by maintaining an NBMA-to-overlay IP address mapping table on the router. This NHRP mapping table is consulted to fill in the required information when sending packets across the DMVPN network.

Just as static routes can be configured for the IP routing table, the NHRP mapping table can be populated using static NHRP mapping command (**ip nhrp map**). However, populating the mapping table this way carries the same drawbacks at scale as configuring static routes. The configuration complexity grows as many more spokes are connected to the same hub router.

The designers of DMVPN take advantage of the NHS/NHC relationship to allow the spokes to **dynamically register** their NHRP mapping information with the hub routers. Spokes are configured with the **ip nhrp nhs** command, which identifies which router functions as the NHS.

In the example topology, Dallas is the hub of the DMVPN and therefore is also the NHS for the NHRP network. Once Houston comes online, it first sends an **NHRP registration request** to Dallas in order to register its NBMA-to-overlay address mapping.

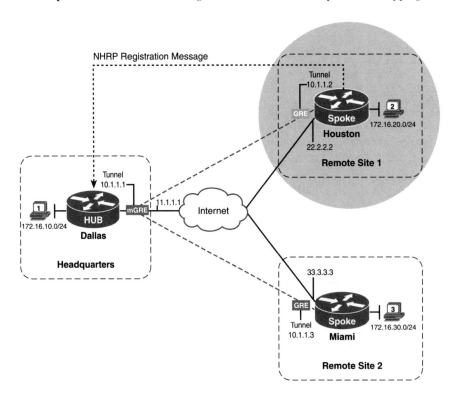

With the help of the **debug nhrp packet** and **debug nhrp detail** commands on both Dallas and Houston, the registration process can be observed in real time. Once Houston's tunnel interface comes online, Houston sends an NHRP registration packet to Dallas. It knows Dallas is the NHS because Dallas's IP address is identified in the **ip nhrp nhs 10.1.1.1** command on Houston's tunnel interface. This NHRP registration packet is shown in the debugging output below:

```
Houston:


NHRP: Send Registration Request via Tunnel1 vrf 0, packet size: 88
 src: 10.1.1.2, dst: 10.1.1.1
 (F) afn: AF_IP(1), type: IP(800), hop: 255, ver: 1
     shtl: 4(NSAP), sstl: 0(NSAP)
     pktsz: 88 extoff: 52
 (M) flags: "unique nat ", reqid: 11
     src NBMA: 22.2.2.2
     src protocol: 10.1.1.2, dst protocol: 10.1.1.1
 (C-1) code: no error(0)
       prefix: 32, mtu: 17916, hd_time: 7200
```

The first two lines of the debugging output indicate that an NHRP registration request packet is being sent to 10.1.1.1 (NHS). The source of the packet is 10.1.1.2 (Houston's tunnel address). The mapping information is split in the src NBMA and src protocol fields of the registration packet. The src NBMA field indicates the NBMA address of the device that is sending the NHRP registration request. In this case, Houston's NBMA address is 22.2.2.2, the address configured as the tunnel source address of its GRE interface connected to the DMVPN. The src protocol address is the overlay IP address of the device sending the registration request. For Houston, this address is its tunnel interface address 10.1.1.2, which is the tunnel IP address assigned to Houston's GRE interface connected to the DMVPN.

These pieces of information combined are received on the hub router, Dallas, as shown below:

```
NHRP: Receive Registration Request via Tunnel1 vrf 0, packet size: 88
  (F) afn: AF_IP(1), type: IP(800), hop: 255, ver: 1
      shtl: 4(NSAP), sstl: 0(NSAP)
      pktsz: 88 extoff: 52
  (M) flags: "unique nat ", reqid: 11
      src NBMA: 22.2.2.2
      src protocol: 10.1.1.2, dst protocol: 10.1.1.1
  (C-1) code: no error(0)
```

```
   prefix: 32, mtu: 17916, hd_time: 7200
          addr_len: 0(NSAP), subaddr_len: 0(NSAP), proto_len: 0, pref: 0
NHRP: Adding Tunnel Endpoints (VPN: 10.1.1.2, NBMA: 22.2.2.2)
NHRP: Successfully attached NHRP subblock for Tunnel Endpoints (VPN:
10.1.1.2, NBMA: 22.2.2.2)
```

Once Dallas receives the mapping, it adds the information to the NHRP mapping table. Notice that the debugging output above indicates the VPN address as 10.1.1.2 for Houston. In this context, VPN indicates the overlay protocol address for the DMVPN.

The resulting mapping on Dallas can be verified using the **show ip nhrp** and **show dmvpn** commands on Dallas:

```
Dallas#show ip nhrp

10.1.1.2/32 via 10.1.1.2
   Tunnel1 created 00:55:33, expire 01:44:27
   Type: dynamic, Flags: unique registered used nhop
   NBMA address: 22.2.2.2

Dallas#show dmvpn

Legend: Attrb --> S - Static, D - Dynamic, I - Incomplete
        N - NATed, L - Local, X - No Socket
        # Ent --> Number of NHRP entries with same NBMA peer
        NHS Status: E --> Expecting Replies, R --> Responding, W -->
Waiting
        UpDn Time --> Up or Down Time for a Tunnel
======================================================================

Interface: Tunnel1, IPv4 NHRP Details
Type:Hub, NHRP Peers:1,

 # Ent   Peer NBMA address Peer Tunnel Add State  UpDn Tm Attrb
 ----- --------------- --------------- ----- -------- -----
     1 22.2.2.2                 10.1.1.2   UP 01:02:32     D
```

The **show ip nhrp** output lists the mapping information for the 10.1.1.2/32 address on the overlay network. The NBMA address is listed as 22.2.2.2, and it is flagged as a **dynamic** entry because it was added as a result of the NHRP registration process.

The **show dmvpn** output shows the entry with the NBMA address 22.2.2.2 as the Peer NBMA address and the overlay address 10.1.1.2 as the Peer Tunnel Add. It lists the state of the tunnel as UP. The tunnel itself can be in many other states, depending on which part of the NHRP registration process the entry is currently going through. The last column, the Attrb column, signifies that the entry was created dynamically.

In response to the NHRP registration request from Houston, Dallas replies to Houston with an **NHRP registration reply** message. The exchange is shown below:

```
On Dallas:


NHRP: Attempting to send packet through interface Tunnel1 via DEST
dst 10.1.1.2
NHRP: Send Registration Reply via Tunnel1 vrf 0, packet size: 108
  src: 10.1.1.1, dst: 10.1.1.2
  (F) afn: AF_IP(1), type: IP(800), hop: 255, ver: 1
      shtl: 4(NSAP), sstl: 0(NSAP)
      pktsz: 108 extoff: 52
  (M) flags: "unique nat ", reqid: 11
      src NBMA: 22.2.2.2
      src protocol: 10.1.1.2, dst protocol: 10.1.1.1
  (C-1) code: no error(0)
        prefix: 32, mtu: 17916, hd_time: 7200
        addr_len: 0(NSAP), subaddr_len: 0(NSAP), proto_len: 0, pref: 0
NHRP: Encapsulation succeeded.  Sending NHRP Control Packet  NBMA
Address: 22.2.2.2
NHRP: 132 bytes out Tunnel1


On Houston:


NHRP: Receive Registration Reply via Tunnel1 vrf 0, packet size: 108
  (F) afn: AF_IP(1), type: IP(800), hop: 255, ver: 1
      shtl: 4(NSAP), sstl: 0(NSAP)
      pktsz: 108 extoff: 52
  (M) flags: "unique nat ", reqid: 11
      src NBMA: 22.2.2.2
      src protocol: 10.1.1.2, dst protocol: 10.1.1.1
  (C-1) code: no error(0)
```

When the process is complete, Houston has successfully registered with Dallas. Dallas has been configured with an mGRE tunnel interface. There is no tunnel destination configured for the GRE tunnel interface to use in its GRE tunnel IP header. With Houston registered, Dallas now has sufficient information to forward packets out its tunnel interface to Houston. The successful ping below demonstrates communication between Dallas and Houston:

```
Dallas#ping 10.1.1.2

Type escape sequence to abort.
Sending 5, 100-byte ICMP Echos to 10.1.1.2, timeout is 2 seconds:
!!!!!
Success rate is 100 percent (5/5), round-trip min/avg/max = 1/4/5 ms
```

Adding a new spoke to the DMVPN is as simple as pasting the same configuration template from Houston on router Miami, taking care to change the tunnel IP address and tunnel source address accordingly:

```
On Miami:

interface Tunnel1
 ip address 10.1.1.3 255.255.255.0
 ip nhrp network-id 1
 ip nhrp nhs 10.1.1.1
 tunnel source 33.3.3.3
 tunnel destination 11.1.1.1
```

The output of the **show dmvpn** command from the hub Dallas verifies that the spoke Miami has registered with it dynamically as well. A ping from Dallas to Miami's tunnel IP address is also shown to succeed:

```
Dallas#show dmvpn

Legend: Attrb --> S - Static, D - Dynamic, I - Incomplete
        N - NATed, L - Local, X - No Socket
        # Ent --> Number of NHRP entries with same NBMA peer
        NHS Status: E --> Expecting Replies, R --> Responding, W -->
Waiting
        UpDn Time --> Up or Down Time for a Tunnel
==========================================================================

Interface: Tunnel1, IPv4 NHRP Details
Type:Hub, NHRP Peers:2,
```

```
 # Ent   Peer NBMA address Peer Tunnel Add State  UpDn Tm Attrb
-----  --------------- --------------- ----- -------- -----
    1 22.2.2.2                10.1.1.2   UP 01:10:58    D
    1 33.3.3.3                10.1.1.3   UP 00:00:07    D

Dallas#ping 10.1.1.3

Type escape sequence to abort.
Sending 5, 100-byte ICMP Echos to 10.1.1.3, timeout is 2 seconds:
!!!!!
Success rate is 100 percent (5/5), round-trip min/avg/max = 1/4/5 ms
```

The DMVPN hub router is not only responsible for the NHRP mapping table but also for the exchange of routing information between the spokes. Above, EIGRP is used as the routing protocol of choice and is enabled on the tunnel interfaces. EIGRP multicast hello packets discover neighbors. In the previous section, these multicasts needed a proper NBMA address to be pseudo-multicasted over the overlay.

NHRP fills this gap in as well by maintaining a multicast mapping table. This table can also be populated dynamically or statically. In DMVPN, routing protocol multicasts are sent only between the hub and spoke routers. This means the spokes need an NHRP multicast mapping only for the hub—and not for the other spokes. It also means the hub router requires an NHRP multicast mapping for every spoke that registers with it on the DMVPN cloud. This information too can be dynamically filled in at the same time the hub creates the dynamic NHRP mapping for NBMA-to-overlay addressing through the **ip nhrp map multicast dynamic** command.

> **Note**   In the case where the spokes are configured with point-to-point GRE tunnels, there is no need to configure the NHRP multicast mapping on the spokes. A point-to-point GRE tunnel has only one destination, to which all packets can be sent: a destination that is hard coded as the **tunnel destination** configuration under the tunnel interface. Therefore, multicast traffic can always be sent out the point-to-point tunnel interfaces to this destination address. This is the case above, where the spokes have point-to-point GRE tunnels configured and the hub uses the mGRE tunnel.
>
> However, multicast mappings would be required in cases where the spokes also use mGRE interfaces—specifically in DMVPN Phase 2 and Phase 3 designs.

With the **ip nhrp map multicast dynamic** command configured on the tunnel interface on Dallas, whenever a spoke registers with Dallas, it automatically adds the spoke's NBMA address to its NHRP multicast table. The output below from **debug nhrp detail** was taken when Houston first registered with Dallas. The **show ip nhrp multicast** command confirms the mapping:

---

**On Dallas:**

```
NHRP: Tu1: Creating dynamic multicast mapping  NBMA: 22.2.2.2
NHRP: Added dynamic multicast mapping for NBMA: 22.2.2.2

Dallas#show ip nhrp multicast

 I/F      NBMA address
Tunnel1   22.2.2.2          Flags: dynamic           (Enabled)
```

---

The same occurs for Miami. With EIGRP configured on the tunnel interfaces, EIGRP packets (multicast and unicast) will now be encapsulated within GRE and unicasted to the NBMA addresses of Houston and Miami by Dallas. The following captures show an example of such packets transmitted by Dallas to the spokes, Houston and Miami.

---

```
Frame 32: 98 bytes on wire (784 bits), 98 bytes captured (784 bits) on
interface 0
Ethernet II, Src: aa:bb:cc:00:01:00 (aa:bb:cc:00:01:00), Dst:
aa:bb:cc:00:04:00 (aa:bb:cc:00:04:00)
Internet Protocol Version 4, Src: 11.1.1.1, Dst: 22.2.2.2
Generic Routing Encapsulation (IP)
Internet Protocol Version 4, Src: 10.1.1.1, Dst: 224.0.0.10
Cisco EIGRP


Frame 33: 98 bytes on wire (784 bits), 98 bytes captured (784 bits) on
interface 0
Ethernet II, Src: aa:bb:cc:00:01:00 (aa:bb:cc:00:01:00), Dst:
aa:bb:cc:00:04:00 (aa:bb:cc:00:04:00)
Internet Protocol Version 4, Src: 11.1.1.1, Dst: 33.3.3.3
Generic Routing Encapsulation (IP)
Internet Protocol Version 4, Src: 10.1.1.1, Dst: 224.0.0.10
Cisco EIGRP
```

---

EIGRP relationships are then formed between Dallas and the spokes, Houston and Miami. The **show ip eigrp neighbors** command output on Dallas verifies these EIGRP neighborships:

**Houston:**

```
Houston#show ip eigrp neighbors
EIGRP-IPv4 Neighbors for AS(1)
H   Address          Interface     Hold Uptime    SRTT    RTO   Q   Seq
                                   (sec)          (ms)        Cnt Num
1   10.1.1.3         Tu1           12 00:09:20      5   1470   0   3
0   10.1.1.2         Tu1           12 00:19:36     13   1470   0   7
```

On completing the above configurations, the routing tables on Houston and Miami confirm that they have EIGRP routes of each other's LAN networks. A ping is issued between the LANs on Houston and Miami to confirm the communication:

**On Houston:**

```
Houston#show ip route eigrp | begin Gate
Gateway of last resort is not set

     172.16.0.0/16 is variably subnetted, 4 subnets, 2 masks
D    172.16.10.0/24 [90/27008000] via 10.1.1.1, 00:21:39, Tunnel1
D     172.16.30.0/24 [90/28288000] via 10.1.1.1, 00:11:23, Tunnel1
```

**On Miami:**

```
Miami#show ip route eigrp | begin Gate
Gateway of last resort is not set

     172.16.0.0/16 is variably subnetted, 4 subnets, 2 masks
D     172.16.10.0/24 [90/27008000] via 10.1.1.1, 00:11:40, Tunnel1
D     172.16.20.0/24 [90/28288000] via 10.1.1.1, 00:11:40, Tunnel1
```

**On Houston:**

```
Houston#ping 172.16.30.1 source 172.16.20.1

Type escape sequence to abort.
Sending 5, 100-byte ICMP Echos to 172.16.30.1, timeout is 2 seconds:
Packet sent with a source address of 172.16.20.1
!!!!!
Success rate is 100 percent (5/5), round-trip min/avg/max = 1/4/5 ms
```

# DMVPN Designs

The word *phase* is almost always connected to DMVPN design discussions. *DMVPN phase* refers to the version of DMVPN implemented in a DMVPN design. DMVPN as a solution was rolled out in different stages as the solution became more widely adopted to address performance issues and additional improvised features. There are three main phases for DMVPN:

> Phase 1 - Hub-and-spoke
>
> Phase 2 - Spoke-initiated spoke-to-spoke tunnels
>
> Phase 3 - Hub-initiated spoke-to-spoke tunnels

The differences between the DMVPN phases are related to routing efficiency and the ability to create spoke-to-spoke tunnels.

## Phase 1: Hub-and-Spoke

Earlier, we discussed the problem of providing WAN connectivity to allow branch sites of a corporation to communicate with each other. To create a scalable and dynamic WAN strategy, a DMVPN solution was implemented as an overlay network. This network used only a single tunnel interface on three routers to create a hub-and-spoke network. The hub router Dallas leverages mGRE and NHRP to dynamically create a tunnel between itself and the branch (spoke) office routers Houston and Miami, which both use traditional point-to-point GRE tunnels.

The resulting overall design mimics a traditional hub-and-spoke network, where all traffic between Miami and Houston first travels through Dallas. In this design, Miami and Houston cannot communicate directly with each other. This design implementation is referred to as **DMVPN Phase 1**.

DMVPN Phase 1 uses mGRE interfaces on the hub router and point-to-point GRE tunnel interfaces on the spoke routers. With point-to-point GRE interfaces on spoke routers, all traffic sent by spokes through the DMVPN overlay is forced through the hub router. In other words, traffic from a spoke to another spoke always traverses the hub. Because traffic is forced through the hub router, there is no reason for the spokes to retain specific routing information for networks behind other spoke routers. The routing tables on the spokes can be optimized to a single default route received from the hub router.

To prove this point, a traceroute is performed below on Houston to the network address 172.16.30.1 on Miami. This network is advertised via EIGRP by the hub router Dallas to Houston. As seen below, the path taken to reach this address is from Houston, then to Dallas, and then to Miami.

```
Houston#show ip route eigrp | begin Gateway


Gateway of last resort is not set

      172.16.0.0/16 is variably subnetted, 4 subnets, 2 masks
D        172.16.10.0/24 [90/27008000] via 10.1.1.1, 01:00:20, Tunnel1
D        172.16.30.0/24 [90/28288000] via 10.1.1.1, 01:00:19, Tunnel1

Houston#traceroute 172.16.30.1 source 172.16.20.1

Type escape sequence to abort.
Tracing the route to 172.16.30.1
VRF info: (vrf in name/id, vrf out name/id)
  1 10.1.1.1 0 msec 5 msec 5 msec
  2 10.1.1.3 1 msec 5 msec 5 msec
```

Since traffic from Houston's LAN segment takes a Houston ➜ Dallas ➜ Miami path, the specific routing information for Miami's connected LAN segment 172.16.30.0/24 is unnecessary in the routing table on Houston. Dallas could send a default route to both spokes and Houston would still take the same Houston ➜ Dallas ➜ Miami path as shown below:

```
Dallas#show run interface tunnel1 | begin int

interface Tunnel1
 ip address 10.1.1.1 255.255.255.0
 no ip redirects
 no ip split-horizon eigrp 1
 ip nhrp map multicast dynamic
 ip nhrp network-id 1
 ip nhrp redirect
 ip summary-address eigrp 1 0.0.0.0 0.0.0.0
 tunnel source 11.1.1.1
 tunnel mode gre multipoint
end

Houston#show ip route eigrp | begin Gateway
Gateway of last resort is 10.1.1.1 to network 0.0.0.0

D*    0.0.0.0/0 [90/27008000] via 10.1.1.1, 00:00:54, Tunnel1
```

```
Houston#traceroute 172.16.30.1 source 172.16.20.1

Type escape sequence to abort.
Tracing the route to 172.16.30.1
VRF info: (vrf in name/id, vrf out name/id)
  1 10.1.1.1 0 msec 5 msec 5 msec
  2 10.1.1.3 1 msec 5 msec 5 msec
```

Using the **ip summary-address eigrp 1** command, Dallas has been instructed to advertise a default summary route out of its tunnel interface. This causes Dallas to suppress all specific routes and only send a single default route to the spokes Houston and Miami. As mentioned, the traffic path remains the same from Houston's 172.16.20.0/24 LAN segment and Miami's 172.16.30.0/24 LAN segment. What has changed is the routing tables on the spokes have been optimized by removing unnecessary specific routing information about remote spoke LAN segments that do not have an effect on the DMVPN traffic flow. Such an optimization is recommended whenever possible in a DMVPN implementation.

## Dynamic Spoke-to-Spoke Tunnels

DMVPN Phase 1 is the simplest phase to implement. As long as the hub has enough resources to service the spokes, the network will perform well. Phase 1 also allows for complete reduction of routing information by sending a default route down to the spoke sites. This way, spoke routing tables can be kept efficient. However, Phase 1 optimizes the routing tables of spoke routers at the cost of routing efficiency between spokes. DMVPN Phases 2 and 3 introduce the concept of **spoke-to-spoke tunnels**.

## The Need for Spoke-to-Spoke Tunnels

The goal for any DMVPN deployment is to provide connectivity between clients connected at remote sites of an organization. In our example, the clients located at the Miami and Houston sites need to be able to communicate not only with the Dallas site but with each other as well.

As the company grows and branch offices are added, those branch offices are also additional spokes in the DMVPN network. With more spokes, the amount of traffic increases across the DMVPN network. If the hub router is overloaded with traffic, overall network performance suffers. Through traffic analysis, network operators can determine whether the majority of the increased traffic is spoke-to-hub or spoke-to-spoke communication. If the majority is spoke-to-hub, the hub router resources may need to be increased. If it is spoke-to-spoke, however, the bottleneck can be relieved by simply allowing spoke sites to communicate with one another directly.

There are two main topologies for allowing spoke-to-spoke connectivity: **full-mesh** and **partial-mesh**. In full-mesh topologies, all routers have direct connections with each other, as shown here:

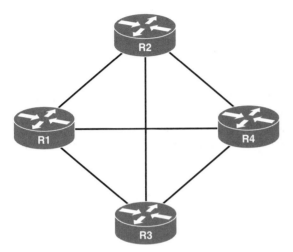

In the above, if R1 needed to reach any router, it can do so directly without using another router as transit. This design is also fault tolerant. If R1 loses its link to R2, it can route around the failure through R3.

The downside of full-mesh topologies is the cost of provisioning the circuits between sites. An alternative is to identify which sites contribute to the majority of direct traffic and directly connect those sites. Such a design, like the one shown here, would be considered to be a **partial-mesh** design:

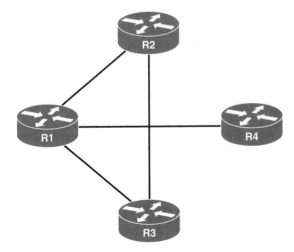

The sites that have direct connections are determined based on traffic patterns and volume at each individual site. The partially meshed sites exchange each other's routing information and can route directly to each other, relieving tension at the hub site.

Partial-mesh solutions provide cost savings over full-mesh solutions, but they still carry costs related to provisioning additional WAN circuits. Also, a direct connection between spokes may only be needed in peak seasons. It might be difficult and costly to provision a direct WAN circuit between sites for seasonal traffic spikes; this is a downside with both partial- and full-mesh designs.

DMVPN addresses this problem by supporting dynamic spoke-to-spoke tunnels between DMVPN spokes. A dynamic spoke-to-spoke tunnel is a temporary tunnel that spoke sites build and use whenever the traffic flows require it. If the tunnel goes unused, it is torn down until it is needed again. Spoke-to-spoke tunnels were first introduced in **DMVPN Phase 2**.

In order to lift the Phase 1 requirement of spoke-hub-spoke traffic patterns, a DMVPN network needs to be modified in two ways:

■ Spokes need the ability to support multiple endpoints on the DMVPN tunnel interface.

■ Mechanisms that trigger direct communication between spokes are needed.

## Enabling Multipoint GRE on Spokes

The first point highlights the major limiting factor of DMVPN Phase 1, which is the point-to-point GRE tunnel configuration on the spokes. With a hub configured as the sole endpoint for the DMVPN tunnel interface, there is no way for the spokes to even form a direct tunnel between each other. Thus, the point-to-point GRE tunnels on the spokes need to be traded out for mGRE tunnels, just like on the hub router. To provide this functionality, the tunnel interfaces on all routers are shut down. Then the **tunnel destination** command is removed, and **tunnel mode gre multipoint** is configured instead on the Houston and Miami routers. Finally, the tunnel interfaces are brought back up, starting with Dallas:

**Note** The sequence of shutting down the tunnel interfaces of all routers, bringing up the hub tunnel interface first, and then bringing up the spokes is vital. If the spoke tunnel interfaces are brought up before the hub, the first registration request sent from the spokes might not be received by the hub, causing delay in bringing up the DMVPN. With the hub interface up first, it is ensured that the first registration request sent from the spokes is received by the hub immediately.

**On Dallas, Houston, and Miami:**

```
interface Tunnel1
 shutdown
 end
```

**On Houston and Miami:**

```
interface Tunnel1
 no tunnel destination
 tunnel mode gre multipoint
```

**On Dallas:**

```
interface Tunnel1
 no shut
```

**On Houston and Miami:**

```
interface Tunnel1
 no shut
```

Once the tunnel interfaces come back up on all routers, a ping is issued from Dallas to Houston to test the configuration:

```
Dallas#ping 10.1.1.2

Type escape sequence to abort.
Sending 5, 100-byte ICMP Echos to 10.1.1.2, timeout is 2 seconds:
.....
Success rate is 0 percent (0/5)
```

As shown above, the ping is unsuccessful. The **show dmvpn** command is issued to check the status of DMVPN spoke registration on the hub, Dallas:

```
Dallas#show dmvpn


Legend: Attrb --> S - Static, D - Dynamic, I - Incomplete
        N - NATed, L - Local, X - No Socket
        # Ent --> Number of NHRP entries with same NBMA peer
        NHS Status: E --> Expecting Replies, R --> Responding, W -->
Waiting
        UpDn Time --> Up or Down Time for a Tunnel
=====================================================================
```

This output confirms that neither Houston nor Miami has registered with the hub, preventing the hub from learning their NBMA-to-overlay mapping information. The **debug ip nhrp packet** output on Houston sheds light on the underlying problem:

```
Houston#debug nhrp packet
NHRP activity debugging is on

 NHRP: Incompatible Destination NBMA (UNKNOWN) for 'Tunnel1'
 NHRP: NHS-DOWN: 10.1.1.1
```

The debugging messages prove that Houston is trying to register with Dallas but is unable to. The failure occurs because the NBMA address for 10.1.1.1 (Dallas) is unknown to Houston. Recall that in order to successfully tunnel DMVPN traffic across the underlay, the router needs to know what NBMA address to use for the destination of the GRE/IP packet sent across the underlay.

Earlier, Houston had a static point-to-point tunnel interface, where this information was explicitly configured with the **tunnel destination** command. Now, Houston has an mGRE tunnel interface that does not accept static tunnel destination commands.

```
Houston(config-if)#tunnel destination 11.1.1.1

Tunnel destination configuration failed on tunnel in mode multi-GRE/
IP configuring 11.1.1.1: tunnel destination cannot be configured under
existing mode
```

When the spoke is unable to register with the hub, the DMVPN network is broken, and communication cannot continue. The solution to this problem is to provide the spoke routers with a static NHRP mapping for the hub. When the **ip nhrp map** command is used to configure the static mapping for the hub, the spoke can properly register with the hub, and the DMVPN network functions as normal. This configuration should be added in the configuration template for future spokes. Below, Houston is configured with the static NHRP mapping for the hub's NBMA address. After the tunnel is flapped on Houston, Dallas receives the mapping, and **ping** succeeds again:

---

**On Houston:**

```
interface tunnel 1
 ip nhrp map 10.1.1.1 11.1.1.1 ! Static IP to NBMA mapping of the hub
 exit

Houston#show dmvpn | begin Interface
Interface: Tunnel1, IPv4 NHRP Details
Type:Spoke, NHRP Peers:1,

 # Ent  Peer NBMA address Peer Tunnel Add State  UpDn Tm Attrb
 ----- --------------- --------------- ----- -------- -----
    1 11.1.1.1               10.1.1.1    UP 00:01:59     S

Houston(config)#interface tunnel1
Houston(config-if)#shut

%LINEPROTO-5-UPDOWN: Line protocol on Interface Tunnel1, changed state
to down
%LINK-5-CHANGED: Interface Tunnel1, changed state to administratively
down

Houston(config-if)#no shut

%LINEPROTO-5-UPDOWN: Line protocol on Interface Tunnel1, changed state
to up
```

**On Dallas:**

```
Dallas#show dmvpn | begin Interface

Interface: Tunnel1, IPv4 NHRP Details
Type:Hub, NHRP Peers:1,
```

```
# Ent  Peer NBMA address Peer Tunnel Add State  UpDn Tm Attrb
----- --------------- --------------- ----- -------- -----
    1 22.2.2.2                  10.1.1.2    UP 00:01:03      D

Dallas#ping 10.1.1.2
Type escape sequence to abort.
Sending 5, 100-byte ICMP Echos to 10.1.1.2, timeout is 2 seconds:
!!!!!
Success rate is 100 percent (5/5), round-trip min/avg/max = 1/4/5 ms
```

Everything appears to be functioning. However, after some time, the following is logged on Houston:

```
Houston:


%DUAL-5-NBRCHANGE: EIGRP-IPv4 1: Neighbor 10.1.1.1 (Tunnel1) is down:
retry limit exceeded


%DUAL-5-NBRCHANGE: EIGRP-IPv4 1: Neighbor 10.1.1.1 (Tunnel1) is up:
new adjacency
```

The EIGRP neighborship to Dallas is flapping. This is the same situation experienced by Dallas regarding its mGRE interface. EIGRP uses multicast for hellos. Earlier, Houston had a point-to-point GRE tunnel and sent multicast EIGRP hello packets to Dallas. Dallas would create a neighbor structure and attempt to bring up the neighborship. Houston ignored Dallas's unicast response because it had not yet seen a multicast hello from Dallas. The neighborship timed out, and the process repeated until Dallas was configured to dynamically populate its NHRP multicast table with NBMA destinations for all spokes that successfully register with it.

In this situation, Dallas is able to send multicast hellos to Houston, but Houston cannot send them to Dallas because the point-to-point tunnel has been converted into an mGRE interface. Like Dallas, Houston also needs a multicast mapping in its NHRP table for Dallas's NBMA address to send multicasts successfully. The NHRP multicast tables on the routers confirm the problem:

```
On Dallas:


Dallas#show ip nhrp multicast


  I/F     NBMA address
Tunnel1    22.2.2.2        Flags: dynamic         (Enabled)
```

**On Houston:**

```
Houston#show ip nhrp multicast
  I/F     NBMA address
```

The solution for Dallas was to enable dynamic multicast mappings by using the **ip nhrp map multicast dynamic** command. Whenever a spoke registers, a multicast mapping is created. This works for DMVPN hub routers but does not work for DMVPN spoke routers. The DMVPN hub will never register its address with a DMVPN spoke router, rendering the **ip nhrp map multicast dynamic** command purposeless. Instead, a static multicast mapping should be enabled on the spoke, using the **ip nhrp map multicast** *[IP address]*. The IP address should be the NBMA address of the hub, as shown here:

**On Houston:**

```
interface Tunnel1
 ip nhrp map multicast 11.1.1.1 ! Static NHRP multicast mapping
```

Following this configuration, the EIGRP neighborship is established between Dallas and Houston, as shown below:

**Houston:**

```
%DUAL-5-NBRCHANGE: EIGRP-IPv4 1: Neighbor 10.1.1.1 (Tunnel1) is up:
new adjacency

Houston#show ip eigrp neighbors

EIGRP-IPv4 Neighbors for AS(1)
H   Address          Interface       Hold Uptime   SRTT   RTO  Q  Seq
                                     (sec)         (ms)       Cnt Num
0   10.1.1.1         Tu1               13 00:00:44    5  1470  0   40
```

The following is a summary of static tunnel configurations that should be included in a template for configuring additional DMVPN spoke routers to enable proper DMVPN functionality:

---

**On Spokes:**

```
interface Tunnel1
 ip nhrp map 10.1.1.1 11.1.1.1
 ip nhrp map multicast 11.1.1.1
 ip nhrp network-id 1
 ip nhrp nhs 10.1.1.1
```

---

The total NHRP configuration takes five configuration commands, three of which are related to the NHS/NHC relationship.

As DMVPN matured, its designers came up with a collapsed command that reflects the same style of configuration but in a single line: **ip nhrp nhs** *overlay-address* **nbma** *nbma-address* **multicast**. This command configures the NHS, maps the NHS overlay address to the NBMA address, and also creates the required multicast mapping for the NHS. By using this command, the above configuration template can be condensed to:

---

**On Spokes:**

```
interface Tunnel1
 ip nhrp network-id 1
 ip nhrp nhs 10.1.1.1 nbma 11.1.1.1 multicast
end
```

---

The same command is then configured on Miami's tunnel interface to complete its conversion to mGRE tunnels:

---

**Miami:**

```
interface Tunnel1
 ip address 10.1.1.3 255.255.255.0
 ip nhrp network-id 1
 ip nhrp nhs 10.1.1.1 nbma 11.1.1.1 multicast
 tunnel source 33.3.3.3
 tunnel mode gre multipoint
end
```

The output below verifies the DMVPN, EIGRP, and IP connectivity between Dallas and Miami and between the networks behind Houston and Miami:

---

**On Dallas:**

```
Dallas#show dmvpn | begin Interface

Interface: Tunnel1, IPv4 NHRP Details
Type:Hub, NHRP Peers:2,

 # Ent  Peer NBMA address Peer Tunnel Add State  UpDn Tm Attrb
 ----- --------------- --------------- ----- -------- -----
     1 22.2.2.2                10.1.1.2    UP 00:29:18     D
     1 33.3.3.3                10.1.1.3    UP 00:02:06     D


Dallas#show ip eigrp neighbors
EIGRP-IPv4 Neighbors for AS(1)

H    Address         Interface          Hold Uptime    SRTT   RTO  Q  Seq
                                        (sec)          (ms)        Cnt
Num
1    10.1.1.3        Tu1                  14 00:02:06     6  1512  0  25
0    10.1.1.2        Tu1                  14 00:12:44    25  1470  0  34

Dallas#ping 10.1.1.3

Type escape sequence to abort.
Sending 5, 100-byte ICMP Echos to 10.1.1.3, timeout is 2 seconds:
!!!!!
Success rate is 100 percent (5/5), round-trip min/avg/max = 1/4/5 ms
```

**On Houston:**

```
Houston#ping 172.16.30.1 source 172.16.20.1

Type escape sequence to abort.
Sending 5, 100-byte ICMP Echos to 172.16.30.1, timeout is 2 seconds:
Packet sent with a source address of 172.16.20.1
!!!!!
Success rate is 100 percent (5/5), round-trip min/avg/max = 1/3/5 ms
```

## Forming Spoke-to-Spoke Tunnels

The spokes are ready to begin forming dynamic spoke-to-spoke tunnels using their mGRE interfaces. There is only one piece of information missing. In order to successfully build a tunnel over the DMVPN network, the spokes require the NBMA address of the destination DMVPN endpoint. This NBMA address is used in the outer GRE/IP header of the packet that is forwarded over the underlay.

Hubs gain this information about the spokes through the NHRP registration process outlined earlier. Spokes, on the other hand, do not register with each other. Upon initialization, a DMVPN spoke has no knowledge of other DMVPN spokes participating in its own DMVPN cloud. Spokes could be statically configured with additional NHRP mapping commands for each neighboring spoke. However, as spokes are added, keeping track of which spokes have static mappings and which spokes do not can become cumbersome. Also, static configurations of this kind remove the dynamic nature of DMVPN. The creators of DMVPN solved this problem by leveraging a relationship each spoke already has: the one with the hub itself.

Since the hub router receives all mapping information for all spokes connected to the DMVPN, spokes can ask the hub for the proper mapping using a process known as **NHRP resolution**. Through NHRP resolution, a spoke queries the hub for the proper NBMA-to-overlay mapping for a corresponding spoke router by sending an NHRP resolution request. With the addition of this relationship, the hub fulfills its full role as an NHS, providing a database of mappings for the spokes that require mapping information for other spokes connected to the DMVPN.

The resolution request sent by the spokes contains the source NBMA address of the spoke initiating the resolution request and the target overlay address for which an NBMA address mapping is needed.

This process can be seen when PC-2 behind Houston pings PC-3 behind Miami for the first time. The target in this case is 10.1.1.3 (indicated in the dst protocol field in the output), and the source is Houston's own NBMA 22.2.2.2:

```
PC-2#ping 172.16.30.2

Type escape sequence to abort.
Sending 5, 100-byte ICMP Echos to 172.16.30.2, timeout is 2 seconds:
.!!!!
Success rate is 80 percent (4/5), round-trip min/avg/max = 1/4/5 ms
```

**Houston:**

```
NHRP: Send Resolution Request via Tunnel1 vrf 0, packet size: 72
  src: 10.1.1.2, dst: 10.1.1.3
  (F) afn: AF_IP(1), type: IP(800), hop: 255, ver: 1
```

```
       shtl: 4(NSAP), sstl: 0(NSAP)
       pktsz: 72 extoff: 52
(M) flags: "router auth src-stable nat ", reqid: 10
       src NBMA: 22.2.2.2
       src protocol: 10.1.1.2, dst protocol: 10.1.1.3
  (C-1) code: no error(0)
        prefix: 32, mtu: 17916, hd_time: 7200
        addr_len: 0(NSAP), subaddr_len: 0(NSAP), proto_len: 0, pref: 0
```

Houston begins by sending a NHRP resolution request to Dallas. Dallas receives the resolution request and forwards the packet out its tunnel interface toward Miami. The hub makes this decision based on the destination protocol address, which in this case is 10.1.1.3:

**Dallas:**

```
--Certain debug outputs have been omitted for brevity--

NHRP: Receive Resolution Request via Tunnel1 vrf 0, packet size: 72

      src NBMA: 22.2.2.2
      src protocol: 10.1.1.2, dst protocol: 10.1.1.3

 NHRP: Forwarding Resolution Request via Tunnel1 vrf 0, packet size:
92
  src: 10.1.1.1, dst: 10.1.1.3
      src NBMA: 22.2.2.2
      src protocol: 10.1.1.2, dst protocol: 10.1.1.3
```

Miami receives the resolution request, which contains the NBMA address of Houston. Using this address, Miami sends a resolution reply directly to Houston:

**Miami:**

```
--Certain debug outputs have been omitted for brevity--

NHRP: Receive Resolution Request via Tunnel1 vrf 0, packet size: 92

      src NBMA: 22.2.2.2
      src protocol: 10.1.1.2, dst protocol: 10.1.1.3
```

```
NHRP: Send Resolution Reply via Tunnel1 vrf 0, packet size: 120
  src: 10.1.1.3, dst: 10.1.1.2

     src NBMA: 22.2.2.2
     src protocol: 10.1.1.2, dst protocol: 10.1.1.3

       client NBMA: 33.3.3.3
       client protocol: 10.1.1.3
```

The resolution reply contains Miami's NHRP client information (highlighted in blue above). Once Houston receives this information, it adds it to its NHRP mapping table. Houston now has all the information needed to send messages directly to Miami without traversing the hub, leading to the formation of a spoke-to-spoke tunnel:

```
Houston:


NHRP: Receive Resolution Reply via Tunnel1 vrf 0, packet size: 120
  (F) afn: AF_IP(1), type: IP(800), hop: 255, ver: 1
      shtl: 4(NSAP), sstl: 0(NSAP)
      pktsz: 120 extoff: 60
  (M) flags: "router auth dst-stable unique src-stable nat ", reqid:
10
      src NBMA: 22.2.2.2
      src protocol: 10.1.1.2, dst protocol: 10.1.1.3
  (C-1) code: no error(0)
        prefix: 32, mtu: 17916, hd_time: 7200
        addr_len: 4(NSAP), subaddr_len: 0(NSAP), proto_len: 4, pref: 0
        client NBMA: 33.3.3.3
        client protocol: 10.1.1.3
```

The **show ip nhrp** command output below shows the contents of the NHRP mapping table on Houston. Notice that it now includes dynamic mapping information for Miami's tunnel interface 10.1.1.3 to the NBMA address 33.3.3.3:

```
Houston#show ip nhrp

10.1.1.1/32 via 10.1.1.1
   Tunnel1 created 00:15:21, never expire
   Type: static, Flags: used
   NBMA address: 11.1.1.1
```

```
10.1.1.2/32 via 10.1.1.2
   Tunnel1 created 00:13:57, expire 01:46:02
   Type: dynamic, Flags: router unique local
   NBMA address: 22.2.2.2
    (no-socket)
10.1.1.3/32 via 10.1.1.3
   Tunnel1 created 00:13:57, expire 01:46:02
   Type: dynamic, Flags: router nhop
   NBMA address: 33.3.3.3
```

Finally, a **traceroute** between the two PCs confirms direct connectivity:

```
PC-2#traceroute 172.16.30.2


Type escape sequence to abort.
Tracing the route to 172.16.30.2
VRF info: (vrf in name/id, vrf out name/id)
  1 172.16.20.1 1 msec 0 msec 6 msec ! Houston
  2 10.1.1.3 6 msec 6 msec 1 msec    ! Miami
  3 172.16.30.2 1 msec 1 msec 0 msec
```

This is the general process used for building the NHRP mapping information between two spokes. Keep in mind that the Miami router performs the same steps when routing the return traffic back to Houston: It sends a resolution request to Dallas, Dallas forwards to Houston, Houston replies directly to Miami, and Miami adds the mapping information for Houston.

**Note**  In earlier implementations of DMVPN, the hub router would respond directly to the spoke sending the resolution request with the proper mapping information. This functionality has been modified in recent IOS versions to provide more scalability and support for hierarchical hub routers in advanced DMVPN designs. Furthermore, allowing the target spoke to respond directly to the requesting spoke ensures that the most up-to-date mapping information is gained in an efficient way in the event that changes are made in other areas of the DMVPN hierarchy.

## Triggering NHRP Resolutions

The NHRP resolution process provides an elegant solution for spokes to learn the required mapping information for creating dynamic spoke-to-spoke tunnels. But how does a spoke know to perform such a function? DMVPN Phases 2 and 3 accomplish this feat in two different ways, which will be explored later.

## Phase 2: Spoke-Initiated Spoke-to-Spoke Tunnels

Spoke-to-spoke tunnels were first introduced in DMVPN Phase 2 as an enhancement to the hub-and-spoke model of DMVPN Phase 1. In Phase 2, the responsibility for knowing when to send NHRP resolution requests was given to each spoke individually, meaning spokes actually initiated the NHRP resolution process when they determined that a packet needed a spoke-to-spoke tunnel.

The spoke would make this decision based on the information contained in its own routing table with the help of Cisco Express Forwarding (CEF). The routing table on Houston provides insight into how this trigger works:

```
Houston#show ip route eigrp | begin Gateway
Gateway of last resort is not set

      172.16.0.0/16 is variably subnetted, 4 subnets, 2 masks
D        172.16.10.0/24 [90/27008000] via 10.1.1.1, 00:20:52, Tunnel1
D        172.16.30.0/24 [90/28185600] via 10.1.1.3, 00:20:36, Tunnel1
```

Notice the second entry in Houston's routing table for 172.16.30.0/24, the Miami LAN. Houston has received the route for that prefix on its Tunnel1 interface, pointing to Miami's overlay address 10.1.1.3 as the next hop. In normal IP routing forwarding, when Houston sends traffic destined to that LAN out the tunnel interface, it performs the following:

1. Houston sends the packet to the tunnel interface.

2. The tunnel interface forces encapsulation of a new GRE/IP header. The source and destination are determined by the tunnel source and tunnel destination configurations made under the tunnel interface.

3. The new GRE/IP packet is routed based on the new destination IP address contained in the outer GRE/IP header. Layer 2 forwarding information is added as well.

4. The new packet is forwarded out an exit interface.

This process applies to normal point-to-point tunnel interfaces. Houston, however, does not have a point-to-point tunnel interface anymore, and it doesn't have sufficient forwarding information to build the outer GRE/IP header. Here is where the CEF table comes in.

CEF precomputes rewrite headers in an *adjacency table*, which contains next hop forwarding information for directly connected devices. The basic process is as follows: Routing table entries are downloaded into the CEF Forwarding Information Base (FIB). At the same time, CEF completes the recursive process in the routing table to determine the appropriate exit interfaces for all routes contained in the routing table. Then, CEF determines whether adjacency information is available for the next hop/exit interface pairs. These are recorded in the adjacency table linked to the corresponding FIB entry by a key.

The **show ip cef internal** command shows this information. Let's compare the **show ip cef internal** output on Houston for Dallas's overlay address to the 172.16.30.2 (PC-3) address behind Miami:

```
Houston#show ip cef 10.1.1.1 internal


10.1.1.1/32, epoch 0, flags attached, refcount 5, per-destination
sharing
  sources: Adj
  subblocks:
   Adj source: IP midchain out of Tunnel1, address 10.1.1.1 F2776928
    Dependent covered prefix type adjfib, cover 10.1.1.0/24
  ifnums:
   Tunnel1(23): 10.1.1.1
  path F2765DF8, path list F2798F84, share 1/1, type adjacency
prefix, for IPv4
  attached to Tunnel1, adjacency IP midchain out of Tunnel1, address
10.1.1.1 F2776928
  output chain: IP midchain out of Tunnel1, address 10.1.1.1 F2776928
IP adj out of Ethernet0/0, address 22.2.2.1 F4EDE6A8


Houston#show ip cef 172.16.30.2 internal


172.16.30.0/24, epoch 0, RIB[I], refcount 5, per-destination sharing
  sources: RIB
  feature space:
   IPRM: 0x00028000
  ifnums:
   Tunnel1(23): 10.1.1.3
  path F527E768, path list F527F924, share 1/1, type attached nexthop,
for IPv4
  nexthop 10.1.1.3 Tunnel1, adjacency IP midchain out of Tunnel1,
address 10.1.1.3 (incomplete)
  output chain: IP midchain out of Tunnel1, address 10.1.1.3
(incomplete) drop
```

The portions highlighted in red reveal a major difference. Houston has calculated the next hop as 10.1.1.1 for Dallas's overlay address. It has also calculated the next hop as 10.1.1.3 for PC-3 (based on the IP routing table) at the Miami site. The difference lies in the adjacency information.

For Dallas's overlay address, the FIB output shows an adjacency as attached, while the adjacency for PC-3 shows as incomplete. The **show adjacency** and **show adjacency encapsulation** commands can be used to gain a little more insight into this:

```
Houston#show adjacency


Protocol Interface                Address
IP       Ethernet0/0              22.2.2.1(18)
IP       Ethernet0/1              172.16.20.2(7)
IP       Tunnel1                  10.1.1.1(11)
IP       Tunnel1                  10.1.1.3(5) (incomplete)


Houston#show adjacency encapsulation | begin 10.1.1.1


IP       Tunnel1                  10.1.1.1(11)
  Encap length 24
  4500000000000000FF2F97C916020202
  0B01010100000800
  Provider: TUNNEL
  Protocol header count in macstring: 2
    HDR 0: ipv4
       dst: static, 11.1.1.1
       src: static, 22.2.2.2
      prot: static, 47
       ttl: static, 255
        df: static, cleared
      per packet fields: tos ident tl chksm
    HDR 1: gre
      prot: static, 0x800
      per packet fields: none
IP       Tunnel1                  10.1.1.3(5) (incomplete)
  adjacency is incomplete
```

This disparity has important ramifications for how Houston will route the packet. In the case of Dallas's overlay address, the adjacency table shows it has completed precalculated forwarding information for its next hop. For Miami's LAN, this information is incomplete. *This incomplete entry in Houston's adjacency table triggers Houston to send an*

*NHRP resolution request* in order to gain the information it needs to form a spoke-to-spoke tunnel. In this case, Houston requires Miami's NBMA address.

The process goes as follows:

1. Houston receives a packet destined for PC-3 from PC-2.

2. Houston checks its FIB for precalculated routing information.

3. The FIB points to incomplete adjacency information.

4. Houston sends an NHRP resolution request to the hub in response to the incomplete adjacency.

5. Houston has a decision to make:

   a. Drop the packet.

   b. Delay forwarding the packet until the NHRP resolution process completes.

   c. Forward the traffic along a known good path.

6. The NHRP resolution process completes, the adjacency is properly populated, and Houston has a spoke-to-spoke tunnel with Miami.

7. Subsequent packets are forwarded directly to Miami through the spoke-to-spoke tunnel.

The key part of this process is that once Houston determines it needs more forwarding information to forward the packet to PC-3 at step 5, there are a number of actions it can take. The designers of DMVPN chose to go with the third option, where, in this case, Houston forwards the packets along a known good path. With this default behavior, rather than simply dropping or delaying the packet, Houston chooses to forward it in a direction where there is a high likelihood of its reaching the proper destination. This direction is toward the hub or, more specifically, the NHRP NHS.

The reasoning behind this behavior is that if Houston is relying on the hub to provide the mapping information, the hub must have the mapping information itself and can forward the packet accordingly. Doing so ensures that traffic to PC-3 routed through Houston still reaches PC-3 while Houston works out the spoke-to-spoke tunnel formation. The result is that the first packet Houston sends that requires a spoke-to-spoke tunnel will always traverse the hub until the spoke-to-spoke tunnel is formed. Subsequent packets will not traverse the hub.

The debug output below shows the NHRP resolution process. Dallas receives the resolution request from Houston. It forwards the request to Miami. Miami receives the resolution request, and sends a resolution reply packet, containing its NBMA to Overlay mapping information, and back to Houston directly (note the source and destination IP addresses in the reply debug). Houston will receive this reply from Miami and add an entry in its NHRP mapping table for Miami's NBMA address.

**On Dallas:**

```
NHRP: Receive Resolution Request via Tunnel1 vrf 0, packet size: 72
  (F) afn: AF_IP(1), type: IP(800), hop: 255, ver: 1
      shtl: 4(NSAP), sstl: 0(NSAP)
      pktsz: 72 extoff: 52
  (M) flags: "router auth src-stable nat ", reqid: 6

NHRP: Forwarding Resolution Request via Tunnel1 vrf 0, packet size:
92
  src: 10.1.1.1, dst: 172.16.30.2
  (F) afn: AF_IP(1), type: IP(800), hop: 254, ver: 1
      shtl: 4(NSAP), sstl: 0(NSAP)
      pktsz: 92 extoff: 52
  (M) flags: "router auth src-stable nat ", reqid: 6
```

**On Miami:**

```
NHRP: Receive Resolution Request via Tunnel1 vrf 0, packet size: 92
  (F) afn: AF_IP(1), type: IP(800), hop: 254, ver: 1
      shtl: 4(NSAP), sstl: 0(NSAP)
      pktsz: 92 extoff: 52
  (M) flags: "router auth src-stable nat ", reqid: 6

NHRP: Send Resolution Reply via Tunnel1 vrf 0, packet size: 120
  src: 10.1.1.3, dst: 10.1.1.2
  (F) afn: AF_IP(1), type: IP(800), hop: 255, ver: 1
      shtl: 4(NSAP), sstl: 0(NSAP)
      pktsz: 120 extoff: 60
  (M) flags: "router auth dst-stable unique src-stable nat ", reqid: 6
      src NBMA: 22.2.2.2
      src protocol: 10.1.1.2, dst protocol: 172.16.30.2
  (C-1) code: no error(0)
      prefix: 24, mtu: 17916, hd_time: 7200
      addr_len: 4(NSAP), subaddr_len: 0(NSAP), proto_len: 4, pref: 0
      client NBMA: 33.3.3.3
      client protocol: 10.1.1.3
```

**On Houston:**

```
Houston#show ip nhrp

10.1.1.1/32 via 10.1.1.1
  Tunnel1 created 00:35:34, never expire
    Type: static, Flags: used
    NBMA address: 11.1.1.1
--- omitted ---
172.16.30.0/24 via 10.1.1.3
    Tunnel1 created 00:11:18, expire 01:48:41
    Type: dynamic, Flags: router rib
    NBMA address: 33.3.3.3
```

## Phase 2 Spoke-to-Spoke Tunnel Caveats

You have seen the basic spoke-to-spoke tunnel formation process in DMVPN Phase 2, and you now need to see the mechanisms that make it possible:

- Spokes are configured with mGRE interfaces.

- A routing table is populated with specific prefixes for remote spoke LANs.

- The next hop for those prefixes points to the specific remote spoke's tunnel IP address.

It is important to realize that all three of these points must be met in order for spoke-to-spoke tunnels to form in DMVPN Phase 2. If any of them is missing, spoke-to-spoke tunnels cannot form. Let's look first at a scenario where the spoke doesn't have an mGRE tunnel but all other points are fulfilled. Say that Houston and Miami have been configured with a standard point-to-point tunnel to the hub and all other configurations have been kept the same on the other routers. The following is Houston's resulting routing table:

```
Houston#show ip route eigrp | begin Gateway
Gateway of last resort is not set

      172.16.0.0/16 is variably subnetted, 4 subnets, 2 masks
D        172.16.10.0/24 [90/27008000] via 10.1.1.1, 00:00:12, Tunnel1
D        172.16.30.0/24 [90/28185600] via 10.1.1.3, 00:00:12, Tunnel1
```

No matter how many times a **traceroute** between the PCs is formed, traffic always goes through the hub (highlighted in red):

```
PC-2#traceroute 172.16.30.2


Type escape sequence to abort.
Tracing the route to 172.16.30.2
VRF info: (vrf in name/id, vrf out name/id)
  1 172.16.20.1 0 msec 5 msec 5 msec
  2 10.1.1.1 0 msec 5 msec 5 msec
  3 10.1.1.3 1 msec 5 msec 5 msec
  4 172.16.30.2 5 msec 0 msec 5 msec


PC-2#traceroute 172.16.30.2


Type escape sequence to abort.
Tracing the route to 172.16.30.2
VRF info: (vrf in name/id, vrf out name/id)
  1 172.16.20.1 0 msec 5 msec 5 msec
  2 10.1.1.1 5 msec 5 msec 5 msec
  3 10.1.1.3 5 msec 1 msec 5 msec
  4 172.16.30.2 1 msec 0 msec 5 msec


PC-2#traceroute 172.16.30.2


Type escape sequence to abort.
Tracing the route to 172.16.30.2
VRF info: (vrf in name/id, vrf out name/id)
  1 172.16.20.1 5 msec 5 msec 5 msec
  2 10.1.1.1 5 msec 0 msec 5 msec
  3 10.1.1.3 0 msec 1 msec 0 msec
  4 172.16.30.2 1 msec 1 msec 0 msec
```

The reason for this lies in the CEF adjacency table for the tunnel interface, shown below on Houston:

```
Houston#show ip cef 172.16.30.2 internal


172.16.30.0/24, epoch 0, RIB[I], refcount 5, per-destination sharing
  sources: RIB
  feature space:
   IPRM: 0x00028000
```

```
  ifnums:
   Tunnel1(23)
  path F527CE50, path list F42B873C, share 1/1, type attached nexthop,
for IPv4
  nexthop 10.1.1.3 Tunnel1, adjacency IP midchain out of Tunnel1
F27757F8
  output chain: IP midchain out of Tunnel1 F27757F8 IP adj out of
Ethernet0/0, address 22.2.2.1 F4EDE6A8

Houston#show adjacency tunnel1

Protocol Interface                Address
IP         Tunnel1                point2point(14)


Houston#show adjacency encapsulation | begin Tunnel1

IP         Tunnel1                point2point(14)
  Encap length 24
  4500000000000000FF2F97C916020202
  0B01010100000800
  Provider: TUNNEL
  Protocol header count in macstring: 2
    HDR 0: ipv4
      dst: static, 11.1.1.1
      src: static, 22.2.2.2
     prot: static, 47
      ttl: static, 255
       df: static, cleared
     per packet fields: tos ident tl chksm
    HDR 1: gre
      prot: static, 0x800
      per packet fields: none
```

Notice that the adjacency for all prefixes out the tunnel interface points to a point-2point adjacency. The point2point adjacency artificially fills in the NBMA address for Dallas as the outer header of the GRE/IP packet. With this configuration, there is no way for Houston to form a spoke-to-spoke tunnel because traffic routed out the tunnel will always go to Dallas, based on these CEF entries. This is why mGRE interfaces are required for spoke-to-spoke tunnels in DMVPN.

To prove the second requirement's importance, Houston and Miami are configured with mGRE interfaces again, but the routing protocol configuration on Dallas has been modified such that only a default route is sent to the spokes. The resulting routing table on Houston is as follows:

```
Houston#show ip route eigrp | begin Gateway

Gateway of last resort is 10.1.1.1 to network 0.0.0.0

D*    0.0.0.0/0 [90/27008000] via 10.1.1.1, 00:00:15, Tunnel1
```

Again, each **traceroute** proves that the hub is still being used at every point to transit traffic:

```
PC-2#traceroute 172.16.30.2

Type escape sequence to abort.
Tracing the route to 172.16.30.2
VRF info: (vrf in name/id, vrf out name/id)
  1 172.16.20.1 5 msec 5 msec 0 msec
  2 10.1.1.1 0 msec 5 msec 0 msec
  3 10.1.1.3 1 msec 3 msec 5 msec
  4 172.16.30.2 1 msec 0 msec 1 msec

PC-2#traceroute 172.16.30.2

Type escape sequence to abort.
Tracing the route to 172.16.30.2
VRF info: (vrf in name/id, vrf out name/id)
  1 172.16.20.1 6 msec 5 msec 5 msec
  2 10.1.1.1 5 msec 5 msec 5 msec
  3 10.1.1.3 0 msec 6 msec 5 msec
  4 172.16.30.2 0 msec 6 msec 2 msec

PC-2#traceroute 172.16.30.2

Type escape sequence to abort.
Tracing the route to 172.16.30.2
VRF info: (vrf in name/id, vrf out name/id)
  1 172.16.20.1 5 msec 4 msec 1 msec
  2 10.1.1.1 0 msec 6 msec 4 msec
  3 10.1.1.3 5 msec 5 msec 5 msec
  4 172.16.30.2 6 msec 4 msec 5 msec
```

The reason again is that the CEF adjacency entry for the default route points to Dallas as the next hop, which is not an incomplete entry. As a result, Houston sends traffic directly to the hub even though a better path can be established directly with Miami. This point highlights the fact that the CEF incomplete entry is what triggers the spoke-to-spoke tunnel formation in DMVPN Phase 2:

```
Houston#show ip cef 172.16.30.2 internal

0.0.0.0/0, epoch 0, flags default route, RIB[I], refcount 5,
per-destination sharing
  sources: RIB, DRH
  feature space:
   IPRM: 0x00028000
  ifnums:
   Tunnel1(23): 10.1.1.1
  path F42B8818, path list F42B99B4, share 1/1, type attached nexthop,
for IPv4
  nexthop 10.1.1.1 Tunnel1, adjacency IP midchain out of Tunnel1,
address 10.1.1.1 F27757F8
  output chain: IP midchain out of Tunnel1, address 10.1.1.1 F27757F8
IP adj out of Ethernet0/0, address 22.2.2.1 F4EDE6A8

Houston#show adjacency tunnel1

Protocol Interface              Address
IP       Tunnel1                10.1.1.1(11)


Houston#show adjacency tunnel1 encapsulation

Protocol Interface              Address
IP       Tunnel1                10.1.1.1(11)
  Encap length 24
  4500000000000000FF2F97C916020202
  0B01010100000800
  Provider: TUNNEL
  Protocol header count in macstring: 2
    HDR 0: ipv4
      dst: static, 11.1.1.1
      src: static, 22.2.2.2
     prot: static, 47
      ttl: static, 255
       df: static, cleared
```

```
per packet fields: tos ident tl chksm
  HDR 1: gre
    prot: static, 0x800
    per packet fields: none
```

To correct this, the hub needs to send specific prefixes for all networks that are reachable behind the spoke sites.

The final case outlines that the above is not the only requirement. Even with specific prefixes and mGRE interfaces, if the next hops do not point to the proper remote spokes, no spoke-to-spoke tunnel will be formed. To demonstrate, the routing protocol on Dallas has been configured to set Dallas itself as the next hop for all prefixes it advertises to the spokes. The resulting routing table on Houston is as follows:

```
Houston#show ip route eigrp | begin Gateway
Gateway of last resort is not set

      172.16.0.0/16 is variably subnetted, 4 subnets, 2 masks
D        172.16.10.0/24 [90/27008000] via 10.1.1.1, 00:00:12, Tunnel1
D        172.16.30.0/24 [90/28185600] via 10.1.1.1, 00:00:12, Tunnel1
```

Again, traceroutes from PC-2 to PC-3 all traverse the hub.

```
PC-2#traceroute 172.16.30.2

Type escape sequence to abort.
Tracing the route to 172.16.30.2
VRF info: (vrf in name/id, vrf out name/id)
  1 172.16.20.1 0 msec 6 msec 5 msec
  2 10.1.1.1 0 msec 5 msec 5 msec
  3 10.1.1.3 0 msec 6 msec 5 msec
  4 172.16.30.2 1 msec 0 msec 6 msec

PC-2#traceroute 172.16.30.2

Type escape sequence to abort.
Tracing the route to 172.16.30.2
VRF info: (vrf in name/id, vrf out name/id)
  1 172.16.20.1 5 msec 5 msec 5 msec
```

```
   2 10.1.1.1 1 msec 5 msec 5 msec
   3 10.1.1.3 0 msec 5 msec 5 msec
   4 172.16.30.2 1 msec 5 msec 5 msec

PC-2#traceroute 172.16.30.2

Type escape sequence to abort.
Tracing the route to 172.16.30.2
VRF info: (vrf in name/id, vrf out name/id)
   1 172.16.20.1 5 msec 5 msec 5 msec
   2 10.1.1.1 1 msec 5 msec 5 msec
   3 10.1.1.3 1 msec 5 msec 5 msec
   4 172.16.30.2 1 msec 1 msec 0 msec
```

Investigating the CEF tables for the destination reveals that the next hop being set to the hub forces Houston to use the hub's adjacency information for forwarding. The CEF entries do not lead to incomplete adjacencies, and spoke-to-spoke tunnels do not form:

```
Houston#show ip cef 172.16.30.2 internal

172.16.30.0/24, epoch 0, RIB[I], refcount 5, per-destination sharing
  sources: RIB
  feature space:
   IPRM: 0x00028000
  ifnums:
   Tunnel1(23): 10.1.1.1
  path F42B87A8, path list F42B99B4, share 1/1, type attached nexthop,
for IPv4
  nexthop 10.1.1.1 Tunnel1, adjacency IP midchain out of Tunnel1,
address 10.1.1.1 F27757F8
  output chain: IP midchain out of Tunnel1, address 10.1.1.1 F27757F8
IP adj out of Ethernet0/0, address 22.2.2.1 F4EDE6A8


Houston#show adjacency tunnel1

Protocol Interface           Address
IP       Tunnel1             10.1.1.1(12)


Houston#show adjacency tunnel1 encapsulation

Protocol Interface           Address
IP       Tunnel1             10.1.1.1(12)
```

```
Encap length 24
4500000000000000FF2F97C916020202
0B01010100000800
Provider: TUNNEL
Protocol header count in macstring: 2
  HDR 0: ipv4
     dst: static, 11.1.1.1
     src: static, 22.2.2.2
    prot: static, 47
     ttl: static, 255
      df: static, cleared
    per packet fields: tos ident tl chksm
  HDR 1: gre
     prot: static, 0x800
    per packet fields: none
```

The results of these requirements carry heavy ramifications on DMVPN Phase 2's spoke-to-spoke mechanics. Specifically, the requirement where the spokes need to have complete routing information for all networks behind remote spokes eliminates the routing table efficiencies gained in DMVPN Phase 1. No longer can the hub send a simple default route down to the spokes. Thus, routing table optimization is traded in favor of data plane optimization.

DMVPN Phase 2 requires mGRE interfaces and specific routes for all spoke networks, and each of those routes should point to the owning spoke. All of this needs to exist in the spoke routing table in order to trigger spoke-to-spoke tunnels. These requirements severely limit the scalability of DMVPN as the number of spoke sites grows. The limiting factor then becomes a combination of the memory on each spoke router dedicated to storing additional routes and CEF entries and the routing protocol processing overhead on the hub router. Luckily, there is an optimization for that: DMVPN Phase 3.

## Phase 3: Hub-Initiated Spoke-to-Spoke Tunnels

DMVPN Phase 3 was engineered to solve the deficiencies of Phase 2. Phase 2 requires specific prefixes on each spoke router in order to properly trigger NHRP resolution for spoke-to-spoke tunnels. With such a configuration, spoke routing tables may contain routes to prefixes the spoke may never use but that they must have just in case a spoke-to-spoke tunnel needs to be formed. Phase 2 also eliminates summarization from the hub to the spokes, although summarization can still be performed from the spokes to the hub.

Without summarization from hub to spoke, the routing protocol overhead on the hub itself increases based on the number of routes each spoke advertises to it.

DMVPN Phase 3 takes a different approach to triggering spoke-to-spoke tunnels. Rather than having the spokes make the determination, Phase 3 DMVPN shifts this responsibility to the hub router. The logic here is that because the first packet is always routed to the hub in the first place, why not have the hub signal the NHRP resolution process itself?

**Note**   There is no official documentation to support the logic presented above. The lab authors assume this conversation was had at some point by Cisco developers.

This feature was introduced with the **NHRP shortcut switching enhancements**. The basic idea is that, by using NHRP messaging, the hub can signal to the spokes whenever the potential for a spoke-to-spoke tunnel exists for specific networks. After the spokes complete the resolution process for a remote spoke, NHRP running on the spoke amends the routing table with special **NHRP shortcut** or **override routes**. These routes lead to the proper CEF entries required to force the spoke to continue to use the established spoke-to-spoke tunnel for subsequent packets sent to that specific network.

Whenever the hub forwards a packet out of the same DMVPN tunnel interface the packet was received on (an indication of a hair pinning the traffic), it sends what is known as an **NHRP traffic indication** message. This process mimics the logic used by the router when it transits traffic it receives on an Ethernet interface out the same Ethernet interface. The difference is that it sends an ICMP redirect message instead.

The NHRP traffic indication message is sent out the hub's tunnel interface toward the source of the hairpinned packet, which ends up at the originating spoke based on the hub's own routing table. The NHRP packet contains the header information from the offending packet, which provides the spoke with the information it needs to send an NHRP resolution request.

It is important to note that the spoke does not send a resolution request for the next-hop address contained in its routing table as in DMVPN Phase 2. The act of receiving an NHRP traffic indication message from the hub signals to the spoke that there is a better next-hop other than the one it is currently using to reach the destination. The spoke doesn't know the address of this "better" next hop. It only knows that the better next hop exists and that it should try to find out what the address is. Thus, instead of resolving a next hop address, the spoke sends a resolution request for the destination network, asking for the mapping information for the device that has the best path to reach that destination.

To see this in action, a traceroute is initiated from PC-2 to PC-3 with Phase 3 enhancements enabled on the DMVPN. The topology was reconfigured using the Phase 1 configuration before the modifications were made to convert the topology to Phase 2. Dallas sends a default route down to the spokes.

```
PC-2#traceroute 172.16.30.2


Type escape sequence to abort.
Tracing the route to 172.16.30.2
VRF info: (vrf in name/id, vrf out name/id)
  1 172.16.20.1 0 msec 5 msec 5 msec
  2 10.1.1.1 0 msec 5 msec 5 msec ! Dallas
  3 10.1.1.3 6 msec 1 msec 0 msec
  4 172.16.30.2 1 msec 5 msec 6 msec
```

The process works as follows:

1. Dallas receives a packet from Houston on its DMVPN tunnel interface. It removes the outer GRE/IP header and examines the inner IP packet.

2. Dallas determines that the packet is destined to another spoke router, the Miami router.

3. Dallas encapsulates the packet appropriately and forwards it out the same DMVPN tunnel interface toward Miami.

4. Realizing that it has sent traffic out the same interface on which it was received (hairpinning the traffic), Dallas sends an NHRP traffic indication message to the source IP address of the offending packet.

```
NHRP: Send Traffic Indication via Tunnel1 vrf 0, packet size: 84
  src: 10.1.1.1, dst: 172.16.20.2
  (F) afn: AF_IP(1), type: IP(800), hop: 255, ver: 1
      shtl: 4(NSAP), sstl: 0(NSAP)
      pktsz: 84 extoff: 68
  (M) traffic code: redirect(0)
      src NBMA: 11.1.1.1
      src protocol: 10.1.1.1, dst protocol: 172.16.20.2
      Contents of nhrp traffic indication packet:
          45 00 00 1C 00 B5 00 00 01 11 2E F8 AC 10 14 02
          AC 10 1E 02 C0 B5 82 A0 00 08 32
```

5. The Houston router receives the traffic indication message and sends an NHRP resolution request to Dallas for the original destination network.

**On Houston:**

```
NHRP: Receive Traffic Indication via Tunnel1 vrf 0, packet size: 84
  (F) afn: AF_IP(1), type: IP(800), hop: 255, ver: 1
      shtl: 4(NSAP), sstl: 0(NSAP)
      pktsz: 84 extoff: 68
  (M) traffic code: redirect(0)
      src NBMA: 11.1.1.1
      src protocol: 10.1.1.1, dst protocol: 172.16.20.2
      Contents of nhrp traffic indication packet:
          45 00 00 1C 00 B5 00 00 01 11 2E F8 AC 10 14 02
          AC 10 1E 02 C0 B5 82 A0 00 08 32

NHRP: Send Resolution Request via Tunnel1 vrf 0, packet size: 72
  src: 10.1.1.2, dst: 172.16.30.2
  (F) afn: AF_IP(1), type: IP(800), hop: 255, ver: 1
      shtl: 4(NSAP), sstl: 0(NSAP)
      pktsz: 72 extoff: 52
  (M) flags: "router auth src-stable nat ", reqid: 6
      src NBMA: 22.2.2.2
      src protocol: 10.1.1.2, dst protocol: 172.16.30.2
  (C-1) code: no error(0)
        prefix: 32, mtu: 17916, hd_time: 7200
        addr_len: 0(NSAP), subaddr_len: 0(NSAP), proto_len: 0, pref: 0
```

6. Dallas receives the resolution request. It looks at the "dst protocol" field. The field lists the 172.16.30.2 address as destination. Dallas performs a routing table lookup for this destination address and forwards the resolution request to Miami. Miami replies directly to Houston with the proper mapping information.

**On Dallas:**

```
NHRP: Receive Resolution Request via Tunnel1 vrf 0, packet size: 72
  (F) afn: AF_IP(1), type: IP(800), hop: 255, ver: 1
      shtl: 4(NSAP), sstl: 0(NSAP)
      pktsz: 72 extoff: 52
  (M) flags: "router auth src-stable nat ", reqid: 6

 NHRP: Forwarding Resolution Request via Tunnel1 vrf 0, packet size:
92
  src: 10.1.1.1, dst: 172.16.30.2
  (F) afn: AF_IP(1), type: IP(800), hop: 254, ver: 1
```

```
       shtl: 4(NSAP), sstl: 0(NSAP)
       pktsz: 92 extoff: 52
  (M) flags: "router auth src-stable nat ", reqid: 6
```

## On Miami:

```
NHRP: Receive Resolution Request via Tunnel1 vrf 0, packet size: 92
  (F) afn: AF_IP(1), type: IP(800), hop: 254, ver: 1
       shtl: 4(NSAP), sstl: 0(NSAP)
       pktsz: 92 extoff: 52
  (M) flags: "router auth src-stable nat ", reqid: 6

NHRP: Send Resolution Reply via Tunnel1 vrf 0, packet size: 120
   src: 10.1.1.3, dst: 10.1.1.2
  (F) afn: AF_IP(1), type: IP(800), hop: 255, ver: 1
       shtl: 4(NSAP), sstl: 0(NSAP)
       pktsz: 120 extoff: 60
  (M) flags: "router auth dst-stable unique src-stable nat ", reqid: 6
       src NBMA: 22.2.2.2
       src protocol: 10.1.1.2, dst protocol: 172.16.30.2
  (C-1) code: no error(0)
        prefix: 24, mtu: 17916, hd_time: 7200
        addr_len: 4(NSAP), subaddr_len: 0(NSAP), proto_len: 4, pref: 0
        client NBMA: 33.3.3.3
        client protocol: 10.1.1.3
```

## On Houston:

```
Houston#show ip nhrp

10.1.1.1/32 via 10.1.1.1
   Tunnel1 created 00:35:34, never expire
   Type: static, Flags: used
   NBMA address: 11.1.1.1
--- omitted ---
172.16.30.0/24 via 10.1.1.3
   Tunnel1 created 00:11:18, expire 01:48:41
   Type: dynamic, Flags: router rib
   NBMA address: 33.3.3.3
```

**7.** Houston installs an NHRP shortcut route in its routing table, pointing to the new network.

```
Houston#show ip route nhrp | begin Gateway
Gateway of last resort is 10.1.1.1 to network 0.0.0.0

      10.0.0.0/8 is variably subnetted, 3 subnets, 2 masks
H         10.1.1.3/32 is directly connected, 00:13:11, Tunnel1
      172.16.0.0/16 is variably subnetted, 3 subnets, 2 masks
H         172.16.30.0/24 [250/1] via 10.1.1.3, 00:13:11, Tunnel1
```

**8.** Subsequent traceroutes from PC-2 to PC-3 are now routed directly between the spoke sites.

```
PC-2#traceroute 172.16.30.2

Type escape sequence to abort.
Tracing the route to 172.16.30.2
VRF info: (vrf in name/id, vrf out name/id)
  1 172.16.20.1 5 msec 5 msec 5 msec
  2 10.1.1.3 5 msec 0 msec 5 msec !Miami
  3 172.16.30.2 0 msec 6 msec 0 msec
```

This process completely prevents the need for Houston and Miami to have complete routing information to form spoke-to-spoke tunnels. It also offloads the configuration complexity from the routing protocol (requiring specific prefixes and preserving the original next hops for those prefixes) to NHRP, which is already in charge of mapping information for the DMVPN network. By providing the specific routing information at step 7, NHRP acts as a routing source—just as an IGP would.

The end result is that certain routing protocol features, such as split horizon and next-hop-self, no longer have to be disabled when implementing DMVPN Phase 3. The DMVPN hub routers can send default routes to all of their spokes and redirect them as necessary to form spoke-to-spoke tunnels.

## Shortcut or Override

In the example above, NHRP was used to solve the incomplete routing information problem. The ultimate goal for NHRP is to make it such that the CEF table entries no longer point to the hub as the next hop for the redirected traffic but rather point to the newly received mapping information for the remote spoke. The reason is that local forwarding decisions are driven by the CEF table and not the IP routing table on Cisco IOS routers. NHRP can solve this in one of two ways:

- Add prefixes to the routing table

- Amend prefixes that already exist in the routing table

With the first option, NHRP simply adds the specific prefix as a routing table entry in the routing table, complete with the proper next hop information. Doing so forces CEF to download the new entry into the FIB and generate new adjacency information. Packets are now forwarded based on this new routing information. This is the approach taken in the example above. Houston installs an NHRP route (signified by the H in the routing table output) for the 172.16.30.0/24 network, pointing to Miami as the next hop.

This first method works well if a specific prefix does not exist for a particular destination, but what if, for some reason, there already exists such a prefix? This scenario can present itself in situations where the routing protocol does not provide adequate means of summarizing or preserving the right next hop information.

In such a case, NHRP takes a different approach. Instead of adding a route to the routing table, it simply overrides the existing routing table entry. An example can help clarify the point. Here the routing protocol EIGRP running on the DMVPN network has been configured to send specific prefixes without proper next hops. Houston's routing table results in the following:

```
Houston#show ip route eigrp | begin Gateway
Gateway of last resort is not set

      172.16.0.0/16 is variably subnetted, 4 subnets, 2 masks
D        172.16.10.0/24 [90/27008000] via 10.1.1.1, 00:01:15, Tunnel1
D        172.16.30.0/24 [90/28185600] via 10.1.1.1, 00:01:02, Tunnel1
```

When PC-2 pings PC-3, the process outlined previously takes place. Originally Houston installed the NHRP route for 172.16.30.0/24 because such a route did not previously exist. In this case, Houston already has such a route, so NHRP overrides the existing next hop and replaces it with 10.1.1.3. This modification is indicated with the % sign in the routing table:

```
Houston#show ip route eigrp | begin Gateway
Gateway of last resort is not set

      172.16.0.0/16 is variably subnetted, 4 subnets, 2 masks
D        172.16.10.0/24 [90/27008000] via 10.1.1.1, 00:03:55, Tunnel1
D    %   172.16.30.0/24 [90/28185600] via 10.1.1.1, 00:03:42, Tunnel1
```

The overridden next hop information can be seen in the routing table in the output of the **show ip route next-hop-override** command and also in the CEF table in the output of the **show ip cef** command:

```
Houston#show ip route next-hop-override | include D|NHO


        D - EIGRP, EX - EIGRP external, O - OSPF, IA - OSPF inter area
        o - ODR, P - periodic downloaded static route, H - NHRP, l -
LISP
D         172.16.10.0/24 [90/27008000] via 10.1.1.1, 00:06:51, Tunnel1
D    %    172.16.30.0/24 [90/28185600] via 10.1.1.1, 00:06:38, Tunnel1
                          [NHO] [90/1] via 10.1.1.3, 00:03:20, Tunnel1

Houston#show ip cef 172.16.30.0

172.16.30.0/24
  nexthop 10.1.1.3 Tunnel1
```

Both methods lead to the same results: Houston follows the spoke-to-spoke route to reach the remote spoke destination 172.16.30.0/24.

# Conclusion

This introduction has served to describe the basics of DMVPN operation, including the motivation behind deploying DMVPN, DMVPN operation, DMVPN basic configuration, and DMVPN mechanics of spoke-to-spoke tunnels across the DMVPN phases. The concepts introduced in this section lay the groundwork for building basic DMVPN solutions.

Once the introductory concepts are understood, they can be applied to create various DMVPN implementations. The designs typically depend on the level of redundancy required for the implementation. There are two pieces of redundancy that can be employed: hub redundancy or transport redundancy.

Hub redundancy is achieved by deploying multiple DMVPN hubs in a single DMVPN cloud. Each spoke registers with each hub over the same or multiple tunnel interfaces. If one hub fails, the second hub can still direct NHRP resolution for the DMVPN.

Transport redundancy is achieved by deploying multiple DMVPN clouds. Each cloud should correspond to a separate transport, forming two separate overlay networks. The routing protocol used across the overlay can help you determine which cloud is used to transit traffic between DMVPN routers.

Hub and transport redundancy options can be combined into many hybrid DMVPN designs. The design introduced in this section is called a single-hub, single-cloud DMVPN design. There is no redundancy for the hub or DMVPN tunnel interfaces in such a design. If the hub goes down, spokes will no longer be able to resolve new spoke destinations. Also, if the single underlay transport connecting the DMVPN routers fails, the DMVPN also cannot function.

To better demonstrate the different routing protocol options and DMVPN designs, the next section begins the guided lab portion of this chapter. Four DMVPN designs are introduced in the following lab, along with routing protocol configuration specifics for OSPF, EIGRP, and BGP through all phases. Each section begins with network design goals for the implementation and rationale for each design goal. With only a few exceptions, the lab focuses on overlay connectivity. It is assumed that the underlay has already been configured properly to allow all routers to communicate with each other.

## Lab 1: Single Hub, Single Cloud

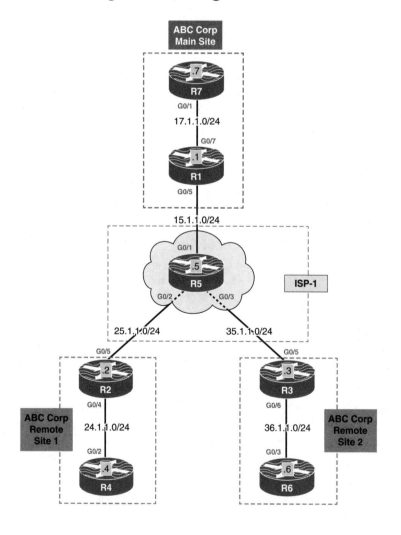

## This lab should be conducted on the Enterprise Rack.

## Lab Setup:

If you are using EVE-NG, and you have imported the EVE-NG topology from the **EVE-NG-Topology** folder, ignore the following and use **Lab-1-Single Hub Single Cloud** in the **DMVPN** folder in EVE-NG.

To copy and paste the initial configurations, go to the **Initial-config** folder → **DMVPN** folder → **Lab-1.**

## Implement Phase 1

## Design Goal

ABC Corp has expanded into two remote sites and needs connectivity between individual hosts at each site. In order to reduce cost, ABC Corp has decided against private WAN connectivity. The network engineers at ABC Corp have decided to leverage the Internet connection to ISP-1 at each site as the underlay for the VPN between the main site and remote sites.

Following are the detailed requirements:

- R4 and R6 should be able to communicate with R7, located at the main campus.

- R4 and R6 should be able to communicate with each other via R1.

- Routing tables should contain the minimal amount of information required to perform routing between sites.

---

### DMVPN Tunnel Configuration

The design goals outline basic connectivity requirements for the VPN. They specify that the main site should have direct connectivity with the remote sites. Any remote-site-to-remote-site traffic should first traverse the main site. These requirements fit perfectly into a Phase 1 DMVPN design. In the design, the main site router, R1, is the DMVPN hub and NHRP NHS. The remote site routers R2 and R3 are the DMVPN spoke routers and NHRP NHCs.

To implement this design, first create an mGRE tunnel on the hub R1. The configuration for this is simple. **interface tunnel 100** creates the logical interface tunnel 100. **ip address 100.1.1.1 255.255.255.0** assigns an IP address to the tunnel 100 interface. **tunnel source 15.1.1.1** specifies the source of the GRE header. **tunnel mode gre multipoint** configures an mGRE tunnel interface on R1 to allow it to connect to both the spokes R2 and R3 over the same tunnel interface.

**On R1:**

```
R1(config)#interface tunnel 100
R1(config-if)#ip address 100.1.1.1 255.255.255.0
R1(config-if)#tunnel source 15.1.1.1
R1(config-if)#tunnel mode gre multipoint
```

With the mGRE tunnel configured, the next step is to configure NHRP to run on the mGRE tunnel interface to glue together the DMVPN. There are two main commands that will be issued on the hub. The first command enables NHRP operation on the mGRE interface, and the second sets up pseudo-multicast to support dynamic routing protocols.

First, **ip nhrp network-id 100** is configured on the mGRE tunnel interface. This command enables NHRP on tunnel 100 on R1 and is locally significant. The command takes in a numerical value that defines an NHRP domain and can be used to differentiate between multiple NHRP domains. This value is only locally significant to the router, meaning it is not transmitted in the NHRP packets exchanged between nodes in the same domain. Therefore, it is not mandatory to use the same network ID on all the members of the same NHRP domain.

In cases where there are multiple NHRP domains on a router, matching NHRP network IDs between the members makes it easy to keep track of which NHRP networks have GRE interfaces configured.

The final NHRP-related command configured on the hub is **ip nhrp map multicast dynamic**. This command configures the hub to automatically add spoke NBMA addresses to the NHRP multicast table whenever a spoke registers. This command is essential to support dynamic routing protocols such as OSPF and EIGRP.

**Note**   The **ip nhrp map multicast dynamic** command and the static version of the same command are not necessary for BGP. BGP does not use multicast to establish peering relationship; rather, it uses explicit unicast communication over peering unicast IP addresses.

**On R1:**

```
R1(config)#interface tunnel 100
R1(config-if)#ip nhrp network-id 100
R1(config-if)#ip nhrp map multicast dynamic
```

With the **ip nhrp network-id** command configured, the hub can now generate NHRP messages.

The next step is to configure R2 and R3 as spoke routers. The configuration commands are similar to that of the hub, with one minor tweak. Unlike hub routers, DMVPN spoke routers do not enable multipoint GRE using the **tunnel mode gre multipoint** command for Phase 1 operation, as the design indicates. Instead, simple point-to-point tunnels are enough for strict Phase 1 operation.

Phase 1 operation does not permit a spoke-to-spoke tunnel, which would require the mGRE tunnel. Without any spoke-to-spoke tunnel, spoke R2 will form only a single spoke-to-spoke tunnel with the hub. Therefore, R2 is configured with the **tunnel destination 15.1.1.1** command:

### On R2:

```
R2(config)#interface tunnel 100
R2(config-if)#ip address 100.1.1.2 255.255.255.0
R2(config-if)#tunnel source 25.1.1.2
R2(config-if)#tunnel destination 15.1.1.1
```

Just as with the hub, after completing the base GRE configuration, NHRP should be enabled on the spokes as well. Much as with the hub, **ip nhrp network-id 100** enables NHRP on the R2's tunnel interface. The **ip nhrp nhs 100.1.1.1** command is then issued to provide R2 with the address of the next hop server, R1. There is no need to configure **ip nhrp map multicast** commands on the spokes. Because the spokes are configured with static point-to-point tunnels, multicast traffic can be routed properly without maintaining NHRP multicast entries.

### On R2:

```
R2(config)#interface tunnel 100
R2(config-if)#ip nhrp network-id 100
R2(config-if)#ip nhrp nhs 100.1.1.1
```

When you issue the **ip nhrp nhs 100.1.1.1** command on the spoke R2, R2 registers with the hub R1.

Much like the above, the following configures a point-to-point GRE tunnel on R3 with the necessary NHRP-related commands to allow it to dynamically register with the hub R1:

**On R3:**

```
R3(config)#interface tunnel 100
R3(config-if)#ip address 100.1.1.3 255.255.255.0
R3(config-if)#ip nhrp network-id 100
R3(config-if)#ip nhrp nhs 100.1.1.1
R3(config-if)#tunnel source 35.1.1.3
R3(config-if)#tunnel destination 15.1.1.1
```

The **show dmvpn** output on R1 confirms that R1 has dynamically (as indicated with a D attribute) learned the NBMA-to-tunnel IP mapping of spokes R2 and R3:

```
R1#show dmvpn | begin Peer
Type:Hub, NHRP Peers:2,

 # Ent  Peer NBMA Addr Peer Tunnel Add State  UpDn Tm Attrb
 ----- --------------- --------------- ----- -------- -----
     1 25.1.1.2                100.1.1.2    UP 00:05:07    D !SPOKE R2
     1 35.1.1.3                100.1.1.3    UP 00:02:41    D !SPOKE R3
```

At this point, a **traceroute** to the tunnel IP addresses in the DMVPN verifies reachability.

The following **traceroute** output confirms reachability between the spokes R2 and R3 to the hub R1:

**On R2:**

```
R2#traceroute 100.1.1.1 probe 1
Type escape sequence to abort.
Tracing the route to 100.1.1.1
VRF info: (vrf in name/id, vrf out name/id)
  1 100.1.1.1 15 msec
```

**On R3:**

```
R2#traceroute 100.1.1.1 probe 1
Type escape sequence to abort.
Tracing the route to 100.1.1.1
VRF info: (vrf in name/id, vrf out name/id)
  1 100.1.1.1 17 msec
```

Similarly, a **traceroute** from R2 to R3 traverses the hub, confirming Phase 1 operation:

**On R2:**

```
R2#traceroute 100.1.1.3 probe 1
Type escape sequence to abort.
Tracing the route to 100.1.1.3
VRF info: (vrf in name/id, vrf out name/id)
  1 100.1.1.1 45 msec
  2 100.1.1.3 10 msec
```

With DMVPN Phase 1 successfully set up between R1, R2, and R3, the next part of the task involves advertising the host networks at each site into an overlay protocol. The following section demonstrates the configuration and implementation of OSPF, EIGRP, and BGP as overlay protocols.

As mentioned in the introduction section, when implementing DMVPN Phase 1, the routing is important only to pull the VPN traffic through the tunnel. Because of the limitations of the point-to-point GRE tunnel on the spoke routers, traffic will always be pulled toward the hub, regardless of what the routing table entries reveal. Spoke routers will not resolve spoke-to-spoke tunnels even if next hops are preserved when advertised from the hub router.

## Implement OSPF

When implementing DMVPN with OSPF as the overlay routing protocol, an engineer needs to be wary of how the different OSPF network types influence the resulting routing table on each OSPF router.

OSPF's network types do not technically play a role in determining the routing in the DMVPN network for Phase 1. Each of the network types can be used to provide the appropriate communication. Also, a main characteristic of DMVPN Phase 1 is the hub and spoke capability only, meaning all traffic destined from a spoke to another spoke always traverses the hub. Because of this, no special consideration needs to be made for preservation of next hops. OSPF network types are categorized as:

- Broadcast

- Point-to-point

- Point-to-multipoint

- Non-broadcast (NBMA)

- Point-to-multipoint, non-broadcast

Any of the OSPF network types can be used to provide the routing in a Phase 1 DMVPN implementation. All non-broadcast network types will be ignored. Their requirement of static neighbor communication does not fit well with the DMVPN design philosophy. Hence, only the broadcast, point-to-point, and point-to-multipoint network types will be implemented in this lab.

### Broadcast Network Type

Before beginning the broadcast network type configuration, two main points need to be addressed:

- Broadcast network type preserves the next hop IP address.

- Broadcast network type elects a DR/BDR.

The broadcast network type preserves the next hop IP address when OSPF adds routes to the routing table. In the topology diagram at the beginning of this lab, this means when R3 advertises 36.1.1.0/24 to the hub R1, R1 retains the actual next hop IP address 100.1.1.3 when advertising the route to the spoke R2 and vice versa. As a result, the network 36.1.1.0/24 is associated with the next hop IP address 100.1.1.3 on R2.

However, in Phase 1 DMVPN with point-to-point GRE tunnels, this does not force a spoke-to-spoke NHRP resolution to occur and hence does not present any problem. What should be considered, though, is the placement of the OSPF DR in the DMVPN.

Spokes only form OSPF adjacencies with the hub and therefore can only become fully adjacent with the hub router. On a broadcast network, routers only become fully adjacent with the DR on the segment. If the hub is not chosen as the DR on the segment, then the spoke routers will be unable to solve the SPF tree. Thus, for a correct design, the hub R1 should be configured as the OSPF DR, and the spoke routers R2 and R3 should be made ineligible to become either DR or BDR. This can be achieved by setting the OSPF priority to 0 on the spokes R2 and R3.

The following configuration establishes OSPF adjacencies between R1 and R2 and between R1 and R3. The default OSPF network type point-to-point on the tunnel is changed to broadcast network type with the **ip ospf network broadcast** command on the tunnel 100 interface. The tunnel interfaces are then assigned to the OSPF process 100 to run in Area 0. Finally, R2 and R3 have their OSPF priorities set to 0, using the **ip ospf priority 0** command on their tunnel interfaces.

---

**On R1:**

```
R1(config)#interface tunnel 100
R1(config-if)#ip ospf network broadcast
R1(config-if)#ip ospf 100 area 0
```

## On R2:

```
R2(config)#interface tunnel 100
R2(config-if)#ip ospf network broadcast
R2(config-if)#ip ospf priority 0
R2(config-if)#ip ospf 100 area 0
```

You should see the following console message:

```
%OSPF-5-ADJCHG: Process 100, Nbr 100.1.1.1 on Tunnel100 from LOADING
to FULL, Loading Done
```

## On R3:

```
R3(config)#interface tunnel 100
R3(config-if)#ip ospf network broadcast
R3(config-if)#ip ospf priority 0
R3(config-if)#ip ospf 100 area 0
```

You should see the following console message:

```
%OSPF-5-ADJCHG: Process 100, Nbr 100.1.1.1 on Tunnel100 from LOADING
to FULL, Loading Done
```

The **show ip ospf neighbor detail** command output on R1 now confirms the OSPF adjacencies between R1 and R2 and R1 and R3, along with certain other key details. Notice how the output indicates that the neighbor priority value is 0, and the DR is 100.1.1.1.

## On R1:

```
R1#show ip ospf neighbor detail

 Neighbor 100.1.1.2, interface address 100.1.1.2
    In the area 0 via interface Tunnel100
    Neighbor priority is 0, State is FULL, 6 state changes
    DR is 100.1.1.1 BDR is 0.0.0.0
    Options is 0x12 in Hello (E-bit, L-bit)
    Options is 0x52 in DBD (E-bit, L-bit, O-bit)
    LLS Options is 0x1 (LR)
    Dead timer due in 00:00:31
    Neighbor is up for 00:04:27
    Index 1/1/1, retransmission queue length 0, number of
retransmission 3
```

```
    First 0x0(0)/0x0(0)/0x0(0) Next 0x0(0)/0x0(0)/0x0(0)
    Last retransmission scan length is 1, maximum is 1
    Last retransmission scan time is 0 msec, maximum is 0 msec
Neighbor 100.1.1.3, interface address 100.1.1.3
    In the area 0 via interface Tunnel100
    Neighbor priority is 0, State is FULL, 6 state changes
    DR is 100.1.1.1 BDR is 0.0.0.0
    Options is 0x12 in Hello (E-bit, L-bit)
    Options is 0x52 in DBD (E-bit, L-bit, O-bit)
    LLS Options is 0x1 (LR)
    Dead timer due in 00:00:39
    Neighbor is up for 00:02:03
    Index 2/2/2, retransmission queue length 0, number of
retransmission 0
    First 0x0(0)/0x0(0)/0x0(0) Next 0x0(0)/0x0(0)/0x0(0)
    Last retransmission scan length is 0, maximum is 0
    Last retransmission scan time is 0 msec, maximum is 0 msec
```

The next step is to advertise the host networks at the main campus and remote sites into OSPF process 100 for area 0. To do so, simply enable OSPF process 100 for area 0 on the respective VLAN interfaces on R1, R2, and R3. These VLANs are connected to end hosts; therefore, other OSPF-speaking routers are not expected to be connected to those LANs. Accidental OSPF adjacencies can be prevented from forming on these interfaces by making them passive using the **passive-interface** command in OSPF configuration mode:

## On R1:

```
R1(config)#interface g0/7
R1(config-if)#ip ospf 100 area 0

R1(config-if)#router ospf 100
R1(config-router)#passive-interface g0/5
```

## On R2:

```
R2(config)#interface g0/4
R2(config-if)#ip ospf 100 area 0

R2(config-if)#router ospf 100
R2(config-router)#passive-interface g0/5
```

## On R3:

```
R3(config)#interface g0/6
R3(config-if)#ip ospf 100 area 0

R3(config-if)#router ospf 100
R3(config-router)#passive-interface g0/5
```

With the above configurations complete, the **show ip route ospf** command at each site shows that the routers have installed OSPF routes for host networks at the remote sites:

## On R1:

```
R1#show ip route ospf | begin Gate
Gateway of last resort is not set

      24.0.0.0/24 is subnetted, 1 subnets
O        24.1.1.0 [110/1001] via 100.1.1.2, 01:12:00, Tunnel100
      36.0.0.0/24 is subnetted, 1 subnets
O        36.1.1.0 [110/1001] via 100.1.1.3, 01:10:30, Tunnel100
```

## On R2:

```
R2#show ip route ospf | begin Gate
Gateway of last resort is not set

      17.0.0.0/24 is subnetted, 1 subnets
O        17.1.1.0 [110/1001] via 100.1.1.1, 01:14:34, Tunnel100
      36.0.0.0/24 is subnetted, 1 subnets
O        36.1.1.0 [110/1001] via 100.1.1.3, 01:11:25, Tunnel100
```

## On R3:

```
R3#show ip route ospf | begin Gate
Gateway of last resort is not set

      17.0.0.0/24 is subnetted, 1 subnets
O        17.1.1.0 [110/1001] via 100.1.1.1, 01:15:24, Tunnel100
      24.0.0.0/24 is subnetted, 1 subnets
O        24.1.1.0 [110/1001] via 100.1.1.2, 01:14:21, Tunnel100
```

As mentioned earlier, the next hop on R2 for R3's host network 36.1.1.0/24 is R3's tunnel IP address 100.1.1.3. Similarly, the next hop on R3 for R2's host network is R2's tunnel IP address 100.1.1.2. The same can be confirmed with the **show ip cef** output on R2 and R3, as shown below:

```
R2#show ip cef 36.1.1.0

36.1.1.0/24
  nexthop 100.1.1.3 Tunnel100

R3#show ip cef 24.1.1.0

24.1.1.0/24
  nexthop 100.1.1.2 Tunnel100
```

Next a **traceroute** is performed from R4 to R7 at the main site and from R4 to R6 at the remote site 2. As evidenced below, the traffic always traverses the hub router, as should occur in Phase 1 DMVPN:

### On R4:

```
R4#traceroute 17.1.1.7 probe 1

Type escape sequence to abort.
Tracing the route to 17.1.1.7
VRF info: (vrf in name/id, vrf out name/id)
  1 24.1.1.2 13 msec
  2 100.1.1.1 9 msec
  3 17.1.1.7 12 msec


R4#traceroute 36.1.1.6 probe 1

Type escape sequence to abort.
Tracing the route to 36.1.1.6
VRF info: (vrf in name/id, vrf out name/id)
  1 24.1.1.2 9 msec
  2 100.1.1.1 11 msec
  3 100.1.1.3 42 msec
  4 36.1.1.6 12 msec
```

## Point-to-Point and Point-to-Multipoint Network Types

The following points should be addressed when configuring the point-to-point network type for DMVPN:

- Next-hop IP addresses are not preserved.

- Point-to-point network type does not allow multiple neighbors on a single interface.

- Point-to-point and point-to-multipoint use different hello interval timers.

Unlike with the broadcast network type, point-to-point and point-to-multipoint network types do not preserve the next hop IP addresses of the spokes. Refer to the topology diagram at the beginning of this lab once again. The next hop IP address for the 36.1.1.0/24 network on R2 will be R1's tunnel IP address 100.1.1.1.

OSPF's point-to-point network type does not allow multiple neighbors on the tunnel interface. So this network type can be used on the spokes as R2 and R3 only form OSPF adjacencies with the hub R1 and not with each other. The hub R1, on the other hand, is required to form multiple OSPF adjacencies—one each with R2 and R3. As such, the point-to-multipoint network type should be configured on R1's tunnel 100 interface.

A slight tweak related to the hello interval is required when combining point-to-point and point-to-multipoint on the same overlay OSPF domain. The default hello and dead intervals differ on these network types, and OSPF requires that these timers match on all nodes. The point-to-multipoint hello timer is 30 seconds by default, whereas the point-to-point hello timer is 10 seconds by default. So, a key configuration change to keep in mind when combining point-to-point and point-to-multipoint network types is ensuring that the hello parameters match. It is easiest to change the hello timer on R1 to match the spokes R2 and R3, since it only requires one configuration command on the hub router.

At the main campus, R1 is configured to run its tunnel 100 interface as point-to-multipoint with the **ip ospf network point-to-multipoint** command. The tunnel is then assigned to OSPF process 100 to run in Area 0. In addition, 17.1.1.0/24, the link that connects R1 to R7, is already advertised into OSPF, and the interface is declared passive.

---

**On R1:**

```
R1(config)#interface tunnel 100
R1(config-if)#ip ospf network point-to-multipoint
```

**To verify the configuration:**

```
R1#show ip ospf interface tunnel 100 | include Network|Timer
```

```
    Process ID 100, Router ID 100.1.1.1, Network Type POINT_TO_
MULTIPOINT, Cost: 1000
    Timer intervals configured, Hello 30, Dead 120, Wait 120, Retransmit 5
```

Note in the **show ip ospf interface tunnel 100** output above that the hello interval is set to 30 seconds, which is the default for point-to-multipoint network type. This timer is changed to match the hello interval of 10 seconds, which is the default on the spokes' point-to-point interface with the **ip ospf hello-interval** command. Modifying the hello interval time automatically resets the dead interval to four times the hello interval timer:

## On R1:

```
R1(config)#interface tunnel 100
R1(config-if)#ip ospf hello-interval 10
```

## To verify the configuration:

```
R1#show ip ospf interface tunnel 100 | include Timer
```

```
    Timer intervals configured, Hello 10, Dead 40, Wait 40, Retransmit 5
```

You should see the following console messages:

```
%OSPF-5-ADJCHG: Process 100, Nbr 100.1.1.3 on Tunnel100 from LOADING
to FULL, Loading Done
```

```
%OSPF-5-ADJCHG: Process 100, Nbr 100.1.1.2 on Tunnel100 from LOADING
to FULL, Loading Done
```

R2's and R3's tunnel interfaces are already configured with **ip ospf 100 area 0**, and the default OSPF network type on GRE tunnel interfaces is point-to-point. However, the network type of the tunnel 100 interface on the spoke routers was changed in the previous scenario to broadcast. It must be changed to point-to-point with the **ip ospf network point-to-point** command:

## On R2 and R3:

```
Rx(config)#interface tunnel 100
Rx(config-if)#ip ospf network point-to-point
```

You should see the following console messages:

```
%OSPF-5-ADJCHG: Process 100, Nbr 100.1.1.1 on Tunnel100 from FULL to
DOWN, Neighbor Down: Interface down or detached
```

```
%OSPF-5-ADJCHG: Process 100, Nbr 100.1.1.1 on Tunnel100 from LOADING
to FULL, Loading Done
```

The **show ip ospf neighbor** output below shows R1's OSPF adjacencies with the spokes R2 and R3 over the tunnel 100 interface:

```
R1#show ip ospf neighbor

Neighbor ID     Pri   State    Dead Time    Address        Interface
100.1.1.2         0   FULL/    00:00:39     100.1.1.2      Tunnel100
100.1.1.3         0   FULL/    00:00:32     100.1.1.3      Tunnel100
```

The **show ip route ospf** command at each site shows that the routers have installed OSPF routes for each other's host networks. R2 and R3 use R1's tunnel IP address 100.1.1.1 as the next hop address for 36.1.1.0/24 and 24.1.1.0/24, respectively. As mentioned, this is a characteristic of point-to-point /point-to-multipoint network types, where the hub does not preserve the true next hop. The **show ip cef** output confirms this:

## On R1:

```
R1#show ip route ospf | begin Gate
Gateway of last resort is not set

      24.0.0.0/24 is subnetted, 1 subnets
O        24.1.1.0 [110/1001] via 100.1.1.2, 00:04:03, Tunnel100
      36.0.0.0/24 is subnetted, 1 subnets
O        36.1.1.0 [110/1001] via 100.1.1.3, 00:01:34, Tunnel100
```

## On R2:

```
R2#show ip route ospf | begin Gate
Gateway of last resort is not set

      17.0.0.0/24 is subnetted, 1 subnets
O        17.1.1.0 [110/1001] via 100.1.1.1, 00:05:06, Tunnel100
      36.0.0.0/24 is subnetted, 1 subnets
O        36.1.1.0 [110/2001] via 100.1.1.1, 00:02:37, Tunnel100
      100.0.0.0/8 is variably subnetted, 3 subnets, 2 masks
O        100.1.1.1/32 [110/1000] via 100.1.1.1, 00:05:06, Tunnel100
```

```
R2#show ip cef 36.1.1.0

36.1.1.0/24
  nexthop 100.1.1.1 Tunnel100
```

### On R3:

```
R3#show ip route ospf | begin Gate
Gateway of last resort is not set

      17.0.0.0/24 is subnetted, 1 subnets
O       17.1.1.0 [110/1001] via 100.1.1.1, 00:03:44, Tunnel100
      24.0.0.0/24 is subnetted, 1 subnets
O       24.1.1.0 [110/2001] via 100.1.1.1, 00:03:44, Tunnel100
      100.0.0.0/8 is variably subnetted, 3 subnets, 2 masks
O       100.1.1.1/32 [110/1000] via 100.1.1.1, 00:03:44, Tunnel100

R3#show ip cef 24.1.1.0

24.1.1.0/24
  nexthop 100.1.1.1 Tunnel100
```

**Note**   Although the spokes form a single adjacency with the hub, the point-to-multi-point network type can be configured on their tunnel interfaces as well. This configuration would not require modifying the hello interval on either the hub or the spokes. Spokes will still show a single adjacency with the hub because, due to the point-to-point GRE tunnel, the spokes will only send multicast hellos to the hub router.

Also, notice the /32 prefixes (100.1.1.1/32) installed in the RIB for the DMVPN tunnel interfaces. This is a side effect of the point-to-multipoint network types. When these network types are used, OSPF models the IP address on the link it is enabled on (in this case, the tunnel interface) as a /32 stub network. Doing so provides connectivity whenever both ends of an OSPF point-to-point link are not in the same subnet. This can occur when unnumbered point-to-point links are used. Broadcast network types do not exhibit this behavior.

### Summarization with OSPF

OSPF forces the network to be segmented into a collection of areas. In order for two routers to become OSPF neighbors, the link connecting them must be in the same area. Routers participating in the same area share complete routing information about all networks that reside in that area in link-state advertisements (LSAs). LSAs are compiled on each individual router to form the link-state database (LSDB). The LSDB of an area contains all routers, all networks connected to those routers, and all router-to-router connections. The result is an accurate graph of the interconnections of the area. To calculate routes in the routing table, the OSPF router runs the SPF algorithm to calculate shortest paths. This is all made possible because of the complete information contained in the LSDB.

OSPF domains can consist of multiple areas creating logical groupings of routers. A router can participate in multiple areas, creating a separate LSDB for each area it participates in. Such routers are called ABRs. ABRs glue together the OSPF domain by advertising routing information from one area to another in distance vector fashion. Such routes are called *inter-area routes*.

Routing information within an area cannot be summarized or reduced as doing so would break the route calculation process. Therefore, the routing tables of all routers within an area will contain all prefixes reachable within that area. This can severely limit the degree of summarization that OSPF can achieve when implementing DMVPN.

Keeping the above in mind, in order to exchange OSPF routing information, the hub R1 and spoke routers R2 and R3 must become OSPF neighbors. To do so, they must all exist in the same OSPF area and carry the limitation with summarization mentioned above. This limits the hub from being able to send summarized information of the host networks at R2 to R3 and vice versa.

There is, however, a workaround to this that involves performing summarization at the spokes. The interfaces connecting to the end hosts at each remote site can be placed into a separate area. As a result, R2 and R3 would now function as ABRs as they are connected to the backbone and non-backbone areas. This would give them the ability to perform inter-area summarization with the **area range** command, as shown below:

To demonstrate this, let's place the link connecting R2 and R4 into Area 2 and the link connecting R3 and R6 into Area 3:

## On R2:

```
R2(config)#interface g0/4
R2(config-if)#ip ospf 100 area 2
```

## On R3:

```
R3(config)#interface g0/6
R3(config-if)#ip ospf 100 area 3
```

Notice how the **show ip ospf** output shows R2 and R3 to be the ABRs:

## On R2:

```
R2#show ip ospf | include It is an

 It is an area border router
```

**On R3:**

```
R3#show ip ospf | include It is an

 It is an area border router
```

Next, the **area range** command summarizes the host networks to /8 on R2 and R3:

**On R2:**

```
R2(config)#router ospf 100
R2(config-router)#area 2 range 24.0.0.0 255.0.0.0
```

**On R3:**

```
R3(config)#router ospf 100
R3(config-router)#area 3 range 36.0.0.0 255.0.0.0
```

On observing the routing tables on R2 and R3, you see that specific 24.1.1.0/24 and 36.1.1.0/24 routes have been suppressed and have been replaced with the /8 summaries for each other's host networks:

```
R3#show ip route ospf | begin Gate
Gateway of last resort is not set

      17.0.0.0/24 is subnetted, 1 subnets
O        17.1.1.0 [110/1001] via 100.1.1.1, 00:02:40, Tunnel100
O IA  24.0.0.0/8 [110/2001] via 100.1.1.1, 00:02:40, Tunnel100
      36.0.0.0/8 is variably subnetted, 3 subnets, 3 masks
O        36.0.0.0/8 is a summary, 00:02:40, Null0
      100.0.0.0/8 is variably subnetted, 3 subnets, 2 masks
O        100.1.1.1/32 [110/1000] via 100.1.1.1, 00:02:40, Tunnel100
```

**On R2:**

```
R2#show ip route ospf | begin Gate
Gateway of last resort is not set

      17.0.0.0/24 is subnetted, 1 subnets
O        17.1.1.0 [110/1001] via 100.1.1.1, 00:03:55, Tunnel100
```

```
        24.0.0.0/8 is variably subnetted, 3 subnets, 3 masks
O          24.0.0.0/8 is a summary, 00:03:55, Null0
O IA  36.0.0.0/8 [110/2001] via 100.1.1.1, 00:03:36, Tunnel100
        100.0.0.0/8 is variably subnetted, 3 subnets, 2 masks
O          100.1.1.1/32 [110/1000] via 100.1.1.1, 00:03:55, Tunnel100
```

### Implement EIGRP

Implementing EIGRP in DMVPN Phase 1 is pretty straightforward. First, EIGRP is enabled on the tunnel 100 interfaces on R1, R2, and R3 with the **network** command under the EIGRP router configuration mode. This results in an EIGRP adjacency between R1 and R2 and between R1 and R3. The host networks at the main campus and remote sites are also advertised into EIGRP with the **network** statement. In addition, the interfaces facing R4, R6, and R7 are made passive interfaces to prevent any EIGRP adjacencies from forming over them. Before you configure EIGRP, you should remove OSPF on these three routers:

**On R1:**

```
R1(config)#no router ospf 100

R1(config)#interface tunnel 100
R1(config-if)#no ip ospf network point-to-multipoint

R1(config)#router eigrp 100
R1(config-router)#network 17.1.1.1 0.0.0.0
R1(config-router)#network 100.1.1.1 0.0.0.0
R1(config-router)#passive-interface g0/5
```

**On R2:**

```
R2(config)#no router ospf 100

R2(config)#router eigrp 100
R2(config-router)#network 100.1.1.2 0.0.0.0
R2(config-router)#network 24.1.1.2 0.0.0.0
R2(config-router)#passive-interface g0/5
```

You should see the following console message:

```
%DUAL-5-NBRCHANGE: EIGRP-IPv4 100: Neighbor 100.1.1.1 (Tunnel100) is
up: new adjacency
```

**On R3:**

```
R3(config)#no router ospf 100

R3(config)#router eigrp 100
R3(config-router)#network 36.1.1.3 0.0.0.0
R3(config-router)#network 100.1.1.3 0.0.0.0
R3(config-router)#passive-interface g0/5
```

You should see the following console message:

```
%DUAL-5-NBRCHANGE: EIGRP-IPv4 100: Neighbor 100.1.1.1 (Tunnel100) is
up: new adjacency
```

The **show ip eigrp 100 neighbor** output on R1 shows the EIGRP neighborships between R1 and R2 and R1 and R3 over the tunnel 100 interface:

**On R1:**

```
R1#show ip eigrp 100 neighbors
EIGRP-IPv4 Neighbors for AS(100)

H    Address            Interface        Hold Uptime    SRTT    RTO   Q  Seq
                                         (sec)          (ms)          Cnt
Num
1    100.1.1.3          Tu100            11 00:02:22    12    1434    0  3
0    100.1.1.2          Tu100            14 00:06:21    10    1434    0  4
```

The routing table on R1 shows that R1 has learned of the host networks 24.1.1.0/24 and 36.1.1.0/24 from R2 and R3, respectively:

**On R1:**

```
R1#show ip route eigrp 100 | begin Gate
Gateway of last resort is not set

      24.0.0.0/24 is subnetted, 1 subnets
D        24.1.1.0 [90/26880256] via 100.1.1.2, 00:03:06, Tunnel100
      36.0.0.0/24 is subnetted, 1 subnets
D        36.1.1.0 [90/26880256] via 100.1.1.3, 00:01:56, Tunnel100
```

However, the routing tables on R2 and R3 reveal that the spokes have only learned a route to the host network 17.1.1.0/24 at the main site. Neither spoke contains the other spoke's host network (36.1.1.0/24 and 24.1.1.0/24):

## On R2:

```
R2#show ip route eigrp 100 | begin Gate
Gateway of last resort is not set

     17.0.0.0/24 is subnetted, 1 subnets
D       17.1.1.0 [90/26880256] via 100.1.1.1, 00:09:43, Tunnel100
```

## On R3:

```
R3#show ip route eigrp 100 | begin Gate
Gateway of last resort is not set

     17.0.0.0/24 is subnetted, 1 subnets
D       17.1.1.0 [90/26880256] via 100.1.1.1, 00:06:45, Tunnel100
```

As mentioned in the introduction section of this lab, EIGRP's split-horizon feature which is enabled by default will prevent the hub router R1 from advertising prefixes between the spokes. The **show ip eigrp 100 interface detail** output below verifies that split horizon is enabled on R1's tunnel interface:

## On R1:

```
R1#show ip eigrp 100 interfaces detail | include Split

  Split-horizon is enabled
```

The spli-horizon feature can be turned off with the **no ip split-horizon eigrp 100** command on the tunnel interface on R1. As a result, R1 advertises the host networks at the remote sites learned via EIGRP to R2 and R3. By default, the hub sets the next hop of advertised prefixes to itself, as shown below:

## On R1:

```
R1(config)#interface tunnel 100
R1(config-if)#no ip split-horizon eigrp 100
```

You should see the following console messages:

```
%DUAL-5-NBRCHANGE: EIGRP-IPv4 100: Neighbor 100.1.1.3 (Tunnel100) is
resync: split horizon changed

%DUAL-5-NBRCHANGE: EIGRP-IPv4 100: Neighbor 100.1.1.2 (Tunnel100) is
resync: split horizon changed
```

**On R2:**

```
R2#show ip route eigrp 100 | begin Gate
Gateway of last resort is not set

     17.0.0.0/24 is subnetted, 1 subnets
D       17.1.1.0 [90/26880256] via 100.1.1.1, 00:16:01, Tunnel100
     36.0.0.0/24 is subnetted, 1 subnets
D       36.1.1.0 [90/28160256] via 100.1.1.1, 00:00:52, Tunnel100
```

**On R3:**

```
R3#show ip route eigrp 100 | begin Gate
Gateway of last resort is not set

     17.0.0.0/24 is subnetted, 1 subnets
D       17.1.1.0 [90/26880256] via 100.1.1.1, 00:12:48, Tunnel100
     24.0.0.0/24 is subnetted, 1 subnets
D       24.1.1.0 [90/28160256] via 100.1.1.1, 00:01:38, Tunnel100
```

The design goals for this lab, however, indicate that R1 should send as much summary information to the spokes as possible. To complete this task, R1 can send a default summary route to the spokes. Routing will continue to function properly because the spokes still send specific prefixes to the hub. Spokes will route to the hub for all prefixes for which they do not have a specific prefix (in this case, each other's LANs), and the hub can properly forward the traffic.

With the hub sending a default summary route, the split-horizon configuration becomes inconsequential. The hub no longer needs to forward spoke prefixes between other spokes to provide proper routing. To prove this point, split horizon is turned back on with the **ip split-horizon eigrp 100** command. R1 is then configured to send a default route via EIGRP to the spokes with the **ip summary-address eigrp 100 0.0.0.0 0.0.0.0** command:

**On R1:**

```
R1(config)#interface tunnel 100
R1(config-if)#ip split-horizon eigrp 100
R1(config-if)#ip summary-address eigrp 100 0.0.0.0 0.0.0.0
```

The following output reveals that the default route entries on R2 and R3 use the tunnel 100 interface as the exit point:

#### On R2 and R3:

```
Rx#show ip route eigrp 100 | begin Gate
Gateway of last resort is 100.1.1.1 to network 0.0.0.0

D*    0.0.0.0/0 [90/26880256] via 100.1.1.1, 00:01:50, Tunnel100
```

Following traceroutes confirm reachability between the sites. Because this is a Phase 1 implementation, traffic between spokes always traverses the hub:

#### On R4:

```
R4#traceroute 17.1.1.7 probe 1
Type escape sequence to abort.

Tracing the route to 17.1.1.7
VRF info: (vrf in name/id, vrf out name/id)
  1 24.1.1.2 6 msec
  2 100.1.1.1 8 msec
  3 17.1.1.7 13 msec
```

#### On R6:

```
R6#traceroute 17.1.1.7 probe 1
Type escape sequence to abort.

Tracing the route to 17.1.1.7
VRF info: (vrf in name/id, vrf out name/id)
  1 36.1.1.3 5 msec
  2 100.1.1.1 11 msec
  3 17.1.1.7 12 msec


R4#traceroute 36.1.1.6 probe 1

Type escape sequence to abort.
Tracing the route to 36.1.1.6
VRF info: (vrf in name/id, vrf out name/id)
  1 24.1.1.2 9 msec
  2 100.1.1.1 11 msec
  3 100.1.1.3 42 msec
  4 36.1.1.6 12 msec
```

## Implement iBGP

Before moving on to configure iBGP peerings between R1 and R2 and between R1 and R3, certain key points need to be addressed:

- iBGP peers do not advertise paths learned from an iBGP peer to another iBGP peer.

- Traditional BGP configurations require static neighbor configurations.

In BGP, the local router will pick the best prefixes and advertise the best path to its neighbors. However, if the prefix has the route type internal, then the local router will not advertise this path to its other internal peers. This is because within an AS, BGP does not update the AS_PATH information when sending updates to internal peers. The fact that the AS_PATH is not updated eliminates BGP's primary loop-prevention mechanism: denying prefixes whose AS_PATH contains the local ASN. As a result, iBGP neighbors do not advertise received iBGP routes with each other.

---

The **show ip route x.x.x.x** output can be used to verify the route type. If a network is learned from an iBGP peer, the type shows up as **internal**, as shown below:

```
R1#show ip route 36.1.1.0

Routing entry for 36.1.1.0/24
  Known via "bgp 100", distance 200, metric 0, type internal
  Last update from 100.1.1.3 00:00:40 ago
  Routing Descriptor Blocks:
  * 100.1.1.3, from 100.1.1.3, 00:00:40 ago
      Route metric is 0, traffic share count is 1
      AS Hops 0
      MPLS label: none
```

If a network is learned from an eBGP peer, the type shows up as **external**, as shown below:

```
R1#show ip route 36.1.1.0

Routing entry for 36.1.1.0/24
  Known via "bgp 100", distance 20, metric 0
  Tag 300, type external
  Last update from 100.1.1.3 00:00:07 ago
  Routing Descriptor Blocks:
  * 100.1.1.3, from 100.1.1.3, 00:00:07 ago
      Route metric is 0, traffic share count is 1
      AS Hops 1
      Route tag 300
      MPLS label: none
```

Correlating this to the design topology, whenever the hub R1 receives host network 24.1.1.0/24 as a BGP prefix from iBGP peer R2, R1 does not advertise the 24.1.1.0/24 network down to the other spoke R3 and vice versa. One of the ways to overcome this constraint is to configure hub R1 as a route reflector to host the control plane for the iBGP topology. As a route reflector, R1 receives the host networks from R2 and R3 at the remote site, selects them as the best path, and advertises them down to each other. This configuration forces a similar operation to setting the OSPF DR from the OSPF section of the configuration.

BGP peers are typically created using static **neighbor** commands for each specific BGP speaker that should become a peer with the local BGP speaker. This configuration presents some problems when applied to DMVPN specifically. The task does not directly address this issue, but it is something that should be thought of when implementing a DMVPN solution using BGP. The reason behind this configuration lies in BGP's use of TCP to form peerings.

BGP uses TCP as its transport for forming peering relationships between routers. When a BGP router attempts to peer with another BGP router, it first must initiate a TCP connection by sending a TCP SYN packet to the remote peer. The SYN will be destined to the well-known BGP TCP port 179. If the remote peer accepts the SYN packet, it responds accordingly with a SYN-ACK. The BGP router that initiated the request responds with an ACK packet, completing the TCP connection. This process is known as the *TCP three-way handshake.*

In a typical BGP configuration, potential BGP peers are manually configured with **neighbor** statements in BGP configuration mode. The BGP router attempts to open a TCP connection with each peer periodically, with the intention of forming a BGP peering relationship.

In the topology diagram at the beginning of this lab, R1 is the DMVPN hub and needs to form iBGP peering sessions with the spoke routers R2 and R3. For scalable designs, R1 does not know how many DMVPN spokes are connected to the DMVPN until the spokes register with it when they come online. While it is fully possible for an administrator to manually configure the peering addresses, doing so would violate the dynamic intention of DMVPN. To circumvent this, there is another feature that can be used: **BGP's dynamic neighbor feature**. With the BGP dynamic neighbor feature, the hub can simply listen for TCP connections from a specified range of IP addresses. When it receives one, it automatically begins a peering session with that neighbor.

The spokes R2 and R3 will be manually configured with the IP address of the hub router. Once this is configured, R2 and R3 will begin sending TCP SYN packets to the hub with the destination port 179.

Taking advantage of the fact that spokes send connection attempts to the hub R1, R1 can be configured to simply listen for such connection attempts from prospective spoke routers and respond accordingly. When spokes send their TCP SYN packets to the hub, they are automatically considered TCP clients for the TCP connection, and the hub is the TCP server.

The **bgp listen-range** command configured on hub R1 will allow the hub router to listen for incoming BGP connection attempts from a specific IP address range. R1 applies a peer group to all connections originating from that IP address range.

With that established, the following configurations allow for iBGP peerings between the route reflector R1 and R2 and R1 and R3.

First, a peer group is created on the hub that contains the appropriate configuration information for the dynamic peers (in this case, the ASN and route reflector client status), which are the spokes. This peer group is linked to the **bgp listen-range** command for the 100.1.1.0/24 subnet (the subnet the peers will come from). R2 and R3 are configured with **neighbor** statements to peer R1's tunnel IP address 100.1.1.1. Finally, the **network** command is used at each site to advertise the host networks into BGP:

---

**On R1, R2, and R3:**

```
Rx(config)#no router eigrp 100
```

**On R1:**

```
R1(config)#router bgp 100
R1(config-router)#neighbor spokes peer-group
R1(config-router)#neighbor spokes remote-as 100
R1(config-router)#bgp listen range 100.1.1.0/24 peer-group spokes

R1(config-router)#address-family ipv4
R1(config-router-af)#neighbor spokes activate
R1(config-router-af)#neighor spokes route-reflector-client
R1(config-router-af)#network 17.1.1.0 mask 255.255.255.0
```

**On R2:**

```
R2(config)#router bgp 100
R2(config-router)#neighbor 100.1.1.1 remote-as 100

R2(config-router)#address-family ipv4
R2(config-router-af)#network 24.1.1.0 mask 255.255.255.0
R2(config-router-af)#neighbor 100.1.1.1 activate
```

You should see the following console message:

```
%BGP-5-ADJCHANGE: neighbor 100.1.1.1 Up
```

## On R3:

```
R3(config)#router bgp 100
R3(config-router)#neighbor 100.1.1.1 remote-as 100

R3(config-router)#address-family ipv4
R3(config-router-af)#neighbor 100.1.1.1 activate
R3(config-router-af)#network 36.1.1.0 mask 255.255.255.0
```

You should see the following console message:

```
%BGP-5-ADJCHANGE: neighbor 100.1.1.1 Up
```

The following output from the **show ip bgp summary** command on R1 shows that peering's to the iBGP neighbors 100.1.1.2 and 100.1.1.3 was dynamically established:

## On R1:

```
R1#show ip bgp summary | begin Nei

Neighbor      V   AS MsgRcvd MsgSent   TblVer  InQ OutQ Up/Down   State/
PfxRcd
*100.1.1.2    4  100      10      10        4    0    0 00:05:04
1
*100.1.1.3    4  100       6      11        4    0    0 00:02:35
1
* Dynamically created based on a listen range command
Dynamically created neighbors: 2, Subnet ranges: 1

BGP peergroup spokes listen range group members:
  100.1.1.0/24

Total dynamically created neighbors: 2/(100 max), Subnet ranges: 1
```

After establishing the peering relationships with the hub and exchanging BGP routing information, R2 and R3 learn each other's host networks via BGP:

## On R1:

```
R1#show ip bgp | begin Net

    Network          Next Hop          Metric LocPrf Weight Path
 *>   17.1.1.0/24      0.0.0.0               0          32768 i
 *>i  24.1.1.0/24      100.1.1.2             0    100      0 i
 *>i  36.1.1.0/24      100.1.1.3             0    100      0 i
```

**On R2:**

```
R2#show ip bgp | begin Net

     Network          Next Hop          Metric LocPrf Weight Path
 *>i  17.1.1.0/24      100.1.1.1              0    100     0 i
 *>   24.1.1.0/24      0.0.0.0                0         32768 i
 *>i  36.1.1.0/24      100.1.1.3              0    100     0 i
```

**On R3:**

```
R3#show ip bgp | begin Net

     Network          Next Hop          Metric LocPrf Weight Path
 *>i  17.1.1.0/24      100.1.1.1              0    100     0 i
 *>i  24.1.1.0/24      100.1.1.2              0    100     0 i
 *>   36.1.1.0/24      0.0.0.0                0         32768 i
```

The BGP and RIB entries on the spokes R2 and R3 for each other's host network point to each other's tunnel IP addresses. This is as expected because route reflectors do not modify the next hop value. As already mentioned in the OSPF section, this shouldn't present any problem because the tunnels on the spokes are point-to-point GRE tunnels:

**On R2:**

```
R2#show ip route bgp | begin Gate
Gateway of last resort is not set

      17.0.0.0/24 is subnetted, 1 subnets
B        17.1.1.0 [200/0] via 100.1.1.1, 00:47:05
      36.0.0.0/24 is subnetted, 1 subnets
B        36.1.1.0 [200/0] via 100.1.1.3, 00:43:43a
```

**On R3:**

```
R3#show ip route bgp | begin Gate
Gateway of last resort is not set

      17.0.0.0/24 is subnetted, 1 subnets
B        17.1.1.0 [200/0] via 100.1.1.1, 00:44:23
      24.0.0.0/24 is subnetted, 1 subnets
B        24.1.1.0 [200/0] via 100.1.1.2, 00:44:23
```

The design requirements state that hub R1 should propagate a default route to the spokes R1 and R2. One of the ways to inject a default route into BGP is to use the **neighbor default-originate** command for a specific BGP neighbor. In R1's case, this command should be added to the spokes peer group configuration using the **neighbor spokes default-originate** command in IPv4 address family configuration mode. With **default-originate** enabled for the peer group, all future spokes that connect to the DMVPN will automatically receive a default route from R1. This configuration alone, however, does not suppress the specific prefixes the hub advertises to the spokes.

To suppress the specific prefixes and ensure that only a default route is propagated to the spokes, a prefix list identifying and permitting the default route 0.0.0.0/0 is created. The prefix list is then referenced in a route map, which is appended to the neighbor statement outbound on the hub R1. The implicit deny statement at the end of a route-map prevents the specific prefixes from being advertised to the spokes:

## On R1:

```
R1(config)#ip prefix-list TST permit 0.0.0.0/0

R1(config)#route-map default permit 10
R1(config-route-map)#match ip address prefix TST

R1(config)#router bgp 100
R1(config-router)#address-family ipv4
R1(config-router-af)#neighbor spokes default-originate
R1(config-router-af)#neighbor spokes route-map default out

R1#clear ip bgp * out
```

The result of the above configuration is seen in the **show ip bgp** output on R2 and R3. R2 and R3 only receive a default route from R1. Since the default route was originated by R1, the next hop IP address for this route is set to R1's tunnel 100 interface address 100.1.1.1:

## On R1:

```
R1#show ip bgp | begin Net

     Network          Next Hop          Metric LocPrf Weight Path
     0.0.0.0          0.0.0.0                               0 i
 *>  17.1.1.0/24      0.0.0.0                0          32768 i
 *>i 24.1.1.0/24      100.1.1.2              0    100      0 i
 *>i 36.1.1.0/24      100.1.1.3              0    100      0 i
```

**On R2:**

```
R2#show ip bgp | begin Net

     Network            Next Hop          Metric LocPrf Weight Path
 *>i  0.0.0.0           100.1.1.1              0    100      0 i
 *>   24.1.1.0/24       0.0.0.0                0         32768 i
```

**On R3:**

```
R3#show ip bgp | begin Net

     Network            Next Hop          Metric LocPrf Weight Path
 *>i  0.0.0.0           100.1.1.1              0    100      0 i
 *>   36.1.1.0/24       0.0.0.0                0         32768 i
```

On completing the above, reachability between the sites is verified with the traceroutes below:

**On R4:**

```
R4#traceroute 17.1.1.7 probe 1
Type escape sequence to abort.

Tracing the route to 17.1.1.7
VRF info: (vrf in name/id, vrf out name/id)
  1 24.1.1.2 6 msec
  2 100.1.1.1 8 msec
  3 17.1.1.7 13 msec
```

**On R6:**

```
R6#traceroute 17.1.1.7 probe 1
Type escape sequence to abort.

Tracing the route to 17.1.1.7
VRF info: (vrf in name/id, vrf out name/id)
  1 36.1.1.3 5 msec
  2 100.1.1.1 11 msec
  3 17.1.1.7 12 msec
```

```
R4#traceroute 36.1.1.6 probe 1

Type escape sequence to abort.
Tracing the route to 36.1.1.6
VRF info: (vrf in name/id, vrf out name/id)
  1 24.1.1.2 9 msec
  2 100.1.1.1 11 msec
  3 100.1.1.3 42 msec
  4 36.1.1.6 12 msec
```

## Implement eBGP

eBGP as an overlay for DMVPN can be implemented in two ways:

- Each spoke can be configured to belong to different autonomous systems.

- All spokes can be configured to belong to the same autonomous system.

### Spokes in Different Autonomous Systems

The first implementation is easy. R1, R2, and R3 use different autonomous system numbers. eBGP peering is established between R1 and R2 and between R1 and R3. The BGP **listen range** command allows for dynamic BGP peerings on R1. Because R2 and R3 belong to two different autonomous systems, the neighbor peer group command on R1 now accepts two ASNs with the alternate-as keyword. R2 and R3 are both configured to peer with R1's tunnel IP address 100.1.1.1. Finally, the **network** command is used to advertise the host networks at each site into BGP:

---

**On R1:**

There is no need to remove the BGP configuration from the previous task from R1. The **neighbor spokes remote-as** command will be overwritten with the new **neighbor spokes remote-as** command.

```
R1(config)#router bgp 100
R1(config-router)#neighbor spokes remote-as 200 alternate-as 300
R1(config-router)#bgp listen range 100.1.1.0/24 peer spokes

R1(config-router)#address-family ipv4

R1(config-router-af)#no neighbor spokes default-originate
R1(config-router-af)#no neighbor spokes route-map default out

R1#clear ip bgp * out
```

### On R2:

```
R2(config)#no router bgp 100

R2(config)#router bgp 200
R2(config-router)#neighbor 100.1.1.1 remote-as 100

R2(config-router)#address-family ipv4
R2(config-router-af)#neighbor 100.1.1.1 activate
R2(config-router-af)#network 24.1.1.0 mask 255.255.255.0
```

You should see the following console message:

```
%BGP-5-ADJCHANGE: neighbor 100.1.1.1 Up
```

### On R3:

```
R3(config)#no router bgp 100

R3(config)#router bgp 300
R3(config-router)#neighbor 100.1.1.1 remote-as 100

R3(config-router)#address-family ipv4
R3(config-router-af)#neighbor 100.1.1.1 activate
R3(config-router-af)#network 36.1.1.0 mask 255.255.255.0
```

You should see the following console message:

```
%BGP-5-ADJCHANGE: neighbor 100.1.1.1 Up
```

As a result of the above configurations, R1, R2, and R3 now learn of each other's host networks via BGP. Key points to note in the output below are the next hop IP address for the network 36.1.1.0/24 on R2 and the network 24.1.1.0/24 on R3:

### On R1:

```
R1#show ip bgp | begin Net

     Network          Next Hop         Metric LocPrf Weight Path
 *>  17.1.1.0/24      0.0.0.0               0          32768 i
 *>  24.1.1.0/24      100.1.1.2             0              0 200 i
 *>  36.1.1.0/24      100.1.1.3             0              0 300 i
```

**On R2:**

```
R2#show ip bgp | begin Net

     Network           Next Hop        Metric LocPrf Weight Path
 *>   17.1.1.0/24       100.1.1.1            0              0 100 i
 *>   24.1.1.0/24       0.0.0.0              0          32768 i
 *>   36.1.1.0/24       100.1.1.3                           0 100
300 i
```

**On R3:**

```
R3#show ip bgp | begin Net

     Network           Next Hop        Metric LocPrf Weight Path
 *>   17.1.1.0/24       100.1.1.1            0              0 100 i
 *>   24.1.1.0/24       100.1.1.2                           0 100 200
i
 *>   36.1.1.0/24       0.0.0.0              0          32768 i
```

In normal circumstances, between eBGP peers, a router changes the next hop value of a BGP route to its own address before sending it out to the next eBGP neighbor. However, the output above shows that the next hop IP address for the 36.1.1.0/24 network on R2 is R3's tunnel IP address, 100.1.1.3. The next hop IP address for the 24.1.1.0/24 network on R3 is R2's tunnel IP address, 100.1.1.2. This means that R1 as an eBGP peer is not modifying the next hop value to itself before advertising paths to eBGP peer spokes R2 and R3.

R3 is not modifying the next hop value to itself because of BGP's **third-party next hop** feature. The third-party next hop feature prevents an eBGP peer from modifying the next-hop information of a received external prefix. It activates when the next hop for an advertised prefix is in the same subnet as the peering address of the eBGP peer. In the design, R1, R2, and R3 all belong to the same subnet 100.1.1.10/24. As such, whenever R1 receives the routing information for 24.1.1.0/24 with the next hop of R2's IP address on the same subnet, it does not modify this information when advertising to R3. The same occurs for prefixes R1 receives from R3.

The third-party next hop feature assumes that if all peers are in the same subnet, then they each have reachability to each other. Retaining the original next hop prevents sub-optimal routing where R3 would send packets destined to R2's LAN to R1 first, when it could send directly to R2. In DMVPN Phase 1, this enhancement does not accomplish this goal and has little effect on the traffic pattern—mainly due to the point-to-point GRE tunnels configured on the spokes. The feature can be turned off with the **neighbor spokes next-hop-self** command on the hub if needed.

### Spokes in the Same AS

The second design choice where the spokes are configured in the same ASN requires a little more work and tweaking than the first. Hub R1 is configured to form eBGP peer sessions for AS 100 with R2 and R3. Spokes R2 and R3 both now belong to AS 230 and are configured to form an eBGP peering session with R1:

```
On R1:


R1(config)#no router bgp 100  !

R1(config)#router bgp 100
R1(config-router)#neighbor spokes peer-group
R1(config-router)#neighbor spokes remote-as 230
R1(config-router)#bgp listen range 100.1.1.0/24 peer-group spokes

R1(config-router)#address-family ipv4
R1(config-router-af)#neighbor spokes activate
R1(config-router-af)#network 17.1.1.0 mask 255.255.255.0


On R2:


R2(config)#no router bgp 200

R2(config)#router bgp 230
R2(config-router)#neighbor 100.1.1.1 remote-as 100

R2(config-router)#address-family ipv4
R2(config-router-af)#neighbor 100.1.1.1 activate
```

You should see the following console message:

```
%BGP-5-ADJCHANGE: neighbor 100.1.1.1 Up


On R3:


R3(config)#no router bgp 300

R3(config)#router bgp 230
R3(config-router)#neighbor 100.1.1.1 remote-as 100
```

```
R3(config-router)#address-family ipv4
R3(config-router-af)#neighbor 100.1.1.1 activate
```

You should see the following console message:

```
%BGP-5-ADJCHANGE: neighbor 100.1.1.1 Up
```

The following verifies the R1/R2 and R1/R3 eBGP peering sessions:

## On R1:

```
R1#show ip bgp summary | begin Nei

Neighbor        V    AS MsgRcvd MsgSent    TblVer   InQ OutQ Up/Down
State/PfxRcd
*100.1.1.2      4   230      10       12         6     0    0 00:04:58
0
*100.1.1.3      4   230       8       13         6     0    0 00:03:48
0
* Dynamically created based on a listen range command
Dynamically created neighbors: 2, Subnet ranges: 1

BGP peergroup spokes listen range group members:
  100.1.1.0/24

Total dynamically created neighbors: 2/(100 max), Subnet ranges: 1
```

Next, you add the host networks at the remote sites into BGP. On R2, **debug ip bgp updates** has been turned on. On advertising the host networks with the **network** command, the debugging messages log says **DENIED due to: AS-PATH contains our own AS;** on R2 for the 36.1.1.0/24 path:

## On R2:

```
R2#debug ip bgp updates
BGP updates debugging is on for address family: IPv4 Unicast

R2(config)#router bgp 230
R2(config-router)#address-family ipv4
R2(config-router-af)#network 24.1.1.0 mask 255.255.255.0

BGP(0): 100.1.1.1 rcv UPDATE about 36.1.1.0/24 -- DENIED due to:
AS-PATH contains our own AS; NEXTHOP is our own address;
```

**On R3:**

```
R3(config)#router bgp 230
R3(config-router)#address-family ipv4
R3(config-router-af)#network 36.1.1.0 mask 255.255.255.0
```

This debugging message is due to BGP's loop-prevention mechanism. BGP updates are denied if the AS_PATH contained in them matches that of the local AS.

Examine the Wireshark capture below. R2 receives a BGP update from 100.1.1.1 for R3's host network 36.1.1.0/24. Because the AS_PATH segment includes its own ASN 230, R2 denies this update as it assumes that the route was advertised back to it. The same happens on R3.

```
► Internet Protocol Version 4, Src: 15.1.1.1, Dst: 25.1.1.2
► Generic Routing Encapsulation (IP)
► Internet Protocol Version 4, Src: 100.1.1.1, Dst: 100.1.1.2
► Transmission Control Protocol, Src Port: 14470, Dst Port: 179,
▼ Border Gateway Protocol – UPDATE Message
    Marker: ffffffffffffffffffffffffffffffff
    Length: 51
    Type: UPDATE Message (2)
    Withdrawn Routes Length: 0
    Total Path Attribute Length: 24
  ▼ Path attributes
    ► Path Attribute – ORIGIN: IGP
    ▼ Path Attribute – AS_PATH: 100 230
       ► Flags: 0x40, Transitive, Well-known, Complete
         Type Code: AS_PATH (2)
         Length: 10
       ► AS Path segment: 100 230
    ► Path Attribute – NEXT_HOP: 100.1.1.3
  ▼ Network Layer Reachability Information (NLRI)
    ► 36.1.1.0/24
```

This can be handled in two ways:

- Configure **allowas-in** on the spokes R2 and R3.

- Send a default route from the hub R1 to R2 and R3.

The **allowas-in** feature disables the loop prevention in BGP. With this featured configured, a BGP speaking router no longer denies any BGP updates that have its own ASN listed. It is applied on a per-neighbor basis with the **neighbor** command. On configuring the feature on the spokes R2 and R3, the debugging outputs show that they now install each other's host network. The **show ip bgp** output confirms this:

## On R2:

```
R2(config)#router bgp 230
R2(config-router)#neighbor 100.1.1.1 allowas-in
```

You should see the following debug output:

```
BGP(0): Revise route installing 1 of 1 routes for 36.1.1.0/24 ->
100.1.1.3(global) to main IP table
```

```
R2#show ip bgp | begin Net

     Network          Next Hop          Metric LocPrf Weight Path
 *>   17.1.1.0/24      100.1.1.1              0              0 100 i
 *>   24.1.1.0/24      0.0.0.0                0          32768 i
 *>   36.1.1.0/24      100.1.1.3                             0 100 230 i
```

## On R3:

```
R3(config)#router bgp 230
R3(config-router)#neighbor 100.1.1.1 allowas-in

BGP(0): Revise route installing 1 of 1 routes for 24.1.1.0/24 ->
100.1.1.2(global) to main IP table
```

```
R3#show ip bgp | begin Net

     Network          Next Hop          Metric LocPrf Weight Path
 *>   17.1.1.0/24      100.1.1.1              0              0 100 i
 *>   24.1.1.0/24      100.1.1.2                             0 100 230 i
 *>   36.1.1.0/24      0.0.0.0                0          32768 i
```

The design requires the hub to send down a default route. So, much as in the iBGP section, the following configuration causes R1 to propagate a default route to the spokes R2 and R3 while suppressing the more specific prefixes. The next hop IP address of the default route is the hub R1's tunnel IP address 100.1.1.1:

### On R1:

The following prefix-list and route-map are likely already configured from an earlier step.

```
R1(config)#ip prefix-list TST seq 5 permit 0.0.0.0/0

R1(config)#route-map default permit 10
R1(config-route-map)#match ip address prefix TST

R1(config)#router bgp 100
R1(config-router)#address-family ipv4
R1(config-router-af)#neighbor spokes default-originate
R1(config-router-af)#neighbor spokes route-map default out

R1#clear ip bgp * out
```

### On R2:

```
R2#show ip bgp | begin Net

     Network          Next Hop            Metric LocPrf Weight Path
 *>  0.0.0.0          100.1.1.1                              0 100 i
 *>  24.1.1.0/24      0.0.0.0                  0         32768 i
```

### On R3:

```
R3#show ip bgp | begin Net

     Network          Next Hop            Metric LocPrf Weight Path
 *>  0.0.0.0          100.1.1.1                              0 100 i
 *>  36.1.1.0/24      0.0.0.0                  0         32768 i
```

As in the other sections, traceroutes between the sites verify proper reachability for both configuration scenarios.

**On R4:**

```
R4#traceroute 17.1.1.7 probe 1
Type escape sequence to abort.

Tracing the route to 17.1.1.7
VRF info: (vrf in name/id, vrf out name/id)
  1 24.1.1.2 6 msec
  2 100.1.1.1 8 msec
  3 17.1.1.7 13 msec
```

**On R6:**

```
R6#traceroute 17.1.1.7 probe 1
Type escape sequence to abort.

Tracing the route to 17.1.1.7
VRF info: (vrf in name/id, vrf out name/id)
  1 36.1.1.3 5 msec
  2 100.1.1.1 11 msec
  3 17.1.1.7 12 msec
```

```
R4#traceroute 36.1.1.6 probe 1

Type escape sequence to abort.
Tracing the route to 36.1.1.6
VRF info: (vrf in name/id, vrf out name/id)
  1 24.1.1.2 9 msec
  2 100.1.1.1 11 msec
  3 100.1.1.3 42 msec
  4 36.1.1.6 12 msec
```

## Implement Phase 2

## Design Goal

When the VPN was first deployed, traffic patterns were mostly between remote sites and the main campus site. Over the years, the network engineers at ABC Corp have noticed the traffic patterns shift to be primarily remote site to remote site. To reduce the load on the main site hub router, the network engineers have decided to extend the network to allow the remote sites to directly communicate with each other.

### DMVPN Tunnel Configuration

Before beginning configuration, the routing protocol and DMVPN tunnel interfaces
are removed and rebuilt on each router. The mGRE tunnel configuration on the hub R1
requires no modifications from the configurations made in Phase 1:

---

**On All Routers**

```
Rx(config)#no interface tunnel 100
```

**On R1:**

```
R1(config)#no router bgp 100
```

**On R1:**

```
R1(config)#interface tunnel 100
R1(config-if)#ip address 100.1.1.1 255.255.255.0
R1(config-if)#ip nhrp map multicast dynamic
R1(config-if)#ip nhrp network-id 100
R1(config-if)#tunnel source GigabitEthernet0/5
R1(config-if)#tunnel mode gre multipoint
```

As mentioned in the introduction section, for DMVPN Phase 2 operation, the spokes
must be configured with multipoint GRE tunnels, just like the hub, to allow dynamic
tunnels to form between them. With such a configuration, in order for the spokes to register with the hub properly, the spokes must be configured with static NHRP mapping
information for the hub, along with appropriate static NHRP multicast mapping information if dynamic routing protocols that use multicast are used.

To configure the static mapping, the **ip nhrp nhs 100.1.1.1 nbma 15.1.1.1 multicast** command is configured on the tunnel interfaces on R2 and R3, along with the **tunnel mode
gre multipoint** command to convert the point-to-point GRE tunnel into an mGRE tunnel. These two commands configure the appropriate static NHRP and NHRP multicast
mappings on the spoke routers:

**On R2:**

```
R2#undebug all
All possible debugging has been turned off

R2(config)#no router bgp 230
```

---

```
R2(config)#interface tunnel 100
R2(config-if)#ip address 100.1.1.2 255.255.255.0
R2(config-if)#ip nhrp network-id 100
R2(config-if)#tunnel source 25.1.1.2
R2(config-if)#tunnel mode gre multipoint
R2(config-if)#ip nhrp nhs 100.1.1.1 nbma 15.1.1.1 multicast
```

## On R3:

```
R3#undebug all
All possible debugging has been turned off

R3(config)#no router bgp 230

R3(config)#interface tunnel 100
R3(config-if)#ip address 100.1.1.3 255.255.255.0
R3(config-if)#ip nhrp network-id 100
R3(config-if)#tunnel source 35.1.1.3
R3(config-if)#tunnel mode gre multipoint
R3(config-if)#ip nhrp nhs 100.1.1.1 nbma 15.1.1.1 multicast
```

The **show dmvpn** output verifies the tunnels between the Hub and Spokes. Notice the "**D**" flag on R1 for each Spoke and the "**S**" flag on R2 and R3 for the Hub. The "**D**" flag signifies the mapping information was dynamically learned. This is because the Hub learns of the Spokes via NHRP registration messages sent to it by the spokes directly. The "**S**" flag on the spokes signifies the mapping information was learned statically, because the spokes have been statically configured with Hub's NBMA-to-tunnel-IP mapping:

## On R1:

```
R1#show dmvpn | begin Peer NBMA

 # Ent  Peer NBMA Addr Peer Tunnel Add State  UpDn Tm Attrb
 ----- --------------- --------------- ----- -------- -----
     1 25.1.1.2                100.1.1.2   UP 00:08:29      D
     1 35.1.1.3                100.1.1.3   UP 00:09:23      D
```

## On R2:

```
R2#show dmvpn | begin Peer NBMA
```

```
 # Ent  Peer NBMA Addr Peer Tunnel Add State  UpDn Tm Attrb
 ----- --------------- --------------- ----- -------- -----
     1 15.1.1.1                100.1.1.1   UP 00:06:56    S
```

## On R3:

```
R3#show dmvpn | begin Peer NBMA

 # Ent  Peer NBMA Addr Peer Tunnel Add State  UpDn Tm Attrb
 ----- --------------- --------------- ----- -------- -----
     1 15.1.1.1                100.1.1.1   UP 00:03:42    S
```

The **show ip nhrp multicast** command on R1, R2, and R3 checks for multicast connectivity and replication. The hub automatically assigns a multicast flag to every spoke that registers with it—hence the flag **dynamic**. The spokes are manually told to send multicast to the configured NHS IP address—hence the flag **nhs**.

## On R1:

```
R1#show ip nhrp multicast

  I/F      NBMA address
Tunnel100  35.1.1.3         Flags: dynamic         (Enabled)
Tunnel100  25.1.1.2         Flags: dynamic         (Enabled)
```

## On R2:

```
R2#show ip nhrp multicast

  I/F      NBMA address
Tunnel100  15.1.1.1         Flags: nhs             (Enabled)
```

## On R3:

```
R3#show ip nhrp multicast

  I/F      NBMA address
Tunnel100  15.1.1.1         Flags: nhs             (Enabled)
```

With DMVPN set up, a **traceroute** from R2 to R3's tunnel IP address 100.1.1.3 is performed to verify reachability:

## On R2:

```
R2#traceroute 100.1.1.3 numeric

Type escape sequence to abort.
Tracing the route to 100.1.1.3
VRF info: (vrf in name/id, vrf out name/id)
  1 100.1.1.1 [AS 100] 11 msec *  18 msec
    100.1.1.3 5 msec 5 msec 5 msec

R2#traceroute 100.1.1.3 numeric

Type escape sequence to abort.
Tracing the route to 100.1.1.3
VRF info: (vrf in name/id, vrf out name/id)
  1 100.1.1.3 [AS 100] 11 msec *  18 msec
```

As shown above, the first **traceroute** to 100.1.1.3 travels to R3 from R2 via the hub R1. The following **traceroute** to the same address escapes the hub and is sent directly from R2 to R3. This is an indication of spoke-to-spoke tunnel formation between R2 and R3. This is further verified with the **show dmvpn** output on R2 and R3. Notice the **D** attribute set against the R2/R3 tunnel, which indicates the dynamic nature of this spoke-to-spoke tunnel:

## On R2:

```
R2#show dmvpn | begin Peer NBMA

 # Ent   Peer NBMA Addr Peer Tunnel Add State  UpDn Tm Attrb
 ----- --------------- --------------- ----- -------- -----
     1 15.1.1.1               100.1.1.1    UP 00:16:38    S
     1 35.1.1.3               100.1.1.3    UP 00:05:07    D
```

## On R3:

```
R3#show dmvpn | begin Peer NBMA

 # Ent   Peer NBMA Addr Peer Tunnel Add State  UpDn Tm Attrb
 ----- --------------- --------------- ----- -------- -----
     1 15.1.1.1               100.1.1.1    UP 00:13:35    S
     1 25.1.1.2               100.1.1.2    UP 00:06:01    D
```

With DMVPN Phase 2 set up successfully between R1, R2, and R3, the next part of the task involves advertising the host networks at each site into an overlay protocol. The following section demonstrates the configuration and implementation of OSPF, EIGRP, and BGP as overlay protocols.

As mentioned in the introduction section, for DMVPN Phase 2, spoke routing tables should be populated with complete routing information for all host networks residing at remote spoke sites. This routing information should contain the original spoke's tunnel IP address as the next hop. Applied to the scenario above, R2 should receive or calculate a route to the 36.1.1.0/24 network with R3's tunnel interface 100.1.1.3 as the next hop. The same applies to R3. The following sections detail how to accomplish this with OSPF, EIGRP, and BGP.

## Implement OSPF

The point-to-point and point-to-multipoint OSPF network types do not preserve the next hop IP addresses. Therefore, these two network types should not be used in DMVPN Phase 2. All non-broadcast network types will be ignored as their requirement of static neighbor configuration does not fit well with the DMVPN design philosophy. This leaves you with the broadcast network type for Phase 2 behavior when using OSPF as the overlay protocol.

The configuration to implement OSPF's broadcast network type for Phase 2 behavior is similar to the configurations made in the Phase 1 section. The network type is set to broadcast with the **ip ospf network broadcast** command on the tunnel 100 interfaces on R1, R2, and R3. OSPF's priority on R2 and R3 is set to 0 with the **ip ospf priority 0** command to prevent them from becoming the DRs or BDRs. Finally, the respective host LAN interfaces at each site are also advertised into OSPF process 100 in Area 0. They are declared as passive interfaces under the OSPF configuration mode:

**On R1:**

```
R1(config)#no router bgp 100

R1(config)#interface tunnel 100
R1(config-if)#ip ospf network broadcast
R1(config-if)#ip ospf 100 area 0

R1(config-if)#interface g0/7
R1(config-if)#ip ospf 100 area 0

R1(config-if)#router ospf 100
R1(config-router)#passive-interface g0/7
```

**On R2:**

```
R2(config)#no router bgp 230

R2(config)#interface tunnel 100
R2(config-if)#ip ospf network broadcast
R2(config-if)#ip ospf 100 area 0
R2(config-if)#ip ospf priority 0

R2(config)#interface g0/4
R2(config-if)#ip ospf 100 area 0

R2(config)#router ospf 100
R2(config-router)#passive-interface g0/4
```

You should see the following console message:

```
%OSPF-5-ADJCHG: Process 100, Nbr 100.1.1.1 on Tunnel100 from LOADING
to FULL, Loading Done
```

**On R3:**

```
R3(config)#no router bgp 230

R3(config)#interface tunnel 100
R3(config-if)#ip ospf network broadcast
R3(config-if)#ip ospf 100 area 0
R3(config-if)#ip ospf priority 0

R3(config)#interface g0/6
R3(config-if)#ip ospf 100 area 0

R3(config)#router ospf 100
R3(config-router)#passive-interface g0/6
```

You should see the following console message:

```
%OSPF-5-ADJCHG: Process 100, Nbr 100.1.1.1 on Tunnel100 from LOADING
to FULL, Loading Done
```

The **show ip ospf neighbor** output on R1 verifies the OSPF adjacencies between R1 and R2 and between R1 and R3:

**On R1:**

```
R1#show ip ospf neighbor
```

```
Neighbor ID      Pri    State          Dead Time    Address      Interface
100.1.1.2          0    FULL/DROTHER   00:00:39     100.1.1.2    Tunnel100
100.1.1.3          0    FULL/DROTHER   00:00:39     100.1.1.3    Tunnel100
```

The **show ip route ospf** output on R1, R2, and R3 verifies the remote host networks at each site:

```
R1#show ip route ospf | begin Gate
Gateway of last resort is not set

      24.0.0.0/24 is subnetted, 1 subnets
O        24.1.1.0 [110/1001] via 100.1.1.2, 00:02:07, Tunnel100
      36.0.0.0/24 is subnetted, 1 subnets
O        36.1.1.0 [110/1001] via 100.1.1.3, 00:02:07, Tunnel100
```

## On R2:

```
R2#show ip route ospf | begin Gate
Gateway of last resort is not set

      17.0.0.0/24 is subnetted, 1 subnets
O        17.1.1.0 [110/1001] via 100.1.1.1, 00:04:01, Tunnel100
      36.0.0.0/24 is subnetted, 1 subnets
O        36.1.1.0 [110/1001] via 100.1.1.3, 00:04:01, Tunnel100
```

## On R3:

```
R3#show ip route ospf | begin Gate
Gateway of last resort is not set

      17.0.0.0/24 is subnetted, 1 subnets
O        17.1.1.0 [110/1001] via 100.1.1.1, 00:02:26, Tunnel100
      24.0.0.0/24 is subnetted, 1 subnets
O        24.1.1.0 [110/1001] via 100.1.1.2, 00:02:26, Tunnel100
```

Notice that the next hops on R2 and R3 for each other's host network point to each other's tunnel IP address. Next, **traceroute** is performed twice from R4 to R6. The first **traceroute** traverses the hub R1. Once the resolution process concludes, the next **traceroute** bypasses the hub, and traffic is sent over the dynamic spoke-to-spoke tunnel between R2 and R3:

**On R4:**

```
R4#traceroute 36.1.1.6

Type escape sequence to abort.
Tracing the route to 36.1.1.6
VRF info: (vrf in name/id, vrf out name/id)
  1 24.1.1.2 4 msec 5 msec 5 msec
  2 100.1.1.1 3 msec 2 msec 1 msec
  3 100.1.1.3 1 msec 0 msec 1 msec
  4 36.1.1.6 0 msec 2 msec 1 msec

R4#traceroute 36.1.1.6

Type escape sequence to abort.
Tracing the route to 36.1.1.6
VRF info: (vrf in name/id, vrf out name/id)
  1 24.1.1.2 1 msec 4 msec 6 msec
  2 100.1.1.3 1 msec 1 msec 0 msec
  3 36.1.1.6 1 msec 1 msec 0 msec
```

The second traceroute shows the traffic from R4 to R7 being routed through the hub:

**On R4:**

```
R4#traceroute 17.1.1.7 probe 1

Type escape sequence to abort.
Tracing the route to 17.1.1.7
VRF info: (vrf in name/id, vrf out name/id)
  1 24.1.1.2 11 msec
  2 100.1.1.1 10 msec
  3 17.1.1.7 12 msec
```

## Implement EIGRP

The EIGRP configuration to implement Phase 2 is simple. EIGRP is enabled on the tunnel interface 100 on R1, R2, and R3 with the **network** command under the EIGRP router configuration mode. Respective host networks at each site are then advertised into EIGRP using the same command. These interfaces are then declared as passive to prevent any neighborships from forming over them.

Two additional EIGRP commands are necessary on the hub R1 for Phase 2 behavior to occur. The **no ip split-horizon eigrp 100** command on R1's tunnel 100 disables split horizon to ensure that R1 advertises specific host networks from R2 to R3 and from R3 to R2. In addition, the **no ip next-hop-self eigrp 100** command prevents R1 from setting itself as the next hop for the advertised prefixes. Before you do all the configurations, you must remove OSPF from the earlier section:

---

**On R1:**

```
R1(config)#no router ospf 100

R1(config)#interface tunnel 100
R1(config-if)#no ip ospf network broadcast

R1(config)#router eigrp 100
R1(config-router)#network 17.1.1.1 0.0.0.0
R1(config-router)#network 100.1.1.1 0.0.0.0
R1(config-router)#passive-interface g0/7

R1(config)#interface tunnel 100
R1(config-if)#no ip next-hop-self eigrp 100
R1(config-if)#no ip split-horizon eigrp 100
```

**On R2:**

```
R2(config)#no router ospf 100

R2(config)#interface tunnel 100
R2(config-if)#no ip ospf network broadcast
R2(config-if)#no ip ospf priority 0

R2(config)#router eigrp 100
R2(config-router)#network 24.1.1.2 0.0.0.0
R2(config-router)#network 100.1.1.2 0.0.0.0
R2(config-router)#passive-interface g0/4
```

You should see the following console message:

```
%DUAL-5-NBRCHANGE: EIGRP-IPv4 100: Neighbor 100.1.1.1 (Tunnel100) is
up: new adjacency
```

**On R3:**

```
R3(config)#no router ospf 100

R3(config)#interface tunnel 100
R3(config-if)#no ip ospf network broadcast
R3(config-if)#no ip ospf priority 0

R3(config)#router eigrp 100
R3(config-router)#network 36.1.1.3 0.0.0.0
R3(config-router)#network 100.1.1.3 0.0.0.0
R3(config-router)#passive-interface g0/6
```

You should see the following console message:

```
%DUAL-5-NBRCHANGE: EIGRP-IPv4 100: Neighbor 100.1.1.1 (Tunnel100) is
up: new adjacency
```

The **show ip eigrp 100 neighbors** command on R1 verifies the EIGRP neighborships between R1 and R2 and between R1 and R3:

**On R1:**

```
R1#show ip eigrp 100 neighbors
EIGRP-IPv4 Neighbors for AS(100)

H   Address           Interface        Hold Uptime    SRTT   RTO
Q   Seq
                                       (sec)          (ms)
Cnt Num
1   100.1.1.3         Tu100            14 00:02:24       4   1470
0   3
0   100.1.1.2         Tu100            11 00:06:22       2   1470
0   4
```

The **show ip route eigrp 100** command shows the EIGRP learned routes on R1, R2, and R3. Much as with OSPF for Phase 2, notice that the next hops for 24.1.1.0/24 and 36.1.1.0/24 on R2 and R3 point to each other's tunnel IP address:

**On R1:**

```
R1#show ip route eigrp 100 | begin Gate
Gateway of last resort is not set

      24.0.0.0/24 is subnetted, 1 subnets
```

```
D          24.1.1.0 [90/26880256] via 100.1.1.2, 00:09:02, Tunnel100
        36.0.0.0/24 is subnetted, 1 subnets
D          36.1.1.0 [90/26880256] via 100.1.1.3, 00:05:04, Tunnel100
```

## On R2:

```
R2#show ip route eigrp 100 | begin Gate
Gateway of last resort is not set

        17.0.0.0/24 is subnetted, 1 subnets
D        17.1.1.0 [90/26880256] via 100.1.1.1, 00:09:52, Tunnel100
        36.0.0.0/24 is subnetted, 1 subnets
D        36.1.1.0 [90/28160256] via 100.1.1.3, 00:05:55, Tunnel100
```

## On R3:

```
R3#show ip route eigrp 100 | begin Gate
Gateway of last resort is not set

        17.0.0.0/24 is subnetted, 1 subnets
D        17.1.1.0 [90/26880256] via 100.1.1.1, 00:06:25, Tunnel100
        24.0.0.0/24 is subnetted, 1 subnets
D        24.1.1.0 [90/28160256] via 100.1.1.2, 00:06:25, Tunnel100
```

The first **traceroute** from R4 to R6 traverses the hub while the NHRP resolution process completes. The following **traceroute** follows the direct path over the spoke-to-spoke tunnel between R2 and R3:

## On R4:

```
R4#traceroute 36.1.1.3 numeric

Type escape sequence to abort.
Tracing the route to 36.1.1.3
VRF info: (vrf in name/id, vrf out name/id)
  1 24.1.1.2 0 msec 5 msec 5 msec
  2 100.1.1.1 5 msec 1 msec 0 msec
  3 100.1.1.3 0 msec 1 msec 0 msec

R4#traceroute 36.1.1.3 numeric
```

```
Type escape sequence to abort.
Tracing the route to 36.1.1.3
VRF info: (vrf in name/id, vrf out name/id)
  1 24.1.1.2 1 msec 5 msec 5 msec
  2 100.1.1.3 1 msec 1 msec 0 msec
```

A **traceroute** from R4 to R7 at the main site is routed through the hub R1:

## On R4:

```
R4#traceroute 17.1.1.7 numeric

Type escape sequence to abort.
Tracing the route to 18.1.1.8
VRF info: (vrf in name/id, vrf out name/id)
  1 24.1.1.2 4 msec 6 msec 4 msec
  2 100.1.1.1 2 msec 4 msec 1 msec
  3 17.1.1.7 0 msec 1 msec 0 msec
```

## Implement iBGP

The configuration for iBGP peering sessions is similar to the iBGP configuration made in the Phase 1 section of this chapter.

R1 is configured as a route-reflector and uses BGP's dynamic Peering feature to allow dynamic peering sessions to be established. Spokes R2 and R3 are configured with **neighbor** statements to form iBGP peering sessions with R1's tunnel IP address 100.1.1.1. The host networks at each site are advertised into BGP with the **network** statement. Before BGP is configured, EIGRP AS 100 must be removed:

## On R1:

```
R1(config)#no router eigrp 100

R1(config)#router bgp 100
R1(config-router)#neighbor spokes peer-group
R1(config-router)#neighbor spokes remote-as 100
R1(config-router)#bgp listen range 100.1.1.0/24 peer-group spokes

R1(config-router)#address-family ipv4
R1(config-router-af)#neighbor spokes activate
R1(config-router-af)#neighbor spokes route-reflector-client
R1(config-router-af)#network 17.1.1.0 mask 255.255.255.0
```

## On R2:

```
R2(config)#no router eigrp 100

R2(config)#router bgp 100
R2(config-router)#neighbor 100.1.1.1 remote-as 100

R2(config-router)#address-family ipv4
R2(config-router-af)#neighbor 100.1.1.1 activate
R2(config-router-af)#network 24.1.1.0 mask 255.255.255.0
```

You should see the following console message:

```
%BGP-5-ADJCHANGE: neighbor 100.1.1.1 Up
```

## On R3:

```
R3(config)#no router eigrp 100

R3(config)#router bgp 100
R3(config-router)#neighbor 100.1.1.1 remote-as 100

R3(config-router)#address-family ipv4
R3(config-router-af)#network 36.1.1.0 mask 255.255.255.0
R3(config-router-af)#neighbor 100.1.1.1 activate
```

You should see the following console message:

```
%BGP-5-ADJCHANGE: neighbor 100.1.1.1 Up
```

The **show ip bgp** output on R1, R2, and R3 shows the host networks each site learns via BGP:

## On R1:

```
R1#show ip bgp | begin Net

     Network          Next Hop         Metric LocPrf Weight Path
 *>   17.1.1.0/24      0.0.0.0               0         32768 i
 *>i  24.1.1.0/24      100.1.1.2             0    100     0 i
 *>i  36.1.1.0/24      100.1.1.3             0    100     0 i
```

**On R2:**

```
R2#show ip bgp | begin Net

     Network          Next Hop          Metric LocPrf Weight Path
 *>i  17.1.1.0/24      100.1.1.1              0    100      0 i
 *>   24.1.1.0/24      0.0.0.0                0          32768 i
 *>i  36.1.1.0/24      100.1.1.3              0    100      0 i
```

**On R3:**

```
R3#show ip bgp | begin Net

     Network          Next Hop          Metric LocPrf Weight Path
 *>i  17.1.1.0/24      100.1.1.1              0    100      0 i
 *>i  24.1.1.0/24      100.1.1.2              0    100      0 i
 *>   36.1.1.0/24      0.0.0.0                0          32768 i
```

Notice the next hop IP address for the 36.1.1.0/24 network on R2 and for the 24.1.1.0/24 network on R3 in the output above and below. Since route reflectors do not modify the next hop attribute, the next hop IP address on R2 and R3 for each other's host networks is retained. The RIB entries on the spokes below confirm this:

**On R2:**

```
R2#show ip route bgp | begin Gate
Gateway of last resort is not set

      17.0.0.0/24 is subnetted, 1 subnets
B        17.1.1.0 [200/0] via 100.1.1.1, 00:08:22
      36.0.0.0/24 is subnetted, 1 subnets
B        36.1.1.0 [200/0] via 100.1.1.3, 00:04:32
```

**On R3:**

```
R3#show ip route bgp | begin Gate
Gateway of last resort is not set

      17.0.0.0/24 is subnetted, 1 subnets
B        17.1.1.0 [200/0] via 100.1.1.1, 00:05:03
      24.0.0.0/24 is subnetted, 1 subnets
B        24.1.1.0 [200/0] via 100.1.1.2, 00:05:03
```

To test reachability, traceroutes are performed between sites. As seen below, traffic from R4 to R6 first traverses the hub, and subsequent traffic uses the direct spoke to spoke tunnel:

## On R4:

```
R4#traceroute 36.1.1.6

Type escape sequence to abort.
Tracing the route to 36.1.1.6
VRF info: (vrf in name/id, vrf out name/id)
  1 24.1.1.2 4 msec 5 msec 5 msec
  2 100.1.1.1 3 msec 2 msec 1 msec
  3 100.1.1.3 1 msec 0 msec 1 msec
  4 36.1.1.6 0 msec 2 msec 1 msec

R4#traceroute 36.1.1.6

Type escape sequence to abort.
Tracing the route to 36.1.1.6
VRF info: (vrf in name/id, vrf out name/id)
  1 24.1.1.2 1 msec 4 msec 6 msec
  2 100.1.1.3 1 msec 1 msec 0 msec
  3 36.1.1.6 1 msec 1 msec 0 msec
```

Traffic from R4 to R7 is routed through the Hub:

## On R4:

```
R4#traceroute 17.1.1.7 probe 1

Type escape sequence to abort.
Tracing the route to 17.1.1.7
VRF info: (vrf in name/id, vrf out name/id)
  1 24.1.1.2 11 msec
  2 100.1.1.1 10 msec
  3 17.1.1.7 12 msec
```

## Implement eBGP

Similar to the case with the eBGP section of Phase 1, eBGP can be implemented in Phase 2 either with the Spokes in:

- Same autonomous system, or

- Different autonomous system

The following configures the spokes R2 and R3 in same autonomous systems, 230. Hub R1 is configured to be in AS 100. The host networks at each site are advertised into BGP with the **network** command.

For Phase 2, the spokes need specific routes with the true next hop IP address to trigger the NHRP resolution process. This means that, unlike with Phase 1, the hub cannot be configured to propagate a default route to the spokes, as that would reset the next hop IP address to the hub's tunnel IP address. For this purpose, it is important to configure the **allowas-in** feature on R2 and R3. The **allowas-in** feature on the spokes R2 and R3 results in them bypassing the loop-prevention check and accepting routes with the ASN 230 in the AS_PATH attribute. Before the routers are configured, you should remove BGP from the previous task/scenario:

### On R1:

```
R1(config)#no router bgp 100

R1(config)#router bgp 100
R1(config-router)#neighbor spokes peer-group
R1(config-router)#neighbor spokes remote-as 230
R1(config-router)#bgp listen range 100.1.1.0/24 peer-group spokes

R1(config-router)#address-family ipv4
R1(config-router-af)#neighbor spokes activate
R1(config-router-af)#network 17.1.1.0 mask 255.255.255.0
```

### On R2:

```
R2(config)#no router bgp 100

R2(config)#router bgp 230
R2(config-router)#neighbor 100.1.1.1 remote-as 100

R2(config-router)#address-family ipv4
R2(config-router-af)#neighbor 100.1.1.1 activate
R2(config-router-af)#neighbor 100.1.1.1 allowas-in
R2(config-router-af)#network 24.1.1.0 mask 255.255.255.0
```

You should see the following console message:

```
%BGP-5-ADJCHANGE: neighbor 100.1.1.1 Up
```

## On R3:

```
R2(config)#no router bgp 100

R3(config)#router bgp 230
R3(config-router)#neighbor 100.1.1.1 remote-as 100

R3(config-router)#address-family ipv4
R3(config-router-af)#neighbor 100.1.1.1 activate
R3(config-router-af)#neighbor 100.1.1.1 allowas-in
R3(config-router-af)#network 36.1.1.0 mask 255.255.255.0
```

You should see the following console message:

```
%BGP-5-ADJCHANGE: neighbor 100.1.1.1 Up
```

The **show ip bgp** output verifies that R1, R2, and R3 learn of each other's host networks via BGP:

## On R1:

```
R1#show ip bgp | begin Net

     Network          Next Hop          Metric LocPrf Weight Path
 *>   17.1.1.0/24     0.0.0.0                0          32768 i
 *>   24.1.1.0/24     100.1.1.2              0              0 230 i
 *>   36.1.1.0/24     100.1.1.3              0              0 230 i
```

## On R2:

```
R2#show ip bgp | begin Net

     Network          Next Hop        Metric LocPrf Weight Path
 *>   17.1.1.0/24     100.1.1.1            0              0 100 i
 *>   24.1.1.0/24     0.0.0.0             0          32768 i
 *>   36.1.1.0/24     100.1.1.3                          0 100 230 i
```

## On R3:

```
R3#show ip bgp | begin Net

     Network          Next Hop          Metric LocPrf Weight Path
```

```
*>    17.1.1.0/24      100.1.1.1            0              0 100 i
*>    24.1.1.0/24      100.1.1.2                           0 100 230 i
*>    36.1.1.0/24      0.0.0.0              0          32768 i
```

The above demonstrated the configuration commands needed to establish eBGP peering between the hub and spokes with the spokes sharing the same ASN. The following implements the second design option, where the spokes R2 and R3 are placed in different autonomous systems—ASN 200 and AS 300, respectively. They are configured to form eBGP peerings with the hub R1 in ASN 100. The host networks are advertised into BGP with the **network** command:

## On R1:

```
R1(config)#router bgp 100
R1(config-router)#no neighbor spokes remote-as 230
R1(config-router)#neighbor spokes remote-as 200 alternate-as 300
```

## On R2:

```
R2(config)#no router bgp 230

R2(config)#router bgp 200
R2(config-router)#neighbor 100.1.1.1 remote-as 100

R2(config-router)#address-family ipv4
R2(config-router-af)#network 24.1.1.0 mask 255.255.255.0
R2(config-router-af)#neighbor 100.1.1.1 activate
```

You should see the following console message:

```
%BGP-5-ADJCHANGE: neighbor 100.1.1.1 Up
```

## On R3:

```
R3(config)#no router bgp 230

R3(config)#router bgp 300
R3(config-router)#neighbor 100.1.1.1 remote-as 100

R3(config-router)#address-family ipv4
R3(config-router-af)#neighbor 100.1.1.1 activate
R3(config-router-af)#network 36.1.1.0 mask 255.255.255.0
```

You should see the following console message:

```
%BGP-5-ADJCHANGE: neighbor 100.1.1.1 Up
```

The **show ip bgp** output on R1, R2, and R3 confirms the host networks learned via BGP. The next hop IP address for 36.1.1.0/24 is R3's tunnel IP address 100.1.1.3 on R2. Similarly, the next hop IP address for the 24.1.1.0/24 network is R2's tunnel IP address 100.1.1.2 on R3. This is a result of BGP third-party next hop feature, which is turned on by default:

**On R1:**

```
R1#show ip bgp | begin Net

     Network          Next Hop          Metric LocPrf Weight Path
 *>  17.1.1.0/24      0.0.0.0                0          32768 i
 *>  24.1.1.0/24      100.1.1.2              0              0 200 i
 *>  36.1.1.0/24      100.1.1.3              0              0 300 i
```

**On R2:**

```
R2#show ip bgp | begin Net

     Network          Next Hop        Metric LocPrf Weight Path
 *>  17.1.1.0/24      100.1.1.1            0            0 100 i
 *>  24.1.1.0/24      0.0.0.0              0        32768 i
 *>  36.1.1.0/24      100.1.1.3                         0 100 300 i
```

**On R3:**

```
R3#show ip bgp | begin Net

     Network          Next Hop          Metric LocPrf Weight Path
 *>  17.1.1.0/24      100.1.1.1              0              0 100 i
 *>  24.1.1.0/24      100.1.1.2                             0 100
200 i
 *>  36.1.1.0/24      0.0.0.0               0          32768 i
```

To test reachability for both scenarios, traceroutes are performed between sites. As seen below, traffic from R4 to R6 first traverses the hub and subsequent traffic uses the direct spoke to spoke tunnel:

**On R4:**

```
R4#traceroute 36.1.1.6
```

```
Type escape sequence to abort.
Tracing the route to 36.1.1.6
VRF info: (vrf in name/id, vrf out name/id)
  1 24.1.1.2 4 msec 5 msec 5 msec
  2 100.1.1.1 3 msec 2 msec 1 msec ! DMVPN Hub R1
  3 100.1.1.3 1 msec 0 msec 1 msec
  4 36.1.1.6 0 msec 2 msec 1 msec

R4#traceroute 36.1.1.6

Type escape sequence to abort.
Tracing the route to 36.1.1.6
VRF info: (vrf in name/id, vrf out name/id)
  1 24.1.1.2 1 msec 4 msec 6 msec
  2 100.1.1.3 1 msec 1 msec 0 msec
  3 36.1.1.6 1 msec 1 msec 0 msec
```

Traffic from R4 to R7 is routed through the Hub:

**On R4:**

```
R4#traceroute 17.1.1.7 probe 1

Type escape sequence to abort.
Tracing the route to 17.1.1.7
VRF info: (vrf in name/id, vrf out name/id)
  1 24.1.1.2 11 msec
  2 100.1.1.1 10 msec
  3 17.1.1.7 12 msec
```

## Implement Phase 3

## Design Goal

During a network design review, the network engineers at ABC Corp evaluate the effect of routing protocol updates and size on the remote site spoke routers as ABC Corp expanded into other locations. They decide that it was not necessary for the remote sites to initially receive all routing information for all other remote sites unless those sites need to directly communicate. The engineering team decides to implement complete summarization from the main site hub router toward the remote site spoke routers while retaining the ability for remote sites to directly communicate with each other.

## DMVPN Tunnel Configuration

To enable Phase 3 enhancements for the DMVPN cloud, the **ip nhrp redirect** command is added to the Phase 2 DMVPN tunnel configuration on the hub, as indicated in the introductory sections. Likewise, the **ip nhrp shortcut** command is added to the Phase 2 DMVPN tunnel configuration on the spokes R2 and R3. These changes are shown below by first removing the current tunnel 100 interfaces on R1, R2, and R3. The tunnel 100 interface is then recreated with the Phase 3 enhancement configuration commands:

```
On R1:

R1(config)#no interface tunnel 100

R1(config)#interface tunnel 100
R1(config-if)#ip address 100.1.1.1 255.255.255.0
R1(config-if)#tunnel source 15.1.1.1
R1(config-if)#tunnel mode gre multipoint
R1(config-if)#ip nhrp redirect
R1(config-if)#ip nhrp network-id 100
R1(config-if)#ip nhrp map multicast dynamic


On R2:

R2(config)#no interface tunnel 100

R2(config)#interface tunnel 100
R2(config-if)#ip address 100.1.1.2 255.255.255.0
R2(config-if)#ip nhrp network-id 100
R2(config-if)#tunnel source 25.1.1.2
R2(config-if)#tunnel mode gre multipoint
R2(config-if)#ip nhrp nhs 100.1.1.1 nbma 15.1.1.1 multicast
R2(config-if)#ip nhrp shortcut


On R3:

R3(config)#no interface tunnel 100

R3(config)#interface tunnel 100
R3(config-if)#ip address 100.1.1.3 255.255.255.0
R3(config-if)#ip nhrp network-id 100
R3(config-if)#tunnel source 35.1.1.3
R3(config-if)#tunnel mode gre multipoint
R3(config-if)#ip nhrp nhs 100.1.1.1 nbma 15.1.1.1 multicast
R3(config-if)#ip nhrp shortcut
```

### To verify the configuration:

The show ip nhrp command is then issued on R1. As seen below, both R2 and R3 have successful registered with the hub:

### On R1:

```
R1#show ip nhrp

100.1.1.2/32 via 100.1.1.2
   Tunnel100 created 00:03:56, expire 00:08:33
   Type: dynamic, Flags: registered nhop
   NBMA address: 25.1.1.2
100.1.1.3/32 via 100.1.1.3
   Tunnel100 created 00:03:57, expire 00:09:08
   Type: dynamic, Flags: registered nhop
   NBMA address: 35.1.1.3
```

## Implement OSPF

Because it is not possible to completely summarize routing information from hub to spokes in OSPF, OSPF is not suitable for the design goals of this section. As such, OSPF will not be implemented in this section.

**Note**   It is important to understand that, as long as the spokes are configured with mGRE interfaces, OSPF's broadcast network type can be used to build direct spoke-to-spoke tunnels. However, this configuration does not necessarily result in true Phase 3 behavior. Due to the next hop being preserved with the use of the broadcast network type, the RIB and CEF entries point to the true next hop: the remote spoke. As a result, the spokes self-trigger a resolution request for the next hop.

In true Phase 3 behavior, the NHRP resolution process should be triggered because of receiving the **traffic indication** messages from the hub.

In actuality, the spoke will perform two resolutions: one for the remote spoke's overlay address (caused by an incomplete CEF adjacency, a Phase 2 construct) and another for the target network (caused by the NHRP traffic indication message it receives from the hub).

Due to this order of operations, the Phase 3 resolution is redundant and may lead to no change in the routing table (depending on how specific the prefixes are).

*Continued*

The fact that the Phase 3 resolution is redundant and can result in no change leads to the conclusion that OSPF's broadcast network and the NBMA network types do not allow for true Phase 3 behavior. At the very best, the Phase 3 enhancements are superfluous if used because the next hop is already pointing to the correct remote spoke.

This leaves point-to-point and point-to-multipoint OSPF network types. These network types can be implemented to achieve true, efficient Phase 3 behavior. The hub R1 is configured with a point-to-multipoint network type as it must be form OSPF adjacencies with both R2 and R3. Spokes R2 and R3 use the point-to-point OSPF network type on their tunnel interfaces to allow them to form OSPF adjacencies with R1. The hello timer on the hub is modified to 10 seconds to match the hello timer of point-to-point interface on the spokes.

Even though the above P2P/P2MP configuration allows for Phase 3 resolution to be implemented properly without redundant Phase 2-style resolution, OSPF cannot take advantage of a fully optimized Phase 3 implementation where minimal routing information is shared between the hub and spokes. This is because of OSPF's limitations with summarization within an single OSPF area. R1, R2, and R3 in the same area must have complete topology information in order to maintain loop-free SPF computations in OSPF. Thus, R1 cannot simply flood a default route and suppress other more-specific routing information from the spokes.

## Implement EIGRP

Implementing full Phase 3 DMVPN designs with summarization from the hub to the spokes is not fully possible with OSPF. This is because OSPF has strict topology and hierarchy rules for it to operate. EIGRP, on the other hand, has no such topological or hierarchical constraints. Thus, it can easily accommodate Phase 3 summarization.

The following enables EIGRP on the tunnel 100 and the host network interfaces on R1, R2, and R3. The **passive-interface** command declares the host-facing interfaces passive, preventing any EIGRP adjacencies from forming over them. Before EIGRP is configured, BGP must be removed from the previous task:

```
On R1:

R1(config)#no router bgp 100

R1(config)#router eigrp 100
R1(config-router)#network 17.1.1.1 0.0.0.0
R1(config-router)#network 100.1.1.1 0.0.0.0
R1(config-router)#passive-interface g0/7
```

## On R2:

```
R2(config)#no router bgp 200

R2(config)#router eigrp 100
R2(config-router)#network 24.1.1.2 0.0.0.0
R2(config-router)#network 100.1.1.2 0.0.0.0
R2(config-router)#passive-interface g0/4
```

You should see the following console message:

```
%DUAL-5-NBRCHANGE: EIGRP-IPv4 100: Neighbor 100.1.1.1 (Tunnel100) is
up: new adjacency
```

## On R3:

```
R3(config)#no router bgp 300

R3(config)#router eigrp 100
R3(config-router)#network 36.1.1.3 0.0.0.0
R3(config-router)#network 100.1.1.3 0.0.0.0
R3(config-router)#passive-interface g0/6
```

You should see the following console message:

```
%DUAL-5-NBRCHANGE: EIGRP-IPv4 100: Neighbor 100.1.1.1 (Tunnel100) is
up: new adjacency
```

After completing the above, the following verifies the EIGRP neighborships between R1 - R2 and R1 - R3. The routing tables on each of these routers also show the host networks at each site learned via EIGRP:

## On R1:

```
R1#show ip eigrp 100 neighbors

EIGRP-IPv4 Neighbors for AS(100)
H   Address          Interface       Hold Uptime     SRTT   RTO  Q   Seq
                                     (sec)           (ms)        Cnt
Num
1   100.1.1.3        Tu100           14 00:02:30    12   1470  0   3
0   100.1.1.2        Tu100           11 00:05:59     5   1470  0   3
```

**On R1:**

```
R1#show ip route eigrp 100 | begin Gate
Gateway of last resort is not set

      24.0.0.0/24 is subnetted, 1 subnets
D        24.1.1.0 [90/26880256] via 100.1.1.2, 00:08:52, Tunnel100
      36.0.0.0/24 is subnetted, 1 subnets
D        36.1.1.0 [90/26880256] via 100.1.1.3, 00:05:22, Tunnel100
```

**On R2:**

```
R2#show ip route eigrp 100 | begin Gate
Gateway of last resort is not set

      17.0.0.0/24 is subnetted, 1 subnets
D        17.1.1.0 [90/26880256] via 100.1.1.1, 00:09:50, Tunnel100
```

**On R3:**

```
R3#show ip route eigrp 100 | begin Gate
Gateway of last resort is not set

      17.0.0.0/24 is subnetted, 1 subnets
D        17.1.1.0 [90/26880256] via 100.1.1.1, 00:07:05, Tunnel100
```

**On R3:**

```
R3#show ip route eigrp 100 | begin Gate
Gateway of last resort is not set

      17.0.0.0/24 is subnetted, 1 subnets
D        17.1.1.0 [90/26880256] via 100.1.1.1, 00:07:05, Tunnel100
```

In the routing table above, notice that the hub has learned of the host networks 24.1.1.0/24 and 36.1.1.0/24 via EIGRP from R2 and R3, respectively. R2 and R3, however, only learn of the host network 17.1.1.0/24 at the main site. The reason for this, as already mentioned, is that the advertisement of the host networks at the remote sites is being prevented by split horizon on the hub R1. However, as per the design requirements, the spokes R2 and R3 do not need the specific routes; rather, the route information should be summarized by the hub. For this purpose, there is no need to disable split horizon at the hub site.

To complete the design, R1 is configured to send a default route via EIGRP to R2 and
R3 with the **ip summary-address eigrp 100 0.0.0.0 0.0.0.0** command in its tunnel 100
interface:

## On R1:

```
R1(config)#interface tunnel 100
R1(config-if)#ip summary-address eigrp 100 0.0.0.0 0.0.0.0
```

Following reveals the routing table on R2 and R3 that is now populated with an EIGRP
default route from the hub R1:

## On R2:

```
R2#show ip route eigrp 100 | begin Gate
Gateway of last resort is 100.1.1.1 to network 0.0.0.0

D*    0.0.0.0/0 [90/26880256] via 100.1.1.1, 00:01:22, Tunnel100
```

## On R3:

```
R3#show ip route eigrp 100 | begin Gate
Gateway of last resort is 100.1.1.1 to network 0.0.0.0

D*    0.0.0.0/0 [90/26880256] via 100.1.1.1, 00:01:49, Tunnel100
```

Traceroutes are then issued to test reachability between the sites. As seen below, traffic
from R4 to R6 first traverses the hub. Once the NHRP resolution process completes,
the same traffic is shown to travel over the spoke to spoke tunnel between R2 and R3.
Traffic from R4 to R7 is sent to the hub:

## On R4:

```
R4#traceroute 36.1.1.6

Type escape sequence to abort.
Tracing the route to 36.1.1.6
VRF info: (vrf in name/id, vrf out name/id)
  1 24.1.1.2 4 msec 5 msec 5 msec
  2 100.1.1.1 3 msec 2 msec 1 msec ! DMVPN Hub R1
  3 100.1.1.3 1 msec 0 msec 1 msec
  4 36.1.1.6 0 msec 2 msec 1 msec
```

```
R4#traceroute 36.1.1.6

Type escape sequence to abort.
Tracing the route to 36.1.1.6
VRF info: (vrf in name/id, vrf out name/id)
  1 24.1.1.2 1 msec 4 msec 6 msec
  2 100.1.1.3 1 msec 1 msec 0 msec
  3 36.1.1.6 1 msec 1 msec 0 msec
```

Traffic from R4 to R7 is routed through the Hub:

## On R4:

```
R4#traceroute 17.1.1.7 probe 1

Type escape sequence to abort.
Tracing the route to 17.1.1.7
VRF info: (vrf in name/id, vrf out name/id)
  1 24.1.1.2 11 msec
  2 100.1.1.1 10 msec ! DMVPN Hub R1
  3 17.1.1.7 12 msec
```

The show ip route nhrp | begin Gate command proves that R2 and R3 have added more-specific NHRP routes to reach each other's remote networks:

## On R2:

```
R2#show ip route nhrp | begin Gate
Gateway of last resort is 100.1.1.1 to network 0.0.0.0

      36.0.0.0/24 is subnetted, 1 subnets
H        36.1.1.0 [250/1] via 100.1.1.3, 00:00:27, Tunnel100
      100.0.0.0/8 is variably subnetted, 3 subnets, 2 masks
H        100.1.1.3/32 is directly connected, 00:00:27, Tunnel100
```

## On R3:

```
R3#show ip route nhrp | begin Gate
Gateway of last resort is 100.1.1.1 to network 0.0.0.0

      24.0.0.0/24 is subnetted, 1 subnets
H        24.1.1.0 [250/1] via 100.1.1.2, 00:00:44, Tunnel100
      100.0.0.0/8 is variably subnetted, 3 subnets, 2 masks
H        100.1.1.2/32 is directly connected, 00:00:44, Tunnel100
```

## Implement iBGP

Just as with EIGRP, BGP has no topological or hierarchical constraints, allowing full Phase 3 summarization to be used. To implement this design, R1 is once again configured to function as a route reflector and is configured for dynamic iBGP peerings with clients R2 and R3. The host networks at each site are advertised into BGP with the network statement. Before BGP is configured, the EIGRP routing protocol must be removed and the NHRP cache should be cleared on R2 and R3:

```
On R1:

R1(config)#no router eigrp 100

R1(config)#router bgp 100
R1(config-router)#neighbor spokes peer-group
R1(config-router)#neighor spokes remote 100
R1(config-router)#bgp listen range 100.1.1.0/24 peer-group spokes

R1(config-router)#address-family ipv4
R1(config-router-af)#neighor spokes activate
R1(config-router-af)#network 17.1.1.0 mask 255.255.255.0


On R2:

R2(config)#no router eigrp 100

R2(config)#router bgp 100
R2(config-router)#neighbor 100.1.1.1 remote-as 100

R2(config-router)#address-family ipv4
R2(config-router-af)#network 24.1.1.0 mask 255.255.255.0
R2(config-router-af)#neighbor 100.1.1.1 activate


R2#clear ip nhrp
You should see the following console message:
%BGP-5-ADJCHANGE: neighbor 100.1.1.1 Up


On R3:

R3(config)#no router eigrp 100

R3#clear ip nhrp
```

```
R3(config)#router bgp 100
R3(config-router)#neighbor 100.1.1.1 remote-as 100

R3(config-router)#address-family ipv4
R3(config-router-af)#network 36.1.1.0 mask 255.255.255.0
R3(config-router-af)#neighbor 100.1.1.1 activate
```

You should see the following console message:

```
%BGP-5-ADJCHANGE: neighbor 100.1.1.1 Up
```

R1 is configured to send a default route to the Spokes R2 and R3. The same prefix-list and route-map combination from earlier is used with the neighbor statement on R1. This ensures that R1 only advertises the default route while suppressing the more specific networks 24.1.1.0/24 and 36.1.1.0/24:

## On R1:

```
R1(config)#ip prefix-list TST permit 0.0.0.0/0

R1(config)#route-map default permit 10
R1(config-route-map)#match ip address prefix TST

R1(config)#router bgp 100
R1(config-router)#address-family ipv4
R1(config-router-af)#neighbor spokes default-originate
R1(config-router-af)#neighbor spokes route-map default out


R1#clear ip bgp * out
```

On completing the above configurations, the routing and BGP tables look as shown below. Notice that the next hop IP address for the default route on R2 and R3 is R1's tunnel IP address, 100.1.1.1.

```
R1#show ip bgp | begin Net

     Network          Next Hop          Metric LocPrf Weight Path
     0.0.0.0          0.0.0.0                               0 i
*>   17.1.1.0/24      0.0.0.0                0         32768 i
*>i  24.1.1.0/24      100.1.1.2              0    100      0 i
*>i  36.1.1.0/24      100.1.1.3              0    100      0 i


R1#show ip route bgp | begin Gate
Gateway of last resort is not set

     24.0.0.0/24 is subnetted, 1 subnets
```

```
B        24.1.1.0 [200/0] via 100.1.1.2, 00:09:51
     36.0.0.0/24 is subnetted, 1 subnets
B        36.1.1.0 [200/0] via 100.1.1.3, 00:06:31
```

## On R2:

R2#**show ip bgp | begin Net**

```
    Network            Next Hop           Metric LocPrf Weight Path
 *>i 0.0.0.0           100.1.1.1              0    100      0 i
 *>  24.1.1.0/24       0.0.0.0                0         32768 i
```

R2#**show ip route bgp | begin Gate**
```
Gateway of last resort is 100.1.1.1 to network 0.0.0.0

B*   0.0.0.0/0 [200/0] via 100.1.1.1, 00:01:34
```

## On R3:

R3#**show ip bgp | begin Net**

```
    Network            Next Hop           Metric LocPrf Weight Path
 *>i 0.0.0.0           100.1.1.1              0    100      0 i
 *>  36.1.1.0/24       0.0.0.0                0         32768 i
```

R3#**show ip route bgp | begin Gate**
```
Gateway of last resort is 100.1.1.1 to network 0.0.0.0

B*   0.0.0.0/0 [200/0] via 100.1.1.1, 00:02:32
```

Traceroutes are then issued to test reachability between the sites. As seen below, traffic from R4 to R6 at 2 first traverses the hub. Once the NHRP resolution process completes, the same traffic is shown to travel over the spoke to spoke tunnel between R2 and R3. Traffic from R4 to R7 is sent to the hub:

## On R4:

R4#**traceroute 36.1.1.6**

```
Type escape sequence to abort.
Tracing the route to 36.1.1.6
VRF info: (vrf in name/id, vrf out name/id)
```

```
  1 24.1.1.2 4 msec 5 msec 5 msec
  2 100.1.1.1 3 msec 2 msec 1 msec
  3 100.1.1.3 1 msec 0 msec 1 msec
  4 36.1.1.6 0 msec 2 msec 1 msec
```

R4#**traceroute 36.1.1.6**

```
Type escape sequence to abort.
Tracing the route to 36.1.1.6
VRF info: (vrf in name/id, vrf out name/id)
  1 24.1.1.2 1 msec 4 msec 6 msec
  2 100.1.1.3 1 msec 1 msec 0 msec
  3 36.1.1.6 1 msec 1 msec 0 msec
```

Traffic from R4 to R7 is routed through the Hub:

## On R4:

R4#**traceroute 17.1.1.7 probe 1**

```
Type escape sequence to abort.
Tracing the route to 17.1.1.7
VRF info: (vrf in name/id, vrf out name/id)
  1 24.1.1.2 11 msec
  2 100.1.1.1 10 msec
  3 17.1.1.7 12 msec
```

Just as in the EIGRP example, the show ip route nhrp output from R2 and R3 below confirms the specific NHRP routes have been added to their respective routing tables for the remote networks and tunnel endpoints:

## On R2:

R2#**show ip route nhrp | begin Gate**
```
Gateway of last resort is 100.1.1.1 to network 0.0.0.0

      36.0.0.0/24 is subnetted, 1 subnets
H        36.1.1.0 [250/1] via 100.1.1.3, 00:00:27, Tunnel100
      100.0.0.0/8 is variably subnetted, 3 subnets, 2 masks
H        100.1.1.3/32 is directly connected, 00:00:27, Tunnel100
```

**On R3:**

```
R3#show ip route nhrp | begin Gate
Gateway of last resort is 100.1.1.1 to network 0.0.0.0

      24.0.0.0/24 is subnetted, 1 subnets
H        24.1.1.0 [250/1] via 100.1.1.2, 00:00:44, Tunnel100
      100.0.0.0/8 is variably subnetted, 3 subnets, 2 masks
H        100.1.1.2/32 is directly connected, 00:00:44, Tunnel100
```

## Implement eBGP

Similar to what was done in Phase 1 and Phase 2, eBGP can be implemented in two ways for Phase 3. The spokes can belong to the same AS or to different ASes.

### Spokes in the Same AS

Below sets the base configuration for this design choice.

R1 in AS 100 will configured to form dynamic eBGP peering sessions with R2 and R3. R2 and R3 are configured in AS 230. The network statement on R1, R2, and R3 is used to advertise their respective host networks into BGP.

The **allowas-in** feature will not be used for Phase 3. This is because the hub R1 will be configured to send a default route to the Spokes R2 and R3. In doing so, it will set itself as the next hop IP address in compliance with the design goals.

**On R1:**

```
R1(config)#no router bgp 100

R1(config)#router bgp 100
R1(config-router)#neighbor spokes peer-group
R1(config-router)#neighbor spokes remote-as 230
R1(config-router)#bgp listen range 100.1.1.0/24 peer-group spokes

R1(config-router)#address-family ipv4
R1(config-router-af)#neighbor spokes activate
R1(config-router-af)#network 17.1.1.0 mask 255.255.255.0
```

### On R2:

```
R2(config)#no router bgp 100

R2(config)#router bgp 230
R2(config-router)#neighbor 100.1.1.1 remote-as 100

R2(config-router)#address-family ipv4
R2(config-router-af)#neighbor 100.1.1.1 activate
R2(config-router-af)#network 24.1.1.0 mask 255.255.255.0
```

You should see the following console message:

```
%BGP-5-ADJCHANGE: neighbor 100.1.1.1 Up
```

### On R3:

```
R3(config)#no router bgp 100

R3(config)#router bgp 230
R3(config-router)#neighbor 100.1.1.1 remote-as 100

R3(config-router)#address-family ipv4
R3(config-router-af)#neighbor 100.1.1.1 activate
R3(config-router-af)#network 36.1.1.0 mask 255.255.255.0
```

You should see the following console message:

```
%BGP-5-ADJCHANGE: neighbor 100.1.1.1 Up
```

To honor the design requirements, using similar methods as in earlier tasks, R1 is configured to advertise BGP default route to Spokes R2 and R3:

### On R1:

```
R1(config)#ip prefix-list TST permit 0.0.0.0/0

R1(config)#route-map default permit 10
R1(config-route-map)# match ip address prefix-list TST

R1(config)#router bgp 100
R1(config-router)#address-family ipv4
R1(config-router-af)#neighbor spokes default-originate
R1(config-router-af)#neighbor spokes route-map default out

R1#clear ip bgp * out
```

Following shows the BGP routes learned on R1, R2, and R3. Both R2 and R3 have a BGP default route from R1:

**On R1:**

R1#**show ip bgp | begin Net**

|     | Network | Next Hop | Metric | LocPrf | Weight | Path |
|-----|---------|----------|--------|--------|--------|------|
|     | 0.0.0.0 | 0.0.0.0 |        |        | 0 | i |
| *>  | 17.1.1.0/24 | 0.0.0.0 | 0 |    | 32768 | i |
| *>  | 24.1.1.0/24 | 100.1.1.2 | 0 |  | 0 | 230 i |
| *>  | 36.1.1.0/24 | 100.1.1.3 | 0 |  | 0 | 230 i |

R1#**show ip route bgp | begin Gate**
Gateway of last resort is not set

```
     24.0.0.0/24 is subnetted, 1 subnets
B        24.1.1.0 [20/0] via 100.1.1.2, 00:08:35
     36.0.0.0/24 is subnetted, 1 subnets
B        36.1.1.0 [20/0] via 100.1.1.3, 00:06:02
```

**On R2:**

R2#**show ip bgp | begin Net**

|     | Network | Next Hop | Metric | LocPrf | Weight | Path |
|-----|---------|----------|--------|--------|--------|------|
| *>  | 0.0.0.0 | 100.1.1.1 |       |        | 0 | 100 i |
| *>  | 24.1.1.0/24 | 0.0.0.0 | 0 |    | 32768 | i |

R2#**show ip route bgp | begin Gate**
Gateway of last resort is 100.1.1.1 to network 0.0.0.0

```
B*   0.0.0.0/0 [20/0] via 100.1.1.1, 00:02:44
```

**On R3:**

R3#**show ip bgp | begin Net**

|     | Network | Next Hop | Metric | LocPrf | Weight | Path |
|-----|---------|----------|--------|--------|--------|------|

```
 *>    0.0.0.0          100.1.1.1                                0 100 i
 *>    36.1.1.0/24      0.0.0.0                     0        32768 i


R3#show ip route bgp | begin Gate
Gateway of last resort is 100.1.1.1 to network 0.0.0.0


B*    0.0.0.0/0 [20/0] via 100.1.1.1, 00:03:18
```

### Spokes in Different Autonomous Systems

The second design option is to configure the spokes R2 and R3 in different autonomous systems—ASNs 200 and 300, respectively. The hub R1 is configured in ASN 100:

**On R1:**

```
R1(config)#router bgp 100
R1(config-router)#no neighbor spokes remote-as 230
R1(config-router)#neighbor spokes remote-as 200 alternate-as 300

R1(config-router)#address-family ipv4
R1(config-router-af)#no neighbor spokes default-originate
R1(config-router-af)#no neighbor spokes route-map default out

R1#clear ip bgp *
```

**On R2:**

```
R2(config)#no router bgp 230

R2(config)#router bgp 200
R2(config-router)#neighbor 100.1.1.1 remote-as 100

R2(config-router)#address-family ipv4
R2(config-router-af)#neighbor 100.1.1.1 activate
R2(config-router-af)#network 24.1.1.0 mask 255.255.255.0
```

You should see the following console message:

```
%BGP-5-ADJCHANGE: neighbor 100.1.1.1 Up
```

## On R3:

```
R3(config)#no router bgp 230

R3(config)#router bgp 300
R3(config-router)#neighbor 100.1.1.1 remote 100

R3(config-router)#address-family ipv4
R3(config-router-af)#neighbor 100.1.1.1 act
R3(config-router-af)#network 36.1.1.0 mask 255.255.255.0
```

Due to the third-party next hop feature, R1 does not specify itself as the next hop when advertising paths to R2 and R3. This means that R2 and R3 see each other's tunnel IP address as the next hop for each other's host networks, preventing them from advertising a true Phase 3 behavior:

## On R1:

```
R1#show ip bgp | begin Net

     Network          Next Hop         Metric LocPrf Weight Path
 *>  17.1.1.0/24      0.0.0.0               0          32768 i
 *>  24.1.1.0/24      100.1.1.2             0              0 200 i
 *>  36.1.1.0/24      100.1.1.3             0              0 300 i
```

## On R2:

```
R2#show ip bgp | begin Net

     Network          Next Hop         Metric LocPrf Weight Path
 *>  17.1.1.0/24      100.1.1.1             0              0 100 i
 *>  24.1.1.0/24      0.0.0.0               0          32768 i
 *>  36.1.1.0/24      100.1.1.3                            0 100 300 i
```

## On R3:

```
R3#show ip bgp | begin Net
     Network          Next Hop         Metric LocPrf Weight Path
 *>  17.1.1.0/24      100.1.1.1             0              0 100 i
 *>  24.1.1.0/24      100.1.1.2                            0 100 200 i
 *>  36.1.1.0/24      0.0.0.0               0          32768 i
```

This default behavior can be turned off with the **neighbor spokes next-hop-self** command. However, the design requires the Hub R1 to propagate a default route to R2 and R3. This means setting the next hop to self on R1 would be unnecessary as the hub would advertise itself as the next hop for the default route it generates. Because the ip prefix-list and the route-map is already configured, it should still be in R1's running configuration; therefore, the only commands necessary on R1 to accomplish this task are to configure the neighbor spokes default-originate and neighbor spokes route-map out commands:

## On R1:

To see the IP prefix list and the route map:

```
R1#show run | include ip prefix
ip prefix-list TST seq 5 permit 0.0.0.0/0

R1#show run | section route-map
  neighbor spokes route-map default out
route-map default permit 10
 match ip address prefix-list TST

R1(config)#router bgp 100

R1(config-router)#address-family ipv4
R1(config-router-af)#neighbor spokes default-originate
R1(config-router-af)#neighbor spokes route-map default out

R1#clear ip bgp * out
```

As seen below, Spokes R2 and R3 have each installed a BGP default route with 100.1.1.1 as the next hop IP address:

## On R2:

```
R2#show ip bgp | begin Net

     Network          Next Hop            Metric LocPrf Weight Path
 *>   0.0.0.0          100.1.1.1                              0 100 i
 *>   24.1.1.0/24      0.0.0.0                  0         32768 i
```

## On R3:

```
R3#show ip bgp | begin Net
```

```
      Network              Next Hop           Metric LocPrf Weight Path
  *>   0.0.0.0             100.1.1.1                          0 100 i
  *>   36.1.1.0/24         0.0.0.0              0          32768 i
```

Finally, traceroutes are issued to test reachability for both design choices. As seen below, traffic from R4 to R6 at first traverses the hub. After the NHRP resolution process completes, the same traffic is shown to travel over the spoke-to-spoke tunnel between R2 and R3. Traffic from R4 to R7 is sent to the hub:

## On R4:

```
R4#traceroute 36.1.1.6

Type escape sequence to abort.
Tracing the route to 36.1.1.6
VRF info: (vrf in name/id, vrf out name/id)
  1 24.1.1.2 4 msec 5 msec 5 msec
  2 100.1.1.1 3 msec 2 msec 1 msec ! DMVPN Hub R1
  3 100.1.1.3 1 msec 0 msec 1 msec
  4 36.1.1.6 0 msec 2 msec 1 msec


R4#traceroute 36.1.1.6

Type escape sequence to abort.
Tracing the route to 36.1.1.6
VRF info: (vrf in name/id, vrf out name/id)
  1 24.1.1.2 1 msec 4 msec 6 msec
  2 100.1.1.3 1 msec 1 msec 0 msec
  3 36.1.1.6 1 msec 1 msec 0 msec
```

Traffic from R4 to R7 is routed through the Hub:

## On R4:

```
R4#traceroute 17.1.1.7 probe 1

Type escape sequence to abort.
Tracing the route to 17.1.1.7
VRF info: (vrf in name/id, vrf out name/id)
  1 24.1.1.2 11 msec
  2 100.1.1.1 10 msec
  3 17.1.1.7 12 msec
```

The routing tables on R2 and R3 will show the same NHRP-added routes as the previous examples and are omitted in this section.

## Lab 2: Single Hub, Dual Cloud

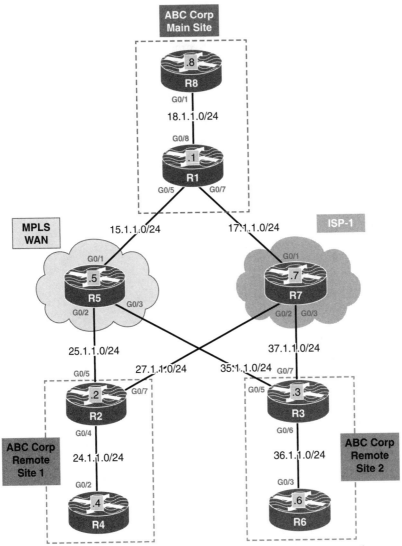

This lab should be conducted on the Enterprise Rack.

Lab Setup:

If you are using EVE-NG, and you have imported the EVE-NG topology from the EVE-NG-Topology folder, ignore the following and use Lab-2-Single Hub Single Cloud in the DMVPN folder in EVE-NG.

To copy and paste the initial configurations, go to the **Initial-config** folder → **DMVPN** folder → **Lab-2**.

## Implement Phase 1

## Design Goal

ABC Corp is expanding into two remote sites. The company has purchased MPLS WAN and Internet service from separate service providers. XYZ Company requires high availability between the remote sites and the main site. The network engineers have decided to use both connections to provide high availability for the remote sites. The primary path taken should be through the MPLS WAN, using the Internet connection through ISP-1 as backup.

### DMVPN Tunnel Configuration

When implementing single-hub, dual-cloud redundancy, the goal is to provide transport redundancy across the solution. With only a single transport, DMVPN connectivity relies on that transport working properly. With two transports, a backup path can be designated by the routing protocol to provide redundancy for both spoke-to-spoke resolutions and the data plane. The type of redundancy will vary depending on the DMVPN phase implemented.

The common thread that connects the configuration across all DMVPN phases, regardless of routing protocol, is how the DMVPN network is set up across the various transports. To complete the design goal stated above, each transport should have its own tunnel interface dedicated to it. From the hub's (R1's) perspective, two tunnel interfaces are created: tunnel 100 and tunnel 200. Tunnel 100 uses R1's IP address 15.1.1.1 as source. 15.1.1.1 on R1 is the IP address of its interface connected to MPLS WAN. Tunnel 200 uses the source IP address 17.1.1.1, which is the IP address of its interface connected to the ISP-1.

The same is true on the spokes R2 and R3. Tunnel 100 will use a source address of their interface towards the MPLS WAN (25.1.1.2 and 35.1.1.3, respectively). Tunnel 200 will use a source address of their interface towards ISP-1 (27.1.1.2 and 37.1.1.3, respectively).

Because the tunnel interfaces on all routers use different source addresses, the routers can distinguish between the two tunnels configured in the lab. Also, each tunnel on each router is configured with a separate NHRP network ID. This configuration allows the routers to keep track of which DMVPN cloud the tunnel interfaces belong. It is not necessary for the network IDs to match between the routers. The configuration is only locally significant. However, similar ID schemes are used for ease of troubleshooting and understanding. Tunnel 100 will be assigned network ID 100 and Tunnel 200 will be assigned network ID 200 on all routers.

The following configures the Tunnel 100 and Tunnel 200 interfaces on R1, R2, and R3:

---

**On R1:**

```
R1(config)#interface tunnel 100
R1(config-if)#ip address 100.1.1.1 255.255.255.0
R1(config-if)#tunnel source 15.1.1.1
R1(config-if)#tunnel mode gre multipoint
R1(config-if)#ip nhrp network-id 100
R1(config-if)#ip nhrp map multicast dynamic

R1(config)#interface tunnel 200
R1(config-if)#ip address 200.1.1.1 255.255.255.0
R1(config-if)#tunnel source 17.1.1.1
R1(config-if)#tunnel mode gre multipoint
R1(config-if)#ip nhrp network-id 200
R1(config-if)#ip nhrp map multicast dynamic
```

**On R2:**

```
R2(config)#interface tunnel 100
R2(config-if)#ip address 100.1.1.2 255.255.255.0
R2(config-if)#tunnel source 25.1.1.2
R2(config-if)#tunnel destination 15.1.1.1
R2(config-if)#ip nhrp network-id 100
R2(config-if)#ip nhrp nhs 100.1.1.1

R2(config)#interface tunnel 200
R2(config-if)#ip address 200.1.1.2 255.255.255.0
R2(config-if)#tunnel source 27.1.1.2
R2(config-if)#tunnel destination 17.1.1.1
R2(config-if)#ip nhrp network-id 200
R2(config-if)#ip nhrp nhs 200.1.1.1
```

**On R3:**

```
R3(config)#interface tunnel 100
R3(config-if)#ip address 100.1.1.3 255.255.255.0
R3(config-if)#tunn source 35.1.1.3
R3(config-if)#tunnel destination 15.1.1.1
R3(config-if)#ip nhrp network-id 100
R3(config-if)#ip nhrp nhs 100.1.1.1
```

```
R3(config-if)#interface tunnel 200
R3(config-if)#ip address 200.1.1.3 255.255.255.0
R3(config-if)#tunnel source 37.1.1.3
R3(config-if)#tunnel destination 17.1.1.1
R3(config-if)#ip nhrp network-id 200
R3(config-if)#ip nhrp nhs 200.1.1.1
```

The show dmvpn command output is then used to verify the status of the tunnels. As seen below, the Tunnel 100 and Tunnel 200 interfaces are both up:

**On R1:**

```
R1#show dmvpn | begin Peer NBMA|Tunnel

      UpDn Time --> Up or Down Time for a Tunnel
========================================================================
===

Interface: Tunnel100, IPv4 NHRP Details
Type:Hub, NHRP Peers:2,

 # Ent  Peer NBMA Addr Peer Tunnel Add State  UpDn Tm Attrb
 ----- --------------- --------------- ----- -------- -----
    1 25.1.1.2            100.1.1.2    UP 00:38:42     D
    1 35.1.1.3            100.1.1.3    UP 00:03:50     D

Interface: Tunnel200, IPv4 NHRP Details
Type:Hub, NHRP Peers:2,

 # Ent  Peer NBMA Addr Peer Tunnel Add State  UpDn Tm Attrb
 ----- --------------- --------------- ----- -------- -----
    1 27.1.1.2            200.1.1.2    UP 00:36:58     D
    1 37.1.1.3            200.1.1.3    UP 00:01:45     D
```

Reachability to the Tunnel 100 interfaces is verified below by issuing traceroutes from R2 to R1 and R3's tunnel 100 interface IP addresses:

**On R2:**

```
R2#traceroute 100.1.1.1 numeric
Type escape sequence to abort.
Tracing the route to 100.1.1.1
VRF info: (vrf in name/id, vrf out name/id)
  1 100.1.1.1 5 msec *  4 msec
```

```
R2#traceroute 100.1.1.3 numeric

Type escape sequence to abort.
Tracing the route to 100.1.1.3
VRF info: (vrf in name/id, vrf out name/id)
  1 100.1.1.1 43 msec 8 msec 8 msec
  2 100.1.1.3 52 msec *  10 msec
```

Reachability to the Tunnel 200 interfaces is verified below by issuing traceroutes from R2 to R1 and R3's tunnel 200 interface IP addresses:

## On R2:

```
R2#traceroute 200.1.1.1 numeric

Type escape sequence to abort.
Tracing the route to 200.1.1.1
VRF info: (vrf in name/id, vrf out name/id)
  1 200.1.1.1 8 msec *  4 msec


R2#traceroute 200.1.1.3 numeric

Type escape sequence to abort.
Tracing the route to 200.1.1.3
VRF info: (vrf in name/id, vrf out name/id)
  1 200.1.1.1 4 msec 6 msec 6 msec
  2 200.1.1.3 9 msec *  6 msec
```

**Note**   While implementing a single hub, dual cloud DMVPN is technically possible. it is not without some inherent limitations that limit its scalability and viability. Most of these issues stem from the fact that two tunnel interfaces are required to implement the DMVPN over two separate transports. In certain failure scenarios, routers may attempt to reach a neighboring DMVPN endpoint over a transport over which that specific neighbor has experienced a failure.

For example, in the Single Hub | Dual Cloud topology diagram, R1, R2, and R3 have two tunnel interfaces over two transports: the MPLS-WAN and the ISP-1. If R2 experiences a failure that disconnects it from the MPLS WAN, depending on the routing protocol and DMVPN phase, this failure may not affect R3's decision when trying to route packets to R2. R3 may still try to reach R2 using the MPLS WAN instead of switching over to the ISP transport.

Solving these connectivity problems is outside of the scope of this lab guide, but some potential solutions will be briefly mentioned where applicable.

## Implement OSPF

This section covers the implementation of DMVPN Phase 1 with OSPF to fulfill the task requirements. This solution is tailored to the specific task above and serves as a guide for solving similar tasks.

The primary difference between the **single hub, single cloud** and **single-hub, dual-cloud** designs is the second tunnel interface for the second DMVPN cloud. From OSPF's perspective, adjacencies will form over both tunnel interfaces. Because there are no next hop considerations in DMVPN Phase 1, broadcast or point-to-point/point-to-multipoint network types can both be used.

OSPF interface costs can then be modified to provide preference to one tunnel interface over the other.

## Broadcast Network Type

The primary concern for the broadcast network type is the placement of the DR for the broadcast segment. The hub should be chosen as the DR for **both** DMVPN tunnel interfaces, and the spokes should be ineligible to become the DR/BDR by having their OSPF priority set to 0 on **both** DMVPN tunnel interfaces.

Below is the initial OSPF configuration for both tunnel 100 and tunnel 200 on the hub R1 and spokes R2 and R3. OSPF process 100 for Area 0 is enabled on the tunnel interfaces. The host networks at each site are advertised into OSPF Area 0, and their network interfaces are declared passive to prevent any OSPF adjacencies over them. Notice the setting of the priority values on each interface on the spokes:

```
On R1:

R1(config)#interface tunnel 100
R1(config-if)#ip ospf network broadcast
R1(config-if)#ip ospf 100 area 0

R1(config)#interface tunnel 200
R1(config-if)#ip ospf network broadcast
R1(config-if)#ip ospf 100 area 0

R1(config-if)#interface g0/8
R1(config-if)#ip ospf 100 area 0

R1(config-if)#router ospf 100
R1(config-router)#passive-interface g0/8
```

**On R2:**

```
R2(config)#interface tunnel 100
R2(config-if)#ip ospf network broadcast
R2(config-if)#ip ospf priority 0
R2(config-if)#ip ospf 100 area 0
```

You should see the following console message:

```
%OSPF-5-ADJCHG: Process 100, Nbr 200.1.1.1 on Tunnel100 from LOADING
to FULL, Loading Done
```

```
R2(config)#interface tunnel 200
R2(config-if)#ip ospf network broadcast
R2(config-if)#ip ospf priority 0
R2(config-if)#ip ospf 100 area 0
```

You should see the following console message:

```
%OSPF-5-ADJCHG: Process 100, Nbr 200.1.1.1 on Tunnel200 from LOADING
to FULL, Loading Done
```

```
R2(config)#interface g0/4
R2(config-if)#ip ospf 100 area 0
```

```
R2(config)#router ospf 100
R2(config-router)#passive-interface g0/4
```

**On R3:**

```
R3(config)#interface tunnel 100
R3(config-if)#ip ospf network broadcast
R3(config-if)#ip ospf priority 0
R3(config-if)#ip ospf 100 area 0
```

You should see the following console message:

```
%OSPF-5-ADJCHG: Process 100, Nbr 200.1.1.1 on Tunnel100 from LOADING
to FULL, Loading Done
```

```
R3(config)#interface tunnel 200
R3(config-if)#ip ospf network broadcast
R3(config-if)#ip ospf priority 0
R3(config-if)#ip ospf 100 area 0
```

You should see the following console message:

```
%OSPF-5-ADJCHG: Process 100, Nbr 200.1.1.1 on Tunnel200 from LOADING
to FULL, Loading Done
```

```
R3(config)#interface g0/6
R3(config-if)#ip ospf 100 area 0
R3(config)#router ospf 100
R3(config-router)#passive-interface g0/6
```

The above configuration results in OSPF adjacencies over both tunnel interfaces between the spokes and the hub router. The show ip ospf neighbor command from the spokes below verifies this:

## On R2:

```
R2#show ip ospf neighbor

Neighbor ID     Pri   State       Dead Time   Address        Interface
200.1.1.1         1   FULL/DR     00:00:39    200.1.1.1      Tunnel200
200.1.1.1         1   FULL/DR     00:00:31    100.1.1.1      Tunnel100
```

## On R3:

```
R3#show ip ospf neighbor

Neighbor ID     Pri   State       Dead Time   Address        Interface
200.1.1.1         1   FULL/DR     00:00:33    200.1.1.1      Tunnel200
200.1.1.1         1   FULL/DR     00:00:35    100.1.1.1      Tunnel100
```

The show ip route ospf command is then issued on R1, R2, and R3. Notice in the output below, with the default OSPF settings, the routers are performing ECMP for each other's LAN networks:

## On R1:

```
R1#show ip route ospf | begin Gate
Gateway of last resort is not set

      24.0.0.0/24 is subnetted, 1 subnets
```

```
O         24.1.1.0 [110/1001] via 200.1.1.2, 00:08:55, Tunnel200
                   [110/1001] via 100.1.1.2, 00:08:55, Tunnel100
          36.0.0.0/24 is subnetted, 1 subnets
O         36.1.1.0 [110/1001] via 200.1.1.3, 00:02:46, Tunnel200
                   [110/1001] via 100.1.1.3, 00:02:46, Tunnel100
```

## On R2:

```
R2#show ip route ospf | begin Gate
Gateway of last resort is not set

          18.0.0.0/24 is subnetted, 1 subnets
O         18.1.1.0 [110/1001] via 200.1.1.1, 00:10:37, Tunnel200
                   [110/1001] via 100.1.1.1, 00:12:04, Tunnel100
          36.0.0.0/24 is subnetted, 1 subnets
O         36.1.1.0 [110/1001] via 200.1.1.3, 00:03:34, Tunnel200
                   [110/1001] via 100.1.1.3, 00:03:34, Tunnel100
```

## On R3:

```
R3#show ip route ospf | begin Gate
Gateway of last resort is not set

          18.0.0.0/24 is subnetted, 1 subnets
O         18.1.1.0 [110/1001] via 200.1.1.1, 00:05:37, Tunnel200
                   [110/1001] via 100.1.1.1, 00:06:44, Tunnel100
          24.0.0.0/24 is subnetted, 1 subnets
O         24.1.1.0 [110/1001] via 200.1.1.2, 00:05:37, Tunnel200
                   [110/1001] via 100.1.1.2, 00:06:44, Tunnel100
```

The routers load share between the two interfaces is because of the default OSPF costs on the tunnel interfaces. By default, GRE tunnels have an artificially high cost of 1000 as shown below. When added to the Gigabit Ethernet cost of 1, the resulting cost of prefixes learned through both tunnels is the 1001 shown in the routing table output above.

## On R1:

```
R1#show ip ospf interface brief

Interface    PID    Area          IP Address/Mask    Cost   State Nbrs
F/C
```

| Gi8 | 100 | 0 | 18.1.1.1/24 | 1 | DR | 0/0 |
| Tu200 | 100 | 0 | 200.1.1.1/24 | 1000 | DR | 2/2 |
| Tu100 | 100 | 0 | 100.1.1.1/24 | 1000 | DR | 2/2 |

## On R2:

```
R2#show ip ospf interface brief
```

| Interface F/C | PID | Area | IP Address/Mask | Cost | State | Nbrs |
| --- | --- | --- | --- | --- | --- | --- |
| Gi4 | 100 | 0 | 24.1.1.2/24 | 1 | DR | 0/0 |
| Tu200 | 100 | 0 | 200.1.1.2/24 | 1000 | DROTH | 1/1 |
| Tu100 | 100 | 0 | 100.1.1.2/24 | 1000 | DROTH | 1/1 |

## On R3:

```
R3#show ip ospf interface brief
```

| Interface F/C | PID | Area | IP Address/Mask | Cost | State | Nbrs |
| --- | --- | --- | --- | --- | --- | --- |
| Gi6 | 100 | 0 | 36.1.1.3/24 | 1 | DR | 0/0 |
| Tu200 | 100 | 0 | 200.1.1.3/24 | 1000 | DROTH | 1/1 |
| Tu100 | 100 | 0 | 100.1.1.3/24 | 1000 | DROTH | 1/1 |

The task requires the MPLS-WAN transport to be preferred over ISP-1. Therefore, the interface cost on all routers for tunnel 100 and tunnel 200 should be modified: Either set the cost lower on tunnel 100 or higher on tunnel 200. The solution here chooses to lower the cost on the tunnel 100 interface with the **ip ospf cost 500** command. Remember that the default cost of a tunnel interface is 1000.

## On R1, R2, and R3:

```
R1(config)#interface tunnel 100
R1(config-if)#ip ospf cost 500
```

With a lower OSPF cost over Tunnel 100, the routing table on R1, R2, and R3 now shows a single path to remote host networks that traverses MPLS-WAN transport. The next hop IP address for the 24.1.1.0/24 network on R3 and the 36.1.1.0/24 network on R2 is set to R2 and R3's tunnel IP address, respectively. This is because the true next hop is retained when using OSPF's broadcast network type. As already mentioned earlier, the preservation of the original next hop does not present any problem since in Phase 1 because the GRE tunnels on the spokes are point-to-point:

**On R1:**

```
R1#show ip route ospf | begin Gate
Gateway of last resort is not set

      24.0.0.0/24 is subnetted, 1 subnets
O        24.1.1.0 [110/501] via 100.1.1.2, 00:02:01, Tunnel100
      36.0.0.0/24 is subnetted, 1 subnets
O        36.1.1.0 [110/501] via 100.1.1.3, 00:02:01, Tunnel100
```

**On R2:**

```
R2#show ip route ospf | begin Gate
Gateway of last resort is not set

      18.0.0.0/24 is subnetted, 1 subnets
O        18.1.1.0 [110/501] via 100.1.1.1, 00:02:45, Tunnel100
      36.0.0.0/24 is subnetted, 1 subnets
O        36.1.1.0 [110/501] via 100.1.1.3, 00:02:45, Tunnel100
```

**On R3:**

```
R3#show ip route ospf | begin Gateway
Gateway of last resort is not set

      18.0.0.0/24 is subnetted, 1 subnets
O        18.1.1.0 [110/501] via 100.1.1.1, 00:03:43, Tunnel100
      24.0.0.0/24 is subnetted, 1 subnets
O        24.1.1.0 [110/501] via 100.1.1.2, 00:03:43, Tunnel100
```

After the configuration changes are made, a **traceroute** from R4 to R8, R6 to R8, and R4 to R6 takes the path through MPLS-WAN (tunnel 100) instead of ISP-1:

**On R4:**

```
R4#traceroute 18.1.1.8 probe 1

Type escape sequence to abort.
Tracing the route to 18.1.1.8
VRF info: (vrf in name/id, vrf out name/id)
  1 24.1.1.2 14 msec
```

```
  2 100.1.1.1 10 msec
  3 18.1.1.8 19 msec
```

## On R6:

```
R6#traceroute 18.1.1.8 probe 1

Type escape sequence to abort.
Tracing the route to 18.1.1.8
VRF info: (vrf in name/id, vrf out name/id)
  1 36.1.1.3 80 msec
  2 100.1.1.1 6 msec
  3 18.1.1.8 12 msec
```

## On R4:

```
R4#traceroute 36.1.1.6 probe 1

Type escape sequence to abort.
Tracing the route to 36.1.1.6
VRF info: (vrf in name/id, vrf out name/id)
  1 24.1.1.2 14 msec
  2 100.1.1.1 8 msec
  3 100.1.1.3 9 msec
  4 36.1.1.6 12 msec
```

Next, to test redundancy, pings are repeated between R4 and R6. **During the pings, the G0/5 interface is shut down on R1 to simulate the primary path via MPLS-WAN failure.** The output below shows the results of the simulation:

## On R4:

```
R4#ping 36.1.1.6 repeat 100000

Type escape sequence to abort.
Sending 100000, 100-byte ICMP Echos to 36.1.1.6, timeout is 2 seconds:
!!!!!!!!!!!!!!!!!!!!!!!!!!!!!!!!!!!!!!!!!!!!!!!!!!!!!!!!!!!!!!!!!!!!!!!!!!!!
!!!!!!!!!!!!!!!!!!!!!!!!!!!!!!!!!!!!!!!!!!!!!!!!!!!!!!!!!!!!!!!!!!!!!!!!!!!!
!!!!!!!!!!!!!!!!!!!!!!!!!!!!!!!!!!!!!!!!!!!!!!!!!!!!!!!!!!!!!!!!!!!!!!!!!!!!
!!!!!!!!!!!!!!!!!!!!!!!!!!!!!!!!!!!!!!!!!!!!!!!!!!!!!!!!!!!!!!!!!!!!!!!!!!!!
```

```
!!!!!!!!!!!!!!!!!!!!!!!!!!!!!!!!!!!!!!!!!!!!!!!!!!!!!!!!!!!!!!!!!!!!!!!!!!!!!!
!!!!!!!!!!!!!!!!!!!!!!!!!!!!!!!!!!!!!!!!!!!!!!!!!!!!!!!!!!!!!!!!!!!!!!!!!!!!!!
!!!!!!!!!!!!!!!!!!!!!!!!!!!!!!!!!!!!!!!!!!!!!!!!!!!!!!!!!!!!!!....!!!!!!!!!!!!
!!!!!!!!!!!!!!!!!!!!!!!!!!!!!!!!!!!!!!!!!!!!!!!!!!!!!!!!!!!!!!!!!!!!!!!!!!!!!!
!!!!!!!!!!!!!!!!!!!!!!!!!!!!!!!!!!!!!!!!!!!!!!!!!!!!!!!!!!!!!!!!!!!!!!!!!!!!!!
!!!!!!!!!!!!!!!!!!!!!!!!!!!!!!!!!!!!!!!!!!!!!
Success rate is 99 percent (666/670), round-trip min/avg/max =
8/21/122 ms
```

The four yellow highlighted dots in between represent the roughly 8 seconds it took for the spoke routers R2 and R3 to switch to the secondary path through their tunnel 200 interface. The output below from R2 and R3 now shows the path to the remote host network on R2 and R3 via the backup tunnel 200:

## On R2:

```
R2#show ip route ospf 123 | begin Gate
Gateway of last resort is not set

      18.0.0.0/24 is subnetted, 1 subnets
O        18.1.1.0 [110/1001] via 200.1.1.1, 00:04:07, Tunnel200
      36.0.0.0/24 is subnetted, 1 subnets
O        36.1.1.0 [110/1001] via 200.1.1.3, 00:04:07, Tunnel200
```

## On R3:

```
R3#show ip route ospf 123 | begin Gate
Gateway of last resort is not set

      18.0.0.0/24 is subnetted, 1 subnets
O        18.1.1.0 [110/1001] via 200.1.1.1, 00:04:42, Tunnel200
      24.0.0.0/24 is subnetted, 1 subnets
O        24.1.1.0 [110/1001] via 200.1.1.2, 00:04:42, Tunnel200
```

### Point-to-Point and Point-to-Multipoint Network Types

To implement this design, the hub R1's tunnel interfaces 100 and 200 are configured to use OSPF's point-to-multipoint network type. Tunnel interfaces 100 and 200 on spokes R2 and R3 run OSPF's point-to-point network type. The OSPF hello interval timer on R1's point-to-multipoint tunnel interfaces is modified to match the hello interval timer of the spokes' point-to-point tunnel interfaces with the **ip ospf hello-interval 10** command:

**On R1:**

```
R1(config)#interface g0/5
R1(config-if)#no shut
```

**On R1, R2, and R3:**

```
Rx(config)#interface tunnel 100
Rx(config-if)#no ip ospf cost 500
```

**On R1:**

```
R1(config)#interface tunnel 100
R1(config-if)#ip ospf network point-to-multipoint
R1(config-if)#ip ospf hello-interval 10

R1(config)#interface tunnel 200
R1(config-if)#ip ospf network point-to-multipoint
R1(config-if)#ip ospf hello-interval 10
```

The OSPF configuration for the host facing interfaces has been retained from the earlier task. As such, this configuration is not required here.

**On R2:**

```
R2(config)#interface tunnel 100
R2(config-if)#ip ospf network point-to-point
```

You should see the following console message:

```
%OSPF-5-ADJCHG: Process 100, Nbr 200.1.1.1 on Tunnel100 from LOADING
to FULL, Loading Done
R2(config)#interface tunnel 200
R2(config-if)#ip ospf network point-to-point
```

You should see the following console message:

```
%OSPF-5-ADJCHG: Process 100, Nbr 200.1.1.1 on Tunnel200 from LOADING
to FULL, Loading Done
```

**On R3:**

```
R3(config)#interface tunnel 100
R3(config-if)#ip ospf network point-to-point
```

You should see the following console message:

```
%OSPF-5-ADJCHG: Process 100, Nbr 200.1.1.1 on Tunnel100 from LOADING
to FULL, Loading Done
```

```
R3(config)#interface tunnel 200
R3(config-if)#ip ospf network point-to-point
```

You should see the following console message:

```
%OSPF-5-ADJCHG: Process 100, Nbr 200.1.1.1 on Tunnel200 from LOADING
to FULL, Loading Done
```

After completing the above, OSPF adjacencies are formed between the spokes and the hub router over both tunnel interfaces. The show ip route ospf command output below shows the host networks from each site learned via OSPF. The routing table on all routers reveals equal cost load sharing between the two tunnel interfaces for the host networks. Similar to the broadcast network type implementation, the load sharing is a result of the equal default cost on the tunnel interfaces.

Also notice the next hop addresses for the 36.1.1.0/24 network on R2 and the 24.1.1.0/24 network on R3 is set to the hub's tunnel IP address. This is the expected behavior when implementing the P2P/P2MP network in the DMVPN where the original next hop addresses are not retained.

## On R1:

```
R1#show ip route ospf | begin Gate
Gateway of last resort is not set

      24.0.0.0/24 is subnetted, 1 subnets
O        24.1.1.0 [110/1001] via 200.1.1.2, 00:00:34, Tunnel200
                  [110/1001] via 100.1.1.2, 00:00:34, Tunnel100
      36.0.0.0/24 is subnetted, 1 subnets
O        36.1.1.0 [110/1001] via 200.1.1.3, 00:00:34, Tunnel200
                  [110/1001] via 100.1.1.3, 00:00:34, Tunnel100
```

## On R2:

```
R2#show ip route ospf | begin Gate
Gateway of last resort is not set

      18.0.0.0/24 is subnetted, 1 subnets
O        18.1.1.0 [110/1001] via 200.1.1.1, 00:01:21, Tunnel200
                  [110/1001] via 100.1.1.1, 00:01:21, Tunnel100
```

```
      36.0.0.0/24 is subnetted, 1 subnets
O        36.1.1.0 [110/2001] via 200.1.1.1, 00:00:59, Tunnel200
                  [110/2001] via 100.1.1.1, 00:00:59, Tunnel100
      100.0.0.0/8 is variably subnetted, 3 subnets, 2 masks
O        100.1.1.1/32 [110/1000] via 200.1.1.1, 00:01:21, Tunnel200
                      [110/1000] via 100.1.1.1, 00:01:21, Tunnel100
      200.1.1.0/24 is variably subnetted, 3 subnets, 2 masks
O        200.1.1.1/32 [110/1000] via 200.1.1.1, 00:01:21, Tunnel200
                      [110/1000] via 100.1.1.1, 00:01:21, Tunnel100
```

## On R3:

```
R3#show ip route ospf | begin Gate
Gateway of last resort is not set

      18.0.0.0/24 is subnetted, 1 subnets
O        18.1.1.0 [110/1001] via 200.1.1.1, 00:02:38, Tunnel200
                  [110/1001] via 100.1.1.1, 00:02:38, Tunnel100
      24.0.0.0/24 is subnetted, 1 subnets
O        24.1.1.0 [110/2001] via 200.1.1.1, 00:01:26, Tunnel200
                  [110/2001] via 100.1.1.1, 00:01:26, Tunnel100
      100.0.0.0/8 is variably subnetted, 3 subnets, 2 masks
O        100.1.1.1/32 [110/1000] via 200.1.1.1, 00:02:38, Tunnel200
                      [110/1000] via 100.1.1.1, 00:02:38, Tunnel100
      200.1.1.0/24 is variably subnetted, 3 subnets, 2 masks
O        200.1.1.1/32 [110/1000] via 200.1.1.1, 00:02:38, Tunnel200
                      [110/1000] via 100.1.1.1, 00:02:38, Tunnel100
```

To complete the task, OSPF cost on the Tunnel 100 interface on R1, R2, and R3 is modi-fied to 500 with the ip ospf cost 500 command. This makes the MPLS-WAN the primary path and the Internet service from ISP-1 as the backup. The OSPF process ID can also be manipulated. In OSPF, the lower process id is a better path for the same type of routes. Another method is to use NHS Cluster; this will be tested in later labs.

## On R1, R2, and R3:

```
Rx(config)#interface tunnel 100
Rx(config-if)#ip ospf cost 500
```

## On R1:

```
R1#show ip route ospf | begin Gate
Gateway of last resort is not set
```

```
       24.0.0.0/24 is subnetted, 1 subnets
O          24.1.1.0 [110/501] via 100.1.1.2, 00:01:05, Tunnel100
       36.0.0.0/24 is subnetted, 1 subnets
O          36.1.1.0 [110/501] via 100.1.1.3, 00:01:05, Tunnel100
```

## On R2:

```
R2#show ip route ospf | begin Gate
Gateway of last resort is not set

       18.0.0.0/24 is subnetted, 1 subnets
O          18.1.1.0 [110/501] via 100.1.1.1, 00:01:26, Tunnel100
       36.0.0.0/24 is subnetted, 1 subnets
O          36.1.1.0 [110/1001] via 100.1.1.1, 00:01:26, Tunnel100
       100.0.0.0/8 is variably subnetted, 3 subnets, 2 masks
O          100.1.1.1/32 [110/500] via 100.1.1.1, 00:01:26, Tunnel100
       200.1.1.0/24 is variably subnetted, 3 subnets, 2 masks
O          200.1.1.1/32 [110/500] via 100.1.1.1, 00:01:26, Tunnel100
```

## On R3:

```
R3#show ip route ospf | begin Gate
Gateway of last resort is not set

       18.0.0.0/24 is subnetted, 1 subnets
O          18.1.1.0 [110/501] via 100.1.1.1, 00:01:56, Tunnel100
       24.0.0.0/24 is subnetted, 1 subnets
O          24.1.1.0 [110/1001] via 100.1.1.1, 00:01:56, Tunnel100
       100.0.0.0/8 is variably subnetted, 3 subnets, 2 masks
O          100.1.1.1/32 [110/500] via 100.1.1.1, 00:01:56, Tunnel100
       200.1.1.0/24 is variably subnetted, 3 subnets, 2 masks
O          200.1.1.1/32 [110/500] via 100.1.1.1, 00:01:56, Tunnel100
```

To test redundancy, pings are repeated from R4 to R6. During the pings, the G0/5 interface is shut down on R1 to simulate a failure. The output below shows the results of the simulation:

## On R4:

```
R4#ping 36.1.1.6 repeat 100000

Type escape sequence to abort.
```

```
Sending 100000, 100-byte ICMP Echos to 36.1.1.6, timeout is 2 seconds:
!!!!!!!!!!!!!!!!!!!!!!!!!!!!!!!!!!!!!!!!!!!!!!!!!!!!!!!!!!!!!!!!!!!!!!!!
!!!!!!!!!!!!!!!!!!!!!!!!!!!!!!!!!!!!!!!!!!!!!!!!!!!!!!!!!!!!!!!!!!!!!!!!
!!!!!!!!!!!!!!!!!!!!!!!!!!!!!!!!!!!!!!!!!!!!!!!!!!!!!!!!!!!!!!!!!!!!!!!!
!!!!!!!!!!!!!!!!!!!!!!!!!!!!!!!!!!!!!!!!!!!!!!!!!!!!!!!!!!!!!!!!!!!!!!!!
!!!!!!!!!!!....!!!!!!!!!!!!!!!!!!!!!!!!!!!!!!!!!!!!!!!!!!!!!!!!!!!!!!!!!
!!!!!!!!!!!!!!!!!!!!!!!!!!!!!!!!!!!!!!!!!!!!!!!!!!!!!!!!!!!!!!!!!!!!!!!!
!!!!!!!!!!!!!!!!!!!!!!!!!!!!!!!!!!!!!!!!!!!!!!!!!!!!!!!!!!!!!!!!!!!!!!!!
!!!!!!!!!!!!!!!!!!!!!!!!!!!!!!!!
Success rate is 98 percent (511/519), round-trip min/avg/max = 9/21/40
ms
```

Much as in the case of the broadcast network type, the yellow highlighted dots above represent roughly the time it took for the spoke routers to switch to the secondary path via ISP-1 through their tunnel 200 interface. The routing tables on R2 and R3 now use the backup path via tunnel 200 over the ISP-1 transport:

## On R2:

```
R2#show ip route ospf | begin Gate
Gateway of last resort is not set

      18.0.0.0/24 is subnetted, 1 subnets
O        18.1.1.0 [110/1001] via 200.1.1.1, 00:02:42, Tunnel200
      36.0.0.0/24 is subnetted, 1 subnets
O        36.1.1.0 [110/2001] via 200.1.1.1, 00:02:42, Tunnel200
      200.1.1.0/24 is variably subnetted, 3 subnets, 2 masks
O        200.1.1.1/32 [110/1000] via 200.1.1.1, 00:02:42, Tunnel200
```

## On R3:

```
R3#show ip route ospf | begin Gate
Gateway of last resort is not set

      18.0.0.0/24 is subnetted, 1 subnets
O        18.1.1.0 [110/1001] via 200.1.1.1, 00:03:12, Tunnel200
      24.0.0.0/24 is subnetted, 1 subnets
O        24.1.1.0 [110/2001] via 200.1.1.1, 00:03:12, Tunnel200
      200.1.1.0/24 is variably subnetted, 3 subnets, 2 masks
O        200.1.1.1/32 [110/1000] via 200.1.1.1, 00:03:12, Tunnel200
```

### Implement EIGRP

EIGRP for Single Hub | Dual Cloud is implemented by enabling the same EIGRP process on both the tunnel interfaces with the network command under the EIGRP router configuration mode. The network command is also used to advertise the host networks at each site into the same EIGRP process. These interfaces are declared as passive interfaces with the passive-interface command under the EIGRP router configuration mode as shown below. However, before this solution is implemented, the OSPF 100 configuration from the earlier task is removed and the G0/5 interface on R1 is brought back up:

---

**On R1, R2, and R3:**

```
Rx(config)#no router ospf 100
```

**On R1:**

```
R1(config)#interface g0/5
R1(config-if)#no shut

R1(config)#router eigrp 100
R1(config-router)#network 18.1.1.1 0.0.0.0
R1(config-router)#network 100.1.1.1 0.0.0.0
R1(config-router)#network 200.1.1.1 0.0.0.0
R1(config-router)#passive-interface g0/8
```

**On R2:**

```
R2(config)#router eigrp 100
R2(config-router)#network 24.1.1.2 0.0.0.0
R2(config-router)#network 100.1.1.2 0.0.0.0
R2(config-router)#network 200.1.1.2 0.0.0.0
R2(config-router)#passive-interface g0/4
```

You should see the following console messages:

```
%DUAL-5-NBRCHANGE: EIGRP-IPv4 100: Neighbor 100.1.1.1 (Tunnel100) is
up: new adjacency

%DUAL-5-NBRCHANGE: EIGRP-IPv4 100: Neighbor 200.1.1.1 (Tunnel200) is
up: new adjacency
```

**On R3:**

```
R3(config)#router eigrp 100
R3(config-router)#network 36.1.1.3 0.0.0.0
```

```
R3(config-router)#network 100.1.1.3 0.0.0.0
R3(config-router)#network 200.1.1.3 0.0.0.0
R3(config-router)#passive-interface g0/6
```

You should see the following console messages:

```
%DUAL-5-NBRCHANGE: EIGRP-IPv4 100: Neighbor 100.1.1.1 (Tunnel100) is
up: new adjacency

%DUAL-5-NBRCHANGE: EIGRP-IPv4 100: Neighbor 200.1.1.1 (Tunnel200) is
up: new adjacency
```

The above results in EIGRP neighborships between R2 and R1 and between R3 and R1 over their tunnel 100 and tunnel 200 interfaces:

**On R2:**

```
R2#show ip eigrp 100 neighbors
EIGRP-IPv4 Neighbors for AS(100)
H   Address          Interface        Hold Uptime    SRTT   RTO  Q
Seq
                                      (sec)          (ms)        Cnt
Num
1   100.1.1.1        Tu100            11 00:03:24     3   1470  0   16
0   200.1.1.1        Tu200            13 00:07:29     9   1470  0   15
```

**On R3:**

```
R3#show ip eigrp 100 neighbors
EIGRP-IPv4 Neighbors for AS(100)
H   Address          Interface        Hold Uptime    SRTT  RTO  Q   Seq
                                      (sec)          (ms)       Cnt
Num
1   100.1.1.1        Tu100            10 00:05:21     5   1470  0   16
0   200.1.1.1        Tu200            13 00:06:23     4   1470  0   17
```

Hub R1 is configured to send EIGRP summary default routes to the spokes over its tunnel interfaces with the **ip summary-address** command:

**On R1:**

```
R1(config)#interface tunnel 100
R1(config-if)#ip summary-address eigrp 100 0.0.0.0 0.0.0.0
```

```
R1(config)#interface tunnel 200
R1(config-if)#ip summary-address eigrp 100 0.0.0.0 0.0.0.0
```

The routing tables on spokes R2 and R3 show that they receive two default routes from the hub R1 over their tunnel 100 and 200 interfaces:

**On R2:**

```
R2#show ip route eigrp 100 | begin Gate
Gateway of last resort is 200.1.1.1 to network 0.0.0.0

D*   0.0.0.0/0 [90/26880256] via 200.1.1.1, 00:01:39, Tunnel200
               [90/26880256] via 100.1.1.1, 00:01:39, Tunnel100
```

**On R3:**

```
R3#show ip route eigrp 100 | begin Gate
Gateway of last resort is 200.1.1.1 to network 0.0.0.0

D*   0.0.0.0/0 [90/26880256] via 200.1.1.1, 00:02:05, Tunnel200
               [90/26880256] via 100.1.1.1, 00:02:05, Tunnel100
```

By default, R2 and R3 perform ECMP for the default routes. The reason for this is that the EIGRP metrics associated with the tunnel 100 and tunnel 200 interfaces are the same as shown below:

**On R2:**

```
R2#show interface tunnel 100 | include DLY
  MTU 9976 bytes, BW 100 Kbit/sec, DLY 50000 usec,

R2#show interface tunnel 200 | include DLY
  MTU 9976 bytes, BW 100 Kbit/sec, DLY 50000 usec,
```

EIGRP uses the above bandwidth and delay metrics as part of its metric calculation algorithm. Because the metrics above have the same values, EIGRP computes equal costs for routes received from both interfaces.

To allow the spokes to use MPLS-WAN as the primary path, the delay on the tunnel 100 interface is lowered. This forces EIGRP to calculate a better metric through the tunnel 100 interface over the tunnel 200 interface, as shown below:

**On R1, R2, and R3:**

```
Rx(config)#interface tunnel 100
Rx(config-if)#delay 500
```

## To verify the configuration:

```
Rx#show interface tunnel 100 | include DLY
  MTU 9976 bytes, BW 100 Kbit/sec, DLY 5000 usec,
```

## On R1:

```
R1#show ip route eigrp 100 | begin Gate
Gateway of last resort is 0.0.0.0 to network 0.0.0.0

D*     0.0.0.0/0 is a summary, 00:09:12, Null0
       24.0.0.0/24 is subnetted, 1 subnets
D         24.1.1.0 [90/25728256] via 100.1.1.2, 00:03:01, Tunnel100
       36.0.0.0/24 is subnetted, 1 subnets
D         36.1.1.0 [90/25728256] via 100.1.1.3, 00:03:01, Tunnel100
```

## On R2:

```
R2#show ip route eigrp 100 | begin Gate
Gateway of last resort is 100.1.1.1 to network 0.0.0.0

D*     0.0.0.0/0 [90/25728256] via 100.1.1.1, 00:03:21, Tunnel100
```

## On R3:

```
R3#show ip route eigrp 100 | begin Gate
Gateway of last resort is 100.1.1.1 to network 0.0.0.0

D*     0.0.0.0/0 [90/25728256] via 100.1.1.1, 00:03:38, Tunnel100
```

With MPLS WAN as the primary path, redundancy is verified by performing a repeated ping from R4 to R6. During the ping, G0/5 interface on R1 is shut down. This results in loss of connectivity between R4 – R6 (evidenced by the yellow highlighted dots below). After a few seconds EIGRP installs the backup route through the Tunnel 200 interface, restoring communication.

**On R4:**

```
R4#ping 36.1.1.6 repeat 100000
Type escape sequence to abort.
Sending 100000, 100-byte ICMP Echos to 36.1.1.6, timeout is 2 seconds:
!!!!!!!!!!!!!!!!!!!!!!!!!!!!!!!!!!!!!!!!!!!!!!!!!!!!!!!!!!!!!!!!!!!!!!!!!!
!!!!!!!!!!!!!!!!!!!!!!!!!!!!!!!!!!!!!!!!!!!!!!!!!!!!!!!!!!!!!!!!!!!!!!!!!!
!!!!!!!!!!!!!!!!!!!!!!!!!!!!!!!!!!!!!!!!!!!!!!!!!!!!!!!!!!!!!!!!!!!!!!!!!!
!!!!!!!!!!!!!!!!!!!!!!!!!!!!!!!!!!!!!!!!!!!!!!!!!!!!!!!!!!......!!!!!!!!!
!!!!!!!!!!!!!!!!!!!!!!!!!!!!!!!!!!!!!!!!!!!!!!!!!!!!!!!!!!!!!!!!!!!!!!!!!!
!!!!!!!!!!!!!!!!!!!!!!!!!!!!!!!!!!!!!!!!!!!!!!!!!!!!!!!!!
Success rate is 98 percent (398/405), round-trip min/avg/max = 8/21/67
ms
```

### Implement iBGP

A major difference in the iBGP configuration for a single hub, dual cloud design lies in the peer group configuration. With such a design, it is desirable to configure different routing policies for each DMVPN cloud to prefer one transport over the other. Peer groups carry the restriction that all members of a peer group must have the same routing policies. As such, it is not possible to utilize a single peer group for the dynamic peering for both tunnel interfaces on the route reflector R1.

Instead, the tunnel 100 peer group is used for iBGP neighbors over tunnel 100 and the tunnel 200 peer group is used for iBGP neighbors over tunnel 200. The tunnel 100 peer group is associated with the dynamic listen range 100.1.1.0/24, the Tunnel 100 DMVPN overlay address. Likewise, the tunnel 200 peer group is associated with the 200.1.1.0/24 dynamic listen range corresponding to the Tunnel 200 DMVPN overlay addresses.

The result is two independent peer groups over which policies can be configured to affect the routing in the DMVPN overlay. The respective host networks at each site are advertised into BGP with the network statement. Before iBGP is configured, the EIGRP 100 configuration and any other leftover OSPF configuration commands from the earlier tasks should be removed on R1, R2, and R3.

**On R1:**

```
R1(config)#no router eigrp 100

R1(config)#interface g0/5
R1(config-if)#no shut
```

```
R1(config)#interface tunnel 100
R1(config-if)#no delay 500
R1(config-if)#no ip ospf network point-to-multipoint
R1(config-if)#no ip ospf hello-interval 10

R1(config)#interface tunnel 200
R1(config-if)#no ip ospf network point-to-multipoint
R1(config-if)#no ip ospf hello-interval 10

R1(config)#router bgp 100
R1(config-router)#neighbor tunnel100 peer-group
R1(config-router)#neighbor tunnel100 remote-as 100

R1(config-router)#neighbor tunnel200 peer-group
R1(config-router)#neighbor tunnel200 remote-as 100

R1(config-router)#bgp listen range 100.1.1.0/24 peer-group tunnel100
R1(config-router)#bgp listen range 200.1.1.0/24 peer-group tunnel200
R1(config-router)#address-family ipv4
R1(config-router-af)#neighbor tunnel100 activate
R1(config-router-af)#neighbor tunnel200 activate
R1(config-router-af)#network 18.1.1.0 mask 255.255.255.0
R1(config-router-af)#neighbor tunnel100 route-reflector-client
R1(config-router-af)#neighbor tunnel200 route-reflector-client
```

## On R2:

```
R2(config)#no router eigrp 100

R2(config)#interface tunnel 100
R2(config-if)#no ip ospf network point-to-point
R2(config-if)#no ip ospf cost 500
R2(config-if)#no delay 500

R2(config)#interface tunnel 200
R2(config-if)#no ip ospf network point-to-point

R2(config)#router bgp 100
R2(config-router)#neighbor 100.1.1.1 remote-as 100
R2(config-router)#neighbor 200.1.1.1 remote-as 100
```

```
R2(config-router)#address-family ipv4
R2(config-router-af)#network 24.1.1.0 mask 255.255.255.0
```

You should see the following console messages:

```
%BGP-5-ADJCHANGE: neighbor 100.1.1.1 Up
%BGP-5-ADJCHANGE: neighbor 200.1.1.1 Up
```

## On R3:

```
R3(config)#no router eigrp 100

R3(config)#interface tunnel 100
R3(config-if)#no ip ospf network point-to-point
R3(config-if)#no ip ospf cost 500
R3(config-if)#no delay 500

R3(config)#interface tunnel 200
R3(config-if)#no ip ospf network point-to-point

R3(config)#router bgp 100
R3(config-router)#neighbor 100.1.1.1 remote 100
R3(config-router)#neighbor 200.1.1.1 remote 100

R3(config-router)#address-family ipv4
R3(config-router-af)#network 36.1.1.0 mask 255.255.255.0
```

You should see the following console messages:

```
%BGP-5-ADJCHANGE: neighbor 100.1.1.1 Up
%BGP-5-ADJCHANGE: neighbor 200.1.1.1 Up
```

The above configuration results in two R1/R2 iBGP peerings and two R1/R3 iBGP peerings, one for each transport:

## On R1:

```
R1#show ip bgp summary | begin Nei

Neighbor      V   AS MsgRcvd MsgSent   TblVer  InQ OutQ Up/Down
State/PfxRcd
*100.1.1.2    4  100      16      19        6    0    0 00:08:12    1
*100.1.1.3    4  100      16      19        6    0    0 00:08:14    1
```

```
*200.1.1.2    4   100     242     245       6    0    0 03:35:21      1
*200.1.1.3    4   100     237     243       6    0    0 03:32:29      1
* Dynamically created based on a listen range command
Dynamically created neighbors: 4, Subnet ranges: 2

BGP peergroup tunnel100 listen range group members:
  100.1.1.0/24
BGP peergroup tunnel200 listen range group members:
  200.1.1.0/24

Total dynamically created neighbors: 4/(100 max), Subnet ranges: 2
```

Next, the hub R1 is then configured to send a BGP default route to the spokes R2 and R3 via the iBGP peering over its tunnel 100 and 200 interfaces. The method used to propagate the default route is similar to what was configured in the earlier BGP designs:

## On R1:

```
R1(config)#ip prefix-list NET permit 0.0.0.0/0

R1(config)#route-map TST permit 10
R1(config-route-map)#match ip address prefix NET

R1(config)#router bgp 100
R1(config-router)#address-family ipv4
R1(config-router-af)#neighbor tunnel100 default-originate
R1(config-router-af)#neighbor tunnel200 default-originate
R1(config-router-af)#neighbor tunnel100 route-map TST out
R1(config-router-af)#neighbor tunnel200 route-map TST out
```

```
R1#clear ip bgp * out
```

The show ip bgp command is then issued on R1, R2, and R3. R1 has chosen the path via tunnel 100 as best for the host networks at the remote sites. R2 and R3 choose the path via tunnel 100 as best for the default route:

## On R1:

```
R1#show ip bgp | begin Net

    Network          Next Hop          Metric LocPrf Weight Path
       0.0.0.0          0.0.0.0                            0 i
```

```
*>     18.1.1.0/24       0.0.0.0               0          32768 i
*>i    24.1.1.0/24       100.1.1.2             0    100      0 i
*  i                     200.1.1.2             0    100      0 i
*>i    36.1.1.0/24       100.1.1.3             0    100      0 i
*  i                     200.1.1.3             0    100      0 i
```

## On R2:

```
R2#show ip bgp | begin Net

      Network           Next Hop          Metric LocPrf Weight Path
*  i  0.0.0.0           200.1.1.1              0    100      0 i
*>i                     100.1.1.1              0    100      0 i
*>     24.1.1.0/24      0.0.0.0                0          32768 i
```

## On R3:

```
R3#show ip bgp | begin Net

      Network           Next Hop          Metric LocPrf Weight Path
*>i  0.0.0.0            100.1.1.1              0    100      0 i
*  i                    200.1.1.1              0    100      0 i
*>     36.1.1.0/24      0.0.0.0                0          32768 i
```

To understand why R2 and R3 choose the path via tunnel 100 as best, the **show ip bgp 0.0.0.0** command is issued on them:

## On R2:

```
R2#show ip bgp 0.0.0.0

BGP routing table entry for 0.0.0.0/0, version 10
Paths: (2 available, best #2, table default)
  Not advertised to any peer
  Refresh Epoch 2
  Local
    200.1.1.1 from 200.1.1.1 (200.1.1.1)
      Origin IGP, metric 0, localpref 100, valid, internal
      rx pathid: 0, tx pathid: 0
  Refresh Epoch 3
  Local
    100.1.1.1 from 100.1.1.1 (200.1.1.1)
```

```
     Origin IGP, metric 0, localpref 100, valid, internal, best
     rx pathid: 0, tx pathid: 0x0
```

## On R3:

```
R3#show ip bgp 0.0.0.0

BGP routing table entry for 0.0.0.0/0, version 11
Paths: (2 available, best #1, table default)
  Not advertised to any peer
  Refresh Epoch 3
  Local
    100.1.1.1 from 100.1.1.1 (200.1.1.1)
      Origin IGP, metric 0, localpref 100, valid, internal, best
      rx pathid: 0, tx pathid: 0x0
  Refresh Epoch 4
  Local
    200.1.1.1 from 200.1.1.1 (200.1.1.1)
      Origin IGP, metric 0, localpref 100, valid, internal
      rx pathid: 0, tx pathid: 0
```

As shown above, R2 and R3 choose the MPLS WAN path as their best path; this is the correct pathing choice, according to the design goals. The only issue is the reason behind the pathing decision. With all other BGP attributes tied, the BGP best-path algorithm reverts to step 13, choosing the lowest neighbor peering address as the deciding factor. R2 and R3 choose the path over tunnel 100 because the peering address is 100.1.1.1, as opposed to the higher address of 200.1.1.1 over tunnel 200.

While this is a deterministic decision, it does not provide stability. If for some reason the DMVPN overlay addresses were changed, the results of the BGP best-path algorithm could change as well. For this reason, it is best to influence a BGP attribute that is considered before the neighbor peering address at step 13. Local preference is a good choice for modification as it is one of the first attributes considered in the best-path algorithm.

To implement this consistent path choice, R1 assigns a local preference of 200 to all paths received from a member of the tunnel 100 peer group, as shown below. Likewise, R2 and R3 apply a local preference of 200 for all prefixes received from R1's tunnel 100 peering address 100.1.1.1:

## On R1:

```
R1(config)#route-map local-pref permit 10
R1(config-route-map)#set local-preference 200
```

```
R1(config)#router bgp 100
R1(config-router)#address-family ipv4
R1(config-router-af)#neighbor tunnel100 route-map local-pref in

R1#clear ip bgp * in
```

### On R2 and R3:

```
Rx(config)#route-map local-pref permit 10
Rx(config-route-map)#set local-pref 200

Rx(config)#router bgp 100
Rx(config-router)#address-family ipv4
Rx(config-router-af)#neighbor 100.1.1.1 route-map local-pref in

Rx#clear ip bgp * in
```

### On R1:

```
R1#show ip bgp | begin Net
```

| | Network | Next Hop | Metric | LocPrf | Weight | Path |
|---|---|---|---|---|---|---|
| | 0.0.0.0 | 0.0.0.0 | | | 0 | i |
| *> | 18.1.1.0/24 | 0.0.0.0 | 0 | | 32768 | i |
| *>i | 24.1.1.0/24 | 100.1.1.2 | 0 | 200 | 0 | i |
| * i | | 200.1.1.2 | 0 | 100 | 0 | i |
| *>i | 36.1.1.0/24 | 100.1.1.3 | 0 | 200 | 0 | i |
| * i | | 200.1.1.3 | 0 | 100 | 0 | i |

### On R2:

```
R2#show ip bgp | begin Net
```

| | Network | Next Hop | Metric | LocPrf | Weight | Path |
|---|---|---|---|---|---|---|
| * i | 0.0.0.0 | 200.1.1.1 | 0 | 100 | 0 | i |
| *>i | | 100.1.1.1 | 0 | 200 | 0 | i |
| *> | 24.1.1.0/24 | 0.0.0.0 | 0 | | 32768 | i |

## On R3:

```
R3#show ip bgp | begin Net

      Network          Next Hop         Metric LocPrf Weight Path
 *>i  0.0.0.0          100.1.1.1             0    200      0 i
 * i                   200.1.1.1             0    100      0 i
 *>   36.1.1.0/24      0.0.0.0               0           32768 i
```

Redundancy can once again be checked by performing a repeated ping from R4 to R6. During the pings, the G0/5 interface on R1 is shut down. The yellow highlighted dots once again represent the time taken for R2 to start using the default route via the secondary path over the MPLS WAN transport through tunnel 200:

## On R4:

```
R4#ping 36.1.1.6 repeat 100000

Type escape sequence to abort.
Sending 100000, 100-byte ICMP Echos to 36.1.1.6, timeout is 2 seconds:
!!!!!!!!!!!!!!!!!!!!!!!!!!!!!!!!!!!!!!!!!!!!!!!!!!!!!!!!!!!!!!!!!!!!!!!!!!
!!!!!!!!!!!!!!!!!!!!!!!!!!!!!!!!!!!!!!!!!!!!!!!!!!!!!!!!!!!!!!!!!!!!!!!!!!
!!!!!!!!!!!!!!!!!!!!!!!!!!!!!!!!!!!!!!!!!!!!!!!!!!!!!!!!!!!!!!!!!!!!!!!!!!
!!!!!!!!!!!!!!!!!!!!!!!!!!!!!!!!!!!!!!!!!!!!!!!!!!!!!!!!!!!!!!!!!!!!!!!....
..................................................................
............!!!!!!!!!!!!!!!!!!!!!!!!!!!!!!!!!!!!!!!!!!!!!!!!!!!!!!!!!!!!!!
!!!!!!!!!!!!!!!!!!!!!!!!!!!!!!!!!!!!!!!!!!!!!!!!!!!!!!!!!!!!!!!!!!!!!!!!!!
!!!!!!!!!!!!!!!!!!!!!!!!!!!!!!!!!!!!!!!!!!!!!!!!!!!!!!!!!!!!!!!!!!!!!!!!!!
!!!!!!!!!!!!!!!!!!!!!!!!!!!!!!!!!!!!!!!!!!!!!!!!!!!!!!!!!!!!!!!!!!!!!!!!!!
!!!!!!!!!!!!!!!!!!!!!!!!!!!!!!!!!!!
Success rate is 87 percent (645/734), round-trip min/avg/max =
9/21/102 ms
```

> **Note**   The convergence time in this case is limited by the BGP keepalive and hold-down timers. The default keepalive timer for BGP is 60 seconds, and the default hold-down timer is 3 times the keepalive, or 180 seconds. With these defaults, it can take up to 3 minutes before BGP declares the neighbor down and begins the reconvergence process. If speedier convergence is the goal, before checking for redundancy, the keepalive timer and the hold-down timer for BGP can be lowered. This configuration would only have to be done on one router since BGP accepts the lower keepalive time between peers when the neighbors establish peering.

With this in mind, the hub is the logical choice for making this change since all other routers peer directly with it. The following configuration on the DMVPN hub router lowers the keepalive timer to 6 seconds and the hold-down timer to 20 seconds. It is applied to the peer group configuration for the spokes connected to a specific transport:

```
R1(config)#router bgp 100
R1(config-router)#neighbor SPOKES timers 6 20
```

The routing tables on R2 and R3 confirm that the secondary path via tunnel 200 over ISP-1 is in use:

### On R2:

```
R2#show ip route bgp | begin Gate
Gateway of last resort is 200.1.1.1 to network 0.0.0.0

B*    0.0.0.0/0 [200/0] via 200.1.1.1, 00:03:33
```

### On R3:

```
R3#show ip route bgp | begin Gate
Gateway of last resort is 200.1.1.1 to network 0.0.0.0

B*    0.0.0.0/0 [200/0] via 200.1.1.1, 00:04:24
```

## Implement eBGP

Much as in the previous BGP sections, two design choices can be used for eBGP peerings between the hub and spokes. Spokes can either be configured to belong to different autonomous systems or to the same autonomous systems.

### Spokes in Different Autonomous Systems

The following configurations implement the first design where the spokes R2 and R3 are placed in different autonomous systems—ASN 200 and ASN 300, respectively. They are configured to peer with the hub R1 (ASN 100) over their tunnel 100 and tunnel 200 interfaces. Respective host networks at each site are advertised into BGP with the **network** statement. In addition, because this is Phase 1, the hub R1 can be configured to propagate a default route to the spokes while suppressing the more specific networks.

**On R1:**

Before configuring this task, you need to remove BGP AS 100 with the no router bgp 100 command and issue a no shut on the G0/5 interface. The prefix list and the route map should already be part of the running configuration because they were configured previously.

```
R1(config)#no router bgp 100

R1(config)#interface g0/5
R1(config-if)#no shut

R1#show run | include ip prefix

ip prefix-list NET seq 5 permit 0.0.0.0/0

R1#show run | section route-map TST

route-map TST permit 10
 match ip address prefix-list NET

R1(config)#router bgp 100
R1(config-router)#neighbor tunnel100 peer-group
R1(config-router)#neighbor tunnel200 peer-group

R1(config-router)#neighbor tunnel100 remote-as 200 alternate-as 300
R1(config-router)#neighbor tunnel200 remote-as 200 alternate-as 300

R1(config-router)#bgp listen range 100.1.1.0/24 peer-group tunnel100
R1(config-router)#bgp listen range 200.1.1.0/24 peer-group tunnel200

R1(config-router)#address-family ipv4
R1(config-router-af)#neighbor tunnel100 activate
R1(config-router-af)#neighbor tunnel200 activate

R1(config-router-af)#neighbor tunnel100 default-originate
R1(config-router-af)#neighbor tunnel200 default-originate

R1(config-router-af)#neighbor tunnel100 route-map TST out
R1(config-router-af)#neighbor tunnel200 route-map TST out

R1(config-router-af)#network 18.1.1.0 mask 255.255.255.0
```

## On R2:

```
R2(config)#no router bgp 100

R2(config)#router bgp 200
R2(config-router)#neighbor 100.1.1.1 remote-as 100
R2(config-router)#neighbor 200.1.1.1 remote-as 100

R2(config-router)#address-family ipv4
R2(config-router-af)#network 24.1.1.0 mask 255.255.255.0
```

You should see the following console messages:

```
%BGP-5-ADJCHANGE: neighbor 100.1.1.1 Up
%BGP-5-ADJCHANGE: neighbor 200.1.1.1 Up
```

## On R3:

```
R3(config)#no router bgp 100

R3(config)#router bgp 300
R3(config-router)#neighbor 100.1.1.1 remote-as 100
R3(config-router)#neighbor 200.1.1.1 remote-as 100

R3(config-router)#address-family ipv4
R3(config-router-af)#network 36.1.1.0 mask 255.255.255.0
```

You should see the following console messages:

```
%BGP-5-ADJCHANGE: neighbor 100.1.1.1 Up
%BGP-5-ADJCHANGE: neighbor 200.1.1.1 Up
```

With the eBGP peering up between the spokes and the hub, the show ip bgp command is issued on them. R1 learns of the host networks from R2 and R3 over tunnel 100 and 200. R2 and R3 receive two default routes from R1 over their tunnel 100 and tunnel 200 interfaces:

## On R1:

```
R1#show ip bgp | begin Net

     Network          Next Hop         Metric LocPrf Weight Path
      0.0.0.0          0.0.0.0                            0 i
 *>   18.1.1.0/24      0.0.0.0               0       32768 i
 *    24.1.1.0/24      200.1.1.2             0           0 200 i
```

```
 *>                      100.1.1.2                 0           0 200 i
 *       36.1.1.0/24     200.1.1.3                 0           0 300 i
 *>                      100.1.1.3                 0           0 300 i
```

## On R2:

```
R2#show ip bgp | begin Net

      Network           Next Hop           Metric LocPrf Weight Path
 *      0.0.0.0          200.1.1.1                              0 100 i
 *>                      100.1.1.1                              0 100 i
 *>     24.1.1.0/24      0.0.0.0                 0          32768 i
```

## On R3:

```
R3#show ip bgp | begin Net

      Network           Next Hop           Metric LocPrf Weight Path
 *      0.0.0.0          200.1.1.1                              0 100 i
 *>                      100.1.1.1                              0 100 i
 *>     36.1.1.0/24      0.0.0.0                 0          32768 i
```

All routers choose paths over their tunnel 100 interfaces as best because of the lower neighbor IP address. Once again, to ensure a deterministic result, the local preference for paths learned and sent over the tunnel 100 interface is modified to 200 on R1, R2, and R3:

## On R1:

You should be able to use an existing route map from one of the previous tasks to verify:

```
R1#show run | section route-map local-pref

route-map local-pref permit 10
 set local-preference 200

R1(config)#router bgp 100
R1(config-router)#address-family ipv4
R1(config-router-af)#neighbor tunnel100 route-map local-pref in

R1#clear ip bgp * in
```

## On R2:

```
R2(config)#route-map local-pref permit 10
R2(config-route-map)#set local-preference 200
R2(config-route-map)#router bgp 200
R2(config-router)#address-family ipv4
R2(config-router-af)#neighbor 100.1.1.1 route-map local-pref in

R2#clear ip bgp * in
```

## On R3:

```
R3(config)#route-map local-pref permit 10
R3(config-route-map)#set local-preference 200

R3(config)#router bgp 300
R3(config-router)#address-family ipv4
R3(config-router-af)#neighbor 100.1.1.1 route-map local-pref in

R3#clear ip bgp * in
```

The **show ip bgp** output on R1, R2, and R3 verifies that the local preference value is set to 200 on the paths learned via tunnel 100, making it the preferred path:

## On R1:

```
R1#show ip bgp | begin Net
```

| | Network | Next Hop | Metric | LocPrf | Weight | Path |
|---|---|---|---|---|---|---|
| | 0.0.0.0 | 0.0.0.0 | | | 0 | i |
| *> | 18.1.1.0/24 | 0.0.0.0 | 0 | | 32768 | i |
| * | 24.1.1.0/24 | 200.1.1.2 | 0 | | 0 | 200 i |
| *> | | 100.1.1.2 | 0 | 200 | 0 | 200 i |
| * | 36.1.1.0/24 | 200.1.1.3 | 0 | | 0 | 300 i |
| *> | | 100.1.1.3 | 0 | 200 | 0 | 300 i |

## On R2:

```
R2#show ip bgp | begin Net
```

| Network | Next Hop | Metric | LocPrf | Weight | Path |
|---|---|---|---|---|---|

```
*      0.0.0.0          200.1.1.1                          0 100 i
*>                      100.1.1.1                  200     0 100 i
*>    24.1.1.0/24       0.0.0.0              0           32768 i
```

### On R3:

```
R3#show ip bgp | begin Net

      Network           Next Hop          Metric LocPrf Weight Path
*      0.0.0.0          200.1.1.1                          0 100 i
*>                      100.1.1.1                  200     0 100 i
*>    36.1.1.0/24       0.0.0.0              0           32768 i
```

## Spokes in the Same AS

The second design choice places the spokes in the same autonomous system—in this case, ASN 230. The hub is placed in AS 100. Because the hub R1 is required to propagate a default route to the spokes and suppress the more specific prefixes, the BGP update messages the spokes received will contain the hub's ASN 100. Therefore, there is no need to use the **allowas-in** feature on the spokes.

### On R1:

You can use the existing IP prefix list and route map:

```
R1#show run | include ip prefix

ip prefix-list NET seq 5 permit 0.0.0.0/0

R1#show run | section route-map TST permit 10

route-map TST permit 10
 match ip address prefix-list NET

R1(config)#no router bgp 100

R1(config)#router bgp 100
R1(config-router)#neighbor tunnel100 peer-group
R1(config-router)#neighbor tunnel200 peer-group
R1(config-router)#neighbor tunnel100 remote-as 230
R1(config-router)#neighbor tunnel200 remote-as 230
```

```
R1(config-router)#bgp listen range 100.1.1.0/24 peer-group tunnel100
R1(config-router)#bgp listen range 200.1.1.0/24 peer-group tunnel200

R1(config-router)#address-family ipv4
R1(config-router-af)#neighbor tunnel100 activate
R1(config-router-af)#neighbor tunnel200 activate
R1(config-router-af)#network 18.1.1.0 mask 255.255.255.0

R1(config-router-af)#neighbor tunnel100 route-map TST out
R1(config-router-af)#neighbor tunnel200 route-map TST out

R1(config-router-af)#neighbor tunnel100 default-originate
R1(config-router-af)#neighbor tunnel200 default-originate

R1#clear ip bgp * out
```

**On R2:**

```
R2(config)#no router bgp 200

R2(config)#router bgp 230
R2(config-router)#neighbor 100.1.1.1 remote-as 100
R2(config-router)#neighbor 200.1.1.1 remote-as 100

R2(config-router)#address-family ipv4
R2(config-router-af)#network 24.1.1.0 mask 255.255.255.0
```

You should see the following console messages:

```
%BGP-5-ADJCHANGE: neighbor 100.1.1.1 Up
%BGP-5-ADJCHANGE: neighbor 200.1.1.1 Up
```

**On R3:**

```
R3(config)#no router bgp 300

R3(config)#router bgp 230
R3(config-router)#neighbor 100.1.1.1 remote-as 100
R3(config-router)#neighbor 200.1.1.1 remote-as 100
R3(config-router-af)#address-family ipv4
R3(config-router-af)#network 36.1.1.0 mask 255.255.255.0
```

You should see the following console messages:

```
%BGP-5-ADJCHANGE: neighbor 100.1.1.1 Up
%BGP-5-ADJCHANGE: neighbor 200.1.1.1 Up
```

R1, R2, and R3 are once again configured to raise the local preference for paths learned over the tunnel 100 interface to make the tunnel 100 path the preferred path:

## On R1:

You can use an existing route map, called **local-pref**:

```
route-map SET_LOCAL_PREFERENCE permit 10
 set local-preference 200

R1(config)#router bgp 100

R1(config-router)#address-family ipv4
R1(config-router-af)#neighbor tunnel100 route-map local-pref in

R1#clear ip bgp * in
```

## On R2:

```
R2(config)#route-map local-pref permit 10
R2(config-route-map)#set local-preference 200

R2(config)#router bgp 230

R2(config-router)#address-family ipv4
R2(config-router-af)#neighbor 100.1.1.1 route-map local-pref in

R2#clear ip bgp * in
```

## On R3:

```
R3(config)#route-map local-pref permit 10
R3(config-route-map)#set local-preference 200

R3(config)#router bgp 230

R3(config-router)#address-family ipv4
R3(config-router-af)#neighbor 100.1.1.1 route-map local-pref in

R3#clear ip bgp * in
```

Notice that the host networks on R1 learned over the tunnel 100 interface have been selected as best due to the higher local preference value 200. The same is true on R2 and R3 for the default route learned over the tunnel 100 interface:

## On R1:

```
R1#show ip bgp | begin Net

     Network          Next Hop          Metric LocPrf Weight Path
     0.0.0.0          0.0.0.0                                 0 i
 *   24.1.1.0/24      200.1.1.2            0                  0 230 i
 *>                   100.1.1.2            0      200         0 230 i
 *>  36.1.1.0/24      100.1.1.3            0      200         0 230 i
 *                    200.1.1.3            0                  0 230 i
```

## On R2:

```
R2#show ip bgp | begin Net

     Network          Next Hop          Metric LocPrf Weight Path
 *   0.0.0.0          200.1.1.1                             0 100 i
 *>                   100.1.1.1                   200       0 100 i
 *>  24.1.1.0/24      0.0.0.0              0           32768 i
```

## On R3:

```
R3#show ip bgp | begin Net

     Network          Next Hop          Metric LocPrf Weight Path
 *>  0.0.0.0          100.1.1.1                   200       0 100 i
 *                    200.1.1.1                             0 100 i
 *>  36.1.1.0/24      0.0.0.0              0           32768 i
```

Redundancy is tested for both designs by performing a repeated ping to the 36.1.1.6 address from R4. During the pings, the G0/5 interface on R1 is shut down. This results in a connectivity loss while BGP switches over to using the default route learned over the secondary path, via tunnel 200:

## On R4:

```
R4#ping 36.1.1.6 rep 100000
```

```
Type escape sequence to abort.
Sending 100000, 100-byte ICMP Echos to 36.1.1.6, timeout is 2 seconds:
!!!!!!!!!!!!!!!!!!!!!!!!!!!!!!!!!!!!!!!!!!!!!!!!!!!!!!!!!!!!!!!!!!!!!!!!!!!
!!!!!!!!!!!!!!!!!!!!!!!!!!!!!!!!!!!!!!!!!!!!!!!!!!!!!!!!!!!!!!!!!!!!!!!!!!!
!!!!!!!!!!!!!!!!!!!!!!!!!!!!!!!!!!!!!!!!!!!!!!!!!!!!!!!!!!!!!!!!!!!!!!!!!!!
!!!!!!!!!!!!!!!!!!!!!!!!!!!!!!!!!!!!!!!!!!!!!!!!!!!!!!!!!!!!!!!!!!!!!!!!!!!
!!!!!!!!!!!!!!!!!!!!!!!!!!!!!!!!..........................................
..............................................!!!!!!!!!!!!!!!!!!!!!!!!!!!!
!!!!!!!!!!!!!!!!!!!!!!!!!!!!!!!!!!!!!!!!!!!!!!!!!!!!!!!!!!!!!!!!!!!!!!!!!!!
!!!!!!!!!!!!!!!!!!!!!!!!!!!!!!!!!!!!!!!!!!!!!!!!!!!!!!!!!!!!!!!!!!!!!!!!!!!
!!!!!!!!!!!!!!!!!!!!!!!!!!!!!!!!!!
Success rate is 85 percent (504/591), round-trip min/avg/max = 9/21/30 ms
```

The output of the command **show ip bgp** on R2 and R3 confirms the switchover to tunnel 200 for the default route:

## On R2:

```
R2#show ip bgp | begin Net

     Network          Next Hop           Metric LocPrf Weight Path
 *>   0.0.0.0          200.1.1.1                         0 100 i
 *>   24.1.1.0/24      0.0.0.0                 0         32768 i
```

## On R3:

```
R3#show ip bgp | begin Net

     Network          Next Hop           Metric LocPrf Weight Path
 *>   0.0.0.0          200.1.1.1                         0 100 i
 *>   36.1.1.0/24      0.0.0.0                 0         32768 i
```

# Implement Phase 2

# Design Goal

The network engineers have received reports of application anomalies for application resources shared between remote sites. Users are experiencing timeouts and delays. The engineers have determined that the main site hub router becomes overloaded during some operations. To alleviate this, the team decides to implement a method to allow the remote sites to bypass the hub for communication.

## DMVPN Tunnel Configuration

Based on the design goals, DMVPN Phase 2 will be implemented for the topology. From the hub's perspective, the base configuration for the DMVPN network remains the same as the Phase 1 single-hub, dual-cloud setup. Two mGRE tunnel interfaces are created on the hub that map to the separate transports. Tunnel 100 is configured with NHRP network ID 100, and tunnel 200 is configured with NHRP network ID 200. The tunnel source for tunnel 100 is the hub's interface facing the MPLS WAN. The tunnel source for tunnel 200 is the hub's interface facing ISP-1. The ip nhrp map multicast dynamic command is also issued to allow the hub to automatically add NHRP multicast entries for every client that registers with it over both tunnel interfaces

The spoke configuration must be modified from the Phase 1 configuration. Instead of using two point-to-point GRE tunnels, the spoke tunnel interfaces should be converted to mGRE tunnels with the **tunnel mode gre multipoint** command. Once the tunnels are converted to mGRE tunnel interfaces, there is no need to configure a **tunnel destination**. Therefore, the spokes will no longer be able to send traffic to the hub natively. They require a static NHRP mapping for the hub to fill in the appropriate NBMA destination address in the resulting GRE/IP packet, as explained in previous sections. To enable multicast transmission of routing protocol hellos, the spokes also need to create a mapping in the NHRP multicast table for the hub in order for the routing protocol adjacencies to form.

In this case, you will examine the static configuration of **ip nhrp nhs x.x.x.x** and the **ip nhrp map multicast** command, which fill in all of the requirements on the spokes.

Before proceeding with the complete base configuration for the DMVPN, the BGP configuration from the earlier task is removed:

---

**On R1:**

```
R1(config)#no router bgp 100

R1(config)#interface g0/5
R1(config-if)#no shut

R1(config)#interface tunnel 100
R1(config-if)#no ip ospf cost 500
R1(config-if)#ip address 100.1.1.1 255.255.255.0
R1(config-if)#tunnel source 15.1.1.1
R1(config-if)#tunnel mode gre multipoint
R1(config-if)#ip nhrp network-id 100
R1(config-if)#ip nhrp map multicast dynamic
```

```
R1(config)#interface tunnel 200
R1(config-if)#ip address 200.1.1.1 255.255.255.0
R1(config-if)#tunnel source 17.1.1.1
R1(config-if)#tunnel mode gre multipoint
R1(config-if)#ip nhrp network-id 200
R1(config-if)#ip nhrp map multicast dynamic
```

## To verify the configuration:

```
R1#show ip nhrp multicast

  I/F      NBMA address
Tunnel100  35.1.1.3       Flags: static    (Enabled)
Tunnel100  25.1.1.2       Flags: static    (Enabled)
Tunnel200  37.1.1.3       Flags: static    (Enabled)
Tunnel200  27.1.1.2       Flags: static    (Enabled)
```

## On R2:

```
R2(config)#no interface tunnel 100
R2(config)#no interface tunnel 200
R2(config)#no router bgp 230

R2(config)#interface tunnel 100
R2(config-if)#ip address 100.1.1.2 255.255.255.0
R2(config-if)#tunnel source 25.1.1.2
R2(config-if)#tunnel mode gre multipoint
R2(config-if)#ip nhrp network-id 100
R2(config-if)#ip nhrp nhs 100.1.1.1
R2(config-if)#ip nhrp map multicast 15.1.1.1
R2(config-if)#ip nhrp map 100.1.1.1 15.1.1.1


R2(config)#interface tunnel 200
R2(config-if)#ip address 200.1.1.2 255.255.255.0
R2(config-if)#tunnel source 27.1.1.2
R2(config-if)#tunnel mode gre multipoint
R2(config-if)#ip nhrp network-id 200
R2(config-if)#ip nhrp nhs 200.1.1.1
R2(config-if)#ip nhrp map multicast 17.1.1.1
R2(config-if)#ip nhrp map 200.1.1.1 17.1.1.1
```

## To verify the configuration:

```
R2#show ip nhrp multicast

  I/F     NBMA address
Tunnel100  15.1.1.1      Flags: static       (Enabled)
Tunnel200  17.1.1.1      Flags: static       (Enabled)
```

## On R3:

```
R3(config)#no router bgp 230
R3(config)#no interface tunnel 100
R3(config)#no interface tunnel 200

R3(config)#interface tunnel 100
R3(config-if)#ip address 100.1.1.3 255.255.255.0
R3(config-if)#tunnel source 35.1.1.3
R3(config-if)#tunnel mode gre multipoint
R3(config-if)#ip nhrp network-id 100
R3(config-if)#ip nhrp nhs 100.1.1.1
R3(config-if)#ip nhrp map multicast 15.1.1.1
R3(config-if)#ip nhrp map 100.1.1.1 15.1.1.1

R3(config)#interface tunnel 200
R3(config-if)#ip address 200.1.1.3 255.255.255.0
R3(config-if)#tunnel source 37.1.1.3
R3(config-if)#tunnel mode gre multipoint
R3(config-if)#ip nhrp network-id 200
R3(config-if)#ip nhrp nhs 200.1.1.1
R3(config-if)#ip nhrp map 200.1.1.1 17.1.1.1
R3(config-if)#ip nhrp map multicast 17.1.1.1
```

## To verify the configuration:

```
R3#show ip nhrp multicast

  I/F     NBMA address
Tunnel100  15.1.1.1      Flags: static       (Enabled)
Tunnel200  17.1.1.1      Flags: static       (Enabled)
```

### On R1:

```
R1#show ip nhrp tunnel 100

100.1.1.2/32 via 100.1.1.2
   Tunnel100 created 00:28:24, expire 00:07:59
   Type: dynamic, Flags: registered nhop
   NBMA address: 25.1.1.2
100.1.1.3/32 via 100.1.1.3
   Tunnel100 created 00:11:29, expire 00:07:33
   Type: dynamic, Flags: registered nhop
   NBMA address: 35.1.1.3

R1#show ip nhrp tunnel 200

200.1.1.2/32 via 200.1.1.2
   Tunnel200 created 00:28:05, expire 00:08:19
   Type: dynamic, Flags: registered nhop
   NBMA address: 27.1.1.2
200.1.1.3/32 via 200.1.1.3
   Tunnel200 created 00:05:05, expire 00:07:47
   Type: dynamic, Flags: registered nhop
   NBMA address: 37.1.1.3
```

One of the key characteristics of Phase 2 implementation is the use of spoke-to-spoke tunnels. Spoke-to-spoke tunnels are resolved based on the incomplete CEF adjacency table entries. These incomplete entries exist whenever a spoke needs to route a packet using a route with a remote spoke as the next-hop address.

The problem with the Single Hub | Dual Cloud design is the use of two tunnel interfaces on the hub. These two tunnel interfaces can cause problems with the third-party next-hop features when the hub advertises routes received from one spoke to another. The problem stems from the fact that the two tunnel interfaces are in different subnets. When the hub advertises routes between the two tunnel interfaces, third-party next-hop features may not take effect, causing the hub to advertise itself as next-hop instead of the originating spoke. This breaks the Phase 2 spoke-to-spoke tunnel resolution process. As these issues are encountered, they are explained below. Some solutions to the various problems may be outside of the scope of this lab.

## Implement OSPF

A key point for DMVPN Phase 2 operation is preservation of the original next hop advertised from the hub to the spokes. The OSPF broadcast network type does this by default. This is the only network type aside from non-broadcast that can be used to implement DMVPN Phase 2 behavior in an OSPF environment.

The following configuration implements DMVPN Phase 2 when using OSPF as an overlay in single-hub, dual-cloud setups. The tunnel 100 and 200 interfaces are configured to run OSPF process 100 for Area 0. The interfaces are also configured to use the OSPF broadcast network type. This allows the hub to preserve the original next hop IP address for the OSPF routes it advertises to the spokes R2 and R3. **ip ospf priority 0** on the tunnel 100 and 200 interfaces on R2 and R3 ensures that the hub R1 is always elected DR. Host networks at each site are enabled for OSPF process 100 for Area 0 and declared passive to prevent unnecessary OSPF adjacencies from forming over them:

**On R1:**

```
R1(config)#interface tunnel 100
R1(config-if)#ip ospf network broadcast
R1(config-if)#ip ospf 100 area 0

R1(config)#interface tunnel 200
R1(config-if)#ip ospf network broadcast
R1(config-if)#ip ospf 100 area 0

R1(config-if)#interface g0/8
R1(config-if)#ip ospf 100 area 0

R1(config-if)#router ospf 100
R1(config-router)#passive-interface g0/8
```

**On R2:**

```
R2(config)#interface tunnel 100
R2(config-if)#ip ospf network broadcast
R2(config-if)#ip ospf priority 0
R2(config-if)#ip ospf 100 area 0
```

You should see the following console message:

```
%OSPF-5-ADJCHG: Process 100, Nbr 200.1.1.1 on Tunnel100 from LOADING
to FULL, Loading Done

R2(config)#interface tunnel 200
```

```
R2(config-if)#ip ospf network broadcast
R2(config-if)#ip ospf priority 0
R2(config-if)#ip ospf 100 area 0

R2(config)#interface g0/4
R2(config-if)#ip ospf 100 area 0

R2(config)#router ospf 100
R2(config-router)#passive-interface g0/4
```

You should see the following console message:

```
%OSPF-5-ADJCHG: Process 100, Nbr 200.1.1.1 on Tunnel200 from LOADING
to FULL, Loading Done
```

## On R3:

```
R3(config)#interface tunnel 100
R3(config-if)#ip ospf network broadcast
R3(config-if)#ip ospf priority 0
R3(config-if)#ip ospf 100 area 0
```

You should see the following console message:

```
%OSPF-5-ADJCHG: Process 100, Nbr 200.1.1.1 on Tunnel100 from LOADING
to FULL, Loading Done
```

```
R3(config)#interface tunnel 200
R3(config-if)#ip ospf network broadcast
R3(config-if)#ip ospf priority 0
R3(config-if)#ip ospf 100 area 0
```

You should see the following console message:

```
%OSPF-5-ADJCHG: Process 100, Nbr 200.1.1.1 on Tunnel200 from LOADING
to FULL, Loading Done
```

```
R3(config)#interface g0/6
R3(config-if)#ip ospf 100 area 0

R3(config-if)#router ospf 100
R3(config-router)#passive-interface g0/6
```

The **show ip ospf neighbor** output shows that R2 and R3 form two OSPF adjacencies each with the hub R1 over their tunnel 100 and 200 interfaces:

### On R2:

```
R2#show ip ospf neighbor

Neighbor ID     Pri   State        Dead Time    Address
Interface
200.1.1.1         1   FULL/DR      00:00:39     200.1.1.1
Tunnel200
200.1.1.1         1   FULL/DR      00:00:31     100.1.1.1
Tunnel100
```

### On R3:

```
R3#show ip ospf neighbor

Neighbor ID     Pri   State        Dead Time    Address
Interface
200.1.1.1         1   FULL/DR      00:00:30     200.1.1.1
Tunnel200
200.1.1.1         1   FULL/DR      00:00:32     100.1.1.1
Tunnel100
```

The **show ip route ospf** command output below verifies the OSPF-learned routes over the tunnel 100 and tunnel 200 interfaces on R1, R2, and R3:

### On R1:

```
R1#show ip route ospf | begin Gate
Gateway of last resort is not set

      24.0.0.0/24 is subnetted, 1 subnets
O        24.1.1.0 [110/1001] via 200.1.1.2, 00:08:19, Tunnel200
                  [110/1001] via 100.1.1.2, 00:08:19, Tunnel100
      36.0.0.0/24 is subnetted, 1 subnets
O        36.1.1.0 [110/1001] via 200.1.1.3, 00:05:18, Tunnel200
                  [110/1001] via 100.1.1.3, 00:05:18, Tunnel100
```

### On R2:

```
R2#show ip route ospf | begin Gate
Gateway of last resort is not set
```

```
        18.0.0.0/24 is subnetted, 1 subnets
O          18.1.1.0 [110/1001] via 200.1.1.1, 00:09:54, Tunnel200
                    [110/1001] via 100.1.1.1, 00:10:36, Tunnel100
        36.0.0.0/24 is subnetted, 1 subnets
O          36.1.1.0 [110/1001] via 200.1.1.3, 00:06:24, Tunnel200
                    [110/1001] via 100.1.1.3, 00:06:24, Tunnel100
```

## On R3:

```
R3#show ip route ospf | begin Gate
Gateway of last resort is not set

        18.0.0.0/24 is subnetted, 1 subnets
O          18.1.1.0 [110/1001] via 200.1.1.1, 00:07:45, Tunnel200
                    [110/1001] via 100.1.1.1, 00:08:09, Tunnel100
        24.0.0.0/24 is subnetted, 1 subnets
O          24.1.1.0 [110/1001] via 200.1.1.2, 00:07:45, Tunnel200
                    [110/1001] via 100.1.1.2, 00:08:09, Tunnel100
```

As evidenced by the output above, all routers are performing equal-cost multipathing for the OSPF-learned routes. **ip ospf cost 500** is used on the tunnel 100 interfaces on R1, R2, and R3 to manipulate the cost to make MPLS-WAN the primary path.

## On R1, R2, and R3:

```
Rx(config)#interface tunnel 100
Rx(config-if)#ip ospf cost 500
```

## To verify the configuration:

## On R1:

```
R1#show ip ospf interface brief
```

| Interface F/C | PID | Area | IP Address/Mask | Cost | State | Nbrs |
|---|---|---|---|---|---|---|
| Gi8 | 100 | 0 | 18.1.1.1/24 | 1 | DR | 0/0 |
| Tu200 | 100 | 0 | 200.1.1.1/24 | 1000 | DR | 2/2 |
| Tu100 | 100 | 0 | 100.1.1.1/24 | 500 | DR | 2/2 |

**On R2:**

```
R2#show ip ospf interface brief
```

| Interface F/C | PID | Area | IP Address/Mask | Cost | State | Nbrs |
|---|---|---|---|---|---|---|
| Gi4 | 100 | 0 | 24.1.1.2/24 | 1 | DR | 0/0 |
| Tu200 | 100 | 0 | 200.1.1.2/24 | 1000 | DROTH | 1/1 |
| Tu100 | 100 | 0 | 100.1.1.2/24 | 500 | DROTH | 1/1 |

**On R3:**

```
R3#show ip ospf interface brief
```

| Interface F/C | PID | Area | IP Address/Mask | Cost | State | Nbrs |
|---|---|---|---|---|---|---|
| Gi6 | 100 | 0 | 36.1.1.3/24 | 1 | DR | 0/0 |
| Tu200 | 100 | 0 | 200.1.1.3/24 | 1000 | DROTH | 1/1 |
| Tu100 | 100 | 0 | 100.1.1.3/24 | 500 | DROTH | 1/1 |

With a lower OSPF cost over the tunnel 100 interface, routing tables on R1, R2, and R3 show tunnel 100 as the exit interface for the remote host networks:

**On R1:**

```
R1#show ip route ospf | begin Gate
Gateway of last resort is not set

      24.0.0.0/24 is subnetted, 1 subnets
O        24.1.1.0 [110/501] via 100.1.1.2, 00:04:11, Tunnel100
      36.0.0.0/24 is subnetted, 1 subnets
O        36.1.1.0 [110/501] via 100.1.1.3, 00:04:11, Tunnel100
```

**On R2:**

```
R2#show ip route ospf | begin Gate
Gateway of last resort is not set

      18.0.0.0/24 is subnetted, 1 subnets
O        18.1.1.0 [110/501] via 100.1.1.1, 00:04:28, Tunnel100
      36.0.0.0/24 is subnetted, 1 subnets
O        36.1.1.0 [110/501] via 100.1.1.3, 00:04:28, Tunnel100
```

**On R3:**

```
R3#show ip route ospf | begin Gate
Gateway of last resort is not set


     18.0.0.0/24 is subnetted, 1 subnets
O        18.1.1.0 [110/501] via 100.1.1.1, 00:04:53, Tunnel100
     24.0.0.0/24 is subnetted, 1 subnets
O        24.1.1.0 [110/501] via 100.1.1.2, 00:04:53, Tunnel100
```

A traceroute from R4 to R8 and to R6 is shown to take the path via the tunnel interface 100. Following this, a second traceroute from R4 to R6 traverses the direct spoke-to-spoke tunnel 100 that was dynamically created between R2 and R3:

```
R4#traceroute 18.1.1.8
Type escape sequence to abort.
Tracing the route to 18.1.1.8
VRF info: (vrf in name/id, vrf out name/id)
  1 24.1.1.2 1 msec 1 msec 0 msec
  2 100.1.1.1 2 msec 2 msec 2 msec
  3 18.1.1.8 2 msec *   3 msec


R4#traceroute 36.1.1.6
Type escape sequence to abort.
Tracing the route to 36.1.1.6
VRF info: (vrf in name/id, vrf out name/id)
  1 24.1.1.2 1 msec 1 msec 1 msec
  2 100.1.1.1 2 msec 2 msec 1 msec
  3 100.1.1.3 3 msec 2 msec 3 msec
  4 36.1.1.6 2 msec *   3 msec


R4#traceroute 36.1.1.6
Type escape sequence to abort.
Tracing the route to 36.1.1.6
VRF info: (vrf in name/id, vrf out name/id)
  1 24.1.1.2 1 msec 1 msec 2 msec
  2 100.1.1.3 2 msec 2 msec 1 msec
  3 36.1.1.6 1 msec *   2 msec
```

Unlike the earlier designs, redundancy will be tested by shutting down the G0/5 interface on R2 instead of R1 like in the previous cases. If the G0/5 interface on R1 is shut down, this will not affect the traffic pattern on the spoke R2. This is because R2 will continue to maintain the NHRP mapping information for the spoke-to-spoke tunnel to R3 from the earlier traceroute from R4 to R6. The same information is retained on R3 as well for the same spoke-to-spoke tunnel.

With R2 and R3's connection to the original MPLS WAN transport active, they can
still transit traffic directly to each other via their Tunnel 100 interfaces without the hub.
This is because the hub is no longer in the data plane path for forwarding as in Phase 1.
In Phase 2, the hub hosts the control plane, helping to orchestrate spoke-to-spoke tunnel formation and only participating in the data plane forwarding if necessary. As such,
unless the NHRP entries are expired, the switchover to using Tunnel 200 will not happen.

To test redundancy, pings are repeated between R4 and R6. During the ping, the G0/5
interface is shut down on R2 to simulate a failure. The output below shows the results
of the simulation. The highlighted dots in between indicate the moment the tunnel 100
interface on R2 goes down. R2 purges the OSPF route over the tunnel 100 interface and
installs the OSPF path via tunnel 200:

### On R4:

```
R4#ping 36.1.1.6 repeat 10000
Type escape sequence to abort.
Sending 10000, 100-byte ICMP Echos to 36.1.1.6, timeout is 2 seconds:
!!!!!!!!!!!!!!!!!!!!!!!!!!!!!!!!!!!!!!!!!!!!!!!!!!!!!!!!!!!!!!!!!!!!!!!!!!!!!
!!!!!!!!!!!!!!!!!!!!!!!!!!!!!!!!!!!!!!!!!!!!!!!!!!!!!!!!!!!!!!!!!!!!!!!!!!!!!
!!!!!!!!!!!!!!!!!!!!!!!!!!!!!!!!!!!!!!!!!!!!!!!!!!!!!!!!!!!!!!!!!!!!!!!!!!!!!
!!!!!!!!!!!!!!!!!!!!!!!!!!!!!!!!!!!!!!!!!!!!!!!!!!!!!!!!!!!!!!!!!!!!!!!!!!!!!
!!!!!!!!!!!!!!!!!!!!!!!!!!!!!!!!!!!!!!!!!!!!!!!!!!!!!!!!!!!!!!!!!!!!!!!!!!!!!
!!!!!!!!!!!!!!!!!!!!!!!!!!!!!!!!!!!!!!!!!!!!!!!!!!!!!!!!!!!!!!!!!!!!!!!!!!!!!
!!!!!!!!!!!!!!!!!!!!!!!!!!!!!!!!!!!!!!!!!!!!!!!!!!!!!!!!!!!!!!!!!!!!!!!!!!!!!
!!!!!!!!!!!!!!!!!!!!!!!!!!!!!!!!!!!!!!!!!!!!!!!!!!!!!!!!!!!!!!!!!!!!!!!!!!!!!
!!!!!!!!!!!!!!!!!!!!!!!!!!!!!!!!!!!!!!!!!!!!!!!!!!!!!!!!.......!!!!!!!!!!!!!!
Success rate is 99 percent (2463/2466), round-trip min/avg/max =
5/19/106 ms
```

The introduction section explained scenarios where having two tunnel interfaces can
break the spoke-to-spoke tunnel resolution for Single Hub | Dual Cloud DMVPN
designs. This happens because the two tunnel interfaces are in different subnets. When
advertising paths between subnets, the hub will set itself as next-hop.

OSPF is a routing protocol that does not suffer from this problem, evidenced by the
following traceroute output from R4 to R6 after the above failure. The NHRP table was
cleared on R2 and R3 prior to retrieving this output:

```
R4#traceroute 36.1.1.6 source 24.1.1.4 probe 1
Type escape sequence to abort.
Tracing the route to 36.1.1.6
VRF info: (vrf in name/id, vrf out name/id)
  1 24.1.1.2 1 msec
  2 200.1.1.1 3 msec
```

```
  3 200.1.1.3 3 msec
  4 36.1.1.6 2 msec
```

```
R4#traceroute 36.1.1.6 source 24.1.1.4 probe 1
Type escape sequence to abort.
Tracing the route to 36.1.1.6
VRF info: (vrf in name/id, vrf out name/id)
  1 24.1.1.2 1 msec
  2 200.1.1.3 3 msec
  3 36.1.1.6 3 msec
```

The previous output shows normal Phase 2 spoke-to-spoke resolution. The first trace-route uses the hub as the first-hop while the spoke-to-spoke tunnel is being resolved. The second traceroute shows the traffic going directly to the remote spoke.

OSPF does not suffer from the aforementioned next-hop issue because of its use of the Link State Database. In OSPF, the Link State Database, or LSDB, is a database that contains a list of all of the router nodes and links connecting those router nodes in the network. When OSPF models the current DMVPN in the LSDB, it creates three router nodes connected by two network nodes.

The three router nodes represent R1, R2, and R3. The network nodes are created by the DR, R1, to represent the 100.1.1.0/24 network and the 200.1.1.0/24 network. Each router advertises a link to both of these network nodes as seen in the show ip ospf database network output on R1:

```
R1#show ip ospf database network

             OSPF Router with ID (200.1.1.1) (Process ID 100)

                   Net Link States (Area 0)

  LS age: 10
  Options: (No TOS-capability, DC)
  LS Type: Network Links
  Link State ID: 100.1.1.1 (address of Designated Router)
  Advertising Router: 200.1.1.1
  LS Seq Number: 80000006
  Checksum: 0xC8CE
  Length: 36
  Network Mask: /24
        Attached Router: 200.1.1.1
        Attached Router: 200.1.1.2
        Attached Router: 200.1.1.3
```

```
LS age: 523
Options: (No TOS-capability, DC)
LS Type: Network Links
Link State ID: 200.1.1.1 (address of Designated Router)
Advertising Router: 200.1.1.1
LS Seq Number: 80000002
Checksum: 0xB77F
Length: 36
Network Mask: /24
        Attached Router: 200.1.1.1
        Attached Router: 200.1.1.2
        Attached Router: 200.1.1.3
```

The output above shows two network LSAs created by the DR R1 representing the 100.1.1.0/24 and 200.1.1.0/24 networks. R1 takes note of all routers it has become fully adjacent with on those networks and adds their router IDs as "attached routers" in the Network LSA. This information is flooded to all routers in the network.

It is important to understand that this means each router has complete topology information for the network. They all know that the 100.1.1.0/24 and 200.1.1.0/24 shared segments exist and which routers are connected to them.

When R2's G0/5 interface is shut down, it loses its adjacency with R1 on the 100.1.1.0/24 shared segment. As a result R1 removes it as an attached router from the corresponding network LSA:

```
R1#

%OSPF-5-ADJCHG: Process 100, Nbr 200.1.1.2 on Tunnel100 from FULL to
DOWN, Neighbor Down: Dead timer expired

R1#show ip ospf database network 100.1.1.1

            OSPF Router with ID (200.1.1.1) (Process ID 100)


                Net Link States (Area 0)


    LS age: 4
    Options: (No TOS-capability, DC)
    LS Type: Network Links
    Link State ID: 100.1.1.1 (address of Designated Router)
    Advertising Router: 200.1.1.1
    LS Seq Number: 80000007
    Checksum: 0xB1B5
    Length: 32
    Network Mask: /24
```

```
     Attached Router: 200.1.1.1
     Attached Router: 200.1.1.3
     ! R2's router ID (200.1.1.2) is missing here
```

This change in the LSDB forces a recalculation of the SPT on all routers, most importantly on R2 and R3. R2 needs to find the shortest path to reach the 36.1.1.0/24 network advertised in R3's router LSA. It looks up the LSA and notices that R3 is attached to both of the two LAN segments:

R2#**show ip ospf database router 200.1.1.3**

```
            OSPF Router with ID (200.1.1.2) (Process ID 100)

            Router Link States (Area 0)

  LS age: 785
  Options: (No TOS-capability, DC)
  LS Type: Router Links
  Link State ID: 200.1.1.3
  Advertising Router: 200.1.1.3
  LS Seq Number: 80000008
  Checksum: 0xD02E
  Length: 60
  Number of Links: 3

    Link connected to: a Stub Network
     (Link ID) Network/subnet number: 36.1.1.0
     (Link Data) Network Mask: 255.255.255.0
      Number of MTID metrics: 0
       TOS 0 Metrics: 1

    Link connected to: a Transit Network
     (Link ID) Designated Router address: 200.1.1.1
     (Link Data) Router Interface address: 200.1.1.3
      Number of MTID metrics: 0
       TOS 0 Metrics: 1000

    Link connected to: a Transit Network
     (Link ID) Designated Router address: 100.1.1.1
     (Link Data) Router Interface address: 100.1.1.3
      Number of MTID metrics: 0
       TOS 0 Metrics: 500
```

R2 looks at the Network LSA for the two shared segments and finds that it is connected to the 200.1.1.0/24 network segment along with R3:

```
R2#show ip ospf database network

              OSPF Router with ID (200.1.1.2) (Process ID 100)

                  Net Link States (Area 0)

  LS age: 358
  Options: (No TOS-capability, DC)
  LS Type: Network Links
  Link State ID: 100.1.1.1 (address of Designated Router)
  Advertising Router: 200.1.1.1
  LS Seq Number: 80000007
  Checksum: 0xB1B5
  Length: 32
  Network Mask: /24
        Attached Router: 200.1.1.1
        Attached Router: 200.1.1.3

  LS age: 1167
  Options: (No TOS-capability, DC)
  LS Type: Network Links
  Link State ID: 200.1.1.1 (address of Designated Router)
  Advertising Router: 200.1.1.1
  LS Seq Number: 80000002
  Checksum: 0xB77F
  Length: 36
  Network Mask: /24
        Attached Router: 200.1.1.1
        Attached Router: 200.1.1.2
        Attached Router: 200.1.1.3
```

With this information, R2 decides that it can use R3's interface connected to this shared segment as its next-hop to reach that network. It installs the route to 36.1.1.0/24 with 200.1.1.3 as next-hop:

```
R2#show ip route 36.1.1.0
Routing entry for 36.1.1.0/24
  Known via "ospf 100", distance 110, metric 1001, type intra area
  Last update from 200.1.1.3 on Tunnel200, 00:08:21 ago
  Routing Descriptor Blocks:
  * 200.1.1.3, from 200.1.1.3, 00:08:21 ago, via Tunnel200
      Route metric is 1001, traffic share count is 1
```

The same occurs on R3 but for the 24.1.1.0/24 network. It looks up and notices that itself and R2 are both connected to the 200.1.1.0/24 network and can therefore install a route to that prefix using 200.1.1.2 as next-hop:

```
R3#show ip route 24.1.1.0
Routing entry for 24.1.1.0/24
  Known via "ospf 100", distance 110, metric 1001, type intra area
  Last update from 200.1.1.2 on Tunnel200, 00:09:30 ago
  Routing Descriptor Blocks:
  * 200.1.1.2, from 200.1.1.2, 00:09:30 ago, via Tunnel200
      Route metric is 1001, traffic share count is 1
```

The result is R2 and R3 both retain each other as next-hop and the Phase 2 spoke-to-spoke tunnel resolution process is retained in failure situations.

OSPF can successfully retain spoke-to-spoke tunnels because each router has a complete view of the network. Routes are calculated by calculating shortest paths between nodes in the LSDB and not based on routes being received directly from neighbors. This is a fundamental property of link-state routing protocols and can be both an advantage and disadvantage in certain situations. In this particular case, it is an advantage.

## Implement EIGRP

To implement EIGRP as an overlay for Single Hub | Dual Cloud Phase 2, EIGRP process 100 is enabled on the tunnel 100, tunnel 200 interfaces and the host networks at each site. The host network interfaces are declared as passive under the EIGRP configuration mode.

Since Phase 2 requires the Hub to advertise the specific routes with the true next hop IP address down to the Spokes, split horizon is disabled on the tunnel 100 and 200 interfaces on the R1 with the **no ip split-horizon** command. The **no ip next-hop-self** is also configured on the tunnel interfaces on R1 to prevent R1 from setting itself as the next hop for EIGRP routes it advertises to R2 and R3:

---

**On R1:**

```
R1(config)#interface g0/5
R1(config-if)#no shut

R1(config)#no router ospf 100

R1(config)#interface tunnel 100
R1(config-if)#no ip ospf 100 area 0
R1(config-if)#no ip ospf network broadcast
R1(config-if)#no ip ospf cost 500
R1(config-if)#no ip next-hop-self eigrp 100
R1(config-if)#no ip split-horizon eigrp 100
```

```
R1(config)#interface tunnel 200
R1(config-if)#no ip split-horizon eigrp 100
R1(config-if)#no ip next-hop-self eigrp 100

R1(config)#router eigrp 100
R1(config-router)#network 18.1.1.1 0.0.0.0
R1(config-router)#network 100.1.1.1 0.0.0.0
R1(config-router)#network 200.1.1.1 0.0.0.0
R1(config-router)#passive-interface g0/8
```

## On R2:

```
R2(config)#no router ospf 100

R2(config)#interface tunnel 100
R2(config-if)#no ip ospf network broadcast
R2(config-if)#no ip ospf priority 0
R2(config-if)#no ip ospf 100 area 0
R2(config-if)#no ip ospf cost 500
```

You should see the following console message:

```
%DUAL-5-NBRCHANGE: EIGRP-IPv4 100: Neighbor 100.1.1.1 (Tunnel100) is
up: new adjacency
```

```
R2(config)#interface tunnel 200
R2(config-if)#no ip ospf network broadcast
R2(config-if)#no ip ospf priority 0
R2(config-if)#no ip ospf 100 area 0
```

```
R2(config)#router eigrp 100
R2(config-router)#network 24.1.1.2 0.0.0.0
R2(config-router)#network 100.1.1.2 0.0.0.0
R2(config-router)#network 200.1.1.2 0.0.0.0R2(config-router)#passive-
interface g0/4
```

You should see the following console messages:

```
%DUAL-5-NBRCHANGE: EIGRP-IPv4 100: Neighbor 200.1.1.1 (Tunnel200) is
up: new adjacency
```

```
%DUAL-5-NBRCHANGE: EIGRP-IPv4 100: Neighbor 100.1.1.1 (Tunnel100) is
up: new adjacency
```

**On R3:**

```
R3(config)#no router ospf 100

R3(config)#interface tunnel 100
R3(config-if)#no ip ospf cost 500
R3(config-if)#no ip ospf priority 0
R3(config-if)#no ip ospf network broadcast

R3(config)#interface tunn 200
R3(config-if)#no ip ospf network broadcast
R3(config-if)#no ip ospf priority 0

R3(config)#router eigrp 100
R3(config-router)#network 36.1.1.3 0.0.0.0
R3(config-router)#network 100.1.1.3 0.0.0.0
R3(config-router)#network 200.1.1.3 0.0.0.0
R3(config-router)#passive-interface g0/6
```

You should see the following console messages:

```
%DUAL-5-NBRCHANGE: EIGRP-IPv4 100: Neighbor 100.1.1.1 (Tunnel100) is
up: new adjacency

%DUAL-5-NBRCHANGE: EIGRP-IPv4 100: Neighbor 200.1.1.1 (Tunnel200) is
up: new adjacency
```

The **show ip eigrp 100 neighbors** shows R2 and R3 form two EIGRP neighborships
with the Hub R1 over their Tunnel 100 and Tunnel 200 interfaces:

**On R2:**

```
R2#show ip eigrp 100 neighbors
EIGRP-IPv4 Neighbors for AS(100)
```

| H | Address | Interface | Hold Uptime | SRTT | RTO | Q | Seq |
|---|---------|-----------|-------------|------|-----|---|-----|
|   |         |           | (sec)       |      | (ms) |  |     |
| Cnt Num |   |     |       |   |      |   |    |
| 1 | 100.1.1.1 | Tu100 | 14 00:02:21 | 7 | 1470 | 0 | 18 |
| 0 | 200.1.1.1 | Tu200 | 11 00:15:23 | 17 | 1470 | 0 | 17 |

**On R3:**

```
R3#show ip eigrp 100 neighbors
EIGRP-IPv4 Neighbors for AS(100)
```

```
H    Address           Interface             Hold Uptime    SRTT   RTO
Q    Seq
                                             (sec)          (ms)
Cnt  Num
1    100.1.1.1         Tu100                 12 00:02:55      7   1470
0    18
0    200.1.1.1         Tu200                 13 00:10:24     17   1470
0    17
```

Host networks from each site are learned via EIGRP as seen in the following routing tables from R1, R2, and R3. All routers are load sharing over the two tunnel interfaces:

## On R1:

```
R1#show ip route eigrp 100 | begin Gate
Gateway of last resort is not set

      24.0.0.0/24 is subnetted, 1 subnets
D        24.1.1.0 [90/26880256] via 200.1.1.2, 00:04:16, Tunnel200
                  [90/26880256] via 100.1.1.2, 00:04:16, Tunnel100
      36.0.0.0/24 is subnetted, 1 subnets
D        36.1.1.0 [90/26880256] via 200.1.1.3, 00:03:45, Tunnel200
                  [90/26880256] via 100.1.1.3, 00:03:45, Tunnel100
```

## On R2:

```
R2#show ip route eigrp 100 | begin Gate
Gateway of last resort is not set

      18.0.0.0/24 is subnetted, 1 subnets
D        18.1.1.0 [90/26880256] via 200.1.1.1, 00:04:51, Tunnel200
                  [90/26880256] via 100.1.1.1, 00:04:51, Tunnel100
      36.0.0.0/24 is subnetted, 1 subnets
D        36.1.1.0 [90/28160256] via 200.1.1.3, 00:04:16, Tunnel200
                  [90/28160256] via 100.1.1.3, 00:04:16, Tunnel100
```

## On R3:

```
R3#show ip route eigrp 100 | begin Gate
Gateway of last resort is not set
```

```
      18.0.0.0/24 is subnetted, 1 subnets
D        18.1.1.0 [90/26880256] via 200.1.1.1, 00:04:47, Tunnel200
                  [90/26880256] via 100.1.1.1, 00:04:47, Tunnel100
      24.0.0.0/24 is subnetted, 1 subnets
D        24.1.1.0 [90/28160256] via 200.1.1.2, 00:04:47, Tunnel200
                  [90/28160256] via 100.1.1.2, 00:04:47, Tunnel100
```

For the Phase 1 configuration, the delay value on the Tunnel100 interface was modified to influence the EIGRP metrics to prefer that interface over the Tunnel 200 interface on the spokes. Another method for implementing this change takes advantage of the per routing peer Administrative Distance (AD) configuration in IOS.

R1, R2, and R3 are configured to set the AD for all prefixes received from a neighbor with a source address in the 100.1.1.0/24 range. When comparing competing routes to a destination, IOS prefers the route with the lower AD. By default, internal EIGRP prefixes are assigned a local AD of 90 when they are imported into the routing table. Using the **distance *[routing-source-IP]* *[routing-source-wildcard]*** command allows the administrator to set the AD for prefixes received from a specific routing source. The routing source can be a specific router or represent an entire subnet using a wildcard mask.

To implement this change the **distance 80 100.1.1.0 0.0.0.255** command is configured in EIGRP configuration mode on all of the routers. The command means "for all prefixes received from a routing source in the 100.1.1.0/24 network, set the AD to 80."

In this topology, the 100.1.1.0/24 network corresponds to the MPLS WAN tunnel interface. This configuration ensures that all routes learned over tunnel 100 interface have an AD of 80 while the ones learned over the Tunnel200 interface have an AD of 90. IOS will choose the lower AD Tunnel 100 routes over the higher AD Tunnel 200 routes as shown below:

## On R1, R2, and R3:

```
Rx(config)#router eigrp 100
Rx(config-router)#distance 80 100.1.1.0 0.0.0.255

R1#show ip route eigrp 100 | begin Gate
Gateway of last resort is not set

      24.0.0.0/24 is subnetted, 1 subnets
D        24.1.1.0 [80/26880256] via 100.1.1.2, 00:00:27, Tunnel100
      36.0.0.0/24 is subnetted, 1 subnets
D        36.1.1.0 [80/26880256] via 100.1.1.3, 00:00:28, Tunnel100
```

## On R2:

```
R2#show ip route eigrp 100 | begin Gate
Gateway of last resort is not set
```

```
      18.0.0.0/24 is subnetted, 1 subnets
D        18.1.1.0 [80/26880256] via 100.1.1.1, 00:00:46, Tunnel100
      36.0.0.0/24 is subnetted, 1 subnets
D        36.1.1.0 [80/28160256] via 100.1.1.3, 00:00:40, Tunnel100
```

## On R3:

```
R3#show ip route eigrp 100 | begin Gate
Gateway of last resort is not set

      18.0.0.0/24 is subnetted, 1 subnets
D        18.1.1.0 [80/26880256] via 100.1.1.1, 00:01:21, Tunnel100
      24.0.0.0/24 is subnetted, 1 subnets
D        24.1.1.0 [80/28160256] via 100.1.1.2, 00:01:21, Tunnel100
```

A traceroute from R4 to R8 and R6 is shown to take the path via the tunnel interface 100. Following this, the second traceroute from R4 to R6 traverses over the direct spoke-to-spoke Tunnel 100 that was dynamically created between R2 and R3:

```
R4#traceroute 18.1.1.8
Type escape sequence to abort.
Tracing the route to 18.1.1.8
VRF info: (vrf in name/id, vrf out name/id)
  1 24.1.1.2 1 msec 1 msec 0 msec
  2 100.1.1.1 2 msec 2 msec 2 msec
  3 18.1.1.8 2 msec *  3 msec


R4#traceroute 36.1.1.6
Type escape sequence to abort.
Tracing the route to 36.1.1.6
VRF info: (vrf in name/id, vrf out name/id)
  1 24.1.1.2 1 msec 1 msec 1 msec
  2 100.1.1.1 2 msec 2 msec 1 msec ! DMVPN Hub R1
  3 100.1.1.3 3 msec 2 msec 3 msec
  4 36.1.1.6 2 msec *  3 msec


R4#traceroute 36.1.1.6
Type escape sequence to abort.
Tracing the route to 36.1.1.6
VRF info: (vrf in name/id, vrf out name/id)
  1 24.1.1.2 1 msec 1 msec 2 msec
  2 100.1.1.3 2 msec 2 msec 1 msec
  3 36.1.1.6 1 msec *  2 msec
```

To test redundancy, pings are repeated between R4 and R6. During the ping, the G0/5 interface is shut down on R2 to simulate a failure. The following output shows the results of the simulation. The yellow highlighted section in between indicates the moment the tunnel 100 interface on R2 goes down. R2 purges the EIGRP route over the tunnel 100 interface and installs the path via tunnel 200:

**On R4:**

```
R4#ping 36.1.1.6 repeat 100000

Type escape sequence to abort.
Sending 100000, 100-byte ICMP Echos to 36.1.1.6, timeout is 2 seconds:
!!!!!!!!!!!!!!!!!!!!!!!!!!!!!!!!!!!!!!!!!!!!!!!!!!!!!!!!!!!!!!!!!!!!!!!!!!
!!!!!!!!!!!!!!!!!!!!!!!!!!!!!!!!!!!!!!!!!!!!!!!!!!!!!!!!!!!!!!!!!!!!!!!!!!
!!!!!!!!!!!!!!!!!!!!!!!!!!!!!!!!!!!!!!!!!!!!!!!!!!!!!!!!!!!!!!!!!!!!!!!!!!
!!!!!!!!!!!!!!!!!!!!!!!!!!!!!!!!!!!!!!!!!!!!!!!!!!!!!!!!!!!!!!!!!!!!!!!!!!
!!!!!!!!!!!!!!!!!!!!!!!!!!!!!!!!!!!!!!!!!!!!!!!!!!!!!!!!!!!!!!!!!!!!!!!!!!
!!!!!!!!!!!!!!!!!!!!!!!!!!!!!!!!!!!!!!!!!!!!!!!!!!!!!!!!!!!!!!!!!!!!!!!!!!
!!!!!!!!!!!!!!!!!!!!!!!!!!!!!!!!!!!!!!!!!!!!!!!!!!!!!!!!!!!!!!!!!!!!!!!!!!
!!!!!!!!!!!!!!!!!!!!!!!!!!!!!!!!!!!!!!!!!!!!!U..!!!!!!!!!!!!!!!!!!!!!!!!!!!
!!!!!!!!!!!!!!!!!!!!!!!!!!!!!!!!!!!!!!!!!!!!!!!!!!!!!!!!!!!!!!!!!!!!!!!!!!
Success rate is 99 percent (1414/1419), round-trip min/avg/max =
6/19/129 ms
```

The previous may lead to the assumption that the spoke-to-spoke tunnel has been formed and all is well in the network; however, this is only partially true. A traceroute from R4 to R6 below uncovers the truth:

```
R4#traceroute 36.1.1.6 source 24.1.1.4 probe 1
Type escape sequence to abort.
Tracing the route to 36.1.1.6
VRF info: (vrf in name/id, vrf out name/id)
  1 24.1.1.2 1 msec
  2 200.1.1.1 3 msec !
  3 100.1.1.3 3 msec
  4 36.1.1.6 3 msec


R4#traceroute 36.1.1.6 source 24.1.1.4 probe 1
Type escape sequence to abort.
Tracing the route to 36.1.1.6
VRF info: (vrf in name/id, vrf out name/id)
  1 24.1.1.2 1 msec
  2 200.1.1.1 2 msec
  3 100.1.1.3 3 msec
  4 36.1.1.6 3 msec
```

```
R4#traceroute 36.1.1.6 source 24.1.1.4 probe 1
Type escape sequence to abort.
Tracing the route to 36.1.1.6
VRF info: (vrf in name/id, vrf out name/id)
  1 24.1.1.2 1 msec
  2 200.1.1.1 2 msec
  3 100.1.1.3 3 msec
  4 36.1.1.6 4 msec
```

In the traceroute output above, the actual path followed to reach R6 from R4 goes through the hub each time. This means a spoke-to-spoke tunnel has not been formed between R2 and R3. Looking at the show ip route eigrp output on R2 and R3 reveals the reason behind this occurrence:

```
R2#show ip route eigrp 100 | begin Gateway
Gateway of last resort is not set

      18.0.0.0/24 is subnetted, 1 subnets
D        18.1.1.0 [90/26880256] via 200.1.1.1, 00:01:05, Tunnel200
      36.0.0.0/24 is subnetted, 1 subnets
D        36.1.1.0 [90/28160256] via 200.1.1.1, 00:01:05, Tunnel200
      100.0.0.0/24 is subnetted, 1 subnets
D        100.1.1.0 [90/28160000] via 200.1.1.1, 00:01:05, Tunnel200


R3#show ip route eigrp 100 | begin Gateway
Gateway of last resort is not set

      18.0.0.0/24 is subnetted, 1 subnets
D        18.1.1.0 [80/26880256] via 100.1.1.1, 00:05:40, Tunnel100
      24.0.0.0/24 is subnetted, 1 subnets
D        24.1.1.0 [80/28160256] via 100.1.1.1, 00:00:41, Tunnel100
```

The critical parts of the sections in the previous output are the next-hop addresses for the routes on R2 and R3. These next-hops point to R1's tunnel IP address as the next-hop. Also, notice that R2 has a route to 100.1.1.0/24 the Tunnel 100 network.

The reason behind this is because, unlike OSPF, EIGRP calculates routes received from neighbors and doesn't have a complete view of the network topology from which it can calculate its own routes.

When R2's G0/5 interface is shut down, its tunnel 100 interface goes down as well. This terminates the neighbor relationship between R2 and R1 over their tunnel 100 interface. Instead, R2 advertises its 24.1.1.0/24 network over its tunnel 200 interface towards R1. R1 receives this network on its tunnel 200 interface with next-hop 200.1.1.2 as shown below:

```
R1#show ip route eigrp 100 | begin Gate
Gateway of last resort is not set
```

```
       24.0.0.0/24 is subnetted, 1 subnets
D         24.1.1.0 [90/26880256] via 200.1.1.2, 00:00:16, Tunnel200
       36.0.0.0/24 is subnetted, 1 subnets
D         36.1.1.0 [80/26880256] via 100.1.1.3, 00:01:04, Tunnel100
```

R1, on the other hand, still has its neighborship with R3 over its tunnel 100 interface, retaining R3's 100.1.1.3 tunnel IP address as next-hop. When R1 advertises the 36.1.1.0/24 route learned from R3 on tunnel 100 to R2 over Tunnel 200, it does not retain the next-hop because the two interfaces are in different subnets. Instead, it sets itself as next-hop. The same happens when R1 advertises the route to the 24.1.1.0/24 network received from R2 over its tunnel 200 interface to R3. Because the next-hop 200.1.1.2 is not in the same subnet as tunnel 100, R1 sets itself as next-hop. The third-party next-hop feature is not activated in either case because the interfaces are in different shared segments. This breaks phase 2 resolution.

**On R2:**

```
R2#show ip route 36.1.1.0
Routing entry for 36.1.1.0/24
  Known via "eigrp 100", distance 90, metric 28160256, type internal
  Redistributing via eigrp 100
  Last update from 200.1.1.1 on Tunnel200, 00:06:09 ago
  Routing Descriptor Blocks:
  * 200.1.1.1, from 200.1.1.1, 00:06:09 ago, via Tunnel200
      Route metric is 28160256, traffic share count is 1
      Total delay is 100010 microseconds, minimum bandwidth is 100
Kbit
      Reliability 255/255, minimum MTU 1476 bytes
      Loading 1/255, Hops 2
```

**On R3:**

```
R3#show ip route 24.1.1.0
Routing entry for 24.1.1.0/24
  Known via "eigrp 100", distance 80, metric 28160256, type internal
  Redistributing via eigrp 100
  Last update from 100.1.1.1 on Tunnel100, 00:05:33 ago
  Routing Descriptor Blocks:
  * 100.1.1.1, from 100.1.1.1, 00:05:33 ago, via Tunnel100
      Route metric is 28160256, traffic share count is 1
      Total delay is 100010 microseconds, minimum bandwidth is 100
Kbit
      Reliability 255/255, minimum MTU 1476 bytes
      Loading 1/255, Hops 2
```

Once again, the reason EIGRP behaves this way is because it is a Distance Vector protocol. EIGRP routers only know about routes and the network as advertised from their neighbors. In this example, R2 and R3 do not know to use the alternate, direct path to reach the spoke networks. In fact, they are not even aware they are connected to the same LAN segments.

This problem can be solved using a variety of techniques such as IP SLA and EEM scripting. These solutions are outside of the scope of this lab.

### Implement iBGP

The following shows the configuration of BGP as the overlay for the single-hub, dual-cloud setup for Phase 2. The configuration uses two peer groups, tunnel100 and tunnel200, for neighbors over the tunnel 100 and tunnel 200 interfaces. R1 as the route reflector is configured for iBGP peerings with clients R2 and R3 over their tunnel 100 and tunnel 200 interfaces. The **listen range** command on R1 includes the 100.1.1.0/24 and 200.1.1.0/24 networks. R2 and R3 are also configured to form two iBGP peerings with R1 over their tunnel 100 and 200 interfaces. The host networks at each site are advertised into BGP using the **network** statement:

---

**On R1, R2, and R3:**

```
Rx(config)#no router eigrp 100

R1(config)#interface g0/5
R1(config-if)#no shut

R1(config)#router bgp 100
R1(config-router)#neighbor tunnel100 peer-group
R1(config-router)#neighbor tunnel200 peer-group
R1(config-router)#neighbor tunnel100 remote 100
R1(config-router)#neighbor tunnel200 remote 100
R1(config-router)#neighbor tunnel100 timers 6 20
R1(config-router)#neighbor tunnel200 timers 6 20

R1(config-router)#bgp listen range 100.1.1.0/24 peer-group tunnel100
R1(config-router)#bgp listen range 200.1.1.0/24 peer-group tunnel200

R1(config-router)#address-family ipv4
R1(config-router-af)#network 18.1.1.0 mask 255.255.255.0
R1(config-router-af)#neighbor tunnel100 route-reflector-client
R1(config-router-af)#neighbor tunnel200 route-reflector-client
```

## On R2:

```
R2(config)#router bgp 100
R2(config-router)#neighbor 100.1.1.1 remote-as 100
R2(config-router)#neighbor 200.1.1.1 remote-as 100

R2(config-router)#address-family ipv4
R2(config-router-af)#network 24.1.1.0 mask 255.255.255.0
```

You should see the following console messages:

```
%BGP-5-ADJCHANGE: neighbor 100.1.1.1 Up
%BGP-5-ADJCHANGE: neighbor 200.1.1.1 Up
```

## On R3:

```
R3(config)#router bgp 100
R3(config-router)#neighbor 100.1.1.1 remote-as 100
R3(config-router)#neighbor 200.1.1.1 remote-as 100

R3(config-router)#address-family ipv4
R3(config-router-af)#network 36.1.1.0 mask 255.255.255.0
```

You should see the following console messages:

```
%BGP-5-ADJCHANGE: neighbor 100.1.1.1 Up
%BGP-5-ADJCHANGE: neighbor 200.1.1.1 Up
```

Once the BGP peerings come up between the iBGP peers, the **show ip bgp** command output shows the networks learned by all routers:

## On R1:

```
R1#show ip bgp | begin Net

     Network          Next Hop          Metric LocPrf Weight Path
 *>    18.1.1.0/24     0.0.0.0               0           32768 i
 *>i  24.1.1.0/24     100.1.1.2             0      100      0 i
 * i                  200.1.1.2             0      100      0 i
 * i   36.1.1.0/24     200.1.1.3             0      100      0 i
 *>i                  100.1.1.3             0      100      0 i
```

**On R2:**

```
R2#show ip bgp | begin Net

     Network            Next Hop          Metric LocPrf Weight Path
 *>i  18.1.1.0/24       100.1.1.1              0    100      0 i
 * i                    200.1.1.1              0    100      0 i
 *>   24.1.1.0/24       0.0.0.0                0         32768 i
 * i  36.1.1.0/24       100.1.1.3              0    100      0 i
 *>i                    100.1.1.3              0    100      0 i
```

```
R2#show ip bgp 36.1.1.0
BGP routing table entry for 36.1.1.0/24, version 3
Paths: (2 available, best #2, table default)
  Not advertised to any peer
  Refresh Epoch 1
  Local
    100.1.1.3 from 200.1.1.1 (200.1.1.1)
      Origin IGP, metric 0, localpref 100, valid, internal
      Originator: 200.1.1.3, Cluster list: 200.1.1.1
      rx pathid: 0, tx pathid: 0
  Refresh Epoch 1
  Local
    100.1.1.3 from 100.1.1.1 (200.1.1.1)
      Origin IGP, metric 0, localpref 100, valid, internal, best
      Originator: 200.1.1.3, Cluster list: 200.1.1.1
      rx pathid: 0, tx pathid: 0x0
```

**On R3:**

```
R3#show ip bgp | begin Net

     Network            Next Hop          Metric LocPrf Weight Path
 * i  18.1.1.0/24       200.1.1.1              0    100      0 i
 *>i                    100.1.1.1              0    100      0 i
 * i  24.1.1.0/24       100.1.1.2              0    100      0 i
 *>i                    100.1.1.2              0    100      0 i
 *>   36.1.1.0/24       0.0.0.0                0         32768 i
```

```
R3#show ip bgp 24.1.1.0
BGP routing table entry for 24.1.1.0/24, version 2
Paths: (2 available, best #2, table default)
  Not advertised to any peer
```

```
Refresh Epoch 2
Local
  100.1.1.2 from 200.1.1.1 (200.1.1.1)
    Origin IGP, metric 0, localpref 100, valid, internal
    Originator: 200.1.1.2, Cluster list: 200.1.1.1
    rx pathid: 0, tx pathid: 0
Refresh Epoch 2
Local
  100.1.1.2 from 100.1.1.1 (200.1.1.1)
    Origin IGP, metric 0, localpref 100, valid, internal, best
    Originator: 200.1.1.2, Cluster list: 200.1.1.1
    rx pathid: 0, tx pathid: 0x0
```

In the output above R2 and R3 routers select the paths learned over the tunnel 100 interface as best. As mentioned in previous cases, the reason for this is the lower neighbor IP address over the tunnel 100 interface. This satisfies the design requirements as traffic destined to R6 from R4 would use the tunnel 100 interface over the MPLS WAN. However, once again, in order to obtain a more deterministic selection method, the solution guide chooses to modify the WEIGHT attribute for prefixes learned over tunnel 100.

The WEIGHT attribute is a Cisco-proprietary attribute, and paths with a higher WEIGHT value are preferred. The default weight for BGP-learned routes is 0. To ensure that R1, R2, and R3 always select tunnel 100 as the primary path for each other's network, the WEIGHT attribute for paths learned from the neighbors over tunnel 100 is set to 100:

## On R1:

```
R1(config)#route-map tst permit 10
R1(config-route-map)#set weight 100

R1(config)#router bgp 100
R1(config-router)#address-family ipv4
R1(config-router-af)#neighbor tunnel100 route-map tst in

R1#clear ip bgp * in
```

## On R2:

```
R2(config)#route-map tst permit 10
R2(config-route-map)#set weight 100
```

```
R2(config)#router bgp 100
R2(config-router)#address-family ipv4
R2(config-router-af)#neighbor 100.1.1.1 route-map tst in
R2#clear ip bgp * in
```

## On R3:

```
R3(config)#route-map tst permit 10
R3(config-route-map)#set weight 100

R3(config)#router bgp 100
R3(config-router)#address-family ipv4
R3(config-router-af)#neighbor 100.1.1.1 route-map tst in

R3#clear ip bgp * in
```

Notice the BGP tables on R1, R2, and R3 below. All paths learned over tunnel 100 have a WEIGHT value of 100, making them more preferable than the paths learned over tunnel 200, which have a default WEIGHT value of 0:

## On R1:

```
R1#show ip bgp | begin Net

     Network          Next Hop         Metric LocPrf Weight Path
 *>   18.1.1.0/24      0.0.0.0              0           32768 i
 *>i  24.1.1.0/24      100.1.1.2            0    100     100 i
 * i                   200.1.1.2            0    100       0 i
 * i  36.1.1.0/24      200.1.1.3            0    100       0 i
 *>i                   100.1.1.3            0    100     100 i
```

## On R2:

```
R2#show ip bgp | begin Net

     Network          Next Hop         Metric LocPrf Weight Path
 *>i  18.1.1.0/24      100.1.1.1            0    100     100 i
 * i                   200.1.1.1            0    100       0 i
 *>   24.1.1.0/24      0.0.0.0              0           32768 i
 * i  36.1.1.0/24      100.1.1.3            0    100       0 i
 *>i                   100.1.1.3            0    100     100 i
```

**On R3:**

```
R3#show ip bgp | begin Net
```

|     | Network     | Next Hop  | Metric | LocPrf | Weight | Path |
|-----|-------------|-----------|--------|--------|--------|------|
| * i | 18.1.1.0/24 | 200.1.1.1 | 0      | 100    | 0      | i    |
| *>i |             | 100.1.1.1 | 0      | 100    | 100    | i    |
| * i | 24.1.1.0/24 | 100.1.1.2 | 0      | 100    | 0      | i    |
| *>i |             | 100.1.1.2 | 0      | 100    | 100    | i    |
| *>  | 36.1.1.0/24 | 0.0.0.0   | 0      |        | 32768  | i    |

A traceroute from R4 to R8 and R6 is shown to take the path via the tunnel interface 100. Following this, the second traceroute from R4 to R6 traverses over the direct spoke to spoke tunnel 100 that was dynamically created between R2 and R3:

```
R4#traceroute 18.1.1.8
Type escape sequence to abort.
Tracing the route to 18.1.1.8
VRF info: (vrf in name/id, vrf out name/id)
  1 24.1.1.2 1 msec 1 msec 0 msec
  2 100.1.1.1 2 msec 2 msec 2 msec
  3 18.1.1.8 2 msec *  3 msec


R4#traceroute 36.1.1.6
Type escape sequence to abort.
Tracing the route to 36.1.1.6
VRF info: (vrf in name/id, vrf out name/id)
  1 24.1.1.2 1 msec 1 msec 1 msec
  2 100.1.1.1 2 msec 2 msec 1 msec ! HUB R1
  3 100.1.1.3 3 msec 2 msec 3 msec
  4 36.1.1.6 2 msec *  3 msec


R4#traceroute 36.1.1.6
Type escape sequence to abort.
Tracing the route to 36.1.1.6
VRF info: (vrf in name/id, vrf out name/id)
  1 24.1.1.2 1 msec 1 msec 2 msec
  2 100.1.1.3 2 msec 2 msec 1 msec
  3 36.1.1.6 1 msec *  2 msec
```

To test redundancy, pings are repeated between R4 and R6. During the ping, the G0/5 interface is shut down on R2 to simulate a failure. The output below shows the results of the simulation:

## On R4:

```
R4#ping 36.1.1.6 repeat 10000
Type escape sequence to abort.
Sending 10000, 100-byte ICMP Echos to 36.1.1.6, timeout is 2 seconds:
UUUUUUUUUUUUUUUUUUUUUUUUUUUUUUUUUUUUUUUUUUUUUUUUUUUUUUUUUUUUUUUUUUUUUU
UUUUUUUUUUUUUUUUUUUUUUUUUUUUUUUUUUUUUUUUUUUUUUUUUUUUUUUUUUUUUUUUUUUUUU
UUUUUUUUUUUUUUUUUUUUUUUUUUUUUUUUUUUUUUUUUUUUUUUUUUUUUUUUUUUUUUUUUUUUUU
UUUUUUUUUUUUUUUUUUUUUUUUUUUUUUUUUUUUUUUUUUUUUUUUUUUUUUUUUUUUUUUUUUUUUU
UUUUUUUUUUUUUUUUUUUUUUUUUUUUUUUUUUUUUUUUUUUUUUUUUUUUUUUUUUUUUUUUUUUUUU
UUUUUUUUUUUUUUUUUUUUUUUUUUUUUUUUUUUUUUUUUUUUUUUUUUUUUUUUUUUUUUUUUUUUUU
UUUUUUUUUUUUUUUUUUUUUUUUUUUUUUUUUUUUUUUUUUUUUUUUUUUUUUUUUUUUUUUUUUUUUU
UUUUUUUUUUUUUUUUUUUUUUUUUUUUUUUUUUUUUUUUUUUUUUUUUUUUUUUUUUUUUUUUUUUUUU
```

The above pings return with a "U" status code meaning the destination is unreachable. Upon further investigation into the BGP table on R2, it is revealed that R2 switches to the path received from R1 on its Tunnel 200 interface for the 36.1.1.0/24 network with next-hop 100.1.1.3.

Upon further investigation into the BGP table on R2, when R2's tunnel 100 interface goes down (as a result of shutting down the G0/5 interface), R2 loses the path via tunnel 100 and switches over to the path learned over its tunnel 200 peering session with R1:

```
R2#show ip bgp 36.1.1.0
BGP routing table entry for 36.1.1.0/24, version 15
Paths: (1 available, no best path)
  Not advertised to any peer
  Refresh Epoch 3
  Local
    100.1.1.3 (inaccessible) from 200.1.1.1 (200.1.1.1)
      Origin IGP, metric 150, localpref 100, valid, internal
      Originator: 200.1.1.3, Cluster list: 200.1.1.1
      rx pathid: 0, tx pathid: 0
```

However, notice the next-hop 100.1.1.3 shows up as inaccessible on R2 in the output above. The reason for this is that the failure on R2 does not change the path preference on R1. R1 continues to mark its path from the R3 tunnel 100 peering address with a next-hop of 100.1.1.3 as its best path. Because it is a route reflector, it reflects the path to 36.1.1.0/24 to R2 with the next-hop of 100.1.1.3.

Upon shutting down the G0/5 interface on R2, the line protocol of tunnel 100 goes down, the peering between R1 and R2 over tunnel 100 is torn down, and R2 loses the route to the 100.1.1.3 prefix. R2 will now mark paths with the next hop of 100.1.1.3 as "inaccessible" because it no longer has a route in its routing table to reach that next-hop. This is proven in the output below:

```
R2#show ip route 100.1.1.3
% Network not in table
```

Paths in the BGP table that have inaccessible next-hops are ineligible to be used as best paths. This fact prevents R2 from installing the path in its routing table causing the unreachable messages when the pings are issued.

There are different ways of solving this problem. One such solution would be the use of IP SLA, Object tracking, and EEM scripting to ensure all routers in the DMVPN domain switch over to tunnel 200 upon a failure on a particular spoke. However, such configurations and tweaks could get complex and convoluted as the DMVPN grows.

## Implement eBGP

Like the previous eBGP examples there are two methods for implementing eBGP, using the spokes in differing autonomous systems or grouping all of the spokes in the same autonomous system.

### Spokes in Different Autonomous Systems

The configuration modifies the BGP peer group remote-as command using the alternate-as command to specify the additional ASNs the spoke sites will be using. Similar to the previous examples, R2 belongs to AS 200 and R3 belongs to AS 300.

A route-map is created on R1 that sets the MED for paths sent and received on R1's peering sessions using the tunnel 200 peering address to 150. BGP prefers lower MED values over higher MED values. Setting the MED for paths sent out tunnel 200 to 150 ensures the routers always prefer the paths through tunnel 100. Paths learned over this interface will either have a missing MED value or a MED value of 0.

**On R1, R2, and R3:**

```
R1(config)#no router bgp 100
```

**On R2:**

```
R2(config)#interface g0/5
R2(config-if)#no shut
```

**On R1:**

```
R1(config)#no route-map tst

R1(config-router)#route-map tst permit 10
R1(config-route-map)#set metric 150
```

```
R1(config)#router bgp 100
R1(config-router)#neighbor tunnel100 peer-group
R1(config-router)#neighbor tunnel200 peer-group
R1(config-router)#neighbor tunnel100 timers 6 20
R1(config-router)#neighbor tunnel200 timers 6 20

R1(config-router)#bgp listen range 100.1.1.0/24 peer-group tunnel100
R1(config-router)#bgp listen range 200.1.1.0/24 peer-group tunnel200

R1(config-router)#neighbor tunnel100 remote-as 200 alternate-as 300
R1(config-router)#neighbor tunnel200 remote-as 200 alternate-as 300

R1(config-router)#address-family ipv4
R1(config-router-af)#neighbor tunnel100 activate
R1(config-router-af)#neighbor tunnel200 activate
R1(config-router-af)#neighbor tunnel200 route-map tst out
R1(config-router-af)#neighbor tunnel200 route-map tst in
R1(config-router-af)#network 18.1.1.0 mask 255.255.255.0

R1#clear ip bgp * out
```

## On R2:

```
R2(config)#router bgp 200
R2(config-router)#neighbor 100.1.1.1 remote 100
R2(config-router)#neighbor 200.1.1.1 remote 100

R2(config-router)#address-family ipv4
R2(config-router-af)#network 24.1.1.0 mask 255.255.255.0
```

You should see the following console messages:

```
%BGP-5-ADJCHANGE: neighbor 100.1.1.1 Up
%BGP-5-ADJCHANGE: neighbor 200.1.1.1 Up
```

## On R3:

```
R3(config)#router bgp 300
R3(config-router)#neighbor 100.1.1.1 remote-as 100
R3(config-router)#neighbor 200.1.1.1 remote-as 100
```

```
R3(config-router)#address-family ipv4
R3(config-router-af)#network 36.1.1.0 mask 255.255.255.0
```

You should see the following console messages:

```
%BGP-5-ADJCHANGE: neighbor 100.1.1.1 Up
%BGP-5-ADJCHANGE: neighbor 200.1.1.1 Up
```

The routing table on R2 and R3 confirms the configuration. Notice the paths received over tunnel 200 have a MED value of 150 assigned to them. The MED value for path to the remote host networks over tunnel 100 is missing. In Cisco IOS, missing and zero values for MED are treated as the lowest possible value for MED. This means the paths over tunnel 100 with missing or zero values are more desirable than the paths with MED of 150 over the tunnel 200 interface:

### On R2:

```
R2#show ip bgp | begin Net

     Network          Next Hop         Metric LocPrf Weight Path
 *   18.1.1.0/24      200.1.1.1          150              0 100 i
 *>                   100.1.1.1            0              0 100 i
 *>  24.1.1.0/24      0.0.0.0              0          32768 i
 *>  36.1.1.0/24      100.1.1.3                           0 100 300 i
 *                    200.1.1.1          150              0 100 300 i
```

### On R3:

```
R3#show ip bgp | begin Net

     Network          Next Hop         Metric LocPrf Weight Path
 *>  18.1.1.0/24      100.1.1.1            0              0 100 i
 *                    200.1.1.1          150              0 100 i
 *   24.1.1.0/24      200.1.1.1          150              0 100 200 i
 *>                   100.1.1.2                           0 100 200 i
 *>  36.1.1.0/24      0.0.0.0              0          32768 i
```

The configuration changes made above are complete and appear to allow for proper Phase 2 operation. There are a few points that are worth mentioning about how the DMVPN is operating in its current state, most notably with regards to BGP's path advertisement behavior.

First, as covered in previous sections of the lab, the third-party next-hop feature allows eBGP neighbors to advertise paths to other eBGP neighbors with the original next-hop retained. With this behavior, the expectation in this lab for Phase 2 is that R1 will advertise paths to the 24.1.1.0/24 network with R2's peering address as next-hop to R3 and paths to the 36.1.1.0/24 network with R3's peering address as next-hop.

Looking at the output above, it may seem contradictory to see the next-hop for some paths to the 36.1.1.0/24 network received from R1 on R2 to have their next-hops set to R1's tunnel 200 peering address (200.1.1.1). The **show ip bgp 36.1.1.0** provides a detailed view of this:

```
R2#show ip bgp 36.1.1.0
BGP routing table entry for 36.1.1.0/24, version 4
Paths: (2 available, best #1, table default)
  Advertised to update-groups:
    1
  Refresh Epoch 1
  100 300
    100.1.1.3 from 100.1.1.1 (200.1.1.1)
      Origin IGP, localpref 100, valid, external, best
      rx pathid: 0, tx pathid: 0x0
  Refresh Epoch 1
  100 300
    200.1.1.1 from 200.1.1.1 (200.1.1.1)
      Origin IGP, metric 150, localpref 100, valid, external
      rx pathid: 0, tx pathid: 0
```

There is no contradiction here. BGP is functioning normally. The reason why the next-hops appear this way is because of how R1 is advertising the prefixes.

R1 has two interfaces with different peering addresses, Tunnel 100 and Tunnel 200. It has a peering session to R2 and R3 that use both peering addresses. The same is true on R2 and R3. They have peering addresses on their Tunnel 100 and Tunnel 200 interfaces as well. R1 establishes a peering with R2 and R3's Tunnel 100 interface using its IP address 100.1.1.1, and with R2 and R3's Tunnel 200 interface using the IP address 200.1.1.1.

When the spokes advertise their connected LANs to R1 through BGP, they advertise the path to both peering sessions (with R1's 100.1.1.1 address and 200.1.1.1 address). Using R3's networks as an example, R1 receives a path to 36.1.1.0/24 from both peering sessions to 100.1.1.3 and 200.1.1.3 as separate paths. The **show ip bgp 36.1.1.0/24** output below proves this:

```
R1#show ip bgp 36.1.1.0/24
BGP routing table entry for 36.1.1.0/24, version 5
Paths: (2 available, best #1, table default)
```

```
Advertised to update-groups:
    1           2
Refresh Epoch 1
300
   100.1.1.3 from *100.1.1.3 (200.1.1.3)
     Origin IGP, metric 0, localpref 100, valid, external, best
     rx pathid: 0, tx pathid: 0x0
Refresh Epoch 1
300
   200.1.1.3 from *200.1.1.3 (200.1.1.3)
     Origin IGP, metric 150, localpref 100, valid, external
     rx pathid: 0, tx pathid: 0
```

BGP on R1 selects a single best-path between two identical best-paths in the BGP table. When R1 selects its best path, it selects the path over the tunnel 100 interface with next-hop 100.1.1.3. R1 then advertises this path to all of its eBGP neighbors, specifically to its peering session with R2's 100.1.1.2 and 200.1.1.2 addresses. When advertised to 100.1.1.2, the next-hop is in the same subnet as R2's peering address. R1 retains the original next-hop assuming that since they reside in the same subnet, they can reach each other directly. This confirms the third-party next hop behavior.

However, when R1 advertises the same path to over its peering session to R2's 200.1.1.2 peering address (Tunnel 200) it sets the next-hop to itself because the next-hop 100.1.1.3 is not in the same subnet as its peer 200.1.1.2. The same happens for the R1/R3 tunnel 200 peering as well. This behavior has a major impact on how the DMVPN traffic flows during failure scenarios.

When all tunnel interfaces are up and active, the network works as intended. A traceroute from 24.1.1.4 to 36.1.1.6 first takes the hub. After the spoke-to-spoke tunnel is resolved in true Phase 2 fashion, all subsequent traffic goes directly to the spokes as shown below:

```
R4#traceroute 36.1.1.6 source 24.1.1.4 probe 1
Type escape sequence to abort.
Tracing the route to 36.1.1.6
VRF info: (vrf in name/id, vrf out name/id)
  1 24.1.1.2 1 msec
  2 100.1.1.1 3 msec
  3 100.1.1.3 2 msec
  4 36.1.1.6 2 msec


R4#traceroute 36.1.1.6 source 24.1.1.4 probe 1
Type escape sequence to abort.
Tracing the route to 36.1.1.6
VRF info: (vrf in name/id, vrf out name/id)
```

```
1 24.1.1.2 2 msec
2 100.1.1.3 2 msec
3 36.1.1.6 3 msec
```

A problem surfaces whenever a failure scenario is presented. To simulate this failure, R2's G0/5 interface is shut down:

```
R2(config)#interface g0/5
R2(config-if)#shut
```

```
%DUAL-5-NBRCHANGE: EIGRP-IPv4 10: Neighbor 25.1.1.5
(GigabitEthernet0/5) is down: interface down
```

```
%LINEPROTO-5-UPDOWN: Line protocol on Interface Tunnel100, changed
state to down
%BGP-5-NBR_RESET: Neighbor 100.1.1.1 reset (Interface flap)
```

The output indicates that R2 has lost its underlay IGP adjacency with R5. Its tunnel 100 interface goes down and it loses its overlay BGP peering session to 100.1.1.1. The current state of the network is as follows:

R1 has a peering with 100.1.1.3, 200.1.1.2, and 200.1.1.3 as shown below:

```
R1#show ip bgp summary | begin Neigh
```

| Neighbor<br>Down  State/PfxRcd | V | AS | MsgRcvd | MsgSent | TblVer | InQ | OutQ | Up/ |
|---|---|---|---|---|---|---|---|---|
| *100.1.1.3<br>00:36:48 | 4<br>1 | 300 | 351 | 391 | 10 | 0 | 0 | |
| *200.1.1.2<br>00:36:54 | 4<br>1 | 200 | 362 | 389 | 10 | 0 | 0 | |
| *200.1.1.3<br>00:36:43 | 4<br>1 | 300 | 352 | 388 | 10 | 0 | 0 | |

R3 has a BGP peering session with 100.1.1.1 and 200.1.1.1, while R2 only has an active peering session to 200.1.1.1:

```
R3#show ip bgp summary | begin Neighbor
```

| Neighbor<br>Down  State/PfxRcd | V | AS | MsgRcvd | MsgSent | TblVer | InQ | OutQ | Up/ |
|---|---|---|---|---|---|---|---|---|
| 100.1.1.1<br>00:36:48 | 4<br>2 | 100 | 391 | 351 | 9 | 0 | 0 | |
| 200.1.1.1<br>00:36:43 | 4<br>2 | 100 | 388 | 352 | 9 | 0 | 0 | |

```
R2#show ip bgp summary | begin Neighbor
```

| Neighbor<br>Down  State/PfxRcd | V | AS | MsgRcvd | MsgSent | TblVer | InQ | OutQ | Up/ |
|---|---|---|---|---|---|---|---|---|
| 100.1.1.1<br>00:02:46 Idle | 4 | 100 | 0 | 0 | 1 | 0 | 0 | |
| 200.1.1.1<br>00:36:54 | 4<br>2 | 100 | 389 | 362 | 14 | 0 | 0 | |

The traceroute from 24.1.1.4 to 36.1.1.6 is repeated 3 times:

**On R4:**

```
R4#traceroute 36.1.1.6 source 24.1.1.4 probe 1
Type escape sequence to abort.
Tracing the route to 36.1.1.6
VRF info: (vrf in name/id, vrf out name/id)
  1 24.1.1.2 1 msec
  2 200.1.1.1 2 msec
  3 100.1.1.3 3 msec
  4 36.1.1.6 3 msec


R4#traceroute 36.1.1.6 source 24.1.1.4 probe 1
Type escape sequence to abort.
Tracing the route to 36.1.1.6
VRF info: (vrf in name/id, vrf out name/id)
  1 24.1.1.2 2 msec
  2 200.1.1.1 2 msec
  3 100.1.1.3 3 msec
  4 36.1.1.6 3 msec


R4#traceroute 36.1.1.6 source 24.1.1.4 probe 1
Type escape sequence to abort.
Tracing the route to 36.1.1.6
VRF info: (vrf in name/id, vrf out name/id)
  1 24.1.1.2 1 msec
  2 200.1.1.1 2 msec
  3 100.1.1.3 2 msec
  4 36.1.1.6 3 msec
```

In the above traceroute, no matter how many times the traceroute is repeated, the path taken always goes through the hub. No spoke-to-spoke tunnel is formed between R2 and R3 as is expected in Phase 2 operation. The reason behind this behavior lies in the overlay BGP operations. The following is the BGP table on all three routers:

```
R1#show ip bgp | begin Network
     Network          Next Hop          Metric LocPrf Weight Path
 *>  18.1.1.0/24      0.0.0.0                0         32768 i
 *>  24.1.1.0/24      200.1.1.2            150             0 200 i
 *>  36.1.1.0/24      100.1.1.3              0             0 300 i
 *                    200.1.1.3            150             0 300 i
```

```
R2#show ip bgp | begin Network
     Network            Next Hop          Metric LocPrf Weight Path
 *>  18.1.1.0/24        200.1.1.1            150              0 100 i
 *>  24.1.1.0/24        0.0.0.0                0          32768 i
 *>  36.1.1.0/24        200.1.1.1            150              0 100 300 i

R3#show ip bgp | begin Network
     Network            Next Hop          Metric LocPrf Weight Path
 *   18.1.1.0/24        200.1.1.1            150              0 100 i
 *>                     100.1.1.1              0              0 100 i
 *   24.1.1.0/24        200.1.1.2            150              0 100 200 i
 *>                     100.1.1.1                             0 100 200 i
 *>  36.1.1.0/24        0.0.0.0                0          32768 i
```

Looking at the above, R1 marks the path with next-hop 200.1.1.2, received over its tunnel 200 peering, as best path to the 24.1.1.0/24 network. It retains its path to the 36.1.1.0/24 network with next-hop 100.1.1.3, received over its tunnel 100 peering, as the best path to the 36.1.1.0/24 network.

R2 has no choice but to mark all paths received over its tunnel 200 peering session as best because it only receives paths from R1.

R3, maintaining its original BGP table best-path selections, chooses the paths received over its tunnel 100 peering address session as best-paths.

The key here is the next-hops on R2 and R3. On R2, 200.1.1.1 is listed as the next-hop for the 36.1.1.0/24 network. This is the routing entry R2 uses to route the traceroute packet from R4 to R6. On R3's end, its next-hop to reach the 24.1.1.0/24 network is 100.1.1.1. This is the routing entry R3 uses to route the traceroute return traffic from R6 to R4.

The summary is R2 and R3 install routes to each other's LANs with R1 as the next-hop. This means when R2 and R3 attempt to route the traffic, they do not trigger spoke-to-spoke tunnel resolution. Instead, all traffic is transited over the hub as seen in the trace-route output.

This happens because even though R1 loses its peering to 100.1.1.2 (R2's Tunnel 100 IP address), it still has a peering to both 100.1.1.3 (R3's Tunnel 100 IP address), 200.1.1.2 (R2's Tunnel 200 IP address), and 200.1.1.3 (R3's Tunnel 200 IP address). R1 selects its best path to the 24.1.1.0/24 network with next-hop 200.1.1.2 and advertises it to both 100.1.1.3 and 200.1.1.3 (R3's peering address). As noted earlier, it sets the next-hop to itself when advertising to 100.1.1.3 because the next-hop 200.1.1.2 is not on the same subnet as 100.1.1.3.

Similarly, R1 advertises its best-path to 36.1.1.0/24 with next-hop 100.1.1.3 to 200.1.1.2 and sets the next-hop to itself because the 100.1.1.3 next-hop is not in the same subnet as the 200.1.1.2 peering address. The result, as mentioned, is R2 and R3 receive paths with R1 set as the next-hop address instead of the original advertising spoke.

This problem presents itself prominently in single hub, dual cloud DMVPN designs where eBGP is the overlay protocol. The problem makes BGP unsuitable for accomplishing the task objectives in this design with the default settings. There are methods for avoiding this problem, but those techniques are outside of the scope of this lab. It is best to know that this failure scenario is possible with eBGP as the overlay protocol in a single hub, dual cloud DMVPN implementation.

## Spokes in the Same AS

The configuration for spokes in the same AS only differs in that it omits the **alternate-as** command on the spoke peer group and adds the **allowas-in** command on the spokes. This way, the spokes accept paths with the shared ASN in the AS_PATH attribute.

**On R2:**

```
R2(config)#no router bgp 200
```

**On R3:**

```
R3(config)#no router bgp 300
```

**On R1:**

```
R1(config)#router bgp 100
R1(config-router)#neighbor tunnel100 remote-as 230
R1(config-router)#neighbor tunnel200 remote-as 230
```

**On R2:**

```
R2(config)#router bgp 230
R2(config-router)#neighbor 100.1.1.1 remote-as 100
R2(config-router)#neighbor 200.1.1.1 remote-as 100

R2(config-router)#address-family ipv4
R2(config-router-af)#neighbor 100.1.1.1 allowas-in
R2(config-router-af)#neighbor 200.1.1.1 allowas-in
R2(config-router-af)#network 24.1.1.0 mask 255.255.255.0
```

You should see the following console messages:

```
%BGP-5-ADJCHANGE: neighbor 100.1.1.1 Up
%BGP-5-ADJCHANGE: neighbor 200.1.1.1 Up
```

## On R3:

```
R3(config)#router bgp 230
R3(config-router)#neighbor 100.1.1.1 remote-as 100
R3(config-router)#neighbor 200.1.1.1 remote-as 100

R3(config-router)#address-family ipv4
R3(config-router-af)#network 36.1.1.0 mask 255.255.255.0
R3(config-router-af)#neighbor 100.1.1.1 allowas-in
R3(config-router-af)#neighbor 200.1.1.1 allowas-in
```

You should see the following console messages:

```
%BGP-5-ADJCHANGE: neighbor 100.1.1.1 Up
%BGP-5-ADJCHANGE: neighbor 200.1.1.1 Up
```

Once again, the routing tables on R2 and R3 confirm the configuration. Notice that the paths with next hop 200.1.1.1 have a MED value of 150:

## On R2:

```
R2#show ip bgp | begin Net

     Network          Next Hop          Metric LocPrf Weight Path
 *   18.1.1.0/24      200.1.1.1            150            0 100 i
 *>                   100.1.1.1              0            0 100 i
 *   24.1.1.0/24      200.1.1.1            150            0 100 230
 i
 *>                   0.0.0.0                0        32768 i
 *   36.1.1.0/24      200.1.1.1            150            0 100 230
 i
 *>                   100.1.1.3                           0 100 230
 i
```

## On R3:

```
R3#show ip bgp | begin Net

     Network          Next Hop          Metric LocPrf Weight Path
 *   18.1.1.0/24      200.1.1.1            150            0 100 i
```

```
*>                      100.1.1.1          0             0 100 i
*      24.1.1.0/24      200.1.1.1        150             0 100 230 i
*>                      100.1.1.2                        0 100 230 i
*      36.1.1.0/24      200.1.1.1        150             0 100 230 i
*>                      0.0.0.0            0         32768 i
```

For both cases—spokes in the same AS and spokes in different autonomous systems—the **traceroute** outputs below confirm that the spoke-to-spoke tunnel is formed:

## On R4:

R4#**traceroute 18.1.1.8 probe 1**

```
Type escape sequence to abort.
Tracing the route to 18.1.1.8
VRF info: (vrf in name/id, vrf out name/id)
  1 24.1.1.2 15 msec
  2 100.1.1.1 10 msec
  3 18.1.1.8 12 msec
```

R4#**traceroute 36.1.1.6 probe 1**

```
Type escape sequence to abort.
Tracing the route to 36.1.1.6
VRF info: (vrf in name/id, vrf out name/id)
  1 24.1.1.2 4 msec
  2 100.1.1.3 59 msec
  3 36.1.1.6 8 msec
```

To verify the redundancy, pings are issued from R4 to R6 while the G0/5 interface on R1 is shut down. As expected, there is a period of no connectivity (indicated by the yellow highlighted dots), followed by connectivity once the network converges.

## On R4:

R4#**ping 36.1.1.6 rep 100000**

```
Type escape sequence to abort.
Sending 100000, 100-byte ICMP Echos to 36.1.1.6, timeout is 2 seconds:
!!!!!!!!!!!!!!!!!!!!!!!!!!!!!!!!!!!!!!!!!!!!!!!!!!!!!!!!!!!!!!!!!!!!!!!!!
!!!!!!!!!!!!!!!!!!!!!!!!!!!!!!!!!!!!!!!!!!!!!!!!!!!!!!!!!!!!!!!!!!!!!!!!!
!!!!!!!!!!!!!!!!!!!!!!!!!!!!!!!!!!!!!!!!!!!!!!!!!!!!!!!!!!!!!!!!!!!!!!!!!
```

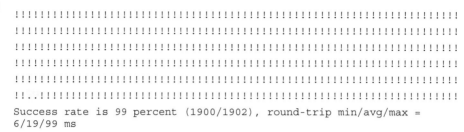

```
Success rate is 99 percent (1900/1902), round-trip min/avg/max =
6/19/99 ms
```

Keep in mind the same failure situation related to next-hop processing detailed in the "Spokes in different AS" section of this lab, apply to this configuration as well. In certain failure scenarios, Phase 2 spoke-to-spoke tunnel resolution will not occur due to the third-party next-hop mechanism and how BGP advertises paths to its peers.

## Potential Solution to Above Problems

The above sections introduced issues the Single Hub | Dual Cloud design can experience in failure scenarios with certain routing protocols and DMVPN phases. The issues are mainly seen whenever the spokes attempt to resolve a spoke-to-spoke tunnel using EIGRP or BGP. Because of the use of two tunnel interfaces, the third-party next-hop feature may not activate and causes the hub to advertise itself as next-hop instead of the original spokes. This breaks the spoke-to-spoke tunnel resolution process.

One way to utilize both transports for redundancy is to implement a Single Hub | Single Cloud design instead of a Single Hub | Dual Cloud design utilizing a single hub. The setup is as follows:

1. R1, R2, and R3 are configured with a loopback address (1.1.1.1, 2.2.2.2, 3.3.3.3 respectively) that is advertised to both underlay transports.

2. A single tunnel interface is configured on each router. The source address for this tunnel interface is the loopback interface previously created.

3. All IGP and DMVPN overlay configurations are applied to the single tunnel interface.

With only a single tunnel interface, third-party next-hop features can be implemented consistently because all of the DMVPN endpoints will be in the same shared segment. Also, because the tunnel endpoint addresses are advertised to both underlay transports, loss of the primary transport causes the routers to switch over to the backup transport transparently. The overlay protocols do not notice the switchover because they are riding on top of the overlay tunnel DMVPN.

The following demonstrates this solution using EIGRP as the overlay. First, the tunnel configurations on each router are shown:

**R1:**

```
interface lo100
 ip address 1.1.1.1 255.255.255.255
!
interface Tunnel100
 ip address 100.1.1.1 255.255.255.0
 no ip next-hop-self eigrp 100
 no ip split-horizon eigrp 100
 ip nhrp map multicast dynamic
 ip nhrp network-id 100
 tunnel source 1.1.1.1
 tunnel mode gre multipoint
```

**R2:**

```
interface lo100
 ip address 2.2.2.2 255.255.255.255
!
interface Tunnel100
 ip address 100.1.1.2 255.255.255.0
 ip nhrp network-id 100
 ip nhrp nhs 100.1.1.1 nbma 1.1.1.1 multicast
 tunnel source 2.2.2.2
 tunnel mode gre multipoint
```

**R3:**

```
interface lo100
 ip address 3.3.3.3 255.255.255.255
!
interface Tunnel100
 ip address 100.1.1.3 255.255.255.0
 ip nhrp network-id 100
 ip nhrp nhs 100.1.1.1 nbma 1.1.1.1 multicast
 tunnel source 3.3.3.3
 tunnel mode gre multipoint
end
```

In the above, the routers are configured with a loopback interface 100. This loopback interface IP address serves as the IP address used as the source of their tunnel interfaces (highlighted in yellow). R2 and R3 are configured to use R1's new NBMA address (1.1.1.1 highlighted in green) as the NBMA address in the ip nhrp nhs command. Finally, R1 is configured with the commands necessary to allow proper Phase 2 operation for EIGRP operation. (NOTE: EIGRP 100 is the routing protocol used in this case. Its complete configuration is not shown but mimics the previous Single Hub | Single Cloud Phase 2 EIGRP configuration).

The routing tables on R2 and R3 show the proper next-hops for the remote spoke networks:

```
R2#show ip route eigrp 100 | begin Gate
Gateway of last resort is not set


      18.0.0.0/24 is subnetted, 1 subnets
D        18.1.1.0 [90/26880256] via 100.1.1.1, 00:06:16, Tunnel100
      36.0.0.0/24 is subnetted, 1 subnets
D        36.1.1.0 [90/28160256] via 100.1.1.3, 00:06:05, Tunnel100


R3#show ip route eigrp 100 | begin Gate
Gateway of last resort is not set


      18.0.0.0/24 is subnetted, 1 subnets
D        18.1.1.0 [90/26880256] via 100.1.1.1, 00:06:16, Tunnel100
      24.0.0.0/24 is subnetted, 1 subnets
D        24.1.1.0 [90/28160256] via 100.1.1.2, 00:06:05, Tunnel100
```

Traceroute output from R4 to R6 confirms Phase 2 operation before failure:

```
R4#traceroute 36.1.1.6 source 24.1.1.4 probe 1
Type escape sequence to abort.
Tracing the route to 36.1.1.6
VRF info: (vrf in name/id, vrf out name/id)
  1 24.1.1.2 2 msec
  2 100.1.1.1 3 msec ! HUB R1
  3 100.1.1.3 3 msec
  4 36.1.1.6 3 msec


R4#traceroute 36.1.1.6 source 24.1.1.4 probe 1
Type escape sequence to abort.
Tracing the route to 36.1.1.6
VRF info: (vrf in name/id, vrf out name/id)
  1 24.1.1.2 1 msec
  2 100.1.1.3 3 msec
  3 36.1.1.6 3 msec
   Tracing the route to 36.1.1.6
```

The NHRP table is cleared on R2 and R3. Then the G0/5 interface on R2 is shut down as in previous failure examples. The routing table on both routers still shows the proper next-hop because the overlay tunnel interface has not been compromised as a result of the failure:

## R2 and R3:

```
Rx#clear ip nhrp

R2:

R2(config)#interface g0/5
R2(config-if)#shut

R2#show ip route eigrp 100 | begin Gate
Gateway of last resort is not set

      18.0.0.0/24 is subnetted, 1 subnets
D        18.1.1.0 [90/26880256] via 100.1.1.1, 00:06:16, Tunnel100
      36.0.0.0/24 is subnetted, 1 subnets
D        36.1.1.0 [90/28160256] via 100.1.1.3, 00:06:05, Tunnel100

R3#show ip route eigrp 100 | begin Gate
Gateway of last resort is not set

      18.0.0.0/24 is subnetted, 1 subnets
D        18.1.1.0 [90/26880256] via 100.1.1.1, 00:06:16, Tunnel100
      24.0.0.0/24 is subnetted, 1 subnets
D        24.1.1.0 [90/28160256] via 100.1.1.2, 00:06:05, Tunnel100
```

Traceroutes repeated from R4 to R6 prove that the spoke-to-spoke tunnel resolution is unaffected by the failure:

```
R4#traceroute 36.1.1.6 source 24.1.1.4 probe 1
Type escape sequence to abort.
Tracing the route to 36.1.1.6
VRF info: (vrf in name/id, vrf out name/id)
  1 24.1.1.2 2 msec
  2 100.1.1.1 3 msec ! HUB R1
  3 100.1.1.3 3 msec
  4 36.1.1.6 3 msec

R4#traceroute 36.1.1.6 source 24.1.1.4 probe 1
Type escape sequence to abort.
```

```
VRF info: (vrf in name/id, vrf out name/id)
  1 24.1.1.2 1 msec
  2 100.1.1.3 3 msec
  3 36.1.1.6 3 msec
```

This solution will work for iBGP and eBGP as well. This is because eliminating the second tunnel from all routers effectively returns the topology to a Single Hub | Single Cloud implementation. The same routing protocol configurations used will work in this case. The difference, however, is that the DMVPN is made resilient by providing redundancy for the tunnel endpoint addresses. This is achieved by setting the tunnel interface source address to a loopback interface IP address and advertising the same loopback IP address to both transport networks (MPLS and ISP in this example).

One caveat with this solution is the choice of which transport is preferred depending upon the routing tables of the DMVPN endpoints. If one transport is preferred over another, adjustments must be made on the physical interface or routing process connected to each transport. For example, if EIGRP were the underlay routing protocol a simple offset list could be employed to make routes learned from the ISP worse than those learned from the MPLS WAN. The router would then choose the MPLS WAN connection over the ISP for the underlying transport.

The details of this specific configuration vary from protocol to protocol and from provider to provider and are outside the scope of this lab. The specific transport being used to reach a particular DMVPN endpoint NBMA address can be verified using the show ip cef output for the endpoint NBMA address. For example, on R2, to find out which transport is being utilized to reach R1's NBMA address 1.1.1.1 the show ip cef 1.1.1.1 output below can be used:

```
R2#show ip cef 1.1.1.1
1.1.1.1/32
  nexthop 27.1.1.7 GigabitEthernet0/5
```

## Implement Phase 3

## Design Goal

ABC Corp has announced internally that it is expanding to 40 additional locations. To prepare for this transition, the network engineering team has decided to redesign the VPN solution for routing table scalability on the remote sites. These sites should receive specific routing information for remote spokes only when they try to communicate with a specific remote spoke.

### DMVPN Tunnel Configuration

The Phase 3 DMVPN tunnel configuration for the hub and spokes resembles the Phase 2 configuration. Both the hub and spokes are configured with mGRE interfaces for tunnel 100 and tunnel 200. R1 uses 15.1.1.1 as the tunnel source (its Ethernet interface toward the MPLS WAN) for its tunnel 100 interface and 17.1.1.1 (its Ethernet interface toward the ISP) for its tunnel 200 interface. R2 uses 25.1.1.2 (its Ethernet interface toward the MPLS WAN) as the tunnel source for tunnel 100 and 27.1.1.2 (its Ethernet interface toward the ISP) for tunnel 200. Likewise, R3 uses 35.1.1.3 (its Ethernet interface toward the MPLS WAN) as the tunnel source of tunnel 100 and 37.1.1.3 (its Ethernet interface toward the ISP) for tunnel 200.

The only difference between this configuration and the Phase 2 configuration is the addition of the ip nhrp redirect command on the hub and the ip nhrp shortcut command on the spokes. The ip nhrp redirect command enables the NHRP redirect (called a traffic indication message) signaling process on the hub. This signaling process triggers when the hub forwards an IP packet out the same NHRP-enabled tunnel interface on which the packet was received. This situation occurs whenever, for example, a host on the R2 LAN pings a host on the R3 LAN. In this process, R1 sends an NHRP traffic indication message that contains the original IP header of the packet that caused the redirect. The ip nhrp shortcut command enables the shortcut switching enhancements on the spokes that allow them to respond to the receipt of an NHRP redirect from the hub. Upon receipt of the redirect message, the spoke will send an NHRP resolution request for the target network indicated in the NHRP redirect packet.

Below is the complete configuration information for the tunnel interfaces on R1, R2, and R3. Before the tunnel interface configuration occurs, BGP and some leftover configurations are removed.

---

**On R1:**

```
R1(config)#no router bgp 100

R1(config)#interface g0/5
R1(config-if)#no shut

R1(config)#interface tunnel 100
R1(config-if)#ip nhrp redirect

R1(config)#interface tunnel 200
R1(config-if)#ip nhrp redirect
R1(config-if)#no ip ospf network broadcast
```

**On R2:**

```
R2(config)#no router bgp 230

R2(config)#interface tunnel 100
R2(config-if)#ip nhrp shortcut
```

```
R2(config)#interface tunnel 200
R2(config-if)#ip nhrp shortcut
```

## On R3:

```
R3(config)#no router bgp 230

R3(config)#interface tunnel 100
R3(config-if)#ip nhrp shortcut

R3(config)#interface tunnel 200
R3(config-if)#ip nhrp shortcut
```

## To verify the configuration:

## On R1:

```
R1#show dmvpn | begin Peer NBMA|Interface

Interface: Tunnel100, IPv4 NHRP Details
Type:Hub, NHRP Peers:2,

 # Ent  Peer NBMA Addr Peer Tunnel Add State  UpDn Tm Attrb
 ----- --------------- --------------- ----- -------- -----
     1 25.1.1.2               100.1.1.2    UP 00:01:10    D
     1 35.1.1.3               100.1.1.3    UP 00:01:40    D

Interface: Tunnel200, IPv4 NHRP Details
Type:Hub, NHRP Peers:2,

 # Ent  Peer NBMA Addr Peer Tunnel Add State  UpDn Tm Attrb
 ----- --------------- --------------- ----- -------- -----
     1 27.1.1.2               200.1.1.2    UP 16:35:45    D
     1 37.1.1.3               200.1.1.3    UP 16:12:45    D
```

Due to OSPF's inability to summarize routing information completely as required by the task, OSPF is not implemented as an overlay protocol in this section. EIGRP and BGP configurations are demonstrated.

## Implement EIGRP

The configuration for EIGRP in Phase 3 is similar to the configuration in Phase 1. EIGRP process 100 is enabled on the tunnel 100 and tunnel 200 interfaces on R1, R2, and R3. Host networks at each site are advertised into EIGRP with the network command. These LAN-facing interfaces are also declared as passive interfaces under the EIGRP configuration mode. R1 is also configured to inject a EIGRP default summary route over both the tunnel interfaces:

---

**On R1:**

```
R1(config)#interface tunnel 100
R1(config-if)#ip summary-address eigrp 100 0.0.0.0 0.0.0.0

R1(config)#interface tunnel 200
R1(config-if)#ip summary-address eigrp 100 0.0.0.0 0.0.0.0

R1(config)#router eigrp 100
R1(config-router)#network 18.1.1.1 0.0.0.0
R1(config-router)#network 100.1.1.1 0.0.0.0
R1(config-router)#network 200.1.1.1 0.0.0.0
R1(config-router)#passive-interface g0/8
```

**On R2:**

```
R2(config)#router eigrp 100
R2(config-router)#network 24.1.1.2 0.0.0.0
R2(config-router)#network 100.1.1.2 0.0.0.0
R2(config-router)#network 200.1.1.2 0.0.0.0
R2(config-router)#passive-interface g0/4
```

You should see the following console messages:

```
%DUAL-5-NBRCHANGE: EIGRP-IPv4 100: Neighbor 100.1.1.1 (Tunnel100) is
up: new adjacency

%DUAL-5-NBRCHANGE: EIGRP-IPv4 100: Neighbor 200.1.1.1 (Tunnel200) is
up: new adjacency
```

**On R3:**

```
R3(config)#router eigrp 100
R3(config-router)#network 36.1.1.3 0.0.0.0
R3(config-router)#network 100.1.1.3 0.0.0.0
```

```
R3(config-router)#network 200.1.1.3 0.0.0.0
R3(config-router)#passive-interface g0/6
```

You should see the following console messages:

```
%DUAL-5-NBRCHANGE: EIGRP-IPv4 100: Neighbor 100.1.1.1 (Tunnel100) is
up: new adjacency

%DUAL-5-NBRCHANGE: EIGRP-IPv4 100: Neighbor 200.1.1.1 (Tunnel200) is
up: new adjacency
```

On completing the above, the **show ip route** command is issued on R1, R2, and R3. R1 is performing ECMP for the host networks at the remote site. The spoke routers are performing ECMP for the EIGRP default route injected by R1:

## On R1:

```
R1#show ip route eigrp 100 | begin Gate
Gateway of last resort is 0.0.0.0 to network 0.0.0.0

D*    0.0.0.0/0 is a summary, 00:08:18, Null0
      24.0.0.0/24 is subnetted, 1 subnets
D        24.1.1.0 [90/26880256] via 200.1.1.2, 00:06:12, Tunnel200
                  [90/26880256] via 100.1.1.2, 00:06:12, Tunnel100
      36.0.0.0/24 is subnetted, 1 subnets
D        36.1.1.0 [90/26880256] via 200.1.1.3, 00:03:44, Tunnel200
                  [90/26880256] via 100.1.1.3, 00:03:44, Tunnel100
```

## On R2:

```
R2#show ip route eigrp 100 | begi Gate
Gateway of last resort is 200.1.1.1 to network 0.0.0.0

D*    0.0.0.0/0 [90/26880256] via 200.1.1.1, 00:06:44, Tunnel200
                [90/26880256] via 100.1.1.1, 00:06:44, Tunnel100
```

## On R3:

```
R3#show ip route eigrp 100 | begin Gate
Gateway of last resort is 200.1.1.1 to network 0.0.0.0

D*    0.0.0.0/0 [90/26880256] via 200.1.1.1, 00:04:49, Tunnel200
                [90/26880256] via 100.1.1.1, 00:04:49, Tunnel100
```

To ensure MPLS-WAN is used as the primary path, the EIGRP's delay is lowered over the tunnel 100 interfaces on R1, R2, and R3:

**On R1, R2, and R3:**

```
R1(config)#interface tunnel 100
R1(config-if)#delay 500
```

**To verify the configuration:**

```
R1#show ip route eigrp 100 | begin Gate
Gateway of last resort is 0.0.0.0 to network 0.0.0.0

D*     0.0.0.0/0 is a summary, 00:12:03, Null0
       24.0.0.0/24 is subnetted, 1 subnets
D         24.1.1.0 [90/25728256] via 100.1.1.2, 00:01:21, Tunnel100
       36.0.0.0/24 is subnetted, 1 subnets
D         36.1.1.0 [90/25728256] via 100.1.1.3, 00:01:21, Tunnel100
```

**On R2:**

```
R2#show ip route eigrp 100 | begin Gate
Gateway of last resort is 100.1.1.1 to network 0.0.0.0

D*     0.0.0.0/0 [90/25728256] via 100.1.1.1, 00:01:18, Tunnel100
```

**On R3:**

```
R3#show ip route eigrp 123 | begin Gateway
Gateway of last resort is 100.1.1.1 to network 0.0.0.0

D*     0.0.0.0/0 [90/25753600] via 100.1.1.1, 00:00:25, Tunnel100
```

To test redundancy, pings are repeated between the R4 to R6. During the ping, the G0/5 interface is shut down on R2 to simulate a failure. The output of the ping should show the results of the simulation:

```
R4#ping 18.1.1.1 repeat 100000
Type escape sequence to abort.
```

```
Sending 100000, 100-byte ICMP Echos to 18.1.1.1, timeout is 2 seconds:
!!!!!!!!!!!!!!!!!!!!!!!!!!!!!!!!!!!!!!!!!!!!!!!!!!!!!!!!!!!!!!!!!!!!!!!!!!
!!!!!!!!!!!!!!!!!!!!!!!!!!!!!!!!!!!!!!!!!!!!!!!!!!!!!!!!!!!!!!!!!!!!!!!!!!
!!!!!!!!!!!!!!!!!!!!!!!!!!!!!!!!!!!!!!!!!!!!!!!!!!!!!!!!!!!!!!!!!!!!!!!!!!
!!!!!!!!!!!!!!!!!!!!!!!!!!!!!!!!!!!!!!!!!!!!!!!!!!!!!!!!!!!!!!!!!!!!!!!!!!
!!!!!!!!!!!!!!!!!!!!!!!!!!!!!!!!!!!!!!!!!!!!!!!!!!!!!!!!!!!!!!!!!!!!!!!!!!
!!!!!!!!!!!!!!!!!!!!!!!!!!!!!!!!!!!!!!!!!!!!!!!!!!!!!!!!!!!!!!!!!!!!!!!!!!
!!!!!!!!!!!!!!!!!!!!!!!!!!!!!!!!!!!!!!!!!!!!!!!!!!!!!!!!!!!!!!!!!!!!!!!!!!
!!!!!!!!!!!!!!!!!!!!!!!!!!!!!!!!!!!!!!!!!!!!!!!!!!!!!!!!!!!!!!!!!!!!!!!!!!
!!!!!!!!!!!!!!!!!!!!!!!!!!!!!!!!!!!!!!!!!!!!!!!!!!!!!!!!!!!!!!!!!!!!!!!!!!
!!!!!!!!!!!!!!!!!!!!!!!!!!!!!!!!!!!!!!!!!!!!!!!!!!!!!!!!!!!!!!!!!!!!!!!!!!
!!!!!!!!!!!!!!!!!!!!!!!!!!!!!!!!!!!!!!!!!!!!!!!!!!!!!!!!!!!!!!!!!!!....
```

In the output above, pings are successful until the G0/5 interface is shut down on R2. At that point, the stream of exclamation points is replaced by periods indicating the pings are failing. It appears the failover is not working as intended. To investigate this issue the routing tables on R2 and R3 should be examined as they are the routers that are making the routing decision:

```
R2#show ip route | begin Gateway
Gateway of last resort is 200.1.1.1 to network 0.0.0.0
D*   0.0.0.0/0 [90/26905600] via 200.1.1.1, 00:02:21, Tunnel200

--- Output Omitted ---
```

The output above shows R2 has properly installed the default route pointing out of its tunnel200 interface. This is expected after the failure. First, the G0/5 interface is shut down. After which the Tunnel 100 interface's line protocol goes down. When the Tunnel 100 interface's line protocol goes down all EIGRP adjacencies learned over that interface are torn down and all routes learned over that interface are removed from the routing table. The default route received on Tunnel 200 is then installed into the routing table.

Looking at R3's routing table below, however, reveals a different story. R3 was unaffected by the failover. It still has the NHRP shortcut route installed for the 24.1.1.0/24 network (R2's LAN). This route was installed whenever traffic from the R2 LAN was sent to the R3 LAN. It is the result of the NHRP redirect process triggered by the hub router. Because NHRP is the routing source, it does not get removed from the routing table whenever R2's Tunnel 100 interface goes down.

```
R3#show ip route nhrp  | begin Gateway
Gateway of last resort is 100.1.1.1 to network 0.0.0.0
      24.0.0.0/24 is subnetted, 1 subnets
H      24.1.1.0 [250/1] via 100.1.1.2, 00:01:15, Tunnel100
      100.0.0.0/8 is variably subnetted, 3 subnets, 2 masks
H      100.1.1.2/32 is directly connected, 00:01:15, Tunnel100
```

What's happening is initially, R4 sends a packet destined for the R3 LAN. R2 routes this packet to R1. R1 sends the received packet back out the same tunnel interface (Tunnel 100) it received it, towards R3. When R1 detects it has sent the packet out the same interface it was received, it sends an NHRP redirect message back to R2. R2 receives the redirect message and sends an NHRP resolution packet back towards R1 to resolve the spoke-to-spoke tunnel.

R1 routes the resolution request to R3 based on its routing table. R3 responds directly to R2 with the proper mapping information. The same process happens in reverse when R3 sends return traffic to the R2 LAN. After the resolution process, R2 and R3 both install an NHRP route learned over their Tunnel 100 interfaces to use for direct spoke-to-spoke communication.

When R2 loses connectivity over its Tunnel 100 interface, that NHRP route still exists on R3. R3 still tries to send packets to R2's LAN using that old NHRP route. All because R3 has no way of knowing R2 has lost communication on its Tunnel 100 interface.

One solution to this problem of R3 continuing to use the old NHRP-learned routing information is to clear the NHRP mapping table on R3 using the clear ip nhrp command. R3 will purge its NHRP cache of all NHRP mapping information. The pings from R4 to R6 now succeed:

```
R3#clear ip nhrp

R3#show ip route nhrp | begin Gateway
Gateway of last resort is 100.1.1.1 to network 0.0.0.0

R4#ping 36.1.1.6 repeat 10000
Type escape sequence to abort.
Sending 10000, 100-byte ICMP Echos to 36.1.1.6, timeout is 2 seconds:
!!!!!!!!!!!!!!!!!!!!!!!!!!!!!!!!!!!!!!!!!!!!!!!!!!!!!!!!!!!!!!!!!!!!!!!!
```

A repeated traceroute performed from R4 to R6 reveals the spoke-to-spoke tunnel does not form between R2 and R3.

```
R4#traceroute 36.1.1.6
Type escape sequence to abort.
Tracing the route to 36.1.1.6
VRF info: (vrf in name/id, vrf out name/id)
  1 24.1.1.2 0 msec 5 msec 5 msec
  2 200.1.1.1 1 msec 1 msec 0 msec
  3 100.1.1.3 1 msec 2 msec 1 msec
  4 36.1.1.6 1 msec 0 msec 1 msec

R4#traceroute 36.1.1.6
Type escape sequence to abort.
Tracing the route to 36.1.1.6
VRF info: (vrf in name/id, vrf out name/id)
  1 24.1.1.2 0 msec 5 msec 5 msec
  2 200.1.1.1 1 msec 1 msec 0 msec
  3 100.1.1.3 1 msec 2 msec 1 msec
  4 36.1.1.6 1 msec 0 msec 1 msec
```

A spoke-to-spoke tunnel will not form in this case because the hub is in charge of trig-gering the spoke-to-spoke tunnel resolution process by sending an NHRP redirect mes-sage. The hub will only send a redirect message if it notices itself sending packets out a tunnel interface on which the traffic was received. Hops 2 and 3 of the traceroute output above proves that the hub isn't sending the packets out of the same tunnel interface. Instead, it is routing the packets from the Tunnel 200 interface (evidenced by 200.1.1.1 in hop 2, indicating R1 received the packet on its Tunnel 200 interface) to the Tunnel 100 interface (evidenced by the 100.1.1.3 in hop 3, indicating R3 received the packet on its Tunnel 100 interface meaning R1 routed the packet to that interface).

Similar to earlier sections, there are other solutions to this problem such as EEM script-ing combined with interface tracking and IP SLA operations (to track the status of reach-ability across the Tunnel 100 interfaces of all routers). Such solutions are outside the scope of this lab.

Additionally, implementing the single cloud solution where tunnel endpoint redundancy is achieved by advertising tunnel endpoint addresses to both transports can be imple-mented as well. The overlay routing configuration is comparable to the single hub, single cloud Phase 3 implementation details.

## Implement iBGP

Base Phase 3 configuration for iBGP mirrors the configuration used for Phase 1 and Phase 2. R1 is configured with a peer group used to designate the spokes as route reflec-tor clients. This peer group is used in the bgp listen range command to allow the hub to dynamically form iBGP peering with R2 and R3. Once again, local preference is used to prefer tunnel 100 over tunnel 200. Finally, to meet the design goals, R1 is configured to send only a BGP default route to the spokes with the **default-originate** command on the peer group combined with a route map. The route map calls a prefix list that permits only the default route. This route map is then applied in the outbound direction to the peer group with the **neighbor** *peer-group-name* **route-map** *route-map-name* **out** command.

### On R1:

```
R1(config)#interface tunnel 100
R1(config-if)#no delay 500
R1(config-if)#no ip summary-address eigrp 100 0.0.0.0 0.0.0.0

R1(config-if)#interface tunnel 200
R1(config-if)#no ip summary-address eigrp 100 0.0.0.0 0.0.0.0

R1(config)#no router eigrp 100
```

```
R1(config)#ip prefix-list NET permit 0.0.0.0/0

R1(config)#route-map tst permit 10
R1(config-route-map)#match ip addr prefix NET

R1(config)#route-map local-pref permit 10
R1(config-route-map)#set local-preference 200

R1(config)#router bgp 100
R1(config-router)#neighbor tunnel100 peer-group
R1(config-router)#neighbor tunnel200 peer-group
R1(config-router)#neighbor tunnel100 remote-as 100
R1(config-router)#neighbor tunnel200 remote-as 100
R1(config-router)#neighbor tunnel100 timers 6 20
R1(config-router)#neighbor tunnel200 timers 6 20

R1(config-router)#bgp listen range 100.1.1.0/24 peer-group tunnel100
R1(config-router)#bgp listen range 200.1.1.0/24 peer-group tunnel200

R1(config-router)#address-family ipv4
R1(config-router-af)#neighbor tunnel100 route-reflector-client
R1(config-router-af)#neighbor tunnel200 route-reflector-client

R1(config-router-af)#neighbor tunnel100 default-originate
R1(config-router-af)#neighbor tunnel200 default-originate

R1(config-router-af)#neighbor tunnel200 route-map tst out
R1(config-router-af)#neighbor tunnel100 route-map local-pref in

R1(config-router-af)#network 18.1.1.0 mask 255.255.255.0
```

## On R2:

```
R2(config)#no router eigrp 100

R2(config)#route-map local-pref permit 10
R2(config-route-map)#set local-preference 200

R2(config)#router bgp 100
R2(config-router)#neighbor 100.1.1.1 remote-as 100
R2(config-router)#neighbor 200.1.1.1 remote-as 100
```

```
R2(config-router)#address-family ipv4
R2(config-router-af)#neighbor 100.1.1.1 route-map local-pref in
R2(config-router-af)#network 24.1.1.0 mask 255.255.255.0
```

You should see the following console messages:

```
%BGP-5-ADJCHANGE: neighbor 100.1.1.1 Up
%BGP-5-ADJCHANGE: neighbor 200.1.1.1 Up
```

## On R3:

```
R3(config)#no router eigrp 100

R3(config)#route-map local-pref permit 10
R3(config-route-map)#set local-preference 200

R3(config)#router bgp 100
R3(config-router)#neighbor 100.1.1.1 remote-as 100
R3(config-router)#neighbor 200.1.1.1 remote-as 100

R3(config-router)#address-family ipv4
R3(config-router-af)#neighbor 100.1.1.1 route-map local-pref in
R3(config-router-af)#network 36.1.1.0 mask 255.255.255.0
```

You should see the following console messages:

```
%BGP-5-ADJCHANGE: neighbor 100.1.1.1 Up
%BGP-5-ADJCHANGE: neighbor 200.1.1.1 Up
```

As a result of modifying the local preference for paths received over tunnel 100, R2 and R3 choose the default route via MPLS-WAN as the best path:

## On R2:

```
R2#show ip bgp | begin Net
```

| | Network | Next Hop | Metric | LocPrf | Weight | Path |
|---|---|---|---|---|---|---|
| *>i | 0.0.0.0 | 100.1.1.1 | 0 | 200 | 0 | i |
| * i | | 200.1.1.1 | 0 | 100 | 0 | i |
| *>i | 18.1.1.0/24 | 100.1.1.1 | 0 | 200 | 0 | i |
| *> | 24.1.1.0/24 | 0.0.0.0 | 0 | | 32768 | i |
| *>i | 36.1.1.0/24 | 100.1.1.3 | 0 | 200 | 0 | i |

## On R3:

```
R3#show ip bgp | begin Net
```

```
     Network           Next Hop           Metric LocPrf Weight Path
 * i  0.0.0.0          200.1.1.1               0    100      0 i
 *>i                   100.1.1.1               0    200      0 i
 *>i  18.1.1.0/24      100.1.1.1               0    200      0 i
 *>i  24.1.1.0/24      100.1.1.2               0    200      0 i
 *>   36.1.1.0/24      0.0.0.0                 0          32768 i
```

A traceroute from R4 to R6 is shown to first traverse the hub over MPLS-WAN. Subsequent traceroute is shown to use the direct spoke to spoke tunnel between R2 and R3:

```
R4#traceroute 36.1.1.6
Type escape sequence to abort.
Tracing the route to 36.1.1.6
VRF info: (vrf in name/id, vrf out name/id)
  1 24.1.1.2 4 msec 5 msec 6 msec
  2 100.1.1.1 6 msec 5 msec 5 msec
  3 100.1.1.3 5 msec 7 msec
    36.1.1.6 5 msec


R4#traceroute 36.1.1.6
Type escape sequence to abort.
Tracing the route to 36.1.1.6
VRF info: (vrf in name/id, vrf out name/id)
  1 24.1.1.2 5 msec 4 msec 5 msec
  2 100.1.1.3 5 msec 6 msec 6 msec
  3 36.1.1.6 6 msec 6 msec 4 msec
```

To test redundancy, repeated pings are performed from R4 to R6 during which the G0/5 interface is shutdown on R2. The same issue as reported above in the EIGRP section occurs in this situation. Because R3 retains the old NHRP route for the destination network 24.1.1.0/24 pointed out of its Tunnel 100 interface, it cannot return traffic to R4. As in the EIGRP case, a clear ip nhrp is issued on R3 causing it to purge its NHRP cache.

```
R3#clear ip nhrp


R3#show ip route nhrp | begin Gateway
Gateway of last resort is 100.1.1.1 to network 0.0.0.0


R4ping 36.1.1.6 repeat 10000
Type escape sequence to abort.
Sending 10000, 100-byte ICMP Echos to 36.1.1.6, timeout is 2 seconds:
!!!!!!!!!!!!!!!!!!!!!!!!!!!!!!!!!!!!!!!!!!!!!!!!!!!!!!!!!!!!!!!!!!!!!!!
!!!!!!!!!!!!!!!!!!!!!!!!!!!!!!!!!!!!!!!!!!!!!!!!!!!!!!!!!!!!!!!!!!!!!!!
!!!!!!!!!!!!!!!!!!!!!!!!!!!!!!!!!!!!!!!!!!!!!!!!!!!!!!!!!!!!!!!!!!!!!!!!
```

```
!!!!!!!!!!!!!!!!!!!!!!!!!!!!!!!!!!!!!!!!!!!!!!!!!!!!!!!!!!!!!!!!!!!!!!!!!!!
!!!!!!!!!!!!!!!!!!!!!!!!!!!!!!!!!!!!!!!!!!!!!!!!!!!!!!!!!!!!!!!!!!!!!!!!!!!
!!!!!!!!!!!!!!!!!!!!............!!!!!!!!!!!!!!!!!!!!!!!!!!!!!!!!!!!!!!!!!!
!!!!!!!!!!!!!!!!!!!!!!!!!!!!!!!!!!!!!!!!!!!!!!!!!!!!!!
```

```
R4#traceroute 36.1.1.6
Type escape sequence to abort.
Tracing the route to 36.1.1.6
VRF info: (vrf in name/id, vrf out name/id)
  1 24.1.1.2 0 msec 5 msec 5 msec
  2 200.1.1.1 1 msec 1 msec 0 msec
  3 100.1.1.3 1 msec 2 msec 1 msec
  4 36.1.1.6 1 msec 0 msec 1 msec
```

The traceroute output above again indicates the spoke-to-spoke tunnel will not form
between R2 and R3 because R1 is not sending the NHRP redirect message, meaning the
hub will be involved in all communication between the R2 and R3 LANs. Additional
methods to mitigate this problem can be employed just as indicated in the EIGRP section, however, these solutions are not detailed in this lab.

## Implement eBGP

Similar to the earlier section, the eBGP implementation below demonstrates two design
choices: Spokes are either placed in the same AS or in a different AS.

### Spokes in the Same AS

Following configures the spokes in AS 230. Local preference for paths learned over the
tunnel 100 interface has been modified to 200. The hub R1 in AS 100 has also been configured to send a default route down to the spokes:

**On R2:**

```
R2(config)#no router bgp 100

R2(config)#route-map local-pref permit 10
R2(config-route-map)#set local-preference 200

R2(config)#router bgp 230
R2(config-router)#neighbor 100.1.1.1 remote-as 100
R2(config-router)#neighbor 200.1.1.1 remote-as 100
```

```
R2(config-router)#address-family ipv4
R2(config-router-af)#network 24.1.1.0 mask 255.255.255.0
R2(config-router-af)#neighbor 100.1.1.1 route-map local-pref in
```

## On R3:

```
R3(config)#no router bgp 100

R3(config)#route-map local-pref permit 10
R3(config-route-map)#set local-preference 200

R3(config)#router bgp 230
R3(config-router)#neighbor 100.1.1.1 remote-as 100
R3(config-router)#neighbor 200.1.1.1 remote-as 100

R3(config-router)#address-family ipv4
R3(config-router-af)#network 36.1.1.0 mask 255.255.255.0
R3(config-router-af)#neighbor 100.1.1.1 route-map local-pref in
```

## On R1:

```
R1(config)#router bgp 100
R1(config-router)#neighbor tunnel100 peer-group
R1(config-router)#neighbor tunnel100 remote-as 230
R1(config-router)#neighbor tunnel100 timers 6 20
R1(config-router)#neighbor tunnel200 peer-group
R1(config-router)#neighbor tunnel200 remote-as 230
R1(config-router)#neighbor tunnel200 timers 6 20

R1(config-router)#bgp listen range 200.1.1.0/24 peer-group tunnel200
R1(config-router)#bgp listen range 100.1.1.0/24 peer-group tunnel100

R1(config-router)#address-family ipv4
R1(config-router-af)#network 18.1.1.0 mask 255.255.255.0
R1(config-router-af)#neighbor tunnel100 default-originate
R1(config-router-af)#neighbor tunnel100 route-map local-pref in
R1(config-router-af)#neighbor tunnel200 default-originate
R1(config-router-af)#neighbor tunnel200 route-map tst out
R1(config-router-af)#neighbor tunnel100 route-map tst out
```

You should see the following console messages:

```
%BGP-5-ADJCHANGE: neighbor *200.1.1.2 Up
%BGP-5-ADJCHANGE: neighbor *100.1.1.3 Up
%BGP-5-ADJCHANGE: neighbor *200.1.1.3 Up
%BGP-5-ADJCHANGE: neighbor *100.1.1.2 Up
```

## To verify the configuration:

```
R1#show ip bgp summ | begin Nei
```

| Neighbor<br>State/PfxRcd | V | AS | MsgRcvd | MsgSent | TblVer | InQ | OutQ | Up/Down | |
|---|---|---|---|---|---|---|---|---|---|
| *100.1.1.2 | 4 | 230 | 88 | 101 | 7 | 0 | 0 | 00:08:54 | 1 |
| *100.1.1.3 | 4 | 230 | 89 | 101 | 7 | 0 | 0 | 00:09:05 | 1 |
| *200.1.1.2 | 4 | 230 | 90 | 97 | 7 | 0 | 0 | 00:09:07 | 1 |
| *200.1.1.3 | 4 | 230 | 90 | 97 | 7 | 0 | 0 | 00:09:05 | 1 |

```
* Dynamically created based on a listen range command
Dynamically created neighbors: 4, Subnet ranges: 2

BGP peergroup tunnel100 listen range group members:
  100.1.1.0/24
BGP peergroup tunnel200 listen range group members:
  200.1.1.0/24

Total dynamically created neighbors: 4/(100 max), Subnet ranges: 2
```

```
R1#show ip bgp | begin Net
```

| | Network | Next Hop | Metric | LocPrf | Weight | Path |
|---|---|---|---|---|---|---|
| | 0.0.0.0 | 0.0.0.0 | | | 0 | i |
| *> | 18.1.1.0/24 | 0.0.0.0 | 0 | | 32768 | i |
| *> | 24.1.1.0/24 | 100.1.1.2 | 0 | 200 | 0 | 230 i |
| * | | 200.1.1.2 | 0 | | 0 | 230 i |
| * | 36.1.1.0/24 | 200.1.1.3 | 0 | | 0 | 230 i |
| *> | | 100.1.1.3 | 0 | 200 | 0 | 230 i |

## On R2:

```
R2#show ip bgp | begin Net
```

| Network | Next Hop | Metric | LocPrf | Weight | Path |
|---|---|---|---|---|---|

```
     *>    0.0.0.0            100.1.1.1                        200        0 100 i
     *                        200.1.1.1                                   0 100 i
     *>    18.1.1.0/24        100.1.1.1               0        200        0 100 i
     *>    24.1.1.0/24        0.0.0.0                 0                32768 i
```

## On R3:

```
R3#show ip bgp | begin Net

        Network            Next Hop            Metric LocPrf Weight Path
     *>    0.0.0.0            100.1.1.1                        200        0 100 i
     *                        200.1.1.1                                   0 100 i
     *>    18.1.1.0/24        100.1.1.1               0        200        0 100 i
     *>    36.1.1.0/24        0.0.0.0                 0                32768 i
```

### Spokes in Different Autonomous Systems

To place spokes in a different AS, the alternate-as command is added to the remote-as peer group configuration on R1. R2 is configured in AS 200 and R3 in AS 300:

## On R2:

The route map called **local-pref** was not deleted.

```
R2(config)#no router bgp 230

R2(config)#router bgp 200
R2(config-router)#neighbor 100.1.1.1 remote-as 100
R2(config-router)#neighbor 200.1.1.1 remote-as 100

R2(config-router)#address-family ipv4
R2(config-router-af)#network 24.1.1.0 mask 255.255.255.0
R2(config-router-af)#neighbor 100.1.1.1 route-map local-pref in
```

## On R3:

```
R3(config)#no router bgp 230

R3(config)#router bgp 300
R3(config-router)#neighbor 100.1.1.1 remote-as 100
R3(config-router)#neighbor 200.1.1.1 remote-as 100
```

```
R3(config-router)#address-family ipv4
R3(config-router-af)#network 36.1.1.0 mask 255.255.255.0
R3(config-router-af)#neighbor 100.1.1.1 route-map local-pref in
```

## On R1:

```
R1(config)#router bgp 100
R1(config-router)#no neighbor tunnel100 remote-as 230
R1(config-router)#no neighbor tunnel200 remote-as 230
R1(config-router)#neighbor tunnel100 remote-as 200 alternate-as 300
R1(config-router)#neighbor tunnel200 remote-as 200 alternate-as 300
```

You should see the following console messages:

```
%BGP-5-ADJCHANGE: neighbor *200.1.1.2 Up
%BGP-5-ADJCHANGE: neighbor *100.1.1.3 Up
%BGP-5-ADJCHANGE: neighbor *200.1.1.3 Up
%BGP-5-ADJCHANGE: neighbor *100.1.1.2 Up
```

## To verify the configuration:

## On R2:

```
R2#show ip bgp | begin Net

     Network          Next Hop         Metric LocPrf Weight Path
 *   0.0.0.0          200.1.1.1                            0 100 i
 *>                   100.1.1.1                    200     0 100 i
 *>  18.1.1.0/24      100.1.1.1            0       200     0 100 i
 *>  24.1.1.0/24      0.0.0.0             0            32768 i
 *>  36.1.1.0/24      100.1.1.3                    200     0 100
300 i
```

## On R3:

```
R3#show ip bgp | begin Net

     Network          Next Hop         Metric LocPrf Weight Path
 *   0.0.0.0          200.1.1.1                            0 100 i
 *>                   100.1.1.1                    200     0 100 i
```

| | | | | | | |
|---|---|---|---|---|---|---|
| *> | 18.1.1.0/24 | 100.1.1.1 | 0 | 200 | 0 100 i | |
| *> | 24.1.1.0/24 | 100.1.1.2 | | 200 | 0 100 | |
| 200 i | | | | | | |
| *> | 36.1.1.0/24 | 0.0.0.0 | 0 | | 32768 i | |

Traceroute from R4 to R6 is shown to first traverse the hub after which it uses the direct spoke to spoke tunnel between R2 and R3:

```
R4#traceroute 36.1.1.6
Type escape sequence to abort.
Tracing the route to 36.1.1.6
VRF info: (vrf in name/id, vrf out name/id)
  1 24.1.1.2 1 msec 0 msec 5 msec
  2 100.1.1.1 2 msec 0 msec 1 msec
  3 100.1.1.3 1 msec 1 msec 1 msec
  4 36.1.1.6 1 msec 1 msec 0 msec


R4#traceroute 36.1.1.6
Type escape sequence to abort.
Tracing the route to 36.1.1.6
VRF info: (vrf in name/id, vrf out name/id)
  1 24.1.1.2 5 msec 1 msec 5 msec
  2 100.1.1.3 6 msec 6 msec 5 msec
  3 36.1.1.6 6 msec 5 msec 5 msec
```

To test redundancy, repeated pings are performed from R4 to R6 during which the G0/5 interface is shut down on R2. The same issue as reported above in the iBGP and EIGRP section occurs in this situation. Because R3 retains the old NHRP route for the destination network 24.1.1.0/24 pointed out of its Tunnel 100 interface, it cannot return traffic to R4. As in the EIGRP case, a clear ip nhrp is issued on R3 causing it to purge its NHRP cache.

```
R3#clear ip nhrp


R3#show ip route nhrp | begin Gateway
Gateway of last resort is 100.1.1.1 to network 0.0.0.0


R4ping 36.1.1.6 repeat 10000
Type escape sequence to abort.
Sending 10000, 100-byte ICMP Echos to 36.1.1.6, timeout is 2 seconds:
!!!!!!!!!!!!!!!!!!!!!!!!!!!!!!!!!!!!!!!!!!!!!!!!!!!!!!!!!!!!!!!!!!!!!!!!!!
!!!!!!!!!!!!!!!!!!!!!!!!!!!!!!!!!!!!!!!!!!!!!!!!!!!!!!!!!!!!!!!!!!!!!!!!!!
!!!!!!!!!!!!!!!!!!!!!!!!!!!!!!!!!!!!!!!!!!!!!!!!!!!!!!!!!!!!!!!!!!!!!!!!!!
!!!!!!!!!!!!!!!!!!!!!!!!!!!!!!!!!!!!!!!!!!!!!!!!!!!!!!!!!!!!!!!!!!!!!!!!!!
!!!!!!!!!!!!!!!!!!!!!!!!!!!!!!!!!!!!!!!!!!!!!!!!!!!!!!!!!!!!!!!!!!!!!!!!!!
!!!!!!!!!!!!!!!!!!......!!!!!!!!!!!!!!!!!!!!!!!!!!!!!!!!!!!!!!!!!!!!!
!!!!!!!!!!!!!!!!!!!!!!!!!!!!!!!!!!!!!!!!!!!!!!!!!!!!
```

```
R4#traceroute 36.1.1.6
Type escape sequence to abort.
Tracing the route to 36.1.1.6
VRF info: (vrf in name/id, vrf out name/id)
  1 24.1.1.2 0 msec 5 msec 5 msec
  2 200.1.1.1 1 msec 1 msec 0 msec
  3 100.1.1.3 1 msec 2 msec 1 msec
  4 36.1.1.6 1 msec 0 msec 1 msec

R4#traceroute 36.1.1.6
Type escape sequence to abort.
Tracing the route to 36.1.1.6
VRF info: (vrf in name/id, vrf out name/id)
  1 24.1.1.2 0 msec 5 msec 5 msec
  2 200.1.1.1 1 msec 1 msec 0 msec
  3 100.1.1.3 1 msec 2 msec 1 msec
  4 36.1.1.6 1 msec 0 msec 1 msec

R4#traceroute 36.1.1.6
Type escape sequence to abort.
Tracing the route to 36.1.1.6
VRF info: (vrf in name/id, vrf out name/id)
  1 24.1.1.2 0 msec 5 msec 5 msec
  2 200.1.1.1 1 msec 1 msec 0 msec
  3 100.1.1.3 1 msec 2 msec 1 msec
  4 36.1.1.6 1 msec 0 msec 1 msec
```

The traceroute output above again indicates the spoke-to-spoke tunnel will not form between R2 and R3 because R1 is not sending the NHRP redirect message, meaning the hub will be involved in all communication between the R2 and R3 LANs. Additional methods to mitigate this problem can be employed just as indicated in the EIGRP section, however, these solutions are not detailed in this lab.

# Lab 3: Dual Hub, Single Cloud

## This lab should be conducted on the Enterprise Rack.

## Lab Setup:

If you are using EVE-NG, and you have imported the EVE-NG topology from the **EVE-NG-Topology** folder, ignore the following and use **Lab-3-Dual Hub Single Cloud** in the **DMVPN** folder in EVE-NG.

To copy and paste the initial configurations, go to the **Initial-config** folder ➔ **DMVPN** folder ➔ **Lab-3**.

The base topology of the main site has changed to include two VPN routers, R1 and R7. R8, which was originally functioning as a host, has been enabled with IP routing to avoid a common problem with such VPN designs regarding asymmetric routing.

Asymmetric routing is when packets take a different return path from the original path taken to reach the destination. In the example above, R8 sits behind R1 and R7. When R8 receives a packet from R1, it could decide to return that traffic to R7 instead of to R1 again.

Asymmetric routing carries some important consequences. The path through R7 may use a separate set of policies—such as firewall rules, SLAs, and QoS mechanisms—than the R1 path. These differences can cause intermittent or sustained connectivity problems in the network.

To mitigate these issues, R8 has been enabled with routing features, and the R1/R7/R8 LAN will run EIGRP in AS 100. R7 has been configured to advertise a default route to R8, and R1 advertises specific prefixes. This way, R8 will prefer the specific prefixes learned from R1 over the default route from R7. When R1 fails, the specific prefixes are removed, and R8 follows the default route through R7. Below is the configuration for the R1/R7/R8LAN.

**On R1:**

```
R1(config)#router eigrp 100
R1(config-router)#network 187.1.1.1 0.0.0.0
```

**On R7:**

```
R7(config)#router eigrp 100
R7(config-router)#network 187.1.1.7 0.0.0.0

R7(config)#interface g0/9
R7(config-if)#ip summary-address eigrp 100 0.0.0.0 0.0.0.0
```

You should see the following console message:

```
%DUAL-5-NBRCHANGE: EIGRP-IPv4 100: Neighbor 187.1.1.1
(GigabitEthernet0/9) is up: new adjacency
```

**On R8:**

```
R8(config)#router eigrp 100
R8(config-router)#network 187.1.1.8 0.0.0.0
R8(config-router)#network 18.1.1.8 0.0.0.0
```

You should see the following console message:

```
%DUAL-5-NBRCHANGE: EIGRP-IPv4 100: Neighbor 187.1.1.1
(GigabitEthernet0/9) is up: new adjacency

%DUAL-5-NBRCHANGE: EIGRP-IPv4 100: Neighbor 187.1.1.7
(GigabitEthernet0/9) is up: new adjacency
```

On completing the above, the show ip route eigrp 100 command is issued on R8. As seen below, R8 learns an EIGRP default route from R7. Since the rest of the DMVPN has not yet been configured, there are no specific prefixes from R1 at this point:

**To verify the configuration:**

```
R8#show ip route eigrp 100  | begin Gate
Gateway of last resort is 187.1.1.7 to network 0.0.0.0

D*     0.0.0.0/0 [90/3072] via 187.1.1.7, 00:10:48, GigabitEthernet0/9
```

This DMVPN design scenario will only discuss Phase 3, since that is the recommended approach to a Dual Hub, Single Cloud design.

## Implement Phase 3

## Design Goal

ABC Corp has grown into ABC Enterprise, with multiple remote sites in addition to the main site. The corporation has outsourced network design and configuration to a network engineering firm. The firm has been tasked with delivering a design proof of concept for connecting the remote sites to the main site without the added expense of a private WAN circuit. The design should allow remote sites to directly communicate with each other with minimal routing overhead. In addition, a failure of a main site device should not prevent the VPN from functioning. Traffic should flow through R1 primarily and use R7 as backup.

### DMVPN Tunnel Configuration

To summarize the design goal stated above, the WAN connectivity design should meet the following criteria:

- The VPN solution should use the existing Internet connection to avoid provisioning expensive private WAN circuits.

- Remote sites should be able to communicate directly with each other with the least possible routing information overhead.

- Failure of a main site device should not prevent the VPN from functioning.

- Traffic should be preferred through R1. R7 is used as backup.

These four requirements can be fulfilled using a dual-hub, single-cloud DMVPN configuration. This type of solution obtains high availability, as failure of any one hub device does not impede the functionality of the DMVPN network. In order to allow remote sites to communicate with minimal routing information, DMVPN Phase 3 should be implemented. Phase 3 allows summarization from the hub to the spokes, relying on NHRP redirect messages from the hub to trigger spoke-to-spoke tunnels.

The following configuration is the basic outline configuration for the DMVPN tunnel interfaces for both hubs, R1 and R7, and spokes R2 and R3. Note that each spoke is configured with both hubs as the NHRP NHS, and a single tunnel interface is configured on each device:

**On Hub R1:**

```
R1(config)#interface tunnel 100
R1(config-if)#ip address 100.1.1.1 255.255.255.0
R1(config-if)#tunnel source 15.1.1.1
R1(config-if)#tunnel mode gre multipoint
R1(config-if)#ip nhrp network-id 100
R1(config-if)#ip nhrp map multicast dynamic
R1(config-if)#ip nhrp redirect
```

**On Hub R7:**

```
R7(config)#interface tunnel 100
R7(config-if)#ip address 100.1.1.7 255.255.255.0
R7(config-if)#tunnel source 57.1.1.7
R7(config-if)#tunnel mode gre multipoint
R7(config-if)#ip nhrp network-id 100
R7(config-if)#ip nhrp map multicast dynamic
R7(config-if)#ip nhrp redirect
```

**On R2:**

```
R2(config)#interface tunnel 100
R2(config-if)#ip address 100.1.1.2 255.255.255.0
R2(config-if)#tunnel source 25.1.1.2
```

```
R2(config-if)#tunnel mode gre multipoint
R2(config-if)#ip nhrp network-id 100
R2(config-if)#ip nhrp nhs 100.1.1.1 nbma 15.1.1.1 multicast
R2(config-if)#ip nhrp nhs 100.1.1.7 nbma 57.1.1.7 multicast
R2(config-if)#ip nhrp shortcut
```

## On R3:

```
R3(config)#interface tunnel 100
R3(config-if)#ip address 100.1.1.3 255.255.255.0
R3(config-if)#tunnel source 35.1.1.3
R3(config-if)#tunnel mode gre multipoint
R3(config-if)#ip nhrp network-id 100
R3(config-if)#ip nhrp nhs 100.1.1.1 nbma 15.1.1.1 multicast
R3(config-if)#ip nhrp nhs 100.1.1.7 nbma 57.1.1.7 multicast
R3(config-if)#ip nhrp shortcut
```

This configuration enables NHRP redirect and shortcut switching enhancements on the tunnel interfaces for the hubs and spokes, respectively. In addition, on each spoke, the **ip nhrp nhs 100.1.1.1 nbma 15.1.1.1 multicast** command has been issued for hub R1, and **ip nhrp nhs 200.1.1.1 nbma 57.1.1.7 multicast** has been issued for hub R7. This allows the spokes to register with both hubs appropriately and use each of them for resolving overlay-to-NBMA mapping information when attempting to form a spoke-to-spoke tunnel.

The **show dmvpn** output on each router confirms the configuration. Notice in the output below, both spokes have successfully registered with Hub R1 and R7:

## On R1:

```
R1#show dmvpn | begin Peer NBMA

 # Ent   Peer NBMA Addr Peer Tunnel Add State  UpDn Tm Attrb
 -----  --------------- --------------- ----- -------- -----
     1 25.1.1.2             100.1.1.2    UP 00:13:16    D
     1 35.1.1.3             100.1.1.3    UP 00:10:01    D

R1#show ip nhrp multicast

   I/F     NBMA address
Tunnel100  25.1.1.2      Flags: dynamic      (Enabled)
Tunnel100  35.1.1.3      Flags: dynamic      (Enabled)
```

## On R7:

```
R7#show dmvpn | begin Peer NBMA

# Ent   Peer NBMA Addr  Peer Tunnel Add  State   UpDn Tm  Attrb
----- --------------- --------------- ----- -------- -----
    1 25.1.1.2                 100.1.1.2    UP 00:15:23    D
    1 35.1.1.3                 100.1.1.3    UP 00:10:16    D


R7#show ip nhrp multicast

  I/F       NBMA address
Tunnel100   25.1.1.2      Flags: dynamic      (Enabled)
Tunnel100   35.1.1.3      Flags: dynamic      (Enabled)
```

## On R2:

```
R2#show dmvpn | begin Peer NBMA

# Ent   Peer NBMA Addr  Peer Tunnel Add  State   UpDn Tm  Attrb
----- --------------- --------------- ----- -------- -----
    1 15.1.1.1                 100.1.1.1    UP 00:14:23    S
    1 57.1.1.7                 100.1.1.7    UP 00:15:59    S


R2#show ip nhrp multicast
  I/F       NBMA address
Tunnel100   57.1.1.7      Flags: nhs          (Enabled)
Tunnel100   15.1.1.1      Flags: nhs          (Enabled)
```

## On R3:

```
R3#show dmvpn | begin Peer NBMA

# Ent   Peer NBMA Addr  Peer Tunnel Add  State   UpDn Tm  Attrb
----- --------------- --------------- ----- -------- -----
    1 15.1.1.1                 100.1.1.1    UP 00:11:50    S
    1 57.1.1.7                 100.1.1.7    UP 00:11:33    S


R3#show ip nhrp multicast

  I/F       NBMA address
```

```
Tunnel100   57.1.1.7        Flags: nhs              (Enabled)
Tunnel100   15.1.1.1        Flags: nhs              (Enabled)
```

The output above verifies that the spokes have registered mapping information with both hubs dynamically, just as in the single-hub, single-cloud configuration. Now, whenever the spoke needs to resolve a spoke-to-spoke overlay-to-NBMA mapping, the spokes can use either R1 or R7 to facilitate the resolution process.

The following commands are used to verify reachability between the hub and spokes using a **traceroute** from R2 to the tunnel 100 address on R1, R7, and R3:

## On R2:

```
R2#traceroute 100.1.1.1 probe 1

Type escape sequence to abort.
Tracing the route to 100.1.1.1
VRF info: (vrf in name/id, vrf out name/id)
  1 100.1.1.1 26 msec

R2#traceroute 100.1.1.7 probe 1

Type escape sequence to abort.
Tracing the route to 100.1.1.7
VRF info: (vrf in name/id, vrf out name/id)
  1 100.1.1.7 22 msec

R2#traceroute 100.1.1.3 probe 1

Type escape sequence to abort.
Tracing the route to 100.1.1.3
VRF info: (vrf in name/id, vrf out name/id)
  1 100.1.1.1 12 msec
  2 100.1.1.3 52 msec

R2#traceroute 100.1.1.3 probe 1

Type escape sequence to abort.
Tracing the route to 100.1.1.3
VRF info: (vrf in name/id, vrf out name/id)
  1 100.1.1.3 4 msec

R2#show dmvpn | begin Peer NBMA
```

```
# Ent  Peer NBMA Addr  Peer Tunnel Add  State  UpDn Tm  Attrb
-----  --------------- ---------------  -----  -------- -----
    1  15.1.1.1              100.1.1.1   UP 00:23:36       S
    1  35.1.1.3              100.1.1.3   UP 00:01:06       D
    1  57.1.1.7              100.1.1.7   UP 00:25:12       S
```

The next sections detail routing protocol configuration for EIGRP and BGP for this design. OSPF is not demonstrated because it is unable to fully meet the requirement of minimal routing information. OSPF's requirement that all routers in the same area must have all routes reachable within the area limits the ability to completely summarize routing information from the hub routers to the spokes.

## Implement EIGRP

The EIGRP configuration here is very similar to the single-hub, single-cloud configuration. EIGRP is enabled on all tunnel interfaces in the network as well as the connected LAN interface of each router. R1 and R7 are configured to send a default route down to the spokes out their tunnel 100 interfaces as well. The following are the initial configurations for EIGRP as the DMVPN overlay:

**On R1:**

```
R1(config)#router eigrp 100
R1(config-router)#network 100.1.1.1 0.0.0.0

R1(config)#interface tunnel 100
R1(config-if)#ip summary-address eigrp 100 0.0.0.0 0.0.0.0
```

**On R7:**

```
R7(config)#router eigrp 100
R7(config-router)#network 100.1.1.7 0.0.0.0

R7(config)#interface tunnel 100
R7(config-if)#ip summary-address eigrp 100 0.0.0.0 0.0.0.0
```

Due to the lack of NHRP multicast mappings for each other, the hub routers R1 and R7 will not become EIGRP neighbors.

```
R7#show ip nhrp 100.1.1.1
R7#
```

## On R2:

```
R2(config)#router eigrp 100
R2(config-router)#network 24.1.1.2 0.0.0.0
R2(config-router)#network 100.1.1.2 0.0.0.0
R2(config-router)#passive-interface g0/4
```

You should see the following console messages:

```
%DUAL-5-NBRCHANGE: EIGRP-IPv4 100: Neighbor 100.1.1.1 (Tunnel100) is
up: new adjacency
```

```
%DUAL-5-NBRCHANGE: EIGRP-IPv4 100: Neighbor 100.1.1.7 (Tunnel100) is
up: new adjacency
```

## On R3:

```
R3(config)#router eigrp 100
R3(config-router)#network 36.1.1.3 0.0.0.0
R3(config-router)#network 100.1.1.3 0.0.0.0
R3(config-router)#passive-interface g0/6
```

You should see the following console messages:

```
%DUAL-5-NBRCHANGE: EIGRP-IPv4 100: Neighbor 100.1.1.1 (Tunnel100) is
up: new adjacency
```

```
%DUAL-5-NBRCHANGE: EIGRP-IPv4 100: Neighbor 100.1.1.7 (Tunnel100) is
up: new adjacency
```

With the console log messages above confirming the EIGRP neighborships between the spokes and hub routers, the show ip route eigrp 100 command is issued on R2 and R3. Both spokes are performing ECMP and have installed the default route advertised by both hubs:

## On R2:

```
R2#show ip route eigrp 100 | begin Gate
Gateway of last resort is 100.1.1.7 to network 0.0.0.0

D*    0.0.0.0/0 [90/26880256] via 100.1.1.7, 00:03:45, Tunnel100
                [90/26880256] via 100.1.1.1, 00:03:45, Tunnel100
```

## On R3:

```
R3#show ip route eigrp 100 | begin Gate
Gateway of last resort is 100.1.1.7 to network 0.0.0.0
```

```
D*    0.0.0.0/0 [90/26880256] via 100.1.1.7, 00:02:11, Tunnel100
                [90/26880256] via 100.1.1.1, 00:02:11, Tunnel100
```

R8's routing table reveals the specific prefixes learned from R1 via EIGRP:

```
R8#show ip route eigrp | begin Gate
Gateway of last resort is 187.1.1.7 to network 0.0.0.0


D*    0.0.0.0/0 [90/3072] via 187.1.1.7, 00:09:59, GigabitEthernet0/9
      24.0.0.0/24 is subnetted, 1 subnets
D        24.1.1.0 [90/26880512] via 187.1.1.1, 00:06:11,
GigabitEthernet0/9
      36.0.0.0/24 is subnetted, 1 subnets
D        36.1.1.0 [90/26880512] via 187.1.1.1, 00:04:07,
GigabitEthernet0/9
      100.0.0.0/24 is subnetted, 1 subnets
D        100.1.1.0 [90/26880256] via 187.1.1.1, 00:11:15,
GigabitEthernet0/9
```

As shown here, R8 retains a default route it received from R7 originally in addition to the specific prefixes from R1. R8 will always prefer the specific prefixes from R1 over the EIGRP default route from R7, preventing the asymmetric routing situation described in the base configuration section.

The design goals specify that R1 should be used as the primary path, and R7 should be backup. To configure the network to comply with this restriction, an offset list is configured in the EIGRP configuration of R7 that adds the delay setting 500 to all prefixes advertised out the tunnel 100 interface. As a result, R2 and R3 now install the default route received from R1 only:

**On R7:**


```
R7(config)#router eigrp 100
R7(config-router)#offset-list 0 out 500 tunnel100
```


**To verify the configuration:**


**On R2:**


```
R2#show ip route eigrp 100 | begin Gate
Gateway of last resort is 100.1.1.1 to network 0.0.0.0


D*    0.0.0.0/0 [90/26880256] via 100.1.1.1, 00:01:09, Tunnel100
```

### On R3:

```
R3#show ip route eigrp 100 | begin Gate
Gateway of last resort is 100.1.1.1 to network 0.0.0.0

D*    0.0.0.0/0 [90/26880256] via 100.1.1.1, 00:01:39, Tunnel100
```

When this configuration is complete, the following traceroute outputs confirm that the network functions as described in the design goals section. A traceroute from R4 to 18.1.1.8 is shown traversing the hub R1. The first traceroute from R4 to R6 traverses the hub while the NHRP resolution process completes. The subsequent traceroute is shown taking the direct spoke-to-spoke tunnel between R2 and R3.

### On R4:

```
R4#traceroute 18.1.1.8 probe 1

Type escape sequence to abort.
Tracing the route to 18.1.1.8
VRF info: (vrf in name/id, vrf out name/id)
  1 24.1.1.2 46 msec
  2 100.1.1.1 8 msec
  3 187.1.1.8 12 msec


R4#traceroute 36.1.1.6 probe 1

Type escape sequence to abort.
Tracing the route to 36.1.1.6
VRF info: (vrf in name/id, vrf out name/id)
  1 24.1.1.2 3 msec
  2 100.1.1.1 6 msec
  3 100.1.1.3 66 msec
  4 36.1.1.6 20 msec


R4#traceroute 36.1.1.6 probe 1

Type escape sequence to abort.
Tracing the route to 36.1.1.6
VRF info: (vrf in name/id, vrf out name/id)
  1 24.1.1.2 2 msec
  2 100.1.1.3 7 msec
  3 36.1.1.6 9 msec
```

The next step is to verify that network redundancy functions as described in the design goals.

Since the DMVPN solution is configured in Phase 3, spoke-to-spoke tunnels that are formed before the hub fails will continue to function. In this case, failure of the hub prevents new spoke-to-spoke tunnels from being formed. To simulate this situation in the topology, the tunnel 100 interface on R1 is shut down. In addition, the **clear ip nhrp** command is issued on R2 and R3 to clear the dynamic NHRP entries from the NHRP mapping tables:

**On R1:**

```
R1(config)#interface tunnel 100
R1(config-if)#shut
```

**On R2:**

```
R2#show dmvpn | begin Peer NBMA

# Ent   Peer NBMA Addr Peer Tunnel Add State  UpDn Tm Attrb
----- --------------- --------------- ----- -------- -----
    2 35.1.1.3                100.1.1.3    UP 00:03:14   DT1
                              100.1.1.3    UP 00:03:14   DT1
    1 15.1.1.1                100.1.1.1    UP 03:40:42    S
    1 57.1.1.7                100.1.1.7    UP 03:42:18    S

R2#clear ip nhrp

R2#show dmvpn | b Peer NBMA

# Ent   Peer NBMA Addr Peer Tunnel Add State  UpDn Tm Attrb
----- --------------- --------------- ----- -------- -----
    1 15.1.1.1                100.1.1.1    UP 03:41:55    S
    1 57.1.1.7                100.1.1.7    UP 03:43:31    S
```

**On R3:**

```
R3#clear ip nhrp
```

With the NHRP mappings cleared, R2 and R3 need to reestablish the spoke-to-spoke tunnel between them. In Phase 3, the spoke-to-spoke tunnel is triggered by the hub. After R1 fails, R2 and R3 install the default route from R7 in their routing tables. The first **traceroute** packet will now go to R7, which will initiate the NHRP redirect process and trigger the R2/R3 spoke-to-spoke tunnel formation:

**On R2:**

```
R2#show ip rou eigrp 100 | begin Gate
Gateway of last resort is 100.1.1.7 to network 0.0.0.0


D*    0.0.0.0/0 [90/26880756] via 100.1.1.7, 00:02:29, Tunnel100

R3#show ip route eigrp 100 | begin Gate
Gateway of last resort is 100.1.1.7 to network 0.0.0.0


D*    0.0.0.0/0 [90/26880756] via 100.1.1.7, 00:03:07, Tunnel100
```

**On R4:**

```
R4#traceroute 18.1.1.8 probe 1


Type escape sequence to abort.
Tracing the route to 18.1.1.8
VRF info: (vrf in name/id, vrf out name/id)
  1 24.1.1.2 16 msec
  2 100.1.1.7 13 msec
  3 187.1.1.8 15 msec


R4#traceroute 36.1.1.6 probe 1


Type escape sequence to abort.
Tracing the route to 36.1.1.6
VRF info: (vrf in name/id, vrf out name/id)
  1 24.1.1.2 4 msec
  2 100.1.1.7 8 msec
  3 100.1.1.3 11 msec
  4 36.1.1.6 13 msec


R4#traceroute 36.1.1.6 probe 1


Type escape sequence to abort.
Tracing the route to 36.1.1.6
VRF info: (vrf in name/id, vrf out name/id)
  1 24.1.1.2 17 msec
  2 100.1.1.3 9 msec
  3 36.1.1.6 15 msec
```

After confirming the failover, the proof of concept prototype has been implemented successfully, using EIGRP as the overlay routing protocol.

## Implement iBGP

The configuration for iBGP as the overlay routing protocol again mimics the single-hub, single-cloud configuration. The difference now is that both R1 and R7 will become route reflectors for the DMVPN spoke routers. Both R1 and R7 are also configured to send a default route down to the spokes through BGP.

The configuration below recreates the BGP peer group for dynamic peering on R1 and R7. It also includes modifications for the default BGP timers to facilitate faster neighbor down detection.

The spokes R2 and R3 are configured to peer with both R1 and R7. Their connected host networks are advertised into BGP with the network command. To implement path preference, the spokes are preloaded to apply a local preference of 150 to all paths learned from R1. Setting the local preference to 150 ensures the spokes will prefer R1's path over R7's as required by the design goals.

---

**On R1:**

```
R1(config)#no router eigrp 100

R1(config)#interface tunnel 100
R1(config-if)#no shut

R1(config)#ip prefix-list TST permit 0.0.0.0/0

R1(config)#route-map default permit 10
R1(config-route-map)#match ip addr prefix TST

R1(config)#router bgp 100
R1(config-router)#neighbor spokes peer-group
R1(config-router)#neighbor spokes remote-as 100
R1(config-router)#neighbor spokes timers 6 20
R1(config-router)#bgp listen range 100.1.1.0/24 peer-group spokes

R1(config-router)#address-family ipv4
R1(config-router-af)#neighbor spokes route-reflector-client
R1(config-router-af)#neighbor spokes default-originate
R1(config-router-af)#neighbor spokes route-map default out
```

**On R7:**

```
R7(config)#no router eigrp 100

R7(config)#ip prefix-list TST permit 0.0.0.0/0
```

```
R7(config)#route-map default permit 10
R7(config-route-map)#match ip address prefix-list TST

R7(config)#router bgp 100
R7(config-router)#neighbor spokes peer-group
R7(config-router)#neighbor spokes remote 100
R7(config-router)#neighbor spokes timers 6 20
R7(config-router)#bgp listen range 100.1.1.0/24 peer-group spokes

R7(config-router)#address-family ipv4
R7(config-router-af)#neighbor spokes route-reflector-client
R7(config-router-af)#neighbor spokes route-map default out
R7(config-router-af)#neighbor spokes default-originate
```

## On R2:

```
R2(config)#no router eigrp 100

R2(config)#route-map local-pref permit 10
R2(config-route-map)#set local-preference 150

R2(config)#router bgp 100
R2(config-router)#neighbor 100.1.1.1 remote-as 100
R2(config-router)#neighbor 100.1.1.7 remote-as 100

R2(config-router)#address-family ipv4
R2(config-router-af)#network 24.1.1.0 mask 255.255.255.0
R2(config-router-af)#neighbor 100.1.1.1 route-map local-pref in

R2#clear ip bgp * in
```

You should see the following console messages:

```
%BGP-5-ADJCHANGE: neighbor 100.1.1.1 Up
%BGP-5-ADJCHANGE: neighbor 100.1.1.7 Up
```

## On R3:

```
R3(config)#no router eigrp 100

R3(config)#route-map local-pref permit 10
R3(config-route-map)#set local-preference 150
```

```
R3(config)#router bgp 100
R3(config-router)#neighbor 100.1.1.1 remote-as 100
R3(config-router)#neighbor 100.1.1.7 remote-as 100

R3(config-router)#address-family ipv4
R3(config-router-af)#neighbor 100.1.1.1 route-map local-pref in
R3(config-router-af)#network 36.1.1.0 mask 255.255.255.0
```

```
R3#clear ip bgp * in
```

You should see the following console messages:

```
%BGP-5-ADJCHANGE: neighbor 100.1.1.1 Up
%BGP-5-ADJCHANGE: neighbor 100.1.1.7 Up
```

After the iBGP peerings are formed between the hub and spoke routers, R2 and R3's BGP table shows the two default routes. The default route from R1 is selected as best because of the higher local preference value of 150 when compared to the default local preference value 100 from R7:

### On R2:

```
R2#show ip bgp | begin Net

     Network          Next Hop          Metric LocPrf Weight Path
 * i  0.0.0.0          100.1.1.7              0    100      0 i
 *>i                   100.1.1.1              0    150      0 i
 *>   24.1.1.0/24      0.0.0.0                0           32768 i


R2#show ip route bgp | begin Gate
Gateway of last resort is 100.1.1.1 to network 0.0.0.0

B*    0.0.0.0/0 [200/0] via 100.1.1.1, 00:09:04
```

### On R3:

```
R3#show ip bgp | begin Net

     Network          Next Hop          Metric LocPrf Weight Path
 * i  0.0.0.0          100.1.1.7              0    100      0 i
 *>i                   100.1.1.1              0    150      0 i
 *>   36.1.1.0/24      0.0.0.0                0           32768 i
```

```
R3#show ip route bgp | begin Gate
Gateway of last resort is 100.1.1.1 to network 0.0.0.0


B*    0.0.0.0/0 [200/0] via 100.1.1.1, 00:05:06
```

To provide proper connectivity to R8, R1 is also configured to redistribute BGP prefixes into EIGRP using the **redistribute bgp** command under the EIGRP configuration mode.

BGP must also be configured to allow iBGP prefixes to be redistributed into an IGP. This is done using the **bgp redistribute-internal** command configured on R1 under the BGP configuration mode. R7 will continue to provide reachability to R8 via the EIGRP default route:

## On R1:

```
R1(config)#router bgp 100
R1(config-router)#address-family ipv4
R1(config-router-af)#bgp redistribute-internal


R1(config)#router eigrp 100
R1(config-router)#network 187.1.1.1 0.0.0.0
R1(config-router)#redistribute bgp 100 metric 1 1 1 1 1
```

## On R7:

```
R7(config)#router eigrp 100
R7(config-router)#network 187.1.1.7 0.0.0.0

R7(config-router)#interface g0/9
R7(config-if)#ip summary-address eigrp 100 0.0.0.0 0.0.0.0
```

## On R8:

Following configuration from R8 has been retained from the earlier task:

```
R8(config)#router eigrp 100
R8(config-router)#network 187.1.1.8 0.0.0.0
R8(config-router)#network 18.1.1.8 0.0.0.0


R8#show ip route | begin Gate
Gateway of last resort is 187.1.1.7 to network 0.0.0.0


D*    0.0.0.0/0 [90/3072] via 187.1.1.7, 00:01:56, GigabitEthernet0/9
      18.0.0.0/32 is subnetted, 1 subnets
```

```
C          18.1.1.8 is directly connected, Loopback1
        24.0.0.0/24 is subnetted, 1 subnets
D EX       24.1.1.0 [170/2560000512] via 187.1.1.1, 00:00:22,
GigabitEthernet0/9
        36.0.0.0/24 is subnetted, 1 subnets
D EX       36.1.1.0 [170/2560000512] via 187.1.1.1, 00:00:22,
GigabitEthernet0/9
        187.1.0.0/16 is variably subnetted, 2 subnets, 2 masks
C          187.1.1.0/24 is directly connected, GigabitEthernet0/9
L          187.1.1.8/32 is directly connected, GigabitEthernet0/9
```

After this configuration, R8 again chooses the specific prefixes over the default route received from R7. Much as in the EIGRP section, redundancy is confirmed by shutting down the tunnel 100 interface on R1, resulting in the spokes using the default route from R7. The dynamic NHRP mapping entries are cleared on R2 and R3 with the **clear ip nhrp** command. Following this, traceroute from R4 to R6 confirms Hub R7 as the active hub in use:

### On R1:

```
R1(config)#interface tunnel 100
R1(config-if)#shut
```

### On R2:

```
R2#show ip bgp | begin Net

     Network          Next Hop          Metric LocPrf Weight Path
 *>i  0.0.0.0          100.1.1.7              0    100      0 i
 *>   24.1.1.0/24      0.0.0.0                0          32768 i

On R2 and R3:

Rx#clear ip nhrp
```

### On R3:

```
R3#show ip route bgp | begin Gate
Gateway of last resort is 100.1.1.7 to network 0.0.0.0

B*     0.0.0.0/0 [200/0] via 100.1.1.7, 00:00:49
```

Traceroute from R4 to R8's loopback address uses Hub R7. Traceroute to the remote spoke network from R4 first transits over Hub R7. Subsequent traceroute is shown to use the spoke-to-spoke tunnel between R2 and R3:

**On R4:**

```
R4#traceroute 18.1.1.8 probe 1

Type escape sequence to abort.
Tracing the route to 18.1.1.8
VRF info: (vrf in name/id, vrf out name/id)
  1 24.1.1.2 13 msec
  2 100.1.1.7 8 msec
  3 187.1.1.8 15 msec


R4#traceroute 36.1.1.6 probe 1

Type escape sequence to abort.
Tracing the route to 36.1.1.6
VRF info: (vrf in name/id, vrf out name/id)
  1 24.1.1.2 14 msec
  2 100.1.1.7 8 msec
  3 100.1.1.3 19 msec
  4 36.1.1.6 20 msec


R4#traceroute 36.1.1.6 probe 1

Type escape sequence to abort.
Tracing the route to 36.1.1.6
VRF info: (vrf in name/id, vrf out name/id)
  1 24.1.1.2 3 msec
  2 100.1.1.3 6 msec
  3 36.1.1.6 13 msec
```

## Implement eBGP

Finally, the eBGP configuration once again mimics the configuration in the single-hub, dual-cloud configuration. BGP can again be configured such that all spokes are configured to be in the same AS or different autonomous systems. Here we outline the configuration steps for both methods, where the path engineering steps are the same for the two methods.

### Spokes in the Same AS

If the spokes are members of the same AS, the peer group configuration for the BGP listen range should set the remote AS to the spoke AS. Notice that there is no need to issue the **allowas-in** command on the spokes. The spokes will not receive each other's prefixes through BGP because the hubs are sending a default route down to the spokes. When the spoke-to-spoke tunnel is formed, an NHRP route is installed that does not carry the AS path information. The following commands configure BGP on R1, R7, R2, and R3 for same AS DMVPN Phase 3 operation:

---

**On R1:**

```
R1(config-router)#interface tunnel 100
R1(config-if)#no shut

R1(config)#router bgp 100
R1(config-router)#no neighbor spokes remote-as 100
R1(config-router)#no neighbor spokes route-reflector-client

R1(config-router)#neighbor spokes remote-as 230
```

**On R7:**

```
R7(config)#router bgp 100
R7(config-router)#no neighbor spokes remote 100
R7(config-router)#no neighbor spokes route-reflector-client

R7(config-router)#neighbor spokes remote-as 230
```

**On R2:**

```
R2(config)#no router bgp 100
```

The **route-map local-pref** from the previous section was not removed and is therefore used in this configuration:

```
R2(config)#router bgp 230
R2(config-router)#neighbor 100.1.1.1 remote 100
R2(config-router)#neighbor 100.1.1.7 remote 100

R2(config-router)#address-family ipv4
R2(config-router-af)#network 24.1.1.0 mask 255.255.255.0
R2(config-router-af)#neighbor 100.1.1.1 route-map local-pref in
```

## On R3:

```
R3(config)#no router bgp 100
```

**NOTE:** The **route-map local-pref** from the previous section was not removed and is therefore used in this configuration:

```
R3(config)#router bgp 230
R3(config-router)#neighbor 100.1.1.1 remote-as 100
R3(config-router)#neighbor 100.1.1.7 remote-as 100

R3(config-router)#address-family ipv4
R3(config-router-af)#network 36.1.1.0 mask 255.255.255.0
R3(config-router-af)#neighbor 100.1.1.1 route-map local-pref in
```

```
R3#clear ip bgp * in
```

Here, local preference is once again modified on the spoke side to prefer R1's paths over R7's. After the configurations have been entered and the peerings come up, R2's and R3's routing tables reflect the preferences. The resulting BGP tables on R2 and R3 are as follows:

## On R2:

```
R2#show ip bgp | begin Net

     Network          Next Hop          Metric LocPrf Weight Path
 *>  0.0.0.0          100.1.1.1                   150      0 100 i
 *                    100.1.1.7                            0 100 i
 *>  24.1.1.0/24      0.0.0.0                0         32768 i
```

## On R3:

```
R3#show ip bgp | begin Net

     Network          Next Hop          Metric LocPrf Weight Path
 *>  0.0.0.0          100.1.1.1                   150      0 100 i
 *                    100.1.1.7                            0 100 i
 *>  36.1.1.0/24      0.0.0.0                0         32768 i
```

## Spokes in Different Autonomous Systems

With the spokes in different autonomous systems, the major configuration change that must be made is on the individual spokes and on the peer group configuration on the hub routers. First, the peer group needs to include the additional spoke ASNs via the **alternate-as** command. The spoke BGP processes need to be configured with the proper ASN as well.

After that configuration, the same path engineering mechanic—modifying the local preference on the spokes is implemented to drive path preference:

---

**On R1:**

```
R1(config)#router bgp 100
R1(config-router)#no neighbor spokes remote-as 230
R1(config-router)#neighbor spokes remote-as 200 alternate-as 300
```

**On R7:**

```
R7(config)#router bgp 100
R7(config-router)#no neighbor spokes remote-as 230
R7(config-router)#neighbor spokes remote 200 alternate-as 300
```

**On R2:**

```
R2(config)#no router bgp 230

R2(config)#router bgp 200
R2(config-router)#bgp log-neighbor-changes
R2(config-router)#neighbor 100.1.1.1 remote-as 100
R2(config-router)#neighbor 100.1.1.7 remote-as 100

R2(config-router)#address-family ipv4
R2(config-router-af)#network 24.1.1.0 mask 255.255.255.0
R2(config-router-af)#neighbor 100.1.1.1 route-map local-pref in
```

You should see the following console messages:

```
%BGP-5-ADJCHANGE: neighbor 100.1.1.7 Up
%BGP-5-ADJCHANGE: neighbor 100.1.1.1 Up
```

---

**On R3:**

```
R3(config)#no router bgp 230

R3(config)#router bgp 300
R3(config-router)#neighbor 100.1.1.1 remote-as 100
R3(config-router)#neighbor 100.1.1.7 remote-as 100

R3(config-router)#address-family ipv4
R3(config-router-af)#network 36.1.1.0 mask 255.255.255.0
R3(config-router-af)#neighbor 100.1.1.1 route-map local-pref in
```

You should see the following console messages:

```
%BGP-5-ADJCHANGE: neighbor 100.1.1.7 Up
%BGP-5-ADJCHANGE: neighbor 100.1.1.1 Up
```

After the configurations above are applied, the BGP tables on R2 and R3 reflect R1's path for the default route as the chosen best path.

**On R2:**

```
R2#show ip bgp | begin Net

     Network          Next Hop          Metric LocPrf Weight Path
 *>   0.0.0.0          100.1.1.1                  150        0 100 i
 *                     100.1.1.7                             0 100 i
 *>   24.1.1.0/24      0.0.0.0                0             32768 i

R2#show ip route bgp | begin Gate
Gateway of last resort is 100.1.1.1 to network 0.0.0.0

B*    0.0.0.0/0 [20/0] via 100.1.1.1, 00:07:01
```

**On R3:**

```
R3#show ip bgp | begin Net

     Network          Next Hop          Metric LocPrf Weight Path
 *    0.0.0.0          100.1.1.7                             0 100 i
```

```
*>                      100.1.1.1                        150      0 100 i
*>    36.1.1.0/24       0.0.0.0                    0            32768 i
```

```
R3#show ip route bgp | begin Gate
Gateway of last resort is 100.1.1.1 to network 0.0.0.0
```

```
B*    0.0.0.0/0 [20/0] via 100.1.1.1, 00:05:40
```

BGP should be redistributed into EIGRP 100 for reachability. This configuration has already been performed in an earlier task. Notice the output from R8 below. It has a EIGRP default route from R7 and specific BGP prefixes for the remote LAN networks from R1:

**On R8:**

```
R8#show ip route eigrp 100 | begin Gate
Gateway of last resort is 187.1.1.7 to network 0.0.0.0
```

```
D*    0.0.0.0/0 [90/3072] via 187.1.1.7, 01:24:20, GigabitEthernet0/9
      24.0.0.0/24 is subnetted, 1 subnets
D EX     24.1.1.0 [170/2560000512] via 187.1.1.1, 00:12:15,
GigabitEthernet0/9
      36.0.0.0/24 is subnetted, 1 subnets
D EX     36.1.1.0 [170/2560000512] via 187.1.1.1, 00:09:42,
GigabitEthernet0/9
```

When routing to the destination remote networks, R8 will always choose the specific path from R1 over the default route from R7.

The traceroute outputs below verifies connectivity between the remote networks. A traceroute to 18.1.1.8 from R4 is sent to R1. Traffic from R4 to the remote network on R6 first traverses the hub R1. Subsequent traceroutes show this traffic using the spoke-to-spoke tunnel between R2 and R3:

**On R4:**

```
R4#traceroute 18.1.1.8 probe 1
```

```
Type escape sequence to abort.
Tracing the route to 18.1.1.8
VRF info: (vrf in name/id, vrf out name/id)
  1 24.1.1.2 15 msec
  2 100.1.1.1 7 msec
  3 187.1.1.8 12 msec
```

```
R4#traceroute 36.1.1.6 probe 1

Type escape sequence to abort.
Tracing the route to 36.1.1.6
VRF info: (vrf in name/id, vrf out name/id)
  1 24.1.1.2 3 msec
  2 100.1.1.1 6 msec
  3 100.1.1.3 18 msec
  4 36.1.1.6 20 msec

R4#traceroute 36.1.1.6 probe 1

Type escape sequence to abort.
Tracing the route to 36.1.1.6
VRF info: (vrf in name/id, vrf out name/id)
  1 24.1.1.2 5 msec
  2 100.1.1.3 6 msec
  3 36.1.1.6 10 msec
```

For both design cases (Spokes in the same AS or in different AS), redundancy is confirmed by shutting down the tunnel 100 interface on R1. A clear ip nhrp is issued on R2 and R3. Following this, traceroutes between remote networks verify the use of Hub R7:

## On R1:

```
R1(config)#interface tunnel 100
R1(config-if)#shut
```

## On R2 and R3:

```
Rx#clear ip nhrp
```

## On R2:

```
R2#show ip bgp | begin Net

    Network          Next Hop          Metric LocPrf Weight Path
 *>  0.0.0.0          100.1.1.7                            0 100 i
 *>  24.1.1.0/24      0.0.0.0                0        32768 i
```

**On R3:**

```
R3#show ip bgp | begin Net

      Network           Next Hop           Metric LocPrf Weight Path
 *>   0.0.0.0           100.1.1.7                            0 100 i
 *>   36.1.1.0/24       0.0.0.0                 0        32768 i
R4#traceroute 18.1.1.8 probe 1
Type escape sequence to abort.
Tracing the route to 18.1.1.8
VRF info: (vrf in name/id, vrf out name/id)
  1 24.1.1.2 1 msec
  2 100.1.1.7 2 msec
  3 187.1.1.8 3 msec


R4#traceroute 36.1.1.6 probe 1
Type escape sequence to abort.
Tracing the route to 36.1.1.6
VRF info: (vrf in name/id, vrf out name/id)
  1 24.1.1.2 1 msec
  2 100.1.1.7 2 msec
  3 100.1.1.3 3 msec
  4 36.1.1.6 7 msec


R4#traceroute 36.1.1.6 probe 1
Type escape sequence to abort.
Tracing the route to 36.1.1.6
VRF info: (vrf in name/id, vrf out name/id)
  1 24.1.1.2 1 msec
  2 100.1.1.3 2 msec
  3 36.1.1.6 3 msec
```

# Lab 4: Dual Hub, Dual Cloud

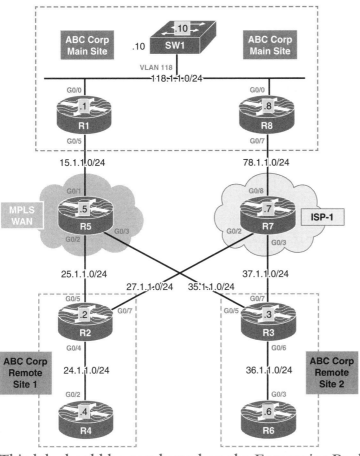

This lab should be conducted on the Enterprise Rack.

Lab Setup:

If you are using EVE-NG, and you have imported the EVE-NG topology from the **EVE-NG-Topology** folder, ignore the following and use **Lab-4-Dual Hub Dual Cloud** in the **DMVPN** folder in EVE-NG.

To copy and paste the initial configurations, go to the **Initial-config** folder → **DMVPN** folder → **Lab-4**.

As with the base configuration in the dual-hub, single-cloud section, the LAN at the main site now includes three devices (R1, R8, SW1) connected to the same LAN interface, as shown in the diagram above.

To prevent asymmetric routing issues that could interfere with efficient routing, EIGRP is once again run on the LAN. R1 advertises specific prefixes, using redistribution if necessary, and R8 advertises a default summary route. SW1 chooses the more specific route through R1 (the MPLS-WAN connection) if R1 is advertising the specific prefixes. If R1's tunnel 100 fails, it withdraws its specific prefix, leaving the default route through R8.

The configuration below sets up this basic routing:

---

**On R1:**

```
R1(config)#router eigrp 100
R1(config-router)#network 118.1.1.1 0.0.0.0
```

**On R8:**

```
R8(config)#router eigrp 100
R8(config-router)#network 118.1.1.8 0.0.0.0
```

You should see the following console message:

```
%DUAL-5-NBRCHANGE: EIGRP-IPv4 100: Neighbor 118.1.1.1
(GigabitEthernet0/0) is up: new adjacency
```

```
R8(config)#interface g0/0
R8(config-if)#ip summary-address eigrp 100 0.0.0.0 0.0.0.0
```

**On SW1:**

```
SW1(config)#router eigrp 100
SW1(config-router)#network 118.1.1.10 0.0.0.0
SW1(config-router)#network 18.1.1.8 0.0.0.0
```

You should see the following console messages:

```
%DUAL-5-NBRCHANGE: EIGRP-IPv4 100: Neighbor 118.1.1.1 (Vlan118) is up:
new adjacency
```

```
%DUAL-5-NBRCHANGE: EIGRP-IPv4 100: Neighbor 118.1.1.8 (Vlan118) is up:
new adjacency
```

The routing table from SW1 is shown below. Since routing hasn't been established over DMVPN yet, the only EIGRP route SW1 learns is the default route from R8:

**To verify the configuration:**

```
SW1#show ip route eigrp 100 | begin Gate
Gateway of last resort is 118.1.1.8 to network 0.0.0.0

D*    0.0.0.0/0 [90/3072] via 118.1.1.8, 00:02:44, Vlan118
```

---

## Implement Phase 3

## Design Goal

After reviewing the previous proposal, ABC Corp, based on its previous experience, questions the network design firm on the reliability of a single Internet connection for transport between the organization's sites. ABC asks for an additional proof of concept for an MPLS WAN circuit as a primary path and the Internet connection as a backup path. The same requirements of site-to-site connectivity are also applied to this design.

### DMVPN Tunnel Configuration

The design goal above expands on the previous design goal by adding an additional ISP transport to the design proposal from the dual-hub, single-cloud configuration. The requirements are the same except that now, each hub will represent a separate DMVPN cloud connected to a specific ISP connection—in order to provide both transport and hub redundancy.

All the other requirements of direct spoke-to-spoke communication and simplified routing tables apply to this design goal as well. DMVPN Phase 3 will be implemented using EIGRP and BGP. OSPF will not be used due to the limitation of summarization from the hub to the spokes.

Below is the proposed configuration for the DMVPN Phase 3. R1 connects solely to the MPLS WAN circuit, and R8 connects solely to ISP-1. R2 and R3 are dual connected, with a single interface toward each transport. Tunnel 100 is configured on R1, R2, and R3 using source IP addresses from the MPLS WAN circuit and network ID 100. Tunnel 200 is configured on R8, R2, and R3 using source IP addresses from ISP-1 and network ID 200.

---

**On Hub R1:**

```
R1(config)#interface tunnel 100
R1(config-if)#ip address 100.1.1.1 255.255.255.0
R1(config-if)#tunnel source 15.1.1.1
R1(config-if)#tunnel mode gre multipoint
R1(config-if)#ip nhrp network-id 100
R1(config-if)#ip nhrp map multicast dynamic
R1(config-if)#ip nhrp redirect
```

**On Hub R8:**

```
R8(config)#interface tunnel 200
R8(config-if)#ip address 200.1.1.8 255.255.255.0
```

```
R8(config-if)#tunnel source 78.1.1.8
R8(config-if)#tunnel mode gre multipoint
R8(config-if)#ip nhrp network-id 200
R8(config-if)#ip nhrp map multicast dynamic
R8(config-if)#ip nhrp redirect
```

## On R2:

```
R2(config)#interface tunnel 100
R2(config-if)#ip address 100.1.1.2 255.255.255.0
R2(config-if)#tunnel source 25.1.1.2
R2(config-if)#tunnel mode gre multipoint
R2(config-if)#ip nhrp network-id 100
R2(config-if)#ip nhrp nhs 100.1.1.1 nbma 15.1.1.1 multicast
R2(config-if)#ip nhrp shortcut

R2(config)#interface tunnel 200
R2(config-if)#ip address 200.1.1.2 255.255.255.0
R2(config-if)#tunnel source 27.1.1.2
R2(config-if)#tunnel mode gre multipoint
R2(config-if)#ip nhrp network-id 200
R2(config-if)#ip nhrp nhs 200.1.1.8 nbma 78.1.1.8 multicast
R2(config-if)#ip nhrp shortcut
```

## On R3:

```
R3(config)#interface tunnel 100
R3(config-if)#ip address 100.1.1.3 255.255.255.0
R3(config-if)#tunnel source 35.1.1.3
R3(config-if)#tunnel mode gre multipoint
R3(config-if)#ip nhrp network-id 100
R3(config-if)#ip nhrp nhs 100.1.1.1 nbma 15.1.1.1 multicast
R3(config-if)#ip nhrp shortcut

R3(config)#interface tunnel 200
R3(config-if)#ip address 200.1.1.3 255.255.255.0
R3(config-if)#tunnel source 37.1.1.3
R3(config-if)#tunnel mode gre multipoint
R3(config-if)#ip nhrp network-id 200
R3(config-if)#ip nhrp nhs 200.1.1.8 nbma 78.1.1.8 multicast
R3(config-if)#ip nhrp shortcut
```

### To verify the configuration:

The following verifies the state of the tunnels on the hub routers. As seen below, both spokes have successfully registered with the hubs R1 and R8:

### On R1:

```
R1#show dmvpn | begin Peer NBMA

 # Ent   Peer NBMA Addr Peer Tunnel Add State   UpDn Tm Attrb
 ----- --------------- --------------- ----- -------- -----
     1 25.1.1.2                100.1.1.2   UP 00:08:10     D
     1 35.1.1.3                100.1.1.3   UP 00:03:21     D
```

### On R8:

```
R8#show dmvpn | begin Peer NBMA

 # Ent   Peer NBMA Addr Peer Tunnel Add State   UpDn Tm Attrb
 ----- --------------- --------------- ----- -------- -----
     1 27.1.1.2                200.1.1.2   UP 00:06:28     D
     1 37.1.1.3                200.1.1.3   UP 00:02:31     D
```

## Implement EIGRP

At this point in the guided lab, the basic EIGRP configuration for Phase 3 DMVPN has been well established. The same configuration principles applied to the previous versions all apply to this design as well. EIGRP should be configured on all tunnel interfaces with the same EIGRP ASN. The hubs R1 and R8 should be configured to send a summary default route down to the spokes out their tunnel 100 and tunnel 200 interfaces. Host networks at the remote site are also advertised into EIGRP 100 with the **network** command. The LAN interfaces are declared as passive interfaces under the EIGRP configuration mode:

### On R1:

```
R1(config)#router eigrp 100
R1(config-router)#network 100.1.1.1 0.0.0.0

R1(config)#interface tunnel 100
R1(config-if)#ip summary-address eigrp 100 0.0.0.0 0.0.0.0
```

#### On R8:

```
R8(config)#router eigrp 100
R8(config-router)#network 200.1.1.8 0.0.0.0

R8(config)#interface tunnel 200
R8(config-if)#ip summary-address eigrp 100 0.0.0.0 0.0.0.0
```

#### On R2:

```
R2(config)#router eigrp 100
R2(config-router)#network 24.1.1.2 0.0.0.0
R2(config-router)#network 100.1.1.2 0.0.0.0
R2(config-router)#network 200.1.1.2 0.0.0.0
R2(config-router)#passive-interface g0/4
```

You should see the following console messages:

```
%DUAL-5-NBRCHANGE: EIGRP-IPv4 100: Neighbor 100.1.1.1 (Tunnel100) is
up: new adjacency

%DUAL-5-NBRCHANGE: EIGRP-IPv4 100: Neighbor 200.1.1.8 (Tunnel200) is
up: new adjacency
```

#### On R3:

```
R3(config)#router eigrp 100
R3(config-router)#network 36.1.1.3 0.0.0.0
R3(config-router)#network 100.1.1.3 0.0.0.0
R3(config-router)#network 200.1.1.3 0.0.0.0
R3(config-router)#passive-interface g0/6
```

You should see the following console messages:

```
%DUAL-5-NBRCHANGE: EIGRP-IPv4 100: Neighbor 100.1.1.1 (Tunnel100) is
up: new adjacency

%DUAL-5-NBRCHANGE: EIGRP-IPv4 100: Neighbor 200.1.1.8 (Tunnel200) is
up: new adjacency
```

#### To verify the configuration:

On completing the above, spokes R2 and R3 each form EIGRP neighborships with both hubs. Their routing tables below show the two EIGRP default routes they learn from both R1 and R8:

```
R3#show ip route eigrp 100 | begin Gate
Gateway of last resort is 200.1.1.8 to network 0.0.0.0

D*    0.0.0.0/0 [90/26880256] via 200.1.1.8, 00:00:56, Tunnel200
                [90/26880256] via 100.1.1.1, 00:00:56, Tunnel100
```

## On R2:

```
R2#show ip route eigrp 100 | begin Gate
Gateway of last resort is 200.1.1.8 to network 0.0.0.0

D*    0.0.0.0/0 [90/26880256] via 200.1.1.8, 00:03:09, Tunnel200
                [90/26880256] via 100.1.1.1, 00:03:09, Tunnel100
```

With EIGRP configured over the DMVPN, the show ip route command is issued on SW1. SW1 receives specific EIGRP prefixes from R1 for the remote host networks and an EIGRP default route from R8:

```
SW1#show ip route eigrp 100 | begin Gate
Gateway of last resort is 118.1.1.8 to network 0.0.0.0

D*    0.0.0.0/0 [90/3072] via 118.1.1.8, 00:58:44, Vlan118
      24.0.0.0/24 is subnetted, 1 subnets
D        24.1.1.0 [90/26880512] via 118.1.1.1, 00:04:27, Vlan118
      36.0.0.0/24 is subnetted, 1 subnets
D        36.1.1.0 [90/26880512] via 118.1.1.1, 00:02:48, Vlan118
      100.0.0.0/24 is subnetted, 1 subnets
D        100.1.1.0 [90/26880256] via 118.1.1.1, 00:07:02, Vlan118
D      200.1.1.0/24 [90/28160256] via 118.1.1.1, 00:04:23, Vlan118
```

SW1 will always prefer the specific prefixes from R1 over the generic default route from R8 to remote host networks. This prevents the asymmetric routing situation described earlier.

As expected, R2 and R3 have decided to perform ECMP for the default summary route they are receiving from R1 and R8. In the previous section, an offset list was applied on the hub to give preference to R1's routes. This topology will employ the same technique. An offset list is configured on R8 that adds 500 to the delay value of routes sent out the tunnel 200 interface to make it less preferrable:

## On R8:

```
R8(config)#router eigrp 100
R8(config-router)#offset-list 0 out 500 tunnel 200
```

## On R2:

```
R2#show ip route eigrp 100 | begin Gate
Gateway of last resort is 100.1.1.1 to network 0.0.0.0

D*    0.0.0.0/0 [90/26880256] via 100.1.1.1, 00:02:24, Tunnel100
```

## On R3:

```
R3#show ip route eigrp 100 | begin Gate
Gateway of last resort is 100.1.1.1 to network 0.0.0.0

D*    0.0.0.0/0 [90/26880256] via 100.1.1.1, 00:03:08, Tunnel100
```

Traceroute from R4 to 18.1.1.8 traverses the primary hub R1. Traceroute from R4 to 36.1.1.6 also first traverses the primary hub R1. Subsequent traceroute is shown to use the direct spoke-to-spoke tunnel between R2 and R3:

## On R4:

```
R4#traceroute 18.1.1.8 probe 1

Type escape sequence to abort.
Tracing the route to 18.1.1.8
VRF info: (vrf in name/id, vrf out name/id)
  1 24.1.1.2 40 msec
  2 100.1.1.1 51 msec
  3 118.1.1.10 11 msec

R4#traceroute 36.1.1.6 probe 1

Type escape sequence to abort.
Tracing the route to 36.1.1.6
VRF info: (vrf in name/id, vrf out name/id)
  1 24.1.1.2 14 msec
  2 100.1.1.1 10 msec
  3 100.1.1.3 10 msec
  4 36.1.1.6 25 msec

R4#traceroute 36.1.1.6 probe 1

Type escape sequence to abort.
Tracing the route to 36.1.1.6
```

```
VRF info: (vrf in name/id, vrf out name/id)
  1 24.1.1.2 4 msec
  2 100.1.1.3 8 msec
  3 36.1.1.6 12 msec
```

To verify the redundancy, following the **traceroute** commands used above, the G0/5 interface is shut down on R1 to simulate a physical link failure. The NHRP table is again cleared on both R2 and R3 to simulate a new registration. Subsequent packets are registered through hub R8 instead of R1 and use the 200.1.1.0/24 DMVPN cloud:

## On R1:

```
R1(config)#interface g0/5
R1(config-if)#shut
```

## On R2:

```
R2#clear ip nhrp

R2#show ip route eigrp 100 | begin Gate
Gateway of last resort is 200.1.1.8 to network 0.0.0.0

D*    0.0.0.0/0 [90/26880756] via 200.1.1.8, 00:00:26, Tunnel200
```

## On R4:

```
R4#traceroute 36.1.1.6 probe 1

Type escape sequence to abort.
Tracing the route to 36.1.1.6
VRF info: (vrf in name/id, vrf out name/id)
  1 24.1.1.2 9 msec
  2 200.1.1.8 10 msec
  3 200.1.1.3 12 msec
  4 36.1.1.6 18 msec


R4#traceroute 36.1.1.6 probe 1

Type escape sequence to abort.
Tracing the route to 36.1.1.6
VRF info: (vrf in name/id, vrf out name/id)
  1 24.1.1.2 3 msec
  2 200.1.1.3 8 msec
  3 36.1.1.6 13 msec
```

## Implement iBGP

To establish basic iBGP connectivity, R1 will be a route reflector for R2 and R3 over the tunnel 100 interface and R8 will do the same for R2 and R3 over the tunnel 200 interface. R1 will listen for peers from the 100.1.1.0/24 network and R8 for the 200.1.1.0/24 network.

Like the earlier iBGP designs, R1 and R8 will be configured as route-reflectors for their peers over the tunnel 100 and tunnel 200 interfaces respectively. Both the hubs will be configured for dynamic iBGP peerings. The listen range for peers over tunnel 100 will be in the 100.1.1.0/24 network range and 200.1.1.0/24 over the tunnel 200. Additionally, similar to earlier sections, R1 and R8 will be configured to propagate a BGP default route to the spokes while suppressing the more specific prefixes. BGP timers are also modified to allow faster convergence during testing.

However, prior to configuring BGP, the G0/5 interface on R1 is brought back up again. Certain EIGRP related configuration is to be removed as seen below:

```
On R1:

R1(config)#interface g0/5
R1(config-if)#no shut
R1(config-if)#interface tunnel 100
R1(config-if)#no ip summary-address eigrp 100 0.0.0.0 0.0.0.0

R1(config)#router eigrp 100
R1(config-router)#no network 100.1.1.1 0.0.0.0


On R8:

R8(config)#interface Tunnel200
R8(config-if)#no ip summary-address eigrp 100 0.0.0.0 0.0.0.0

R8(config-if)#router eigrp 100
R8(config-router)#no network 200.1.1.8 0.0.0.0
R8(config-router)#no offset-list 0 out 500 Tunnel200


On R2:

R2(config)#no router eigrp 100


On R3:

R3(config)#no router eigrp 100
```

**BGP Configuration on R1:**

```
R1(config)#ip prefix-list TST permit 0.0.0.0/0

R1(config)#route-map default permit 10
R1(config-route-map)#match ip address prefix-list TST

R1(config)#router bgp 100
R1(config-router)#neighbor spokes peer-group
R1(config-router)#neighbor spokes remote 100
R1(config-router)#neighbor spokes timers 6 20
R1(config-router)#bgp listen range 100.1.1.0/24 peer-group spokes
R1(config-router)#address-family ipv4
R1(config-router-af)#neighbor spokes route-reflector-client
R1(config-router-af)#neighbor spokes default-originate
R1(config-router-af)#neighbor spokes route-map default out
```

**BGP Configuration on R8:**

```
R8(config)#ip prefix-list TST permit 0.0.0.0/0

R8(config)#route-map default permit 10
R8(config-route-map)#match ip address prefix-list TST

R8(config)#router bgp 100
R8(config-router)#neighbor spokes peer-group
R8(config-router)#neighbor spokes remote 100
R8(config-router)#neighbor spokes timers 6 20
R8(config-router)#bgp listen range 200.1.1.0/24 peer-group spokes
R8(config-router)#address-family ipv4
R8(config-router-af)#neighbor spokes route-reflector-client
R8(config-router-af)#neighbor spokes default-originate
R8(config-router-af)#neighbor spokes route-map default out
```

**On R2:**

```
R2(config)#router bgp 100
R2(config-router)#neighbor 100.1.1.1 remote-as 100
R2(config-router)#neighbor 200.1.1.8 remote-as 100
R2(config-router)#network 24.1.1.0 mask 255.255.255.0
```

## On R3:

```
R3(config)#router bgp 100
R3(config-router)#neighbor 100.1.1.1 remote-as 100
R3(config-router)#neighbor 200.1.1.8 remote-as 100
R3(config-router)#network 36.1.1.0 mask 255.255.255.0
```

As in the previous case, to provide proper connectivity to SW1, R1 is also configured to redistribute BGP prefixes into EIGRP using the redistribute bgp command in EIGRP configuration mode. In certain IOS versions, iBPG routes are not redistributed into an IGP by default. The bgp redistribute-internal command in BGP configuration mode can be used to instruct the router to redistribute iBGP prefixes as well:

## On R1:

```
R1(config)#router eigrp 100
R1(config-router)#redistribute bgp 100 metric 1 1 1 1 1
```

```
R1(config)#router bgp 100
R1(config-router)#bgp redistribute-internal
```

SW1's routing table now verifies the EIGRP routes it learns. It learns the specific remote host networks from R1 and the less specific default route from R8:

## On SW1:

```
SW1#show ip route eigrp 100 | begin Gate
Gateway of last resort is 118.1.1.8 to network 0.0.0.0

D*    0.0.0.0/0 [90/3072] via 118.1.1.8, 01:36:03, Vlan118
      24.0.0.0/24 is subnetted, 1 subnets
D        24.1.1.0 [90/26880512] via 118.1.1.1, 00:20:14, Vlan118
      36.0.0.0/24 is subnetted, 1 subnets
D        36.1.1.0 [90/26880512] via 118.1.1.1, 00:20:22, Vlan118
      100.0.0.0/24 is subnetted, 1 subnets
D        100.1.1.0 [90/26880256] via 118.1.1.1, 00:21:01, Vlan118
D     200.1.1.0/24 [90/28160256] via 118.1.1.1, 00:20:14, Vlan118
```

R2 and R3 BGP table shows default routes from R1 and R8.

**On R2:**

```
R2#show ip bgp | begin Neighbor
     Network          Next Hop         Metric LocPrf Weight Path
 * i 0.0.0.0          200.1.1.8             0    100      0 i
 *>i                  100.1.1.1             0    100      0 i
 *>  24.1.1.0/24      0.0.0.0               0         32768 i
```

**On R3:**

```
R3#show ip bgp | begin Neighbor
     Network          Next Hop         Metric LocPrf Weight Path
 *>i 0.0.0.0          100.1.1.1             0    100      0 i
 * i                  200.1.1.8             0    100      0 i
 *>  36.1.1.0/24      0.0.0.0               0         32768 i
```

Though the current path is through the primary hub R1, to achieve a more deterministic path selection, the local preference value is modified for the path learned from R1 to 150 on R2 and R3.

**On R2:**

```
R2(config)#route-map local-pref permit 10
R2(config-route-map)#set local-preference 150

R2(config)#router bgp 100
R2(config-router)#address-family ipv4
R2(config-router-af)#neighbor 100.1.1.1 route-map local-pref in

R2#clear ip bgp * in
```

**On R3:**

```
R3(config)#route-map local-pref permit 10
R3(config-route-map)#set local-preference 150

R3(config)#router bgp 100
R3(config-router)#address-family ipv4
R3(config-router-af)#neighbor 100.1.1.1 route-map local-pref in

R3#clear ip bgp * in
```

The outputs below verify the local preference value for path over the tunnel 100 is 150:

**On R2:**

```
R2#show ip bgp | begin Neighbor
     Network          Next Hop          Metric LocPrf Weight Path
 * i 0.0.0.0          200.1.1.8              0    100      0 i
 *>i                  100.1.1.1              0    150      0 i
 *>  24.1.1.0/24      0.0.0.0                0          32768 i
```

**On R3:**

```
R3#show ip bgp | begin Neighbor
     Network          Next Hop          Metric LocPrf Weight Path
 *>i 0.0.0.0          100.1.1.1              0    150      0 i
 * i                  200.1.1.8              0    100      0 i
 *>  36.1.1.0/24      0.0.0.0                0          32768 i
```

Traceroutes from R4 are issued to verify connectivity between remote sites. As seen below, a traceroute to 18.1.1.8 traverses the primary hub R1. The first traceroute to the remote host network 36.1.1.6 traverses the hub R1. Subsequent traceroute uses the spoke-to-spoke tunnel between R2 and R3:

**On R4:**

```
R4#traceroute 18.1.1.8 probe 1

Type escape sequence to abort.
Tracing the route to 18.1.1.8
VRF info: (vrf in name/id, vrf out name/id)
  1 24.1.1.2 12 msec
  2 100.1.1.1 7 msec
  3 118.1.1.10 6 msec

R4#traceroute 36.1.1.6 probe 1

Type escape sequence to abort.
Tracing the route to 36.1.1.6
VRF info: (vrf in name/id, vrf out name/id)
  1 24.1.1.2 4 msec
  2 100.1.1.1 8 msec
  3 100.1.1.3 16 msec
  4 36.1.1.6 22 msec

R4#traceroute 36.1.1.6 probe 1
```

```
Type escape sequence to abort.
Tracing the route to 36.1.1.6
VRF info: (vrf in name/id, vrf out name/id)
  1 24.1.1.2 9 msec
  2 100.1.1.3 22 msec
  3 36.1.1.6 16 msec
```

Redundancy is verified by shutting down the G0/5 interface on R1. The traceroute below verifies tunnel 200 via the secondary hub R8 in use:

## On R1:

```
R1(config)#interface g0/5
R1(config-if)#shut
```

## On R2:

```
R2#show ip bgp | begin Net

     Network          Next Hop          Metric LocPrf Weight Path
 r>i  0.0.0.0         200.1.1.8              0    100      0 i
 *>   24.1.1.0/24     0.0.0.0                0         32768 i
```

## On R3:

```
R3#show ip bgp | begin Net

     Network          Next Hop          Metric LocPrf Weight Path
 r>i  0.0.0.0         200.1.1.8              0    100      0 i
 *>   36.1.1.0/24     0.0.0.0                0         32768 i
```

## On R4:

```
R4#traceroute 18.1.1.8 probe 1

Type escape sequence to abort.
Tracing the route to 18.1.1.8
VRF info: (vrf in name/id, vrf out name/id)
  1 24.1.1.2 20 msec
  2 200.1.1.8 13 msec
  3 118.1.1.10 12 msec
```

```
R4#traceroute 36.1.1.6 probe 1

Type escape sequence to abort.
Tracing the route to 36.1.1.6
VRF info: (vrf in name/id, vrf out name/id)
  1 24.1.1.2 4 msec
  2 200.1.1.8 10 msec
  3 200.1.1.3 24 msec
  4 36.1.1.6 17 msec

R4#traceroute 36.1.1.6 probe 1

Type escape sequence to abort.
Tracing the route to 36.1.1.6
VRF info: (vrf in name/id, vrf out name/id)
  1 24.1.1.2 3 msec
  2 200.1.1.3 7 msec
  3 36.1.1.6 12 msec
```

## Implement eBGP

### Spokes in the Same AS

eBGP configuration using the spokes in the same AS follows the iBGP configuration
almost exactly. The notable differences are that R1 and R8 are not route reflectors for
the spokes. The same local preference modification can be performed on R2 and R3 to
prefer R1's paths over R8's. Below is the complete eBGP same-AS configuration for the
DMVPN.

**Note**  As mentioned previously, because the hub routers are sending a default route only,
there is no need to use the **allowas-in** command on the spokes. NHRP will install specific
or override prefixes in the routing table for those specific prefixes when resolving spoke-
to-spoke tunnels.

**On R1:**

The route map for the default route is still applied.

```
R1(config)#interface g0/5
R1(config-if)#no shut
```

```
R1(config)#router bgp 100
R1(config-router)#no neighbor spokes remote-as 100
R1(config-router)#neighbor spokes remote-as 230

R1(config-router)#address-family ipv4
R1(config-router)#no bgp redistribute-internal
R1(config-router-af)#no neighbor spokes route-reflector-client
```

## On R8:

```
R8(config)#router bgp 100
R8(config-router)#no neighbor spokes remote-as 100
R8(config-router)#neighbor spokes remote-as 230

R8(config-router)#address-family ipv4
R8(config-router-af)#no neighbor spokes route-reflector-client
```

## On R2:

```
R2(config)#no router bgp 100
```

The route map for the local preference is still applied.

```
R2(config)#router bgp 230
R2(config-router)#neighbor 100.1.1.1 remote-as 100
R2(config-router)#neighbor 200.1.1.8 remote-as 100

R2(config-router)#address-family ipv4
R2(config-router-af)#network 24.1.1.0 mask 255.255.255.0
R2(config-router-af)#neighbor 100.1.1.1 route-map local-pref in
```

You should see the following console messages:

```
%BGP-5-ADJCHANGE: neighbor 100.1.1.1 Up
%BGP-5-ADJCHANGE: neighbor 200.1.1.8 Up
```

## On R3:

```
R3(config)#no router bgp 100

R3(config)#router bgp 230
R3(config-router)#neighbor 100.1.1.1 remote-as 100
R3(config-router)#neighbor 200.1.1.8 remote-as 100
```

```
R3(config-router)#address-family ipv4
R3(config-router-af)#network 36.1.1.0 mask 255.255.255.0
R3(config-router-af)#neighbor 100.1.1.1 route-map local-pref in
```

You should see the following console messages:

```
%BGP-5-ADJCHANGE: neighbor 100.1.1.1 Up
%BGP-5-ADJCHANGE: neighbor 200.1.1.8 Up
```

As in the previous case, to provide proper connectivity to SW1, R1 is still configured to redistribute BGP prefixes into EIGRP using the redistribute bgp command in EIGRP configuration mode. The routing table from SW1 below shows the more specific prefixes from R1 and a default route from R8:

## On SW1:

```
SW1#show ip route eigrp 100 | begin Gate
Gateway of last resort is 118.1.1.8 to network 0.0.0.0

D*      0.0.0.0/0 [90/3072] via 118.1.1.8, 02:31:36, Vlan118
        24.0.0.0/24 is subnetted, 1 subnets
D EX      24.1.1.0 [170/2560000512] via 118.1.1.1, 00:03:19, Vlan118
        36.0.0.0/24 is subnetted, 1 subnets
D EX      36.1.1.0 [170/2560000512] via 118.1.1.1, 00:03:27, Vlan118
        100.0.0.0/24 is subnetted, 1 subnets
D         100.1.1.0 [90/26880256] via 118.1.1.1, 00:03:34, Vlan118
D       200.1.1.0/24 [90/28160256] via 118.1.1.1, 00:03:19, Vlan118
```

The BGP table on the spoke routers confirms the path via R1 has been chosen as best:

## On R2:

```
R2#show ip bgp | begin Net

     Network          Next Hop          Metric LocPrf Weight Path
 *>  0.0.0.0          100.1.1.1                  150        0 100 i
 *                    200.1.1.8                             0 100 i
 *>  24.1.1.0/24      0.0.0.0                0           32768 i
```

## On R3:

```
R3#show ip bgp | begin Net

     Network          Next Hop          Metric LocPrf Weight Path
 *>  0.0.0.0          100.1.1.1                  150        0 100 i
 *                    200.1.1.8                             0 100 i
 *>  36.1.1.0/24      0.0.0.0                0           32768 i
```

## Spokes in Different Autonomous Systems

The configuration for eBGP with the spokes in a different AS utilizes the same base configuration from earlier sections. The difference being the inclusion of the alternate-as command to specify the other ASNs with each spoke is configured. The same BGP local preference and default route advertising methods are utilized in this example as well.

---

### On R1:

The route map for the default route is still applied.

```
R1(config)#router bgp 100
R1(config-router)#no neighbor spokes remote-as 230
R1(config-router)#neighbor spokes remote 200 alternate-as 300
```

### On R8:

```
R8(config)#router bgp 100
R8(config-router)#no neighbor spokes remote-as 230
R8(config-router)#neighbor spokes remote 200 alternate-as 300
```

### On R2:

```
R2(config)#no router bgp 230

R2(config)#router bgp 200
R2(config-router)#neighbor 100.1.1.1 remote-as 100
R2(config-router)#neighbor 200.1.1.8 remote-as 100

R2(config-router)# address-family ipv4
R2(config-router-af)#network 24.1.1.0 mask 255.255.255.0
R2(config-router-af)#neighbor 100.1.1.1 route-map local-pref in
```

You should see the following console messages:

```
%BGP-5-ADJCHANGE: neighbor 100.1.1.1 Up
%BGP-5-ADJCHANGE: neighbor 200.1.1.8 Up
```

**On R3:**

```
R3(config)#no router bgp 230

R3(config)#router bgp 300
R3(config-router)#neighbor 100.1.1.1 remote-as 100
R3(config-router)#neighbor 200.1.1.8 remote-as 100

R3(config-router)#address-family ipv4
R3(config-router-af)#network 36.1.1.0 mask 255.255.255.0
R3(config-router-af)#neighbor 100.1.1.1 route-map local-pref in
```

You should see the following console messages:

```
%BGP-5-ADJCHANGE: neighbor 100.1.1.1 Up
%BGP-5-ADJCHANGE: neighbor 200.1.1.8 Up
```

The show ip bgp output confirms the configuration, showing R2 and R3 preferring the path with the higher local preference value of 150 from R1.

**On R2:**

```
R2#show ip bgp | begin Net

     Network          Next Hop           Metric LocPrf Weight Path
 *>  0.0.0.0          100.1.1.1                 150       0 100 i
 *                    200.1.1.8                           0 100 i
 *>  24.1.1.0/24      0.0.0.0                0        32768 i
```

**On R3:**

```
R3#show ip bgp | begin Net

     Network          Next Hop           Metric LocPrf Weight Path
 *>  0.0.0.0          100.1.1.1                 150       0 100 i
 *                    200.1.1.8                           0 100 i
 *>  36.1.1.0/24      0.0.0.0                0        32768 i
```

Traceroutes confirm that the pathing is working as described in the design goals:

**On R4:**

```
R4#traceroute 18.1.1.8 probe 1

Type escape sequence to abort.
Tracing the route to 18.1.1.8
VRF info: (vrf in name/id, vrf out name/id)
  1 24.1.1.2 19 msec
  2 100.1.1.1 11 msec
  3 118.1.1.10 14 msec


R4#traceroute 36.1.1.6 probe 1

Type escape sequence to abort.
Tracing the route to 36.1.1.6
VRF info: (vrf in name/id, vrf out name/id)
  1 24.1.1.2 4 msec
  2 100.1.1.1 7 msec
  3 100.1.1.3 17 msec
  4 36.1.1.6 31 msec


R4#traceroute 36.1.1.6 probe 1

Type escape sequence to abort.
Tracing the route to 36.1.1.6
VRF info: (vrf in name/id, vrf out name/id)
  1 24.1.1.2 7 msec
  2 100.1.1.3 10 msec
  3 36.1.1.6 10 msec
```

Same procedure as before is once again used to verify the hub redundancy between the two DMVPN clouds. On shutting down the G0/5 interface on R1, the spokes switch over to using the default route from R8:

**On R1:**

```
R1(config)#interface g0/5
R1(config-if)#shut
```

**On R2:**

```
R2#show ip bgp | begin Net
```

| Network | Next Hop | Metric | LocPrf | Weight | Path |
|---------|----------|--------|--------|--------|------|
| *>  0.0.0.0 | 200.1.1.8 | | | 0 | 100 i |
| *>  24.1.1.0/24 | 0.0.0.0 | 0 | | 32768 | i |

## On R3:

R3#**show ip bgp | begin Net**

| Network | Next Hop | Metric | LocPrf | Weight | Path |
|---------|----------|--------|--------|--------|------|
| *>  0.0.0.0 | 200.1.1.8 | | | 0 | 100 i |
| *>  36.1.1.0/24 | 0.0.0.0 | 0 | | 32768 | i |

## On R4:

Traceroutes below verify R8 as the hub in transit and the spoke to spoke tunnel between R2 and R3:

R4#**traceroute 18.1.1.8 probe 1**

```
Type escape sequence to abort.
Tracing the route to 18.1.1.8
VRF info: (vrf in name/id, vrf out name/id)
  1 24.1.1.2 15 msec
  2 200.1.1.8 11 msec
  3 118.1.1.10 11 msec
```

R4#**traceroute 36.1.1.6 probe 1**

```
Type escape sequence to abort.
Tracing the route to 36.1.1.6
VRF info: (vrf in name/id, vrf out name/id)
  1 24.1.1.2 3 msec
  2 200.1.1.8 8 msec
  3 200.1.1.3 16 msec
  4 36.1.1.6 24 msec
```

R4#**traceroute 36.1.1.6 probe 1**

```
Type escape sequence to abort.
Tracing the route to 36.1.1.6
VRF info: (vrf in name/id, vrf out name/id)
  1 24.1.1.2 32 msec
  2 200.1.1.3 16 msec
  3 36.1.1.6 23 msec
```

# Lab 5: DMVPN NHS Clustering

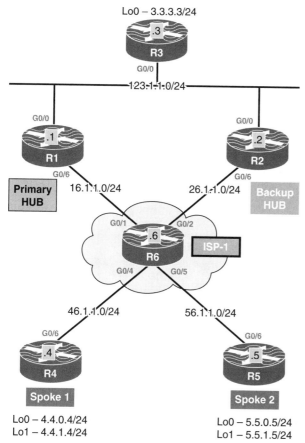

Lo0 – 3.3.3.3/24

R3
G0/0
123.1.1.0/24

G0/0
R1
.1
G0/6
**Primary HUB**  16.1.1.0/24

G0/0
R2
.2
G0/6
26.1.1.0/24  **Backup HUB**

G0/1   G0/2
.6
R6
ISP-1
G0/4   G0/5

46.1.1.0/24        56.1.1.0/24

G0/6
.4
R4
**Spoke 1**

G0/6
.5
R5
**Spoke 2**

Lo0 – 4.4.0.4/24
Lo1 – 4.4.1.4/24

Lo0 – 5.5.0.5/24
Lo1 – 5.5.1.5/24

This lab introduces advanced ways a functional DMVPN can be engineered to control how traffic is forwarded in the DMVPN network outside of editing routing protocol metrics. This section introduces concepts of NHS Clustering and DMVPN with DHCP. The first topic will be DMVPN NHS Clustering.

## This lab should be conducted on the Enterprise Rack.

## Lab Setup:

If you are using EVE-NG, and you have imported the EVE-NG topology from the **EVE-NG-Topology** folder, ignore the following and use **Lab-5-DMVPN NHS Clustering** in the **DMVPN** folder in EVE-NG.

To copy and paste the initial configurations, go to the **Initial-config** folder → **DMVPN** folder → **Lab-5**.

## Task 1

Configure DMVPN Phase 3 on R1, R2, R4, and R5:

**1.** R1 and R2 should be configured as NHRP NHSs.

R4 and R5 should be configured as spokes.

This task uses a single-cloud, dual-hub Phase 3 DMVPN design, with R1 and R2 serving as the hubs. These hubs are connected to a shared LAN segment with R3, which is also attached to another subnet, 3.3.3.0/24. Remote sites at R4 and R5 should have connectivity to the 3.3.3.0/24 subnet.

To complete the task and configure the hub and spoke routers, the following configurations should be applied on the hubs R1 and R2:

**On R1:**

```
R1(config)#interface tunnel 100
R1(config-if)#ip address 100.1.1.1 255.255.255.0
R1(config-if)#tunnel source 16.1.1.1
R1(config-if)#tunnel mode gre multipoint
R1(config-if)#ip nhrp network-id 100
R1(config-if)#ip nhrp map multicast 46.1.1.4
R1(config-if)#ip nhrp map multicast 56.1.1.5
R1(config-if)#ip nhrp redirect
```

**On R2:**

```
R2(config)#interface tunnel 100
R2(config-if)#ip address 100.1.1.2 255.255.255.0
R2(config-if)#tunnel source 26.1.1.2
R2(config-if)#tunnel mode gre multipoint
R2(config-if)#ip nhrp network-id 100
R2(config-if)#ip nhrp map multicast 46.1.1.4
R2(config-if)#ip nhrp map multicast 56.1.1.5
R2(config-if)#ip nhrp redirect
```

These configurations lay the ground for DMVPN communication. Next, spokes R4 and R5 are configured to register with the hubs R1 and R2 and dynamically join the DMVPN:

**On R4:**

```
R4(config)#interface tunnel 100
R4(config-if)#ip address 100.1.1.4 255.255.255.0
```

```
R4(config-if)#tunnel source 46.1.1.4
R4(config-if)#tunnel mode gre multipoint
R4(config-if)#ip nhrp network-id 100
R4(config-if)#ip nhrp nhs 100.1.1.1 nbma 16.1.1.1 multicast
R4(config-if)#ip nhrp nhs 100.1.1.2 nbma 26.1.1.2 multicast
R4(config-if)#ip nhrp shortcut
```

### On R5:

```
R5(config)#interface tunnel 100
R5(config-if)#ip address 100.1.1.5 255.255.255.0
R5(config-if)#tunnel source 56.1.1.5
R5(config-if)#tunnel mode gre multipoint
R5(config-if)#ip nhrp network-id 100
R5(config-if)#ip nhrp nhs 100.1.1.1 nbma 16.1.1.1 multicast
R5(config-if)#ip nhrp nhs 100.1.1.2 nbma 26.1.1.2 multicast
R5(config-if)#ip nhrp shortcut
```

### To verify the configuration:

On completing the above configurations, outputs below from R1 and R2 confirm the spokes have successfully registered with both hubs:

### On R1:

```
R1#show ip nhrp

100.1.1.4/32 via 100.1.1.4
   Tunnel100 created 00:02:57, expire 00:07:02
   Type: dynamic, Flags: registered nhop
   NBMA address: 46.1.1.4
100.1.1.5/32 via 100.1.1.5
   Tunnel100 created 00:00:59, expire 00:09:00
   Type: dynamic, Flags: registered nhop
   NBMA address: 56.1.1.5

R1#show ip nhrp multicast

  I/F     NBMA address
Tunnel100  56.1.1.5        Flags: static       (Enabled)
Tunnel100  46.1.1.4        Flags: static       (Enabled)
```

```
On R2:


R2#show dmvpn | begin Peer NBMA

 # Ent   Peer NBMA Addr Peer Tunnel Add State  UpDn Tm Attrb
 ----- --------------- --------------- ----- -------- -----
     1 46.1.1.4               100.1.1.4     UP 00:03:29    D
     1 56.1.1.5               100.1.1.5     UP 00:01:40    D

R2#show ip nhrp multicast


  I/F      NBMA address
Tunnel100  46.1.1.4        Flags: dynamic       (Enabled)
Tunnel100  56.1.1.5        Flags: dynamic       (Enabled)
```

## Task 2

Configure EIGRP AS 1 based on the following policy:

**1.** R1 and R2: G0/0 and tunnel interfaces

**2.** R3: G0/0 and Lo0

R4 and R5: Tunnel 100 interfaces and Lo0 and Lo1

As specified in the task, the following configures EIGRP as the overlay routing protocol on R1, R2, R3, R4, and R5. EIGRP is enabled on the tunnel interfaces and the loopback interfaces specified in the task with the **network** statement:

**On R1:**

```
R1(config)#router eigrp 1
R1(config-router)#network 100.1.1.1 0.0.0.0
R1(config-router)#network 123.1.1.1 0.0.0.0
```

**On R2:**

```
R2(config)#router eigrp 1
R2(config-router)#network 100.1.1.2 0.0.0.0
R2(config-router)#network 123.1.1.2 0.0.0.0
```

You should see the following console message:

```
%DUAL-5-NBRCHANGE: EIGRP-IPv4 1: Neighbor 123.1.1.1
(GigabitEthernet0/0) is up: new adjacency
```

## On R4:

```
R4(config)#router eigrp 1
R4(config-router)#network 100.1.1.4 0.0.0.0
R4(config-router)#network 4.4.0.4 0.0.0.0
R4(config-router)#network 4.4.1.4 0.0.0.0
```

You should see the following console messages:

```
%DUAL-5-NBRCHANGE: EIGRP-IPv4 1: Neighbor 100.1.1.2 (Tunnel100) is up:
new adjacency

%DUAL-5-NBRCHANGE: EIGRP-IPv4 1: Neighbor 100.1.1.1 (Tunnel100) is up:
new adjacency
```

## On R5:

```
R5(config)#router eigrp 1
R5(config-router)#network 100.1.1.5 0.0.0.0
R5(config-router)#network 5.5.0.5 0.0.0.0
R5(config-router)#network 5.5.1.5 0.0.0.0
```

You should see the following console messages:

```
%DUAL-5-NBRCHANGE: EIGRP-IPv4 1: Neighbor 100.1.1.2 (Tunnel100) is up:
new adjacency

%DUAL-5-NBRCHANGE: EIGRP-IPv4 1: Neighbor 100.1.1.1 (Tunnel100) is up:
new adjacency
```

## On R3:

```
R3(config)#router eigrp 1
R3(config-router)#network 123.1.1.3 0.0.0.0
R3(config-router)#network 3.3.3.3 0.0.0.0
```

You should see the following console messages:

```
%DUAL-5-NBRCHANGE: EIGRP-IPv4 1: Neighbor 123.1.1.2
(GigabitEthernet0/10) is up: new adjacency

%DUAL-5-NBRCHANGE: EIGRP-IPv4 1: Neighbor 123.1.1.1
(GigabitEthernet0/10) is up: new adjacency
```

**To verify the configuration:**

The show ip route eigrp command output below verifies the EIGRP routes learned over the DMVPN network:

**On R4:**

```
R4#show ip route eigrp 1 | begin Gate
Gateway of last resort is not set

      3.0.0.0/24 is subnetted, 1 subnets
D        3.3.3.0 [90/27008256] via 100.1.1.2, 00:03:32, Tunnel100
                 [90/27008256] via 100.1.1.1, 00:03:32, Tunnel100
      123.0.0.0/24 is subnetted, 1 subnets
D        123.1.1.0 [90/26880256] via 100.1.1.2, 00:09:59, Tunnel100
                   [90/26880256] via 100.1.1.1, 00:09:59, Tunnel100
```

**On R5:**

```
R5#show ip route eigrp 1 | begin Gate
Gateway of last resort is not set

      3.0.0.0/24 is subnetted, 1 subnets
D        3.3.3.0 [90/27008256] via 100.1.1.2, 00:03:57, Tunnel100
                 [90/27008256] via 100.1.1.1, 00:03:57, Tunnel100
      123.0.0.0/24 is subnetted, 1 subnets
D        123.1.1.0 [90/26880256] via 100.1.1.2, 00:08:31, Tunnel100
                   [90/26880256] via 100.1.1.1, 00:08:31, Tunnel100
```

**On R1:**

```
R1#show ip route eigrp 1 | begin Gate
Gateway of last resort is not set

      3.0.0.0/24 is subnetted, 1 subnets
D        3.3.3.0 [90/130816] via 123.1.1.3, 00:04:44,
GigabitEthernet0/10
      4.0.0.0/24 is subnetted, 2 subnets
D        4.4.0.0 [90/27008000] via 100.1.1.4, 00:11:05, Tunnel100
D        4.4.1.0 [90/27008000] via 100.1.1.4, 00:11:01, Tunnel100
      5.0.0.0/24 is subnetted, 2 subnets
```

```
D          5.5.0.0 [90/27008000] via 100.1.1.5, 00:09:12, Tunnel100
D          5.5.1.0 [90/27008000] via 100.1.1.5, 00:09:08, Tunnel100
```

## On R2:

```
R2#show ip route eigrp 1 | begin Gate
Gateway of last resort is not set

     3.0.0.0/24 is subnetted, 1 subnets
D        3.3.3.0 [90/130816] via 123.1.1.3, 00:05:12,
GigabitEthernet0/10
     4.0.0.0/24 is subnetted, 2 subnets
D        4.4.0.0 [90/27008000] via 100.1.1.4, 00:11:33, Tunnel100
D        4.4.1.0 [90/27008000] via 100.1.1.4, 00:11:29, Tunnel100
     5.0.0.0/24 is subnetted, 2 subnets
D        5.5.0.0 [90/27008000] via 100.1.1.5, 00:09:41, Tunnel100
D        5.5.1.0 [90/27008000] via 100.1.1.5, 00:09:36, Tunnel100
```

Notice that R4 and R5 do not contain the specific prefixes for each other's networks. This is because, by default, split horizon is enabled under the tunnel interfaces. To remedy this issue, use the **no ip split-horizon eigrp 1** command in the tunnel 100 interface on R1 and R2:

## On R1 and R2:

```
Rx(config)#interface tunnel 100
Rx(config-if)#no ip split-horizon eigrp 1
```

With split horizon disabled, R4 and R5 now learn the remaining specific routes from the hubs.

## To verify the configuration:

## On R4:

```
R4#show ip route eigrp 1 | begin Gate
Gateway of last resort is not set

     3.0.0.0/24 is subnetted, 1 subnets
D        3.3.3.0 [90/27008256] via 100.1.1.2, 00:05:01, Tunnel100
                 [90/27008256] via 100.1.1.1, 00:05:01, Tunnel100
     5.0.0.0/24 is subnetted, 2 subnets
```

```
D          5.5.0.0 [90/28288000] via 100.1.1.2, 00:01:10, Tunnel100
                    [90/28288000] via 100.1.1.1, 00:01:10, Tunnel100
D          5.5.1.0 [90/28288000] via 100.1.1.2, 00:01:10, Tunnel100
                    [90/28288000] via 100.1.1.1, 00:01:10, Tunnel100
        123.0.0.0/24 is subnetted, 1 subnets
D          123.1.1.0 [90/26880256] via 100.1.1.2, 00:05:01, Tunnel100
                      [90/26880256] via 100.1.1.1, 00:05:01, Tunnel100
```

**On R5:**

```
R5#show ip route eigrp 1 | begin Gate
Gateway of last resort is not set

        3.0.0.0/24 is subnetted, 1 subnets
D          3.3.3.0 [90/27008256] via 100.1.1.2, 00:04:20, Tunnel100
                    [90/27008256] via 100.1.1.1, 00:04:20, Tunnel100
        4.0.0.0/24 is subnetted, 2 subnets
D          4.4.0.0 [90/28288000] via 100.1.1.2, 00:01:43, Tunnel100
                    [90/28288000] via 100.1.1.1, 00:01:43, Tunnel100
D          4.4.1.0 [90/28288000] via 100.1.1.2, 00:01:43, Tunnel100
                    [90/28288000] via 100.1.1.1, 00:01:43, Tunnel100
        123.0.0.0/24 is subnetted, 1 subnets
D          123.1.1.0 [90/26880256] via 100.1.1.2, 00:04:20, Tunnel100
                      [90/26880256] via 100.1.1.1, 00:04:20, Tunnel100
```

## Task 3

Configure R1 to be the primary hub and R2 to be the backup. You must use NHRP clustering to accomplish this task.

This task involves traffic engineering using clustering instead of manipulating routing protocol metrics. The routing table on R4 has two equal-cost paths to reach all the networks over the DMVPN tunnel:

```
R4#show ip route eigrp 1 | begin Gate
Gateway of last resort is not set

        3.0.0.0/24 is subnetted, 1 subnets
D          3.3.3.0 [90/27008256] via 100.1.1.2, 00:17:46, Tunnel100
                    [90/27008256] via 100.1.1.1, 00:17:46, Tunnel100
        5.0.0.0/24 is subnetted, 2 subnets
D          5.5.0.0 [90/28288000] via 100.1.1.2, 00:00:06, Tunnel100
                    [90/28288000] via 100.1.1.1, 00:00:06, Tunnel100
```

```
D        5.5.1.0 [90/28288000] via 100.1.1.2, 00:00:06, Tunnel100
                 [90/28288000] via 100.1.1.1, 00:00:06, Tunnel100
     123.0.0.0/24 is subnetted, 1 subnets
D        123.1.1.0 [90/26880256] via 100.1.1.2, 00:17:46, Tunnel100
                   [90/26880256] via 100.1.1.1, 00:17:46, Tunnel100
```

R1 and R2 are advertising equal-cost paths to R4 across the DMVPN network. According to the task, R4 should prefer to use R1's route over R2's unless it loses the route to R1 due to a failure. In the current configuration, R4 will load share traffic between the two destinations. Typically, as in the earlier tasks of this lab, this problem was solved by engineering routing protocol metrics. This task, however, requires the use of **NHRP NHS clustering**, a feature introduced in **IOS 15.1.2T**.

With NHRP NHS clustering, NHSs serving the same DMVPN cloud are placed into groups designated by a **cluster ID**. Under normal operating circumstances, spokes register with all hubs in the cluster. Failover redundancy is implemented by limiting the number of NHSs in a given cluster to which the spokes can build connections to only connect with a subset of all NHSs at a time. Within each NHS cluster, the member NHSs are given priority values between 1 and 255. Priority value 1 is the highest preference, and value 255 is the lowest preference. The spoke will attempt a connection with the highest-priority NHSs within each cluster up to the defined maximum connection limit. These will be the NHSs with the numerically lowest priority values.

This configuration is all accomplished on the spoke interfaces. Therefore, the NHRP NHS clustering configuration is only locally significant to the spoke on which it is configured. Different spokes can group available NHSs to different clusters and priority values, depending on the desired policies.

An NHS is assigned to a cluster using the interface configuration command **ip nhrp nhs** *ip-address-of-nhs* **priority** *priority-value* **cluster** *cluster-id* on the spoke tunnel interface. To limit the number of NHSs to which a spoke will open connections, use the **ip nhrp nhs cluster** *cluster-id* **max-connections** *number-of-connections* command. The following configures this feature on spokes R4 and R5:

### On R4 and R5:

```
Rx(config)#interface tunnel 100
Rx(config-if)#ip nhrp nhs 100.1.1.1 priority 1 cluster 1
Rx(config-if)#ip nhrp nhs 100.1.1.2 priority 2 cluster 1
```

After entering the above on the spokes, the original **ip nhrp nhs x.x.x.x nbma x.x.x.x multicast** command is replaced with the above command. Only one version of this command can be entered in the tunnel interface. This results in the mapping statements from the tunnel interfaces being automatically removed by IOS. You need to reconfigure mapping statements on the spokes with the legacy NHRP mapping statements.

The following reconfigures the static NHRP mapping for hubs R1 and R2 along with multicast mappings on both spokes:

```
Rx(config-if)#ip nhrp map multicast 16.1.1.1
Rx(config-if)#ip nhrp map multicast 26.1.1.2

Rx(config-if)#ip nhrp map 100.1.1.1 16.1.1.1
Rx(config-if)#ip nhrp map 100.1.1.2 26.1.1.2
```

The following configuration limits the spokes to only connect with a single NHS in cluster 1 and configures a registration timeout limit:

```
Rx(config-if)#ip nhrp nhs cluster 1 max-connections 1
Rx(config-if)#ip nhrp registration timeout 5
```

After making the above configuration changes, R4 and R5 are configured with NHRP NHS cluster 1. They are also configured to only create a connection with a single NHS from cluster 1 due to the **ip nhrp nhs cluster x max-connections 1** command. As a result, R4 and R5 will attempt to register with the highest-priority cluster in NHS cluster 1 first. If there is no response after 5 seconds (the configured timeout value), it will move to the next-lowest-priority NHS. In this case, R4 and R5 will attempt a connection with R1 first. If the connection is completed, the routers will not connect with R2. This prevents R2 from advertising a second set of routes to the spokes and makes R1 the preferred next hop for all DMVPN traffic, as shown below:

## On R4:

```
R4#show ip route eigrp 1 | begin Gate
Gateway of last resort is not set

      3.0.0.0/24 is subnetted, 1 subnets
D        3.3.3.0 [90/27008256] via 100.1.1.1, 00:18:52, Tunnel100
      5.0.0.0/24 is subnetted, 2 subnets
D        5.5.0.0 [90/28288000] via 100.1.1.1, 00:18:52, Tunnel100
D        5.5.1.0 [90/28288000] via 100.1.1.1, 00:18:52, Tunnel100
      123.0.0.0/24 is subnetted, 1 subnets
D        123.1.1.0 [90/26880256] via 100.1.1.1, 00:18:52, Tunnel100
```

## On R5:

```
R5#show ip route eigrp 1 | begin Gate
Gateway of last resort is not set

      3.0.0.0/24 is subnetted, 1 subnets
D        3.3.3.0 [90/27008256] via 100.1.1.1, 00:19:08, Tunnel100
      4.0.0.0/24 is subnetted, 2 subnets
```

```
D          4.4.0.0 [90/28288000] via 100.1.1.1, 00:19:52, Tunnel100
D          4.4.1.0 [90/28288000] via 100.1.1.1, 00:19:52, Tunnel100
       123.0.0.0/24 is subnetted, 1 subnets
D          123.1.1.0 [90/26880256] via 100.1.1.1, 00:19:08, Tunnel100
```

The advantage of this setup is that, if R1 fails, the spokes will automatically bring up the connection with the backup hub, R2, and reestablish IGP connectivity. To demonstrate, a ping is issued from R4's Lo0 interface to the Lo0 interface on R3 with a high repeat count. While the ping is executed, the G0/1 interface on R6 is shut down:

### On R4:

```
R4#ping 3.3.3.3 source lo0 repeat 100000

Type escape sequence to abort.
Sending 100000, 100-byte ICMP Echos to 3.3.3.3, timeout is 2 seconds:
Packet sent with a source address of 4.4.0.4
!!!!!!!!!!!!!!!!!!!!!!!!!!!!!!!!!!!!!!!!!!!!!!!!!!!!!!!!!!!!!!!!!!!!!!!!
!!!!!!!!!!!!!!!!!!!!!!!!!!!!!!!!!!!!!!!!!!!!!!!!!!!!!!!!!!!!!!!!!!!!!!!!
```

### On R6:

```
R6(config)#interface g0/1
R6(config-if)#shut
```

### On R4:

```
!!!!!!!!!!!!!!!!!!!!!!!!!!!!!!!!!!!!!!!!!!!!!!!!!!!!!!!!!!!!!!!!!!!!!!!!
!!!!!!!!!!!!!!!!!!!!!!!!!!!!!!!!!!!!!!!!!!!!!!!!!!!!!!!!!!!!!!!!!!!!!!!!
!!!!!!!!!!!!!!!!!!!!!!!!!!!!!!!!!!!!!!!!!!!!!!!!!!!!!!!!!!!.......!!!!!!!!
!!!!!!!!!!!!!!!!!!!!!!!!!!!!!!!!!!!!!!!!!!!!!!!!!!!!!!!!!!!!!!!!!!!!!!!!
!!!!!!!!!!!!!!!!!!!!!!!!!!!!!!!!!!!!!!!!!!!!!!!!!!!!!!!!!!!!!!!!!!
```

In the above, the highlighted missed pings indicate the time it took for R4 to switch over to using R2 as its hub. With the ping timeout of 2 seconds, this equates to about 14 seconds of downtime. The **show ip route eigrp 1 | begin Gate** and **traceroute** output verifies that R4 has switched to using R2 as its next hop for the EIGRP routes:

### To verify the configuration:

### On R4:

```
R4#show ip route eigrp 1 | begin Gate
Gateway of last resort is not set
```

```
        3.0.0.0/24 is subnetted, 1 subnets
D          3.3.3.0 [90/27008256] via 100.1.1.2, 00:06:48, Tunnel100
        5.0.0.0/24 is subnetted, 2 subnets
D          5.5.0.0 [90/28288000] via 100.1.1.2, 00:06:46, Tunnel100
D          5.5.1.0 [90/28288000] via 100.1.1.2, 00:06:46, Tunnel100
        123.0.0.0/24 is subnetted, 1 subnets
D          123.1.1.0 [90/26880256] via 100.1.1.2, 00:06:48, Tunnel100


R4#traceroute 3.3.3.3 source lo0 probe 1

Type escape sequence to abort.
Tracing the route to 3.3.3.3
VRF info: (vrf in name/id, vrf out name/id)
  1 100.1.1.2 65 msec
  2 123.1.1.3 10 msec
```

The **ip nhrp nhs fallback** command controls how long the router will take to switch back over to the original NHS whenever it is recovered. To test this, the **ip nhrp nhs fallback 5** command is issued on R4 and R5. This means the routers will wait 5 seconds before using R1 as the higher-priority NHS when connectivity to R1 is restored. The same ping test is repeated, this time with the G0/1 interface on R6 being **no shut** to simulate the connection being restored:

**On R4 and R5:**

```
Rx(config)#interface tunnel 100
Rx(config-if)#ip nhrp nhs fallback 5
```

This configuration is tested by repeating the same ping and bringing R6's G0/1 interface back up:

**On R4:**

```
R4#ping 3.3.3.3 source lo0 rep 100000

Type escape sequence to abort.
Sending 100000, 100-byte ICMP Echos to 3.3.3.3, timeout is 2 seconds:
Packet sent with a source address of 4.4.0.4
!!!!!!!!!!!!!!!!!!!!!!!!!!!!!!!!!!!!!!!!!!!!!!!!!!!!!!!!!!!!!!!!!!!!!!!!
!!!!!!!!!!!!!!!!!!!!!!!!!!!!!!!!!!!!!!!!!!!!!!!!!!!!!!!!!!!!!!!!!!!!!!!!
!!!!!!!!!!!!!!!!!!!!!!!!!!!!!!!!!!!!!!!!!!!!!!!!!!!!!!!!!!!!!!!!!!!!!!!!
```

### On R6:

```
R6(config)#interface g0/1
R6(config-if)#no shut
```

Notice in the above that no pings were missed. The **show ip route eigrp 1 | begin Gate** and accompanying **traceroute** command on R4 verify that R1 has indeed come back up.

### On R4:

```
R4#show ip route eigrp 1 | begin Gate
Gateway of last resort is not set

      3.0.0.0/24 is subnetted, 1 subnets
D        3.3.3.0 [90/27008256] via 100.1.1.1, 00:00:04, Tunnel100
      5.0.0.0/24 is subnetted, 2 subnets
D        5.5.0.0 [90/28288000] via 100.1.1.1, 00:00:07, Tunnel100
D        5.5.1.0 [90/28288000] via 100.1.1.1, 00:00:07, Tunnel100
      123.0.0.0/24 is subnetted, 1 subnets
D        123.1.1.0 [90/26880256] via 100.1.1.1, 00:00:04, Tunnel100
```

```
R4#traceroute 3.3.3.3 source lo0 probe 1

Type escape sequence to abort.
Tracing the route to 3.3.3.3
VRF info: (vrf in name/id, vrf out name/id)
  1 100.1.1.1 5 msec
  2 123.1.1.3 7 msec
```

The pings weren't missed because there was no connection failure during fallback; it was a connection restoration. Because R2 is up during the entire process, R4 can continue to forward traffic through R2 while the EIGRP neighbor relationship comes up between itself and R1. R1 comes up and establishes an adjacency with R4. R4 adds the new routing information for the prefixes transparently during fallback.

The key to making all of this work is the **ip nhrp nhs cluster 1 max-connections 1** command issued on the spoke tunnel interfaces. This is what limits the connection to only a single NHS at a time. Without this command, the spokes would connect to both NHSs at the same time, and the traffic engineering goals would not be met.

The **show ip nhrp nhs redundancy** command can be issued on the spokes to reveal the status of every NHS configured. Following is example output from R4:

```
R4#show ip nhrp nhs redundancy

Legend: E=Expecting replies, R=Responding, W=Waiting

No.  Interface  Cluster        NHS Priority  Cur-State  Cur-Queue
Prev-State Prev-Queue
  1  Tunnel100     1    100.1.1.1   1     RE   Running     E     Running
  2  Tunnel100     1    100.1.1.2   2     W    Waiting     RE    Running

No.  Interface  Cluster  Status  Max-Con  Total-NHS Registering/UP
Expecting  Waiting Fallback
  1  Tunnel100      1    Enable       1        2                  1
0       1        0
```

The output above shows that R4 has a connection to 100.1.1.1 (**R1**) over its tunnel 100 interface. This NHS is in cluster 1 with priority 1. The **Curr-State** field contains the **RE** flag, meaning the NHS is responding to probes, and the local spoke is expecting replies. The **Cur-Queue** status is **Running** because it is the active NHS. It also lists similar information for NHS 100.1.1.2 (**R2**); however, in this case, the priority is 2, and the state is **W**, which means it is waiting for connections.

The bottom part of the output provides details on the configured clusters. Notice that the **Max-Con** field is set to **1** for cluster 1. This is verification that only one NHS from that cluster will be used for communication.

## Task 4

Erase the startup configuration of the routers and reload them before proceeding to the next lab.

# Lab 6: DMVPN and DHCP

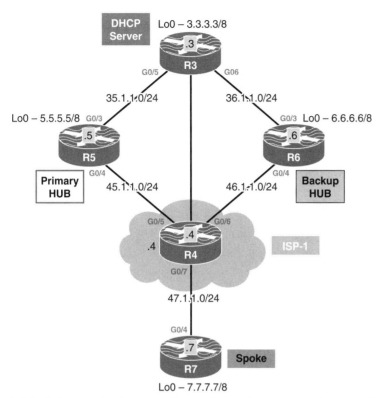

## This lab should be conducted on the Enterprise Rack.

## Lab Setup:

If you are using EVE-NG, and you have imported the EVE-NG topology from the EVE-NG-Topology folder, ignore the following and use **Lab-6-DMVPN and DHCP** in the **DMVPN** folder in EVE-NG.

To copy and paste the initial configurations, go to the **Initial-config** folder → **DMVPN** folder → **Lab-6**.

This lab introduces concepts that can be used for situations in which the spokes of the DMVPN network do not have statically assigned tunnel IP addresses. In this case, the spokes are configured to receive their IP addressing information from a DHCP server located at a central main site location. The hub is then configured to act as a DHCP relay agent to pass the DHCP DISCOVER packets from the spokes to the DHCP server. The DMVPN network shown below will be configured to demonstrate this functionality:

## Task 1

Configure DMVPN Phase 3 such that R5 is the primary hub, R6 is the backup hub, and R7 is configured as the spoke. You should use EIGRP AS 1 to provide reachability to the NBMA IP addresses and EIGRP AS 100 for the tunnel and the loopback interfaces.

---

In this task, Phase 3 DMVPN is configured between R5, R6, and R7. R5 and R6 are the hubs, R7 is the spoke, and R4 represents the cloud. This task requires R5 to be the primary hub and R6 to be the backup hub. However, prior to any DMVPN-related configuration, IP reachability needs to be established for underlying NBMA addresses on R5, R6, and R7. This reachability is advertised over the underlay using EIGRP AS 1, as shown below:

### On R5:

```
R5(config)#router eigrp 1
R5(config-router)#network 45.1.1.5 0.0.0.0
```

### On R6:

```
R6(config)#router eigrp 1
R6(config-router)#network 46.1.1.6 0.0.0.0
```

### On R7:

```
R7(config)#router eigrp 1
R7(config-router)#network 47.1.1.7 0.0.0.0
```

### On R4:

```
R4(config)#router eigrp 1
R4(config-router)#network 0.0.0.0 0.0.0.0
```

You should see the following console messages:

```
%DUAL-5-NBRCHANGE: EIGRP-IPv4 1: Neighbor 45.1.1.5
(GigabitEthernet0/5) is up: new adjacency

%DUAL-5-NBRCHANGE: EIGRP-IPv4 1: Neighbor 46.1.1.6
(GigabitEthernet0/6) is up: new adjacency
```

```
%DUAL-5-NBRCHANGE: EIGRP-IPv4 1: Neighbor 47.1.1.7
(GigabitEthernet0/7) is up: new adjacency
```

The next step is to complete the DMVPN Phase 3 configuration on the hubs R5 and R6. The following configuration commands set up these routers as hubs for DMVPN Phase 3:

**On R5:**

```
R5(config)#interface tunnel 100
R5(config-if)#ip address 100.1.1.5 255.255.255.0
R5(config-if)#tunnel source g0/4
R5(config-if)#tunnel mode gre multipoint
R5(config-if)#ip nhrp network 100
R5(config-if)#ip nhrp map multicast dynamic
R5(config-if)#ip nhrp redirect
```

**On R6:**

```
R6(config)#interface tunnel 100
R6(config-if)#ip address 100.1.1.6 255.255.255.0
R6(config-if)#tunnel source g0/4
R6(config-if)#tunnel mode gre multipoint
R6(config-if)#ip nhrp network 111
R6(config-if)#ip nhrp map multicast dynamic
R6(config-if)#ip nhrp redirect
```

The hub configuration is pretty straightforward. One peculiarity is the **ip nhrp network-id** setting used on the two hubs. R5 uses the ID 100, while R6 uses the ID 111. The NHRP IDs are locally significant to the routers and have no effect on the function of the DMVPN network. The network ID is used by the local router to distinguish between multiple NHRP databases when configured with multiple tunnels.

The configuration on R7, the spoke, deserves some explanation. To implement the requirement that R5 should be the primary hub and R6 should be the secondary hub, R7 is configured with NHRP clustering. R5 and R6 are both configured as potential DMVPN NHS hubs in R7's configuration. The two hubs are given separate priority values in the same cluster, with R5 being preferred over R6. Then R7 is limited to only a single NHS connection for the same cluster, using the **ip nhrp nhs cluster 1 max-connections 1** command:

**On R7:**

```
R7(config)#interface tunnel 100
R7(config-if)#ip address 100.1.1.7 255.255.255.0
```

```
R7(config-if)#tunnel source g0/4
R7(config-if)#tunnel mode gre multipoint
R7(config-if)#ip nhrp network 100
R7(config-if)#ip nhrp map multicast 45.1.1.5
R7(config-if)#ip nhrp map multicast 46.1.1.6
R7(config-if)#ip nhrp map 100.1.1.5 45.1.1.5

R7(config-if)#ip nhrp map 100.1.1.6 46.1.1.6
R7(config-if)#ip nhrp nhs 100.1.1.5 priority 1 cluster 1
R7(config-if)#ip nhrp nhs 100.1.1.6 priority 2 cluster 1
R7(config-if)#ip nhrp shortcut
R7(config-if)#ip nhrp nhs cluster 1 max-connections 1
```

## To verify the configuration:

## On R5:

```
R5#show ip nhrp

100.1.1.7/32 via 100.1.1.7
   Tunnel100 created 00:01:56, expire 00:09:58
   Type: dynamic, Flags: registered nhop
   NBMA address: 47.1.1.7

R5#show ip nhrp multicast

  I/F     NBMA address
Tunnel100  47.1.1.7       Flags: dynamic         (Enabled)
```

## On R6:

Since R6 is the backup NHS, the spoke R7 will not send a NHRP registration to it unless the primary hub R5 fails. As a result, the **show ip nhrp** output on R6 does not produce any output:

```
R6#show ip nhrp
R6#
```

## On R7:

```
R7#show ip nhrp
```

```
100.1.1.5/32 via 100.1.1.5
   Tunnel100 created 00:03:04, never expire
   Type: static, Flags:
   NBMA address: 45.1.1.5
100.1.1.6/32 via 100.1.1.6
   Tunnel100 created 00:02:53, never expire
   Type: static, Flags:
   NBMA address: 46.1.1.6
     (no-socket)
```

Here, R6 does not have an entry for R7's mapping information because R7 is only configured to send a registration request to the highest-priority hub in NHRP cluster 1, R5. As such, R7's **show ip nhrp** output lists R6 as a static mapping but with the **no-socket** status because R7 is using it as a backup and hasn't yet initiated a session directly with R6.

Next, in keeping with the task requirements, EIGRP 100 is used as the overlay routing protocol to advertise the Loopback0 interfaces across the DMVPN network. This should be configured on R3, R5, R6, and R7:

### On R3:

```
R3(config)#router eigrp 100
R3(config-router)#network 3.3.3.3 0.0.0.0
R3(config-router)#network 35.1.1.3 0.0.0.0
R3(config-router)#network 36.1.1.3 0.0.0.0
```

### On R5:

```
R1(config)#router eigrp 100
R5(config-router)#network 5.5.5.5 0.0.0.0
R5(config-router)#network 100.1.1.5 0.0.0.0
R5(config-router)#network 35.1.1.5 0.0.0.0
```

You should see the following console message:

```
%DUAL-5-NBRCHANGE: EIGRP-IPv4 100: Neighbor 35.1.1.3
(GigabitEthernet0/3) is up: new adjacency
```

### On R6:

```
R6(config)#router eigrp 100
R6(config-router)#network 6.6.6.6 0.0.0.0
R6(config-router)#network 36.1.1.6 0.0.0.0
R6(config-router)#network 100.1.1.6 0.0.0.0
```

You should see the following console message:

```
%DUAL-5-NBRCHANGE: EIGRP-IPv4 100: Neighbor 36.1.1.3
(GigabitEthernet0/3)is up: new adjacency
```

### On R7:

```
R7(config)#router eigrp 100
R7(config-router)#network 7.7.7.7 0.0.0.0
R7(config-router)#network 100.1.1.7 0.0.0.0
```

You should see the following console message:

```
%DUAL-5-NBRCHANGE: EIGRP-IPv4 100: Neighbor 100.1.1.5 (Tunnel100) is
up: new adjacency
```

### To verify the configuration:

```
R7#show ip route eigrp 100 | begin Gate
Gateway of last resort is not set

D     3.0.0.0/8 [90/27008256] via 100.1.1.5, 00:00:53, Tunnel100
D     5.0.0.0/8 [90/27008000] via 100.1.1.5, 00:00:53, Tunnel100
D     6.0.0.0/8 [90/27008512] via 100.1.1.5, 00:00:53, Tunnel100
      35.0.0.0/24 is subnetted, 1 subnets
D        35.1.1.0 [90/26880256] via 100.1.1.5, 00:00:53, Tunnel100
      36.0.0.0/24 is subnetted, 1 subnets
D        36.1.1.0 [90/26880512] via 100.1.1.5, 00:00:53, Tunnel100
```

## Task 2

Configure R3 as a DHCP server. R7 should be reconfigured as a DHCP client. In the event that R5 is down, R7 should go through R6 to acquire an IP address.

Typically, in DMVPN setups, both the spokes and the hubs are configured with specific static IP addresses. Manually configuring the IP address for each DMVPN spoke is difficult because the spoke configurations will vary based on the IP address configuration. In order to make the spoke configurations easier and require less interaction, the spokes can obtain their IP addresses automatically, through DHCP. This task is designed to demonstrate how a spoke can be configured to obtain an IP address from a DHCP server before participating in a DMVPN using the DHCP tunnel feature.

Pulling off this configuration requires modifications to the typical DMVPN registration process. In a normal DMVPN network, where the spokes are configured with static IP addresses, when the GRE tunnel interface comes up, the spoke immediately begins sending NHRP registration messages to the hub. The hub builds a dynamic NHRP mapping for the spoke that registered with it, and the tunnel between the hub and spoke comes up. When the spoke is configured to obtain an IP address through DHCP, the spoke needs to obtain an IP address before bringing its tunnel interface up and beginning the NHRP registration process.

If this discussion were about normal DHCP operation, the spoke would broadcast a DHCPDISCOVER message onto the LAN. This broadcast would be picked up by a DHCP server, which would send a DHCPOFFER message. The spoke would confirm that it accepted the offer by sending a DHCPREQUEST packet back to the DHCP server. The DHCP server would then reply with a DHCPACK packet. This process is known as the DHCP DORA (discover, offer, request, acknowledge) process.

The problem with this process when applied to a DMVPN network is that DMVPN networks are NBMA networks, which means broadcasts cannot be forwarded across them. When a spoke needs to send its DHCPDISCOVER packet out, the spoke cannot send it as a native broadcast. Instead, the spoke must convert the DHCPDISCOVER packet into a unicast packet that can be tunneled over the underlay network. In addition to having to forward as unicast over the DMVPN network to obtain an IP address, the spoke needs to know the NBMA address of the device to which it should send the unicasted broadcast DHCP packet in order to successfully tunnel it over the underlay network.

The only device spoke router that is typically preloaded with NBMA mapping information is the hub router. A basic spoke configuration includes the tunnel-to-NBMA IP address mapping information. This indicates the default location to which the spoke will send its DHCPDISCOVER packet.

When the spoke tunnel interface is enabled, it first realizes it is supposed to receive an IP address through DHCP. Having no IP address, the spoke cannot send NHRP register packets to the hub, so it suppresses the NHRP registration process. During this suppression time, it sends its DHCPDISCOVER packet to the NBMA address of the hub router. It is now up to the hub to take action.

At this point in the process, the spoke has sent a DHCPDISCOVER packet to the hub, in the hopes that the hub can do one of two things:

- Provide the spoke with IP address configuration information
- Forward the DHCPDISCOVER packet to another device that can provide IP address configuration information

To perform the first function, the DMVPN hub itself needs to be functioning as a DHCP server. Depending on the IOS version in use, the hub may not be able to be both the DMVPN hub and the DHCP server; some documentation explicitly states that such a configuration is not possible, while other documentation allows this type of configuration.

To perform the second function, the DMVPN hub acts as a DHCP relay agent. A DHCP relay agent is a device that is preconfigured with the unicast IP address of a functioning DHCP server that exists somewhere on the network. The DHCP relay agent has full unicast reachability to these devices and acts as a proxy between DHCP clients and DHCP servers. The job of the DHCP relay agent is to connect DHCP clients with DHCP servers that are in other subnets. The DHCP relay agent does so by converting the broadcast DHCPDISCOVER packet into a unicast DHCPDISCOVER packet sent directly to one of its preconfigured DCHP servers.

The hub's actions after receiving the DHCPDISCOVER from a spoke depend on how it's configured. If the hub is a DHCP server, then it will process the DHCPDISCOVER packet by taking an IP address from its configured pool of addresses. It will create a temporary NBMA-to-tunnel IP address mapping for the spoke and forward the DHCPOFFER packet to the client. The client, if it accepts the IP address, responds with a DHCPREQUEST formally requesting the IP address in the offer. The hub responds with a DHCPACK.

If the hub is configured as a DHCP relay agent, it needs another way of keeping track of the exchange between the spoke and the DHCP server. If multiple spokes are sending DHCPDISCOVER packets at the same time, the hub needs to be sure to return the right DHCPOFFER packets to the right spokes. To do this, on newer IOS versions, the hub adds the NBMA address of the spoke that sent the DHCPDISCOVER to the relay information option 82 field of the DHCP packet it sends to the DHCP server. This way, the information persists when the DHCP server sends a DHCPOFFER packet in response to the DHCPDISCOVER. The hub can send the DHCPOFFER to the spoke by reading the encoded NBMA address of the spoke in the option 82 relay information field. The DHCP DORA process completes, and the spoke obtains its IP addressing information.

After receiving its IP addressing information, the spoke can finally officially bring up its GRE tunnel interface. Once this occurs, the spoke stops suppressing the NHRP registration process and registers its newly acquired tunnel IP address with the hub, as normal.

You have just seen a basic outline of how a spoke obtains an IP address for its DMVPN tunnel interface through DHCP. Because some IOS versions do not support DHCP servers on the hub, this lab uses a model in which the hub is a DHCP relay agent. The DHCP server is located on another subnet that is reachable for the DMVPN hub. The configuration to enable the DHCP tunnel feature involves three steps:

1. Configure the hub to send unicast DHCP messages.

2. Configure the hub as a relay agent with the **ip helper-address** command.

3. Configure the spokes to clear the broadcast flag in DHCPDISCOVER messages.

The DHCP tunnel feature does not work with broadcast communication. Because of this, any hub that is to act as a relay agent must be configured to send unicast DHCP replies to the appropriate spoke. This is accomplished with the **ip dhcp support tunnel unicast** command in global configuration mode.

Second, after the hub has been configured to send unicast DHCP replies, it is configured with the **ip helper-address** command to enable its relay agent features.

Finally, the spoke itself may interfere with the DHCP reply process. By default, DHCP clients set a flag in the DHCPOFFER packet that forces DHCP communication to use broadcast instead of unicast. This needs to be disabled on the spoke routers with the **ip dhcp client broadcast-flag clear** command in interface configuration mode for the DMVPN tunnel interface.

These steps will be demonstrated below. R3, the DHCP server, is configured first with a DHCP pool using the **ip dhcp pool** command. The **network** command is used to specify the subnet network number and mask of the address pool. **ip dhcp excluded-address** ensures that the hub's IP address is not allocated to any spokes:

**To configure the DHCP server:**

**On R3:**

```
R3(config)#ip dhcp pool TST
R3(dhcp-config)#network 100.1.1.0 255.255.255.0
```

Exclude the IP addresses assigned to the hub's tunnel interfaces:

```
R3(config)#ip dhcp excluded-address 100.1.1.1 100.1.1.6
```

The DHCP configuration can be verified using the **show ip dhcp pool TST** command:

```
R3#show ip dhcp pool TST

Pool TST :
 Utilization mark (high/low)    : 100 / 0
 Subnet size (first/next)       : 0 / 0
 Total addresses                : 254
 Leased addresses               : 0
 Pending event                  : none
 1 subnet is currently in the pool :
 Current index    IP address range                      Leased addresses
 100.1.1.1        100.1.1.1        - 100.1.1.254         0
```

Before leaving R3, another thing needs to be sorted. With the current configuration, there are two paths R3 can use to reach the 100.1.1.0/24 network—through R5 or through R6—as shown below:

```
R3#show ip route eigrp 100 | begin Gate
Gateway of last resort is not set


D     5.0.0.0/8 [90/130816] via 35.1.1.5, 02:21:46, GigabitEthernet0/5
D     6.0.0.0/8 [90/130816] via 36.1.1.6, 02:21:28, GigabitEthernet0/6
D     7.0.0.0/8 [90/27008256] via 35.1.1.5, 02:18:08,
GigabitEthernet0/5
      100.0.0.0/24 is subnetted, 1 subnets
D        100.1.1.0 [90/26880256] via 36.1.1.6, 02:21:25,
GigabitEthernet0/6
                   [90/26880256] via 35.1.1.5, 02:21:25,
GigabitEthernet0/5
```

With two paths, R3 may decide to send DHCP reply packets through the backup hub instead of through R5, breaking the DHCP exchange. To remedy this, EIGRP delay is modified on the path via R6 to be artificially higher than the path via R5:

### Before:

```
R3#show interface g0/6 | include DLY

  MTU 1500 bytes, BW 1000000 Kbit/sec, DLY 10 usec,


R3(config)#interface g0/6
R3(config-if)#delay 100
```

### After:

```
R3#show interface g0/6 | include DLY

  MTU 1500 bytes, BW 1000000 Kbit/sec, DLY 1000 usec,


R3#show ip route eigrp 100 | begin Gate
Gateway of last resort is not set


D     5.0.0.0/8 [90/130816] via 35.1.1.5, 00:01:07, GigabitEthernet0/5
D     6.0.0.0/8 [90/156160] via 36.1.1.6, 00:00:44, GigabitEthernet0/6
D     7.0.0.0/8 [90/27008256] via 35.1.1.5, 00:01:07,
GigabitEthernet0/5
      100.0.0.0/24 is subnetted, 1 subnets
D        100.1.1.0 [90/26880256] via 35.1.1.5, 00:00:44,
GigabitEthernet0/5
```

The result of the EIGRP delay modification can be seen in the **show ip route eigrp 100** output above, where only a single path now exists for the 100.1.1.0/24 network. As long as the primary hub is up and running, DHCP reply packets will now be routed to R5 only.

Now that R3 is configured, the two hubs R5 and R6 are configured to allow DHCP. First, the **ip dhcp support tunnel unicast** command is used to enable unicast DHCP messaging for the tunnel interfaces. Then the relay agent is configured for the tunnel 100 DMVPN tunnel interface with the **ip helper-address 3.3.3.3** command (where 3.3.3.3 is the address of the DHCP server at R3):

### On R5:

```
R5(config)#ip dhcp support tunnel unicast
```
The following command configures R5 to function as a relay agent:
```
R5(config)#interface tunnel 100
R5(config-if)#ip helper-address 3.3.3.3
```

### On R6:

```
R6(config)#ip dhcp support tunnel unicast

R6(config)#interface tunnel 100
R6(config-if)#ip helper-address 3.3.3.3
```
The final step is configuration of the DHCP client R7. To begin, tunnel 100 is shut down on R7. Next, some housekeeping is performed. The original EIGRP **network** statement for the overlay referenced R7's specific IP address 100.1.1.7/32. Once configured for DHCP, R7 will not know what address its tunnel interface will receive. So, in order to make sure EIGRP is enabled on the tunnel interface, R7's **network** command for EIGRP AS 100 needs to be changed to match the entire 100.1.1.0/24 subnet.

The tunnel is first shut down for stability:

### On R7:

```
R7(config)#interface tunnel 100
R7(config-if)#shut
```
The **network eigrp** command is modified to include the entire 100.1.1.0/8 subnet:
```
R7(config)#router eigrp 100
R7(config-router)#no network 100.1.1.7 0.0.0.0
R7(config-router)#network 100.1.1.0 0.0.0.255
```

The last step is to use the **ip dhcp client broadcast-flag clear** command to configure R7 to clear the broadcast flag in the DHCPOFFER message and then use the **ip address dhcp** command to acquire an IP address through DHCP:

```
R7(config)#interface tun100
R7(config-if)#ip dhcp client broadcast-flag clear
R7(config-if)#ip address dhcp
```

Now, R7's tunnel 100 interface is brought back up. Notice the log message below, which indicates that it has been assigned the IP address 100.1.1.100 by the DHCP server:

```
R7(config)#interface tunnel 100
R7(config-if)#no shut
```

You should see the following console messages:

```
%LINEPROTO-5-UPDOWN: Line protocol on Interface Tunnel100, changed
state to up

%LINK-3-UPDOWN: Interface Tunnel100, changed state to up

%DUAL-5-NBRCHANGE: EIGRP-IPv4 100: Neighbor 100.1.1.5 (Tunnel100) is
up: new adjacency

%DHCP-6-ADDRESS_ASSIGN: Interface Tunnel100 assigned DHCP address
100.1.1.100, mask 255.255.255.0, hostname R7
```

## Task 3

Erase the startup configuration of the routers and reload them before proceeding to the next lab.

# Chapter 8

# MPLS and L3VPNs

## Lab 1: Configuring Label Distribution Protocol

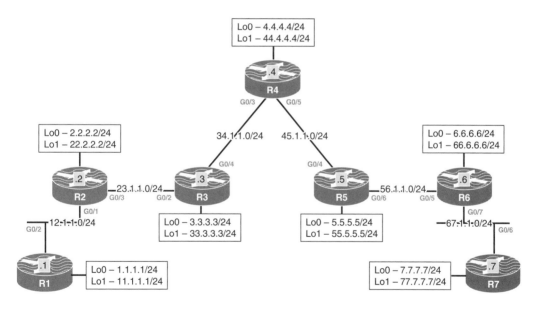

This lab should be conducted on the Enterprise POD.

## Lab Setup:

If you are using EVE-NG, and you have imported the EVE-NG topology from the EVE-NG-Topology folder, ignore the following tasks and use **Lab-1- Configuring Label Distribution Protocol** in the **MPLS** folder in EVE-NG.

To copy and paste the initial configurations, go to the **Initial-config** folder → **MPLS** folder → **Lab-1**.

## Task 1

Configure OSPF Area 0 on all links in the previous topology except the Loopback1 interfaces. Configure the OSPF router IDs of these routers to be 0.0.0.$x$, where $x$ is the router number.

## Task 2

Configure Label Distribution Protocol on the links interconnecting the routers in this topology. Ensure that the LDP ID is based on the IP address assigned to the Loopback0 interfaces of these routers. You may override a command from the previous task to accomplish this task.

## Task 3

Configure the interval for LDP neighbor discovery to be 15 seconds, with a hold timer of 45 seconds on all LSRs.

## Task 4

Configure the session keepalives and hold timers of all routers to 30 and 90 seconds, respectively.

## Task 5

Configure the LDP router ID of R1 to be its Loopback1 interface. You should not reload the router to accomplish this task.

## Task 6

The MPLS label space on a router is platform dependent. By default, the routers begin numbering the labels from 16 up to 100,000. Change the MPLS label space such that the routers use the following label ranges:

| Router | Label Range |
| --- | --- |
| R1 | 100–199 |
| R2 | 200–299 |
| R3 | 300–399 |
| R4 | 400–499 |
| R5 | 500–599 |
| R6 | 600–699 |
| R7 | 700–799 |

## Task 7

Examine and describe the control plane for the 7.7.7.7/32 prefix.

## Task 8

Examine and describe the data plane for the 7.7.7.7/32 prefix, starting from R1.

## Task 9

Configure LDP conditional label advertising to exclude the links that interconnect the routers in this topology.

## Task 10

To test the effects of TTL propagation, remove the **mpls ip** command from the G0/6 interface of R7, the G0/7 interface of R6, the G0/2 interface of R1, and the G0/1 interface of R2. R1 and R7 will pose as customer routers that do not have MPLS enabled. From R7, you will test the connection to 1.1.1.1 by using a traceroute.

## Task 11

Reconfigure the appropriate router/s such that a traceroute from R7 to 1.1.1.1 or from R1 to 7.7.7.7 will not display the links from the provider's network.

## Task 12

Remove the **mpls ip** command from all interfaces of the routers within the cloud—that is, R2, R3, R4, R5, and R6. Verify the configuration.

## Task 13

Enable LDP on all the links connecting the routers to each other. Do not use the **mpls ip** interface configuration command or a global configuration command to accomplish this task.

## Task 14

Configure a GigabitEthernet connection between R3 and R5, using the following parameters and policy:

- R3: G0/5, 35.1.1.3 /24
- R5: G0/3, 35.1.1.5 /24

These links should be included in OSPF Area 0.

## Task 15

Configure the appropriate router/s such that a failure in one of the links between R3 and R5 does not tear down the LDP session between the two LSRs. Do not configure a GRE or an IPnIP tunnel to accomplish this task.

## Task 16

Erase the startup configuration of the routers and reload the devices before proceeding to the next lab.

# Lab 2: Static and RIPv2 Routing in a VPN

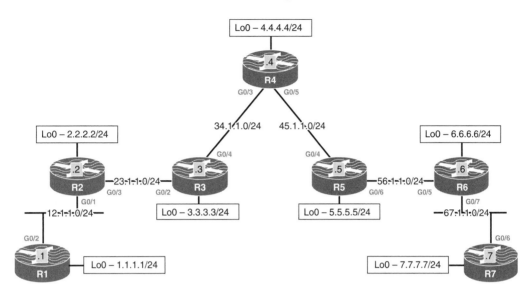

## Lab Setup:

If you are using EVE-NG, and you have imported the EVE-NG topology from the EVE-NG-Topology folder, ignore the following tasks and use Lab-2- Static and RIPv2 Routing in a VPN in the MPLS folder in EVE-NG.

To copy and paste the initial configurations, go to the Initial-config folder → MPLS folder → Lab-2.

## Task 1

Configure OSPF on the core MPLS routers, R2 through R6. Run OSPF Area 0 on the Lo0 interfaces and the links that connect these routers to each other. Configure the OSPF router IDs of R2, R3, R4, R5, and R6 as 0.0.0.2, 0.0.0.3, 0.0.0.4, 0.0.0.5, and 0.0.0.6, respectively.

## Task 2

Configure LDP between the core routers (R2 through R6). Ensure that each of these routers uses its Loopback0 interface as its LDP router ID. The core MPLS routers (R2 through R6) should use the following label ranges:

- R2: 200–299
- R3: 300–399

■ R4: 400–499

■ R5: 500–599

■ R6: 600–699

## Task 3

Configure MP-iBGP between R2 and R6 as they represent the provider edge routers in this topology in AS 100. Do not allow the BGP peers to share IPv4 routing information by default. The only BGP peering relationship should be VPNv4.

## Task 4

Configure virtual routing and forwarding (VRF) instances on R2 and R6 with the following RD and RT values:

■ On R2, a VRF instance named CA for Customer A (R1)

  ■ Route distinguisher (RD): 1:10

  ■ Route target (RT): 1:100

■ On R6, a VRF instance named CB for Customer A (R2)

  ■ Route distinguisher (RD): 1:20

  ■ Route target (RT): 1:100

## Task 5

Configure a static default route on each customer router located in VRF instances CA and CB. Configure these static routes to point to their respective PE router (R2 for R1 and R6 for R7). The PE routers (R2 and R6) should each be configured with a static route that reaches the loopback and the GigabitEthernet interface of the customer router. R2 and R6 should be able to see both static routes in their BGP tables.

## Task 6

Remove the static routes and replace the current method of routing between the PEs and customers with the RIPv2 routing protocol.

## Task 7

Erase the startup configuration of these routers and reload the devices before proceeding to the next lab.

# Lab 3: EIGRP Routing in a VPN

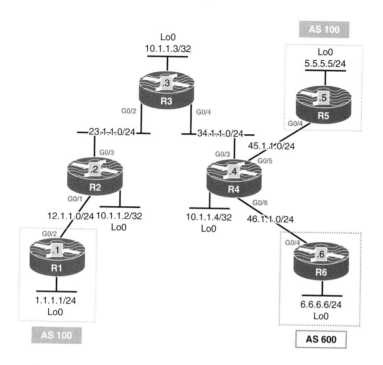

## Lab Setup:

If you are using EVE-NG, and you have imported the EVE-NG topology from the **EVE-NG-Topology** folder, ignore the following tasks and use **Lab-3- EIGRP Routing in a VPN** in the **MPLS** folder in EVE-NG.

To copy and paste the initial configurations, go to the **Initial-config** folder → **MPLS** folder → **Lab-3**.

## Task 1

Configure OSPF on the core MPLS routers R2(PE-2), R3(P-3), and R4(PE-4). Run OSPF Area 0 on the:

- G0/3 interface of R2

- G0/3 interface of R4

- G0/2 and G0/4 interfaces of R3

- Loopback interfaces of these three routers

The OSPF router IDs of these routers should be set to 0.0.0.$x$, where $x$ is the router number.

## Task 2

Configure LDP between the core routers. These routers should use their Loopback0 interfaces as their LDP router IDs. The core MPLS routers (R2, R3, and R4) should use the following label ranges:

- R2: 200–299
- R3: 300–399
- R4: 400–499

## Task 3

Configure an MP-BGP peer session for AS 100 between R2 and R4 as they represent the provider edge routers in this topology. Do not allow the BGP peers to share IPv4 routing information by default. The only BGP peering relationship should be VPNv4.

## Task 4

Configure VRF instances on R2 and R4 and enable VRF forwarding on the interfaces of these two routers based on the following chart:

| PE | VRF | RD | RT | Interface |
|----|-----|------|-------|-----------|
| R2 | 11 | 1:10 | 1:156 | G0/1 |
| R4 | 55 | 1:50 | 1:156 | G0/5 |
|    | 66 | 1:60 | 1:156 | G0/6 |

You should configure an address family when configuring VRF 66.

## Task 5

Configure the following:

1. EIGRP AS 100 between R1 and R2 (PE-2)
2. EIGRP AS 100 between R4 (PE-4) and R5
3. EIGRP 600 between R4 (PE-4) and R6

## Task 6

Configure the PE routers (R2 and R4) so the CE routers (R1, R5, and R6) can see EIGRP routes advertised from the other CE routers and have reachability to them.

## Task 7

Erase the startup configuration of these routers and reload the devices before proceeding to the next lab.

# Lab 4: EIGRP Site-of-Origin

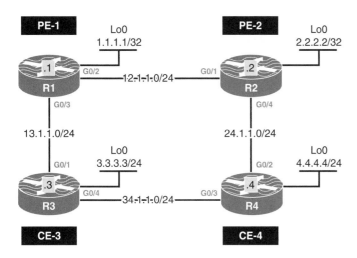

## Lab Setup:

If you are using EVE-NG, and you have imported the EVE-NG topology from the EVE-NG-Topology folder, ignore the following tasks and use **Lab-4- EIGRP Site-of-Origin** in the **MPLS** folder in EVE-NG.

To copy and paste the initial configurations, go to the **Initial-config** folder → **MPLS** folder → **Lab-4**.

## Task 1

Configure OSPF Area 0 on the following interfaces:

- R1: Lo0 and G0/2
- R2: Lo0 and G0/1

Configure the OSPF router IDs of these two routers as 0.0.0.$x$, where $x$ is the router number.

Configure EIGRP AS 100 in named mode on the following interfaces:

- R3: Lo0 and G0/4
- R4: Lo0 and G0/3

## Task 2

Configure the PE routers (R1 and R2) to support MPLS VPN using AS 65001 and using their Loopback0 interfaces. Use the following parameters for VRF configuration:

| | |
|---|---|
| **VRF name** | TST |
| **RD on R1** | 1:10 |
| **RD on R2** | 1:20 |
| **Route target on both** | 34:34 |
| **PE-CE routing protocol** | EIGRP 100 |

Ensure full connectivity between the customer's (R3 and R4) routes. You should configure named mode where possible.

## Task 3

Configure the appropriate routers to prevent the local routes from being learned from the backbone. _Do not_ configure R3 or R4, access lists, or prefix lists to accomplish this task.

## Task 4

After configuring the previous task, it is obvious that there is no redundancy. If the CE routers (R3 and R4) lose their directly connected link, they will have no reachability to each other's routes. Configure the appropriate router/s based on the following policy:

- If the link between R3 and R4 is up, they should use each other as the next hop to reach the routes they are advertising.

- If the link between R3 and R4 is down, they should go through the MPLS cloud to reach each other's routes.

You should configure and test two different solutions to accomplish this task.

## Task 5

Erase the startup configuration of the routers and reload the devices before proceeding to the next lab.

# Lab 5: OSPF Routing in a VPN

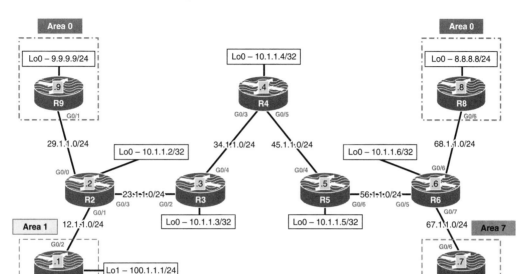

## Lab Setup:

If you are using EVE-NG, and you have imported the EVE-NG topology from the
**EVE-NG-Topology** folder, ignore the following tasks and use **Lab-5- OSPF Routing in a VPN** in the **MPLS** folder in EVE-NG.

To copy and paste the initial configurations, go to the **Initial-config** folder → **MPLS** folder → **Lab-5**.

## Task 1

Configure OSPF on the core MPLS routers (R2, R3, R4, R5, and R6). Run OSPF Area 0 on the following:

- G0/3 interface of R2
- G0/2 and G0/4 interfaces of R3
- G0/3 and G0/5 interfaces of R4
- G0/4 and G0/6 interfaces of R5
- G0/5 interface of R6
- Loopback0 interfaces of these routers

Configure the OSPF router IDs of these routers to be 0.0.0.$x$, where $x$ is the router number.

## Task 2

Configure LDP on the core routers. These routers should use their Loopback0 interfaces as their LDP router IDs. The core MPLS routers (R2, R3, R4, R5, and R6) should use the following label ranges:

- R2: 200–299

- R3: 300–399

- R4: 400–499

- R5: 500–599

- R6: 600–699

## Task 3

Configure MP-BGP peer session between R2 and R6 as they represent the provider edge routers in this topology in AS 100. Do not allow the BGP peers to share IPv4 routing information by default. The only BGP peering relationship should be VPNv4.

## Task 4

Configure VRF instances on R2 and R6 and enable VRF forwarding on the interfaces of these two routers based on the following chart:

| Router | VRF | RD | RT | Interface |
|--------|-----|------|-------|-----------|
| R2 | 99 | 1:90 | 1:100 | G0/0 |
| | 11 | 1:10 | 1:100 | G0/1 |
| R6 | 88 | 1:80 | 1:100 | G0/8 |
| | 77 | 1:70 | 1:100 | G0/7 |

## Task 5

Configure customers R1, R9, R7, and R8 with a VRF service that incorporates OSPF as the routing protocol. R2 should use OSPF process IDs 11 and 99 for R1 and R9, respectively. R6 should use process IDs 77 and 88 for R7 and R8, respectively.

- All directly connected interfaces of R1 should be configured in Area 1 except R1's Lo1 interface. R1 should redistribute its Lo1 interface in this routing domain.

- All directly connected interfaces of R9 should be configured in Area 0.

- All directly connected interfaces of R7 should be configured in Area 7.

- All directly connected interfaces of R8 should be configured in Area 8.

## Task 6

Erase the startup configuration of the routers and reload the devices before proceeding to the next lab.

# Lab 6: Backdoor Links and OSPF

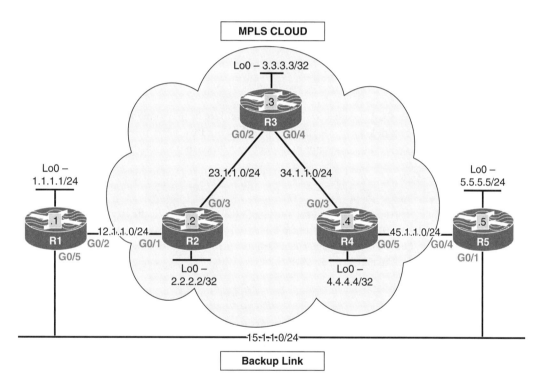

## Lab Setup:

If you are using EVE-NG, and you have imported the EVE-NG topology from the **EVE-NG-Topology** folder, ignore the following tasks and use **Lab-6- Backdoor Links and OSPF** in the **MPLS** folder in EVE-NG.

To copy and paste the initial configurations, go to the **Initial-config** folder → **MPLS** folder → **Lab-6**.

## Task 1

Configure OSPF on the core MPLS routers (R2, R3, and R4). Run OSPF Area 0 on the links and Lo0 interfaces interconnecting these routers. Configure the OSPF router IDs of these routers to be 0.0.0.$x$, where $x$ is the router number.

## Task 2

Configure LDP between the core routers. These routers should use their Loopback0 interfaces as their LDP router IDs. The core MPLS routers (R2, R3, and R4) should use the following label ranges:

- R2: 200–299

- R3: 300–399

- R4: 400–499

## Task 3

Configure MP-BGP peer session between R2 and R4 as they represent the provider edge routers in this topology in AS 100. Do not allow the BGP peers to share IPv4 routing information by default. The only BGP peering relationship should be VPNv4.

## Task 4

Configure a virtual routing and forwarding (VRF) instance with the name aa, the route distinguisher (RD) 1:10, and the route target (RT) 1:100 for R1 (the customer) on R2 (the PE router). On R4, use the same route targets for the VRF instance but configure the RD to be 1:50 and the name of the VRF to be aa.

## Task 5

Configure OSPF using the same process ID on the customer routers (R1 and R5). Configure MP-BGP such that the customer routers can see each other's routes. Customer routers should advertise their Lo0 interfaces with the correct mask.

## Task 6

Configure the G0/5 interface of the customer router R1 and the G0/1 interface of the customer router R5 as a backup link. Ensure that the MPLS service is preferred over the backup link.

## Task 7

Provide another solution to the problem that is different from the one in the previous task.

## Task 8

To satisfy the customer, who is complaining about two additional routes in their routing table, remove them. These are the IP addresses assigned to the Lo24 interface of R2 and Lo42 interface of R4.

## Task 9

Erase the startup configuration of the routers and reload the devices before proceeding to the next lab.

# Lab 7: BGP Routing in a VPN

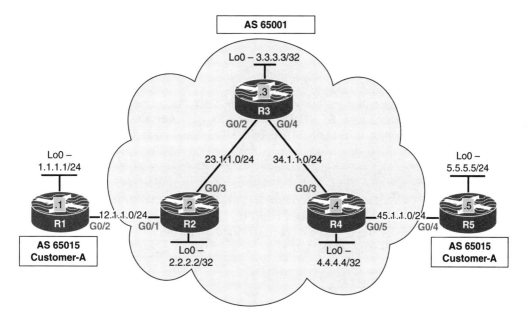

## Lab Setup:

If you are using EVE-NG, and you have imported the EVE-NG topology from the **EVE-NG-Topology** folder, ignore the following tasks and use **Lab-7- BGP Routing in a VPN** in the **MPLS** folder in EVE-NG.

To copy and paste the initial configurations, go to the **Initial-config** folder → **MPLS** folder → **Lab-7.**

## Task 1

Configure OSPF on the core MPLS routers (R2, R3, and R4). Run OSPF Area 0 on the links and Lo0 interfaces interconnecting these routers. Configure the OSPF router IDs of these routers to be 0.0.0.$x$, where $x$ is the router number.

## Task 2

Configure LDP between the core routers. These routers should use their Loopback0 interfaces as their LDP router IDs. The core MPLS routers (R2, R3, and R4) should use the following label ranges:

- R2: 200–299

- R3: 300–399

- R4: 400–499

## Task 3

Configure MP-BGP peer session between R2 and R4 as they represent the provider edge routers in this topology in AS 100. Do not allow the BGP peers to share IPv4 routing information by default. The only BGP peering relationship should be VPNv4.

## Task 4

Configure a virtual routing and forwarding (VRF) instance with the name aa, the route distinguisher (RD) 1:10, and the route target (RT) 1:100 for R1 (the customer) on R2 (the PE router). On R4, use the same route targets for the VRF instance but configure the RD to be 1:50 and the name of the VRF to be aa.

## Task 5

Configure BGP as the MPLS routing protocol between the CEs (R1 and R5) and their respective PEs (R2 and R4). The customer AS of 65015 should be assigned to both customer sites.

## Task 6

Erase the startup configuration of the routers and reload the devices before proceeding to the next lab.

# Lab 8: MPLS and NAT

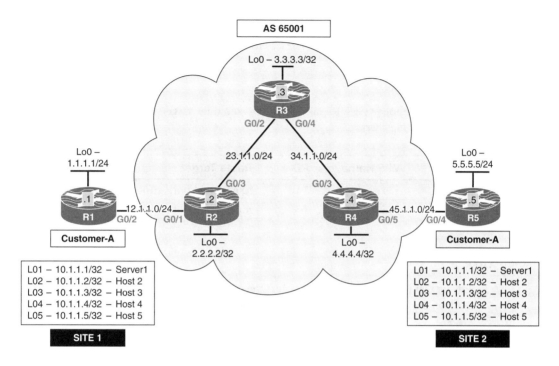

## Lab Setup:

If you are using EVE-NG, and you have imported the EVE-NG topology from the **EVE-NG-Topology** folder, ignore the following tasks and use **Lab-8- MPLS and NAT** in the **MPLS** folder in EVE-NG.

To copy and paste the initial configurations, go to the **Initial-config** folder → **MPLS** folder → **Lab-8**.

## Task 1

Configure OSPF on the core MPLS routers (R2, R3, and R4). Run OSPF Area 0 on the links and Lo0 interfaces interconnecting these routers. Configure the OSPF router IDs of these routers to be 0.0.0.$x$, where $x$ is the router number. Configure the CE routers, R1 and R5, with a static default route pointing to their next hop router.

## Task 2

Configure LDP between the core routers. These routers should use their Loopback0 interfaces as their LDP router IDs.

## Task 3

Configure MP-BGP between R2 and R4 as they represent the provider edge routers in this topology in AS 100. The only BGP peering relationship should be VPNv4. These two neighbors should use their Lo0 interfaces for their peering.

## Task 4

Configure the following VRF instances, RDs, and route targets on the PE routers, based on the following chart:

| Router | VRF Name | RD | Route Target | Interface |
|--------|----------|------|------------------------|-----------|
| R2 | 111 | 1:10 | route-target both 1:100 | G0/1 |
| R4 | 555 | 1:50 | route-target both 1:100 | G0/5 |

## Task 5

Ensure that the hosts in Site-1 can access the server in Site-2 and vice versa. Configure NAT on the CE routers (R1 and R5). Use the following translation chart:

| Router | Inside Local | Inside Global |
|--------|--------------------|----------------------|
| R1 | 10.1.1.1 | 100.1.1.1 |
|    | 10.1.1.2–10.1.1.5 | 100.1.1.2–100.1.1.5 |
| R5 | 10.1.1.1 | 200.1.1.1 |
|    | 10.1.1.2–10.1.1.5 | 200.1.1.2–200.1.1.5 |

## Task 6

Erase the startup configuration of the routers and reload the devices before proceeding to the next lab.

# Lab 9: Route Targets, Import Maps, and Export Maps

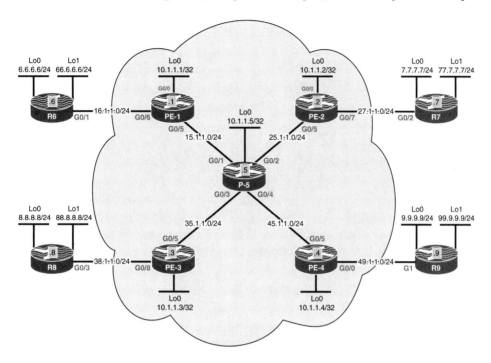

## Lab Setup:

If you are using EVE-NG, and you have imported the EVE-NG topology from the **EVE-NG-Topology** folder, ignore the following tasks and use **Lab-9-Route-Targets-Import maps and Export maps** in the **MPLS** folder in EVE-NG.

To copy and paste the initial configurations, go to the **Initial-config** folder → **MPLS** folder → **Lab-9**.

## Task 1

Configure OSPF on the core MPLS routers (PE-1, PE-2, PE-3, PE-4, and P-5). Run OSPF Area 0 on the G0/5 interfaces of PE-1(R1), PE-2(R2), PE-3 (R3), and PE-4(R4), the G0/1, G0/2, G0/3, and G0/4 interfaces of P-5(R5), and the loopback interfaces of these routers. Configure the OSPF router IDs of these routers to be 0.0.0.$x$, where $x$ is the router number.

## Task 2

Configure LDP between the core routers. These routers should use their Loopback0 interfaces as their LDP router IDs. The core MPLS routers (PE-1, PE-2, PE-3, PE-4, and P-5) should use the following label ranges:

1. PE-1: 100–199

2. PE-2: 200–299

3. PE-3: 300–399

4. PE-4: 400–499

5. P-5: 500–599

## Task 3

Configure MP-BGP peer session between all PE routers using AS 100. Do not allow the BGP peers to share IPv4 routing information by default. The only BGP peering relationship should be VPNv4.

## Task 4

Configure VRF instances and RDs on the PE routers and enable VRF forwarding on the interfaces of these routers based on the following chart:

| Router | VRF | RD | Interface |
| --- | --- | --- | --- |
| PE-1 | 66 | 1:60 | G0/6 |
| PE-2 | 77 | 1:70 | G0/7 |
| PE-3 | 88 | 1:80 | G0/8 |
| PE-4 | 99 | 1:90 | G0/0 |

Do not configure route targets.

## Task 5

Configure routing between the CE and the PE routers, based on the following chart:

| CE Router | PE Router | Routing Protocol |
| --- | --- | --- |
| R6 | PE-1 | EIGRP 100 |
| R7 | PE-2 | OSPF area 0 |
| R8 | PE-3 | RIPv2 |
| R9 | PE-4 | BGP AS 200 |

## Task 6

Configure the appropriate PE/s such that routers R6 and R7 can exchange routes and be in the same VPN.

## Task 7

Configure the appropriate PE/s such that routers R7 and R9 can exchange routes and be in the same VPN.

## Task 8

Configure the appropriate PE/s such that routers R8 and R9 can exchange routes and be in the same VPN.

## Task 9

Configure the appropriate PE/s such that routers R6 and R8 can exchange routes and be in the same VPN.

## Task 10

Configure PE-1 such that R6 only receives networks 7.7.7.7/32 and 8.8.8.0/24. This may affect the reachability achieved in some of the previous tasks.

## Task 11

Configure the following loopback interfaces on R6, R7, and R8:

- R6: Loopback200, 200.1.1.6/32
- R7: Loopback200, 200.1.1.7/32
- R8: Loopback200, 200.1.1.8/32

## Task 12

Erase the startup configuration of the routers and reload the devices before proceeding to the next lab.

# Lab 10: Internet Access Methods: Partial Internet Routes

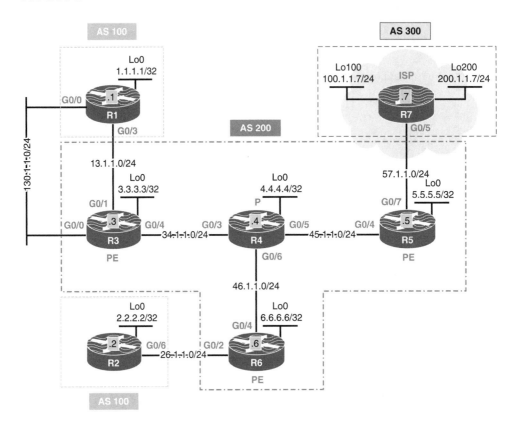

## Lab Setup:

If you are using EVE-NG, and you have imported the EVE-NG topology from the **EVE-NG-Topology** folder, ignore the following tasks and use **Lab-10- Internet Access Methods Partial Internet Routes** in the **MPLS** folder in EVE-NG.

To copy and paste the initial configurations, go to the **Initial-config** folder → **MPLS** folder → **Lab-10**.

## Task 1

Configure the core routers (R3, R4, R5, and R6) to support MPLS VPN using AS 200.

■ R5 in AS 200 should be configured with an IPv4 peering to the physical interface of R7 in AS 300. R7 should advertise its Lo100 and Lo200 interfaces in this AS.

■ R3 in AS 200 should be configured with an IPv4 peering to the G0/0 interface of R1 in AS 100.

## Task 2

Configure a VRF instance called aaa on R3 and R6 (the PE routers).

- Apply this VRF instance to the G0/1 interface of R3 facing R1 and the G0/2 interface of R6 facing R2 (the CE routers).

- Use the RD 1:10 and the route target 1:100 on R3 and the RD 1:20 with the same RT configured on R3.

## Task 3

Ensure the customers R1 and R2 only receive partial Internet routes using the following policies:

- *Only* R1 should receive the partial Internet routes.

- R2 should go through R1 to reach the partial routes.

## Task 4

Erase the startup configuration on all routers and reload the devices before proceeding to the next lab.

# Chapter 9

# IPv6

## Lab 1: Acquiring an IPv6 Address

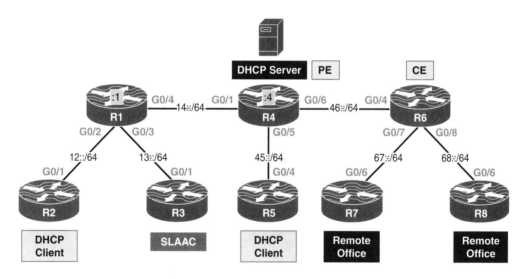

This lab should be conducted on the Enterprise POD.

## Task 1

Configure the segment connecting R1 to R3. Do not assign an IPv6 address to R3. R3 should acquire the network portion of its global unicast IPv6 address through SLAAC process from R1 and R1 *only*. Configure R1's link-local address to be FE80::1. Use the following MAC addresses for these two routers:

■ R1: 0000.1111.1111

■ R3: 0000.3333.3333

## Task 2

Configure the link connecting R4 to R5. Do not assign an IPv6 address to the G0/4 interface of R5. Ensure that R5 is configured as a DHCP client, acquiring an IPv6 address from R4. Ensure that R5 gets its domain name, MicronicsTraining.com, and the DNS server's IPv6 address, 2001:5555::5, from R4.

## Task 3

Configure the link connecting R1 to R4 based on the diagram at the beginning of this lab. Configure the link connecting R1 to R2 based on the following policy:

■ Do not configure an IPv6 address on R2's G0/1 interface. Ensure that this router is configured to acquire an IPv6 address from the DHCP server (R4). R1 should be configured as a DHCP relay agent.

■ Ensure that R4 supplies the following to the client, R2:

■ An IPv6 address from the 12::/64 network range

■ The DNS server address 2001:2222::2

■ The domain name www.R2.com

## Task 4

Configure R3 to get the DNS server and its domain name from the DHCP server, R4, but it should continue using SLAAC for its IPv6 address.

## Task 5

Reconfigure R5 to acquire its IPv6 address from R4 (the DHCP server) using two DHCPv6 messages instead of four.

## Task 6

Configure R4 based on the following:

- Do not assign an IPv6 address to R6, R7, or R8.

- Configure the G0/6 interface of R4 with the 46::4/64 IPv6 address and the MAC address 0000.4444.4444.

## Task 7

ISP-A has the IPv6 prefix 46:1:1::/48, and it needs to subnet this network to /56 subnets and use subnet 1 for its client R6. The CE router, R6, has 2 sites that are connected through its G0/7 and G0/8 interfaces, but soon this company will have 16 remote sites.

- Ensure that R6 acquires a subnet from R4, the CE router, as it adds more remote sites.

- Ensure that the first nonzero subnet is automatically assigned to its G0/8 interface with the host portion of its IPv6 address as ::88. Ensure that R8 uses R6 as its default gateway.

- Ensure that R6's G0/7 interface is automatically assigned the second nonzero subnet with the host portion ::77. Ensure that R7 uses R6 as its default gateway.

- Ensure that R7 and R8 automatically acquire the network portion of their IPv6 addresses from R6 and auto-generate the host portion of their IPv6 addresses.

- Ensure that both R7 and R8 have reachability to R4's G0/6 IPv6 address.

Do not configure any static route or configure static IPv6 address(es) to accomplish this task.

## Task 8

Erase the startup configuration on all routers and reload the devices before proceeding to the next lab.

## Lab 2: DMVPN and IPv6

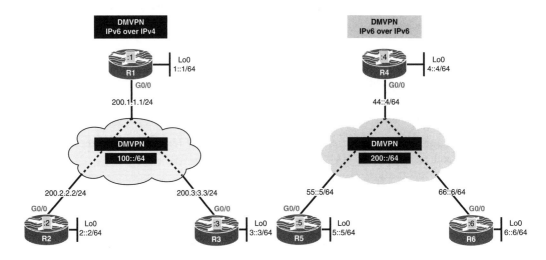

### Task 1

SW1 represents the Internet. Configure a static default route on R1, R2, and R3, pointing to the appropriate interface on SW1. If this configuration is performed correctly, these three routers should be able to ping and have reachability to the G0/0 interfaces of R1, R2, and R3. Ensure that the switch interface to which these routers are connected has a .10 in the host portion of the IP address for that subnet. Shut down all the ports on SW1 and set the duplex mode to half. Only use the ports in the above topology.

### Task 2

Configure DMVPN such that R1 is the hub, and R2 and R3 are configured as the spokes. Use 100::*x*/64 range, where *x* is the router number for the tunnel interfaces of these three routers. Configure the link-local IPv6 address of these routers to the FE80::*x* format, where *x* is the router number. If this configuration is performed correctly, these three routers should have reachability to all tunnel endpoints. When configuring the DMVPN, use static mappings. Ensure that the tunnel interfaces are configured in a multipoint manner to accomplish this task.

### Task 3

Configure the Loopback0 interfaces of these three routers based on the topology. Configure OSPFv3 Area 0 on the Loopback0 and the tunnel 1 interfaces of these three routers. If this configuration is done successfully, these routers should have reachability to the IPv6 addresses of the other routers. Ensure that the router IDs of these routers are using the 0.0.0.*x* format, where *x* is the router number. Ensure that the loopback interfaces are advertised with the correct mask. Configure the OSPF network type for the tunnel interfaces as broadcast.

## Task 4

SW1 represents the Internet. Configure an IPv6 static default route on R4, R5, and R6, pointing to the appropriate interfaces on SW1. If this configuration is performed correctly, these routers should be able to ping and have reachability to the IPv6 address of the G0/0 interfaces of all routers in this topology. Ensure that the switch interface to which the routers are connected is configured with the link-local IPv6 address fe80::10 and the global unicast IPv6 addresses 44::10, 55::10, and 66::10 for the connections to R4, R5, and R6, respectively.

## Task 5

Configure the second DMVPN network using the following policy:

- R4, R5, and R6 must use the IPv6 addresses of their G0/0 interfaces as the source of the tunnel.

- Ensure that the tunnel mode is configured as GRE Multipoint.

- Ensure that the IPv6 addresses of the tunnel interfaces are configured using the $200::x/64$ format, where $x$ is the router number.

- Configure the IPv6 addresses of the loopback interfaces based on the topology. These loopback interfaces must be advertised with the correct mask.

- Run OSPFv3 Area 0 on the tunnel and their Loopback0 interfaces. Ensure that the OSPF network type of the tunnel interface is configured as point-to-multipoint on the hub and point-to-point on the spokes. Use an address family to accomplish this task.

- Ensure that R4 is configured to be the NHS.

- Ensure that this DMVPN network is configured in Phase 3.

## Task 6

Erase the startup configuration on all routers and reload the devices before proceeding to the next lab.

## Lab 3: Configuring OSPFv3

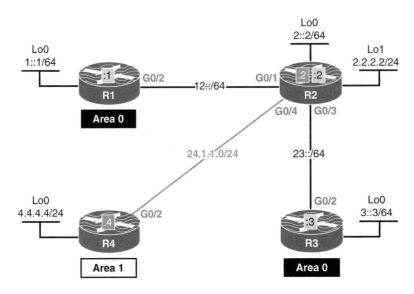

### Task 1

Configure the above topology. Do not configure any routing protocol.

### Task 2

Configure OSPF for IPv4 and IPv6 on the routers in this topology, based on the following policy:

- Configure the GigabitEthernet and Loopback0 interfaces of R1 and R2 in Area 0.

- Configure R4's G0/2 and its loopback interface in Area 1.

- Configure R2's G0/4 interface in Area 1 and R2's G0/3 interface in Area 0.

- Ensure that only R2 and R4 use the address family configuration method to accomplish this task.

- Configure R3's G0/2 and Loopback0 interfaces in Area 0.

- Ensure that the loopback interfaces are configured with the correct mask.

- Ensure that the router ID of each of these routers is configured to use the 0.0.0.$x$ format, where $x$ is the router number.

## Task 3

Erase the startup configuration on all routers and reload the devices before proceeding to the next lab.

# Lab 4: Summarization of Internal and External Networks

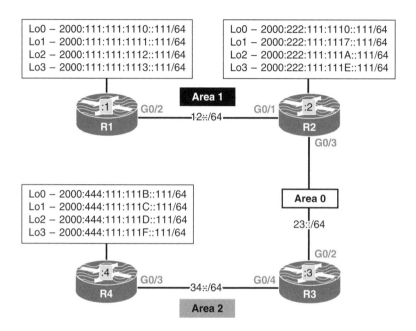

## Task 1

Configure the above topology. Do not configure any routing protocol(s). Configure the IPv6 link-local addresses of these routers as shown below:

- R1: FE80::1

- R2: FE80::2

- R3: FE80::3

- R4: FE80::4

## Task 2

Configure OSPFv3 based on the following requirements:

- Configure OSPFv3 on R1 and run all its directly connected interfaces in Area 1. Do not use an address family to configure this router. Configure the loopback interfaces with the correct mask. Ensure that the router ID of this router is set to 0.0.0.1.

■ Configure OSPFv3 on R2 using an address family. Ensure that this router runs OSPFv3 Area 1 on its G0/1 and OSPFv3 Area 0 on its G0/3. Ensure that the loop-back interface of this router is configured in Area 0. Configure the loopback inter-faces with the correct mask. Ensure that the router ID of this router is set to 0.0.0.2.

■ Configure OSPFv3 on R3 and run its G0/2 interface in Area 0 and its G0/4 interface in Area 2. Do not use an address family to configure this router. Ensure that the router ID of this router is set to 0.0.0.3.

■ Configure OSPFv3 on R4 using an address family. Ensure that this router runs OSPFv3 Area 2 on its G0/3 interface. Ensure that the loopback interface of this router is advertised into OSPFv3 Area 2. Ensure that the router ID of this router is set to 0.0.0.4.

## Task 3

Summarize the loopback interfaces configured on R1 and R2. Ensure that these routers advertise a single route for their loopback interfaces. Do not configure more than three summary routes to accomplish this task.

## Task 4

Summarize the external routes redistributed on R4. If this is configured correctly, the rest of the routers should see a single summary route for the four networks redistributed into the OSPF routing domain.

## Task 5

The policy for summarizing external routes has changed. The routers in Area 2 should see all specific external routes, whereas the routers in the other areas should see a single sum-mary route for the four external routes.

## Task 6

Ensure that none of the routers have a discard route in their routing table.

## Task 7

Erase the startup configuration on the routers, the config.text file, and the VLAN.dat file for the switches and reload the devices before proceeding to the next lab.

# Lab 5: OSPFv3 Broadcast Networks

```
        Lo0                              Lo0
        1::1/64                          2::2/64
         |     _____               |     _____
         |____|   :1      |              |____|   :2      |
              |    R1     |                   |    R2     |
              |_____|                   |_____|
                   | G0/0                          | G0/0
                   |                               |
    _____|_____1234::/64_____|_____
    |                              |
    | G0/0                         | G0/0
 ___|_____                    __|_____
|   :3      |___                |   :4      |___
|    R3     |  | Lo0            |    R4     |  | Lo0
|_____|  | 3::3/64        |_____|  | 4::4/64

    Lo0                              Lo0
    3::3/64                          4::4/64
```

## Task 1

Configure the routers based on the above topology. Do not configure any routing protocol. If this configuration is performed successfully, these routers should be able to ping
their directly connected routers. Ensure that the link-local IPv6 addresses of the routers
are set to fe80::1, fe80::2, fe80::3, and fe80::4 for routers R1, R2, R3, and R4, respectively.
Ensure that all ports on this switch are configured with half duplex. Ensure that the
unused ports are in an administratively down state.

## Task 2

Configure OSPF Area 0 on all routers' directly connected interfaces. Ensure that loopback interfaces are advertised with the correct mask. The router IDs must be configured
with 0.0.0.$x$ format, where $x$ is the router number.

- For R3 and R4, use an address family to accomplish this task.

- Ensure that R4 is the DR for this segment.

## Task 3

## Lab Setup:

If you are using EVE-NG, and you have imported the EVE-NG topology from the
**EVE-NG-Topology** folder, ignore the following tasks and use **Lab-5-Task-3 OSPFv3
Broadcast Networks** in the **IPv6** folder in EVE-NG.

Reload all the devices, and then, to copy and paste the initial configurations, go to the
**initial-config** folder → **IPv6** folder → **Lab-5-Task-3**.

Configure OSPFv3 on the tunnel and Loopback0 interfaces of all routers, based on the
following policy:

- R1 is the hub, and R2, R3, and R4 are configured as spokes. Do not change the topology.

- Configure the tunnel interfaces to be OSPFv3 broadcast network type. Configure R3 and R4 using an address family.

- Ensure that the loopback interfaces are advertised with the correct mask.

- Configure the router IDs of the routers to use the 0.0.0.x format, where x is the router number.

- Ensure that the DMVPN network is not configured with dynamic mapping.

## Task 4

Erase the startup configuration on the routers, the config.text file, and the VLAN.dat file for the switches and reload the devices before proceeding to the next lab.

# Lab 6: OSPFv3 Non-Broadcast Networks

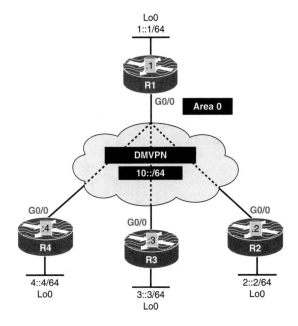

# Lab Setup:

If you are using EVE-NG, and you have imported the EVE-NG topology from the **EVE-NG-Topology** folder, ignore the following and use **Lab-6-OSPFv3 Non-Broadcast Networks** in the **IPv6** folder in EVE-NG.

To copy and paste the initial configurations, go to the **initial-config** folder → **IPv6** folder → **Lab-6**.

## Task 1

Configure OSPFv3 on the tunnel and Loopback0 interfaces of all routers based on the following policy:

- R1 is the hub, and R2, R3, and R4 are configured as spokes. Do not change the topology.

- Configure the tunnel interfaces of all routers to be OSPFv3 non-broadcast network type. Ensure that these routers are configured without an address family.

- Ensure that the loopback interfaces are advertised with the correct mask.

- Configure the router IDs of the routers to use the 0.0.0.$x$ format, where $x$ is the router number.

- The DMVPN network is configured by the initial configuration file. Do not configure dynamic mapping. The DMVPN network must remain as a hub and spoke. Do not change the tunnel mode on any of the routers.

## Task 2

Erase the startup configuration on the routers, the config.text file, and the VLAN.dat file for the switches and reload the devices before proceeding to the next lab.

## Lab 7: OSPFv3 Point-to-Point Networks

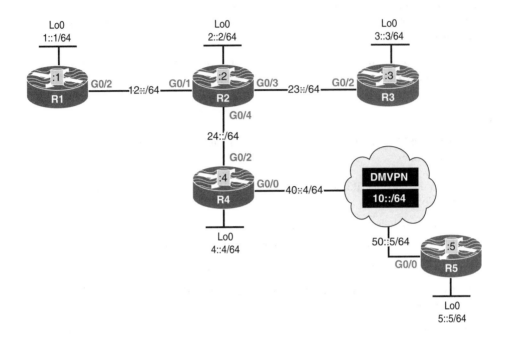

## Lab Setup:

If you are using EVE-NG, and you have imported the EVE-NG topology from the
EVE-NG-Topology folder, ignore the following and use **Lab-7-OSPFv3 Point-to-Point
Networks** in the **IPv6** folder in EVE-NG.

To copy and paste the initial configurations, go to the **initial-config** folder → **IPv6**
folder → **Lab-7**.

## Task 1

Configure OSPFv3 based on the following policy:

- Configure OSPFv3 Area 0 on all routers and their directly connected interfaces.

- Configure the router IDs to be 0.0.0.$x$, where $x$ is the router number.

- Ensure that the loopback interfaces are advertised using the correct mask.

- Ensure that there is not a DR in any of the segments in the above topology.

## Task 2

Erase the startup configuration on the routers, the config.text file, and the VLAN.dat file
for the switches and reload the devices before proceeding to the next lab.

# Lab 8: OSPFv3 Point-to-Multipoint Networks

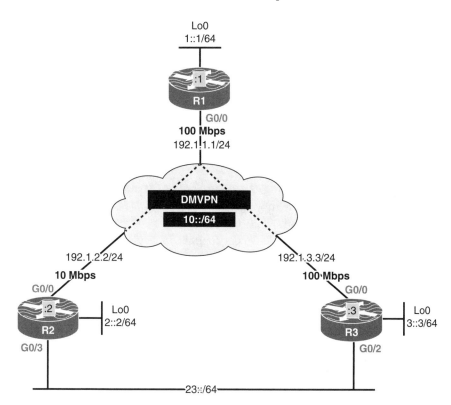

This lab should be conducted on the Enterprise POD.

Lab Setup:

If you are using EVE-NG, and you have imported the EVE-NG topology from the
EVE-NG-Topology folder, ignore the following and use Lab-8-OSPFv3 Point-to-
Multipoint Networks in the IPv6 folder in EVE-NG.

To copy and paste the initial configurations, go to the initial-config folder → IPv6
folder → Lab-8.

## Task 1

Configure OSPFv3 based on the following policy:

- Configure the DMVPN network in a hub-and-spoke manner, where R1 is the hub,
  and R2 and R3 are spoke routers.

- Configure OSPFv3 Area 0 on all routers and their directly connected interfaces except the G0/0 interface of these three routers.

- Use the OSPF router IDs 0.0.0.1, 0.0.0.2, and 0.0.0.3 for R1, R2, and R3, respectively.

- Ensure that the loopback interfaces are advertised using the correct mask.

- Ensure that there is not a DR/BDR in any segment of this topology.

- Ensure that the tunnel interfaces of these routers are configured with the point-to-multipoint OSPF network type.

- Do not map multicast dynamically on the hub router.

### Task 2

Since R2's connection to the cloud is 10 Mbps, and R3's connection is 100, ensure that R1 does not perform equal-cost load sharing for the network 23::/64. Ensure that R1 goes through R3 to reach the 23::/64 network. Do not configure policy-based routing (PBR) or use the **ip ospf cost** command to accomplish this task.

### Task 3

Erase the startup configuration on all routers before proceeding to the next lab.

## Lab 9: OSPFv3 Cost and Auto-Cost

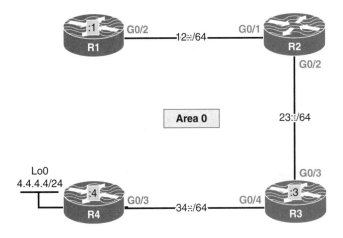

## Lab Setup:

If you are using EVE-NG, and you have imported the EVE-NG topology from the **EVE-NG-Topology** folder, ignore the following and use **Lab-9-OSPFv3 Cost and Auto-Cost** in the **IPv6** folder in EVE-NG.

To copy and paste the initial configurations, go to the **initial-config** folder → **IPv6** folder → **Lab-9**.

## Task 1

Configure OSPFv3 Area 0 on all routers and their directly connected interfaces. Ensure that the loopback interface of R4 is advertised with the correct mask. Configure 0.0.0.1, 0.0.0.2, 0.0.0.3, and 0.0.0.4 as the router IDs of R1, R2, R3, and R4, respectively.

## Task 2

Configure OSPF such that the cost of a GigabitEthernet interface is 20. Do not use the **ipv6 ospf cost** command to accomplish this task.

## Task 3

Erase the startup configuration on all routers and reload the devices before proceeding to the next lab.

## Lab 10: LSAs in OSPFv3

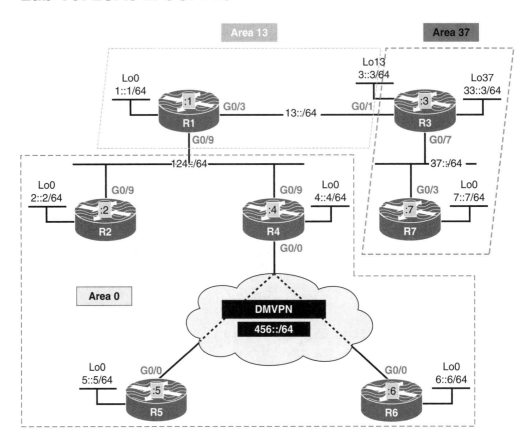

## Lab Setup:

If you are using EVE-NG, and you have imported the EVE-NG topology from the EVE-NG-Topology folder, ignore the following and use **Lab-10-LSAs in OSPFv3** in the **IPv6** folder in EVE-NG.

To copy and paste the initial configurations, go to the **initial-config** folder → **IPv6** folder → **Lab-10**.

## Task 1

Configure OSPF Area 0 on the G0/9 and Loopback0 interfaces of R1, R2, and R4. Ensure that the router IDs are set to using the $0.0.0.x$ format, where $x$ is the router number.

## Task 2

Configure OSPF Area 13 on the G0/3 interface of R1 and G0/1 and the Loopback13 interfaces of R3.

## Task 3

Configure OSPF Area 37 on the G0/7 and Lo37 interfaces of R3 and the G0/3 and Lo0 interfaces of R7. Ensure that these routers see all the prefixes from the other areas in this routing domain.

## Task 4

Configure OSPF Area 0 on the DMVPN network. Ensure that the OSPFv3 network type for the DMVPN network is configured as broadcast.

## Task 5

Erase the startup configuration on all routers and reload the devices before proceeding to the next lab.

# Lab 11: OSPFv3 Area Types

## Lab Setup:

If you are using EVE-NG, and you have imported the EVE-NG topology from the **EVE-NG-Topology** folder, ignore the following and use **Lab-11-OSPFv3 Area Types** in the **IPv6** folder in EVE-NG.

To copy and paste the initial configurations, go to the **initial-config** folder → **IPv6** folder → **Lab-11**.

## Task 1

Configure OSPFv3 on the routers in Area 0 based on the above diagram. Ensure reachability to all prefixes advertised within this area. Ensure that the router ID of each of these routers is set to using the 0.0.0.$x$ format, where $x$ is the router number. Ensure that the loopback interfaces of this area are advertised with the correct mask.

## Task 2

Redistribute the Lo1, Lo2, and Lo3 interfaces of R1 into the OSPF routing domain.

## Task 3

Configure OSPFv3 on the routers in Area 1 and advertise the loopback interfaces with the correct mask. Ensure that the router ID of R5 is set to 0.0.0.5.

## Task 4

Configure OSPFv3 on the routers in Area 2. The loopback interfaces in this area must be advertised with the correct mask. Ensure that the router ID of R8 is set to 0.0.0.8. Configure an address family on R8 to accomplish this task.

## Task 5

Configure OSPFv3 on the routers/switches in Area 3 and advertise the loopback interface on R7 with the correct mask. Ensure that the router ID of SW3 is set to 0.0.0.33. Configure an address family on R7 to accomplish this task. Ensure that SW3 redistributes the three loopback interfaces (Lo0, Lo1, and Lo2) in this routing domain as metric type 1.

## Task 6

Configure OSPFv3 on the routers in Area 4. Ensure that the router ID of SW2 is set to 0.0.0.22. Ensure that SW2 redistributes the three loopback interfaces (Lo0, Lo1, and Lo2) in this routing domain.

## Task 7

Configure OSPFv3 on the routers in Area 5. Ensure that the router ID of SW1 is set to 0.0.0.11. Ensure that SW1 redistributes the three loopback interfaces (Lo1, Lo2, and Lo3) in this routing domain. Ensure that the Loopback0 interface of SW1 is configured in Area 5 with the correct mask.

## Task 8

Configure Area 1 based on the following policy:

- Ensure that the routers in this area see the inter-area and intra-area prefixes.

- Ensure that the routers in this area do not see external prefixes but do have reachability to the external prefixes via a default route with a cost of 99 injected by R4 (the ABR).

- Ensure that the routers in this area do not have inter-area router LSAs.

- Ensure that the routers in this area are not able to redistribute any prefixes in this area.

## Task 9

Configure Area 2 based on the following policy:

- Ensure that the routers in this area do not have inter-area prefixes but do have reachability to all inter-area prefixes via a default route injected by R6 (the ABR).

- Ensure that the routers in this area do not have external prefixes but do have reachability to the external prefixes via a default route injected by R6 (the ABR).

- Ensure that the routers in this area do not have inter-area router LSAs.

- Ensure that routers in this area are not able to redistribute any prefixes in this area.

## Task 10

Configure Area 3 as an NSSA. Ensure that the routers in this area do not get a default route from their ABR (R7).

## Task 11

Configure Area 4 as an NSSA. Ensure that the routers in this area get a default route from their ABR (R3) so they can reach the external routes that are redistributed in other areas of this routing domain. Ensure that this area has inter-area prefixes.

## Task 12

Configure Area 5 as an NSSA. Ensure that this area does not have inter-area prefixes but does have a default route injected by the ABR (R2).

## Task 13

Configure the Lo1 interface on R6 based on the following policy:

- Ensure that the IPv6 address is 61::6/64.

- Ensure that this loopback interface or any future routes redistributed by R6 into OSPF are not injected into Area 3 but ensure that the routers in Area 0 see the redistributed routes.

- Do not configure a distribute list, an ACL, or a prefix list to accomplish this task.

## Task 14

Erase the startup configuration on all routers and switches and reload the devices before proceeding to the next lab.

# Lab 12: OSPFv3 Authentication

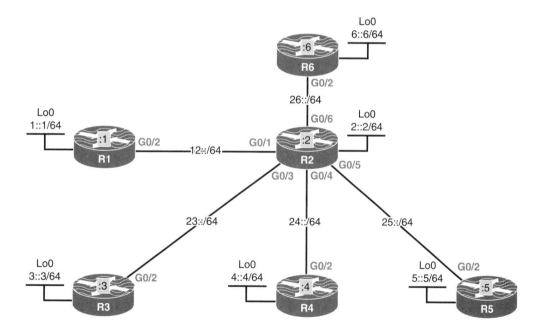

## Lab Setup:

If you are using EVE-NG, and you have imported the EVE-NG topology from the **EVE-NG-Topology** folder, ignore the following and use **Lab-12-OSPFv3 Authentication** in the **IPv6** folder in EVE-NG.

To copy and paste the initial configurations, go to the **initial-config** folder → **IPv6** folder → **Lab-12**.

## Task 1

Configure OSPFv3 Area 12 on the Loopback0 and G0/2 interfaces of R1 and the G0/1 interface of R2.

## Task 2

Configure OSPFv3 Area 26 on the Loopback0 and the G0/2 interfaces of R6 and the G0/6 interface of R2.

## Task 3

Configure OSPFv3 Area 0 on the Loopback0 and G0/3, G0/4, and G0/5 interfaces of R2 and G0/2 and the Loopback0 interfaces of R3, R4, and R5.

## Task 4

Configure OSPFv3 authentication on the link between R1 and R2, based on the following policy:

- Authentication: MD5

- Authentication key: Key 1234567890123456789012334567890AB

- SPI: 1200

- Use interface configuration mode with no encryption to accomplish this task.

## Task 5

Configure OSPFv3 authentication for all the links in Area 0 based on the following policy:

- Authentication: MD5

- Authentication key: Key 1234567890123456789012334567890AB

- SPI: 2345

- Use router configuration mode with no encryption to accomplish this task.

## Task 6

Configure OSPFv3 authentication on the link between R2 and R6 based on the following policy:

- Encryption

  - IPsec

  - SPI: 2600

  - Encryption scheme: 3DES

  - Key: 1234567890123456789012345678901234567890abcdef12

- Authentication

  - MD5

  - Key: 1234567890123456789012345678901234567890ab

## Task 7

Erase the startup configuration on all routers and switches and reload the devices before proceeding to the next lab.

## Lab 13: EIGRPv6

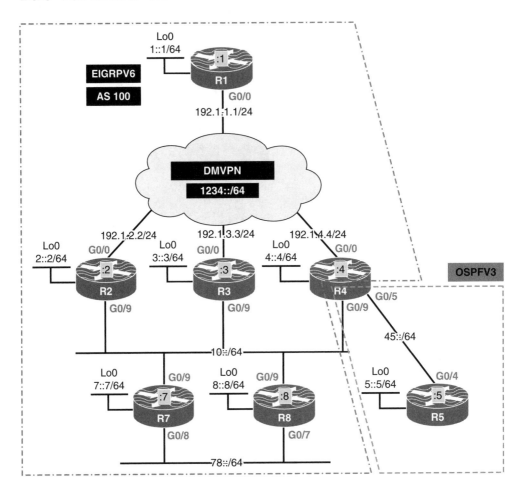

## Lab Setup:

If you are using EVE-NG, and you have imported the EVE-NG topology from the **EVE-NG-Topology** folder, ignore the following and use **Lab-13-EIGRPv6** in the **IPv6** folder in EVE-NG.

To copy and paste the initial configurations, go to the **initial-config** folder → **IPv6** folder → **Lab-13**.

## Task 1

Configure OSPFv3 Area 0 on the Loopback0 and G0/4 interfaces of R5 and the G0/5 interface of R4. Ensure that the Loopback0 interface of R5 is advertised with the correct mask.

## Task 2

Configure EIGRPv6 AS 100 on the Loopback0, G0/8, and G0/9 interfaces of R7 and on the G0/9 and G0/7 interfaces of R8.

## Task 3

Configure EIGRPv6 on all directly connected interfaces of R1, R2, and R3 and the Loopback0, G0/9, and tunnel interfaces of R4.

## Task 4

Configure R4 to redistribute OSPFv3 into EIGRPv6 and inject a default route into the OSPFv3 routing domain.

## Task 5

Configure the hello interval and hold timer of R7 and R8 to 10 and 40 seconds, respectively. Ensure that this policy is enforced on only the Gi0/8 interface of R7 and the Gi0/7 interface of R8.

## Task 6

Configure the Loopback1 interface on R2 using the 2:2::2/64 IPv6 address. Ensure that this loopback interface is advertised in EIGRPv6 AS 100. Ensure that all routers in AS 100 have reachability and redundancy to this network if multiple path(s) are available.

## Task 7

Ensure that R4 never uses more than 25% of its bandwidth for EIGRPv6 traffic on its tunnel and G0/9 interfaces. Use an EIGRP-specific command to accomplish this task.

## Task 8

Configure a Loopback1 interface on R1, using 1:1::1/64 as its IPv6 address. Ensure that every router has reachability to this network. Do not advertise or redistribute this network in EIGRP to provide reachability.

## Task 9

Configure MD5 authentication on all routers connected to the 10::/64 segment; use Micronics as the password to accomplish this task.

## Task 10

Configure authentication on the 78::/64 segment. Use the strongest authentication mechanism possible to accomplish this task. Use Cisco as the password. Do not configure a keychain to accomplish this task.

## Task 11

Configure R4 such that it checks the hop counts for all incoming EIGRP packets. If the hop count is larger than 50 hops, ensure that the local router discards the packet(s). In addition, ensure that this router is configured to wait 10 minutes for replies to its queries when its successor for a router is down and there are no feasible successors.

## Task 12

Configure R2 such that it filters existing and future external routes. Do not use a prefix list, an access list, or a route map to accomplish this task.

## Task 13

Ensure that R3 is configured to filter prefix 2:2::/64.

## Task 14

Erase the startup configuration and reload the routers before proceeding to the next lab.

# Lab 14: BGP Configuration

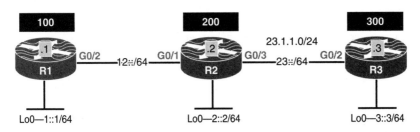

This lab should be conducted on the Enterprise POD.

## Task 1

Configure the above topology. Do not run any routing protocol. Provide IPv6 routing capability to the routers in the above topology.

## Task 2

Configure BGP on R1 and R2. Ensure that these two routers can establish a peer session using the IPv6 address of their directly connected GigabitEthernet interface and advertise their Lo0 interfaces in their assigned AS.

## Task 3

Configure BGP on R2 and R3. Ensure that these two routers can establish a peer session using the IPv4 address of their directly connected interface. Ensure that R3 can advertise its Lo0 interface in AS 300.

## Task 4

Erase the startup configuration on all routers and reload the devices before proceeding to the next lab.

# Chapter 10

# SD-WAN

Embracing the future of networking infrastructure needed to support the migration of applications to the cloud has driven Cisco to create faster, more reliable connectivity solutions. Additionally, the advent of the Internet of Things (IoT) has dictated that networks provide more performance as the number of consumers of applications (endpoints) expands. Traditionally this scaling out of endpoints would tax bandwidth and expose networks to new threats and vulnerabilities due the increase in the number of mobile users in the workforce.

In an effort to navigate this challenging landscape Cisco SD-WAN combines software-defined efficiency with a single pane of glass visibility across the WAN creating a secure extensible network that changes the way we look at networking today.

## The following topology will be used for all the SD-WAN labs:

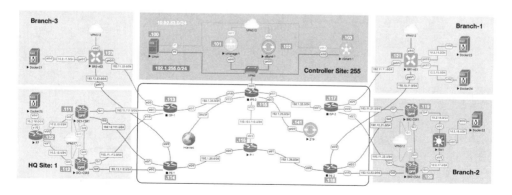

## Lab 1: Onboarding WAN Edge Devices

Navigate to **Configuration > Devices > WAN Edge List > Upload WAN Edge List.**

In the resulting popup window, click **Browse.** In the UI that appears, navigate to **root > Downloads.**

Select the file called **serialfile-SDWAN-ENT.viptela.**

Click **Open.**

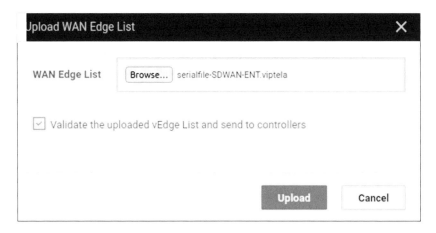

Check **Validate the uploaded vEdge List and send to controllers** and click **Upload**. The system asks one final time whether you actually want to install the list.

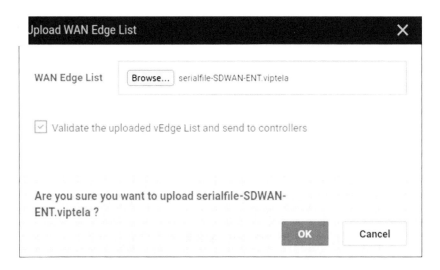

Click **OK**. The following message appears:

Click **OK**. You should see the following output as a result of this process:

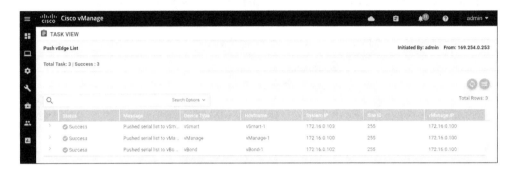

To verify the installation of the vEdge list, navigate to **Configuration > Devices > WAN Edge List,** where you should see a list of devices that have been whitelisted as a result of the steps you have already taken. These devices and only these devices can be added to your SEN fabric.

If you explore this list, you will find a combination of CSR1000v and Viptela cloud routers.

Now that you have installed the list of WAN edge devices, you need to focus on performing baseline configuration on all of the WAN edge devices for this lab. Begin by onboarding the devices in HQ Site 1:

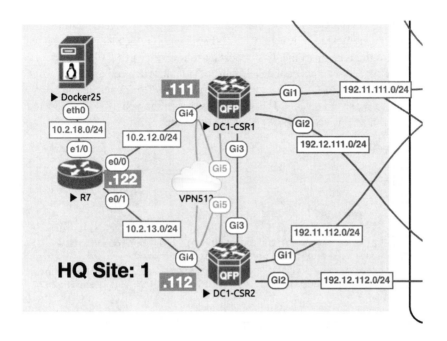

The only devices that will be onboarded during this portion of the lab are DC1-CSR1 and DC1-CSR2. These devices are running IOS XE SD-WAN, and they can therefore be configured as part of the SD-WAN infrastructure. To accomplish this, you need to assign a baseline configuration to each of these devices via the CLI much as you would for controllers.

Next, you need to change the mode of the CSR from autonomous mode to controller mode:

```
Router>enable
Router# controller-mode enable
Enabling controller mode will erase the nvram filesystem, remove all
configuration files, and reload the box!
Ensure the BOOT variable points to a valid image
Continue? [confirm] enter
% Warning: Bootstrap config file needed for Day-0 boot is missing
Do you want to abort? (yes/[no]): enter
```

This forces the device to reload. Once the CSR has finished reloading, you need to configure the information it needs to operate as part of the SEN, including the following:

- System IP address
- Site ID
- Organizational name
- Identity of the vBond controller

You can focus on reachability and tunnel configuration after you provide the information required by the SD-WAN controllers. You can begin with DC1-CSR1, where you will access this CSR for the very first time. It is important to note that a CSR1000v device comes with a one-time login credential pair admin and admin. After you use these credentials, you need to configure a new username and password. Don't panic if you see a message that uses a password 0 value. This just means the syntax you used is considered deprecated. This is how you access the CSR for the first time:

```
User Access Verification

Username: admin
Password: admin


Router>
*Feb 15 16:57:58.205: SDWAN INFO: WARNING: Please configure a new
username and password; one-time user admin is removed.
*Feb 15 16:57:58.227: %SEC_LOGIN-5-LOGIN_SUCCESS: Login Success [user:
admin] [Source: LOCAL] [localport: 0] at 16:57:58 UTC Sat Feb 15 2020
Router>
*Feb 15 16:58:06.320: %SYS-5-CONFIG_P: Configured programmatically by
process iosp_vty_100001_dmi_nesd from console as NETCONF on vty32131
*Feb 15 16:58:06.321: %DMI-5-CONFIG_I: R0/0: nesd: Configured from
NETCONF/RESTCONF by system, transaction-id 32
```

Now you can make some basic changes before you focus on SD-WAN. Set up the hostname and create a new set of credentials for the administrator account:

```
Router# config-transaction

admin connected from 127.0.0.1 using console on Router
Router(config)# hostname DC1-CSR1
Router(config)# username admin privilege 15 secret admin
Router(config)# commit
Commit complete.
DC1-CSR1(config)#
*Feb 15 17:01:16.043: %AAA-5-USER_RESET: User admin failed attempts
reset by NETCONF on vty32131
*Feb 15 17:01:16.043: % AAAA-4-CLI_DEPRECATED: WARNING: Command has
been added to the configuration using a type 5 password
. However, type 5 passwords which are considered weak are now depre-
cated.
*Feb 15 17:01:16.048: %SYS-5-CONFIG_P: Configured programmatically by
process iosp_vty_100001_dmi_nesd from console as NETCONF on vty32131
*Feb 15 17:01:16.049: %DMI-5-CONFIG_I: R0/0: nesd: Configured from
NETCONF/RESTCONF by admin, transaction-id 253
```

This example works, but the proper format would be to use the secret keyword rather than the password option. To illustrate that this example works, you can log out and then log back in before using the non-deprecated syntax:

```
DC1-CSR1(config)# exit
DC1-CSR1# exit
```

Now try to log in again:

```
User Access Verification

Username: admin
Password: admin


DC1-CSR1>
*Feb 15 17:06:14.247: %SEC_LOGIN-5-LOGIN_SUCCESS: Login Success [user:
admin] [Source: LOCAL] [localport: 0] at 17:06:14 UTC Sat Feb 15 2020
DC1-CSR1>enable
DC1-CSR1# config-transaction


admin connected from 127.0.0.1 using console on DC1-CSR1
DC1-CSR1(config)#
```

This works. Now you can configure the system information needed to add this cEdge device to the SEN fabric as part of the onboarding process:

```
DC1-CSR1# config-transaction


admin connected from 127.0.0.1 using console on DC1-CSR1
DC1-CSR1(config)# system
DC1-CSR1(config-system)# system-ip 10.1.1.111
DC1-CSR1(config-system)# site-id 1
DC1-CSR1(config-system)# organization-name micronicslab.com
DC1-CSR1(config-system)# vbond 192.1.255.102
DC1-CSR1(config-system)# commit
Commit complete.
DC1-CSR1(config-system)#
```

To verify that this configuration works, you can use the following command to look at part of the running configuration associated to the SD-WAN settings:

```
DC1-CSR1# show sdwan running-config
system
 system-ip            10.1.1.11
 site-id              101
 admin-tech-on-failure
```

```
organization-name    micronicslab.com
vbond 192.1.255.102
!
<output omitted>
```

Now that the basic SD-WAN configuration is done, you need to set up all the reachability information needed to attach DC1-CSR1 to the SD-WAN infrastructure. Here we focus on the information necessary to establish connectivity to the underlay. This will involve connectivity to both the MPLS and INET transports in the lab. You can use the EVE-NG topology drawing to find all the relevant information regarding IP addresses and gateways.

As shown below, configure the IP addresses on the interfaces that face the transport networks—specifically GigabitEthernet1 (MPLS) and GigabitEthernet2 (INET):

```
DC1-CSR1# config-transaction

admin connected from 127.0.0.1 using console on DC1-CSR1
DC1-CSR1(config)# interface GigabitEthernet1
DC1-CSR1(config-if)# no shutdown
DC1-CSR1(config-if)# ip address 192.11.111.111 255.255.255.0
DC1-CSR1(config-if)# exit
DC1-CSR1(config)# interface GigabitEthernet2
DC1-CSR1(config-if)# no shutdown
DC1-CSR1(config-if)# ip address 192.12.111.111 255.255.255.0
DC1-CSR1(config-if)# exit
DC1-CSR1(config)# ip route 0.0.0.0 0.0.0.0 192.11.111.113
DC1-CSR1(config)# ip route 0.0.0.0 0.0.0.0 192.12.111.114
DC1-CSR1(config)# ip name-server 8.8.8.8
DC1-CSR1(config)# commit
Commit complete.
DC1-CSR1(config)#
```

Now test reachability by trying to ping both gateways and the IP addresses of the controllers:

```
DC1-CSR1# ping 192.11.111.113 ← INET Gateway
Type escape sequence to abort.
Sending 5, 100-byte ICMP Echos to 192.11.111.113, timeout is 2 seconds:
!!!!!
Success rate is 100 percent (5/5), round-trip min/avg/max = 1/1/1 ms

DC1-CSR1# ping 192.12.111.114 ← MPLS Gateway
Type escape sequence to abort.
Sending 5, 100-byte ICMP Echos to 192.12.111.114, timeout is 2 seconds:
!!!!!
Success rate is 100 percent (5/5), round-trip min/avg/max = 1/1/2 ms
```

```
DC1-CSR1# ping 192.1.255.101  ← vManage-1
Type escape sequence to abort.
Sending 5, 100-byte ICMP Echos to 192.1.255.101, timeout is 2 seconds:
!!!!!
Success rate is 100 percent (5/5), round-trip min/avg/max = 1/1/1 ms

DC1-CSR1# ping 192.1.255.102  ← vBond-1
Type escape sequence to abort.
Sending 5, 100-byte ICMP Echos to 192.1.255.102, timeout is 2 seconds:
!!!!!
Success rate is 100 percent (5/5), round-trip min/avg/max = 20/28/31 ms

DC1-CSR1# ping 192.1.255.103  ← vSmart-1
Type escape sequence to abort.
Sending 5, 100-byte ICMP Echos to 192.1.255.103, timeout is 2 seconds:
!!!!!
Success rate is 100 percent (5/5), round-trip min/avg/max = 1/1/2 ms
DC1-CSR1#
```

You have all the reachability you need to proceed, but keep in mind that the configuration of SD-WAN requires the use of tunnels. In a Cisco device, you need an actual tunnel interface configured to allow the initiation and termination of DTLS tunnels. You will create discreet tunnel interfaces and associate those interfaces with the actual physical interfaces you use to attach to the transport networks. In SD-WAN, you will use **ip unnumbered** and a new (to you) tunnel mode that was specifically designed to support DTLS, with **tunnel mode sdwan**.

Before you do that, you need to copy the ROOTCA files that you created on vManage to the bootflash of DC1-CSR1. This will facilitate the onboarding of the CSR1000v and position all the files necessary to add the resource to the SD-WAN fabric. To do this, you need to access DC1-CSR1 and copy those files by using the following CLI commands:

```
DC1-CSR1# copy scp: bootflash:
Address or name of remote host []? 192.1.255.100
Source username [admin]? user
Source filename []? /home/user/Downloads/ROOTCA.pem
Destination filename [ROOTCA.pem]?
Password: Test123
 Sending file modes: C0644 1521 ROOTCA.pem
!
1521 bytes copied in 4.040 secs (376 bytes/sec)
DC1-CSR1#
```

Verify that the file was placed in the bootflash of DC1-CSR1:

```
DC1-CSR1# dir bootflash:ROOTCA.pem
Directory of bootflash:/ROOTCA.pem
```

```
40323    -rw-              1521   Aug 26 2020 15:17:10 +00:00   ROOTCA.pem

6286540800 bytes total (5007073280 bytes free)
DC1-CSR1#
```

Now you can build the tunnels on DC1-CSR1 that are needed to communicate with the controllers so that you can complete the onboarding process for this device:

```
DC1-CSR1# config-transaction

admin connected from 127.0.0.1 using console on DC1-CSR1
DC1-CSR1(config)# interface Tunnel 1
DC1-CSR1(config-if)# no shut
DC1-CSR1(config-if)# ip unnumbered GigabitEthernet1
DC1-CSR1(config-if)# tunnel source GigabitEthernet1
DC1-CSR1(config-if)# tunnel mode sdwan
DC1-CSR1(config-if)# exit
DC1-CSR1(config)# interface Tunnel 2
DC1-CSR1(config-if)# no shut
DC1-CSR1(config-if)# ip unnumbered GigabitEthernet2
DC1-CSR1(config-if)# tunnel source GigabitEthernet2
DC1-CSR1(config-if)# tunnel mode sdwan
DC1-CSR1(config-if)# exit
DC1-CSR1(config)#
```

Specify the configuration associated with these physical interfaces and logical tunnels under the sdwan configuration section of the IOS XE operating system:

```
DC1-CSR1(config)# sdwan
DC1-CSR1(config-sdwan)# interface GigabitEthernet1
DC1-CSR1(config-interface-GigabitEthernet1)# tunnel-interface
DC1-CSR1(config-tunnel-interface)# encapsulation ipsec
DC1-CSR1(config-tunnel-interface)# color biz-internet
DC1-CSR1(config-tunnel-interface)# exit
DC1-CSR1(config-interface-GigabitEthernet1)# exit
DC1-CSR1(config-sdwan)# interface GigabitEthernet2
DC1-CSR1(config-interface-GigabitEthernet2)# tunnel-interface
DC1-CSR1(config-tunnel-interface)# encapsulation ipsec
DC1-CSR1(config-tunnel-interface)# color MPLS
DC1-CSR1(config-tunnel-interface)# exit
DC1-CSR1(config-interface-GigabitEthernet2)# exit
DC1-CSR1(config-sdwan)# exit
DC1-CSR1(config)# commit


*Feb 15 18:04:01.181: %SYS-5-CONFIG_P: Configured programmatically by
process iosp_vty_100001_dmi_nesd from console as NETCONF on vty32131
```

```
*Feb 15 18:04:01.182: %DMI-5-CONFIG_I: R0/0: nesd: Configured from
NETCONF/RESTCONF by admin, transaction-id 381Commit complete.
*Feb 15 18:04:02.003: %LINEPROTO-5-UPDOWN: Line protocol on Interface
Tunnel1, changed state to up
*Feb 15 18:04:02.116: %LINEPROTO-5-UPDOWN: Line protocol on Interface
Tunnel2, changed state to up
DC1-CSR1(config)#
```

Next, you need the CSRs to join the SEN fabric in order to facilitate the turn up of the secure control plane. Each device needs to be able to authenticate to the vBond controller, and once that has taken place, each device can learn the identity of the vSmart controller in vManage. To do this, you need to use the ROOTCA.pem certificate you created to authenticate the controllers. You already copied that ROOTCA.pem certificate to DC1-CSR1. Now you need to use that certificate to facilitate the onboarding process.

Install the certificate as shown below:

```
DC1-CSR1# request platform software sdwan root-cert-chain install
bootflash:ROOTCA.pem
Uploading root-ca-cert-chain via VPN 0
Copying ... /bootflash/ROOTCA.pem via VPN 0
Updating the root certificate chain..
Successfully installed the root certificate chain
DC1-CSR1#
```

Based on how this lab is architected, you need to manually activate this specific cEdge router. You can accomplish this by using one of the chassis number/OTP pair values you uploaded using the serial file. You can arbitrarily select the lines to use, but it is a good idea to go in numerical order from the top. To find these whitelisted devices, you can look at the vManage dashboard and navigate to **Configuration > Devices > WAN Edge List.**

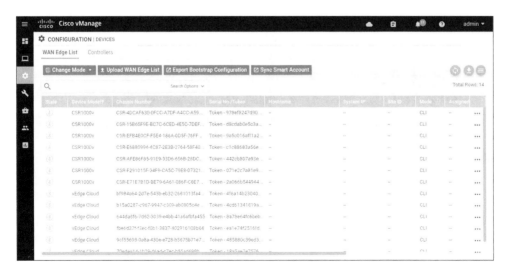

**NOTE** Expand the Chassis Number and Serial No./Token columns so that you can see all the text in them. The information in these columns will be used to onboard the WAN edge devices.

To onboard CSR1 use the following syntax:

To onboard CSR1 use the following syntax: request platform software sdwan vedge_cloud activate chassis-number <UUID> token <OTP>

On DC1-CSR1, it looks like this:

```
DC1-CSR1# request platform software sdwan vedge_cloud activate
chassis-number CSR-20B67640-53EB-EBA1-58E2-84EDFF99D121 token
d51771230bad2d1b14192c2dd61e420f
*Feb 21 14:37:18.478: %DMI-5-AUTH_PASSED: R0/0: dmiauthd: User
'vmanage-admin' authenticated successfully from 10.1.255.101:36403 and
was authorized for netconf over ssh. External groups:
*Feb 21 14:37:26.795: %Cisco-SDWAN-DC1-CSR1-action_notifier-
6-INFO-1400002: R0/0: VCONFD_NOTIFIER: Notification: 2/21/2020
14:37:26 security-install-csr severity-level:minor host-name:default
system-ip:10.1.1.11
*Feb 21 14:37:36.437: %Cisco-SDWAN-DC1-CSR1-action_notifier-
6-INFO-1400002: R0/0: VCONFD_NOTIFIER: Notification: 2/21/2020
14:37:36 security-install-rcc severity-level:minor host-name:default
system-ip:10.1.1.11
*Feb 21 14:37:36.943: %DMI-5-AUTH_PASSED: R0/0: dmiauthd: User
'vmanage-admin' authenticated successfully from 10.1.255.101:36414 and
was authorized for netconf over ssh. External groups:
*Feb 21 14:37:51.347: %Cisco-SDWAN-DC1-CSR1-action_notifier-6-INFO-
1400002: R0/0: VCONFD_NOTIFIER: Notification: 2/21/2020 14:37:51
security-install-rcc severity-level:minor host-name:default
system-ip:10.1.1.11
*Feb 21 14:37:53.753: %DMI-5-AUTH_PASSED: R0/0: dmiauthd: User
'vmanage-admin' authenticated successfully from 10.1.255.101:36420 and
was authorized for netconf over ssh. External groups:
*Feb 21 14:37:59.186: %DMI-5-AUTH_PASSED: R0/0: dmiauthd: User
'vmanage-a
*Feb 21 14:39:11.830: %OSPF-6-DFT_OPT: Protocol timers for fast
convergence are Enabled.
*Feb 21 14:39:11.789: %Cisco-SDWAN-RP_0-OMPD-3-ERRO-400002: R0/0:
OMPD: vSmart peer 10.1.255.103 state changed to Init
*Feb 21 14:39:14.113: %Cisco-SDWAN-RP_0-OMPD-6-INFO-400002: R0/0:
OMPD: vSmart peer 10.1.255.103 state changed to Handshake
*Feb 21 14:39:14.123: %Cisco-SDWAN-RP_0-OMPD-5-NTCE-400002: R0/0:
OMPD: vSmart peer 10.1.255.103 state changed to Up
*Feb 21 14:39:14.124: %Cisco-SDWAN-RP_0-OMPD-6-INFO-400005: R0/0:
OMPD: Number of vSmarts
connected : 1
<output omitted for clarity>
```

You can clearly see that DTLS peering has taken place, based on this output, but to be on the safe side, you can verify it from the command line of DC1-CSR1 as shown below:

```
DC1-CSR1# show sdwan control local-properties
personality                      vedge
sp-organization-name             micronicslab.com
organization-name                micronicslab.com
root-ca-chain-status             Installed

certificate-status               Installed
certificate-validity             Valid
certificate-not-valid-before     Feb 21 14:37:27 2020 GMT
certificate-not-valid-after      Feb 18 14:37:27 2030 GMT

enterprise-cert-status           Not-Applicable
enterprise-cert-validity         Not Applicable
enterprise-cert-not-valid-before Not Applicable
enterprise-cert-not-valid-after  Not Applicable

dns-name                         192.1.255.102
site-id                          1
domain-id                        1
protocol                         dtls
tls-port                         0
system-ip                        10.1.1.11
chassis-num/unique-id            CSR-20B67640-53EB-EBA1-58E2-
                                 84EDFF99D121
serial-num                       1CEF1CA8
token                            Invalid
keygen-interval                  1:00:00:00
retry-interval                   0:00:00:18
no-activity-exp-interval         0:00:00:20
dns-cache-ttl                    0:00:02:00
port-hopped                      TRUE
time-since-last-port-hop         0:00:30:04
embargo-check                    success
number-vbond-peers               1
number-active-wan-interfaces     2


  NAT TYPE: E -- indicates End-point independent mapping
            A -- indicates Address-port dependent mapping
            N -- indicates Not learned
            Note: Requires minimum two vbonds to learn the NAT type
```

```
                         PUBLIC            PUBLIC  PRIVATE        PRIVATE
             PRIVATE                               MAX    RESTRICT/        LAST
SPI TIME   NAT  VM
INTERFACE                IPv4             PORT   IPv4           IPv6
             PORT   VS/VM COLOR                  STATE CNTRL CONTROL/   LR/LB  CONNECTION
REMAINING  TYPE CON


                                                          STUN
                  PRF
---------------------------------------------------------------------------------------
GigabitEthernet1         172.1.1.11       12366  172.1.1.11       ::
             12366   1/0  mpls                    up    2      no/yes/no  No/No  0:00:00:18
 0:11:51:53  N    5
GigabitEthernet2         172.2.2.11       12366  172.2.2.11       ::
             12366   1/1  biz-internet        up    2      no/yes/no  No/No  0:00:00:00
 0:11:51:38  N    5


DC1-CSR1#
```

You can see that the certificate is installed, the organization name is correct, and the connections to mpls and biz-internet are up. In addition, you can see that you have OMP peering going toward the vSmart device:

```
DC1-CSR1# show sdwan omp peers
R -> routes received
I -> routes installed
S -> routes sent

                         DOMAIN  OVERLAY  SITE
PEER            TYPE    ID      ID       ID    STATE  UPTIM   E    R/I/S
----------------------------------------------------------------------------
10.1.255.103    vsmart  1       1        255   up     0:19:   59:22  0/0/0

DC1-CSR1#
```

You should now see something like this in the **Configuration > Devices > WAN Edge List** section of the vManage dashboard:

The interface shows the certificate symbol to the left of the line item, and you can see the hostname DC1-CSR1. This tells you that everything worked. To see if you can view the WAN devices on the main dashboard, go to **Dashboard > Main Dashboard:**

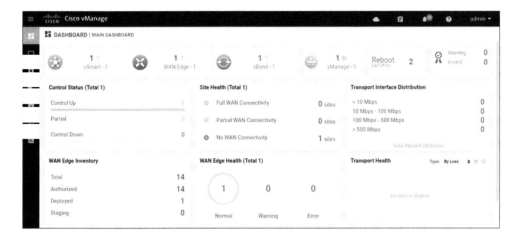

You can now see a number 1 with a green arrow pointing up next to the WAN edge field. This means you did everything correctly.

Rather than itemize every step involved in onboarding DC1-CSR2, this streamlines the process as the steps are identical to what you did on DC1-CSR1. Later, you will find that some sites have limited connectivity, and you will need to handle those situations. You will look at that more closely when you onboard devices in different sites.

You need to enable controller mode and then provide the baseline configuration for DC1-CSR2:

```
Router> enable
Router# controller-mode enable
Enabling controller mode will erase the nvram filesystem, remove all
configuration files, and reload the box!
```

```
Ensure the BOOT variable points to a valid image
Continue? [confirm] enter
% Warning: Bootstrap config file needed for Day-0 boot is missing
Do you want to abort? (yes/[no]): enter
```

The router reloads into controller mode. After that, you can finish the configuration as shown below:

```
User Access Verification

Username: admin
Password: admin


Default admin password needs to be changed.


Enter new password: admin
Confirm password: admin
Router> enable
Router# config-transaction
Router(config)# hostname DC1-CSR2
Router(config)# username admin privilege 15 secret admin
Router(config)# system
Router(config-system)# system-ip 10.1.1.112
Router(config-system)# site-id 1
Router(config-system)# organization-name micronicslab.com
Router(config-system)# vbond 192.1.255.102
Router(config-system)# interface GigabitEthernet1
Router(config-if)# no shutdown
Router(config-if)# ip address 192.11.112.112 255.255.255.0
Router(config-if)# exit
Router(config)# interface GigabitEthernet2
Router(config-if)# no shutdown
Router(config-if)# ip address 192.12.112.112 255.255.255.0
Router(config-if)# exit
Router(config)# ip route 0.0.0.0 0.0.0.0 192.11.112.113
Router(config)# ip route 0.0.0.0 0.0.0.0 192.22.101.114
Router(config)# ip name-server 8.8.8.8
Router(config)# commit
```

Move the ROOTCA.pem as shown below:

```
DC1-CSR2# copy scp: bootflash:
Address or name of remote host []? 192.1.255.100
Source username [DC1-CSR2]? user
```

```
Source filename []? /home/user/Downloads/ROOTCA.pem
Destination filename [ROOTCA.pem]?

Password: Test123
 Sending file modes: C0644 1521 ROOTCA.pem
!
1521 bytes copied in 2.826 secs (518 bytes/sec)
DC1-CSR2#
```

Configure the tunnel as shown below:

```
DC1-CSR2(config)# interface Tunnel 1
DC1-CSR2(config-if)# no shut
DC1-CSR2(config-if)# ip unnumbered GigabitEthernet1
DC1-CSR2(config-if)# tunnel source GigabitEthernet1
DC1-CSR2(config-if)# tunnel mode sdwan
DC1-CSR2(config-if)# exit
DC1-CSR2(config)# interface Tunnel 2
DC1-CSR2(config-if)# no shut
DC1-CSR2(config-if)# ip unnumbered GigabitEthernet2
DC1-CSR2(config-if)# tunnel source GigabitEthernet2
DC1-CSR2(config-if)# tunnel mode sdwan
DC1-CSR2(config-if)# exit
DC1-CSR2(config)# sdwan
DC1-CSR2(config-sdwan)# interface GigabitEthernet1
DC1-CSR2(config-interface-GigabitEthernet1)# tunnel-interface
DC1-CSR2(config-tunnel-interface)# encapsulation ipsec
DC1-CSR2(config-tunnel-interface)# color biz-internet
DC1-CSR2(config-tunnel-interface)# exit
DC1-CSR2(config-interface-GigabitEthernet1)# exit
DC1-CSR2(config-sdwan)# interface GigabitEthernet2
DC1-CSR2(config-interface-GigabitEthernet2)# tunnel-interface
DC1-CSR2(config-tunnel-interface)# encapsulation ipsec
DC1-CSR2(config-tunnel-interface)# color MPLS
DC1-CSR2(config-tunnel-interface)# exit
DC1-CSR2(config-interface-GigabitEthernet2)# exit
DC1-CSR2(config-sdwan)# commit
*Feb 21 19:04:16.027: %LINEPROTO-5-UPDOWN: Line protocol on Interface
Tunnel0, changed state to up
*Feb 21 19:04:16.068: %LINEPROTO-5-UPDOWN: Line protocol on Interface
Tunnel1, changed state to up
*Feb 21 19:04:16.087: %SYS-5-CONFIG_P: Configured programmatically by
process iosp_vty_100
001_dmi_nesd from console as NETCONF on vty32131
```

```
*Feb 21 19:04:16.088: %DMI-5-CONFIG_I: R0/0: nesd: Configured from
NETCONF/RESTCONF by admin, transaction-id 412
Commit complete.
DC1-CSR2(config-sdwan)# end
```

Install the root certificate as shown below:

```
DC1-CSR2# request platform software sdwan root-cert-chain install
bootflash:ROOTCA.pem
Uploading root-ca-cert-chain via VPN 0
Copying ... /bootflash/ROOTCA.pem via VPN 0
Updating the root certificate chain..
Successfully installed the root certificate chain
DC1-CSR2#
```

Now you need to manually register the CSR1000v using the next available CSR chassis and token combination in the vManage list of devices:

```
DC1-CSR2# request platform software sdwan vedge_cloud activate
chassis-number CSR-FF5D8B16-1C11-C3A8-5CFD-495CA090CD2C token
c07dda65c7a29728f4b3f083a28f72b7
DC1-CSR2#
<output omitted for clarity>
*Feb 21 19:15:04.608: %OSPF-6-DFT_OPT: Protocol timers for fast
convergence are Enabled.
*Feb 21 19:15:04.554: %Cisco-SDWAN-RP_0-OMPD-3-ERRO-400002: R0/0:
OMPD: vSmart peer 10.1.255.103 state changed to Init
*Feb 21 19:15:06.802: %Cisco-SDWAN-RP_0-OMPD-6-INFO-400002: R0/0:
OMPD: vSmart peer 10.1.255.103 state changed to Handshake
*Feb 21 19:15:06.804: %Cisco-SDWAN-RP_0-OMPD-5-NTCE-400002: R0/0:
OMPD: vSmart peer 10.1.255.103 state changed to Up
*Feb 21 19:15:06.804: %Cisco-SDWAN-RP_0-OMPD-6-INFO-400005: R0/0:
OMPD: Number of vSmarts connected : 1
DC1-CSR2#
```

After a short time, you should see the CSR registered with the SD-WAN fabric inside the user interface, as shown below:

In addition, you should now see two WAN edge devices on the main dashboard, as shown below:

You have finished the setup for Site 1.

You can now bring up the other sites. The configurations are provided here for your reference. You need to onboard all of the WAN edge devices.

## Site 2: CSR 1000v Onboarding

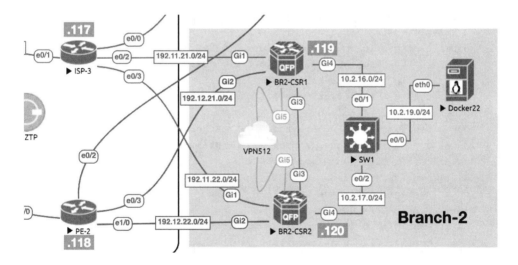

We will now repeat the onboarding operations on BR2-CSR1 by following this process:

```
Router>enable
Router# controller-mode enable
Enabling controller mode will erase the nvram filesystem, remove all
configuration files, and reload the box!
Ensure the BOOT variable points to a valid image
Continue? [confirm] enter
% Warning: Bootstrap config file needed for Day-0 boot is missing
```

```
Do you want to abort? (yes/[no]): enter

<Device will reload!!!!!>

Router>en
Router# config-transaction
binos connected from 127.0.0.1 using console on Router
Router(config)# hostname BR2-CSR1
Router(config)# username admin privilege 15 secret admin
Router(config)# system
Router(config-system)# system-ip 10.1.1.21
Router(config-system)# site-id 2
Router(config-system)# organization-name micronicslab.com
Router(config-system)# vbond 192.1.255.102
Router(config-system)# interface GigabitEthernet1
Router(config-if)# no shutdown
Router(config-if)# ip address 192.11.21.119 255.255.255.0
Router(config-if)# exit
Router(config-system)# interface GigabitEthernet2
Router(config-if)# no shutdown
Router(config-if)# ip address 192.12.21.119 255.255.255.0
Router(config-if)# exit
Router(config)# ip route 0.0.0.0 0.0.0.0 192.11.21.117
Router(config)# ip route 0.0.0.0 0.0.0.0 192.12.21.118
Router(config)# ip name-server 8.8.8.8
Router(config)# interface Tunnel 1
Router(config-if)# no shut
Router(config-if)# ip unnumbered GigabitEthernet1
Router(config-if)# tunnel source GigabitEthernet1
Router(config-if)# tunnel mode sdwan
Router(config-if)# exit
Router(config)# interface Tunnel 2
Router(config-if)# no shut
Router(config-if)# ip unnumbered GigabitEthernet2
Router(config-if)# tunnel source GigabitEthernet2
Router(config-if)# tunnel mode sdwan
Router(config-if)# exit
Router(config)# sdwan
Router(config-sdwan)# interface GigabitEthernet1
Router(config-interface-GigabitEthernet1)# tunnel-interface
Router(config-tunnel-interface)# encapsulation ipsec
Router(config-tunnel-interface)# color biz-internet
Router(config-tunnel-interface)# allow-service all
Router(config-tunnel-interface)# exit
Router(config-interface-GigabitEthernet1)# exit
```

```
Router(config-sdwan)# interface GigabitEthernet2
Router(config-interface-GigabitEthernet2)# tunnel-interface
Router(config-tunnel-interface)# encapsulation ipsec
Router(config-tunnel-interface)# color mpls
Router(config-tunnel-interface)# allow-service all
Router(config-tunnel-interface)# exit
Router(config-interface-GigabitEthernet2)# exit
Router(config-sdwan)# commit
*Feb 21 19:39:34.118: %AAA-5-USER_RESET: User admin failed attempts
reset by NETCONF on vty32131
*Feb 21 19:39:34.118: %AAAA-4-CLI_DEPRECATED: WARNING: Command has
been added to the configuration using a type 5 password. However, type
5 passwords which are considered weak are now deprecated.
*Feb 21 19:39:34.481: %SYS-5-CONFIG_P: Configured programmatically by
process iosp_vty_100001_dmi_nesd from console as NETCONF on vty32131
*Feb 21 19:39:34.482: %DMI-5-CONFIG_I: R0/0: nesd: Configured from
NETCONF/RESTCONF by admin, transaction-id 278
*Feb 21 19:39:35.306: %LINEPROTO-5-UPDOWN: Line protocol on Interface
Tunnel1, changed state to up
*Feb 21 19:39:35.419: %LINEPROTO-5-UPDOWN: Line protocol on Interface
Tunnel2, changed state to up
*Feb 21 19:39:35.748: %Cisco-SDWAN-RP_0-OMPD-5-NTCE-400003: R0/0:
OMPD: Operational state changed to UP
Commit complete.
BR2-CSR1(config-sdwan)# end
```

Install the root certificate as shown below:

```
BR2-CSR1# copy scp: bootflash:
Address or name of remote host []? 192.1.255.100
Source username [admin]? user
Source filename []? /home/user/Downloads/ROOTCA.pem
Destination filename [ROOTCA.pem]?

Password: Test123
 Sending file modes: C0644 1521 ROOTCA.pem
!
1521 bytes copied in 2.627 secs (557 bytes/sec)


R31# request platform software sdwan root-cert-chain install
bootflash:ROOTCA.pem
Uploading root-ca-cert-chain via VPN 0
Copying ... /bootflash/ROOTCA.pem via VPN 0
Updating the root certificate chain..
Successfully installed the root certificate chain
```

```
BR2-CSR1# request platform software sdwan vedge_cloud activate chas-
sis-number CSR-D345642E-2A20-ADE1-90B9-AA97B37B25B5 token 5ad05603a12c
044c0cad7439168546de
*Feb 21 20:04:05.205: %Cisco-SDWAN-RP_0-OMPD-3-ERRO-400002: R0/0:
OMPD: vSmart peer 10.1.255.103 state changed to Init
*Feb 21 20:04:07.885: %CRYPTO-6-ISAKMP_ON_OFF: ISAKMP is ON
*Feb 21 20:04:07.415: %Cisco-SDWAN-RP_0-OMPD-6-INFO-400002: R0/0:
OMPD: vSmart peer 10.1.255.103 state changed to Handshake
*Feb 21 20:04:07.417: %Cisco-SDWAN-RP_0-OMPD-5-NTCE-400002: R0/0:
OMPD: vSmart peer 10.1.255.103 state changed to Up
*Feb 21 20:04:07.417: %Cisco-SDWAN-RP_0-OMPD-6-INFO-400005: R0/0:
OMPD: Number of vSmarts connected : 1
BR2-CSR1#
```

vManage shows that the addition has taken place:

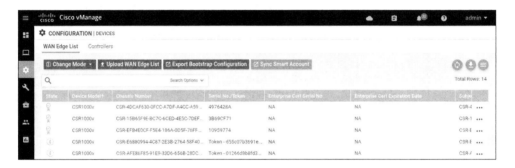

In addition:

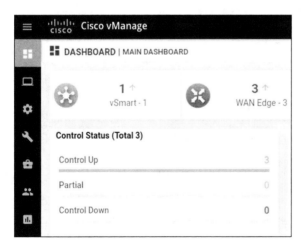

Onboard BR2-CSR2 as shown below:

```
Router>en
Router# controller-mode enable
Enabling controller mode will erase the nvram filesystem, remove all
configuration files, and reload the
box!
Ensure the BOOT variable points to a valid image
Continue? [confirm] enter
% Warning: Bootstrap config file needed for Day-0 boot is missing
Do you want to abort? (yes/[no]): enter

<Device will reload!!!!!>

Router(config)# hostname BR2-CSR2
Router(config)# username admin privilege 15 secret admin
Router(config)# system
Router(config-system)# system-ip 10.1.1.22
Router(config-system)# site-id 2
Router(config-system)# organization-name micronicslab.com
Router(config-system)# vbond 192.1.255.102
Router(config-system)# interface GigabitEthernet1
Router(config-if)# no shutdown
Router(config-if)# ip address 192.11.22.120 255.255.255.0
Router(config-if)# exit
Router(config-system)# interface GigabitEthernet2
Router(config-if)# no shutdown
Router(config-if)# ip address 192.12.22.120 255.255.255.0
Router(config-if)# exit
Router(config)# ip route 0.0.0.0 0.0.0.0 192.11.22.117
Router(config)# ip route 0.0.0.0 0.0.0.0 192.12.22.118
Router(config)# ip name-server 8.8.8.8
Router(config)# interface Tunnel 1
Router(config-if)# no shut
Router(config-if)# ip unnumbered GigabitEthernet1
Router(config-if)# tunnel source GigabitEthernet1
Router(config-if)# tunnel mode sdwan
Router(config-if)# exit
Router(config)# interface Tunnel 2
Router(config-if)# no shut
Router(config-if)# ip unnumbered GigabitEthernet2
Router(config-if)# tunnel source GigabitEthernet2
Router(config-if)# tunnel mode sdwan
Router(config-if)# exit
Router(config)# sdwan
```

```
Router(config-sdwan)# interface GigabitEthernet1
Router(config-interface-GigabitEthernet1)# tunnel-interface
Router(config-tunnel-interface)# encapsulation ipsec
Router(config-tunnel-interface)# color biz-internet
Router(config-tunnel-interface)# allow-service all
Router(config-tunnel-interface)# exit
Router(config-interface-GigabitEthernet1)# exit
Router(config-sdwan)# interface GigabitEthernet2
Router(config-interface-GigabitEthernet1)# tunnel-interface
Router(config-tunnel-interface)# encapsulation ipsec
Router(config-tunnel-interface)# color MPLS
Router(config-tunnel-interface)# allow-service all
Router(config-tunnel-interface)# exit
Router(config-interface-GigabitEthernet1)# exit
Router(config-sdwan)# commit
*Feb 21 19:39:34.118: %AAA-5-USER_RESET: User admin failed attempts
reset by NETCONF on vty32131
*Feb 21 19:39:34.118: %AAAA-4-CLI_DEPRECATED: WARNING: Command has
been added to the configuration using a type 5 password. However, type
5 passwords which are considered weak are now deprecated.
*Feb 21 19:39:34.481: %SYS-5-CONFIG_P: Configured programmatically by
process iosp_vty_100001_dmi_nesd from console as NETCONF on vty32131
*Feb 21 19:39:34.482: %DMI-5-CONFIG_I: R0/0: nesd: Configured from
NETCONF/RESTCONF by admin, transaction-id 278
*Feb 21 19:39:35.306: %LINEPROTO-5-UPDOWN: Line protocol on Interface
Tunnel1, changed state to up
*Feb 21 19:39:35.419: %LINEPROTO-5-UPDOWN: Line protocol on Interface
Tunnel2, changed state to up
*Feb 21 19:39:35.748: %Cisco-SDWAN-RP_0-OMPD-5-NTCE-400003: R0/0:
OMPD: Operational state changed to UP
Commit complete.
BR2-CSR2(config-sdwan)#
```

Install the root certificate as shown below:

```
BR2-CSR2# copy scp: bootflash:
Address or name of remote host []? 192.1.255.100
Source username [admin]? user
Source filename []? /home/user/Downloads/ROOTCA.pem
Destination filename [ROOTCA.pem]?

Password: Test123
 Sending file modes: C0644 1521 ROOTCA.pem
!
1521 bytes copied in 2.627 secs (557 bytes/sec)
BR2-CSR2#
```

```
BR2-CSR2# request platform software sdwan root-cert-chain install
bootflash:ROOTCA.pem
Uploading root-ca-cert-chain via VPN 0
Copying ... /bootflash/ROOTCA.pem via VPN 0
Updating the root certificate chain..
Successfully installed the root certificate chain

BR2-CSR2# request platform software sdwan vedge_cloud activate chas-
sis-number CSR-D345642E-2A20-ADE1-90B9-AA97B37B25B5 token 5ad05603a12c
044c0cad7439168546de
*Feb 21 20:04:05.205: %Cisco-SDWAN-RP_0-OMPD-3-ERRO-400002: R0/0:
OMPD: vSmart peer 10.1.255.103 state changed to Init
*Feb 21 20:04:07.885: %CRYPTO-6-ISAKMP_ON_OFF: ISAKMP is ON
*Feb 21 20:04:07.415: %Cisco-SDWAN-RP_0-OMPD-6-INFO-400002: R0/0:
OMPD: vSmart peer 10.1.255.103 state changed to Handshake
*Feb 21 20:04:07.417: %Cisco-SDWAN-RP_0-OMPD-5-NTCE-400002: R0/0:
OMPD: vSmart peer 10.1.255.103 state changed to Up
*Feb 21 20:04:07.417: %Cisco-SDWAN-RP_0-OMPD-6-INFO-400005: R0/0:
OMPD: Number of vSmarts connected : 1
BR2-CSR2#
```

You can see that the addition has taken place:

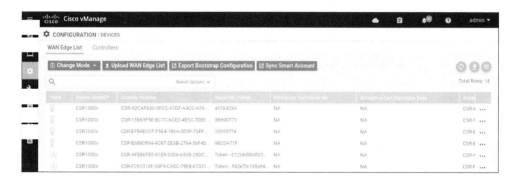

In addition:

### Branch 1: vEdge Cloud Router Onboarding

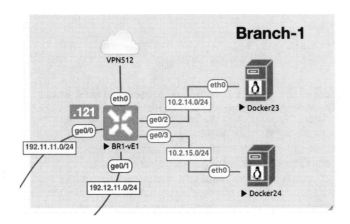

We will prepare BR1-vE1 for onboarding using the following process:

```
vedge# config
Entering configuration mode terminal
vedge(config)# system
vedge(config-system)# host-name  BR1-vE1
vedge(config-system)# system-ip 10.1.1.11
vedge(config-system)# site-id 11
vedge(config-system)# organization-name micronicslab.com
vedge(config-system)# vbond 192.1.255.102
vedge(config-system)# exit
vedge(config)# vpn 0
vedge(config-vpn-0)# dns 8.8.8.8 primary
vedge(config-vpn-0)# ip route 0.0.0.0/0 192.11.11.117
vedge(config-vpn-0)# ip route 0.0.0.0/0 192.12.11.118
vedge(config-vpn-0)# interface ge0/0
vedge(config-interface-ge0/0)# ip address 192.11.11.121/24
vedge(config-interface-ge0/0)# no shut
vedge(config-interface-ge0/0)# tunnel-interface
vedge(config-tunnel-interface)# allow-service all
vedge(config-tunnel-interface)# color biz-internet
vedge(config-tunnel-interface)# encapsulation ipsec
vedge(config-tunnel-interface)# exit
vedge(config-interface-ge0/0)# exit
vedge(config-vpn-0)# interface ge0/1
vedge(config-interface-ge0/1)# no shut
vedge(config-interface-ge0/1)# ip address 192.12.1.121/24
vedge(config-interface-ge0/1)# tunnel-interface
vedge(config-tunnel-interface)# allow-service all
vedge(config-tunnel-interface)# color MPLS
```

```
vedge(config-tunnel-interface)# encapsulation ipsec
vedge(config-tunnel-interface)# commit and-quit
Commit complete.
```

Install the root certificate as shown below:

```
BR1-vE1# vshell
BR1-vE1:~$ scp user@192.1.255.100:/home/user/Downloads/ROOTCA.pem .
The authenticity of host '192.1.255.101 (192.1.255.101)' can't be
established.
ECDSA key fingerprint is SHA256:p9PbfLdHBQvHCIAkZMzFgSmgAI4zOLhf9i2rSp
Fw4UA.
Are you sure you want to continue connecting (yes/no)? yes
Warning: Permanently added '192.1.255.100' (ECDSA) to the list of
known hosts.
user@192.1.255.101's password: Test123
ROOTCA.pem                                    100% 1521      1.5MB/s
00:00
BR1-vE1:~$ ls
ROOTCA.pem   archive_id_rsa.pub
BR1-vE1:~$ exit
BR1-vE1# request root-cert-chain install /home/admin/ROOTCA.pem
Uploading root-ca-cert-chain via VPN 0
Copying ... /home/admin/ROOTCA.pem via VPN 0
Updating the root certificate chain..
Successfully installed the root certificate chain
BR1-vE1#
```

Activate the vEdge device by using the chassis number and token for one of the vEdge
cloud routers from the user interface:

```
BR1-vE1# request vedge-cloud activate chassis-number 32758328-6a9a-
2360-99ba-dc35d16db6aa token 4e2c986f5664ea27e76385698142127d
BR1-vE1#
```

Verify that the device has joined the SD-WAN fabric:

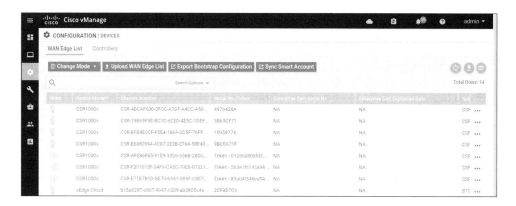

In addition:

# Lab 2: Exploring Unicast Routing

To explore unicast concepts, you need to configure some routing in your topology. You can start with the HQ site, assigning interface IP addresses and configuring routing protocols and corresponding L3 virtual routing and forwarding (VRF) contexts.

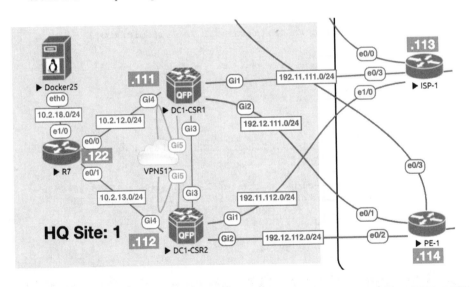

Let's look at what happens when you create an interface that is part of the service-side, or LAN-side, configuration on a vEdge device. Here you will do this using GigabitEthernet4 on DC1-CSR1. This interface will be assigned an IP address. To see the process of advertising information to the vSmart device, you will see what transpires in the control plane as you configure this device.

First, look at the vSmart OMP routing table by entering this command:

```
vSmart-1# show omp routes vpn 0
vSmart-1#
```

Note that there are no OMP routes being learned by the vSmart device. As shown below, you can change that when you create a new VRF instance on DC1-CSR1 called VRF 100. You can then apply an IP address to the GigabitEthernet 4 interface of that same router and place it in VRF 100.

```
DC1-CSR1# config-transaction
DC1-CSR1(config)# vrf definition 100
DC1-CSR1(config-vrf)# address-family ipv4
DC1-CSR1(config-ipv4)# exit
DC1-CSR1(config-vrf)# exit
DC1-CSR1(config)# interface GigabitEthernet4
DC1-CSR1(config-if)# vrf forwarding 100
DC1-CSR1(config-if)# ip address 10.2.12.111 255.255.255.0
DC1-CSR1(config-if)# no shut
DC1-CSR1(config-if)# commit
Commit complete.
```

Now look at the vSmart device to see if anything has changed:

```
vSmart-1# show omp routes | tab
Code:
C   -> chosen
I   -> installed
Red -> redistributed
Rej -> rejected
L   -> looped
R   -> resolved
S   -> stale
Ext -> extranet
Inv -> invalid
Stg -> staged
U   -> TLOC unresolved
```

| | | PATH | | | | | ATTRIBUTE | | | |
|---|---|---|---|---|---|---|---|---|---|---|
| VPN | PREFIX | FROM PEER | ID | LABEL | STATUS | TYPE | TLOC IP | COLOR | ENCAP | PREFERENCE |
| 100 | 10.2.12.0/24 | 10.1.1.111 | 66 | 1003 | C,R | installed | 10.1.1.111 | mpls | ipsec | - |
| | | 10.1.1.111 | 68 | 1003 | C,R | installed | 10.1.1.111 | biz-internet | ipsec | - |

```
vSmart-1#
```

*<output omitted>*

You can see a new VPN entry called VPN100. Note that this is the same name you provided for your VRF instance in DC1-CSR1. You can explore this more closely by specifying the network 10.2.12.0/24 that you configured on GigibitEthernet3:

```
vSmart-1# show omp routes 10.2.12.0/24
Code:
C   -> chosen
I   -> installed
Red -> redistributed
Rej -> rejected
L   -> looped
R   -> resolved
S   -> stale
Ext -> extranet
Inv -> invalid
Stg -> staged
U   -> TLOC unresolved
```

| VPN | PREFIX | FROM PEER | PATH ID | LABEL | STATUS | TYPE | ATTRIBUTE TLOC IP | COLOR | ENCAP | PREFERENCE |
|-----|--------|-----------|---------|-------|--------|------|--------------------|-------|-------|------------|
| 100 | 10.2.12.0/24 | 10.1.1.111 | 66 | 1003 | C,R | installed | 10.1.1.111 | mpls | ipsec | - |
| | | 10.1.1.111 | 68 | 1003 | C,R | installed | 10.1.1.111 | biz-internet | ipsec | - |

```
vSmart-1#
```

Note that the network 10.2.12.0/24 (see the green highlight above) network is being advertised as being reachable from the interfaces on DC1-CSR1, facing the transport networks. Specifically, you can see that the network 172.101.1.0/24 can be reached via both mpls and biz-internet (see the yellow highlight above). You can also see that the device that advertised this information (the originator) has the system IP address 10.1.1.11 (see the blue highlight above).

Now you can add another device to the equation. To do so, you can create the same configuration on DC1-CSR2 that you just created, including creating VRF 100 and applying that VRF instance to interface GigabitEthernet4, along with assigning the IP address on that interface. All this is shown below:

```
DC1-CSR2# config-transaction

admin connected from 127.0.0.1 using console on DC1-CSR2
DC1-CSR2(config)# vrf definition 100
DC1-CSR2 (config-vrf)# address-family ipv4
DC1-CSR2 (config-ipv4)# exit
DC1-CSR2 (config-vrf)# exit
```

```
DC1-CSR2 (config)# interface GigabitEthernet4
DC1-CSR2 (config-if)# vrf forwarding 100
DC1-CSR2 (config-if)# ip address 10.2.13.112 255.255.255.0
DC1-CSR2 (config-if)# no shut
DC1-CSR2 (config-if)# commit
Commit complete.
```

Return to the vSmart device as shown below:

```
vSmart-1# show omp routes | tab
Code:
C   -> chosen
I   -> installed
Red -> redistributed
Rej -> rejected
L   -> looped
R   -> resolved
S   -> stale
Ext -> extranet
Inv -> invalid
Stg -> staged
U   -> TLOC unresolved


                          PATH               ATTRIBUTE

VPN  PREFIX       FROM PEER     ID  LABEL  STATUS  TYPE       TLOC IP     COLOR         ENCAP  PREFERENCE
-----------------------------------------------------------------------------------------------------------
100  10.2.12.0/24  10.1.1.111  66  1003   C,R     installed  10.1.1.111  mpls          ipsec  -
                   10.1.1.111  68  1003   C,R     installed  10.1.1.111  biz-internet  ipsec  -
100  10.2.13.0/24  10.1.1.112  66  1003   C,R     installed  10.1.1.112  mpls          ipsec  -
                   10.1.1.112  68  1003   C,R     installed  10.1.1.112  biz-internet  ipsec  -

vSmart-1#
```

Now you can see the network 10.2.13.0/24 advertised from system IP address 10.1.1.12 via mpls and biz-internet. What you really need to see here, though, is what the vSmart device did. Remember that the vSmart device acts like a route reflector: It advertises prefixes it learns for specific VPNs (or VRF instances, in the case of IOS XE SD-WAN devices) to other devices where those VPNs (or VRF instances) exist. You will explore this on the command line. But first I want to discuss my logic.

You know that DC1-CSR1 is advertising 10.2.12.0/24 to the vSmart device. You also know that DC1-CSR2 is advertising 10.2.13.0/24 to the vSmart device. Also, based on what we discussed earlier, you also know that the vSmart device should "reflect" those routes to DC1-CSR1 and DC1-CSR2 because they both are configured in the VPN/VRF 100. You can verify this as shown below:

```
DC1-CSR2# show ip route vrf 100


Routing Table: 100
Codes: L - local, C - connected, S - static, R - RIP, M - mobile,
B - BGP
        D - EIGRP, EX - EIGRP external, O - OSPF, IA - OSPF inter area
        N1 - OSPF NSSA external type 1, N2 - OSPF NSSA external type 2
        E1 - OSPF external type 1, E2 - OSPF external type 2, m - OMP
        n - NAT, Ni - NAT inside, No - NAT outside, Nd - NAT DIA
        i - IS-IS, su - IS-IS summary, L1 - IS-IS level-1, L2 - IS-IS
level-2
        ia - IS-IS inter area, * - candidate default, U - per-user
static route
        H - NHRP, G - NHRP registered, g - NHRP registration summary
        o - ODR, P - periodic downloaded static route, l - LISP
        a - application route
        + - replicated route, % - next hop override, p - overrides from
PfR
        & - replicated local route overrides by connected


Gateway of last resort is not set


      10.0.0.0/8 is variably subnetted, 2 subnets, 2 masks
C        10.2.13.0/24 is directly connected, GigabitEthernet4
L        10.2.13.112/32 is directly connected, GigabitEthernet4
DC1-CSR2#
```

Seeing this might make you question what we discussed earlier. It seems as though you would see some mention of 10.2.12.0/24 on DC1-CSR2 if the vSmart device is acting as a route reflector. But that is not the case. To more clearly understand this process, you need to consider how this information is exchanged. Remember that you use OMP as the protocol in the overlay. Given this, you might be able to see the prefixes you are looking for if you look in the OMP routing table. To reduce the amount of output you get, you can look specifically for 10.2.12.0/24 on DC1-CSR2:

```
DC1-CSR2# show sdwan omp routes 10.2.12.0/24
Code:
C   -> chosen
I   -> installed
```

```
Red -> redistributed
Rej -> rejected
L   -> looped
R   -> resolved
S   -> stale
Ext -> extranet
Inv -> invalid
Stg -> staged
IA  -> On-demand inactive
U   -> TLOC unresolved
                           PATH          ATTRIBUTE

VPN PREFIX        FROM PEER      ID LABEL STATUS TYPE      TLOC IP        COLOR      ENCAP PREFERENCE
-----------------------------------------------------------------------------------------------------
100 10.2.12.0/24 10.1.255.103  1  1003   Inv,U  installed 10.1.1.111     mpls       ipsec -

                  10.1.255.103  2  1003   Inv,U  installed 10.1.1.111     biz-internet ipsec -


DC1-CSR2#
```

This is fantastic! You can see route 10.2.12.0/24, and you can see that it was originated on 10.1.1.11 (DC1-CSR1), and it can be reached via both mpls and biz-internet. Also, you learned it from 10.1.255.103 (vSmart-1). All this happened without you needing to do anything. But can you reach this prefix from DC1-CSR2? Remember that you have to specify the VRF (100), as shown below:

```
DC1-CSR2# ping vrf 100 10.2.12.111
Type escape sequence to abort.
Sending 5, 100-byte ICMP Echos to 172.101.1.1, timeout is 2 seconds:
.....
Success rate is 0 percent (0/5)
DC1-CSR2#
```

You can see here that you do not have reachability. But this makes sense. Remember that the routing table for the VRF instance must have the prefix in it, or it must have a default route of some kind to afford reachability. You can determine whether the table includes the prefix as shown below:

```
DC1-CSR2# show ip route vrf 100

Routing Table: 100
Codes: L - local, C - connected, S - static, R - RIP, M - mobile,
B - BGP
        D - EIGRP, EX - EIGRP external, O - OSPF, IA - OSPF inter area
        N1 - OSPF NSSA external type 1, N2 - OSPF NSSA external type 2
```

```
        E1 - OSPF external type 1, E2 - OSPF external type 2, m - OMP
        n - NAT, Ni - NAT inside, No - NAT outside, Nd - NAT DIA
        i - IS-IS, su - IS-IS summary, L1 - IS-IS level-1, L2 - IS-IS
level-2
        ia - IS-IS inter area, * - candidate default, U - per-user
static route
        H - NHRP, G - NHRP registered, g - NHRP registration summary
        o - ODR, P - periodic downloaded static route, l - LISP
        a - application route
        + - replicated route, % - next hop override, p - overrides from
PfR
        & - replicated local route overrides by connected

Gateway of last resort is not set

        10.0.0.0/8 is variably subnetted, 2 subnets, 2 masks
C          10.2.13.0/24 is directly connected, GigabitEthernet4
L          10.2.13.112/32 is directly connected, GigabitEthernet4
DC1-CSR2#
```

You can see that there is no prefix, so there is no reachability.

You have routes in OMP, and you want to get those routes to appear in VRF 100. The issue here is that both DC1-CSR1 and DC1-CSR2 belong to Site-1. To prevent loops, you can't place the routes learned from DC1-CSR1 into the routing table of VRF 100. It stands to reason that there should be no circumstance where you would prefer the overlay network to reach a prefix that originated within the site where your devices are located. To drive this point home, you can go to DC1-CSR1 and temporarily change the site ID to 100. This should facilitate making the prefix appear on DC1-CSR2, as shown below:

```
DC1-CSR1# config-transaction

admin connected from 127.0.0.1 using console on DC1-CSR1
DC1-CSR1(config)# system
DC1-CSR1(config-system)# site-id 100
DC1-CSR1(config-system)# commit
Commit complete.
```

Now that you have done this, you can see if the prefix for 10.2.12.0/24 appears in the routing table of DC1-CSR2, as shown below:

```
DC1-CSR2# show ip route vrf 100

Routing Table: 100
Codes: L - local, C - connected, S - static, R - RIP, M - mobile,
B - BGP
        D - EIGRP, EX - EIGRP external, O - OSPF, IA - OSPF inter area
        N1 - OSPF NSSA external type 1, N2 - OSPF NSSA external type 2
```

```
        E1 - OSPF external type 1, E2 - OSPF external type 2, m - OMP
        n - NAT, Ni - NAT inside, No - NAT outside, Nd - NAT DIA
        i - IS-IS, su - IS-IS summary, L1 - IS-IS level-1, L2 - IS-IS
level-2
        ia - IS-IS inter area, * - candidate default, U - per-user
static route
        H - NHRP, G - NHRP registered, g - NHRP registration summary
        o - ODR, P - periodic downloaded static route, l - LISP
        a - application route
        + - replicated route, % - next hop override, p - overrides from
PfR
        & - replicated local route overrides by connected


Gateway of last resort is not set

      10.0.0.0/8 is variably subnetted, 3 subnets, 2 masks
m       10.2.12.0/24 [251/0] via 10.1.1.111, 00:00:08, Sdwan-system-intf
C       10.2.13.0/24 is directly connected, GigabitEthernet4
L       10.2.13.112/32 is directly connected, GigabitEthernet4
DC1-CSR2#
```

Now you have some progress. You can see a route for 10.2.12.0/24 learned via 10.1.1.111 (DC1-CSR1) with the routing code m, which corresponds to OMP. Now you can see if the prefix is reachable, as shown below:

```
DC1-CSR2# ping vrf 100 10.2.12.111
Type escape sequence to abort.
Sending 5, 100-byte ICMP Echos to 10.2.12.111, timeout is 2 seconds:
!!!!!
Success rate is 100 percent (5/5), round-trip min/avg/max = 1/1/2 ms
DC1-CSR2#
```

This is the output you want, but you don't want to leave the configuration like this. In fact, you should take this one step further and build the OSPF infrastructure in Site-1. To do so, you need to apply IP addresses and configure OSPF DC1-CSR1, DC1-CSR2, and R7.

You can put DC1-CSR1 back into site ID 101. In addition, you can use the process ID 100 for the OSPF configuration to match the VRF/VPN number 100:

```
DC1-CSR1# config-transaction

admin connected from 127.0.0.1 using console on DC1-CSR1
DC1-CSR1(config)# system
DC1-CSR1(config-system)# site-id 1
DC1-CSR1(config-system)# exit
DC1-CSR1(config)# router ospf 100 vrf 100
```

```
DC1-CSR1(config-router)# router-id 0.0.0.111
DC1-CSR1(config-router)# commit
Commit complete.
```

Now you can configure HQ-R7 as shown below:

```
Router# conf t
Enter configuration commands, one per line.  End with CNTL/Z.
Router(config)# hostname HQ-R7
HQ-R7(config)# no ip domain lookup
HQ-R7(config)# line con 0
HQ-R7(config-line)# logg synchronous
HQ-R7(config-line)# no exec-timeout
HQ-R7(config-line)# exit
HQ-R7(config)# interface e0/0
HQ-R7(config-if)# ip address 10.2.12.7 255.255.255.0
HQ-R7(config-if)# no shut
HQ-R7(config-if)# int e0/1
HQ-R7(config-if)# ip address 10.2.13.7 255.255.255.0
HQ-R7(config-if)# no shut
HQ-R7(config-if)# int lo 0
HQ-R7(config-if)# ip address 183.1.7.7 255.255.255.255
HQ-R7(config-if)# exit
HQ-R7(config)# router ospf 100
HQ-R7(config-router)# router-id 0.0.0.7
HQ-R7(config-router)# network 10.2.0.0 0.0.255.255 area 0
HQ-R7(config-router)# network 183.1.100.100 0.0.0.0 area 0
```

You would expect to see an adjacency form here if the configuration is set up correctly. You can verify that all three interfaces are configured to operate in OSPF Area 0 and that 10.2.12.111 (DC1-CSR1) is reachable:

```
HQ-R7# show ip ospf int bri
Interface    PID   Area        IP Address/Mask    Cost  State Nbr
s F/C
Lo0          100   0           183.1.7.7/24       1     LOOP  0/0
Et1/0        100   0           10.2.18.7/24       10    DR    0/0
Et0/1        100   0           10.2.13.7/24       10    DR    0/0
Et0/0        100   0           10.2.12.7/24       10    DR    0/0
HQ-R7# ping 10.2.12.111
Type escape sequence to abort.
Sending 5, 100-byte ICMP Echos to 10.2.12.111, timeout is 2 seconds:
.!!!!
Success rate is 80 percent (4/5), round-trip min/avg/max = 1/1/1 ms
HQ-R7#
```

You have reachability, but obviously nothing is set up on DC1-CSR1, so you enter the command shown below:

```
DC1-CSR1# show ip ospf int brief
DC1-CSR1#
```

You can see that this is not right. You need the router to have the interface GigabitEthernet3 to run OSPF and form the missing adjacency. To fix this, you can simply use the **interface** command as shown below:

```
DC1-CSR1(config)# interface GigabitEthernet 4
DC1-CSR1(config-if)# ip ospf 100 area 0
DC1-CSR1(config-if)# commit
Commit complete.
*Mar 28 15:12:54.688: %OSPF-5-ADJCHG: Process 100, Nbr 0.0.0.7 on
GigabitEthernet4 from LOADING to FULL, Loading Done
```

Finally, you can move to DC1-CSR2 and enter the commands shown below:

```
DC1-CSR2# config-transaction

admin connected from 127.0.0.1 using console on DC1-CSR2
DC1-CSR2(config)# router ospf 100 vrf 100
DC1-CSR2(config-router)# exit
DC1-CSR2(config)# interface GigabitEthernet 4
DC1-CSR2(config-if)# ip ospf 100 area 0
DC1-CSR2(config-if)# commit
Commit complete.
DC1-CSR2(config-if)#
*Aug 27 18:57:31.173: %OSPF-5-ADJCHG: Process 100, Nbr 0.0.0.7 on
GigabitEthernet4 from LOADING to FULL
```

Now you have built an OSPF environment in Site-1. All devices are again in the same site, and therefore you will not see any prefixes learned from OMP, as shown below:

```
DC1-CSR2# show ip route vrf 100 omp

Routing Table: 100
Codes: L - local, C - connected, S - static, R - RIP, M - mobile,
B - BGP
        D - EIGRP, EX - EIGRP external, O - OSPF, IA - OSPF inter area
        N1 - OSPF NSSA external type 1, N2 - OSPF NSSA external type 2
        E1 - OSPF external type 1, E2 - OSPF external type 2, m - OMP
        n - NAT, Ni - NAT inside, No - NAT outside, Nd - NAT DIA
        i - IS-IS, su - IS-IS summary, L1 - IS-IS level-1, L2 - IS-IS
level-2
        ia - IS-IS inter area, * - candidate default, U - per-user
static route
```

```
              H - NHRP, G - NHRP registered, g - NHRP registration summary
              o - ODR, P - periodic downloaded static route, l - LISP
              a - application route
              + - replicated route, % - next hop override, p - overrides from
    PfR

    Gateway of last resort is not set


    DC1-CSR2#
```

To remedy this situation, you can go to Branch-1 and add BR1-vE1 to VPN 100. You can just create a physical interface for this lab, as shown below:

```
BR1-vE1# config
Entering configuration mode terminal
BR1-vE1(config)# vpn 100
BR1-vE1(config-vpn-100)# interface ge0/2
BR1-vE1(config-interface-ge0/2)# ip address 10.2.14.121/24
BR1-vE1(config-interface-ge0/2)# no shut
BR1-vE1(config-interface-ge0/2)# commit and-quit
Commit complete.
BR1-vE1#
```

If you did this correctly, you should expect BR1-vE1 to learn something from the vSmart device regarding the VPN 100 routes in Site-1. To see if this is the case, you can investigate what's happening on BR1-vE1, as shown below:

```
BR1-vE1# show ip route vpn 100
Codes Proto-sub-type:
  IA -> ospf-intra-area, IE -> ospf-inter-area,
  E1 -> ospf-external1, E2 -> ospf-external2,
  N1 -> ospf-nssa-external1, N2 -> ospf-nssa-external2,
  e -> bgp-external, i -> bgp-internal
Codes Status flags:
  F -> fib, S -> selected, I -> inactive,
  B -> blackhole, R -> recursive
```

| | | | PROTOCOL | NEXTHOP | NEXTHOP | NEXTHOP | | | | | |
|-----|------------|-----------|----------|---------|---------|---------|-------------|-------------|------|--------|
| VPN | PREFIX | PROTOCOL | SUB TYPE | IF NAME | ADDR | VPN | TLOC IP | COLOR | ENCAP | STATUS |
| 100 | 10.2.12.0/24 | omp | - | - | - | - | 10.1.1.111 | mpls | ipsec | F,S |
| 100 | 10.2.12.0/24 | omp | - | - | - | - | 10.1.1.111 | biz-internet | ipsec | F,S |
| 100 | 10.2.13.0/24 | omp | - | - | - | - | 10.1.1.112 | mpls | ipsec | F,S |
| 100 | 10.2.13.0/24 | omp | - | - | - | - | 10.1.1.112 | biz-internet | ipsec | F,S |
| 100 | 10.2.14.0/24 | connected | - | ge0/2 | - | - | - | - | - | F,S |

```
100    10.2.18.0/24   omp   -    -    -    -    10.1.1.111  mpls        ipsec  F,S
100    10.2.18.0/24   omp   -    -    -    -    10.1.1.111  biz-internet ipsec F,S
100    10.2.18.0/24   omp   -    -    -    -    10.1.1.112  mpls        ipsec  F,S
100    10.2.18.0/24   omp   -    -    -    -    10.1.1.112  biz-internet ipsec F,S
100    183.1.7.7/32   omp   -    -    -    -    10.1.1.111  mpls        ipsec  F,S
100    183.1.7.7/32   omp   -    -    -    -    10.1.1.111  biz-internet ipsec F,S
100    183.1.7.7/32   omp   -    -    -    -    10.1.1.112  mpls        ipsec  F,S
100    183.1.7.7/32   omp   -    -    -    -    10.1.1.112  biz-internet ipsec F,S

BR1-vE1#
```

Here, you are learning about the prefixes in Site-1 that are directly attached to the routers DC1-CSR1 and DC1-CSR2—and you are learning a lot of other things. Specifically, you can see the Loopback0 interface of HQ-R7 (183.1.7.7) and the physical links on DC1-CSR1 and DC1-CSR2. You can test reachability as shown below:

```
BR1-vE1# ping 10.2.12.111 vpn 100 count 5
Ping in VPN 100
PING 10.2.12.111 (10.2.12.111) 56(84) bytes of data.
64 bytes from 10.2.12.111: icmp_seq=1 ttl=255 time=0.971 ms
64 bytes from 10.2.12.111: icmp_seq=2 ttl=255 time=1.29 ms
64 bytes from 10.2.12.111: icmp_seq=3 ttl=255 time=1.09 ms
64 bytes from 10.2.12.111: icmp_seq=4 ttl=255 time=0.997 ms
64 bytes from 10.2.12.111: icmp_seq=5 ttl=255 time=1.29 ms

--- 10.2.12.111 ping statistics ---
5 packets transmitted, 5 received, 0% packet loss, time 4003ms
rtt min/avg/max/mdev = 0.971/1.131/1.299/0.143 ms
BR1-vE1# ping 10.2.13.112 vpn 100 count 5
Ping in VPN 100
PING 10.2.13.112 (10.2.13.112) 56(84) bytes of data.
64 bytes from 10.2.13.112: icmp_seq=1 ttl=255 time=1.17 ms
64 bytes from 10.2.13.112: icmp_seq=2 ttl=255 time=3.28 ms
64 bytes from 10.2.13.112: icmp_seq=3 ttl=255 time=1.12 ms
64 bytes from 10.2.13.112: icmp_seq=4 ttl=255 time=1.02 ms
64 bytes from 10.2.13.112: icmp_seq=5 ttl=255 time=0.882 ms

--- 10.2.13.112 ping statistics ---
5 packets transmitted, 5 received, 0% packet loss, time 4003ms
rtt min/avg/max/mdev = 0.882/1.499/3.285/0.898 ms
BR1-vE1#
```

This looks great, but you might also want to try something past the physical interfaces of DC1-CSR1 and DC1-CSR2, as shown below:

```
BR1-vE1# ping 10.2.12.7 vpn 100 count 5
Ping in VPN 100
PING 10.2.12.7 (10.2.12.7) 56(84) bytes of data.


--- 10.2.12.7 ping statistics ---
5 packets transmitted, 0 received, 100% packet loss, time 4001ms

BR1-vE1# ping 10.2.13.7 vpn 100 count 5
Ping in VPN 100
PING 10.2.13.7 (10.2.13.7) 56(84) bytes of data.


--- 10.2.13.7 ping statistics ---
5 packets transmitted, 0 received, 100% packet loss, time 3999ms

BR1-vE1# ping 183.1.7.7 vpn 100 count 5
Ping in VPN 100
PING 183.1.7.7 (183.1.7.7) 56(84) bytes of data.


--- 183.1.7.7 ping statistics ---
5 packets transmitted, 0 received, 100% packet loss, time 4001ms


BR1-vE1#
```

This is not what you want. But you now have a rough idea of where to go to see what is happening. All pings to resources on DC1-CSR1 and DC1-CSR2 that are in VRF 100 work fine, but nothing past those CSRs seems to be functional. You can move to DC1-CSR1 and make a similar check, as shown below:

```
DC1-CSR1# show ip route vrf 100


Routing Table: 100
Codes: L - local, C - connected, S - static, R - RIP, M - mobile,
B - BGP
       D - EIGRP, EX - EIGRP external, O - OSPF, IA - OSPF inter area
       N1 - OSPF NSSA external type 1, N2 - OSPF NSSA external type 2
       E1 - OSPF external type 1, E2 - OSPF external type 2, m - OMP
       n - NAT, Ni - NAT inside, No - NAT outside, Nd - NAT DIA
       i - IS-IS, su - IS-IS summary, L1 - IS-IS level-1, L2 - IS-IS
level-2
       ia - IS-IS inter area, * - candidate default, U - per-user
static route
```

```
        H - NHRP, G - NHRP registered, g - NHRP registration summary
        o - ODR, P - periodic downloaded static route, l - LISP
        a - application route
        + - replicated route, % - next hop override, p - overrides from
PfR
        & - replicated local route overrides by connected

Gateway of last resort is not set

      10.0.0.0/8 is variably subnetted, 5 subnets, 2 masks
C        10.2.12.0/24 is directly connected, GigabitEthernet4
L        10.2.12.111/32 is directly connected, GigabitEthernet4
O        10.2.13.0/24 [110/11] via 10.2.12.7, 00:21:35,
GigabitEthernet4
m        10.2.14.0/24 [251/0] via 10.1.1.11, 00:12:23, Sdwan-system-
intf
O        10.2.18.0/24 [110/11] via 10.2.12.7, 00:21:35,
GigabitEthernet4
      183.1.0.0/32 is subnetted, 1 subnets
O        183.1.7.7 [110/2] via 10.2.12.7, 00:21:35, GigabitEthernet4
DC1-CSR1#
```

Now you can see why the ping to DC1-CSR1 works. The device knows how to reach the source IP address 10.2.14.0/24. But is this information being advertised to the rest of the devices in Site-1? You need to find out, as shown below:

HQ-R7# **show ip route ospf**

```
Codes: L - local, C - connected, S - static, R - RIP, M - mobile,
B - BGP
        D - EIGRP, EX - EIGRP external, O - OSPF, IA - OSPF inter area
        N1 - OSPF NSSA external type 1, N2 - OSPF NSSA external type 2
        E1 - OSPF external type 1, E2 - OSPF external type 2
        i - IS-IS, su - IS-IS summary, L1 - IS-IS level-1, L2 - IS-IS
level-2
        ia - IS-IS inter area, * - candidate default, U - per-user
static route
        o - ODR, P - periodic downloaded static route, H - NHRP,
l - LISP
        a - application route
        + - replicated route, % - next hop override

Gateway of last resort is not set

HQ-R7#
```

Here you can see that HQ-R7 has no visibility out Site-1. You need to correct this. The issue is that DC1-CSR1 is learning the OMP prefixes but it is not advertising them into OSPF. In addition, note that DC1-CSR1 is in fact advertising the OSPF prefixes into OMP by default. You did not configure this. You should explore both of these outcomes, as shown below:

```
DC1-CSR1# show sdwan running-config sdwan
sdwan
 interface GigabitEthernet1
  tunnel-interface
   encapsulation ipsec
   color biz-internet
   no allow-service bgp
   allow-service dhcp
   allow-service dns
   allow-service icmp
   allow-service sshd
   no allow-service netconf
   no allow-service ntp
   no allow-service ospf
   no allow-service stun
   no allow-service snmp
  exit
 exit
 interface GigabitEthernet2
  tunnel-interface
   encapsulation ipsec
   color mpls
   no allow-service bgp
   allow-service dhcp
   allow-service dns
   allow-service icmp
   no allow-service sshd
   no allow-service netconf
   no allow-service ntp
   no allow-service ospf
   no allow-service stun
   no allow-service snmp
  exit
 exit
 omp
  no shutdown
  graceful-restart
  no as-dot-notation
  address-family ipv4
```

```
    advertise connected
    advertise static
   !
  address-family ipv6
    advertise connected
    advertise static
   !
 !
!
DC1-CSR1#
```

Notice that under **address-family ipv4** for OMP, there is no mention of advertising OSPF. But it is happening, as evidenced by BR1-vE1 learning the prefixes that are running in Site-1 in OSPF. Look at the configuration for your OSPF routing process, as shown below:

```
DC1-CSR1# show run | sec router ospf
router ospf 100 vrf 100
 router-id 0.0.0.111
```

What if you redistribute the OMP prefixes into OSPF, as shown below?

```
DC1-CSR1# config-transaction

admin connected from 127.0.0.1 using console on R11
DC1-CSR1(config)# router ospf 100 vrf 100
DC1-CSR1(config-router)# redistribute omp subnets
DC1-CSR1(config-router)# commit
Commit complete.
```

Now you can verify that HQ-RQ is learning about the network 172.103.1.0/24, as shown below:

```
HQ-R7# show ip route ospf

Codes: L - local, C - connected, S - static, R - RIP, M - mobile,
B - BGP
       D - EIGRP, EX - EIGRP external, O - OSPF, IA - OSPF inter area

       N1 - OSPF NSSA external type 1, N2 - OSPF NSSA external type 2
       E1 - OSPF external type 1, E2 - OSPF external type 2
       i - IS-IS, su - IS-IS summary, L1 - IS-IS level-1, L2 - IS-IS
level-2
       ia - IS-IS inter area, * - candidate default, U - per-user
static route
       o - ODR, P - periodic downloaded static route, H - NHRP,
l - LISP
```

```
        a - application route
        + - replicated route, % - next hop override

Gateway of last resort is not set

      10.0.0.0/8 is variably subnetted, 7 subnets, 2 masks
O E2     10.2.14.0/24 [110/16777214] via 10.2.12.111, 00:00:08, Ether
net0/0
HQ-R7#
```

Excellent. Now you need to see if BR1-vE1 can reach all the addresses it is learning, so try these pings:

```
BR1-vE1# ping 10.2.12.7 vpn 100 count 5
Ping in VPN 100
PING 10.2.12.7 (10.2.12.7) 56(84) bytes of data.
64 bytes from 10.2.12.7: icmp_seq=1 ttl=254 time=1.24 ms
64 bytes from 10.2.12.7: icmp_seq=2 ttl=254 time=1.70 ms
64 bytes from 10.2.12.7: icmp_seq=3 ttl=254 time=2.09 ms
64 bytes from 10.2.12.7: icmp_seq=4 ttl=254 time=1.75 ms
64 bytes from 10.2.12.7: icmp_seq=5 ttl=254 time=1.76 ms

--- 10.2.12.7 ping statistics ---
5 packets transmitted, 5 received, 0% packet loss, time 4004ms
rtt min/avg/max/mdev = 1.240/1.711/2.095/0.274 ms

BR1-vE1# ping 10.2.13.7 vpn 100 count 5
Ping in VPN 100
PING 10.2.13.7 (10.2.13.7) 56(84) bytes of data.
64 bytes from 10.2.13.7: icmp_seq=1 ttl=254 time=1.60 ms
64 bytes from 10.2.13.7: icmp_seq=2 ttl=254 time=1.61 ms
64 bytes from 10.2.13.7: icmp_seq=3 ttl=254 time=1.41 ms
64 bytes from 10.2.13.7: icmp_seq=4 ttl=254 time=1.27 ms
64 bytes from 10.2.13.7: icmp_seq=5 ttl=254 time=1.21 ms

--- 10.2.13.7 ping statistics ---
5 packets transmitted, 5 received, 0% packet loss, time 4004ms
rtt min/avg/max/mdev = 1.218/1.423/1.611/0.168 ms

BR1-vE1# ping 183.1.7.7 vpn 100 count 5
Ping in VPN 100
PING 183.1.7.7 (183.1.7.7) 56(84) bytes of data.
64 bytes from 183.1.7.7: icmp_seq=1 ttl=254 time=1.54 ms
64 bytes from 183.1.7.7: icmp_seq=2 ttl=254 time=1.50 ms
64 bytes from 183.1.7.7: icmp_seq=3 ttl=254 time=1.66 ms
```

```
64 bytes from 183.1.7.7: icmp_seq=4 ttl=254 time=1.53 ms
64 bytes from 183.1.7.7: icmp_seq=5 ttl=254 time=1.41 ms

--- 183.1.7.7 ping statistics ---
5 packets transmitted, 5 received, 0% packet loss, time 4004ms
rtt min/avg/max/mdev = 1.413/1.531/1.666/0.095 ms
BR1-vE1#
```

Now things are working the way you want them to. At this point, you can advertise the OMP prefixes into OSPF on DC1-CSR2:

```
DC1-CSR2# config-transaction

binos connected from 127.0.0.1 using console on R12
DC1-CSR2(config)# router ospf 100 vrf 100
DC1-CSR2(config-router)# redistribute omp subnets
DC1-CSR2(config-router)# commit
Commit complete.
```

With the help of the following command, you can see the OMP routes:

```
BR1-vE1# show ip routes omp
Codes Proto-sub-type:
  IA -> ospf-intra-area, IE -> ospf-inter-area,
  E1 -> ospf-external1, E2 -> ospf-external2,
  N1 -> ospf-nssa-external1, N2 -> ospf-nssa-external2,
  e -> bgp-external, i -> bgp-internal
Codes Status flags:
  F -> fib, S -> selected, I -> inactive,
  B -> blackhole, R -> recursive
```

| VPN | PREFIX | PROTOCOL | PROTOCOL SUB TYPE | NEXTHOP IF NAME | NEXTHOP ADDR | NEXTHOP VPN | TLOC IP | COLOR | ENCAP | STATUS |
|-----|--------|----------|-------------------|-----------------|--------------|-------------|---------|-------|-------|--------|
| 100 | 10.2.12.0/24 | omp | - | - | - | - | 10.1.1.111 | mpls | ipsec | F,S |
| 100 | 10.2.12.0/24 | omp | - | - | - | - | 10.1.1.111 | biz-internet | ipsec | F,S |
| 100 | 10.2.13.0/24 | omp | - | - | - | - | 10.1.1.112 | mpls | ipsec | F,S |
| 100 | 10.2.13.0/24 | omp | - | - | - | - | 10.1.1.112 | biz-internet | ipsec | F,S |
| 100 | 10.2.18.0/24 | omp | - | - | - | - | 10.1.1.111 | mpls | ipsec | F,S |
| 100 | 10.2.18.0/24 | omp | - | - | - | - | 10.1.1.111 | biz-internet | ipsec | F,S |
| 100 | 10.2.18.0/24 | omp | - | - | - | - | 10.1.1.112 | mpls | ipsec | F,S |
| 100 | 10.2.18.0/24 | omp | - | - | - | - | 10.1.1.112 | biz-internet | ipsec | F,S |
| 100 | 183.1.7.7/32 | omp | - | - | - | - | 10.1.1.111 | mpls | ipsec | F,S |
| 100 | 183.1.7.7/32 | omp | - | - | - | - | 10.1.1.111 | biz-internet | ipsec | F,S |
| 100 | 183.1.7.7/32 | omp | - | - | - | - | 10.1.1.112 | mpls | ipsec | F,S |
| 100 | 183.1.7.7/32 | omp | - | - | - | - | 10.1.1.112 | biz-internet | ipsec | F,S |

```
BR1-vE1#
```

Here you can see all of the OMP routes as they are being learned on BR1-vE1. It would be a good idea to explore exactly what is being advertised, how, and why. To accomplish this, you need to take a closer look at the concept of TLOC routes; you will do this in the next lab.

# Lab 3: Configuring Segmentation in All Sites Using VRF 100 and VRF 200

In this lab, you will create a multi-segment infrastructure. The goal will be to configure each site to support two business units. The first is VRF 100, which will support the Engineering department of your business. In addition, you will use VRF 200 to support Human Resources. You have also been assigned the task of configuring an "Out Of Band" infrastructure for each device using VRF 512.

You can start with Site-1, shown below:

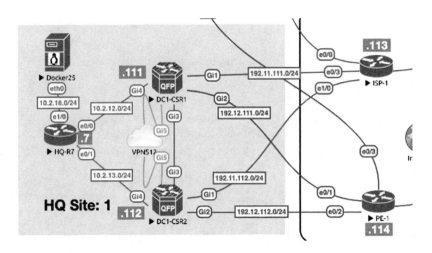

In this site, you have two physical sets of interfaces and devices that will be functioning in each of the two described VRF instances.

You already configured VRF 100 in Lab 2, so now you can simply configure VRF 200 and manage connectivity to your legacy devices in each site. Start with the following:

```
DC1-CSR1# config-transaction

admin connected from 127.0.0.1 using console on DC1-CSR1
DC1-CSR1(config)# vrf definition 200
DC1-CSR1(config-vrf)# address-family ipv4
```

```
DC1-CSR1(config-ipv4)# exit
DC1-CSR1(config-vrf)# exit
DC1-CSR1(config)# interface GigabitEthernet3
DC1-CSR1(config-if)# vrf forwarding 200
DC1-CSR1(config-if)# ip address 172.101.2.111 255.255.255.0
DC1-CSR1(config-if)# no shut
DC1-CSR1(config-if)# commit
Commit complete.
```

Configure DC1-CSR2 as shown below:

```
DC1-CSR2# config-transaction

admin connected from 127.0.0.1 using console on DC1-CSR2
DC1-CSR2(config)# vrf definition 200
DC1-CSR2(config-vrf)# address-family ipv4
DC1-CSR2(config-ipv4)# exit
DC1-CSR2(config-vrf)# interface GigabitEthernet3
DC1-CSR2(config-if)# vrf forwarding 200
DC1-CSR2(config-if)# ip address 172.101.2.112 255.255.255.0
DC1-CSR2(config-if)# no shut
DC1-CSR2(config-if)# commit
Commit complete.
```

You need to know if the two prefixes are being learned by the vSmart device and if they are being reflected. Currently, you can only verify reflected prefixes by using BR1-vE1, as shown below:

```
vSmart-1# show omp routes vpn 200 | tab
Code:
C   -> chosen
I   -> installed
Red -> redistributed
Rej -> rejected
L   -> looped
R   -> resolved
S   -> stale
Ext -> extranet
Inv -> invalid
Stg -> staged
U   -> TLOC unresolved
```

```
                           PATH              ATTRIBUTE

VPN  PREFIX        FROM PEER    ID  LABEL  STATUS  TYPE      TLOC IP       COLOR        ENCAP  PREFERENCE
-------------------------------------------------------------------------------------------------------
200  172.101.2.0/24 10.1.1.111  66  1004   C,R     installed 10.1.1.111  mpls          ipsec  -
                    10.1.1.111  68  1004   C,R     installed 10.1.1.111  biz-internet  ipsec  -
                    10.1.1.112  66  1004   C,R     installed 10.1.1.112  mpls          ipsec  -
                    10.1.1.112  68  1004   C,R     installed 10.1.1.112  biz-internet  ipsec  -


vSmart-1#
```

Verify that the prefixes are being reflected, as shown below:

```
BR1-vE1# show omp routes | tab
Code:
C   -> chosen
I   -> installed
Red -> redistributed
Rej -> rejected
L   -> looped
R   -> resolved
S   -> stale
Ext -> extranet
Inv -> invalid
Stg -> staged
U   -> TLOC unresolved


                           PATH              ATTRIBUTE

VPN  PREFIX        FROM PEER    ID  LABEL  STATUS   TYPE      TLOC IP     COLOR        ENCAP  PREFERENCE
-------------------------------------------------------------------------------------------------------
100  10.2.12.0/24  10.1.255.103 3  1003   C,I,R    installed 10.1.1.111  mpls          ipsec  -
                   10.1.255.103 4  1003   C,I,R    installed 10.1.1.111  biz-internet  ipsec  -
100  10.2.13.0/24  10.1.255.103 1  1003   C,I,R    installed 10.1.1.112  mpls          ipsec  -
                   10.1.255.103 2  1003   C,I,R    installed 10.1.1.112  biz-internet  ipsec  -
100  10.2.14.0/24  0.0.0.0      66 1003   C,Red,R  installed 10.1.1.11   mpls          ipsec  -
                   0.0.0.0      68 1003   C,Red,R  installed 10.1.1.11   biz-internet  ipsec  -
100  10.2.18.0/24  10.1.255.103 9  1003   C,I,R    installed 10.1.1.111  mpls          ipsec  -
                   10.1.255.103 10 1003   C,I,R    installed 10.1.1.111  biz-internet  ipsec  -
                   10.1.255.103 11 1003   C,I,R    installed 10.1.1.112  mpls          ipsec  -
                   10.1.255.103 12 1003   C,I,R    installed 10.1.1.112  biz-internet  ipsec  -
100  183.1.7.7/32  10.1.255.103 5  1003   C,I,R    installed 10.1.1.111  mpls          ipsec  -
                   10.1.255.103 6  1003   C,I,R    installed 10.1.1.111  biz-internet  ipsec  -
                   10.1.255.103 7  1003   C,I,R    installed 10.1.1.112  mpls          ipsec  -
                   10.1.255.103 8  1003   C,I,R    installed 10.1.1.112  biz-internet  ipsec  -


BR1-vE1#
```

Why isn't the vSmart device reflecting the routes to BR1-vE1? Because BR1-vE1 has no knowledge of the VPN/VRF instance, so it has no need to learn prefixes for it. You can look more closely, as shown below:

```
BR1-vE1# show omp routes vpn 200
        show omp routes-table family ipv4 entries vpn 200 *
-------------------------------------------------^
syntax error: unknown argument
Error executing command: CLI command error -
BR1-vE1#
```

This means the system is intelligent enough to recognize that BR1-vE1 has no need to learn about prefixes in the VPN/VRF 200. You can create VPN 200 on this platform as shown below and see what happens:

```
BR1-vE1# config
Entering configuration mode terminal
BR1-vE1(config)# vpn 200
BR1-vE1(config-vpn-200)# commit
Commit complete.
```

Now BR1-vE1 knows about and has an instance of VPN 200 configured on it. You have not yet added any interfaces; you have just created the VPN/VRF instance. So now you need to verify whether BR1-vE1 has a need to know about VPN 200:

```
BR1-vE1# show omp routes vpn 200 | tab
Code:
C   -> chosen
I   -> installed
Red -> redistributed
Rej -> rejected
L   -> looped
R   -> resolved
S   -> stale
Ext -> extranet
Inv -> invalid
Stg -> staged
U   -> TLOC unresolved
```

| VPN PREFIX | FROM PEER | PATH ID | LABEL | STATUS | ATTRIBUTE TYPE | TLOC IP | COLOR | ENCAP | PREFERENCE |
|---|---|---|---|---|---|---|---|---|---|
| 200 172.101.2.0/24 | 10.1.255.103 | 13 | 1004 | C,I,R | installed | 10.1.1.111 | mpls | ipsec | - |
| | 10.1.255.103 | 14 | 1004 | C,I,R | installed | 10.1.1.111 | biz-internet | ipsec | - |
| | 10.1.255.103 | 15 | 1004 | C,I,R | installed | 10.1.1.112 | mpls | ipsec | - |
| | 10.1.255.103 | 16 | 1004 | C,I,R | installed | 10.1.1.112 | biz-internet | ipsec | - |

BR1-vE1#

You can clearly see that the device is learning the IP routes:

```
BR1-vE1# show omp routes vpn 200 | tab
Code:
C   -> chosen
I   -> installed
Red -> redistributed
Rej -> rejected
L   -> looped
R   -> resolved
S   -> stale
Ext -> extranet
Inv -> invalid
Stg -> staged
U   -> TLOC unresolved
```

| VPN PREFIX | FROM PEER | PATH ID | LABEL | STATUS | ATTRIBUTE TYPE | TLOC IP | COLOR | ENCAP | PREFERENCE |
|---|---|---|---|---|---|---|---|---|---|
| 200 172.101.2.0/24 | 10.1.255.103 | 13 | 1004 | C,I,R | installed | 10.1.1.111 | mpls | ipsec | - |
| | 10.1.255.103 | 14 | 1004 | C,I,R | installed | 10.1.1.111 | biz-internet | ipsec | - |
| | 10.1.255.103 | 15 | 1004 | C,I,R | installed | 10.1.1.112 | mpls | ipsec | - |
| | 10.1.255.103 | 16 | 1004 | C,I,R | installed | 10.1.1.112 | biz-internet | ipsec | - |

BR1-vE1#

Now you need to configure BR1-vE1 in Branch-1 such that it will run OSPF with the router RM-R1, using the 172.103.1.0/24 network. You will create a loopback on RM-R1 for testing purposes. This interface will continue to operate in VPN/VRF 100.

## Branch-1

In this part of the lab, you will create a multi-segment infrastructure. The goal will be to configure Branch-1 to support two business units. The first is VRF 100, which will support the Engineering department of your business. In addition, you will use VRF 200 to support Human Resources. You have also been assigned the task of configuring an OOB infrastructure for each device using VRF 512.

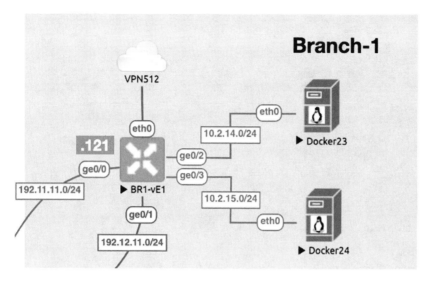

```
BR1-vE1# config
Entering configuration mode terminal
BR1-vE1(config)# vpn 100
BR1-vE1(config-vpn-100)# interface ge0/4
BR1-vE1(config-interface-ge0/4)# ip address 10.2.99.121/24
BR1-vE1(config-interface-ge0/4)# no shut
BR1-vE1(config-interface-ge0/4)# exit
BR1-vE1(config-vpn-100)# router ospf
BR1-vE1(config-ospf)# area 0
BR1-vE1(config-area-0)# interface ge0/4
BR1-vE1(ospf-if-ge0/4)# commit and-quit
Commit complete.
BR1-vE1#
```

You have completed the OSPF configuration on BR1-vE1. Now you just need to see if the configuration is correct and whether the interface is waiting for an OSPF neighbor to form, as shown below:

```
BR1-vE1# show ospf interface vpn 100 | tab
```

| OS PF | | | | | | | | | |
|---|---|---|---|---|---|---|---|---|---|
| | | | BACKUP | | | BACKUP | | | |
| | ADJ | HELLO | MD5 | | | | | | |
| | | IF | IF | | | BROADCAST | AREA | | |
| MTU | | | | | IF | | | | |
| | | DESIGNATED | DESIGNATED | DESIGNATED | | DESIGNATED | LSA | | |
| HELLO | DEAD | RETRANSMIT | NEI | | | | | | |
| GHBOR | NEIGHBOR | DUE | OPER | KEY | MD5 | | | | |

```
VPN   IF ADDR            INDEX  NAME   MTU    BANDWIDTH  ADDR        ADDR
MISMATCH   ROUTER ID   IF TYPE     COST  DELAY  ST
ATE   PRIORITY  ROUTER ID    ROUTER ID   ROUTER IP    ROUTER IP   SEQNUM
MEMBERS     TIMER   INTERVAL  TIMER      COU
NT     COUNT     TIME    STATE  ID   KEY
-------------------------------------------------------------------
100   10.2.99.121/24  0      ge0/4  1500   0          -           0
true      10.1.1.11  broadcast  10     1        if
-dr   1           10.1.1.11   -               10.2.99.121  -         -
designated  10    40        5               0
          0         9       true   -    -
```

```
BR1-vE1#
```

Now you can configure RM-R1 as shown below:

```
Router# conf t
Enter configuration commands, one per line.  End with CNTL/Z.
Router(config)# hostname RM-R1
RM-R1(config)# int e0/0
RM-R1(config-if)# ip address 10.2.99.100 255.255.255.0
RM-R1(config-if)# no shut
RM-R1(config-if)# exit
RM-R1(config)# int lo 0
RM-R1(config-if)# ip address 183.1.1.1 255.255.255.255
RM-R1(config-if)# exit
RM-R1(config)# router ospf 1
RM-R1(config-router)# router-id 0.0.0.1
RM-R1(config-router)# network 183.1.1.1 0.0.0.0 area 0
RM-R1(config-router)# network 10.2.99.100 0.0.0.0 area 0
*Mar 28 16:35:52.216: %OSPF-5-ADJCHG: Process 1, Nbr 10.1.1.11 on
Ethernet0/0 from LOADING to FULL, Loading Done
```

Remember that BR1-vE1 is not redistributing the prefixes into OSPF, and you need to address this issue. As shown below, RM-R1 is not learning any OSPF prefixes:

```
RM-R1# show ip route ospf
Codes: L - local, C - connected, S - static, R - RIP, M - mobile,
B - BGP
        D - EIGRP, EX - EIGRP external, O - OSPF, IA - OSPF inter area
        N1 - OSPF NSSA external type 1, N2 - OSPF NSSA external type 2
        E1 - OSPF external type 1, E2 - OSPF external type 2
        i - IS-IS, su - IS-IS summary, L1 - IS-IS level-1, L2 - IS-IS
level-2
```

```
       ia - IS-IS inter area, * - candidate default, U - per-user
static route
       o - ODR, P - periodic downloaded static route, H - NHRP,
l - LISP
       a - application route
       + - replicated route, % - next hop override


Gateway of last resort is not set


RM-R1#
```

As anticipated, nothing is being learned from the overlay network, as shown below:

```
BR1-vE1# config
Entering configuration mode terminal
BR1-vE1(config)# vpn 100
BR1-vE1(config-vpn-100)# router ospf
BR1-vE1(config-ospf)# redistribute omp
BR1-vE1(config-ospf)# commit and-quit
Commit complete.
BR1-vE1#
```

Now you can expect to see routes being learned via OMP:

```
RM-R1# show ip route ospf
Codes: L - local, C - connected, S - static, R - RIP, M - mobile,
B - BGP
       D - EIGRP, EX - EIGRP external, O - OSPF, IA - OSPF inter area

       N1 - OSPF NSSA external type 1, N2 - OSPF NSSA external type 2
       E1 - OSPF external type 1, E2 - OSPF external type 2
       i - IS-IS, su - IS-IS summary, L1 - IS-IS level-1, L2 - IS-IS
level-2
       ia - IS-IS inter area, * - candidate default, U - per-user
static route
       o - ODR, P - periodic downloaded static route, H - NHRP,
l - LISP
       a - application route
       + - replicated route, % - next hop override


Gateway of last resort is not set


      10.0.0.0/8 is variably subnetted, 5 subnets, 2 masks
O E2    10.2.12.0/24 [110/16777214] via 10.2.99.121, 00:01:24,
Ethernet0/0
```

```
O E2     10.2.13.0/24 [110/16777214] via 10.2.99.121, 00:01:24,
Ethernet0/0
O E2     10.2.18.0/24 [110/16777214] via 10.2.99.121, 00:01:24,
Ethernet0/0
      183.1.0.0/32 is subnetted, 2 subnets
O E2     183.1.7.7 [110/16777214] via 10.2.99.121, 00:01:24,
Ethernet0/0
RM-R1#
```

This leaves the issue of VPN 200. You can configure the interface ge0/2 and place it in VPN 200, as shown below:

```
BR1-vE1# config
Entering configuration mode terminal
BR1-vE1(config)# vpn 200
BR1-vE1(config-vpn-200)# interface ge0/2
BR1-vE1(config-interface-loopback200)# ip address 10.2.14.121/24
BR1-vE1(config-interface-loopback200)# no shut
BR1-vE1(config-interface-loopback200)# commit
Commit complete.
```

Now that the interface has been created and made part of VPN 200, you can look to see if BR1-vE1 is advertising the prefix to the vSmart devices, as shown below:

```
BR1-vE1# show omp routes vpn 200 advertised
Code:
C   -> chosen
I   -> installed
Red -> redistributed
Rej -> rejected
L   -> looped
R   -> resolved
S   -> stale
Ext -> extranet
Inv -> invalid
Stg -> staged
U   -> TLOC unresolved

VPN    PREFIX
-------------------------
200    10.2.14.0/24

BR1-vE1#
```

You can check to see if the vSmart devices are learning about the prefixes as shown below:

```
vSmart-1# show omp routes vpn 200 10.2.14.0/24 | tab
Code:
C    -> chosen
I    -> installed
Red -> redistributed
Rej -> rejected
L    -> looped
R    -> resolved
S    -> stale
Ext -> extranet
Inv -> invalid
Stg -> staged
U    -> TLOC unresolved


             PATH                    ATTRIBUTE
FROM PEER    ID   LABEL STATUS TYPE     TLOC IP     COLOR        ENCAP  PREFERENCE
--------------------------------------------------------------------------------
10.1.1.11    66   1004  C,R    installed  10.1.1.11 mpls         ipsec  -
10.1.1.11    68   1004  C,R    installed  10.1.1.11 biz-internet ipsec  -


Code:
C    -> chosen
I    -> installed
Red -> redistributed
Rej -> rejected
L    -> looped
R    -> resolved
S    -> stale
Ext -> extranet
Inv -> invalid
Stg -> staged
U    -> TLOC unresolved


TO PEER
-----------------
10.1.1.111
10.1.1.112


vSmart-1#
```

The last test is to see if the route is being reflected. You can check this on cEDGE2 as shown below:

```
DC1-CSR2# show ip route vrf 200 omp


Routing Table: 200
Codes: L - local, C - connected, S - static, R - RIP, M - mobile,
B - BGP
       D - EIGRP, EX - EIGRP external, O - OSPF, IA - OSPF inter area
       N1 - OSPF NSSA external type 1, N2 - OSPF NSSA external type 2
       E1 - OSPF external type 1, E2 - OSPF external type 2, m - OMP
       n - NAT, Ni - NAT inside, No - NAT outside, Nd - NAT DIA
       i - IS-IS, su - IS-IS summary, L1 - IS-IS level-1, L2 - IS-IS
level-2
       ia - IS-IS inter area, * - candidate default, U - per-user
static route
       H - NHRP, G - NHRP registered, g - NHRP registration summary
       o - ODR, P - periodic downloaded static route, l - LISP
       a - application route
       + - replicated route, % - next hop override, p - overrides from
PfR
       & - replicated local route overrides by connected

Gateway of last resort is not set

      10.0.0.0/24 is subnetted, 1 subnets
m        10.2.14.0 [251/0] via 10.1.1.11, 00:08:11, Sdwan-system-intf
DC1-CSR2#
```

Now you need to see if HQ-R7 is learning the prefix learned via VPN 100 and test reachability. You should not see the route to 10.2.14.0/24 due to the segmentation you configured in your devices:

```
HQ-R7# show ip route ospf
Codes: L - local, C - connected, S - static, R - RIP, M - mobile,
B - BGP
       D - EIGRP, EX - EIGRP external, O - OSPF, IA - OSPF inter area
       N1 - OSPF NSSA external type 1, N2 - OSPF NSSA external type 2
       E1 - OSPF external type 1, E2 - OSPF external type 2
       i - IS-IS, su - IS-IS summary, L1 - IS-IS level-1, L2 - IS-IS
level-2
       ia - IS-IS inter area, * - candidate default, U - per-user
static route
       o - ODR, P - periodic downloaded static route, H - NHRP,
l - LISP
```

```
       a - application route
       + - replicated route, % - next hop override

Gateway of last resort is not set

     10.0.0.0/8 is variably subnetted, 7 subnets, 2 masks
O E2     10.2.99.0/24 [110/16777214] via 10.2.13.112, 00:51:10,
Ethernet0/1
                       [110/16777214] via 10.2.12.111, 00:51:10,
Ethernet0/0
     183.1.0.0/16 is variably subnetted, 3 subnets, 2 masks
O E2     183.1.1.1/32 [110/16777214] via 10.2.13.112, 00:43:29,
Ethernet0/1
                       [110/16777214] via 10.2.12.111, 00:43:29,
Ethernet0/0
HQ-R7#
```

Indeed, you are learning the prefix (183.1.1.1/32). Note that you can leverage ECMP because all characteristics in the SEN overlay are being treated as equal.

Finally, you can try a ping, as shown below:

```
HQ-R7# ping 183.1.1.1
Type escape sequence to abort.
Sending 5, 100-byte ICMP Echos to 183.1.1.1, timeout is 2 seconds:
!!!!!
Success rate is 100 percent (5/5), round-trip min/avg/max = 1/1/2 ms
HQ-R7#
```

The configuration of Branch-1 is now complete.

## Branch-2

In this part of the lab, you will create a multi-segment infrastructure. The goal will be to configure Branch-2 to support two business units. The first is VRF 100, which will support the Engineering department of your business. In addition, you will use VRF 200 to support Human Resources.

For the time being, you are just going to create subinterfaces on the Gi2 physical interfaces of both BR2-CSR1 and BR2-CSR2. You will create them in VRF 100 and VRF 200, respectively. We need to use VLANs of VRF 100 and VRF 200 on SW1 to complete this task.

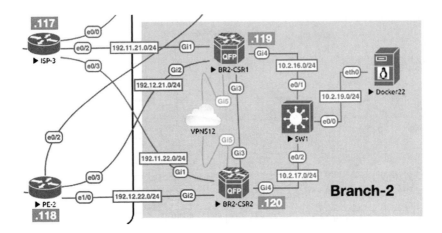

Next we will prepare BR2-CSR1 to support the necessary modifications:

```
BR2-CSR1# config-transaction

admin connected from 127.0.0.1 using console on BR2-CSR1
BR2-CSR1(config)# vrf definition 100
BR2-CSR1(config-vrf)# address-family ipv4
BR2-CSR1(config-ipv4)# exit
BR2-CSR1(config-vrf)# exit
BR2-CSR1(config)# interface GigabitEthernet 4.100
BR2-CSR1(config-if)# vrf forwarding 100
BR2-CSR1(config-if)# encapsulation dot1Q 100
BR2-CSR1(config-if)# ip address 10.2.100.119 255.255.255.0
BR2-CSR1(config-if)# ip mtu 1496
BR2-CSR1(config-if)# no shut
BR2-CSR1(config-if)# exit
BR2-CSR1(config)# vrf definition 200
BR2-CSR1(config-vrf)# address-family ipv4
BR2-CSR1(config-ipv4)# exit
BR2-CSR1(config-vrf)# exit
BR2-CSR1(config)# interface GigabitEthernet 4.200
BR2-CSR1(config-if)# vrf forwarding 200
BR2-CSR1(config-if)# encapsulation dot1Q 200
BR2-CSR1(config-if)# ip address 10.2.200.119 255.255.255.0
BR2-CSR1(config-if)# ip mtu 1496
BR2-CSR1(config-if)# no shut
BR2-CSR1(config-if)# commit
Commit complete.
```

Next, you can configure SW1 in Branch-2 with the necessary trunking and SVI configurations to support BR2-CSR1 and BR2-CSR2:

```
Switch# config t
Enter configuration commands, one per line.  End with CNTL/Z.
Switch(config)# no ip domain lookup
Switch(config)# line con 0
Switch(config-line)# logg synch
Switch(config-line)# no exec-timeout
Switch(config-line)# exit
Switch(config)# vlan 100
Switch(config-vlan)# name VPN100
Switch(config-vlan)# vlan 200
Switch(config-vlan)# name VPN200
Switch(config-vlan)# exit
Switch(config)# int range eth 0/1-2
Switch(config-if-range)# switchport trunk encapsulation dot1q
Switch(config-if-range)# switchport mode trunk
Switch(config-if-range)# no shut
Switch(config-if-range)# exit
Switch(config)# hostname BR2-SW1
BR2-SW1(config)# interface vlan 100
BR2-SW1(config-if)# ip address 10.2.100.111 255.255.255.0
BR2-SW1(config-if)# no shut
BR2-SW1(config-if)# interface vlan 200
BR2-SW1(config-if)# ip address 10.2.200.111 255.255.255.0
BR2-SW1(config-if)# no shut
BR2-SW1(config-if)# do wr
Building configuration...
Compressed configuration from 1095 bytes to 726 bytes[OK]
```

Now you need to test reachability to the interfaces on BR2-CSR1:

```
BR2-SW1# ping 10.2.100.119
Type escape sequence to abort.
Sending 5, 100-byte ICMP Echos to 10.2.100.119, timeout is 2 seconds:
.!!!!
Success rate is 80 percent (4/5), round-trip min/avg/max = 1/1/1 ms
BR2-SW1# ping 10.2.200.119
Type escape sequence to abort.
Sending 5, 100-byte ICMP Echos to 10.2.200.119, timeout is 2 seconds:
.!!!!
Success rate is 80 percent (4/5), round-trip min/avg/max = 1/1/1 ms
BR2-SW1#
```

Now you can make the same configuration on BR2-CSR2:

```
BR2-CSR2# config-transaction

admin connected from 127.0.0.1 using console on BR2-CSR2
BR2-CSR2(config)# vrf definition 100
BR2-CSR2(config-vrf)# address-family ipv4
BR2-CSR2(config-ipv4)# exit
BR2-CSR2(config-vrf)# exit
BR2-CSR2(config)# interface GigabitEthernet 4.100
BR2-CSR2(config-if)# vrf forwarding 100
BR2-CSR2(config-if)# encapsulation dot1Q 100
BR2-CSR2(config-if)# ip address 10.2.100.120 255.255.255.0
BR2-CSR2(config-if)# ip mtu 1496
BR2-CSR2(config-if)# no shut
BR2-CSR2(config-if)# exit
BR2-CSR2(config)# vrf definition 200
BR2-CSR2(config-vrf)# address-family ipv4
BR2-CSR2(config-ipv4)# exit
BR2-CSR2(config-vrf)# exit
BR2-CSR2(config)# interface GigabitEthernet 4.200
BR2-CSR2(config-if)# vrf forwarding 200
BR2-CSR2(config-if)# encapsulation dot1Q 200
BR2-CSR2(config-if)# ip address 10.2.200.120 255.255.255.0
BR2-CSR2(config-if)# ip mtu 1496
BR2-CSR2(config-if)# no shut
BR2-CSR2(config-if)# commit
Commit complete.
```

See if you can ping SW1 and BR2-CSR1 from BR2-CSR2:

```
BR2-CSR2# ping vrf 100 10.2.100.111
Type escape sequence to abort.
Sending 5, 100-byte ICMP Echos to 10.2.100.111, timeout is 2 seconds:
!!!!!
Success rate is 100 percent (5/5), round-trip min/avg/max = 1/1/2 ms
BR2-CSR2# ping vrf 100 10.2.100.119
Type escape sequence to abort.
Sending 5, 100-byte ICMP Echos to 10.2.100.119, timeout is 2 seconds:
!!!!!
Success rate is 100 percent (5/5), round-trip min/avg/max = 1/1/1 ms
BR2-CSR2# ping vrf 200 10.2.200.111
Type escape sequence to abort.
Sending 5, 100-byte ICMP Echos to 10.2.200.111, timeout is 2 seconds:
!!!!!
```

```
Success rate is 100 percent (5/5), round-trip min/avg/max = 1/1/1 ms
BR2-CSR2# ping vrf 200 10.2.200.119
Type escape sequence to abort.
Sending 5, 100-byte ICMP Echos to 10.2.200.119, timeout is 2 seconds:
!!!!!
Success rate is 100 percent (5/5), round-trip min/avg/max = 1/1/1 ms
```

Now you need to run routing protocols between the WAN edge routers and the BR2-SW1 switch. You can run EIGRP in VRF/VPN 100 and OSPF in VRF/VPN 200, starting with VPN 100 on BR2-SW1:

```
BR2-SW1# configure terminal
Enter configuration commands, one per line.  End with CNTL/Z.
BR2-SW1(config)# router eigrp MICRONICS
BR2-SW1(config-router)# address-family ipv4 autonomous-system 100
BR2-SW1(config-router-af)# network 10.2.100.0 0.0.0.255
BR2-SW1(config-router-af)# network 183.2.111.111 0.0.0.0
BR2-SW1(config-router-af)# end
```

To provide a way of testing the process, you can create a Loopback100 interface to advertise into EIGRP:

```
BR2-SW1(config)# int lo 100
BR2-SW1(config-if)# ip address 183.2.111.111 255.255.255.255
BR2-SW1(config-if)# end
```

As shown below, verify that you have two interfaces participating in EIGRP:

```
BR2-SW1# show ip eigrp interfaces
EIGRP-IPv4 VR(MICRONICS) Address-Family Interfaces for AS(100)
                         Xmit Queue  PeerQ        Mean  Pacing Time  Multicast  Pending
Interface        Peers   Un/Reliable Un/Reliable  SRTT  Un/Reliable  Flow Timer Routes
Vl100            0       0/0         0/0          0     0/0          0          0
Lo100            0       0/0         0/0          0     0/0          0          0
BR2-SW1#
```

Now you can configure EIGRP on BR2-CSR1:

```
BR2-CSR1# config-transaction

admin connected from 127.0.0.1 using console on BR2-CSR1
BR2-CSR1(config)# router eigrp MICRONICS
BR2-CSR1(config-router)# address-family ipv4 vrf 100 autonomous-system
100
```

```
BR2-CSR1(config-router-af)# network 10.2.100.119 0.0.0.0
BR2-CSR1(config-router-af)# topology base
BR2-CSR1(config-router-af-topology)# commit
Commit complete.

*Aug 28 14:05:06.209: %DUAL-5-NBRCHANGE: EIGRP-IPv4 100: Neighbor
10.2.100.111 (GigabitEthernet4.
100) is up: new adjacency
```

Now you can do the same configuration on BR2-CSR2:

```
BR2-CSR2# config-transaction

admin connected from 127.0.0.1 using console on BR2-CSR2
BR2-CSR2(config)# router eigrp MICRONICS
BR2-CSR2(config-router)# address-family ipv4 vrf 100 autonomous-system
100
BR2-CSR2(config-router-af)# network 10.2.100.120 0.0.0.0
BR2-CSR2(config-router-af)# topology base
BR2-CSR2(config-router-af-topology)# commit
Commit complete.
*Aug 28 14:08:56.632: %DUAL-5-NBRCHANGE: EIGRP-IPv4 100: Neighbor
10.2.100.111 (GigabitEthernet4.100)
 is up: new adjacency
```

As shown below, verify that BR2-SW1 is learning prefixes in VPN 100 as a part of its
EIGRP relationship with BR2-CSR1 and BR2-CSR2:

```
BR2-SW1# show ip route eigrp
Codes: L - local, C - connected, S - static, R - RIP, M - mobile,
B - BGP
       D - EIGRP, EX - EIGRP external, O - OSPF, IA - OSPF inter area
       N1 - OSPF NSSA external type 1, N2 - OSPF NSSA external type 2
       E1 - OSPF external type 1, E2 - OSPF external type 2
       i - IS-IS, su - IS-IS summary, L1 - IS-IS level-1, L2 - IS-IS
level-2
       ia - IS-IS inter area, * - candidate default, U - per-user
static route
       o - ODR, P - periodic downloaded static route, H - NHRP, l -
LISP
       a - application route
       + - replicated route, % - next hop override, p - overrides from
PfR

Gateway of last resort is not set


BR2-SW1#
```

BR2-SW1 is not learning anything. But you should understand why at this point in your studies. Obviously, OMP is not being redistributed into EIGRP on the WAN edge devices. You can fix this as shown below:

```
BR2-CSR1# config-transaction

admin connected from 127.0.0.1 using console on BR2-CSR1
BR2-CSR1(config)# router eigrp MICRONICS
BR2-CSR1(config-router)# address-family ipv4 unicast vrf 100
autonomous-system 100
BR2-CSR1(config-router-af)# topology base
BR2-CSR1(config-router-af-topology)# redistribute omp
BR2-CSR1(config-router-af-topology)# commit
Commit complete.
```

Enter the following on BR2-CSR2:

```
BR2-CSR2# config-transaction

admin connected from 127.0.0.1 using console on BR2-CSR2
BR2-CSR2(config)# router eigrp MICRONICS
BR2-CSR2(config-router)# address-family ipv4 unicast vrf 100
autonomous-system 100
BR2-CSR2(config-router-af)# topology base
BR2-CSR2(config-router-af-topology)# redistribute omp
BR2-CSR2(config-router-af-topology)# commit
Commit complete.
```

Return to BR2-SW1 and check for those prefixes, as shown below:

```
BR2-SW1# show ip route eigrp
Codes: L - local, C - connected, S - static, R - RIP, M - mobile,
B - BGP
       D - EIGRP, EX - EIGRP external, O - OSPF, IA - OSPF inter area
       N1 - OSPF NSSA external type 1, N2 - OSPF NSSA external type 2
       E1 - OSPF external type 1, E2 - OSPF external type 2
       i - IS-IS, su - IS-IS summary, L1 - IS-IS level-1, L2 - IS-IS
level-2
       ia - IS-IS inter area, * - candidate default, U - per-user
static route
       o - ODR, P - periodic downloaded static route, H - NHRP,
l - LISP
       a - application route
       + - replicated route, % - next hop override, p - overrides from
PfR

Gateway of last resort is not set
```

```
        10.0.0.0/8 is variably subnetted, 8 subnets, 2 masks
D EX    10.2.12.0/24 [170/5120] via 10.2.100.120, 00:01:01, Vlan100
                     [170/5120] via 10.2.100.119, 00:01:01, Vlan100
D EX    10.2.13.0/24 [170/5120] via 10.2.100.120, 00:01:01, Vlan100
                     [170/5120] via 10.2.100.119, 00:01:01, Vlan100
D EX    10.2.18.0/24 [170/5120] via 10.2.100.120, 00:01:01, Vlan100
                     [170/5120] via 10.2.100.119, 00:01:01, Vlan100
D EX    10.2.99.0/24 [170/5120] via 10.2.100.120, 00:01:01, Vlan100
                     [170/5120] via 10.2.100.119, 00:01:01, Vlan100
      183.1.0.0/32 is subnetted, 2 subnets
D EX    183.1.1.1 [170/5120] via 10.2.100.120, 00:01:01, Vlan100
                  [170/5120] via 10.2.100.119, 00:01:01, Vlan100
D EX    183.1.7.7 [170/5120] via 10.2.100.120, 00:01:01, Vlan100
                  [170/5120] via 10.2.100.119, 00:01:01, Vlan100
BR2-SW1#
```

You have them! Now test reachability as shown below:

```
BR2-SW1# ping 183.1.1.1
Type escape sequence to abort.
Sending 5, 100-byte ICMP Echos to 183.1.1.1, timeout is 2 seconds:
.!!!!
Success rate is 80 percent (4/5), round-trip min/avg/max = 1/1/2 ms
BR2-SW1# ping 183.1.7.7
Type escape sequence to abort.
Sending 5, 100-byte ICMP Echos to 183.1.7.7, timeout is 2 seconds:
!!!!!
Success rate is 100 percent (5/5), round-trip min/avg/max = 1/1/2 ms
BR2-SW1# ping 10.2.99.100
Type escape sequence to abort.
Sending 5, 100-byte ICMP Echos to 10.2.99.100, timeout is 2 seconds:
!!!!!
Success rate is 100 percent (5/5), round-trip min/avg/max = 1/1/2 ms
BR2-SW1#
```

This is great!

Now, for the OSPF configuration on VRF/VPN 200, you can start on BR2-SW1, where you will also create a new SVI interface that you will advertise into OSPF:

```
BR1-SW1# conf t
Enter configuration commands, one per line.  End with CNTL/Z.
BR1-SW1(config)# int loopback 200
BR1-SW1(config-if)# ip address 183.200.111.111 255.255.255.255
BR1-SW1(config-if)# exit
BR1-SW1(config)# router ospf 1
```

```
BR1-SW1(config-router)# router-id 0.0.0.111
BR1-SW1(config-router)# network 183.200.111.111 0.0.0.0 area 0
BR1-SW1(config-router)# network 10.2.200.111 0.0.0.0 area 0
BR1-SW1(config-router)# end
```

Check to see if you have two interfaces running OSPF:

```
BR1-SW1# show ip ospf interface brief
Interface   PID   Area        IP Address/Mask     Cost   State Nbrs F/C
Lo200        1     0          183.200.111.111/32  1      LOOP  0/0
Vl200        1     0          10.2.200.111/24     1      DR    0/0
BR1-SW1#
```

Great! Now you can configure VRF/VPN 200 on the WAN edge devices:

```
BR2-CSR1# config-transaction

admin connected from 127.0.0.1 using console on BR2-CSR1
BR2-CSR1(config)# router ospf 1 vrf 200
BR2-CSR1(config-router)# router-id 0.0.0.119
BR2-CSR1(config-router)# network 10.2.200.119 0.0.0.0 area 0
BR2-CSR1(config-router)# redistribute omp subnets
BR2-CSR1(config-router)# commit
Commit complete.
```

Now enter the following on BR2-CSR2:

```
BR2-CSR2# config-transaction

admin connected from 127.0.0.1 using console on BR2-CSR2
BR2-CSR2(config)# router ospf 1 vrf 200
BR2-CSR2(config-router)# router-id 0.0.0.120
BR2-CSR2(config-router)# network 10.2.200.120 0.0.0.0 area 0
BR2-CSR2(config-router)# redistribute omp subnets
BR2-CSR2(config-router)# commit
Commit complete.
```

You have done the configuration, but if you take the time to inspect the results from the perspective of BR2-SW1, you will find that you have an issue related to the lack of OSPF neighbor adjacencies, as shown below:

```
BR1-SW1# show ip ospf neighbor

Neighbor ID   Pri   State         Dead Time   Address        Interface
0.0.0.119      1    EXCHANGE/DR   00:00:36    10.2.200.119   Vlan200
0.0.0.120      1    EXCHANGE/BDR  00:00:37    10.2.200.120   Vlan200
BR1-SW1#
```

You can see that BR2-SW1 is in the EXCHANGE state. Further inspection from the BR2 WAN edge routers shows that they are stuck in EXSTART:

```
BR2-CSR2# show ip ospf neighbor

Neighbor ID    Pri   State           Dead Time   Address       Interface
0.0.0.111       1    EXSTART/DROTHER 00:00:39    10.2.200.111  GigabitEthernet4.200
0.0.0.119       1    FULL/DR         00:00:31    10.2.200.119  GigabitEthernet4.200
BR2-CSR2#
```

Notice that BR2-CSR2 has formed a full relationship with BR2-CSR1 but has failed to form a neighborship with BR2-SW1. This is because of the MTU mismatch between the devices. The WAN edges agree on the MTU (1496), but the switch is running 1500. You need to correct this issue. There are two ways you can do this. One way is to change the MTU to 1496:

```
BR1-SW1# conf t
Enter configuration commands, one per line.  End with CNTL/Z.
BR1-SW1(config)# int vlan 200
BR1-SW1(config-if)# ip mtu 1496
BR1-SW1(config-if)# exit
BR1-SW1(config)#
*Aug 28 15:11:46.928: %OSPF-5-ADJCHG: Process 1, Nbr 0.0.0.120 on
Vlan200 from LOADING to FULL, Loading Done
BR1-SW1(config)#
*Aug 28 15:12:16.293: %OSPF-5-ADJCHG: Process 1, Nbr 0.0.0.119 on
Vlan200 from LOADING to FULL, Loading Done
```

Now as a last verification, you need to see if BR1-SW1 is learning OSPF routes:

```
BR1-SW1# show ip route ospf
Codes: L - local, C - connected, S - static, R - RIP, M - mobile,
B - BGP
        D - EIGRP, EX - EIGRP external, O - OSPF, IA - OSPF inter area
        N1 - OSPF NSSA external type 1, N2 - OSPF NSSA external type 2
        E1 - OSPF external type 1, E2 - OSPF external type 2
        i - IS-IS, su - IS-IS summary, L1 - IS-IS level-1, L2 - IS-IS
level-2
        ia - IS-IS inter area, * - candidate default, U - per-user
static route
        o - ODR, P - periodic downloaded static route, H - NHRP,
l - LISP
        a - application route
        + - replicated route, % - next hop override, p - overrides from
PfR

Gateway of last resort is not set
```

```
      10.0.0.0/8 is variably subnetted, 9 subnets, 2 masks
O E2    10.2.14.0/24 [110/16777214] via 10.2.200.120, 00:03:19,
Vlan200
                      [110/16777214] via 10.2.200.119, 00:03:19,
Vlan200
      172.101.0.0/24 is subnetted, 1 subnets
O E2    172.101.2.0 [110/16777214] via 10.2.200.120, 00:03:19, Vlan200
                     [110/16777214] via 10.2.200.119, 00:03:19, Vlan200
```

When you test for learned routes, you also want to see reachability, as shown below:

```
BR1-SW1# ping 10.2.14.121
Type escape sequence to abort.
Sending 5, 100-byte ICMP Echos to 10.2.14.121, timeout is 2 seconds:
!!!!!
Success rate is 100 percent (5/5), round-trip min/avg/max = 1/1/1 ms
BR1-SW1# ping 172.101.2.111
Type escape sequence to abort.
Sending 5, 100-byte ICMP Echos to 172.101.2.111, timeout is 2 seconds:
.!!!!
Success rate is 80 percent (4/5), round-trip min/avg/max = 1/1/2 ms
BR1-SW1# ping 172.101.2.112
Type escape sequence to abort.
Sending 5, 100-byte ICMP Echos to 172.101.2.112, timeout is 2 seconds:
!!!!!
Success rate is 100 percent (5/5), round-trip min/avg/max = 1/1/2 ms
BR1-SW1#
```

You have completed the unicast routing configuration for Branch-2.

# Lab 4: Configuring vEdge Using a Feature Template

For this lab, you need to configure BR1-vE1 by using a vManage template using the information in the matrix provided below. The following pages walk through how to do this.

| Device | Feature Template | Template – Name | Values |
|--------|------------------|-----------------|--------|
| BR1-vE1 | System | BR1-vE1-SYSTEM-temp | Site-id: 11<br>System-ip: Device Specific<br>Hostname: BR1-vE1<br>Baud Rate: 115200 |
| | VPN | BR1-vE1-VPN0-template | VPN ID: 0<br>DNS: 8.8.8.8<br>GW1: 0.0.0.0/0 192.11.11.117<br>GW2: 0.0.0.0/0 192.12.11.118 |

| Device | Feature Template | Template – Name | Values |
|---|---|---|---|
| | VPN Interface Ethernet | BR1-vE1-VPN0-ge0_0-template | Shutdown: **No** Interface Name: **ge0/0** Static: **192.11.11.121/24** Tunnel Interface: **On** Color: **Biz-Internet** Allow Service: **All** |
| | VPN Interface Ethernet | BR1-vE1-VPN0-ge0_1-template | Shutdown: **No** Interface Name: **ge0/1** Static: **192.12.11.121/24** Tunnel Interface: **On** Color: **MPLS** Allow Service: **All** |
| | VPN | BR1-vE1-VPN100-template | VPN ID: **100** |
| | VPN Interface Ethernet | BR1-vE1-VPN100-int-ge0_4-template | Shutdown: **No** Interface Name: **ge0/4** Static: **10.2.99.121/24** Tunnel: **Off** |
| | OPSF | BR1-vE1-VPN100-OSPF-template | Redistribute: **Connected, Static & OMP** Area: **0** Interface: **ge0/4** |
| | VPN | BR1-vE1-VPN200-template | VPN ID: **200** |
| | VPN Interface Ethernet | BR1-vE1-VPN200-int-ge0_2-template | Shutdown: **No** Interface Name: **ge0/2** Static: **10.2.24.121/24** Tunnel: **Off** |
| | VPN | BR1-vE1-vpn512-temp | VPN ID: **512** |
| | VPN Interface Ethernet | BR1-vE1-vpn512-int-temp | Shutdown: **No** Interface Name: **eth0** Static: **10.82.83.121/24** |
| Device | Device Template | Template-Name | Values |
| BR1-vE1 | vEdge Cloud | BR1-vE1-Device-Template | Use all feature templates created above |

Navigate to **Configuration > Templates > Feature** in the vManage UI and click **Add Template**.

In the screen that appears, scroll down and select **vEdge Cloud** in the left-hand working pane. Then click **System** in the **Select Template > BASIC INFORMATION** section in the right-hand working pane, as shown below:

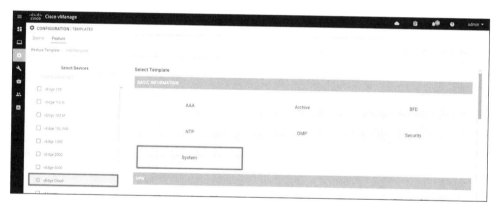

In the following steps, you will provide the information specified in the matrix at the beginning of this lab.

Name the template as shown below:

Provide the basic configuration shown below and click **Save:**

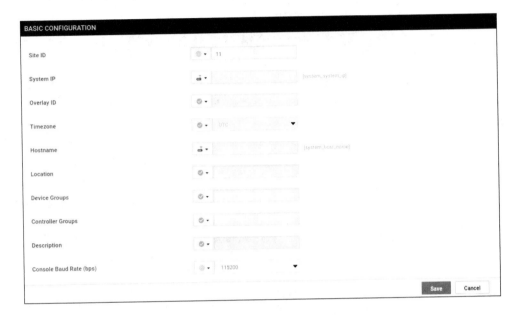

Click **Add Template**. In the screen that appears, scroll down and select **vEdge Cloud** in the left-hand working pane. Then choose **VPN** in the **Select Template > VPN** section in the right-hand working pane, as shown below:

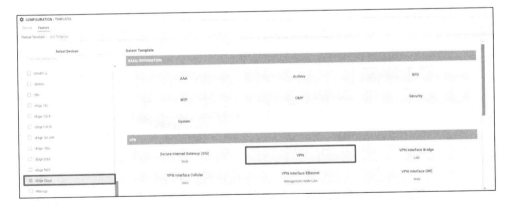

Name the template as shown on the next page:

Select **Basic Configuration** and provide the VPN ID **0**, as shown below:

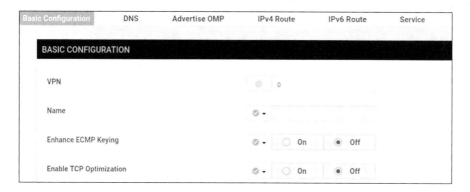

Select **DNS** and provide the DNS IP address **8.8.8.8**, as shown below:

Click **IPv4 Route** and then click **New IPv4 Route**, as shown below:

Enter the **0.0.0.0/0** prefix and click **Add Next Hop**, as shown below:

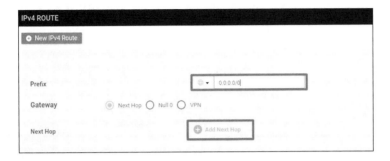

Click **Add Next Hop**, as shown below:

Modify the Next Hop screen as shown below and click **Add**.

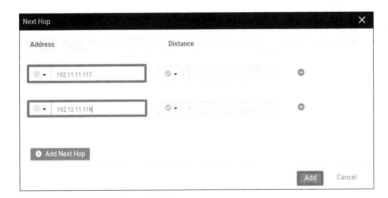

Verify that your screen looks as shown on the next page and click **Add**:

You should see the following information:

Click **Save**:

Click **Add Template**. In the screen that appears, scroll down and select **vEdge Cloud** in the left-hand working pane. Then click **VPN Interface Ethernet** in the **Select Template > VPN** section in the right-hand working pane, as shown below:

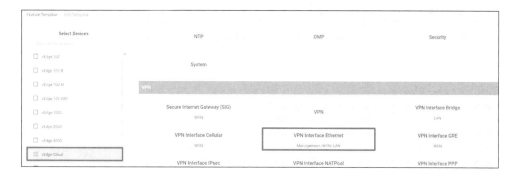

Name the template as shown below:

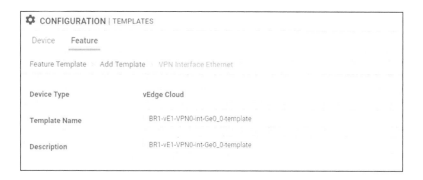

Select **Basic Configuration**, set Shutdown to No, and enter the interface name **ge0/0**. Then provide the static IP address 192.11.11.121/24 for this interface, as shown below:

Select **Tunnel**, set Tunnel Interface to On, and select biz-internet from the Color dropdown, as shown below:

Scroll down to the **Allow Service** section and set All to On, as shown below:

Click **Save**.

Click **Add Template**. In the screen that appears, scroll down and select **vEdge Cloud** in the left-hand working pane. Then click **VPN Interface Ethernet** in the **Select Template > VPN** section in the right-hand working pane, as shown below:

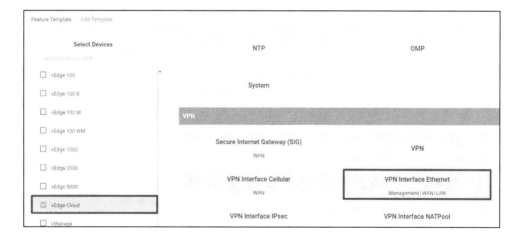

Name the template as shown below:

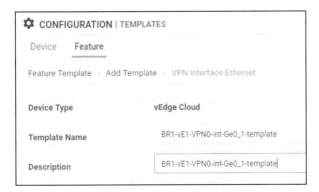

Select **Basic Configuration**, set Shutdown to No, and enter the interface name **ge0/1**. Then provide the static IP address **192.12.11.121/24** for this interface, as shown below:

Select **Tunnel**, set Tunnel Interface to On, and select mpls from the Color dropdown, as shown below:

Scroll down to the Allow Service section and set All to On, as shown below:

Click **Save**.

Click **Add Template**. In the screen that appears, scroll down and select **vEdge Cloud** in the left-hand working pane. Then click **VPN** in the **Select Template > VPN** section in the right-hand working pane, as shown below:

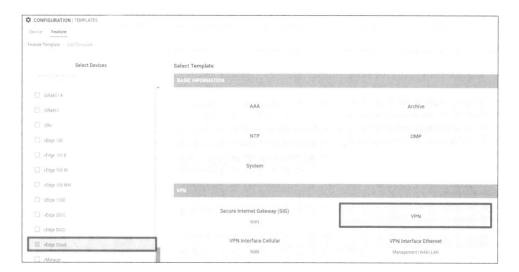

Name the template as shown below:

Select **Basic Configuration** and provide the VPN ID **100**, as shown below:

Click **Save**.

Click **Add Template**. In the screen that appears, scroll down and select **vEdge Cloud** in the left-hand working pane. Then click **OSPF** in the **Select Template > OTHER TEMPLATES** section in the right-hand working pane, as shown below:

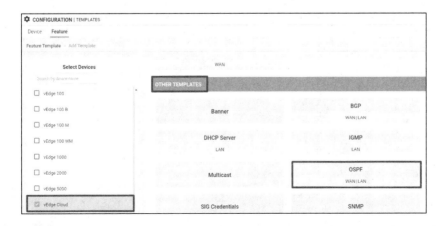

Name the template as shown below:

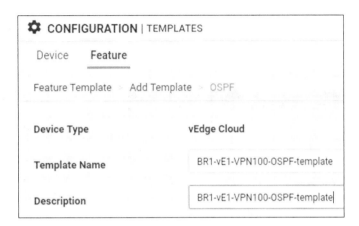

Select **Redistribute** and then click **New Redistribution**, as shown below:

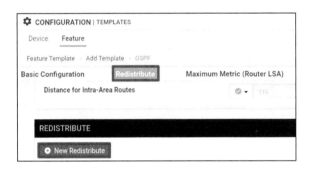

Set Protocol to **omp** and click **Add:**

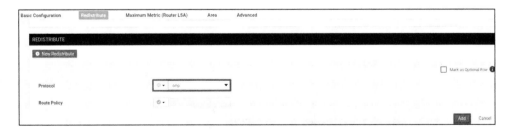

Select **Area** and click **New Area**:

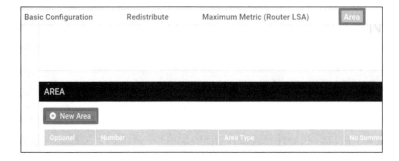

Enter the area number of **0** and click **Add Interface**, as shown below:

Click **Add Interface**, as shown below:

Provide the interface name **ge0/4** and click **Add:**

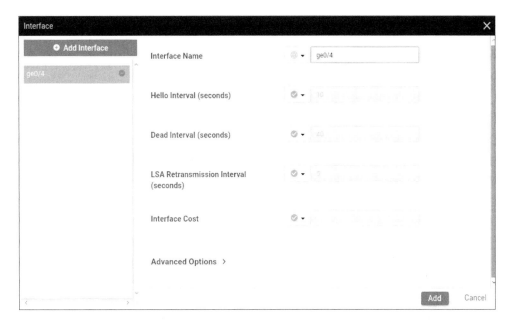

Click **Add** again:

Click **Save.**

Click **Add Template**. In the screen that appears, scroll down and select **vEdge Cloud** in the left-hand working pane. Then click **VPN Interface Ethernet** in the **Select Template > VPN** section in the right-hand working pane, as shown below:

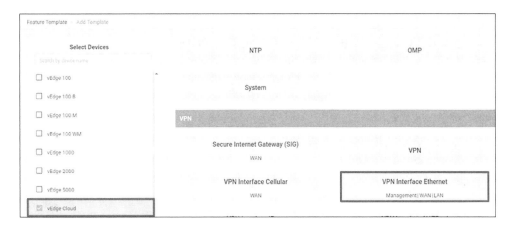

Name the template as shown below:

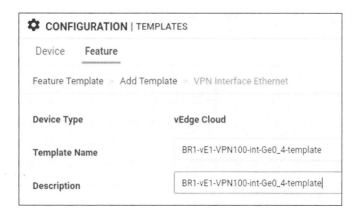

Select **Basic Configuration**, set Shutdown to No, and enter the interface name **ge0/4**. Then provide the static IP address 10.2.99.121/24 for this interface, as shown below:

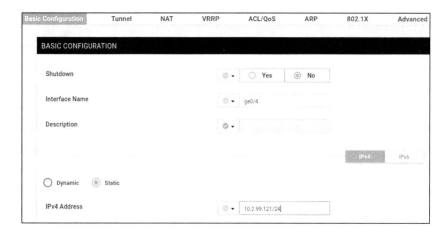

Click **Save**.

Click **Add Template**. In the screen that appears, scroll down and select **vEdge Cloud** in the left-hand working pane. Then click **VPN** in the **Select Template > VPN** section in the right-hand working pane, as shown on the next page:

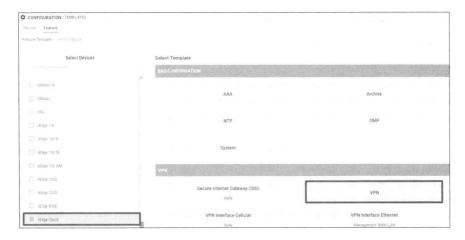

Name the template as shown below:

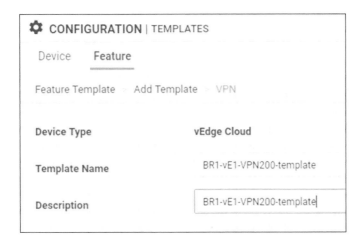

Select **Basic Configuration** and provide the VPN ID **200**, as shown below:

Click **Save**.

Click **Add Template**. In the screen that appears, scroll down and select **vEdge Cloud** in the left-hand working pane. Then click **VPN Interface Ethernet** in the **Select Template > VPN** section in the right-hand working pane, as shown below:

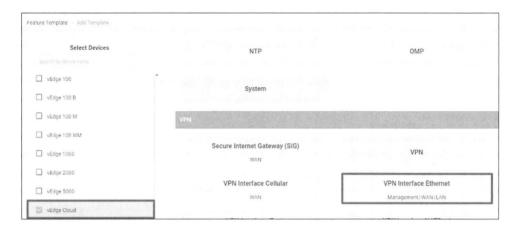

Name the template as shown below:

Select **Basic Configuration**, set Shutdown to No, and enter the interface name **ge0/2**. Then provide the static IP address 10.2.14.121/24 for this interface, as shown on the next page:

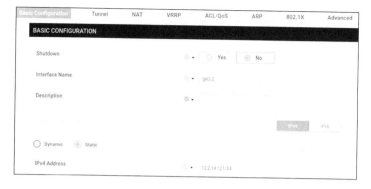

Click **Save**.

Click **Add Template**. In the screen that appears, scroll down and select **vEdge Cloud** in the left-hand working pane. Then click **VPN** in the **Select Template > VPN** section in the right-hand working pane, as shown below:

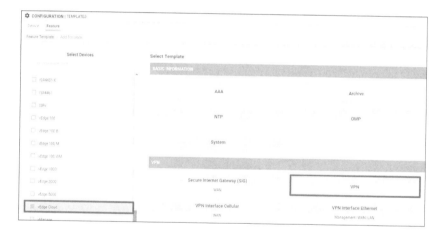

Name the template as shown below:

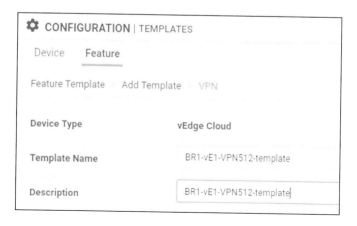

Select **Basic Configuration** and provide the VPN ID **512**, as shown below:

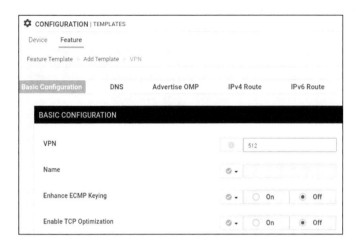

Click **Save**.

Click **Add Template**. In the screen that appears, scroll down and select **vEdge Cloud** in the left-hand working pane. Then click **VPN Interface Ethernet** in the **Select Template > VPN** section in the right-hand working pane, as shown below:

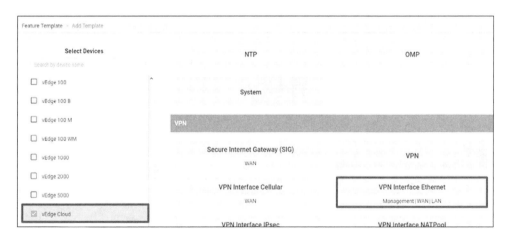

Name the template as shown below:

Select **Basic Configuration**, set Shutdown to No, and enter the interface name **eth0**. Then provide the static IP address 10.82.83.121/24 for this interface, as shown below:

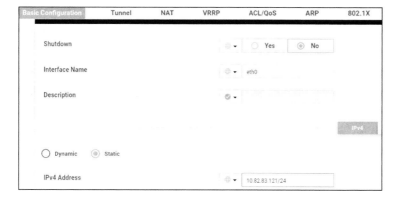

Click **Save**.

Navigate to **Configuration > Templates > Device > Create Template** and select **From Feature Template**. Select **vEdge Cloud** from the Device Model List dropdown and name the template as shown below:

Select **Basic Information** and make the changes shown below:

Select **Transport & Management VPN** and make the changes shown below:

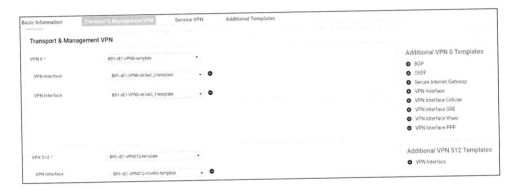

Select **Service VPN** and click **Add VPN**:

In the Available VPN Templates pane, select BR1-vE1-VPN100-template and click the right-pointing arrow to move selected template to the right-hand working pane:

Click **Next**.

Modify the Add VPN window as shown below:

Click **Add**.

Click **Add VPN** again:

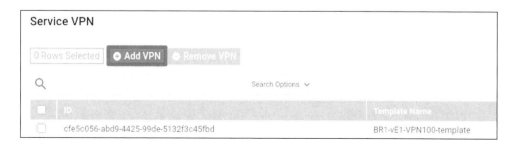

In the Available VPN Templates pane, select BR1-vE1-VPN200-template and click the right-pointing arrow to move it to the right-hand working pane:

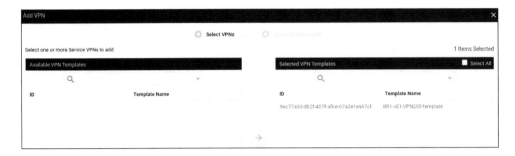

Modify the Add VPN window as shown below:

Click **Add**.

To complete the device template, click **Create**:

Attach this template to BR1-vE1 by clicking the ... icon at the right of the following line and selecting **Attach Devices**, as shown below:

In the Attach Devices window select BR1-vE1 in the Available Devices pane and click the right-pointing arrow to move the device to the Selected Devices pane. Then click **Attach:**

You now see the device template listed on the next screen. You should see a green circle with a check mark at the far-left side of the screen, as shown below. If you see it, click **Next:**

In the list of devices, select BR1-vE1 and verify the configuration that will be pushed to the device. When you are satisfied with the configuration, click **Configure Devices.**

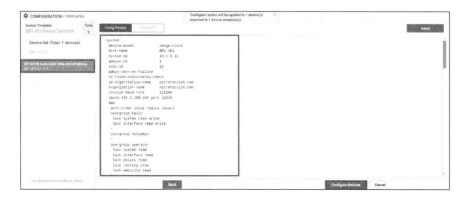

After a few moments, you should see the following:

To test this deployment to make sure everything works, you can enter the pings shown below on Docker23 to see if you can reach VPN 200 resources in the other sites:

```
root@Docker23:~# ping 10.2.200.111 -c 5 ← Loopback of BR2-SW1
PING 10.2.200.111 (10.2.200.111) 56(84) bytes of data.
64 bytes from 10.2.200.111: icmp_seq=1 ttl=253 time=1.28 ms
64 bytes from 10.2.200.111: icmp_seq=2 ttl=253 time=1.32 ms
64 bytes from 10.2.200.111: icmp_seq=3 ttl=253 time=1.09 ms
64 bytes from 10.2.200.111: icmp_seq=4 ttl=253 time=1.48 ms
64 bytes from 10.2.200.111: icmp_seq=5 ttl=253 time=1.31 ms

--- 10.2.200.111 ping statistics ---
5 packets transmitted, 5 received, 0% packet loss, time 4003ms
rtt min/avg/max/mdev = 1.098/1.301/1.481/0.122 ms


root@Docker23:~# ping 172.101.2.111 -c 5 ← DC1-CSR1 Gi3
PING 172.101.2.111 (172.101.2.111) 56(84) bytes of data.
64 bytes from 172.101.2.111: icmp_seq=1 ttl=254 time=1.85 ms
64 bytes from 172.101.2.111: icmp_seq=2 ttl=254 time=1.59 ms
64 bytes from 172.101.2.111: icmp_seq=3 ttl=254 time=1.56 ms
64 bytes from 172.101.2.111: icmp_seq=4 ttl=254 time=1.62 ms
64 bytes from 172.101.2.111: icmp_seq=5 ttl=254 time=1.17 ms

--- 172.101.2.111 ping statistics ---
5 packets transmitted, 5 received, 0% packet loss, time 4006ms
rtt min/avg/max/mdev = 1.175/1.562/1.852/0.218 ms


root@Docker23:~# ping 172.101.2.112 -c 5 ← DC1-CSR2 Gi3
PING 172.101.2.112 (172.101.2.112) 56(84) bytes of data.
64 bytes from 172.101.2.112: icmp_seq=1 ttl=254 time=1.88 ms
64 bytes from 172.101.2.112: icmp_seq=2 ttl=254 time=1.38 ms
64 bytes from 172.101.2.112: icmp_seq=3 ttl=254 time=3.19 ms
64 bytes from 172.101.2.112: icmp_seq=4 ttl=254 time=1.22 ms
64 bytes from 172.101.2.112: icmp_seq=5 ttl=254 time=1.03 ms

--- 172.101.2.112 ping statistics ---
5 packets transmitted, 5 received, 0% packet loss, time 4002ms
rtt min/avg/max/mdev = 1.030/1.742/3.192/0.779 ms
root@Docker23:~#
```

Now you can test reachability in VRF/VPN 100 from RM-R1:

```
RM-R1# ping 183.1.7.7 ← Loopback of HQ-R7
Type escape sequence to abort.
Sending 5, 100-byte ICMP Echos to 183.1.7.7, timeout is 2 seconds:
!!!!!
Success rate is 100 percent (5/5), round-trip min/avg/max = 1/1/2 ms
RM-R1# ping 10.2.100.111 ← SVI VLAN100 of BR2-SW1
Type escape sequence to abort.
Sending 5, 100-byte ICMP Echos to 10.2.100.111, timeout is 2 seconds:
!!!!!
Success rate is 100 percent (5/5), round-trip min/avg/max = 1/1/2 ms
RM-R1#
```

You can see that all reachability has been resolved in Branch-1.

# Lab 5: Configuring vEdge Using a vManage Feature Template

For this lab, you need to configure BR1-vE1 by using a vManage template using the information in the matrix provided below. The following pages walk through how to do this.

| Device | Feature Template | Template – Name | Values |
|---|---|---|---|
| BR1-vE1 | System | BR1-vE1-SYSTEM-temp | Site-id: **11** <br> System-ip: **Device Specific** <br> Hostname: **BR1-vE1** <br> Baud Rate: **115200** |
| | VPN | BR1-vE1-VPN0-template | VPN ID: **0** <br> DNS: **8.8.8.8** <br> GW1: **0.0.0.0/0 192.11.11.117** <br> GW2: **0.0.0.0/0 192.12.11.118** |
| | VPN Interface Ethernet | BR1-vE1-VPN0-ge0_0-template | Shutdown: **No** <br> Interface Name: **ge0/0** <br> Static: **192.11.11.121/24** <br> Tunnel Interface: **On** <br> Color: **Biz-Internet** <br> Allow Service: **All** |

| Device | Feature Template | Template – Name | Values |
|---|---|---|---|
| | VPN Interface Ethernet | BR1-vE1-VPN0-ge0_1-template | Shutdown: **No** <br> Interface Name: **ge0/1** <br> Static: **192.12.11.121/24** <br> Tunnel Interface: **On** <br> Color: **MPLS** <br> Allow Service: **All** |
| | VPN | BR1-vE1-VPN100-template | VPN ID: **100** |
| | VPN Interface Ethernet | BR1-vE1-VPN100-int-ge0_4-template | Shutdown: **No** <br> Interface Name: **ge0/4** <br> Static: **10.2.99.121/24** <br> Tunnel: **Off** |
| | OPSF | BR1-vE1-VPN100-OSPF-template | Redistribute: **Connected, Static & OMP** <br> Area: **0** <br> Interface: **ge0/4** |
| | VPN | BR1-vE1-VPN200-template | VPN ID: **200** |
| | VPN Interface Ethernet | BR1-vE1-VPN200-int-ge0_2-template | Shutdown: **No** <br> Interface Name: **ge0/2** <br> Static: **10.2.24.121/24** <br> Tunnel: **Off** |
| | VPN | BR1-vE1-vpn512-temp | VPN ID: **512** |
| | VPN Interface Ethernet | BR1-vE1-vpn512-int-temp | Shutdown: **No** <br> Interface Name: **eth0** <br> Static: **10.82.83.121/24** |
| **Device** | **Device Template** | **Template-Name** | **Values** |
| BR1-vE1 | vEdge Cloud | BR1-vE1-Device-Template | Use all feature templates created above |

Navigate to **Configuration > Templates > Feature** in the vManage UI and click **Add Template:**

In the screen that appears, scroll down and select **vEdge Cloud** in the left-hand working pane. Then click **System** in the **Select Template > BASIC INFORMATION** section in the right-hand working pane, as shown below:

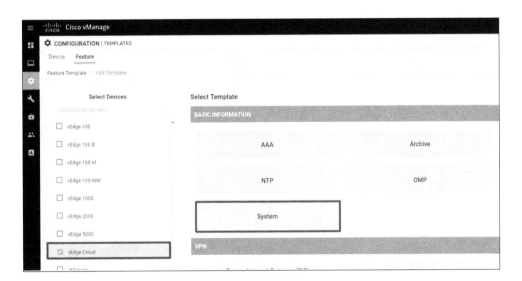

In the following steps, you will provide the information specified in the matrix at the beginning of this lab.

Name the template as shown below:

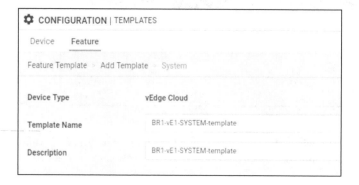

Provide the basic configuration information shown below and click **Save**:

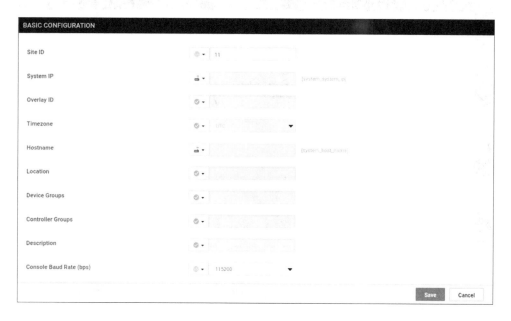

Click **Add Template**. In the screen that appears, scroll down and select **vEdge Cloud** in the left-hand working pane. Then click **VPN** in the **Select Template > VPN** section in the right-hand working pane, as shown on the next page:

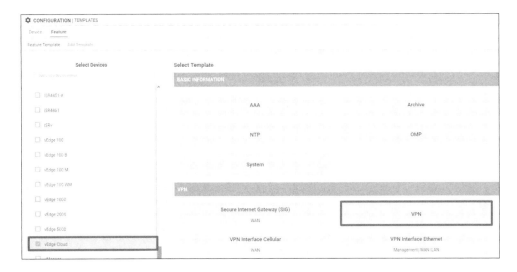

Name the template as shown below:

Select **Basic Configuration** and provide the VPN ID **0**, as shown below:

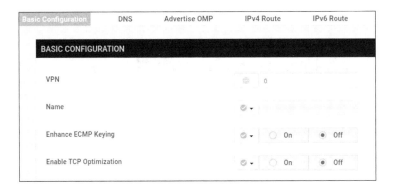

Select **DNS** and provide the DNS IP address **8.8.8.8**, as shown below:

Select **IPv4 Route** and click **New IPv4 Route**:

Enter the **0.0.0.0/0** prefix and click **Add Next Hop**:

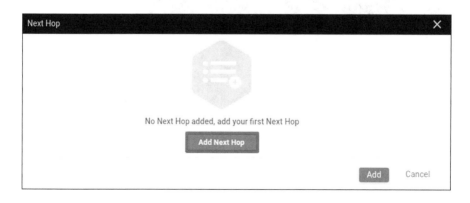

Click **Add Next Hop**:

Modify the Next Hop screen as shown below and click **Add**:

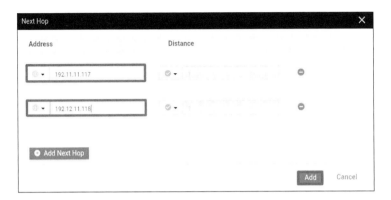

Verify that your screen looks as shown below and click **Add**:

You should see the following information:

Click **Save**.

Click **Add Template**. In the screen that appears, scroll down and select **vEdge Cloud** in the left-hand working pane. Then click **VPN Interface Ethernet** in the **Select Template > VPN** section in the right-hand working pane, as shown below:

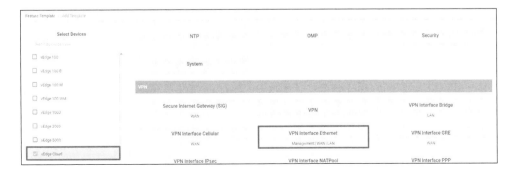

Name the template as shown below:

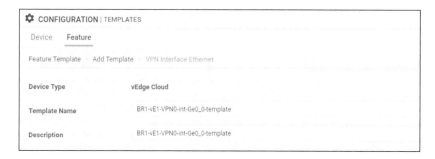

Select **Basic Configuration,** set Shutdown to No, and enter the interface name **ge0/0.** Then provide the static IP address 192.11.11.121/24 for this interface, as shown below:

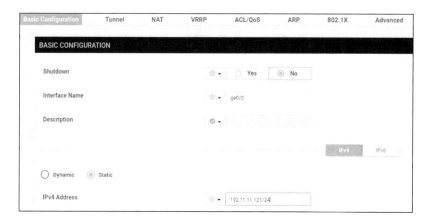

Select **Tunnel,** set Tunnel Interface to On, and select biz-internet from the Color drop-down, as shown below:

Scroll down to the Allow Service section and set All to On, as shown below:

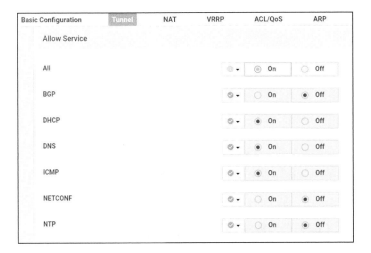

Click **Save.**

Click **Add Template.** In the screen that appears, scroll down and select **vEdge Cloud** in the left-hand working pane. Then click **VPN Interface Ethernet** in the **Select Template > VPN** section in the right-hand working pane, as shown below:

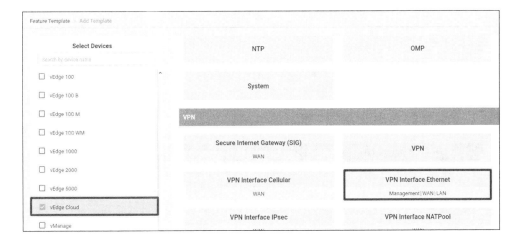

Name the template as shown below:

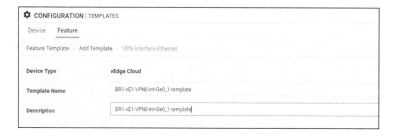

Select **Basic Configuration**, set Shutdown to No, and enter the interface name **ge0/1**. Then provide the static IP address **192.12.11.121/24** for this interface, as shown below:

Select **Tunnel**, set Tunnel Interface to On, and select mpls from the Color dropdown, as shown below:

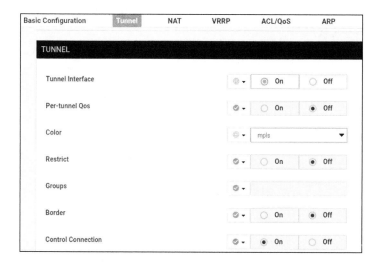

Scroll down to the Allow Service section and set All to On, as shown below:

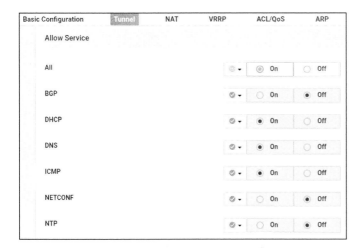

Click **Save.**

Click **Add Template.** In the screen that appears, scroll down and select **vEdge Cloud** in the left-hand working pane. Then click **VPN** in the **Select Template > VPN** section in the right-hand working pane, as shown below:

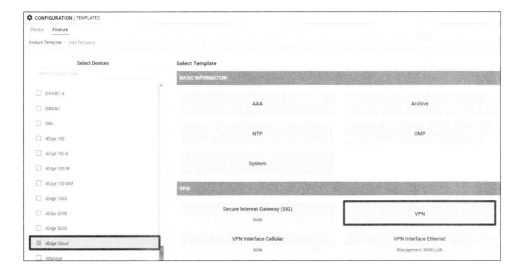

Name the template as shown below:

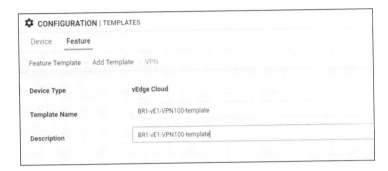

Select **Basic Configuration** and provide the VPN ID **100**, as shown below:

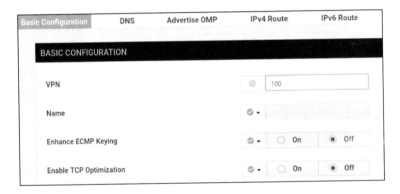

Click **Save.**

Click **Add Template.** In the screen that appears, scroll down and select **vEdge Cloud** in the left-hand working pane. Then click **OSPF** in the **Select** Template > **OTHER TEMPLATES** section in the right-hand working pane, as shown below:

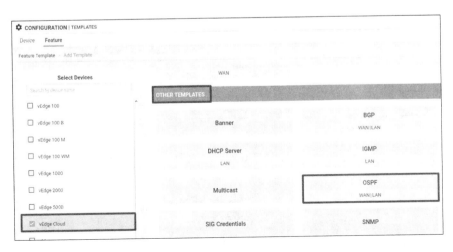

Name the template as shown below:

Select **Redistribute** and click **New Redistribution:**

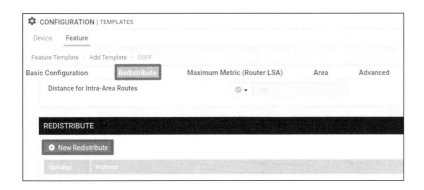

Select omp from the Protocol dropdown and click **Add:**

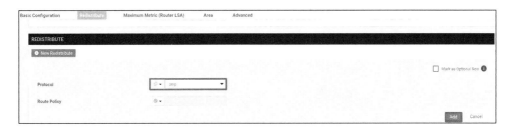

Select **Area** and click **New Area:**

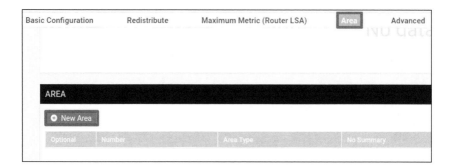

Enter the area number **0** and click **Add Interface:**

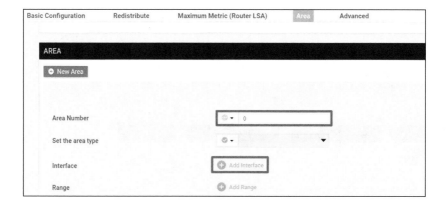

Click **Add Interface**, as shown below:

Provide the interface name **ge0/4** and click **Add**:

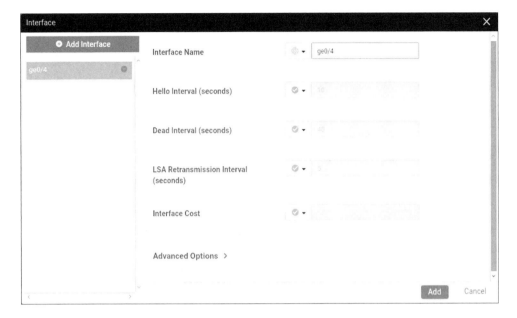

Click **Add** again.

Click **Save**.

Click **Add Template**. In the screen that appears, scroll down and select **vEdge Cloud** in the left-hand working pane. Then click **VPN Interface Ethernet** in the **Select Template > VPN** section in the right-hand working pane, as shown below:

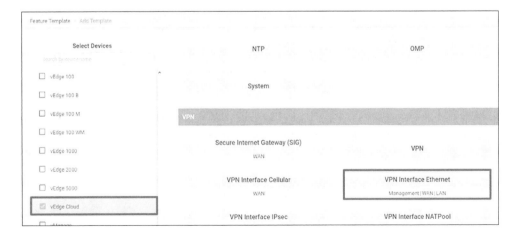

Name the template as shown below:

Select **Basic Configuration**, set Shutdown to No, and enter the interface name **ge0/4**. Then provide the static IP address 10.2.99.121/24 for this interface, as shown below:

Click **Save**.

Click **Add Template**. In the screen that appears, scroll down and select **vEdge Cloud** in the left-hand working pane. Then click **VPN** in the **Select Template > VPN** section in the right-hand working pane, as shown below:

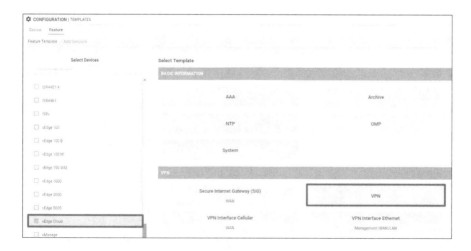

Name the template as shown below:

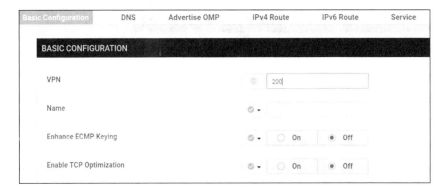

Select **Basic Configuration** and provide the VPN ID **200**, as shown below:

Click **Save.**

Click **Add Template.** In the screen that appears, scroll down and select **vEdge Cloud** in the left-hand working pane. Then click **VPN Interface Ethernet** in the **Select Template > VPN** section in the right-hand working pane, as shown below:

Name the template as shown below:

Select **Basic Configuration**, set Shutdown to No, and enter the interface name **ge0/2**. Then provide the static IP address 10.2.14.121/24 for this interface, as shown below:

Click **Save**.

Click **Add Template**. In the screen that appears, scroll down and select **vEdge Cloud** in the left-hand working pane. Then click **VPN** in the **Select Template > VPN** section in the right-hand working pane, as shown below:

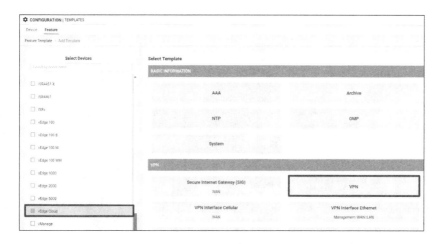

Name the template as shown below:

Select **Basic Configuration** and provide the VPN ID **512**, as shown below:

Click **Save**.

Click **Add Template**. In the screen that appears, scroll down and select **vEdge Cloud** in the left-hand working pane. Then click **VPN Interface Ethernet** in the **Select Template > VPN** section in the right-hand working pane, as shown below:

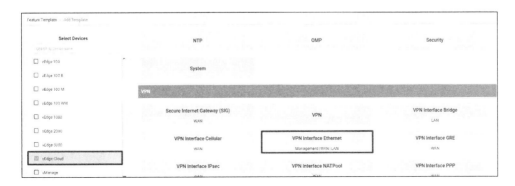

Name the template as shown below:

Select **Basic Configuration**, set Shutdown to No, and enter the interface name **eth0**. Then provide the static IP address 10.82.83.121/24 for this interface, as shown below:

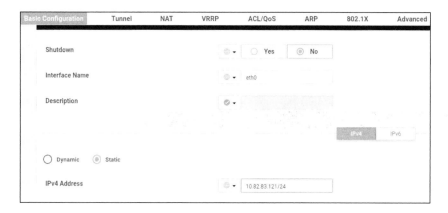

Click **Save**.

Navigate to **Configuration > Templates > Device > Create Template** and select **From Feature Template**. Select **vEdge Cloud** from the Device Model dropdown and name the template as shown below:

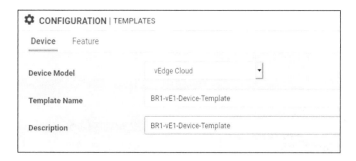

Select **Basic Information** and make the changes shown below:

Select **Transport & Management VPN** and make the changes shown below:

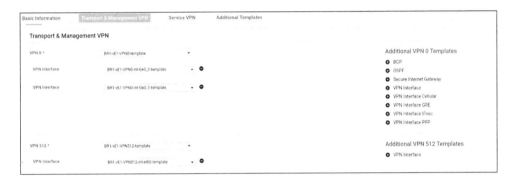

Select **Service VPN** and click **Add VPN**:

In the Available VPN Templates pane, select BR1-vE1-VPN100-template and click the right-pointing arrow to move selected template to the right-hand working pane:

Click **Next.**

Modify the Add VPN window as shown below:

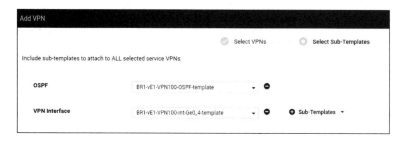

Click **Add.**

Click **Add VPN** again.

In the Available VPN Templates pane, select BR1-vE1-VPN200-template and click the right-pointing arrow to move selected template to the right-hand working pane:

Modify the Add VPN window as shown below:

Click **Add**.

To complete the device template, click **Create**.

Attach this template to BR1-vE1 by clicking the **...** icon at the right of the following line and selecting **Attach Devices**, as shown below:

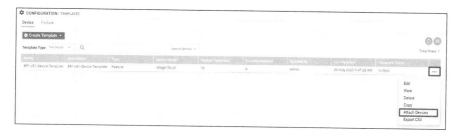

In the Attach Devices window select BR1-vE1 in the Available Devices pane and click the right-pointing arrow to move the device to the Selected Devices pane. Then click **Attach**:

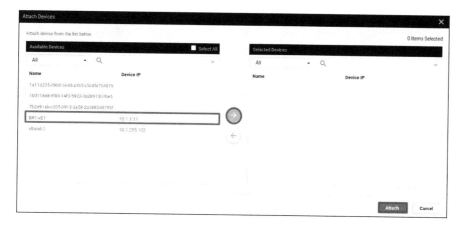

You now see the device template listed on the next screen. You should see a green circle with a check mark at the far-left side of the screen, as shown below. If you see it, click **Next**:

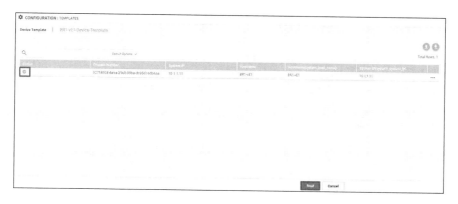

In the list of devices, select BR1-vE1 and verify the configuration that will be pushed to the device. When you are satisfied with the configuration, click **Configure Devices.**

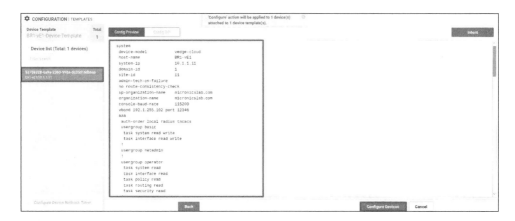

After a few moments, you should see the following:

To test this deployment to make sure everything works, you can enter the pings shown below on Docker23 to see if you can reach VPN 200 resources in the other sites:

```
root@Docker23:~# ping 10.2.200.111 -c 5 ← Loopback of BR2-SW1
PING 10.2.200.111 (10.2.200.111) 56(84) bytes of data.
64 bytes from 10.2.200.111: icmp_seq=1 ttl=253 time=1.28 ms
64 bytes from 10.2.200.111: icmp_seq=2 ttl=253 time=1.32 ms
64 bytes from 10.2.200.111: icmp_seq=3 ttl=253 time=1.09 ms
64 bytes from 10.2.200.111: icmp_seq=4 ttl=253 time=1.48 ms
64 bytes from 10.2.200.111: icmp_seq=5 ttl=253 time=1.31 ms

--- 10.2.200.111 ping statistics ---
5 packets transmitted, 5 received, 0% packet loss, time 4003ms
rtt min/avg/max/mdev = 1.098/1.301/1.481/0.122 ms


root@Docker23:~# ping 172.101.2.111 -c 5 ← DC1-CSR1 Gi3
PING 172.101.2.111 (172.101.2.111) 56(84) bytes of data.
64 bytes from 172.101.2.111: icmp_seq=1 ttl=254 time=1.85 ms
64 bytes from 172.101.2.111: icmp_seq=2 ttl=254 time=1.59 ms
64 bytes from 172.101.2.111: icmp_seq=3 ttl=254 time=1.56 ms
64 bytes from 172.101.2.111: icmp_seq=4 ttl=254 time=1.62 ms
64 bytes from 172.101.2.111: icmp_seq=5 ttl=254 time=1.17 ms
```

```
--- 172.101.2.111 ping statistics ---
5 packets transmitted, 5 received, 0% packet loss, time 4006ms
rtt min/avg/max/mdev = 1.175/1.562/1.852/0.218 ms

root@Docker23:~# ping 172.101.2.112 -c 5 ← DC1-CSR2 Gi3
PING 172.101.2.112 (172.101.2.112) 56(84) bytes of data.
64 bytes from 172.101.2.112: icmp_seq=1 ttl=254 time=1.88 ms
64 bytes from 172.101.2.112: icmp_seq=2 ttl=254 time=1.38 ms
64 bytes from 172.101.2.112: icmp_seq=3 ttl=254 time=3.19 ms
64 bytes from 172.101.2.112: icmp_seq=4 ttl=254 time=1.22 ms
64 bytes from 172.101.2.112: icmp_seq=5 ttl=254 time=1.03 ms

--- 172.101.2.112 ping statistics ---
5 packets transmitted, 5 received, 0% packet loss, time 4002ms
rtt min/avg/max/mdev = 1.030/1.742/3.192/0.779 ms
root@Docker23:~#
```

Now test reachability in VRF/VPN 100 from RM-R1:

```
RM-R1# ping 183.1.7.7 ← Loopback of HQ-R7
Type escape sequence to abort.
Sending 5, 100-byte ICMP Echos to 183.1.7.7, timeout is 2 seconds:
!!!!!
Success rate is 100 percent (5/5), round-trip min/avg/max = 1/1/2 ms
RM-R1# ping 10.2.100.111 ← SVI VLAN100 of BR2-SW1
Type escape sequence to abort.
Sending 5, 100-byte ICMP Echos to 10.2.100.111, timeout is 2 seconds:
!!!!!
Success rate is 100 percent (5/5), round-trip min/avg/max = 1/1/2 ms
RM-R1#
```

You can see that all reachability has been resolved in Branch-1.

# Lab 6: Configuring cEdge Using a BR-2–Specific vManage Feature Template

For this lab, you need to configure BR2-CSR by using a vManage template using the information in the matrix provided on the next page. The following pages walk through how to do this.

| Device | Feature Template | Template – Name | Values |
|---|---|---|---|
| BR2-Site-CSRs | System | BR2-CSR-SYSTEM-temp | Site-id: **2**<br>System-ip: **Device Specific**<br>Hostname: **Device Specific**<br>Baud Rate: **115200** |
| | VPN | BR2-CSR-VPN0-template | VPN ID: **0**<br>DNS: **8.8.8.8**<br>GW1: **0.0.0.0/0 device specific gw-inet**<br>GW2: **0.0.0.0/0 device specific gw-mpls** |
| | VPN Interface Ethernet | BR2-CSR-VPN0-int-g1-template | Shutdown: **No**<br>Interface Name: **GigabitEthernet1**<br>Static: **device specific g1-ip**<br>Tunnel Interface: **On**<br>Color: **Biz-Internet**<br>Allow Service: **All** |
| | VPN Interface Ethernet | BR2-CSR-VPN0-int-g2-template | Shutdown: **No**<br>Interface Name: **GigabitEthernet2**<br>Static: **device specific g2-ip**<br>Tunnel Interface: **On**<br>Color: **MPLS**<br>Allow Service: **All** |
| | VPN | BR2-CSR-VPN100-template | VPN ID: **100** |
| | VPN Interface Ethernet | BR2-CSR-VPN100-int-g4.100-template | Shutdown: **No**<br>Interface Name: **GigabitEthernet4.100**<br>MTU: **1496**<br>Static: **device specific g4_100-ip**<br>Tunnel: **Off** |
| | EIGRP | BR2-CSR-VPN100-EIGRP-template | Redistribute: **OMP**<br>Interface: **GigabitEthernet4.100** |
| | VPN | BR2-CSR-VPN200-template | VPN ID: **200** |

| Device | Feature Template | Template – Name | Values |
|---|---|---|---|
| | VPN Interface Ethernet | BR2-CSR-VPN200-int-g3.200-template | Shutdown: No<br>Interface Name: GigabitEthernet4.200<br>MTU: 1496<br>Static: device specific g4_100-ip<br>Tunnel: Off |
| | OPSF | BR2-CSR-VPN200-OSPF-template | Redistribute: OMP<br>Area: 0<br>Interface: GigabitEthernet4.200 |
| | VPN | BR2-CSR-vpn512-temp | VPN ID: 512 |
| | VPN Interface Ethernet | BR2-CSR-vpn512-int-temp | Shutdown: No<br>Interface Name: GigabitEthernet5<br>Static: device-specific g5-ip |
| **Device** | **Device Template** | **Template-Name** | **Values** |
| BR2-CSR | CSR1000v | BR2-CSR-Device-Template | Use all feature templates created above |

Navigate to **Configuration > Templates > Feature** in the vManage UI and click **Add Template**:

In the screen that appears, scroll down and select **CSR1000v** in the left-hand working pane. Then choose **Cisco System** in the **Select Template > BASIC INFORMATION** section in the right-hand working pane.

In the following steps, you will provide the information specified in the matrix at the beginning of this lab.

Name the template as shown below:

Provide the basic configuration shown below and click **Save**:

Click **Add Template.** In the screen that appears, scroll down and select **CSR1000v** in the left-hand working pane. Then click **VPN** in the **Select Template > VPN** section in the right-hand working pane, as shown below:

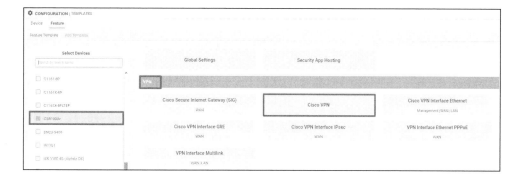

Name the template as shown below:

Select **Basic Configuration** and provide the VPN ID **0**:

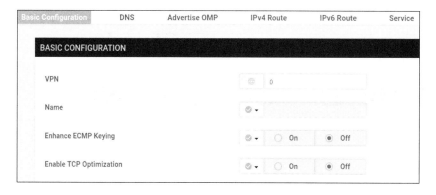

Select **DNS** and provide the DNS IP address **8.8.8.8**:

Select **IPv4 Route** and click **New IPv4 Route**:

Now enter the prefix **0.0.0.0/0** and click **Add Next Hop**:

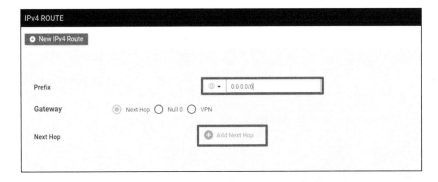

Click **Add Next Hop**:

Modify the Next Hop screen as shown below and click **Add.**

Verify that your screen looks as shown below and click **Add:**

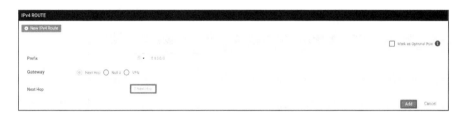

You should see the following information:

Click **Save.**

Click **Add Template.** In the screen that appears, scroll down and select **CSR1000v** in the left-hand working pane. Then click **Cisco VPN Interface Ethernet** in the **Select Template > VPN** section in the right-hand working pane, as shown below:

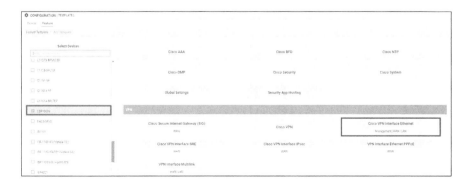

Name the template as shown below:

Select **Basic Configuration**, set Shutdown to No, and enter the interface name **GigabitEthernet1**. Then select **Static** and configure a device-specific variable this interface, as shown below:

Select **Tunnel**, set Tunnel Interface to On, and select biz-internet from the Color dropdown, as shown below:

Scroll down to the Allow Service section and set All to On, as shown below:

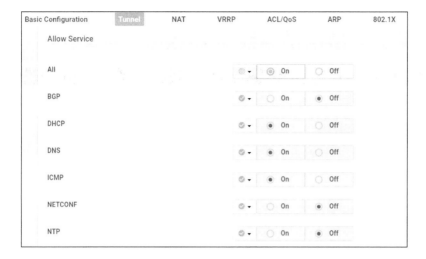

Click **Save**.

Click **Add Template**. In the screen that appears, scroll down and select **CSR1000v** in the left-hand working pane. Then click **Cisco VPN Interface Ethernet** in the **Select Template > VPN** section in the right-hand working pane, as shown below:

Name the template as shown below:

Select **Basic Configuration**, set Shutdown to No, and enter the interface name **GigabitEthernet2**. Then select **Static** and configure a device-specific variable this interface, as shown below:

Select **Tunnel**, set Tunnel Interface to On, and select mpls from the Color dropdown, as shown below:

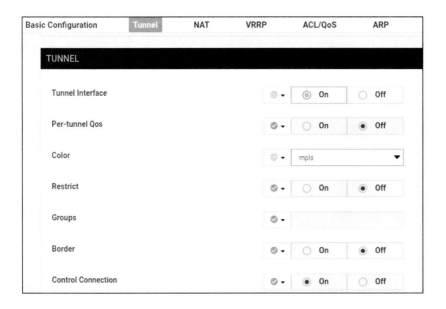

Scroll down to the Allow Service section and set All to On, as shown below:

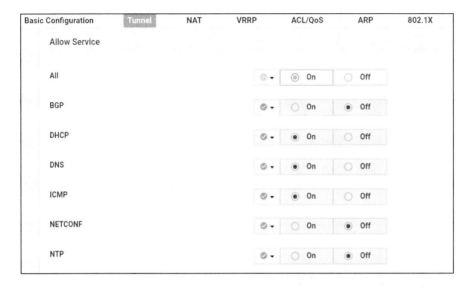

Click **Save.**

Click **Add Template.** In the screen that appears, scroll down and select **CSR1000v** in the left-hand working pane. Then click **Cisco VPN** in the **Select Template > VPN** section in the right-hand working pane, as shown below:

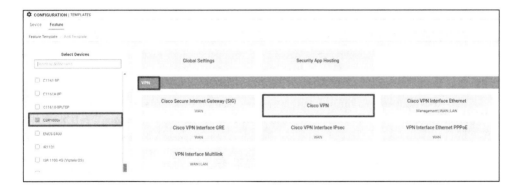

Name the template as shown below:

Select **Basic Configuration** and provide the VPN ID **100**:

Click **Save**.

Click **Add Template**. In the screen that appears, scroll down and select **CSR1000v** in the left-hand working pane. Then click **EIGRP** in the **Select Template > OTHER TEMPLATES** section in the right-hand working pane, as shown below:

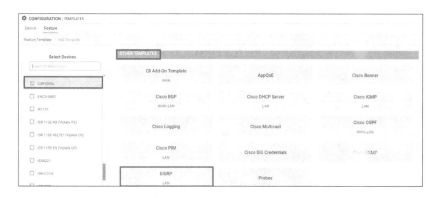

Name the template as shown below:

Select **IPv4 Unicast Address Family** and click **New Redistribution:**

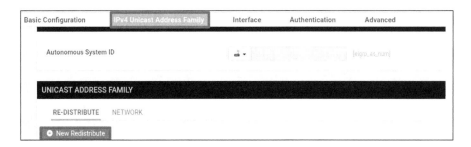

Set Protocol to omp and click **Add:**

Select **Network** and click **New Network:**

Click **Add**:

Select **Interface** and click **Interface**:

Provide the information shown below and click **Add**:

Select **Advanced** and provide the IP MTU **1496**:

| Basic Configuration | Tunnel | NAT | VRRP | ACL/QoS | ARP | Advanced |
|---|---|---|---|---|---|---|
| **ADVANCED** | | | | | | |
| Duplex | | | | ⊘ ▾ | | ▾ |
| MAC Address | | | | ⊘ ▾ | | |
| IP MTU | | | | ⊘ ▾ | 1496 | |
| TCP MSS | | | | ⊘ ▾ | | |

Click **Save**.

Click **Add Template**. In the screen that appears, scroll down and select **CSR1000v** in the left-hand working pane. Then click **Cisco VPN Interface Ethernet** in the **Select Template > VPN** section in the right-hand working pane, as shown on the next page:

Name the template as shown below:

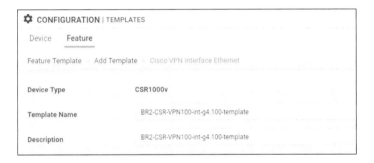

Select **Basic Configuration**, set Shutdown to No, and enter the interface name **GigabitEthernet4.100**. Then select **Static** and configure a device-specific variable this interface, as shown below:

Click **Save**.

Click **Add Template**. In the screen that appears, scroll down and select **CSR1000v** in the left-hand working pane. Then click **Cisco VPN** in the **Select Template > VPN** section in the right-hand working pane, as shown on the next page:

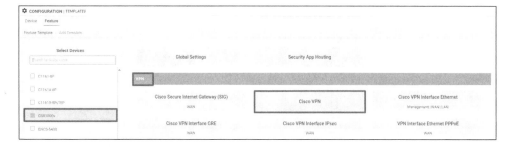

Name the template as shown below:

Select **Basic Configuration** and provide the VPN ID **200**:

Click **Save**.

Click **Add Template**. In the screen that appears, scroll down and select **CSR1000v** in the left-hand working pane. Then click **Cisco OSPF** in the **Select Template > OTHER TEMPLATES** section in the right-hand working pane, as shown on the next page:

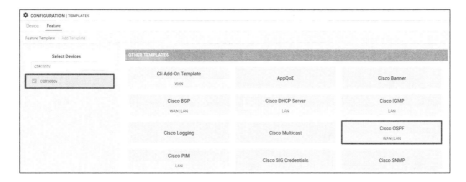

Name the template as shown below:

Select **Redistribute** and click **New Redistribute**:

Set Protocol to omp and click **Add**:

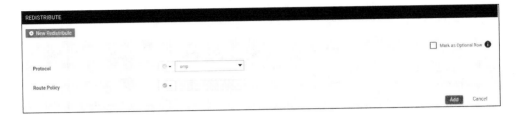

Select **Area** and click **New Area**:

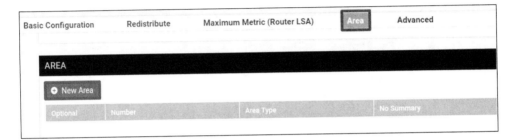

Set Area to 0 and click **Add Interface**:

Click **Add Interface**:

On the Interface screen enter the interface name **GigabitEthernet4.200** and click **Add**:

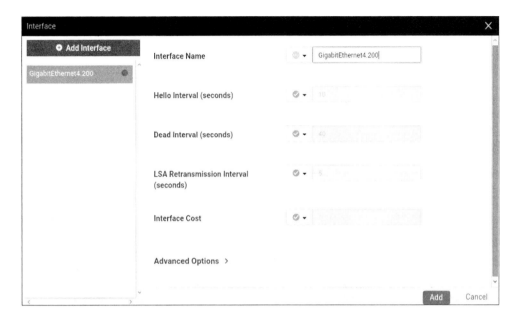

Click **Add** again and then click **Save**.

Click **Add Template**. In the screen that appears, scroll down and select **CSR1000v** in the left-hand working pane. Then click **Cisco VPN Interface Element** in the **Select Template > VPN** section in the right-hand working pane, as shown below:

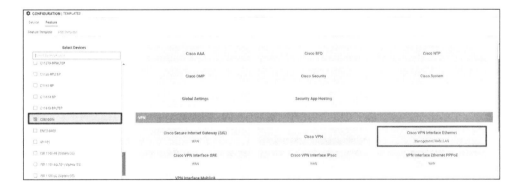

Name the template as shown below:

Select **Basic Configuration**, set Shutdown to No, and enter the interface name **GigabitEthernet4.200**. Then select **Static** and configure a device-specific variable this interface, as shown below:

Select **Advanced** and provide the IP MTU **1496**:

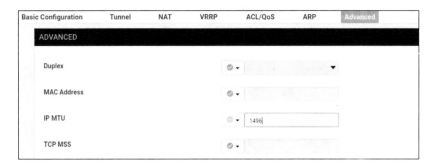

Click **Save**.

Click **Add Template.** In the screen that appears, scroll down and select **CSR1000v** in the left-hand working pane. Then click **Cisco VPN** in the **Select Template > VPN** section in the right-hand working pane, as shown below:

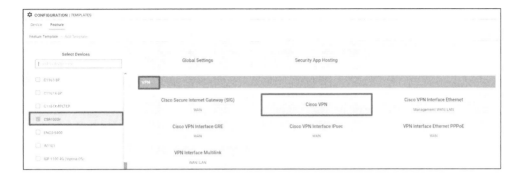

Name the template as shown below:

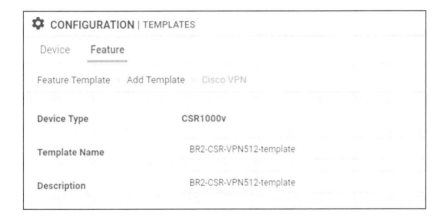

Select **Basic Configuration** and provide the VPN ID **512**:

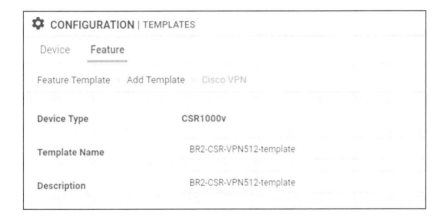

Click **Save.**

Click **Add Template**. In the screen that appears, scroll down and select **CSR1000v** in the left-hand working pane. Then click **Cisco VPN Interface Ethernet** in the **Select Template > VPN** section in the right-hand working pane, as shown below:

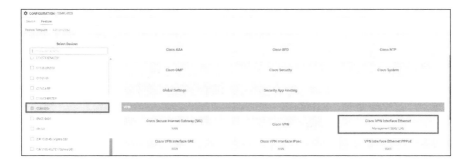

Name the template as shown below:

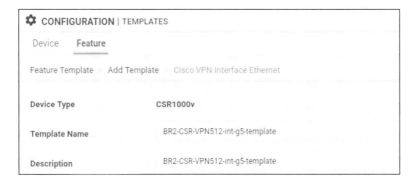

Select **Basic Configuration**, set Shutdown to No, and enter the interface name **GigabitEthernet5**. Then select **Static** and configure a device-specific variable this interface, as shown below:

Click **Save**.

Navigate to **Configuration > Templates > Device > Create Template** and select **From Feature Template**. Select **CSR1000v** from the Device Model dropdown and name the template as shown below:

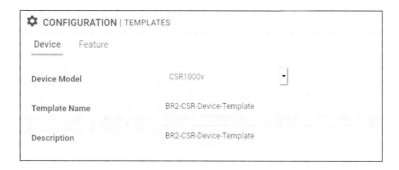

Select **Basic Information** and make the changes shown below:

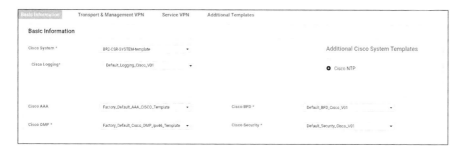

Select **Transport & Management VPN** and make the changes shown below:

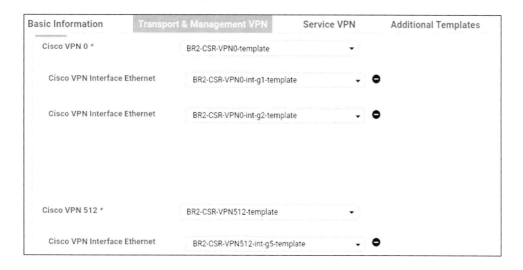

Select **Service VPN** and click **Add VPN**:

In the Available VPN Templates pane, select BR2-CSR-VPN100-template and click the right-pointing arrow to move selected template to the right-hand working pane:

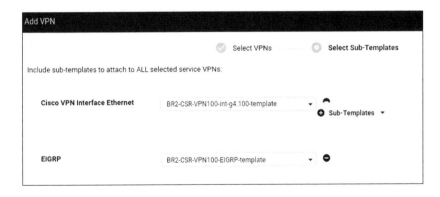

Click **Next**.

Modify the Add VPN window as shown below:

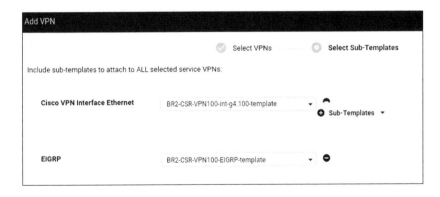

Click **Add**.

Click **Add VPN** again:

In the Available VPN Templates pane, select BR2-CSR-VPN200-template, click the right-pointing arrow to move selected template to the right-hand working pane, and click **Next**:

Modify the Add VPN window as shown below:

Click **Add**.

To complete the device template, click **Create**.

Attach this template to BR2-CSRs by clicking the ... icon at the right of the following line and selecting **Attach Devices**, as shown below:

In the Attach Devices window select B1-CSR1 and B2-CSR2 in the Available Devices pane and click the right-pointing arrow to move the device to the Selected Devices pane. Then click **Attach**:

You should see the device template listed in the next screen. Identify the DC1-CSR1 device and click the ... icon to the right. Then click **Edit Device Template**.

In the Update Device Template page, provide the information shown on the next page and click **Update**:

Find the device BR2-CSR2 and click the ... icon, and click **Edit Device Template**:

On the Update Device Template screen, provide the information shown below and click **Update**:

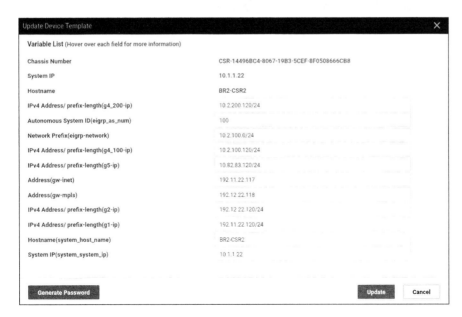

Click **Next.**

In the list of devices, select BR2-CSR1 and verify the configuration that will be pushed to the device. Repeat the process for BR2-CSR2. When you are satisfied with the configuration, click **Configure Devices.**

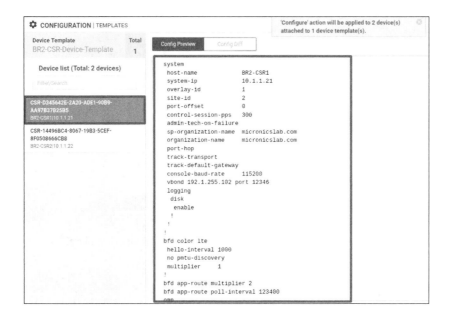

Check **Confirm configuration changes on 2 devices** and click **OK.**

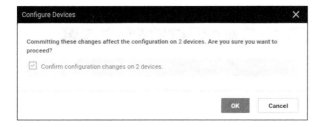

After a few moments, you should see the following:

To test this deployment to make sure everything works, you can enter the pings shown below on Docker23 to see if you can reach VPN 200 resources in the other sites:

```
root@Docker23:~# ping 10.2.200.111 -c 5 ← Loopback of BR2-SW1
PING 10.2.200.111 (10.2.200.111) 56(84) bytes of data.
64 bytes from 10.2.200.111: icmp_seq=1 ttl=253 time=1.28 ms
64 bytes from 10.2.200.111: icmp_seq=2 ttl=253 time=1.32 ms
64 bytes from 10.2.200.111: icmp_seq=3 ttl=253 time=1.09 ms
64 bytes from 10.2.200.111: icmp_seq=4 ttl=253 time=1.48 ms
64 bytes from 10.2.200.111: icmp_seq=5 ttl=253 time=1.31 ms

--- 10.2.200.111 ping statistics ---
5 packets transmitted, 5 received, 0% packet loss, time 4003ms
rtt min/avg/max/mdev = 1.098/1.301/1.481/0.122 ms

root@Docker23:~# ping 172.101.2.111 -c 5 ← DC1-CSR1 Gi3
PING 172.101.2.111 (172.101.2.111) 56(84) bytes of data.
64 bytes from 172.101.2.111: icmp_seq=1 ttl=254 time=1.85 ms
64 bytes from 172.101.2.111: icmp_seq=2 ttl=254 time=1.59 ms
64 bytes from 172.101.2.111: icmp_seq=3 ttl=254 time=1.56 ms
64 bytes from 172.101.2.111: icmp_seq=4 ttl=254 time=1.62 ms
64 bytes from 172.101.2.111: icmp_seq=5 ttl=254 time=1.17 ms

--- 172.101.2.111 ping statistics ---
5 packets transmitted, 5 received, 0% packet loss, time 4006ms
rtt min/avg/max/mdev = 1.175/1.562/1.852/0.218 ms

root@Docker23:~# ping 172.101.2.112 -c 5 ← DC1-CSR2 Gi3
PING 172.101.2.112 (172.101.2.112) 56(84) bytes of data.
64 bytes from 172.101.2.112: icmp_seq=1 ttl=254 time=1.88 ms
64 bytes from 172.101.2.112: icmp_seq=2 ttl=254 time=1.38 ms
64 bytes from 172.101.2.112: icmp_seq=3 ttl=254 time=3.19 ms
64 bytes from 172.101.2.112: icmp_seq=4 ttl=254 time=1.22 ms
64 bytes from 172.101.2.112: icmp_seq=5 ttl=254 time=1.03 ms

--- 172.101.2.112 ping statistics ---
5 packets transmitted, 5 received, 0% packet loss, time 4002ms
rtt min/avg/max/mdev = 1.030/1.742/3.192/0.779 ms
root@Docker23:~#
```

Test reachability in VRF/VPN 100 from RM-R1:

```
RM-R1# ping 183.1.7.7 ← Loopback of HQ-R7
Type escape sequence to abort.
Sending 5, 100-byte ICMP Echos to 183.1.7.7, timeout is 2 seconds:
!!!!!
```

```
Success rate is 100 percent (5/5), round-trip min/avg/max = 1/1/2 ms
RM-R1# ping 10.2.100.111 ← SVI VLAN100 of BR2-SW1
Type escape sequence to abort.
Sending 5, 100-byte ICMP Echos to 10.2.100.111, timeout is 2 seconds:
!!!!!
Success rate is 100 percent (5/5), round-trip min/avg/max = 1/1/2 ms
RM-R1#
```

You can see that all reachability has been resolved in HQ Site-1.

# Lab 7: Configuring vEdge Using a vManage Feature Template and ZTP

For this lab, you need to configure BR3-vE3 by using a vManage template using the information in the matrix provided below. The following pages walk through how to do this.

| Device | Feature Template | Template – Name | Values |
|--------|------------------|-----------------|--------|
| BR3-vE3 | System | BR3-vE3-SYSTEM-temp | Site-id: **3**<br>System-ip: **Device Specific**<br>Hostname: **BR3-vE3**<br>Baud Rate: **115200** |
| | VPN | BR3-vE3-VPN0-template | VPN ID: **0**<br>DNS: **8.8.8.8**<br>GW1: **0.0.0.0/0 192.11.33.113**<br>GW2: **0.0.0.0/0 192.12.33.114** |
| | VPN Interface Ethernet | BR3-vE3-VPN0-ge0_0-template | Shutdown: **No**<br>Interface Name: **ge0/0**<br>Static: **192.11.33.123/24**<br>Tunnel Interface: **On**<br>Color: **Biz-Internet**<br>Allow Service: **All** |
| | VPN Interface Ethernet | BR3-vE3-VPN0-ge0_1-template | Shutdown: **No**<br>Interface Name: **ge0/1**<br>Static: **192.12.33.123/24**<br>Tunnel Interface: **On**<br>Color: **MPLS**<br>Allow Service: **All** |

| Device | Feature Template | Template – Name | Values |
|---|---|---|---|
| | VPN | BR3-vE3-VPN100-template | VPN ID: **100** |
| | VPN Interface Ethernet | BR3-vE3-VPN100-int-lo100-template | Shutdown: **No** <br> Interface Name: **Loopback100** <br> Static: **10.3.100.123/24** <br> Tunnel: **Off** |
| | VPN | BR3-vE3-VPN200-template | VPN ID: **200** |
| | VPN Interface Ethernet | BR3-vE3-VPN200-int-lo200-template | Shutdown: **No** <br> Interface Name: **Loopback200** <br> Static: **10.3.200.121/24** <br> Tunnel: **Off** |
| | VPN | BR3-vE3-VPN300-template | VPN ID: 300 |
| | VPN Interface Ethernet | BR3-vE3-VPN200-int-lo200-template | Shutdown: **No** <br> Interface Name: **ge0/2** <br> Static: **10.2.11.121/24** <br> Tunnel: **Off** |
| | VPN | BR3-vE3-vpn512-temp | VPN ID: **512** |
| | VPN Interface Ethernet | BR3-vE3-vpn512-int-temp | Shutdown: **No** <br> Interface Name: **eth0** <br> Static: **10.82.83.121/24** |
| **Device** | **Device Template** | **Template-Name** | **Values** |
| BR3-vE3 | vEdge Cloud | BR3-vE3-Device-Template | Use all feature templates created above |

Navigate to **Configuration > Templates > Feature** in the vManage UI and click **Add Template**:

In the screen that appears, scroll down and select **vEdge Cloud** in the left-hand working pane. Then click **System** in the **Select Template > BASIC INFORMATION** section in the right-hand working pane, as shown below:

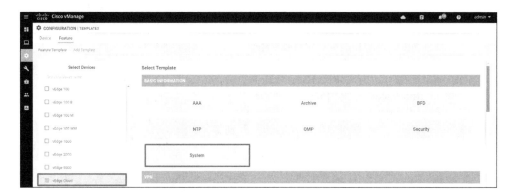

In the following steps, you will provide the information specified in the matrix at the beginning of this lab.

Name the template as shown below:

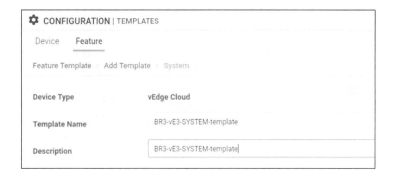

Provide the basic configuration shown below and click **Save:**

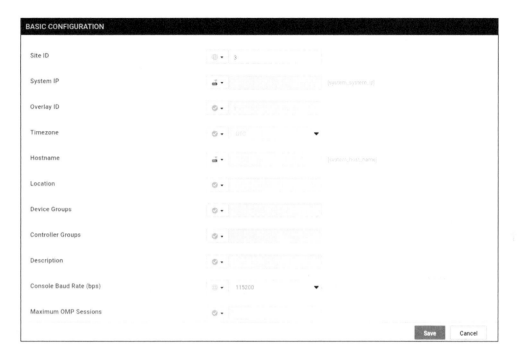

Click **Add Template.** In the screen that appears, scroll down and select **vEdge Cloud** in the left-hand working pane. Then click **VPN** in the **Select Template > VPN** section in the right-hand working pane, as shown below:

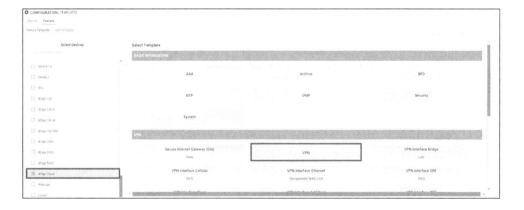

Name the template as shown below:

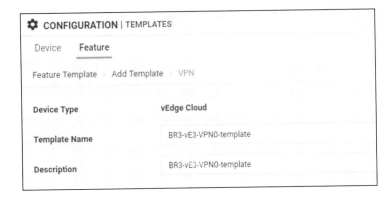

Select **Basic Configuration** and provide the VPN ID **0**:

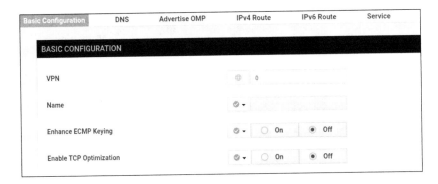

Select **DNS** and provide the DNS IP address **8.8.8.8**:

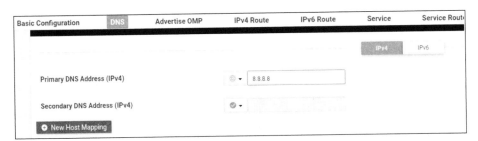

Select **IPv4 Route** and click **New IPv4 Route**:

Enter the prefix **0.0.0.0/0** and click **Add Next Hop:**

Click **Add Next Hop:**

Modify the Next Hop screen as shown below and click **Add:**

Verify that your screen looks as shown below and click **Add**:

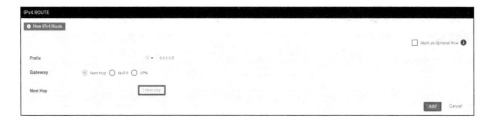

You should see the following information:

Click **Save**.

Click **Add Template**. In the screen that appears, scroll down and select **vEdge Cloud** in the left-hand working pane. Then click **VPN Interface Ethernet** in the **Select Template > VPN** section in the right-hand working pane, as shown below:

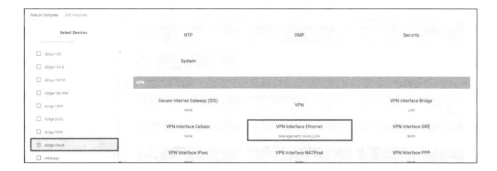

Name the template as shown below:

Select **Basic Configuration**, set Shutdown to No, and enter the interface name **ge0/0**. Then provide the static IP address 192.11.33.123/24 for this interface, as shown on the next page:

Select **Tunnel**, set Tunnel Interface to On, and select biz-internet from the Color dropdown, as shown below:

Scroll down to the Allow Service section and set All to On, as shown below:

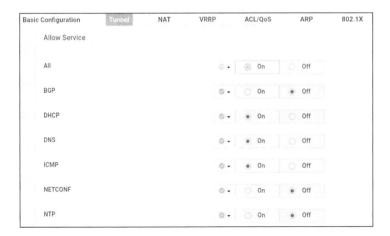

Click **Save**.

Click **Add Template**. In the screen that appears, scroll down and select **vEdge Cloud** in the left-hand working pane. Then click **VPN Interface Ethernet** in the **Select Template > VPN** section in the right-hand working pane, as shown below:

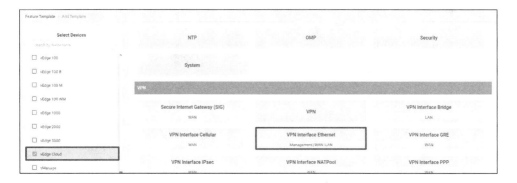

Name the template as shown below:

Select **Basic Configuration**, set Shutdown to No, and enter the interface name **ge0/1**. Then provide the static IP address 192.12.33.123/24 for this interface, as shown below:

Select **Tunnel**, set Tunnel Interface to On, and select mpls from the Color dropdown, as shown below:

Scroll down to the Allow Service section and set All to On, as shown below:

Click **Save.**

Click **Add Template.** In the screen that appears, scroll down and select **vEdge Cloud** in the left-hand working pane. Then click **VPN** in the **Select Template > VPN** section in the right-hand working pane, as shown below:

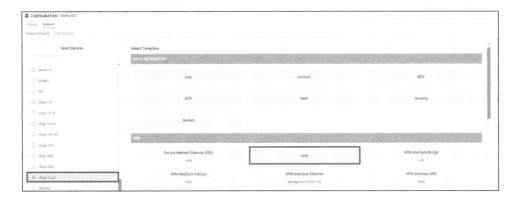

Name the template as shown below:

Select **Basic Configuration** and provide the VPN ID **100**:

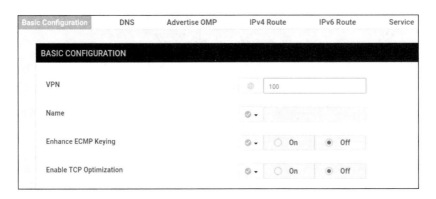

Click **Save.**

Click **Add Template**. In the screen that appears, scroll down and select **vEdge Cloud** in the left-hand working pane. Then click **VPN Interface Ethernet** in the **Select Template > VPN** section in the right-hand working pane, as shown below:

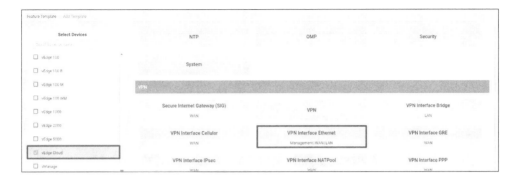

Name the template as shown below:

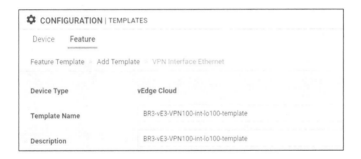

Select **Basic Configuration**, set Shutdown to No, and enter the interface name **loopback100**. Then provide the static IP address 10.3.100.123/24 for this interface, as shown below:

Click **Save**.

Click **Add Template**. In the screen that appears, scroll down and select **vEdge Cloud** in the left-hand working pane. Then click **VPN** in the **Select Template > VPN** section in the right-hand working pane, as shown below:

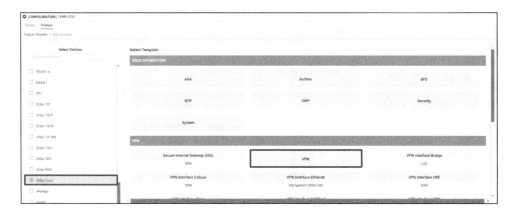

Name the template as shown below:

Select **Basic Configuration** and provide the VPN ID **200**:

Click **Save**.

Click **Add Template**. In the screen that appears, scroll down and select **vEdge Cloud** in the left-hand working pane. Then click **VPN Interface Ethernet** in the **Select Template > VPN** section in the right-hand working pane, as shown below:

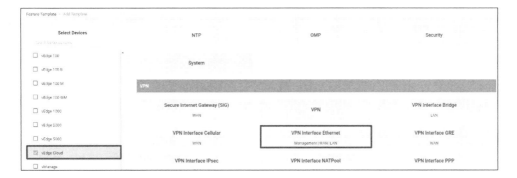

Name the template as shown below:

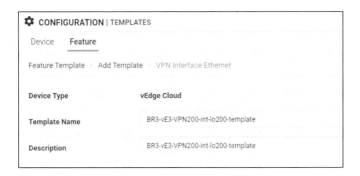

Select **Basic Configuration**, set Shutdown to No, and enter the interface name **loopback200**. Then provide the static IP address 10.3.200.123/24 for this interface, as shown below:

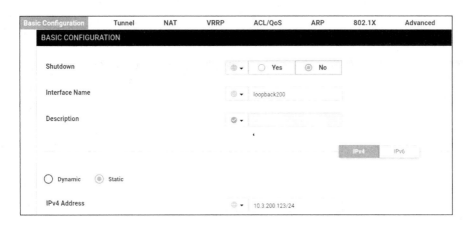

Click **Save**.

Click **Add Template**. In the screen that appears, scroll down and select **vEdge Cloud** in the left-hand working pane. Then click **VPN** in the **Select Template > VPN** section in the right-hand working pane, as shown below:

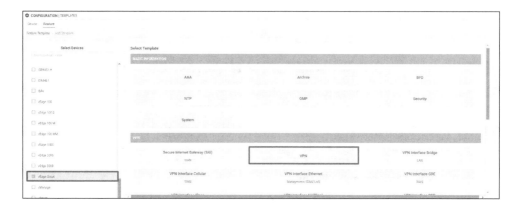

Name the template as shown below:

Select **Basic Configuration** and provide the VPN ID **300**:

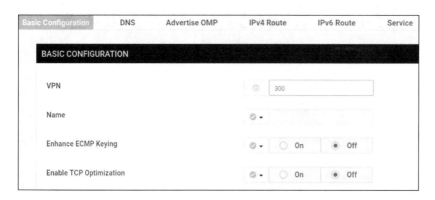

Click **Save**.

Click **Add Template**. In the screen that appears, scroll down and select **vEdge Cloud** in the left-hand working pane. Then click **VPN Interface Ethernet** in the **Select Template > VPN** section in the right-hand working pane, as shown below:

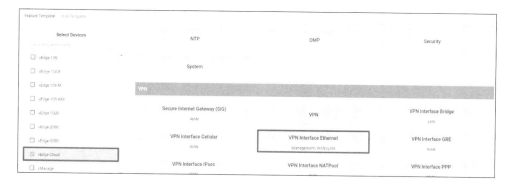

Name the template as shown below:

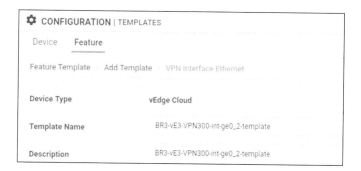

Select **Basic Configuration**, set Shutdown to No, and enter the interface name **ge0/2**. Then provide the static IP address 10.2.11.123/24 for this interface, as shown below:

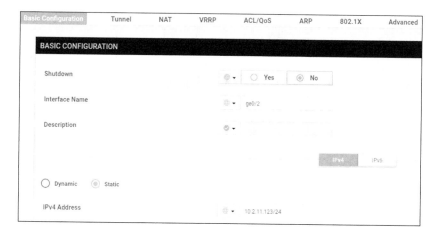

Click **Save**.

Click **Add Template**. In the screen that appears, scroll down and select **vEdge Cloud** in the left-hand working pane. Then click **VPN** in the **Select Template > VPN** section in the right-hand working pane, as shown below:

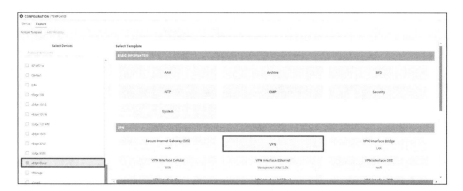

Name the template as shown below:

Select **Basic Configuration** and provide the VPN ID **512**:

Click **Save**.

Click **Add Template**. In the screen that appears, scroll down and select **vEdge Cloud** in the left-hand working pane. Then click **VPN Interface Ethernet** in the **Select Template > VPN** section in the right-hand working pane, as shown below:

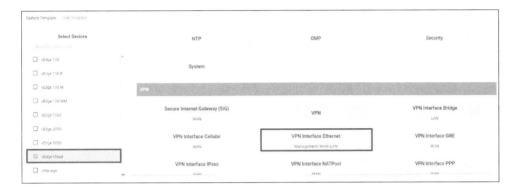

Name the template as shown below:

Select **Basic Configuration**, set Shutdown to No, and enter the interface name **eth0**. Then provide the static IP address 10.82.83.123/24 for this interface, as shown below:

Click **Save**.

Navigate to **Configuration > Templates > Device > Create Template** and select **From Feature Template**. Select **vEdge Cloud** from the Device Model dropdown and name the template as shown below:

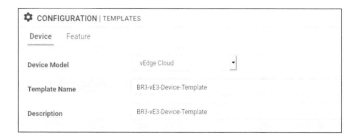

Select **Basic Information** and make the changes shown below:

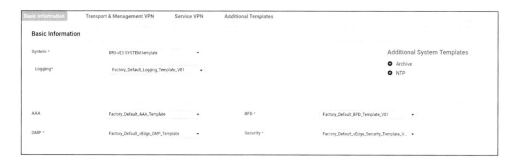

Select **Transport & Management VPN** and make the changes shown below:

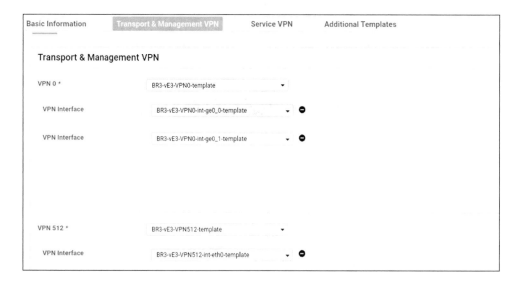

Select **Service VPN** and click **Add VPN**:

In the Available VPN Templates pane, select BR3-vE3-VPN100-template and click the right-pointing arrow to move selected template to the right-hand working pane:

Click **Next**.

Modify the Add VPN window as shown below:

Click **Add**.

Click **Add VPN** again:

In the Available VPN Templates pane, select BR3-vE3-VPN200-template and click the right-pointing arrow to move selected template to the right-hand working pane:

Modify the Add VPN window as shown below:

Click **Add**.

Click **Add VPN** again:

In the Available VPN Templates pane, select BR3-vE3-VPN300-template and click the right-pointing arrow to move selected template to the right-hand working pane:

Modify the Add VPN window as shown below:

Click **Add**.

To complete the device template, click **Create**.

Attach this template to BR3-vE3 by clicking the ... icon at the right of the following line and selecting **Attach Devices**, as shown below:

In the Attach Devices window select 1a11d205-0 in the Available Devices pane and click the right-pointing arrow to move the device to the Selected Devices pane. Then click **Attach**:

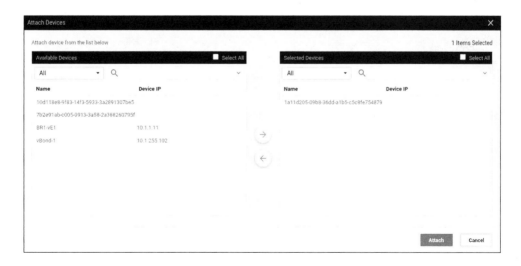

You now see the device template listed on the next screen. You should see that there is no green circle with a check mark at the far-left side of the screen. To correct this, click the ... icon and then click **Edit Device Template**:

Fill in the Update Device Template window as shown below and then click **Update**:

You should now see the screen shown below. If you do, click **Next**.

In the list of devices, select the chassis number shown on the next page and verify the configuration that will be pushed to the device. When you are satisfied with the configuration, click **Configure Devices**.

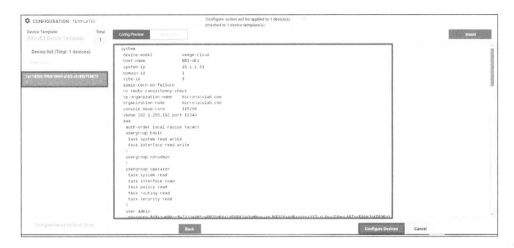

After a few moments, you should see the following:

This is not what you have seen before when onboarding WAN edge devices. You see something different now because there is currently no configuration on BR3-vE3, and you have opted to deploy Branch-3 using Zero Touch Provisioning (ZTP). You have lots of work to do to get this device to attach to this device template that you just created.

You will need to make some modifications to your INET infrastructure. You know that for BR3-vE3 to communicate to any resource in the SEN fabric, it needs an IP address. You can use DHCP on ISP-1 to support this operation.

## Creating a DHCP Server on ISP-1

Next, you need to access BR3-vE3 and look at its factory default configuration. First, you can look at VPN 0:

```
viptela 20.1.1

vedge login: admin
Password: admin
Welcome to Viptela CLI
admin connected from 127.0.0.1 using console on vedge
You must set an initial admin password.
Password: admin
Re-enter password: admin
```

```
vedge# show running-config vpn 0 interface ge0/0
vpn 0
 interface ge0/0
  ip dhcp-client
  ipv6 dhcp-client
  tunnel-interface
   encapsulation ipsec
   no allow-service bgp
   allow-service dhcp
   allow-service dns
   allow-service icmp
   no allow-service sshd
   no allow-service netconf
   no allow-service ntp
   no allow-service ospf
   no allow-service stun
   allow-service https
  !
  no shutdown
 !
!
vedge#
```

You can see that interface ge0/0 is (from the factory) configured for DHCP support and that it is part of VPN 0 by default. You can leverage this to your advantage.

Next, you need to perform a basic DHCP configuration on ISP-1, as shown below:

```
ISP-1>en
ISP-1# conf t
Enter configuration commands, one per line.  End with CNTL/Z.
ISP-1(config)# ip dhcp excluded-address 192.11.33.1 192.11.33.200
ISP-1(config)# ip dhcp pool ZTP-OPERATIONS
ISP-1(dhcp-config)# network 192.11.33.0 /24
ISP-1(dhcp-config)# default-router 192.11.33.113
```

You should see that an IP address was issued to BR3-vE3:

```
ISP-1# show ip dhcp binding
Bindings from all pools not associated with VRF:
IP address          Client-ID/      Lease expiration         T
ype
    Hardware address/
    User name
192.11.33.201       0150.0000.0e00.01        Aug 31 2020 10:20 AM    A
utomatic
ISP-1#
```

You can also verify this on BR3-vE3, as shown below:

```
vedge# show interface description

                                    IF       IF       IF
                       AF           ADMIN    OPER     TRACKER
VPN   INTERFACE   TYPE  IP ADDRESS   STATUS   STATUS   STATUS   DESC
------------------------------------------------------------------------
0     ge0/0       ipv4  192.11.33.201/24  Up       Up       NA       -
0     ge0/1       ipv4  -            Down     Down     NA       -
0     ge0/2       ipv4  -            Down     Down     NA       -
0     ge0/3       ipv4  -            Down     Down     NA       -
512   eth0        ipv4  -            Up       Up       NA       -

vedge#
```

As a result of this configuration, BR3-vE3 now has reachability into the infrastructure. You can validate this as shown below:

```
vedge# ping 192.1.255.101 count 5 ← vManage
Ping in VPN 0
PING 192.1.255.101 (192.1.255.101) 56(84) bytes of data.
64 bytes from 192.1.255.101: icmp_seq=1 ttl=62 time=1.16 ms
64 bytes from 192.1.255.101: icmp_seq=2 ttl=62 time=0.902 ms
64 bytes from 192.1.255.101: icmp_seq=3 ttl=62 time=1.01 ms
64 bytes from 192.1.255.101: icmp_seq=4 ttl=62 time=0.647 ms
64 bytes from 192.1.255.101: icmp_seq=5 ttl=62 time=0.516 ms

--- 192.1.255.101 ping statistics ---
5 packets transmitted, 5 received, 0% packet loss, time 4002ms
rtt min/avg/max/mdev = 0.516/0.847/1.162/0.238 ms
vedge#


vedge# ping 192.1.255.102 count 5 ← vBond
Ping in VPN 0
PING 192.1.255.102 (192.1.255.102) 56(84) bytes of data.
64 bytes from 192.1.255.102: icmp_seq=1 ttl=62 time=30.4 ms
64 bytes from 192.1.255.102: icmp_seq=2 ttl=62 time=30.7 ms
64 bytes from 192.1.255.102: icmp_seq=3 ttl=62 time=30.4 ms
64 bytes from 192.1.255.102: icmp_seq=4 ttl=62 time=29.4 ms
64 bytes from 192.1.255.102: icmp_seq=5 ttl=62 time=22.4 ms

--- 192.1.255.102 ping statistics ---
5 packets transmitted, 5 received, 0% packet loss, time 4002ms
rtt min/avg/max/mdev = 22.417/28.701/30.723/3.173 ms
vedge#
```

```
vedge# ping 192.1.255.103 count 5 ← vSmart
Ping in VPN 0
PING 192.1.255.103 (192.1.255.103) 56(84) bytes of data.
64 bytes from 192.1.255.103: icmp_seq=1 ttl=62 time=1.03 ms
64 bytes from 192.1.255.103: icmp_seq=2 ttl=62 time=0.747 ms
64 bytes from 192.1.255.103: icmp_seq=3 ttl=62 time=0.666 ms
64 bytes from 192.1.255.103: icmp_seq=4 ttl=62 time=0.604 ms
64 bytes from 192.1.255.103: icmp_seq=5 ttl=62 time=0.566 ms

--- 192.1.255.103 ping statistics ---
5 packets transmitted, 5 received, 0% packet loss, time 3999ms
rtt min/avg/max/mdev = 0.566/0.724/1.037/0.168 ms
vedge#
```

Now you have the reachability issue out of the way, but there is another issue. Note that when you run the **show run system** command, as shown below, you see that the device is using ztp.viptela.com as the identity of the vBond device:

```
vedge# show running-config system
system
 host-name              vedge
 admin-tech-on-failure
 no route-consistency-check
 vbond ztp.viptela.com
 aaa
  auth-order local radius tacacs
  usergroup basic
   task system read write
   task interface read write
  !
<output omitted for brevity>
```

```
vedge# ping ztp.viptela.com
Ping in VPN 0
ping: ztp.viptela.com: Temporary failure in name resolution
vedge#
```

This is because ZTP configuration works like PNP configuration. The device connects and authenticates to Viptela's ZTP server, and if it is whitelisted, it is redirected to the organizational vBond controller. You need to provide a DNS solution to facilitate this lookup and at the same time redirect that request to your internal ZTP server.

To accomplish this, use the following syntax:

```
ISP-1(config)# ip host ztp.viptela.com 192.1.20.141
ISP-1(config)# ip dns server
```

```
ISP-1(config)# ip domain lookup
ISP-1(config)# ip dhcp pool ZTP-OPERATIONS
ISP-1(dhcp-config)# dom
ISP-1(dhcp-config)# dns-server 192.11.33.113
ISP-1(dhcp-config)# int e0/0
ISP-1(config-if)# shut
ISP-1(config-if)# no shut
ISP-1(config-if)#
```

Now you want to see if BR3-vE3 will resolve the IP address 192.11.20.141 for ztp.viptela.com. You have not configured the ZTP server yet, so a ping should fail. But you can use the command shown below to see if it resolves:

```
vedge# ping ztp.viptela.com
Ping in VPN 0
PING ztp.viptela.com (192.1.20.141) 56(84) bytes of data.
```

You can see that BR3-vE3 resolves the IP address. Now you can make the basic configuration on the ZTP server for reachability:

```
viptela 20.1.1

vedge login: admin
Password:
Welcome to Viptela CLI
admin connected from 127.0.0.1 using console on vedge
You must set an initial admin password.
Password: admin
Re-enter password: admin
vedge# config
Entering configuration mode terminal
vedge(config)# vpn 0
vedge(config-vpn-0)# interface ge0/0
vedge(config-interface-ge0/0)# ip address 192.1.20.141/24
vedge(config-interface-ge0/0)# no shut
vedge(config-interface-ge0/0)# exit
vedge(config-vpn-0)# ip route 0.0.0.0/0 192.1.20.115
vedge(config-vpn-0)# commit
Commit complete.
```

When you use the command shown below, you should see that BR3-vE3 has reachability to the ZTP server:

```
vedge# ping ztp.viptela.com
Ping in VPN 0
PING ztp.viptela.com (192.1.20.141) 56(84) bytes of data.
```

```
From ztp.viptela.com (192.1.20.141) icmp_seq=332 Destination Net
Unreachable
64 bytes from ztp.viptela.com (192.1.20.141): icmp_seq=337 ttl=62
time=1.39 ms
64 bytes from ztp.viptela.com (192.1.20.141): icmp_seq=338 ttl=62
time=0.681 ms
64 bytes from ztp.viptela.com (192.1.20.141): icmp_seq=339 ttl=62
time=0.591 ms
64 bytes from ztp.viptela.com (192.1.20.141): icmp_seq=340 ttl=62
time=0.598 ms
64 bytes from ztp.viptela.com (192.1.20.141): icmp_seq=341 ttl=62
time=0.634 ms
64 bytes from ztp.viptela.com (192.1.20.141): icmp_seq=342 ttl=62
time=1.14 ms
<control-c>
```

The next step is to get the ZTP server configured and to get a certificate signed for it. Because you are using self-signed certificates, you need to manually complete this process. The easiest way to accomplish this is to add the ZTP server to the vManage UI, sign its certificate, and then decommission the device. To do this, you need to apply the appropriate configuration to the ZTP server:

```
vedge(config)# system
vedge(config-system)# host-name ZTP-Server
vedge(config-system)# system-ip 10.1.1.141
vedge(config-system)# site-id 255
vedge(config-system)# organization-name micronicslab.com
vedge(config-system)# vbond 192.1.20.141 local ztp-server
vedge(config-system)# commit
Commit complete.
```

Download ROOTCA.pem and install it as you did for the previous controllers:

```
ZTP-Server(config-system)# exit
ZTP-Server(config)# vpn 0
ZTP-Server(config-vpn-0)# interface ge0/0
ZTP-Server(config-interface-ge0/0)# no tunnel-interface
ZTP-Server(config-interface-ge0/0)# commit
Commit complete.
ZTP-Server(config-interface-ge0/0)# end
ZTP-Server# vshell
ZTP-Server:~$ scp user@192.1.255.100:/home/user/Downloads/ROOTCA.pem
.
The authenticity of host '192.1.255.100 (192.1.255.100)' can't be est
ablished.
ECDSA key fingerprint is SHA256:Zz7IDU5Bkxvuh2GiVVWx8C9+OKr0U8ZC99BQe
icDmCc.
Are you sure you want to continue connecting (yes/no)? yes
```

```
Warning: Permanently added '192.1.255.100' (ECDSA) to the list of kno
wn hosts.
user@192.1.255.100's password: Test123
ROOTCA.pem                                        0%    0     0.0KB/s
ROOTCA.pem                                      100% 1521    24.7KB/s
 00:00
ZTP-Server:~$ exit
exit
ZTP-Server# request root-cert-chain install /home/admin/ROOTCA.pem
Uploading root-ca-cert-chain via VPN 0
Copying ... /home/admin/ROOTCA.pem via VPN 0
Updating the root certificate chain..
Successfully installed the root certificate chain
ZTP-Server#
```

Now you can verify that the root certificate was installed, as shown below:

```
ZTP-Server# show control local-properties
personality                      vedge
sp-organization-name             micronicslab.com
organization-name                micronicslab.com
root-ca-chain-status             Installed

certificate-status               Not-Installed
<output omitted for brevity>
```

To onboard the ZTP server, in the vManage UI, navigate to **Configuration > Devices > Controllers > Add Controller > vBond**. In the Add vBond screen, provide the information shown below. Ensure that the Generate CSR checkbox is not checked and click **Add**.

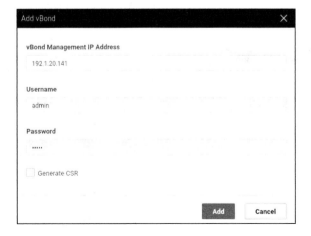

Navigate to **Configuration > Certificates > Controllers** and then find the vBond controller that says **No certificate installed**, click the ... icon to the right of that controller, and select **Generate CSR**, as shown below:

On the CSR screen, click **Download**:

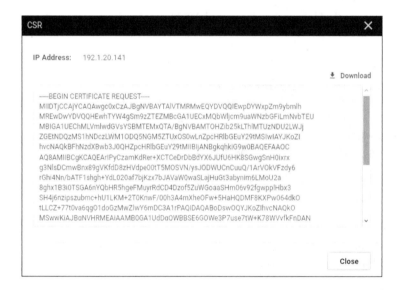

Save undefined.csr to your Downloads folder, as shown below:

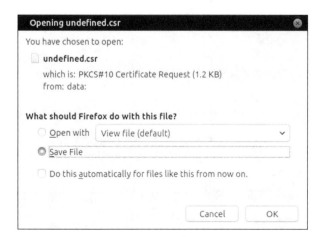

In a terminal session, change the name undefined.csr to ztp-server.csr. Then sign it as shown below:

```
user@user-pc:~/Downloads$ mv undefined.csr ztp-server.csr
user@user-pc:~/Downloads$ openssl x509 -req -in ztp-server.csr -CA
ROOTCA.pem -CAkey ROOTCA.key -CAcreateserial -out ztp-server.crt -days
2000 -sha256
Signature ok
subject=C = US, ST = California, L = San Jose, OU = micronicslab.com,
O = Viptela LLC, CN = vbond-8e153456-bcda-4431-a473-c58494c9e519-1.
viptela.com, emailAddress = support@viptela.com
Getting CA Private Key
```

Print the contents of ztp-server.crt and copy it into the vManage UI dashboard:

```
user@user-pc:~/Downloads$ cat ztp-server.crt
-----BEGIN CERTIFICATE-----
MIID+jCCAuICFBL3Y9wF3DXgSL18Rg4QhtKLK+tTMA0GCSqGSIb3DQEBCwUAMIGk
MQswCQYDVQQGEwJVUzELMAkGA1UECAwCVkExEDAOBgNVBAcMB1JhZGlhbnQxGTAX
BgNVBAoMEG1pY3Jvbmljc2xhYi5jb20xGTAXBgNVBAsMEG1pY3Jvbmljc2xhYi5j
b20xGTAXBgNVBAMMEG1pY3Jvbmljc2xhYi5jb20xJTAjBgkqhkiG9w0BCQEWFmFk
bWluQG1pY3Jvbmljc2xhYi5jb20wHhcNMjAwODMxMjE0MDA4WhcNMjYwMjIxMjE0
MDA4WjCBzTELMAkGA1UEBhMCVVMxEzARBgNVBAgTCkNhbGlmb3JuaWExETAPBgNV
BAcTCFNhbiBKb3NlMRkwFwYDVQQLExBtaWNyb25pY3NsYWIuY29tMRQwEgYDVQQK
EwtWaXB0ZWxhIExMQzFBMD8GA1UEAxM4dmJvbmQtOGUxNTM0NTYtYmNkYS00NDMx
LWE0NzMtYzU4NDk0YzllNTE5LTEudmlwdGVsYS5jb20xIjAgBgkqhkiG9w0BCQEW
E3N1cHBvcnRAdmlwdGVsYS5jb20wggEiMA0GCSqGSIb3DQEBAQUAA4IBDwAwggEK
AoIBAQCsg/ILNqYp1F6v5cJMJ4OsNsF1hfolR9TocrxIbCBKcfSLGvGDc2WwMKbA
GfHz2BUp90PzMdV2l7TS1Pkw5JU3/Kwk4NZQKcK65D/UCtU6RUXN3LqsaGLg2f9s
BMXWyGCH5h0vTbRp/tuMrPHtskBVpbTBpItqMe4a3dpvKeKbosyhTZryCHHUHeLR
NIYDqdhBsdHmGB4Uy7KtF0IPgPOh/lm5YahppIebTq/3Z+DCmmUdvHdIfiPqfOKm
zO5uZz6FTUsoz7ZPQqfAX/TSHcDiZeF44XD7kdodAMwXwpc/DTrh2Q60ssJn7vu3
S9rqqA7V2gbMzBmXBjqYMLcDWs8BAgMBAAEwDQYJKoZIhvcNAQELBQADggEBAGYi
XlKDV0hXguvghA1JJ5t987oAgmVeyFk1QA5g4jVz8zzK63HOrdk8J76XtzBvfn6W
imaLggd7yOAPlhjY+rndJaAMKOvT56Ez0MCQmcua3b3MMrgR18mlly1JfLQEf0M/
pOIM8up52VPrfWBZ5gG1s+5Gr6rH9k4JIxFsWIuIPUOHCPOEwjuF15dU5kFlNxxU
DyP34CPgtyE3ZPA6Ek0mKECHm/WsxBQ0XYVmgnEq3cEomz8tbN8g0HVSRIDwxn5h
AtPdtk4I6rnIEabUVPUEb5+T/udVckEKy3fpq++MzlMFkp/0Vqmm5hVx7PM0CJlC
r7rK8bYmFn5wMEmDxPc=
-----END CERTIFICATE-----
user@user-pc:~/Downloads$
```

Click **Install**.

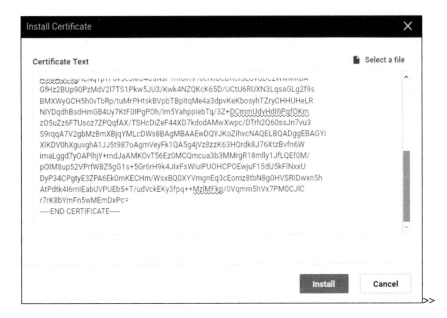

When the process is complete, you should see the following:

Now you need to provide the necessary configuration on ztp-server to support the registration of the BR3-vE3 edge device. To do this, you need to enter the whitelist of valid chassis numbers that will be allowed to join the fabric. To keep this example simple, you will add just one device.

Open the console of the ZTP server and enter the following information:

```
ZTP-Server# request device add chassis-number 1a11d205-09b8-36dd-a1b5-
c5c8fe754879 serial-number df052bedd3cf3a951fd708ecc92b935e validity
 valid vbond 192.1.255.102 org-name micronicslab.com
Chassis number 10D118E8-9F83-14F3-5933-3A2891307BE5 successfully added
to the database

ZTP-Server# show ztp entries
ztp entries 1
  chassis-number  10D118E8-9F83-14F3-5933-3A2891307BE5  ← CN of the next
vedge
  serial-number   1AFD615E6B7752AB8DB10A30ACD7F8B8  ←OTP Token for that
vedge
```

```
 validity          valid
 vbond-ip          192.1.255.102 ← IP Address of our organizational
vBond
 vbond-port        12346
 organization-name micronicslab.com ← exact organizational name in our
labs
 root-cert-path    default
ZTP-Server#
```

Install the root-ca-certificate on BR3-vE3:

```
vedge# config
Entering configuration mode terminal
vedge(config)# vpn 0
vedge(config-vpn-0)# interface ge0/0
vedge(config-interface-ge0/0)# tunnel-interface
vedge(config-tunnel-interface)# encapsulation ipsec
vedge(config-tunnel-interface)# allow-service sshd
vedge(config-tunnel-interface)# commit and-quit
Commit complete.
vedge# vshell
vedge:~$ scp user@192.1.255.100:/home/user/Downloads/ROOTCA.pem .
The authenticity of host '192.1.255.100 (192.1.255.100)' can't be est
ablished.
ECDSA key fingerprint is SHA256:Zz7IDU5Bkxvuh2GiVVWx8C9+OKr0U8ZC99BQe
icDmCc.
Are you sure you want to continue connecting (yes/no)? yes
Warning: Permanently added '192.1.255.100' (ECDSA) to the list of kno
wn hosts.
user@192.1.255.100's password: Test123
ROOTCA.pem                                   0%    0      0.0KB/s
ROOTCA.pem                                   100% 1505   1.0MB/s
 00:00
vedge:~$exit
exit
vedge# request root-cert-chain install /home/admin/ROOTCA.pem
Uploading root-ca-cert-chain via VPN 0
Copying ... /home/admin/ROOTCA.pem via VPN 0
Updating the root certificate chain..
Successfully installed the root certificate chain
vedge#
```

Request that the SEN fabric activate the chassis and token:

```
vedge# request vedge-cloud activate chassis-number 1a11d205-09b8-36dd-
a1b5-c5c8fe754879 token df052bedd3cf3a951fd708ecc92b935e
```

After a few moments, the vEdge device successfully joins the fabric.

To test this deployment to make sure everything works, you can enter the pings shown below on Docker23 to see if you can reach the VPN 200 resources at Branch-3:

```
root@Docker23:~# ping 10.3.200.123 -c 5
PING 10.3.200.123 (10.3.200.123) 56(84) bytes of data.
64 bytes from 10.3.200.123: icmp_seq=1 ttl=63 time=0.932 ms
64 bytes from 10.3.200.123: icmp_seq=2 ttl=63 time=1.16 ms
64 bytes from 10.3.200.123: icmp_seq=3 ttl=63 time=1.25 ms
64 bytes from 10.3.200.123: icmp_seq=4 ttl=63 time=0.827 ms
64 bytes from 10.3.200.123: icmp_seq=5 ttl=63 time=0.917 ms

--- 10.3.200.123 ping statistics ---
5 packets transmitted, 5 received, 0% packet loss, time 4015ms
rtt min/avg/max/mdev = 0.827/1.019/1.253/0.164 ms
```

Test reachability in VRF/VPN 100 from RM-R1:

```
RM-R1# ping 10.3.100.123
Type escape sequence to abort.
Sending 5, 100-byte ICMP Echos to 10.3.100.123, timeout is 2 seconds:
!!!!!
Success rate is 100 percent (5/5), round-trip min/avg/max = 1/1/2 ms
RM-R1#
```

You can see that all reachability has been resolved in Branch-1.

# Lab 8: Configuring an Application-Aware Routing Policy

Open vManage in another tab to create the policy.

Select **Configuration > Policies**, as shown below:

click **Add Policy:**

Click **SLA Class** as shown below:

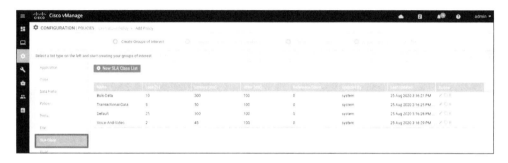

Click **New SLA Class List:**

Set SLA Class List Name to SLA, set Latency to 100, and click **Add.**

Click **Next.**

Click **Next** again.

Under **Application Aware Routing,** click **Add Policy** and select **Create New,** as shown below:

Configure both Name and Description as **AAR:**

Click **Sequence Type** and click **Sequence Rule** to create a new rule:

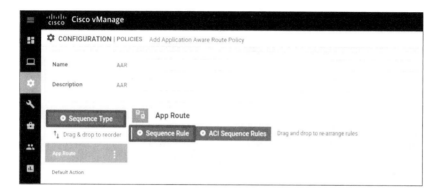

Select **Source Data Prefix**, use the IP prefix **10.0.0.0/8**, click **DSCP**, and set DSCP to **46**, as shown below:

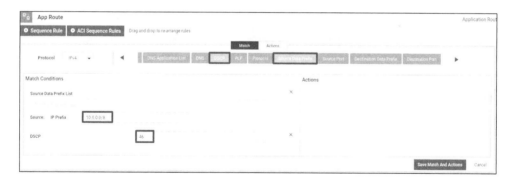

Under Actions, click **SLA Class List**:

Choose **SLA** under SLA Class:

Set Preferred Color to **mpls**:

Click **Backup SLA Preferred Color**, as shown below:

Set Backup SLA Preferred Color to **biz-internet**, as shown below:

Click **Save Match and Actions.**

Save the policy by clicking **Save Application Aware Routing Policy,** as shown below:

When you see that the AAR policy has been created, as shown below, click **Next:**

Under Apply Policies to Sites and VPNs, set Policy Name to **Micronics-AAR-Policy** and set Policy Description to **Micronics-AAR-Policy,** as shown below:

In the Application-Aware Routing section, click **New Site List and VPN List**:

Select **Branch-2**:

Select **VPN100** and then click **Add**:

Save the policy by clicking **Save Policy**:

To view the policy, find **Micronics-AAR-Policy**, click the **...** icon to the right of it, and select **Preview**:

Your policy should look as shown below:

```
viptela-
  policy:policy
  sla-class SLA
    latency 100
  !
app-route-policy
 _VPN100_AAR vpn-list
 VPN100
   sequence
     1 match
      source-ip
      10.0.0.0/8 dscp
      46
      !
      action
       sla-class SLA preferred-color mpls
       backup-sla-preferred-color biz-
       internet
       !
      !
 !
lists
 site-list
  Branch-2 site-
  id 2
 !
 vpn-list
  VPN100 vpn
  100
  !
 !
!
```

```
viptela-policy:apply-
 policy site-list
 Branch-2
  app-route-policy _VPN100_AAR
 !
!
```

To activate the policy, find **Micronics-AAR-Policy**, click the ... icon to the right of it, and select **Activate**:

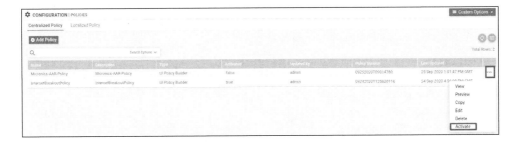

The policy is applied to vSmart. Click **Activate**:

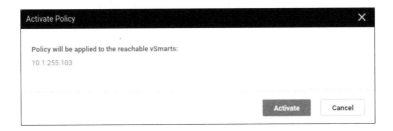

Wait until the policy push is successful.

You have now created and activated an AAR policy.

# Chapter 11

# SD-Access

The Introduction to SD-Access and DNA Center to enterprise network deployments gives the organization access to Cisco's latest features to automate common administrative tasks on security-focused programmable network infrastructures. This chapter will demonstrate the concept of a "Network Fabric" and the different node types that form it (Fabric Edge Nodes, Control Plane Nodes, Border Nodes). It demonstrates the roles of LISP in the Control Plane and VXLAN in the Data Plane for SD-Access Solutions and how DNA Center uses them to automate security and network access.

The following topology will be used for all the SDA labs:

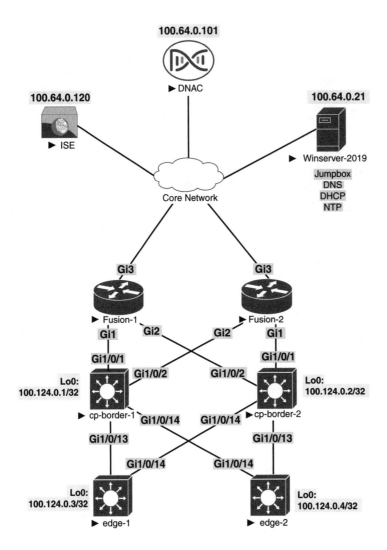

# Lab 1: Configuring the SDA Policy Engine

## Task 1: ISE Integration with DNA Center

Log in to ISE using a browser by navigating to https://ise.micronicslab.com/. The IP address of ISE is 100.64.0.120. Use the following credentials:

Username: **admin**

Password: **ISEisCOOL**

Navigate to **Administration > System > Deployment** and then click **OK** when you see the informational message shown below:

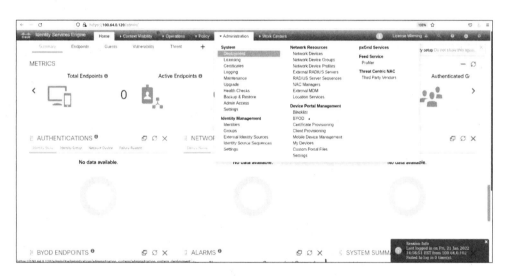

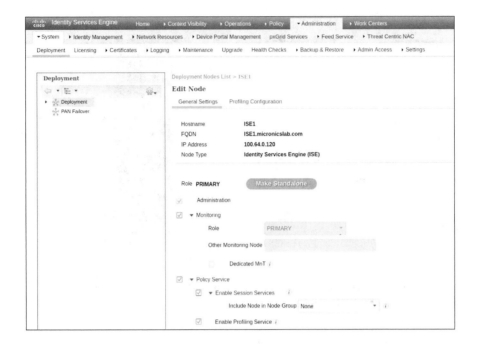

Enable the services SXP Service, Device Admin Service, Passive Identity Service, and pxGrid, as shown below, and click **Save**.

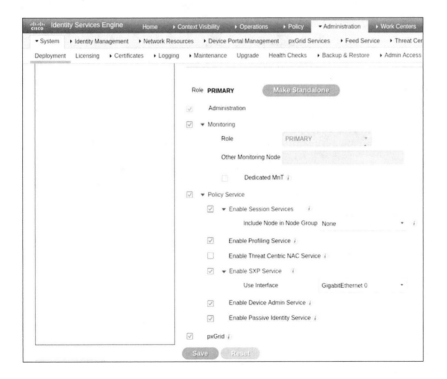

Navigate to **Administration > pxGrid Services** and check the banner in the lower half of the screen. You should see "connected via XMPP" followed by the FQDN of ISE, as shown below. Make note of the FQDN, which you will need later. Keep in mind that this banner might be red in color initially because pxGrid services take some time to initialize. You can check the status of the services by logging in to ISE via the CLI and typing the command **show application status ise**.

Connected via XMPP ISE1.micronicslab.com

You should see output like the following:

```
ise01/admin# show application status ise

ISE PROCESS NAME                    STATE            PROCESS ID
---------------------------------------------------------------------
Database Listener                   running          5235
Database Server                     running          138 PROCESSES
Application Server                  running          13618
Profiler Database                   running          8083
ISE Indexing Engine                 running          15878
AD Connector                        running          17756
M&T Session Database                running          7892
M&T Log Processor                   running          13816
Certificate Authority Service       running          17042
EST Service                         running          29564
SXP Engine Service                  running          17589
Docker Daemon                       running          9407
TC-NAC Service                      disabled

Wifi Setup Helper Container         disabled
pxGrid Infrastructure Service       running          30552
pxGrid Publisher Subscriber Service running          30708
pxGrid Connection Manager           running          30655
pxGrid Controller                   running          30776
PassiveID WMI Service               disabled
PassiveID Syslog Service            disabled
```

Navigate to **Administration > System > Settings > ERS Settings**. Then, under ERS Setting for Primary Administration Node, select **Enable ERS for Read/Write** and click **OK** in any dialog box that appears.

Under ERS Setting for All Other Nodes, select Enable ERS for Read, and under CRSF Check, select **Disable CSRF for ERS Request**, and then click **Save**.

Click **OK** in any additional dialog boxes that appear.

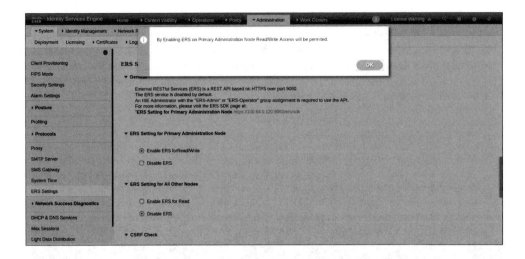

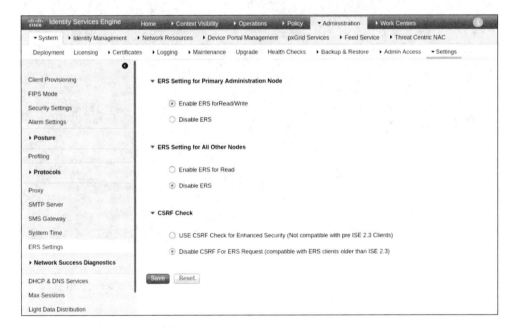

## Task 2: Finalize the Integration on DNA Center

Log in to the DNA Center web interface (https://100.64.0.101), at the top-right corner select the gear icon, and select **System Settings.** Use the following credentials:

Username: **admin**

Password: **ISEisC00L**

Navigate to **Settings > Authentication and Policy Servers** and then click **Add:**

In the Add AAA/ISE Server display shown below, enter the ISE node (Primary PAN) IP address along with the details shown below:

| | |
|---|---|
| Server IP Address | 100.64.0.120 |
| Shared Secret | ISEisC00L |
| ISE Selector | Toggle it to the on position |
| ISE Username | admin |
| ISE Password | ISEisC00L |
| ISE FQDN | Ise1.micronicslab.com |
| Subscriber Name | DNAC1.3.1.7 |
| SSH Key | <Leave Blank> |
| View Advanced Settings | Check TACACS and RADIUS |

**Note**   For this lab you will be using TACACS for network authentication and RADIUS for client authentication.

Click **Apply**.

Log in to ISE and navigate to **Administration > pxGrid Services**. The client named dnac1.3.1.7_dnac_ndp is now showing **Pending** in the Status column.

Choose **Total Pending Approval (1)**, click **Approve All**, and click **Approve All** again to confirm.

A success message appears.

If ISE is integrated with DNA Center after scalable groups are already created in ISE, in addition to the default groups, any existing ISE groups will also be visible. You can see these entries by logging in to DNA Center and navigating to **Policy > Group-Based Access Control > Scalable Groups**, as shown below:

For this exercise, you will use DNA Center to implement group-based access control. Click **Start Migration**, observe the warning message, shown below, and click **Yes**.

When the process is complete you will see the following success message.

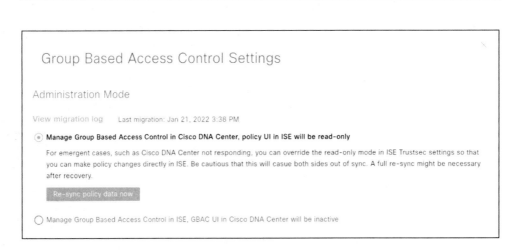

You should now see some additional Scalable Groups added (ACCT, HR, Campus Quarantine).

# Lab 2: SDA Design

## Task 1: Design the Network Hierarchy

Log in to ISE by using a browser to navigate to the IP address 100.64.0.120. Use the following credentials:

Username: **admin**

Password: **ISEisC00L**

Log in to DNA Center by using a browser to navigate to https://100.64.0.101. Use the following credentials:

Username: **admin**

Password: **ISEisC00L**

In DNA Center, go to **DESIGN > Network Hierarchy**, click **Add Site**, and select **Add Area**, as shown below:

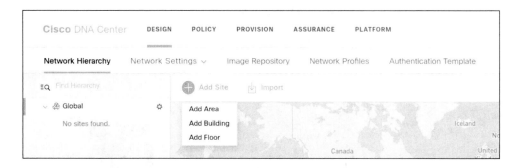

Enter **US** for the area name and click **Add**:

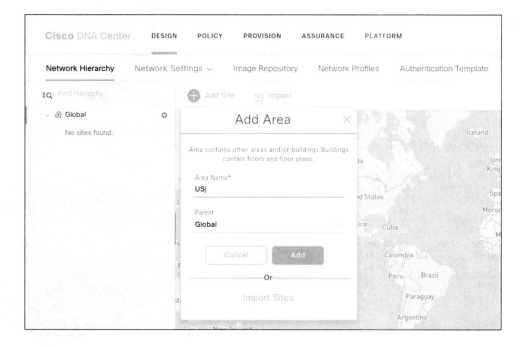

Click the cog wheel next to US in the navigation pane and choose **Add Area**. In the Add Area window, as shown on the next page, enter **San Jose** for the area name and click **Add**.

To add a building, select the cog wheel next to **San Jose** in the navigation pane and click **Add Building**. Enter the building name **HQ** and begin to enter the street address shown on the next page. Click on the correct option from among the street address recommendations that appear to autopopulate the Latitude and Longitude fields. Click **Add** when you're done with this.

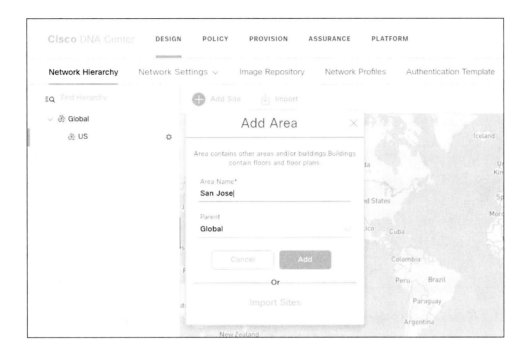

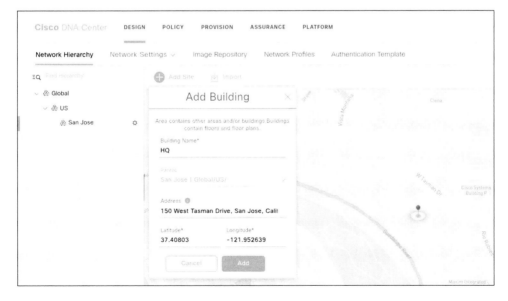

With the building now defined, select **HQ** in the navigation pane, click the gear icon, and select **Add Floor**, as shown on the next page:

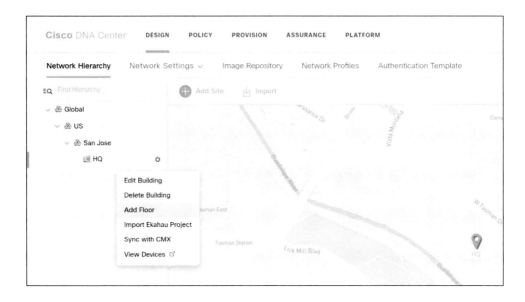

In the Add Floor window, enter **HQ-1** as the floor name and click **Upload File**.

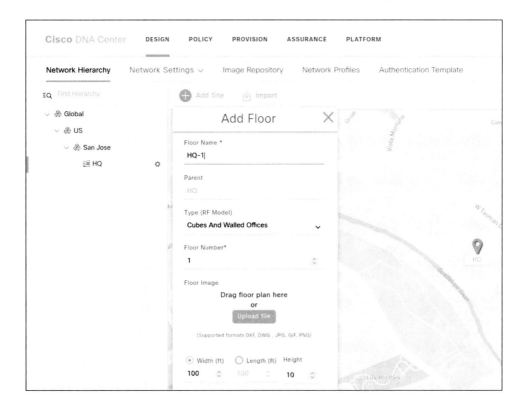

**Note**   You should have floor plans and other files in the **Downloads folder**. Open it and select the **Floor Plan** folder. Look for **HQ-1.png** in this the folder and click **Open** to upload it.

DNA Center presents the floor plan file, as shown below.

Click **Add** to create the floor.

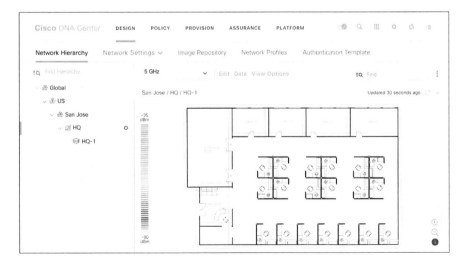

Return to **HQ** in the navigation pane, click the gear icon, and select **Add Floor** again to create another floor.

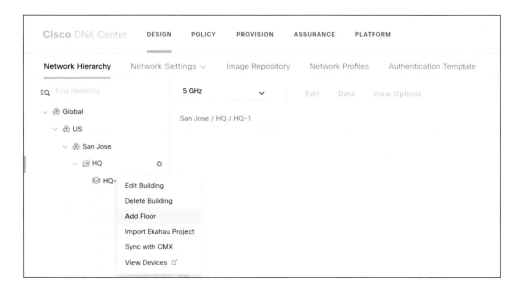

Name the new floor **HQ-MDF** and click **Add.** (You do not need to upload a floor plan in this case.)

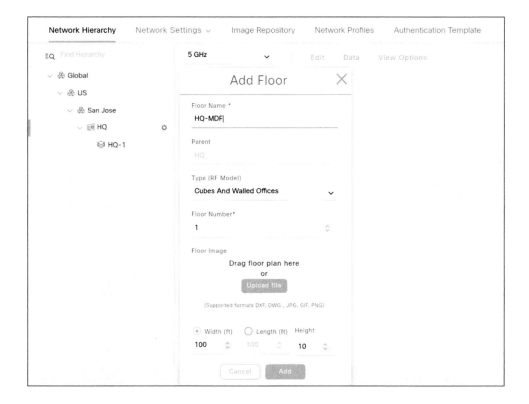

Click **OK** to acknowledge the warning message and proceed without a floor plan for this floor.

At this point, the building and floors necessary for this lab have been created. Observe the hierarchy you have built in the navigation pane shown below:

## Task 2: Configure Common Network Settings

In DNA Center, navigate to **DESIGN > Network Settings > Network**, as shown below.

Ensure that **Global** is selected in the navigation pane and click **Add Servers**.

Check the **AAA** and for **NTP** boxes and click **OK**:

Notice that the AAA Server section is present. If you scroll to the bottom of the page, you also see an NTP section. Check the **Network** and **Client/Endpoint** boxes under AAA Server to reveal more options, as shown on the next page.

As shown below, in the Network section, select the ISE server **100.64.0.120** under both Network and IP Address (Primary).

In the CLIENT/ENDPOINT section the **ISE** radio button under Servers and the **RADIUS** radio button under Protocol.

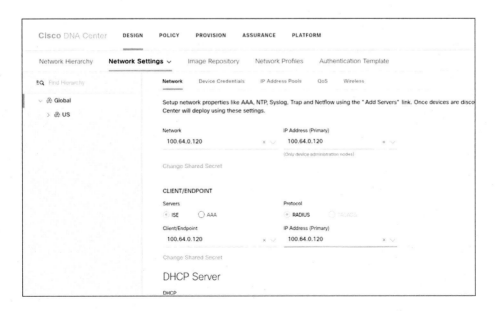

Set the DHCP server to **100.64.0.2**, as shown below, and carefully enter the domain name **micronics.com** and the internal DNS server **100.64.0.2**.

Under NTP Server, enter **100.64.0.2** as the time source. Keep in mind that this is the CSR in the cloud that is providing time for the devices in the setup.

With all the Network Settings input at the Global Level, as shown below, click **Save**.

Confirmation messages like the ones below appear briefly at the bottom right of the screen:

## Task 3: Configure Device Credentials

Navigate to **DESIGN > Network Settings > Device Credentials**, click **Add Credentials**. In the CLI Credentials box, shown below, enter the following credentials:

CLI credentials name: **IOS Device Admin Account**

Username: **netadmin**

Password/enable password: **ISEisC00L**

Click **Save**.

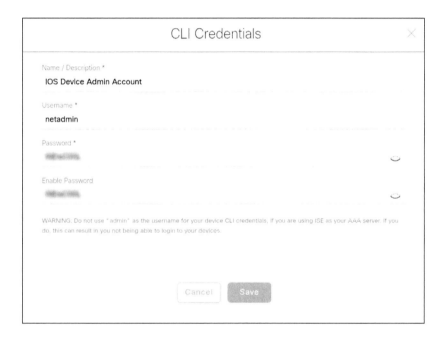

Click **SNMP v2c** and **Read** and enter the following credentials:

Name: **ro**

Read community: **ro**

Click **Save**.

Click **SNMP v2c** and **Write**, as shown on the next page, and enter the following credentials:

Name: **rw**

Write community: **rw**

Click **Save**.

To set the CLI credentials and the SNMP read and write community strings that just you added as global, click on the radio button to the left of **CLI Credentials** and click the radio button to the left of **SNMP Credentials**. (This first click will be for the read-only credentials.)

Next, click the **SNMPV2C Write** link in the center in the SNMP Credentials section. (When you click this link, notice that ro switches to rw in the Name/Description field.)

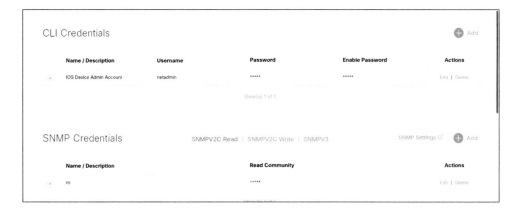

Click the radio button to the left of **rw** to select the read/write credentials.

Click **Save**.

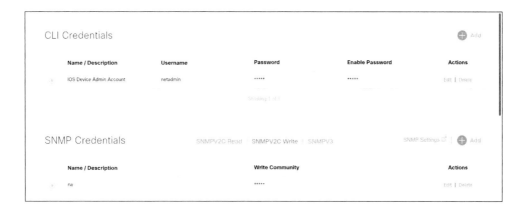

Watch for the small success message that appears briefly in the bottom right of the screen:

## Task 4: Create and Reserve IP Address Pools

To create an IP address pool, go to **DESIGN > Network Settings > IP Address Pools**. Make sure **Global** is selected in the navigation pane and click **Add**.

The Add IP Pool dialog box shown below appears:

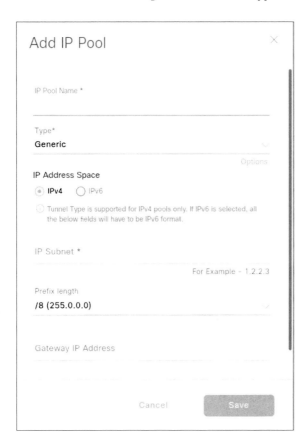

Populate the fields of the Add IP Pool dialog box as shown on the next page, using the following details:

IP Pool Name: **Global-Pool-1**

Type: **Generic**

IP Subnet: **100.96.0.0**

CIDR Prefix: **/11 (255.224.0.0)**

Gateway: **100.96.0.1**

Click **Save.**

It is not necessary to populate DHCP and DNS servers at the global pool level.

To reserve IP pools, in DNA Center, go to **DESIGN > Network Settings > IP Address Pools** and, as shown on the next page, navigate to **San Jose** in the navigation pane. The message shown on the next page appears, describing how the hierarchy works. Check the **Don't show again** box and click **OK** to prevent this message from appearing again in the future.

If you misconfigure a pool reservation, ensure that you **release** the IP pool and re-create it.

With San Jose still selected, click **Reserve** the IP Address Pools.

In the Reserve IP Pool dialog box that appears, as shown on the next page, enter the following information to create a new reservation within the global IP pool you just created:

IP pool name: **SJC-Border-Handoff**

Type: **Generic**

Global Pool: **100.96.0.0/11 (Global-Pool-1)**

Prefix Length: **/24**

IPv4 Subnet: **100.126.1.0**

Gateway: **100.126.1.1**

Click **Reserve.**

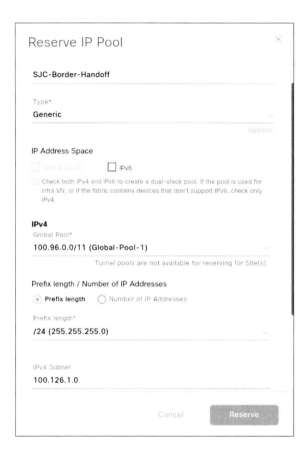

Enter the following information to create a new reservation within the global IP pool you just created:

IP pool name: **SJC-Campus-Users**

Type: **Generic**

Global Pool: **100.96.0.0/11 (Global-Pool-1)**

Prefix Length: **/20**

IPv4 Subnet: **100.100.0.0**

Gateway IP Address: **100.100.0.1**

DHCP Server: **100.64.0.2**

DNS Server: **100.64.0.2**

Click **Reserve.**

Enter the following information to create a new reservation within the global IP pool you just created:

IP pool name: **SJC-Guest-Users**

Type: **Generic**

Global Pool: **100.96.0.0/11 (Global-Pool-1)**

Prefix Length: **/20**

IPv4 Subnet: **100.99.0.0**

Gateway: **100.99.0.1**

DHCP Server: **100.64.0.2**

DNS Server: **100.64.0.2**

Click **Reserve.**

Enter the following information to create a new reservation within the global IP pool you just created:

IP pool name: **SJC-Lan-Automation**

Type: **Lan**

Global Pool: **100.96.0.0/11 (Global-Pool-1)**

Prefix Length: **/20**

IPv4 Subnet: **100.124.128.0**

Gateway: **100.124.128.1**

Click **Reserve**.

At this point, you have created all the IP pools you need to build out the SDA fabric in this lab. You can see them listed in the screen shown below:

# Lab 3: Building the SDA Campus Fabric

## Task 1: Discover Devices

Log in to DNA Center using a browser by navigating to the IP address https://100.64.0.101/ and entering the following credentials:

Username: **admin**

Password: **ISEisC00L**

In DNA Center, click the gear icon and select **Discovery**, as shown below:

On the Discovery Dashboard, click **Add Discovery**. Note that you can get a snapshot of the devices along with details associated with discovery jobs. The aim of this discovery job is to discover the devices that you are going to add to DNA Center manually. Once the devices are added, you will begin configuring them.

Enter **HQ_Devices** as the name of the discovery job and select the **IP Address/Range** radio button. Enter the **From** and **To** IP address range **100.124.0.1** to **100.124.0.2**, as shown on the next page. This will encompass the cp-border-1 and cp-border-2 devices. Under Preferred Management, select **UseLoopBack**.

Scroll down until you see the credentials that were populated in Lab 2 appear as selectable parameters that can be used for this discovery job. (During Lab 2, you made these credentials globally available for all discovery jobs by selecting the radio button.) The credentials should already be selected for use, and the slider can be toggled on or off.

Scroll down further, until you see the **Advanced** option. Expand this option and select **Telnet** as well as **SSH**, in case there are devices that aren't configured for SSH.

When you see the warning about enabling Telnet, click on **OK**.

You can change the order of the protocols in this window, moving Telnet above SSH, if required.

Click **Discover** and, in the window shown below, choose **Now** and click **Start.**

The Discovery starts, and DNA Center reaches out to the network, using a ping sweep on the IP address range you enumerated.

When the discovery job has completed and you see the side panel that lists the discovered devices, as shown below, make note of the green check marks.

Green is good. If you see any red icons, however, a failure has occurred, and the device will not be onboarded into DNA Center as a managed device. For example, if the SNMP credentials were incorrect, DNA Center would let you know that SNMP validation failed.

Navigate to the DNA Center home page and go to the **PROVISION** Page. Notice that the devices show up on this page as **Unassigned Devices** in the navigation pane. You will be fixing this soon. For now, set the Device Role for the CP border devices to **Border Router** if the status of these devices is listed and **UNKNOWN** otherwise. Give the system time to identify the devices. The system will discover these switches as **ACCESS** devices.

## Task 2: Provisioning the Devices

From the jumphost, open a session to **cp-border-1**. This is a reverse Telnet console session to cp-border-1. Use the following credentials, if requested

Username: **netadmin**

Password: **ISEisC00L**

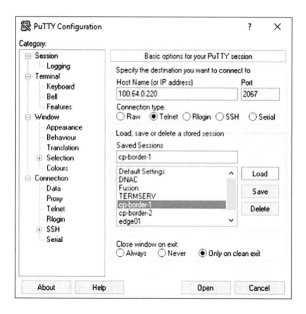

Run a quick check on the configuration of the cp-border-1 device before initiating the provisioning process from DNA Center. To do so, issue the following commands:

>**show run | sec lisp**

>**show run | sec isis**

>**show run | sec vrf**

>**show run | sec aaa**

```
cp-border-1#
cp-border-1#
cp-border-1#
cp-border-1#
*Mar 24 16:33:42.517: %SYS-5-LOGOUT: User netadmin has exited tty session 3(100.
64.0.101)
cp-border-1#
cp-border-1#
cp-border-1#show run | sec lisp
cp-border-1#show run | sec isis
 redistribute isis level-1
router isis
cp-border-1#show run | sec vrf
vrf definition Mgmt-vrf
 !
 address-family ipv4
 exit-address-family
 !
 address-family ipv6
 exit-address-family
 vrf forwarding Mgmt-vrf
cp-border-1#show run | sec aaa
no aaa new-model
cp-border-1#
```

Notice that there is no LISP-related configuration, no additional VRF instances have been created, and there is a rudimentary ISIS configuration. In addition, there is no AAA configuration on this device at this point.

Log in to the Edge01 device via Putty, using the following credentials:

Username: **netadmin**

Password: **ISEisC00L**

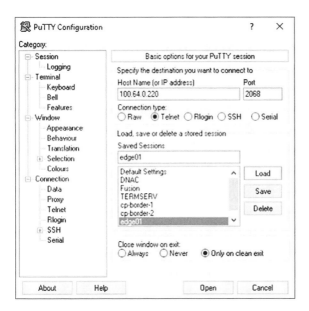

When you are presented with a screen asking you to start the initial configuration, like the one shown below, *do not press any keys*. It is expected that this device will be in a factory default state because you will be onboarding your edge devices via LAN automation:

```
% Please answer 'yes' or 'no'.
Would you like to enter the initial configuration dialog? [yes/no]: 
```

To quickly review the configuration from Lab 2, navigate to **DESIGN > Network Hierarchy** in DNA Center, as shown on the next page:

Recall that in Lab 2, you set up a **Network Hierarchy** and configured various **common network settings** (such as **AAA**). As part of the provisioning process, you need to assign a site to each network device. The network device will inherit settings from that site. Edges will be assigned to the floor HQ-1, and border routers will be assigned to the floor HQ-MDF. They will inherit the common network settings accordingly (the same settings in this case).

Navigate to the **PROVISION** page on DNA Center. Notice, as shown below, that there aren't any devices at the lower levels (for example, San Jose), but there are two unassigned devices.

Click on **Unassigned Devices** in the navigation pane. You now see all the devices that were discovered in this section, as shown below.

Select all the devices, as shown below, and select **Action**, click **Provision**, and click **Provision Device**.

Allocate the devices to the respective sites by clicking **Choose a Site**. Assign devices as follows:

Assign cp-border-1 to **Global/US/San Jose/HQ/HQ-MDF**

Assign cp-border-2 to **Global/US/San Jose/HQ/HQ-MDF**

Click **Next**.

Click **Next** on the Advanced Configuration page. This page is used to deploy templates to devices via the Template Editor tool (which allows you to push custom configuration to the devices during provisioning). Click **Deploy** on the Summary page.

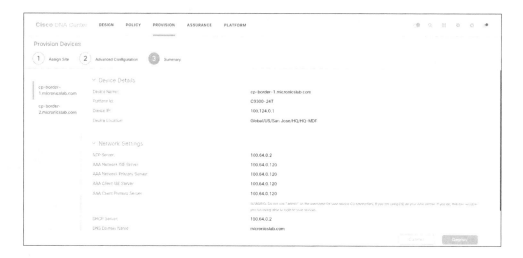

Select **Now** and click **Apply** to apply the configuration immediately.

Give the devices some time to be provisioned. When the provisioning process is complete, you should see a temporary notification in the bottom-right corner, indicating that provisioning was successful.

Now that the devices have been provisioned, you can add the fabric and add the devices to the fabric. To add a new fabric, as shown below, navigate to **PROVISION > Fabric** and, in the top-right corner, click **Add Fabric or Transit/Peer Network** and then click **Fabric**:

In the side panel that appears, select the **San Jose** site as your fabric site.

> **Note**  Keep in mind that the site should be selected appropriately so that network settings (such as IP pools) from that site can be used. If the fabric site is at a level higher than the site where configuration parameters like IP pools have been allocated, they will not be usable.

Name the fabric **CiscoFabric** and select the **San Jose** site. Click **Next**. Make sure both virtual networks created so far (built-in virtual networks) are selected, as shown on the next page, and click **Add**.

Click on the **CiscoFabric** fabric that you just created, as shown below, to start configuring devices in it.

Click on **San Jose** in the navigation pane and then click on **cp-border-1**.

In the sliding panel that appears, set the slider for Border Node to the **On** position. This should bring up a panel where you need to enter the AS number **65534** and check the **Default to all Virtual Networks** checkbox. Click **Add**.

Set the slider for Control Plane to the **On** position. Click **Add**.

Repeat the previous operations for **cp-border-2**, as shown below:

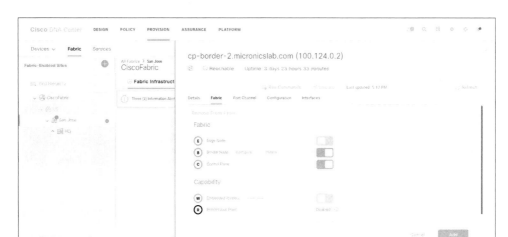

Ensure that the devices that you have configured have a blue outline around them now. This is an indication that these devices will be configured when you click **Save**. Also make sure there is a pointer that specifies the role(s) configured on that device.

Click **Save**, select **Now**, and click **Apply**.

You should see a notification indicating that the devices were successfully configured in the fabric domain.

Issue **show run | sec lisp** on any of your devices, and you should see the LISP configuration shown on the next page. (Keep in mind that the configuration will be different for devices with different roles.)

```
router lisp
 locator-table default
 locator-set rloc_5e7a1eaf-71f7-4b8b-8278-fe92ec9b8229
  IPv4-interface Loopback0 priority 10 weight 10
  exit-locator-set
 !
 service ipv4
  encapsulation vxlan
  itr map-resolver 100.124.0.1
  itr map-resolver 100.124.0.2
  etr map-server 100.124.0.1 key 7 101F0F1A554744
  etr map-server 100.124.0.1 proxy-reply
  etr map-server 100.124.0.2 key 7 11581F0647425D
  etr map-server 100.124.0.2 proxy-reply
  etr
  sgt
  no map-cache away-eids send-map-request
  proxy-itr 100.124.0.1
  map-server
  map-resolver
  exit-service-ipv4
 !
 service ethernet
  database-mapping limit dynamic 5000
  itr map-resolver 100.124.0.1
  itr map-resolver 100.124.0.2
  itr
  etr map-server 100.124.0.1 key 7 065709221C1E5F
  etr map-server 100.124.0.1 proxy-reply
  etr map-server 100.124.0.2 key 7 014200070B5B50
  etr map-server 100.124.0.2 proxy-reply
  etr
  map-server
  map-resolver
  exit-service-ethernet
 !
 site site_uci
  description map-server configured from Cisco DNA-Center
  authentication-key 7 0055150554085D
  exit-site
 !
 ipv4 locator reachability exclude-default
 ipv4 source-locator Loopback0
```

# Lab 4: LAN Automation

In this lab we will explore how to conduct a LAN Automation exercise.

Log in to DNA Center by using a browser to navigate to the IP address https://100.64.0.101/ and entering the following credentials:

Username: **netadmin**

Password: **ISEisC00L**

From the jumphost, open a console session to cp-border-1 so you can use LAN automation for the devices edge-01 and edge-02.

In DNA Center, navigate to **DESIGN > Network Settings > Device Credentials.** Verify that the CLI and SNMP ro and rw credentials have been selected, as partially shown below:

Verify that an IP pool has been reserved for LAN automation, as shown below:

You need to ensure IP connectivity from DNA Center to the LAN automation pool addresses. This can be achieved in multiple ways, such as by using a routing protocol to advertise the subnet from the border(s) out to the fusion, using static routing to DNA Center, or using border automation.

Go to **PROVISION > Actions > Provision > LAN Automation,** as shown on the next page, to start the LAN automation procedure.

Enter the following details in the LAN Automation slide-out panel:

| CONFIGURATION PARAMETER | VALUE |
| --- | --- |
| Primary Site | Global/US/San Jose/HQ/HQ-MDF |
| Primary Device (primary seed device) | cp-border-01.micronicslab.com |
| Peer Site | Global/US/San Jose/HQ/HQ-MDF |
| Peer Device (peer seed device) | cp-border-02.micronicslab.com |
| Choose primary device ports | Gi1/0/13 and Gi1/0/14 |
| Discovered device site | Global/US/San Jose/HQ/HQ-1 |
| IP Pool | SJC-Lan-Automation |
| IS-IS Domain Password | Cisco |

Click on **Start** to start the LAN automation procedure.

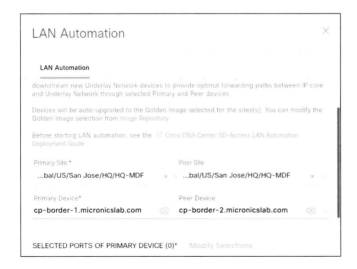

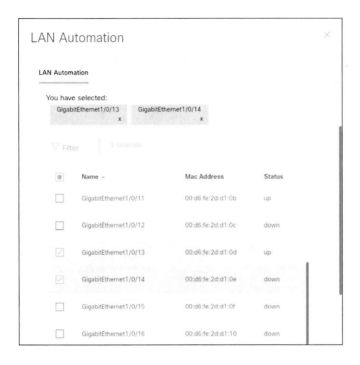

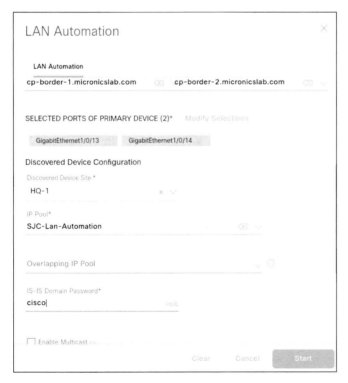

Wait for approximately 120 seconds and view the LAN automation status by navigating to **PROVISION > Actions > Provision > LAN Auto Status.**

You should see some action in the LAN Automation Status screen. In the figure below, a device has been discovered via LAN automation, and the procedure for it is in progress.

**Note** You should see Gi1/0/13 and Gi1/0/14 as the primary device interfaces.

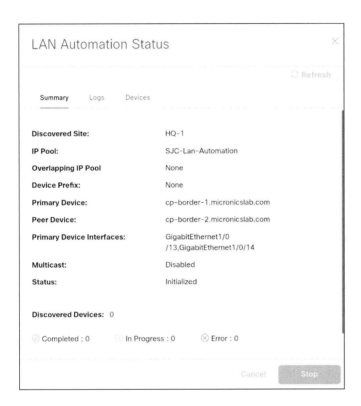

Check the console session for edge-01 and edge-02. You should see some activity with respect to PnP.

Check the LAN automation status after some time, and you should see two devices listed as Completed (edge-01 and edge-02), as shown on the next page:

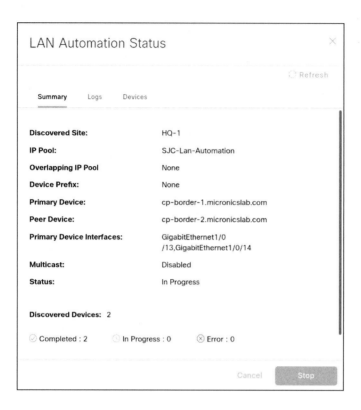

Go to the **PROVISION** page, and you should now see your LAN automated devices popping up. It might take a while before all the devices show up because DNA Center collects information from the devices during the automation process and tries to bring them into a managed state before populating all the information. In the interim, some devices might show up as N/A.

After a while, notice that both devices are added to the inventory and are being managed by DNA Center.

Since you are confident at this point that LAN automation has completed successfully, close out the process by choosing **STOP** on the DNA Center LAN Automation Status screen. You see that ISIS neighborships are now established on the physical interfaces, and IP addresses are being assigned to the interfaces from the LAN automation IP pool created on DNA Center. IP addresses from VLAN 1 and the DHCP pool are removed:

```
cp-border-1#show running-config | sec dhcp
class-map match-any system-cpp-police-dhcp-snooping
  description DHCP snooping
snmp-server enable traps dhcp
cp-border-1#
cp-border-1#show run int vlan 1
Building configuration...

Current configuration : 38 bytes
!
interface Vlan1
 no ip address
end

cp-border-1#show isis neighbors

System Id       Type Interface   IP Address     State Holdtime Circuit Id
Switch-100-124- L2   Gi1/0/13    100.124.130.11 UP    27       15
Switch-100-124- L2   Gi1/0/14    100.124.130.15 UP    20       15
cp-border-1#
```

```
Current configuration : 38 bytes
!
interface Vlan1
 no ip address
end

Switch-100-124-130-12#
Switch-100-124-130-12#show run int g1/0/14
Building configuration...

Current configuration : 342 bytes
!
interface GigabitEthernet1/0/14
 description Fabric Physical Link
 no switchport
 dampening
 ip address 100.124.130.11 255.255.255.254
 no ip redirects
 ip router isis
 ip lisp source-locator Loopback0
 logging event link-status
 load-interval 30
 bfd interval 500 min_rx 500 multiplier 3
 clns mtu 1400
 isis network point-to-point
end

Switch-100-124-130-12#show isis neighbor

System Id       Type Interface   IP Address     State Holdtime Circuit Id
cp-border-1     L2   Gi1/0/14    100.124.130.10 UP    27       15
Switch-100-124-130-12#
```

To provision the LAN automated devices and add them to the fabric as edge nodes, go to the **PROVISION** page, select both of the LAN automated devices, and choose **Actions > Provision > Provision Device**, as shown below:

Assign both devices to **Global/US/San Jose/HQ/HQ-1** and click **Next**.

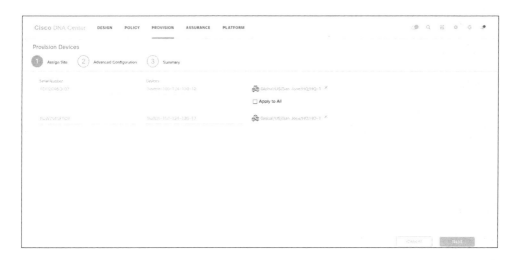

Click **Next** in the Advanced Configuration screen and then click **Deploy** on the Summary page. Select **Now** and click **Apply**.

To set the role of all LAN automated devices to **Access**, go on the **PROVISION** page.

Navigate to the **Fabric** tab, click the **CiscoFabric** fabric, click **San Jose**, and notice the three LAN automated devices there. Click on them one by one and set the role to **Edge Node**. Click **Add**.

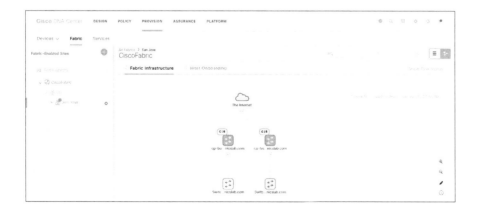

When the devices have been added to the fabric, ensure that the fabric view is similar to what is displayed below (notice the blue shade on the devices, which means they have been added to the fabric successfully):

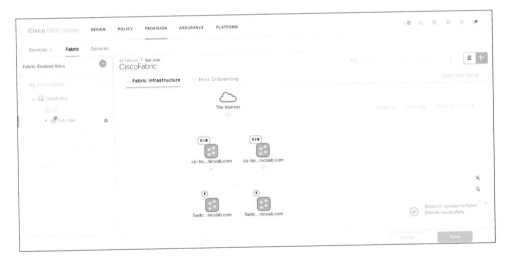

Validate the configuration by using the command **show lisp service ipv4**, as shown below:

```
Switch-100-124-130-12#show lisp service ipv4
Information applicable to all EID instances:
  Router-lisp ID:                     0
  Locator table:                      default
  Ingress Tunnel Router (ITR):        disabled
  Egress Tunnel Router (ETR):         enabled
  Proxy-ITR Router (PITR):            enabled RLOCs: 100.124.130.12
  Proxy-ETR Router (PETR):            disabled
  NAT-traversal Router (NAT-RTR):     disabled
  Mobility First-Hop Router:          disabled
  Map Server (MS):                    disabled
  Map Resolver (MR):                  disabled
  Delegated Database Tree (DDT):      disabled
  ITR Map-Resolver(s):                100.124.0.1, 100.124.0.2
  ETR Map-Server(s):                  100.124.0.1, 100.124.0.2
  xTR-ID:                             0x5AF44867-0xAF974FB1-0xF51ED758-0xA0F39068
  site-ID:                            unspecified
  ITR local RLOC (last resort):       *** NOT FOUND ***
  ITR use proxy ETR RLOC(s):          100.124.0.1, 100.124.0.2
  ITR Solicit Map Request (SMR):      accept and process
    Max SMRs per map-cache entry:     8 more specifics
    Multiple SMR suppression time:    20 secs
  ETR accept mapping data:            disabled, verify disabled
  ETR map-cache TTL:                  1d00h
  Locator Status Algorithms:
    RLOC-probe algorithm:             disabled
    RLOC-probe on route change:       N/A (periodic probing disabled)
    RLOC-probe on member change:      disabled
    LSB reports:                      process
    IPv4 RLOC minimum mask length:    /32
    IPv6 RLOC minimum mask length:    /0
  Map-cache:
    Map-cache limit:                  25000
    Map-cache activity check period:  60 secs
    Persistent map-cache:             disabled
  Global Top Source locator configuration:
    Loopback0 (100.124.130.12)
  Source locator configuration:
    GigabitEthernet1/0/14: 100.124.130.12 (Loopback0)
  Database:
    Dynamic database mapping limit:   5000
Switch-100-124-130-12#
```

# Index

## Numerics

## A

## B

# D

# J-K-L

# U

underlay network, 270

unicast routing, 664–682

unknown unicast flooding, 17

# V

verifying, DMVPN Phase 3 tunnel configuration, 388–389

virtual links, GRE tunnels and, 83–85

virtual network, 270

VMA (VTP membership advertisement), 8

vManage template, 729–753–782

VPN (virtual private network)

  BGP routing in a, 599–600

EIGRP routing in a, 591–593

OSPF routing in a, 595–597

static and RIPv2 routing in a, 589–590

VTP pruning, 5–7

  pruning ineligible, 9, 11

  show interfaces trunk command, 8, 10

  switchport trunk pruning vlan command, 10, 11

  VMA (VTP membership advertisement), 8

# W-X-Y-Z

WEIGHT attribute, 140–147

ZTP server configuration, 809–816